ISBN 978-0-282-99990-2
PIBN 10876209

1 MONTH OF
FREE
READING

at
www.ForgottenBooks.com

By purchasing this book you are eligible for one month membership to ForgottenBooks.com, giving you unlimited access to our entire collection of over 1,000,000 titles via our web site and mobile apps.

To claim your free month visit:
www.forgottenbooks.com/free876209

English
Français
Deutsche
Italiano
Español
Português

www.forgottenbooks.com

Mythology Photography **Fiction**
Fishing Christianity **Art** Cooking
Essays Buddhism Freemasonry
Medicine **Biology** Music **Ancient
Egypt** Evolution Carpentry Physics
Dance Geology **Mathematics** Fitness
Shakespeare **Folklore** Yoga Marketing
Confidence Immortality Biographies
Poetry **Psychology** Witchcraft
Electronics Chemistry History **Law**
Accounting **Philosophy** Anthropology
Alchemy Drama Quantum Mechanics
Atheism Sexual Health **Ancient History**
Entrepreneurship Languages Sport
Paleontology Needlework Islam
Metaphysics Investment Archaeology
Parenting Statistics Criminology
Motivational

THE NEW YORK

GENEALOGICAL AND BIOGRAPHICAL

RECORD.

DEVOTED TO THE INTERESTS OF AMERICAN
GENEALOGY AND BIOGRAPHY.

ISSUED QUARTERLY.

VOLUME XXXIX, 1908.

PUBLISHED BY THE
NEW YORK GENEALOGICAL AND BIOGRAPHICAL SOCIETY,
226 WEST 58TH STREET, NEW YORK.

Publication Committee:

GEORGE AUSTIN MORRISON, JR., *Editor.*

DR. HENRY R. STILES, *Editor Emeritus.*

E. DOUBLEDAY HARRIS.   JOSIAH C. PUMPELLY.

HOPPER STRIKER MOTT.   TOBIAS A. WRIGHT.

Melatiah E. Dwight

THE NEW YORK
Genealogical and Biographical Record.

VOL. XXXIX.   NEW YORK, JANUARY, 1908.   No. 1

REV. MELATIAH EVERETT DWIGHT, M. D., D. D.

BY THOMAS A. ....

Dr. Dwight was born in South Hadley, Mass, ...
and died Sept. 15, 1907, on the heights of .... Me.
where his summer home overlooked the pla............
was the eldest son of John Dwight of New York ....
son of Dr. Elihu Dwight of South Hadley, Mass, ...
eldest son of Justus Dwight and grandson of Capt. ....
Dwight, both of Belchertown, Mass. The latter was ....
descent from John Dwight of D............ His mother was N............
Shaw Everett, daughter of Melatiah Everett of Foxboro, Mass.
the son of John Everett and Melatiah Metcalf, daughter of
Samuel Metcalf of Wrentham, M............

Dr. Dwight's boyhood and .... were spent in New York
City, where his father was laying .... under .... of a business
prosperity that became the so............ city d............ ted be............
lend. He studied in the public s............ of this city, and ....
New York University Grammar S............ graduated from ....
College of the City of New Y............ he a............ ded ....
Thirteenth Street Medical College, gra............ with th............
of M. D. from the latter in 188............ .... at ....
Theological Seminary, and was grad............ in ....
appointment by the American Board of C............
Foreign Missions as missionary to ....
medical studies at Bellevue Hospi............
travelled in Europe, Egypt and the ....
.... his return was consumed by th............
pointment as foreign missionary, a............
field. He was ordained and insta............
Congregational Church of Char............
until 1870, and was then called .... rch
Fairfield, Iowa, of which he was .... 88, when he
resigned on account of po............ .... in ....
relinquish the active work of tr............ d............ church
under me head treatment, he rea............ .... field, N. J., where
he remained for eleven years. .... was called to New
York City to be the companion of .... ther, ... of ....

THE NEW YORK

Genealogical and Biographical Record.

Vol. XXXIX.   NEW YORK, JANUARY, 1908.   No. 1

REV. MELATIAH EVERETT DWIGHT, M. D., D. D.

By Tobias A. Wright.

Dr. Dwight was born in South Hadley, Mass., Oct. 15, 1841, and died Sept. 15, 1907, on the heights of Mt. Holyoke, Mass., where his summer home overlooked the place of his birth. He was the eldest son of John Dwight of New York City, and grandson of Dr. Elihu Dwight of South Hadley, Mass., who was the eldest son of Justus Dwight and grandson of Capt. Nathaniel Dwight, both of Belchertown, Mass. The latter was fourth in descent from John Dwight of Dedham. His mother was Nancy Shaw Everett, daughter of Metcalf Everett of Foxboro, Mass., the son of John Everett and Melatiah Metcalf, daughter of Samuel Metcalf of Wrentham, Mass.

Dr. Dwight's boyhood and youth were spent in New York City, where his father was laying the foundation of a business prosperity that became the source of widely distributed benevolence. He studied in the public schools of this city, and the New York University Grammar School; graduated from the College of the City of New York in 1860; studied medicine at Thirteenth Street Medical College, graduating with the degree of M. D. from the latter in 1864; studied theology at Andover Theological Seminary, and was graduated in 1866. Being under appointment by the American Board of Commissioners for Foreign Missions as missionary to Turkey, he continued his medical studies at Bellevue Hospital Medical College, 1866–1867, travelled in Europe, Egypt and the Holy Land, 1867–1868, but on his return was constrained by ill health to give up his appointment as foreign missionary, and seek a home-missionary field. He was ordained and installed February, 1869, over the Congregational Church of Onarga, Illinois, where he remained until 1879, and was then called to the Congregational Church of Fairfield, Iowa, of which he was the pastor until 1888, when he resigned on account of pulmonary trouble. Being obliged to relinquish the active work of the ministry, and place himself under medical treatment, he removed to Plainfield, N. J., where he remained for eleven years. In 1900 he was called to New York City to be the companion of his aged father, (whose death occurred in November, 1903,) and continued his winter residence here, summering at Northampton, Mass., until the time of his death.

During the years of his pastorate in churches and his missionary work, he not only won a strong and commanding influence in the communities where he lived, but came to wide recognition in ecclesiastical affairs in the local and State associations of his denomination. He was made a trustee in the Congregational Church Building Society in 1906, and received that same year the degree of D. D. from Parsons College.

Dr. Dwight took a very active interest in the "National Federation of Churches and Christian Workers" and gave much of his time and means to the Inter-Church Conference on Federation, held in New York City in 1905, acting as Chairman of Committee on Meetings. In fact it was largely through his efforts and financial contribution that an exhaustive report of that organization was published in book form.

The leading religious Journals of this country have published extended obituaries of Dr. Dwight, paying high tribute to his zeal, to the beauty of his character, and his successful labors in the service of his divine Master, and it is not the purpose of this memorial to enlarge upon the record of the noble service of this man in the Church—abler pens have told the story of his devotion—but rather to treat of his work in our own Society.

When in 1894 he became a member of the New York Genealogical and Biographical Society, and began attending its meetings, no one could have predicted that this modest gentleman, small in stature and pale of face, bearing evidence of ill-health and constitutional feebleness, was destined soon to lead in the work of the Society, become the strong, loyal and trusted friend of every member, and largely instrumental in the upbuilding of our cause. Becoming interested in genealogical and historical studies, Dr. Dwight began giving to the world the results of his researches in 1898 by publishing a genealogical record and history of "*The Kirbys of New England*," followed in 1901, by "*The Journal of Nathaniel Dwight, 1775.*" Recognizing the assistance he had received in the preparation of these works from our Society's publications and Library, he began devoting himself to increasing and enlarging their resources, by giving of his own time and means, and by his enthusiasm and energy stimulating his fellow members to greater efforts, appealing to the strong, encouraging the weak, and harmonizing all with the matchless grace of his charming personality. He recognized the need of cooperation, and with magical diplomacy he brought men together and held them for good. Who could resist the kindly smile and the flashes of subtle humor that made his presence so agreeable? Who could go out of that presence without feeling that he had been in touch with a nobility without ostentation, a royalty without arrogance? In 1901 he was elected a member of the Board of Trustees, and in the following year editor of the NEW YORK GENEALOGICAL AND BIOGRAPHICAL RECORD. Though his predecessors had been such learned and eminent genealogists as Dr. Henry Reed Stiles and the late Dr. Samuel S. Purple, the magazine grew in importance and dignity under his guidance, wielding a wider influence. He took special pride in this publication, defraying the expense of illustrations out of his private means, contributing to the cost of indexing its volumes each year, and paying the entire outlay of making a complete index of subjects of thirty-eight volumes of the RECORD from the beginning of its publication in 1869, down to 1907, which the Society printed. This was the work he loved, and perhaps no where did his abilities show to better advantage.

To him genealogy was as legitimate a study as any other branch of history, leading him into the past in quest of types of pure manhood. It was a great storehouse from which to draw examples of goodness and greatness to be emulated and imitated, and of vice and vileness to be abhorred and avoided. The gartered knight and the crest of royalty had no special charm for him; "The simple annals of the poor" developed fields as rich in christian virtues, and the blood of simple, honest yeomen transmitted traits as worthy of emulation.

In 1905 he was unanimously elected President of the Society in which capacity he served with marked ability until the time of his demise. For many years he served as the Society's necrologist, and it will long be remembered by those who attended the annual meetings with what reverence and sympathy he read the brief memoirs which he had carefully prepared of the Society's dead.

His benevolence was boundless, and his daily generosity proved the very love he had of giving. The extent of his charity will never be known, for it was absolutely without ostentation. He waited not for appeals but watched for opportunities to assist the poor and needy, and found them in plenty. Of such was this man whose gentle spirit has gone to the Great Eternal and whose kindly face we shall see no more.

Dr. Dwight was a member of the New England Historic-Genealogical Society, the New York Academy of Science, the Rhode Island Chapter of the Society of the Cincinnati, and the New York Gamma Chapter of the Phi Beta Kappa Society. He married in Jacksonville, Ill., June 23, 1870, Helen McClure Kirby, daughter of Rev. William Kirby and Hannah McClure Wolcott, who with three sons and two daughters survive him.

The action of the Board of Trustees of the New York Genealogical and Biographical Society, the Committee of the Congregational Church of Fairfield, Iowa, the Congregational Church Building Society, and the City College Club of New York, form an appropriate addition to this tribute to Dr. Dwight:

At a joint meeting of the Board of Trustees and of the Executive Committee of the New York Genealogical and Biographical Society held in the Society's office, November 12, 1907, it being the first formal Fall meeting of the Board of Trustees following the death of our late President, Rev. Melatiah Everett

Dwight, D. D., M. D., the following resolutions were unanimously passed, viz.:

WHEREAS, death has removed from our midst our late President, Rev. Melatiah Everett Dwight, D. D., M. D., who in addition to his office as President, Trustee and Necrologist of the Society, and Editor of the RECORD, had for many years served as a member of the Executive Committee, and:

WHEREAS, his excellent judgment, genial disposition and uniform gentleness and courtesy of manner, had endeared him to all members of the Board of Trustees and of the Executive Committee:

RESOLVED, that in his death the Society, Board of Trustees and Executive Committee have lost a most valuable associate whose memory will always be dear to those with whom he was brought in contact:

RESOLVED, that these Resolutions be engrossed and a copy sent to the family of Doctor Dwight; and that they be spread upon the minutes of this Society, and that a copy of them be published in the January, 1908, issue of THE NEW YORK GENEA-LOGICAL AND BIOGRAPHICAL RECORD.

FAIRFIELD, IOWA, September 26, 1907.

DEAR MRS. DWIGHT AND FAMILY:

We, as a church, desire to express our sympathy for you in your deep affliction. It is only a few days since we heard that our beloved pastor of former days has been called to be with our Heavenly Father in the Home above. We hope that you will be sustained, and that strength will be given you to bear this great loss. We feel that it is our loss too, for we remember his kindness of heart toward every one, his broad sympathies. His life with us was a blessing and a benediction and we are thankful to our Heavenly Father that we had him with us in the years that are past.   Very sincerely yours,

MRS. A. S. JORDAN,
F. J. L. BLACK,
MRS. JOHN WELLS,
Committee in behalf of the Church.

At a meeting of the Board of Trustees of The Congregational Church Building Society, held on Wednesday, September 18, 1907, the following resolutions were presented by the Rev. Charles L. Goodrich, pastor of the First Congregational Church of Plainfield, N. J., of which Mr. Dwight was a member, and they were unanimously adopted:

WHEREAS it has pleased Almighty God in his wise providence to take out of this world our fellow-Trustee, Rev. Melatiah Everett Dwight, D. D.,

RESOLVED: That we, the Board of Trustees of the Congregational Church Building Society, do hereby express our sense of the great loss which the Board sustains in this removal, gratefully recognizing the able as well as faithful and interested service which he rendered this Society; that we put on record our appreciation of his personal character, the genial and cheery temperament with its gleams of humor, the mind keen and alert with unusual originality of thought and expression, the spirit devout, consecrated, singularly unworldly, the heart full of human kindness, the hands rich in helpfulness, finding many ways even in years of partial illness to minister to humanity. A brother beloved, one of God's chosen ones has gone from us.

RESOLVED: That we extend to the bereaved family our respectful sympathy and pray for them the consolations of the Son of God.

VOTED: That this minute be spread upon the records of this Society and a copy sent to his family.

WILLIAM HAYES WARD, Chairman.

Attest: CHARLES H. RICHARDS, Secretary.

CH. E. HOPE, Recording Secretary.

TO THE FAMILY OF REV. MELATIAH E. DWIGHT:

At the last meeting of the City College Club, it was unanimously resolved that in the death of Rev. Melatiah E. Dwight, long and honorably known as a loyal and distinguished alumnus of the College of the City of New York, the club has suffered the loss of one of its noblest members.

The City College Club sends its sympathy to you in your bereavement and trusts that the memory of a good name and work done efficiently will be a source of consolation.

JOHN LIEBERMAN, Secretary.

FERDINAND SHACK, President.

THE DUTCH TITUS FAMILY.

BY FRANK H. TITUS, M.D., DOVER, N. H.

This might with propriety be called the American Titus family, as it originated, as far as the name is concerned in Kings Co., N. Y.

The founder of the family was Titus Syrachs De Vries, who according to Bergen's *Register of Early Settlers of Kings County*, and Riker's *Annals of Newtown*, immigrated to this country at an early date. He was part owner of a gristmill operated by horsepower in New Utrecht in 1660. He was Lieut. of an Infantry Co. of Flatbush in 1673, and was probably promoted, as he is also styled Captain. That he was probably of the noble De Vries family of Holland is indicated not only by his name, which should have been Titus Syrachs simply had he been of the commonalty, but more suggestively that some of his children at least were baptized as Tryntje Titus De Vries, Syrach Titus De Vries, etc.

For some reason difficult to conjecture his children all seem to have dropped the name of de Vries and adhered to the less euphonious one, which, in accordance with the untrammeled custom of the time, they spelled as the fancy of the moment suggested Tetus, Tietus, Tites, Titos, Tytus or more often Titus. There still remains one branch which uses the spelling "Tytus," but the other forms seem to have disappeared.

Possibly the change of the name was in the nature of protective imitation as practiced by various forms of animated creatures lower than the human. Dutch blood was probably not as highly esteemed just after the land had passed from Dutch into English control as it is in our day, and the Britons have never been specially noted for tender consideration of the susceptibilities of those unwise enough to have been born under other skies. So the proximity of the large Titus family of English descent, who were numerous in the adjoining county, may have suggested the adoption of the father's given name according to the Dutch usage as a means of escaping the undesirable advertisement of their foreign blood. Or they may have felt the incongruity a noble name and the plebian occupations necessary for wringing a livelihood out of a new country. Be that as it may, De Vries they were; Titus their descendants are.

1.   TITUS[1] SYRACHS DE VRIES, resided in Flatbush, where he d. 1688 (Bergen), or 1690 (Riker); he m. Jannetje Teunise, dau. of Teunis Janse Coeverts (Covert) and Barbara (Lucas or Jans). Children:

    2   i. Tryntje,[2] bap. 1663.
          ii. Teunis, m. 1699, Mary Barre, went to Mansfield Tp., Burlington Co., N. J., and from there, about 1714, to parts unknown, possibly Virginia.
    3   iii. Francis, d. 1764, Bushwick, N. Y.
    4   iv. Syrach, b. 1679; d. 1761, Bensalem, Pa.
          v. Janetje, b. 1682.
         vi. Arays, signed "Tietus," was in Flatbush in 1693.
       vii. Phebe, m. Johannes Simensz, son of Sigismund Lucas. (Riker, *Hist. Harlem.*)
      viii. Femmetje, m. 1692, John Hegeman of Flatbush.

2.   TRYNTJE[2] TITUS (Titus Syrachs De Vries[1]), bap. 1663; m. 1683, Johannes Van Ekelen, who d. about 1697. Children:

          i. Johannes.[3]
         ii. Johanna.
       iii. Geesje.
       iv. Jannetje, b. 1689; d. inf.
          v. Jannetje, b. 1691.
       vi. Anna.
      vii. Helena.

3.   FRANCIS[2] TITUS (Titus[1]) d. 1764, Bushwick, N. Y.; m. (1) Antie Fonteyn. She was the widow, first of Jacob Jansen, by whom she had two children, Annetie and Catherine; and second of Maurits Covert, by whom she had: Tunis, b. 1691; m. another Antie Fonteyn; Charles, b. 1693; Mauritz, b. 1696; Sarah, b. 1697. They probably had no children. He m. (2) Elizabeth ——, and had:

5   i. Francis,* b. 1728; d. 1802, Bushwick, N. Y.
6   ii. Antie.
     iii. Helena.
7   iv. Elizabeth.
      v. Arientje.
     vi. John, was Capt. in Col. Van Brunt's Regt., Kings Co.
         Militia, in the Revolution.
8   vii. Janetje, was dead in 1792.
9   viii. Johannes, d. 1799.
10   ix. Charles, d. 1802.
      x. Titus.
11   xi. Christina, b. 1747; d. 1816, New York City.

4. SYRACH* TITUS (Titus¹), b. 1679; d. 1761, Bensalem, Bucks
Co., Pa.; m. Aeltje Webs.   Children:
      i. Geertie, b. 1698.
12   ii. Francis, d. 1784.
    iii. Cornelis, b. 1722.
13   iv. Syrach (prob).

5. FRANCIS* TITUS (Francis,* Titus¹), b. 1728; d. 1802, Bushwick,
N. Y.; m. (1) 1757, Cornelia Duryea, dau. of Chas. and Cornelia
(Schenck); in 1781 he m. (2) Catherine Voortman, a widow.
Children, probably all by first wife:
      i. Francis,⁴ m. (1) Maritie Bennet. In March, 1804, they
         were "of Newtown."   He m. (2) Eyda (perhaps
         Debevoise) and signs deeds with her from April,
         1805, to Nov., 1833, being described as a farmer of
         Bushwick. In Aug., 1835, he signs alone. Francis
         was appointed Lieut. of the Kings Co. troops in 1787,
         promoted to Capt. 1796, to 1st Maj. 1807, and in 1815
         he resigned as Lt.-Col. He served in the War of 1812.
     .ii. Elizabeth⁴⸴ } one of these m. Jno. Meserole.
    iii. Cornelia,
     iv. Harampie, b. 1762; d. 1814; m. David Van Cott.

     Lucretia or "Cretia," who according to *N. Y. Marriages* m.
Abraham Polhemus in 1770, is said to be of this family. This can
hardly be, as Francis was first m. in 1757, and could not have a
marriageable dau. in 1770. Besides which, a granddau. of Abraham
Polhemus now (1907) living in New York City, hale and lively at
the age of 91, knows of her grandmother, and states that she was
Christina* (Francis,* Titus¹), as given elsewhere.

6. ANTIE* TITUS (Francis,* Titus¹), m. Johannes (or Isaac) Blank.
Children:
      i. Elizabeth,⁴ b. 1762.
     ii. Frans Titus, b. 1764.

7. ELIZABETH* TITUS (Francis,* Titus¹), m. 1754, Dirk Duryea,
who was dead in 1794.   Children:
      i. John.⁴
     ii. Carel, bap. 1755.

8. JANETJE* TITUS (Francis,* Titus¹), d. before 1792; m. 1763(?),
Thos. Skillman, b. 1736, son of Joseph and Sarah (Meserole); was
a Lieut. of Militia in the Revolution.   Children:

14   i. Joseph,[4] b. 1763; d. 1809.
15   ii. Francis, b. 1764.
        iii. Sarah, b. 1766; m. Martin Schenck, son of Martin and
             Ida (Suydam).
16   iv. Thomas, b. 1770; d. 1833, Smithville, N. Y.

9. JOHANNES[3] TITUS (Francis,[2] Titus[1]), d. 1799; m. 1755, Lena
Andries (Leah Anderson), dau. of Herman. He was 1st Maj. in
Col. Van Brunt's Regt. of Kings Co. Militia in the Revolution.
Children:
17   i. Francis J.[4]
        ii. Mary, m. Jonathan Williams.
        iii. Elizabeth, m. Peter Miller.
        iv. Leah, m. Chas. De Bevoise.

10. CHARLES[3] TITUS (Francis,[2] Titus[1]), d. 1802; m. Sarah
Rapelye, dau. of Folkert. Children:
        i. Folkert.[4]
        ii. Jane.
        iii. Charles, d. 1807; m. Anne Jenkins; no children.
        iv. Sarah, b. 1776; d. 1838; m. John Schenck.
        v. Elizabeth, m. Jno. De Bevoise.
        vi. Matilda.

11. CHRISTINA[3] TITUS (Francis,[2] Titus[1]), b. 1747; d. 1816, New
York City; m. 1770, Abraham Polhemus, who was b. 1742.
Children:
        i. Theodorus,[4] b. 1771; d. unm. 1802.
        ii. Elizabeth, b. 1772; d. 1839; m. Thos. Stagg, b. 1771; d.
             1837; son of Thomas and Jane (Stagg), 2d wife.
             No children.
18   iii. Francis, b. 1775; d, 1818.
        iv. Ann, b. 1777; d. unm.
19   v. Helena, b. 1783.
        vi. Abraham Brinkerhoff, b. 1789; d. 1798.   [4]

12. FRANCIS[3] TITUS (Syrach,[2] Titus[1]), d. 1784, Middletown,
Bucks Co., Pa.; m. 1734, Mary Clark. Children:
20   i. Francis,[4] d. 1800.
        ii. Martha, d. 1816; m. Abraham Slack; no children men-
             tioned in her will. Lower Mansfield Tp., Bucks
             Co., Pa.
21   iii. Elizabeth, m. —— Hellings.
22   iv. John.
23   v. Timothy, d. 1779.
        vi. Samuel.
24   vii. Tunis, d. before 1784.

13. SYRACH[3] TITUS (Syrach,[2] Titus[1]), served in Bensalem Militia
in the Revolutionary War. (Serick.) Child:
25   i. William,[4] b. 1779-80.

14. JOSEPH[4] SKILLMAN (Janetje[3] Titus, Francis,[2] Titus[1]), b. 1763;
d. 1809; m. 1790, Mary Scudder, dau. of Jos. and Mary (Budd).
Children:
        i. John Scudder,[5] b. 1791.
        ii. Thos., b. 1793; d. 1793.

15. FRANCIS[4] SKILLMAN (Jannetje[3] Titus, Francis,[2] Titus[1]), b. 1764; m. 1785, Anne Schenck, b. 1768, dau. of Martin and Ida (Suydam), of the 5th generation from Joris Jansen de Rapeljé. Children:
    i. Jane,[5] b. 1786.
    ii. Martin, b. 1789; d. 1800, of yellow fever.
    iii. Thomas, 1791.
    iv. Abigail, b. 1794; d. unm. 1861.
    v. John, b. 1797.
16. THOMAS[4] SKILLMAN (Janetje[3] Titus, Francis,[2] Titus[1]), b. 1770; d. 1833, Smithville, N. Y.; m. 1788, Jerusha Rogers. Children:
    i. Thomas,[5] b. 1789.
    ii. Rachel, b. 1792; d. 1876; m. Danl. Hudson, b. 1779; d. 1875, Northport, N. Y.
    iii. Josiah, b. 1794.
    iv. Sarah, b. 1797; d. 1847; m. Isaac Sanzy.
    v. Joseph, b. 1802.
    vi. Maria, b. 1804; m. Elisha Green.
    vii. Jane, twin to last, m. 1827, F. T. Spees.
    viii. Elsey, b. 1808; d. unm. 1837.
    ix. Francis Martin, b. 1812.
(For further data of the Skillmans see the article on that family now running in the RECORD.)
17. FRANCIS J.[4] TITUS (Johannes,[3] Francis,[2] Titus[1]), was of Williamsburgh in 1848; m. Iddy ——. He is said to have m. for second wife Rimay De Bevoise, who afterward m. a Cutting, but Iddy survived him, and Rimay is elsewhere mentioned as the widow of one J. Titus. Children:
    i. Francis J.,[5] m. Harriet A. ——; not mentioned in will.
    ii. Johannes.
    iii. George.
    iv. Helene, m. Wm. G. Hoffman, and had: Wm. G.; John H.; Mary E., who m. Wm. C. Herbert; and Louisa, or Eloisa L., m. Jas. Grogan.
18. FRANCIS[4] POLHEMUS (Christina[3] Titus, Francis,[2] Titus[1]), b. 1775; d. 1818; m. 1797, Phebe Caseman, b. 1778; d. 1823. Children:
    i. Abraham F.,[5] b. 1797; d. 1847.
    ii. Eliza Ann, b. 1799; m. (1) Jno. Bradshaw, New York City; m. (2) —— Bausher.
    iii. Christina Maria, b. and d. 1805.
    iv. Christina Titus, b. 1807; d. 1821.
    v. Theodorus, b. and d. 1811.
    vi. Cornelia Van Wyck, b. 1813; m. Wm. E. Stagg, and had: Geo. Webb; Anna; Virginia; Wm., who m. Sarah Guinup; Charles, and Cornelia.
    vii. Phebe Duryea, b. 1816; m. 1837, Benj. F. Stagg, and had: Cornelia; Emma G., who m. Henry Gallagher; and Marie Louise. Mrs. Stagg still lives (July, 1907) in New York City with her second daughter, to whom the writer is indebted for much of the foregoing data.
19. HELENA[4] POLHEMUS (Christina[3] Titus, Francis,[2] Titus[1]), b. 1783; m. 1804; Daniel Riker of New York City. Children:

    i. Jane Rapelyea,[1] b. 1807; m. Robt. M. De Witt.
    ii. Abraham Polhemus, b. 1809; d. 1884; m. Harriet M. Vaughn, and had: Chas. E., a wellknown dealer in surgical instruments in New York; Oscar, and Albert Porter.
    iii. Christina Titus, b. 1811; unm.
    iv. Henry, b. 1813; m. —— Campbell; no children.
    v. Edwin, b. 1815; d. young.
    vi. Edgar, b. 1816.
    vii. Elizabeth Stagg, b. 1819; m. (1) Alpheus Stocking, by whom she had two daus.; m. (2) Moses Tapley, no children.
    viii. Ann Polhemus, b. 1822; m. Wm. Ross Wallace (poet), and had one son.
    ix. Helen, b. 1826; m. Harvey Stocking, and had several children.

20. FRANCIS[4] TITUS (Francis,[3] Syrach,[2] Titus[1]), d. 1800, Bucks Co., Pa. He was a Lieut. of the 4th Co., 3d Battalion of Associators (Col. Wm. Robb), in 1780; m. 1763, Jean H. (or K.) Fagen. Children:
    i. Francis.[5]
    ii. Rebecca, m. —— Van Arsdalen.
    iii. Mary, m. —— Vansant.
    iv. Margaret, m. —— Wilcoxe.

21. ELIZABETH[4] TITUS (Francis,[3] Syrach,[2] Titus[1]), m. —— Hellings. Children:
    i. John.[5]
    ii. Tunis, m. ——; had dau. Martha, who m. —— White.
    iii. Samuel.
    iv. Jesse.
    v. Jacob.

22. JOHN[4] TITUS (Francis,[3] Syrach,[2] Titus[1]). Children:
    i. John.[5]
    ii. Abraham.

23. TIMOTHY[4] TITUS (Francis,[3] Syrach,[2] Titus[1]), d. 1801, Bristol Tp., Bucks Co., Pa.; m. 1764, Martha Wright, who d. between Feb. and Nov., 1801. Children:
    i. Edith, m. Geo. Bergen, and had son Chas. Titus.
    ii. Sarah, m. 1787, Jas. Van Hart.
    iii. Mary, m. —— Stacklehouse, who d. 1801. They had: Rachel; Martha, and Sarah.
    iv. Ira.

24. TUNIS[4] TITUS (Francis,[3] Syrach,[2] Titus[1]), was dead in 1784. Children:
    i. Archible,[5] had dau. Martha.
    ii. Tunis.
    iii. Mary, m. —— Bennet.
    iv. Elizabeth, m. —— Van Horn.
    v. Martha.

25. WILLIAM[4] TITUS (Syrach,[3] Syrach,[2] Titus[1]), b. 1779-80, Buckingham Tp., Bucks Co., Pa. Children:
    i. Syrach (Seruch),[5] had two daus. who lived in Md.

  ii. John, b. 1812; d. 1876; m. Martha J., dau. of Josiah
    Shaw Buck, and had: Henry C., and Amanda Welsh,
    who lived in Philadelphia in 1880.

(In this same township in 1823 d. a widow, Deborah Titus,
possibly widow of this Wm. She mentions in her will her
children David, William, *Seruch*, who had children, Elizabeth,
who had children, Deborah and Mary.)

  HARMAN TITUS of Bensalem, Bucks Co., Pa., who d. 1822, was
perhaps a son of one of the brothers of Francis (No. 12). He m.
Susan ——. Children:

  i. Harman, b. 1778; d. 1858; m. Edith Lewis. Had:
    1. Jacob, b. 1826; d. 1903, Tacony, Pa.; m. Harriet
     Ashton; had seven children.
    2. Wm. R., b. 1821; d. 1890, Holmesburg, Pa.; m.
     Ellen Soley; left many descendants, among
     them Harry and Emerson Titus of Holmesburg.
    3. David, b. 1823; d. 1890; m. Rachel Snyder, and
     had three children.
    4. Howard, b. 1817; d. 1871; m. Mary E. Hughes,
     and had twelve children, among them atty.
     Frank, of Kansas City, and Lincoln G., of
     Columbus, O.
    5. Jane, b. 1829; m. Francis Le Pierre, and now
     lives in Camden, N. J. She had three chil-
     dren, one, Harriet A., a teacher in Camden.
    6. Elizabeth, b. 1818; m. Jos. Jackson, of Holmes-
     burg, Pa. Had twelve children.
  ii. Edward or Edmond, unm.
  iii. Jacob, m. ——.
  iv. Catherine, unm.
  v. Nancy, m. —— Scott, and had three children.
  vi. Susan, m. Isaac Johnson.
  vii. Uzine, unm.
  viii. Elizabeth, m. —— Worthington; no children.
  ix. Sarah, m. Tunis Le Bon.
  x. Tunis, unm.
  xi. Minah.
  xii. Ann.

  In Loudoun Co., Va., are a number of the family, probably
descended from Teunis. They trace back to a family of brothers
and sisters as follows:

  i. Tunis, d. 1848, in Goresville, Va. He m. Sarah Pur-
    dem, and had:
    1. Nancy, m. Geo. Woolford, Bolington, Va.
    2. Edith, m. Jno. Fawley, Taylorstown, Va.
    3. Jeremiah, d. 1896, Coles Co., Ill.; m. Susan
     Goodhart.
    4. Wm., d. 1852, Goresville, Va.; m. Jane Brown;
     had six children.
    5. Louis, d. young.
    6. Elizabeth, unm.
    7. Emeline, m. Solomon Cooper, Bolington, Va.

> 8. Tunis, b. 1816; d. 1899, Leesburg, Va.; m. 1841, Mary Hunter, and had eight children; among them Thos. S. Titus of Leesburg, to whom the writer is indebted for many courtesies.
> 9. Amanda, m. Josiah Shoemaker, Leesburg, Va.
> 10. Margaret, m. John L. Stout, also of Leesburg.

ii. Itom, whose children were:

> 1. Rev. Timothy Tillman, Gettysburg, Pa., m. Rachel M. L. Witherow, and had seven children.
> 2. Samuel, m. Mrs. McNeer, and had two children.
> 3. Armistead, Neersville Va., m. Hannah Virts; seven children.
> 4. Washington.
> 5. Mary Ann, unm.
> 6. Catherine.
> 7. Julia, d. unm.
> 8. Deborah, d. unm.
> 9. Sabra, d. young.

iii. John, unm.
iv. Elizabeth, unm.
v. Deborah, unm.
vi. Dau., name unknown, m. ——, and had a dau. who m. —— Wilson, and had a dau. who m. —— Yates.

Francis Tytus, son of John, was b. in this same Co. in 1742; in 1763 he m. Margaret Winecoop, and d. in 1803-12. They had:

i. Elizabeth, b. 1764; m. John Dungan in Hampshire Co., Va.; moved to Circleville, Ohio; had: Tytus Dungan.
ii. Tunis, b. 1767; m. (1) Mary Kelley, 1793, in Loudoun Co.; she d. 1798; no children; he m. (2) about 1800, Jane Torbert. Children:

> 1. Elizabeth, b. 1801; m. about 1820, Peter Bruner; four children.
> 2. Margaret, b. 1803; m. 1823, Moses Collis, and had one son.
> 3. Francis J., b. 1806; moved to Middletown, Ohio; m. (1) 1831, Sarah Martin; she d. 1841; no adult children; he m. (2) Sarah Butler, and had: Emma J., b. 1844; m. Rev. C. Monjean, Topeka, Kan. Edward, b. 1845; m. Tillie Davis, New Haven, Conn. Lizzie P., m. C. Gardner, Cincinnati, Ohio. John B., b. 1849; m. Minnie Ewing, Middletown, Ohio.
> 4. Harriet, b. 1809; m. Wm. Russell; five children.
> 5. Evaline, b. 1816; m. John McLean; no children.

The first wife of Francis d. and in 1768, he m. Jane Patterson. They had:

iii. Ann, b. 1779; m. (1) John Simpson; m. (2) Jos. Carter.
iv. Sarah, b. 1781; m. —— Kendrick; moved to Ohio.
v. Rebecca, b. 1783; m. Jas. Craig, Loudoun Co., Va.

This line adheres to the spelling "Tytus;" but the recurrence of the family names is a good indication that they were of the same stock as the "Titus" family in the same neighborhood;

and the County records reveal the fact that they did not always adhere to the one spelling, but used both indiscriminately.

Titus Titus seemed to have been a favorite name with the older generation. Besides Titus[3] (Francis,[2] Titus[1]), there are known to have been five others if not more.

Tites Tites and his wife, Mary Morgan, were sponsors at a baptism, 1726.

Titus Titus m. Jane Boudet, 1726; had dau. Antje.

Titus Titus m. Blandina Van Pelt about 1722, and had:

    i. Aeltje, b. 1724; m .Cornelus Bouman, and had dau. Aeltje, b. 1745.

    ii. Sara, b. 1726.

    iii. Maria, b. 1728.

    iv. Antje, b. 1734.

    v. Marytje, b. 1736.

    vi. Teunis, b. 1740.

Tetus Tetus m. Rebecca Boerum, 1770.

Tetus Tetus m. Jemima Townsend of Oyster Bay, 1775.

Tetus Titus, b. about 1750; d. about 1824; m. Polly Johnson; lived in Beaver Co., Pa., and Tioga Co., N. Y.; d. in Scotio Co., Ohio. Children:

    i. Lydia, b. 1792; d. 1888; m. Michael Coryell; seven children, thirty grandchildren.

    ii. Anna, d. in childhood.

    iii. Samuel, b. 1796; d. 1859, Scioto Co., Ohio; m. Clarisa Coryell; eleven children, forty grandchildren, among them Dr. Arthur Titus of Portsmouth, Ohio, father of the present writer.

    iv. John, Penn Yan, N. Y.; had children.

    v. James, m. Lydia Collis; six children.

    vi. Arthur, b. 1808; d. 1875; m. Elizabeth Willis; nine children, thirty-seven grandchildren.

    vii. Susan, d. unm.

    viii. Hannah, m. John Snodgrass; nine children, forty-two grandchildren.

    ix. Stephen, d. 1848; m. Susan Rockwell; six children, nine grandchildren.

    x. Sally, m. Halleck Mapes; four children, twelve grandchildren.

    xi. Betsey, m. James Collis; three children.

    xii. Rebecca, d. about 20 years old.

There are also Titus families in Brooklyn, N. Y., and in Camden, N. J., evidently of this stock, but whose connection with the parent stem cannot at present be demonstrated.

From the foregoing it will be seen that the available information of this family is very fragmentary, and as a search through the usual channels fails to yield further data, this article is published not only to put on record in a tangible shape. the little already known, but in the hope that it may be the means of eliciting further information from sources hitherto undiscovered. Any additional items of the family history will be gladly welcomed by the writer.

NEW BRUNSWICK LOYALISTS OF THE WAR OF THE AMERICAN REVOLUTION.

COMMUNICATED BY D. R. JACK, HISTORIAN OF THE NEW BRUNSWICK LOYALISTS' SOCIETY; COR.-SECT. OF THE NEW BRUNSWICK HISTORICAL SOCIETY; AUTHOR CENTENNIAL PRIZE ESSAY, HISTORY OF ST. JOHN; EDITOR ACADIENSIS ETC.

NOTE.—The reference letter in the second column in the list of New Brunswick Loyalists indicates, it will be remembered, the source of the information from which the list has been compiled. The readers of the RECORD are requested to note the following additions to the schedule which appeared in the January, 1904, issue.

"P." Roll of Loyalists, etc.. settled in Belle Vue in Beavor Harbor, Charlotte County, 10th July, 1784.

"Q." Muster of passengers on transport *Cyrus* on 21st Aug., 1783, upon her trip from New York to the Saint John River. On the 6th of Sept., she was at sea, and on the 14th of Sept., she was in the Saint John River. Copy of return furnished by H. A. Powell, Esq., of Sackville, N. B. (See *Collections of New Brunswick Historical Society*, No. 5, 1904. pp. 277-8-9.)

"R." New Brunswick Loyalists, 1709 in number, whose names appear in the Passamaquoddy section of Major General Campbell's Muster of Loyalists and Disbanded Soldiers, from an original copy initialed by Col. Edward Winslow—of the expulsion of the Acadians fame—compiled 1784 (see *Canadian History Readings* by G. U. Hay, said original copy being now the property of Ward C. Hazen of Saint John, N. B.). The names appearing in this compilation have been copied from the said original by the compiler of this record.

"S." Loyalists who settled on Kemble Manor, Saint John River, N. B., mentioned by Jonas Howe in his article upon that subject, (see *New Brunswick Magazine*, Vol. 1, p. 157.

— This sign indicates that the individual was *less* than 10 years of age in 1783.
+ This sign indicates that the individual was a child but *more* than ten years of age in 1783.

(Continued from Vol. XXXVIII., p. 256, of the RECORD.)

NAME	REF. LETTER	FROM	SETTLED	NOTE
Pears, Ann.............	Q			
Pears, Sarah..	Q			
Peat, Epenetus.........	Q			
Pebbles, John...........	A			
Pebbles, George........	A			
Peck, Timothy.........	A		St. John	
Peck, James...........	A K		"	
Peck, David..........	K		"	
Peck, Henry..........	A K		St. John	
Peck, William.........	A		"	{ Returned to U. S. A. Freeman, St. J., 1785
Peel, Robert...........	B		"	
Peel, Humphrey........	B		Carleton	
Pecker, Jeremiah.......	K		St. John	Blockmaker. Freeman, St. J.,1790
Pendlebury, James......	G	Haverhill, Mass.	Schoodic Falls, N. B.	{ Freeman, St. J., 1785. Described as "gentleman." Grad. Harvard, 1757

Name	Ref. Letter	From	Settled	Note
Pepper, Benjamin	C		St. Andrews	
Percy, James	C		"	
Perkins, Azariah	K		Kings Co.	d. 1825, aet. 83, at Kings Co.
Perry, John	K		St. John	d. 1803 at St. John
Perrine, William	A		"	
Pete, Gilbert	A			
Pete, Margaret	A			
Peters, James	A K	New York	Fredericton	Member N. B. House of Assembly d. at F., 1813, aet. 64
Peters, Thomas	A K		St. John	{ Probably Chas. I., who settled at Gagetown, N. B.
Peters, Charles	A		"	d. Woodstock, N. B., Jan., 1835
Peters, William	A K	New York	St. Andrews	
Peters, Andrew	C H		Queens Co.	Son of Jas. P., Member of Council d. Kings Co., 1805
Peters, Harry	K		Kings Co.	
Peters, William	K		St. John	
Peterson, John	A		"	
Peterson, C. John	A K			d. St. J., 1817, aet. 81
Pettingill, Matthew	K	Newburyport, Mass.	"	
Pettingill, Thomas	O	"	"	} Sons of Matthew P.
Pettingill, Daniel	O	"		
Phair, Andrew	K		Fredericton	Adjutant Arnold's American Legion in 1782. Postmaster at Fredericton
Phelps, Edward	A		St. John	
Philips, James	A		"	
Philips, Nathan (Phillips)	H		Charlotte County	Member the Penobscot Association
Philips, Thomas	C		St. Andrews	
Phillips, James	C H		"	
Picket, John (Pickett)	A K M	Norwalk, Conn.	St. John	Freeman St. J., 1799, d. 1813
Picket, James (Pickett)	K M	Stamford, Conn.	Kings Co.	{ Treasurer K. C., Judge Court of Common Pleas, d. 1826
Pickett, David (Picket)	K M	"	"	
Pickett, Lewis	O	"	"	
Pickett, Gould	O	"	"	} Children of David and Sarah Pickett
Pickett, Hannah	O	"	"	
Pickett, John Lewis	O	"	"	
Picket, David	O	"	"	

Name	Ref. Letter	From	Settled	Note
Pickett, Sarah	O	Stamford, Conn.	Kings Co.	} Children of David and Sarah Pickett
Pickett, Peter	O	"	"	
Pickett, Abram Munson	O	"	"	
Pickle, Nicholas	K		Upham, Kings Co.	d. at U., 1848, aet. 98
Pierce, James	P		Belle Vue, Beaver Har.	
Pike, Joshua	A		St. John	
Pine, Hybecker	C		St. Andrews	Member Cape Ann Assoc'n
Pine, Abraham	L	New York	Charlotte County	
Pine, Ichabod	D	Pine's Ferry, N. Y.	St. Stephen	Freeman, St. J., 1800 " 1804
Pine, Alpheus	K		St. John	
Pine, Stephen	L		"	Member Cape Ann Assoc'n d. Sussex, 1827, aet. 78
Piper, William	K		Charlotte County	
Pitfield, George	A		Sussex, Kings Co.	
Place, Aaron	A P		St. John	
Place, William	B		Carleton	
Place, James	P+		Charlotte County	
Place, Eliz	P+			
Place, Smith	B		Carleton	
Plamart, Francis	P+		Charlotte County	
Place, Rosetta	A		St. John	
Plantain, John	C H		St. Andrews	
Pomeroy, Benjamin	C			
Pomeroy, Richard	A		St. John	
Porteous, John	A		"	
Porter, Anna	C D		St. Andrews	
Post, Miles	C D		"	
Post, Dennis	D		St. Stephen	
Post, David	C H K	Falmouth, Me.	St. Andrews	d. St. A., 23 Nov. 1796, aet. 71 yrs.
Pote, Jeremiah	K	"	"	
Pote, Robert	A	"	St. John	Son of Jeremiah Pote
Potter, Robert	A		"	
Potinger, Abraham	A		"	
Potts, Stephen	A			
Powel, Stephen	A			

(To be continued.)

RECORDS OF THE UNITED BRETHREN CONGREGA-TION, COMMONLY CALLED MORAVIAN CHURCH, STATEN ISLAND, N. Y.

BAPTISMS AND BIRTHS.

ABBREVIATIONS.

Sr.—Sister—A Communicant.   M. M.—Married Man.   M. W.—Married Woman.
Br.—Brother—A Communicant.   S. M.—Single Man.   S. W.—Single Woman.
Wid.—Widow.

(Continued from Vol. XXXVIII., p. 272 of THE RECORD.)

DATE	PARENTS	CHILD	SPONSORS
1837.	BAPTISMS BY REV. A. RONDSHALER.		
July 23. 1835. Nov. 19.	Johann T. Shaber & wife, maiden name Shaber	Catharine Margar- etha	The parents
1837. Aug. 16. 1836. Feb. 2.	Jo n Van Duzer Sarah Vanderbilt, his wife	Daniel Theodore	Bp. at parents' house, Tompkinsville
1837. Sept. 2. 1829. May 1.	Howard Vooris Mary Rhine, his wife	Mary Eliza- beth	In house of Cornelius Vanderbilt, the girl's step-father
1834. b. April 1.	Same as above	Julia Parmer	
1837. Sept. 2. July 27.	Cornelius Vander- bilt Mary, his wife, late Vooris, maiden n. Rhine	Elijah Rhine	
Oct. 13. June 7.	Johann Ruppinger Catharine Frieder- ica Rengaten, his wife	Catharine Friederica	Christian & Barbara Mann, Johannes & Maria Essig
Dec. 25. 1835. June 3.	John Widsworth Elizabeth Wids- worth	Margaretha Ann	The parents
1837. Dec. 25. July 1.	Leonard Fountain Mary Widsworth, his wife	Elizabeth Ann	The gr.-parents John & Elizabeth Wids- worth, & Mary Fountain, the mother
1838. Feb. 1. 1837. May 26.	Carl A u g u s t e Frende Augusta Caroline R u d i n g e r, his wife	Mary Blanche	

DATE	PARENTS	CHILD	SPONSORS
1838.			
May 9.	Abraham E. Miller	George Al-	
1837.	Jane Simonson, his	bert	
Oct. 1.	wife		
1838.			
Dec. 25.	William Egbert	Catharine	
1835.	Mary Ann Lake,	Ann	
April 25.	his wife		
1838.			
Dec. 9.	Cornelius Egbert	Henrietta	
July 2.	Catharine Lake, his		
	wife		

"During the Year 1838 Br. Ronshaler baptized several children belonging to other churches, these were of course entered in the church book of their respective churches."

DATE	PARENTS	CHILD	SPONSORS
1839.			
March 21.	Jacob Burckerdt	Anthon	
1838.	Teresa Schutzen-	Friederich	
Nov. 16.	bach, his wife		
1839.			
Jan. 6.	Ambr. Rondshaler	Edward	
1838.	Matilda Caroline	Henry	
Nov. 30.	Busse, his wife		
1839.			
March 21.	Isaac Butler	Mary Cath.	
1837.	Martha Swain, his		
Aug. 31.	wife		
1839.			
March 21.	William Crips	John	
1837.	Jane Butler, his		
Sept. 6.	wife		
1839.			
March 26.	Oliver Vanderbilt	Sarah	
1837.	Catharine Ann, his	Louisa	
May 12.	wife		
1838.			
Feb. 9.	John Egbert	John	
1837.	Lydia Seguine, his		
Oct. 8.	wife		
1839.			
March 26.	John Van Duzer	Daniel	
1838.	Sarah Vanderbilt,	Theodore	
Sept. 23.	his wife		
1839.			
March 31.	Cornelius Vander-	Oliver H.	
Feb. 25.	bilt		
	Mary, his wife, late		
	Vooris [nee Rhine]		
March 18.	James Thompson	Samuel	Bp. in house of John
1838.	Charity Rome, his	Lewis	Baker, the uncle of
Sept. 10.	wife	Ryess	child

DATE	PARENTS	CHILD	SPONSORS
1839.			
April 23.	Daniel Butler	Tunis Eg-	Bp. in house of Mr.
1838.	Elisabeth Egbert,	bert	Edw. Vanderbilt
Sept. 26.	his wife		
1839.			
April 23.	Edward Johnson	John Ed-	Bp. as above
1838.	Hannah Housman,	ward	
March 22.	his wife		
1839.			
April 23.	EdwardVanderbilt	Cornelius	Bp. as above
1838.	Mary Ann Egbert,	Egbert	
July 7.	his wife		
1839.			
April 28.	Ferdinand Thun	Margaretha	Martin and Sophia
Jan. 14.	Jacobina Small, his		Schmidt
	wife		
April 29.	Anthony Y. Stewart	Sarah Eliz-	
1838.	Mary Lipincott, his	abeth	
March 3.	wife		
1839.			
April 29.	James Gilbert	Elizabeth	
1838.	Abigail Black, his	Frances	
Sept. 4.	wife		

BAPTISMS BY H. G. CLAUDER.

DATE	PARENTS	CHILD	SPONSORS
1839.			
June 9.	Lawrence H. Cor-	Eugene	The parents
1838.	telyou	Augustus	
Dec. 2.	Eliza Hekel, his		
1839.	wife		
Sept. 26.	Joseph Sharrott	David Mer-	
1838.	Cornelia Mer-	cereau	
April 16.	cereau, his wife		
1839.			
Oct. 11.	William Egbert	Mary Eliza-	Bp. in house of parents
March 21.	Mary Elizabeth	beth	in North Quarter.
	Lake, his wife		Sponsors, parents
			& gr.-mother
Nov. 10.	Abraham Bodine	Abraham	Bp. at parsonage,
Feb. 28.	Abby Kinsy, his	Brown	parents sponsors
	wife		
Dec. 18.	Edward Egbert	Ester Ellen	The parents
1837.	Hannah Price, his		
Aug. 31.	wife		
1839.			
b. July 10.	Same parents	Caroline	The parents & Miss
		Atkins	Atkins of N. York
1840.			
Jan. 28.	John Baker	James	James Romer & wife,
	Eliza Romer, his	Henry	gr.-parents, at
	wife		whose house bap-
			tism took place

DATE	PARENTS	CHILD	SPONSORS

1840.
April 23.
1839.
Sept. 22.
	Moses Alston
	Sarah Ann Decker,
	  his wife
		Sarah Ann	Bp. at house of gr.-
			  mother Sr. Ann
			  Decker at Long
			  Neck

1840.
June 21.
1839.
Sept. 6.
	Peter Hibbets from
	  N. Y.
	Catharine Merrile
		Euphemia	Parents & gr.-mother
			  sponsors

1840.
Aug. 16.
	J o h a n n Martin
	  Lutz
	Christina Rokere,
	  his wife
		Christiana	Gallus Gahner of N.Y.,
			  Catharina Lutz &
			  the parents

Aug. 29.
1839.
Sept. 7.
	Jacob F r e d e r i c
	  Jakle of Wurtem-
	  burg, Germany
	Eva Maria Sicking
		Carolina
		Louise	

1840.
Oct. 1.
1837.
Oct. 25.
1839.
b. Dec. 1.
	James Romer, Jr.
	Sarah Maria Lewis,
	  his wife
	
	Same parents
		Sarah Jane
		
		James Isaac
			The gr.-parents James
			  Romer, Sr., & his
			  wife, at whose house
			  ch. was bap.

1840.
Oct. 18.
Aug. 31.
	Cornelius Vander-
	  bilt
	Mary R h i n e, his
	  wife
		Lydia Ann	The parents

Nov. 18. 1841.	Edward Beatty A n n Denice, his wife	Ellenor Louisa	The parents

Jan. 8.
1839.
April 10.
1841.
	C a p t. Cornelius
	  Vanderbilt
	Sophia Johnson, his
	  wife
		George
		Washing-
		ton
			The parents, ch. bap.
			  at house of parents
			  at Quarantine

April 11.
Feb. 21.
	Rev. H. G. Clauder
	Charlott Elizabeth
	  Ruede, his wife
		Henry
		Theophil-
		us, 4th son
			J o h n Gottlieb Her-
			  man, Anna Pauline
			  Herman of Bethle-
			  hem, Pa., Louisa C.
			  Kranisch, s i n g l e,
			  Lydia B e n z i e n,
			  single, both of Beth-
			  lehem, Pa.

April 11.
Feb. 21.
	Rev. H. G. Clauder
	Charlotte Elizabeth
	  Ruede, his wife
		Charlotte
		J a n e, 4th
		dau., twin
		of H e n r y
		Theop.
			Chas. A. B l e c k &
			  Sophia, his wife of
			  N. Y., Lawrence H.
			  & wife Eliza Cor-
			  telyou of S. I., Sr.
			  Jane Matilda Car-
			  gile, single, of N. Y.

DATE	PARENTS	CHILD	SPONSORS
1841. June 27. 1840. Dec. 21.	John Vanduzer Sarah Vanderbilt, his wife	Elisabeth Ann	Bp. in house of John Vanderbilt
1841. June 27. 1840. Dec. 3.	Jacob Van Duzer Mary Holden, his wife	Mary Louisa	
1841. June 30. 1840. Sept. 8.	Oliver Vanderbilt Catharine Morris, his wife	Edward Ward	Mrs. Ward of N. Y., & the parents. Bp. at parents' house at Quarantine
1841. Oct. 18. 1840. July 28.	(James)Thompson, ship carpenter at Quarantine Charity Romer, his wife	Joseph Lake	James & Ann Romer
1841. Nov. 7.	Adam Fugel, Catharine Thum, his wife, both of Wurtemberg, Germany, now at Castleton	Hans Jorg	Hans Jorg Fritz & wife, Maria Wolfen & the parents
Dec. 25. Nov. 30. 1842.	Lawrence H. Cor- telyou Eliza Hekkel, his wife	David Hekkel	The parents. Living at Freshkill
Jan. 2.	Abraham Bodine Abby, his wife	Sarah Ann Kinsey	The parents
Jan. 16. 1841. July 4.	Martin Schmidt, a German farmer now near Capt. Connor's Wife not given	Louis	The parents, Louis Göntz, single
1842. Jan. 30. 1839. April 19. 1841. b. July 24. 1842.	Edward Burbank Jane Britton, his wife	EdwardEg- bert Sarah Ann	The gr.-parents Isaac & Sarah Burbank, at whose house ch. was bap.
Feb. 8.	Joseph Decker Sarah, his wife	Amanda Malvina	The parents
March 6. Jan. 4.	Ferdinand Thum Jacobina "	Christina	Adam Wagener,Chris- tina Bisbalin, his wife
March 18. 1841. July 25.	Paul Schmidt Catharine Miller, his wife	Eliza Bar- rett	The parents, residing at Factoryville

2A

DATE	PARENTS	CHILD	SPONSORS
1842.			
March 27.	Anthony Stewart	William	The parents
March 8.	Mary "	Thomas	
1840.			
b. March 28.	Same parents	Julia Ann	
1842.			
March 27.	W i l l i a m Neats, wheelwright Di., his wife	John Rich- ard Shelton	Bp. at house of Anthony Stewart
July 24. 1840. Oct. 6.	Joseph Sharrott C o r n e l i a Mer- sereau, his wife	Catharine Eliza	The parents. Bp. at minister's
1842.			
Aug. 1. 1841. June 3.	William Egbert Catharine, his wife	Henry	The parents, residing on North Side
1842.			
Sept. 2. Aug. 19.	Theodore O. Sier- sina Meda Lenting, his wife	Marianne Emily	The ch. was evidently near its last & was bp. in house of parents
Sept. 5. Jan. 3.	John Baker Eliza Romer, his wife	Mary Ellen	Bp. in house of E. Johnson
Sept. —. March 11.	Edward Johnson Hannah Housman, his wife	Richard	"
Nov. 18. Aug. 30.	Wm. Neats, wheel- wright at North- side, & wife	Sarah Fran- ces	The parents
Sept. 18. 1840. Sept. 18.	Wm. De Groot Mary Sharrott, his wife	Lenah Ann	The parents, living at North side
1842.			
Oct. 9. 1840. July 29.	Philip Leiser Hetwig, his wife	Ernst Franz	The parents, living at Factoryville
1842.			
Oct. 28. 1841. Jan. 20.	J a m e s Gibett of N. Y. Abigail Ann Black, his wife	James Augustus	Both this ch. & fol- lowing bp. in ch. on S. Island
1842.			
Oct. 28.	Wm. Julin, residing at 80 Oliver St., N. Y. Sarah Jane Stewart, his wife	James Thomas	
Nov. 6. March 7.	Daniel Butler Eliza "	Daniel	

DATE	PARENTS	CHILD	SPONSORS
1842.			
Nov. 28. Aug. 28.	Abraham Garrett-son Eliza Sanders, his wife	John Jacob	
Dec. 10. 1841. Dec. 14. 1843.	Barney Hughes & wife	George Washington	Residing in Jersey City where he has a situation in R. R. office
Jan. 17.	James Brittain Frances Oakly, his wife	Elizabeth Ann Violetta Harriet Amanda	Grocer & shoemaker in this vicinity
	All ch. of same parents	Mary Theresia	
May 16. Feb. 11.	John Rathyen Anna Rotsen, his wife	Mathin, inf. son	Bootmaker at Pt. Richmond
June 18.	Robert Sommers, carpenter Susan Ann "	Robert Gray	Parents sponsors
July 22. 1840. Sept. 11. 1843.	Jo n G. Lake Violetta Spear, his wife	Mary Gifford	Bp. at house of John G. Lake. Parents sponsors
b. Jan. 19.	Same parents	Adriana Britton	
Sept. 10.	Adam Fugel Catharine Thum, his wife	Michael	
Sept. 27.	T. O. Siersina Meda "	Unatais	
Oct. 20. Sept. 30.	Wm. Julin, residing in N.Y. Sarah Jane Steward	Hanna Ann Elizabeth	
	Richard Housman, Jr., & wife Martha, late Butler, nee Swaim	Alfred	This ch. & one above bp. in house of widow Steward
Nov. 12. May 16. 1844.	J. Thompson Charity Romer, his wife	James	Ship carpenter at Tompkinsville
Jan. 6.	James Pollworth, farmer near the Blackhorse, from Berkshire, Scotland	William & Peter	
Jan. 31. 1843. Jan. 7.	Edward Egbert Hannah Price, his wife	Henrietta Prall	Bp. at house of Joseph Lake, Manor

DATE	PARENTS	CHILD	SPONSORS
1844.			
Feb. 4.	H. G. Clauder	Sarah Ade-	Rev. D. Bigler & Ade-
1843.	Charlotte Elizabeth	laide	laide, his wife,
Nov. 20.	Ruede, his wife		maiden name Fin-
			auf, of N. Y., Br.
			Isaac Burbank, Sr.
			Burbank, nee Eg-
			bert, Sr. Lydia Rice,
1844.			wid., of Bethlehem
March 31.	Anthony Stewart,	Samuel	Bp. at Parents' house
Feb. 29.	brushmaker		near Abr. Egbert's.
	Mary "		The parents & Br.
			& Sr. Clauder
April 14.	Capt. Jacob H. Van-	Ellen	Bp. in presence of
1838.	derbilt, residing		Mrs. Charlotte De-
July 30.	at Tompkinsville		forest Egbert & Miss
	Maria Banta, his		Phoebe Vanderbilt
1841.	wife		
b. July 28.	Same parents	Jacob Ellis	
1844.			
April 28.	Peter Cozine	James Ed-	The parents & Eliza
Jan. —.	Hannah Maria Van-	ward	Ann Vanderbilt
	bilt, his wife		
May 5.	James Wood	Mary Ann	Bp. in church
March 16.	Emily Britton		
May 26.	George Schmidt,	Magdalena	The parents & Magda.
1842.	tailor & draper at		Schmidt, single, dau.
Dec. 14.	Tompkinsville		of Martin Schmidt
	Barbara Heusler,		
1844.	his wife		
July 6.	Alexander Boyd,	Margaret	
May 8.	laborer at Col.	Ann, Re-	
	Connors	beccaJane,	
	Rebecca Mc Nab,	twins	
	his wife		
1844.			
Aug. 5.	Joseph Romer	Sarah Jane	Bp. in house of Br.
	Jane Moore, his		John Sharrott. Par-
	wife		ents sponsors
Sept. 10.	Oliver R. Martin	Sarah Ann	These five children are
1839.	Sarah Ann Vander-		gr.-grandchildren of
b. 29 Sept.	bilt, his wife		Br. John & Eliza-
1844.			beth Vanderbilt &
b. March 5.	Same parents	Oliver Rollin	baptized at their
1839.			house
b. July 25.	Henry Flagler	John Walter	
1841.	Isabella Vander-		
b. Dec. 19.	bilt, his wife	Constance	
1844.		Maria	
b. May 26.	Henry & Isabella	Isabella	
	Flagler		

DATE	PARENTS	CHILD	SPONSORS
1844.			
Sept. 15.	Abraham Bodine	Jacob	
April 8.	Abby Ann Kinsy, his wife	Howard	
Sept. 23.	Paul S c h m i d t, laborer at Factoryville	Catharine	
Jan. 6.		Christiana	
	Catharine Schmidt		
Oct. 13.	Robert Summers, carpenter in this vicinity	Albert	
	Susan Ann Stilwell		
Nov. 8.	James Armstrong of Ireland, farmer & laborer, residing on this Island	Amelia	
Oct. 7.			
	Rose, his wife		
Nov. 16.	Augustus Saddler of Port Richmond	Mary Elizabeth	The mother, Sr. D. Neat, Sr. Ann Neat
June 16.	Ann Eliza		
Dec. 29.	Cornelius Egbert	Louisa	Parents & gr.-mother
June 25.	Catharine Lake, his wife		
1845.			
March 4.	Ernst Senne,	Charles	The parents & August Senne, single
1844.	G e s i n e Schiegel,	Henry	
Dec. 28.	his wife, both of Germany	Augustus	
1845.			
March 30.	T. O. Siersema	Phoebe Ann	The parents
1844.	Meda Leiting, his		
Oct. 10.	wife		
1845.			
May 21.	Wandel Baker	Susan &	
	Betsy Haughwout, his wife	Mary	
June 8.	George W. Blake	Emily Anna	
Jan. 16.	Mary Ann Wood, his wife	Christopher	
June 17.	Barney Hughes of Jersey City	Ellen Jane	Bp. in parents' dwelling. Parents sponsors
1843.			
Dec. 30.			
1845.			
July 13.	Joseph Corron	Alfred	
1843.	Jane Burgher, his		
May 31.	wife		
1845.	Ch. of above parents	Nicolas	
July 13.	Abraham Stewart	Mathias	
	Mary Ann Burger, his wife	Burger	

DATE	PARENTS	CHILD	SPONSORS
1845.			
July 24. April 1.	John Baker, mason, near Pt. Richmond Elizabeth Romer	John William	
Aug. 24. 1844. Nov. 21. 1845.	William Wilson, residing in N. Y. Catharine Ann Noble, his wife	Abraham Noble	The parents & gr.-parents, Abr. Noble
Sept. 25. 1841. Jan. 25. 1842.	Jacob Fred. Jackle at Factoryville Eva Maria Jackle	Maria Catharine	
b. Dec. 28. 1845.		Emma Amalia	
b. 16 Jan.	All ch. of above parents	Jacob Frederick	
Nov. 17. July 1.	Mathias Swaim Margaret Jane Egbert, his wife	George Abraham	The parents
Nov. 20. June 17.	James G. Britten Frances Oakley, his wife	George Washington Oakley	The parents
Nov. 23. July 19.	John Mills of Tompkinsville Eliza Egbert, his wife	Moses Newel	The parents & gr.-mother Mrs. Mary Mills
Nov. 23. 1842. Nov. 26. 1845.	Robert Johnston, seaman at Tompkinsville Adaline Holden, his wife	Clara Holden	The mother & her sister Mrs. Jacob Vanduzer
b. 17 May.	Same parents	Robert Clyde	
Dec. 30. April 20.	Richard Conner, Junr. Ann Smith, his wife	Dewitt Clinton	The parents
1846. Feb. 5.	Oliver Vanderbilt, of Tompkinsville Elizabeth Morris, his wife	James Oliver	
Jan. 9. 1845. Oct. 21. 1846.	John Rathyen at Port Richmond Anna Rothen, his wife	Henry	The parents & Henry Gans
Feb. 11. 1842. March 1. 1845.	Thomas Holmes Egbert Elizabeth Ann Merril, his wife	John Merril	Bp. at parents' house, North side
b. 14 June.	Same parents	Elizabeth Mary	

DATE	PARENTS	CHILD	SPONSORS
1846.			
March 27.	Adam F u g e l of	Maria Cath-	
1845.	W u r t e m b e r g,	arine Bar-	
Nov. 25.	Germany, now at	bara	
	F a c t o r y v i l l e,		
	Staten Island		
	Catharine S h u m,		
1846.	his wife		
April 8.	T. O. Siersema, re-	John Theo-	The parents & John
1845.	siding near Edw.	dore	Siersema, unmd.
Nov. 6.	Bodine's in the		
	Manor		
	Meda Lenting, his		
1846.	wife		
May 24.	William W i n a n t,	George	
1845.	carpenter	Henry	
Sept. 1.	Hannah B u r g e r,	Tyson	
	his wife		
1846.			
June 7.	Oliver R. Martin at	Chauncy St.	The gr.-parents, Br.
Jan. 25.	Port Richmond	John	J o h n & Priscilla
	Sarah Martin		V anderbilt
April 2.		Georg Cor-	
		telyou	
Aug. 16.	Robert Summers	George	
Jan. 18.	Susan A n n Still-	James	
	well, his wife		
Aug. 19.	J o h n Perine, of	Richard	T h e gr.-mother, at
1845.	New York	Taylor	whose house ch. was
Oct. 2.	R e b e c c a Jane		bap.
1846.	Lewis, his wife		
Aug. 19.	James Romer	Mary Eliza-	
1844.	Sarah Maria Lewis,	beth	
March 25.	his wife		
1845.			
b. July 22.	Same parents	Thomas	
1846.		Simpson	
Aug. 30.	Alexander B o y d,	Mary	
July 21.	laborer		
	Rebecca M c N a b,		
	his wife		
Aug. 31.	Abr. S. E g b e r t,	Henrietta	Bp. at house of Mrs.
Jan. 23.	hackman		L y d i a E g b e r t,
	Eliza Bird, his wife		Tompkinsville
Aug. 31.	Wm. Vroome	Georgianna	
April 15.	Catharine M a r i a		
1845.	Egbert, his wife		
b. 22 Oct.	Jacob Arnold, shoe-	Maria Louisa	
	maker, & wife Su-		
	san Ann, late Bird		
	nee Perine		

DATE	PARENTS	CHILD	SPONSORS
1846.			
Oct. 11. April 12.	Paul Schmidt, lab- orer, Catharine, his wife, both from Ger- many	Jacob Ed- ward	Parents & Jacob Stoll
b.April 22.	John Kirtche Elizabeth	Henry	The parents. Both these reside at Fac- toryville
Oct. 20. June 30.	William Maines Ellen Baker, his wife	David Wooley	Residing at North shore
Oct. 25. 1845. Oct. 24.	John V. Vanduzer, Junr. Frances Louisa Roff, his wife	Sarah Catharina	The parents & Sr. Sarah Vanduzer
1846. Nov. 4. Oct. 16.	Abraham Bodine Abby Kinsy, his wife	James Ed- ward	The parents, at whose house at 4 corners the ch. was bap.
Nov. 7. Oct. 16.	David Mersereau of Richmond Anneke Lake, his wife	Marieta Gifford, 1st ch.	.
Nov. 22. Oct. 15.	Henry G. Clauder Charlotte Eliza- beth, his wife	Ottelia Vir- ginia	Bp. in ch. on Sunday by her father
Dec. 6. July 6.	William Julin, sailor Sarah Jane, his wife	Catharine Maria Stewart	Bp. at house of An- thony Stewart
Dec. 6. Oct. 11.	Anthony Stewart Mary "	George An- thony	" "
1847. Feb. 5. 1846. Dec. 4.	Ernst Senne Kissine Schiegel, his wife	LouisaMar- garetha Christiana	Living at Northfield when baptism was administered
1847. April 4.	John Mills of Tomp- kinsville Eliza Ann Mills	Mary Eliza- beth Van- derbilt	
April 25. 1846. Oct. 12.	William Wilson, re- siding in N. Y. Catharine Noble, his wife	Grace Noble	
1847. July 23. May —.	Abraham Van- duzer, residing at Quarantine Eliza Vanderbilt, his wife	Sarah Eliz- abeth	

DATE	PARENTS	CHILD	SPONSORS
1847.			
Oct. 3.	Joseph Decker,	Theodore	
July 25.	blacksmith	Hampton	
	Sarah Fitzgerald,		
1848.	his wife		
April 9.	George Fritz at	Henrietta	Conrad Barton, Elisa-
1844.	Factoryville	Elisabeth	beth Schlect
Jan. 13.	Anna Maria Wolf,		
1848.	his wife		
April 23.	Peter Cozine	Mary Pris-	
March 6.	Hanna Maria Van-	cilla	
	derbilt, his wife		
July 30.	John Biaron, form-	Henry	
1847.	erly of Easton,		
Aug. 31.	Pa., now at Fac-		
	toryville		
	Caroline Weiden-		
1848.	miller, his wife		
Aug. 3.	Raymond Augustus	Ellen Ma-	Bp. at parsonage in
June 7.	Dominge of N.Y.	tilda	presence of the gr.-
	Ellen, his wife		mother Mrs. Dun-
			ham
Aug. 17.	John Rathyen of	Anna	
July 15.	Port Richmond		
	Ann Rathyen		
Sept. 17.	Jacob Schneider, at	Anna	
1844.	Factoryville	Emilia	
Aug. 18.	Maria Clara		
1848.	Schneider		
Sept. 28.	Isaac M. Brown	Charles	Bp. at dwelling of Br.
1847.	Mary Romer, his	Henry	James Romer at
June 8.	wife		North side
1848.			
Oct. 6.	Wm. Vroome, re-	Maria	Bothe these ch. bap.
Aug. 22.	siding at Quaran-	Louise	at the house & in
	tine		the presence of their
	Catharine Maria		gr.-mother Lydia
	Egbert, his wife		Egbert
Oct. 6.	Abrm. S. Egbert of	Madora	
1847.	Tompkinsville		
Nov. 28.	Eliza Bird, his wife		
1848.			
Oct. 15.	Thomas Sharrott	Thomas	The parents & gr.-
Sept. 20.	Mary Elizabeth	Howard	mother Mrs. Mary
	Voorhis, his wife		Vanderbilt, at whose
1849.			house ch. was bap.
Jan. 21.	Louis Geiser,	Johannes	John Walter, single,
1848.	Maria Kollman, his		the parents
Dec. 24.	wife, natives of		
	Germany, now at		
	Pt. Richmond		

DATE	PARENTS	CHILD	SPONSORS
1849.			
April 8.	Paul Schmidt of	George	The parents, George
1848.	Factoryville	Sommers	Sommers, Margt.
Nov. 13.	Catharine Schmidt	Marks	Baltzer
1849.			
b. Jan. 29.	Adam Fugel	John	The parents, John
	Catharine Fugel		Schlect, Ros. Rapp

These two ch. were bp. at D. Ref. Ch. at Pt. Richmond, by H. G. Clauder

July 29.	Ernst Senne,	Amalia	Alke Marg. Schiegel,
April 26.	Gesiene Senne, Germans	Sophie Matilda	Sophie Lange, Louise Senne

Bp. in D. Ref. Ch. at Pt. Richmond

July 29.	Theodore Siersema	Frederick	
	Meda Siersema	Henry	
July 29.	John Mills, carpenter	Gilbert Tunis Egbert	
	Eliza Ann Egbert, his wife, deceased		
Aug. 30.	Abraham S. Egbert,	William St.	
April 3.	coachman, son of Jon, residing at Tompkinsville	Clair	
	Eliza Bird, his wife		
Sept. 6.	Mathias Burger	John	
1847.	Hetty Vanderbilt,		
Dec. 11.	his wife		
1849.			
Sept. 9.	John Rathyen,	Anna	The parents, Anna
Aug. 3.	Anna, his wife, Germans at Port Richmond		Reiners, mother, Anna Reiners, daughter
Sept. 9.	Wm. Mains	Elizabeth	
April 23.	Ellen Baker, his wife	Virginia	
Oct. 21.	John Housman &	Martha	Residing near 4 Corners
1845.	his wife Susan	Jane	
Aug. 29.	Ann [Houghwout]		
1849.			
Oct. 21.	Abraham Bodine	Benjamin	This ch. & above one
Jan. 7.	Abby Ann "	JohiaKinsy	were bap. at house of Abr. Bodine
Nov. 18.	Johann Fisher,	Johann	The father & John
May 13.	Christina Rothfus, his wife, Germans		Rothfus, single
Dec. 17.	Benjamin Lydle &	Gilbert Osborne	Residing at Richmond
1843.	wife Ann, late Pierson, formerly Fredericks		
Aug. 24.			
1849.			
b. June 30.		Wm. Wallace	
1847.	All ch. of above		
b. Nov. 21.	parents	MaryElizabeth	

DATE	PARENTS	CHILD	SPONSORS
1849.			
Dec. 24. 1838. Jan. 31.	John Johnson, boot & shoemaker at Quarantine Adelaide Eggers,	Anna Maria	Christian Block, Anna Mary Leating
1850.	his wife		
Jan. 7. 1843. May 17. 1848.	Wm. Egbert at Grantville Mary Ann Lake, his wife	Joseph	
b. March 6. 1850.	Son of same parents both members of our congregation	Wesley	
March 31. 1849. Sept. 27. 1850.	Henry Prall of Port Richmond Elizabeth Neats, his wife	William Henry	
March 31. 1849. Sept. 27. 1850.	Wm. Neats at Port Richmond Di Neats	Lester Palmer	
March 31. 1849. Nov. 25. 1850.	Anthony Stewart, brushmaker Mary Stewart	Mary Alina	
June 5. 1847. Oct. 6. 1849.	John Vanduzer Louisa Roff, his wife	Ellen Louisa	
b. Dec. 24. 1850.	Abrm. Vanduzer Eliza Ann Vanduzer	Sarah Elizabeth	Both these ch. bp. at house of Sr. Sarah Vanduzer at Tompkinsville
July 7. April 12.	Christian Block Rebecca Kniep, his wife	Henry Christn. Ludwig	
Aug. 11. April 30.	Wm. B. Seawood at Pt. Richmond Ann Neats, his wife	Eva Harrison	The parents & Miss Elizabeth H. Palmer of N. Y.
Sept. 11. May 8.	John Bieran of Factoryville Caroline Weidmuller, his wife	Elizabeth	
Oct. 20. Aug. 15.	James B. Wood Emily Britton, his wife	Henrietta	
Jan. 6.	"Garrit Vroome, a *single* young man & [son of Christopher Vroom] Maria Housman *his wife* was baptized into the death of Jesus"		
Jan. 20.	Mathias Burger, md., son of Mathias Burger & Hannah, his wife		

DATE	PARENTS	CHILD	SPONSORS
1849.			
Nov. 18.	Martha Hauseman, late Butler, nee Swaim, wid.		
1850.			
Dec. 15.	John Christian,	Heinrich,	
Aug. 30.	Margaret Ahrens, Germans at Port Richmond	infant	
Nov. 10	John Simonson Catharine, his wife	Catharine, & Ellen, wife of John V. Egbert	
Dec. 29.	John Schlect,	Catharine	Paul & Cath. Schmidt
May 7.	Rosina Raff, his wife, Germans,		
1851.	near Factoryville		
Jan. 12.	John V. Egbert	Louisa Sid-	
1844.	Ellen [Simonson],	ney	
July 11.	his wife		
1847.	Same parents	John Sim-	
b. Nov. 3.		onson	
1851.			
Jan. 26.	John Düringer,	John Henry	The parents, John
1850.	miller		Herman Kniper,
Sept. 16.	Nancy Lubers, his wife		first mate on steam-er Washington, &
1851.			Heinrich Ohl
April 13.	Christopher	Mary Ann	
1830.	Vroome & wife		
April 13.	—— Housman		
1851.			
June 21.	John V. Egbert	Abraham	
Jan. 31.	Ellen Simonson	Tunis	
June 26.	John Oldfield, re-	George	
1847.	siding in Troy,		
Sept. 16.	formerly in N. York		
	Martha Levinia		
1851.	Merril, his wife		
b. July 7.	Same parents	Egbert	
June 29.	John Hatsche & his	Elizabeth	Elizabeth Schmidt,
	wife, at Factory-ville	Georgiana	George Hatsche
Aug. 26.	August Kiesele,	Louisa	John Lambert, Eliza
1845.	Tompkinsville		Schoenberg, George
b. Sept. 12.	Louisa Julia Dimp-		Louis Dimpfel,
1847.	fel		Augustus Plessing,
b. April 28.		Emilie	Elizabeth Dimpfel,
1849.			Emilie Plessing
b. Sept 18.		Lilia	
1851.	All ch. of above	Augusta	
b. July 22.	parents	Eliza Anna	

(To be continued.)

THE KNICKERBOCKER FAMILY.

By William B. Van Alstyne, M.D.

The Knickerbocker family of New York, rendered famous by the genius of Washington Irving, has never to our knowledge been printed in genealogical form. This we now endeavor to do for the first four or five generations. Pains have been taken to secure accuracy and authorities are given for most statements. Traditions are current in the family concerning its origin and history in Holland, but these the writer, not finding leisure to verify them, has omitted. He has encountered many early spellings of the name of the family, such as Knikkerbakker, Knikkelbakker, and Knikkenbakker, but has adhered to the present spellings, Knickerbacker and Knickerbocker. Authorities differ as to the origin of the name Knickerbocker. William Arthur (*Derivation of Family Names*, p. 177) derives it from knacker, a cracker, and backer, a baker; while Edward M. Smith (*History of Rhinebeck, N. Y.*, p. 174) derives it from knikker, a marble, and bakker, a baker. Consensus of opinion favors the latter explanation.

Harmen Jansen Knickerbocker, the ancestor of the family, came to this country from Holland prior to 1683 and settled at Albany, N. Y. Occasionaly he added the termination Van Wie to his name indicating that he came from Wie, the present Wyhe, a few miles south of Zwolle, in the Province of Overyssel, Holland.

In 1683, Harman Jansz Knickelbacker and Lysbet Harmensz were members of the Dutch Reformed Church at Albany (*Year Book, 1904, of the Holland Society of New York*, p. 5).

On 6 May, 1684, Harmen Jansen Knickerbocker deeded land in Albany to Mews Hogeboom (Book 531, *Public Records of Albany Co.*). On 2 June, 1688, Peter Schuyler received a grant of land in Dutchess County near Red Hook. In 1689 he sold one-half of one-fourth of the patent to Harme Gansevoort of Albany, the fourth laying north of a line due east from a point on the river opposite the south end of Slipstein Island, the small island north of Cruger's. On 1 May, 1704, Gansevoort sold his moiety to Harme Jans Knickerbocker. In 1722· Schuyler divided the upper fourth of his patent into thirteen lots, seven of which he deeded to Lawrence, Cornelius, Evert and Pieter Knickerbocker of Dutchess County, Anthony Bogardus of Albany, and Jannetje, his wife, Jan Vosburgh of Dutchess County, and Cornelia, his wife, sons and daughters of Harmen Janse Knickerbocker, late of Dutchess County, deceased (Smith's *History of Rhinebeck, N. Y.*, pp. 23, 80).

In April, 1698, the Earl of Bellomont succeeded Fletcher as Governor; in July he made a journey in great state to Albany and Schenectady, staying two weeks in the former and two days in the latter place, "My Lady" accompanying him. Among the

3

items of expense were "£1 17s. to Harme Janse Knickerbacker for his Waggen and horses to Shinnectady" (Jonathan Pearson's *History of the Schenectady Patent*, p. 283).

On 16 March, 1706–7, the brothers, Daniel and David Ketelhuyn "of the city of Albany," bought of Harme Janse Knickerbacker, "late of the county of Albany," for one hundred and eighty-four pounds and ten shillings, "each one equall half of all that certain tract or parcel of land . . . on the west side of Hudson's river above the land commonly called the Half Moon, being about four English miles above the farm or boundary of Gerrit Hendrickse, which said land begins at the kill or creek that runs into Hudson's river between the Wijhe Vlackje and the said Harme Janse's house, and from thence along the river, on the west side of Hudson's river, and strikes from the river westward into the woods on the south and along the north side of the said kill or creek so as the same runs until you come to the high hills, which said hills run along the fly of the Half Moon and stretch as far as Sarachtogue; and on the north side from the northern end of the said Stonje Island with a direct west line into the woods till you come to the said high hills aforesaid." On 20 March that year, Daniel Ketelhuyn sold his share in this tract to his brother David, for one hundred and one pounds and five shillings (Deeds, book F, No. 6, pp. 3, 41, in the office of the Clerk of Albany County).

In 1711 Harmen Knickerbocker deeded lands in the south part of Amenia, N. Y., to Cornelius Knickerbocker (Isaac Huntting's *Little Nine Partners*, p. 366).

The will of Harmen Jansen Knickerbacker "of Dutchess County, in Province of New York," was made 17 Jan., 1707–8, and recorded in Albany County Wills, Lib. 1, p. 175. In it he mentions wife Elizabeth and "my seven children," namely, Johannes, Lourens, Cornelis, Evert, Peter, Jannetje Lansing, widow of Hendrick Lansing, junior, and Cornelia Knickerbacker; "eldest son Johannes." The will is written in Dutch and mentions real and personal estate. Executors: wife and sons Johannes and Lourens. Witnesses: Jan Ploeg and Pieter Pile.

In 1723 the widow of Harmon Knickerbacker residing in Dutchess County was taxed five pounds and five pence (Smith's *History of Rhinebeck, N. Y.*, p. 45).

1. HARMEN JANSEN[1] KNICKERBOCKER, m. about 1681, Lysbet Janse Bogaert, b. in 1659, in Holland, dau. of Jan Laurensen Bogaert and Cornelia Evertse. Jan Laurensen Bogaert with his wife and two children, seven and four years old, came from Schoonderwoerd, a town in South Holland, in the ship *Spotted Cow*, 16 April, 1663, and it is probable that Lysbet was born there. Harmen Jansen Knickerbocker died prior to 1722, and his widow was living in Dutchess County in 1723. All of their children were born in this country, probably at Albany, where the younger children were baptised.

2   i. Johannes,[2] b. in the Colony of Rensselaerwyck; m. 19 Oct., 1701, at Albany, Anna Quackenbos.

3   ii. Lourens, m. about 1707, Marike Dyckman.

4   iii. Jannetie, b. in the Colony of Rensselaerwyck; m. (1)
            22 March, 1704, at Albany, Hendrick Lansing, Jr.;
            m. (2) 6 March, 1709, at Albany, Anthony Bogardus.
      iv. Cornelis, bap. 2 Sept., 1688; spon.: Jacob Cornelisz
            and Jannetje Jacobsz; d. y.
5   v. Cornelis, bap. 6 Jan., 1692; spon.: Takel Dirksz and
            Aaltje Van Esch; d. 30 March, 1776, at Sharon, Conn.;
            m. about 1721, Johanna Schut.
6   vi. Cornelia, bap. 21 July, 1695; spon.: Evert Van Esch
            and Cornelia Bogart; m. about 1715, Jan Vosburgh.
7   vii. Evert, bap. 3 Sept., 1699; spon.: Evart Ridder and
            Antje Ridders; m. 23 May, 1725, at Albany, Geertruy
            Vosburgh.
8   viii. Pieter, bap. 19 April, 1702; spon.: Wouter and Antje
            Quakkenbosch; m. 1725, Neeltjen Freer.

2. JOHANNES HARMENSEN[2] KNICKERBOCKER (Harmen Jansen[1]),
m. 19 Oct., 1701, at Albany, Anna Quackenbos, dau. of Wouter
Pietersen Quackenbos* and Neeltje Gysbertse. Johannes and
his bride were born and living in the Colony of Rensselaerwyck.
   On 10 July, 1708, the Common Council of the city of Albany
announced the conditions on which the eight plantations on the
south side of Schaghticoke Creek would be assigned to the ap-
plicants accepted by the corporation. Each farm, as determined
by the municipal authorities, was to comprise twenty-five morgens, or fifty acres, of low or meadow land under the hill by the
creek, and five morgens, or ten acres, of upland, toward the said
hill, and all to lie connectedly together in a tract. Twenty
persons severally desired to be assigned one. In order to avoid
partiality in the assignment of the plantations, the clerk of the
Common Council was ordered to prepare eight billets, severally
bearing the number of the farm to be conveyed, and twelve blank
ones, and place them in the mayor's hat, and let each one draw
one, which was accordingly done. Johannes Harmense Knickerbacker was a successful applicant (Arthur J. Weise's *Swartwout
and Ketelhuyn Chronicles*, pp. 543, 544).
   On 22 Nov., 1712, Johannes Barentsen Bratt exchanged twelve
morgens of land with that of Johannes Harmense Knickerbocker,
that particular part of his farm, on the west side of Tamhenick
Creek, for an equal quantity of land on the east side of that
stream (above authority, p. 553).
   12 Nov., 1709, Johannis Knickerbocker granted to Martin
Dellemont five morgens of land at Schaghticoke (deed recorded
1 Feb., 1717–18, Public Records of Albany County, book 5, p. 386);
22 Nov., 1712, he granted to Daniel Ketelhuyn twelve morgens of
land at Schaghticoke (deed recorded 1 Feb., 1717/18, above
authority, book 5, p. 387); 2 July, 1735, he granted to Johannes
Christianse eighteen morgens of land on Anthony Kill, Albany
Co. (deed recorded 22 Feb., 1782, above authority, book 10, p. 311),

---

* Wouter Pietersen Quackenbos of Albany, N. Y., m. (1) Neeltje Gysberts
m. (2) 4 Oct., 1696, at Albany, Cornelia Bogaert, dau. of Jan Lourensen Bogaer
and Cornelia Evertse.

and 9 July, 1737, he deeded to Neeltje Bradt and John Schuyler land on the east side of Hudson River, in the Manor of Rensselaerwyck (deed unrecorded). The following children were baptised at Albany:

9   i. Lysbet,* bap. 1 Nov., 1702; spon.: Harmon and Lysbeth Knikkelbakker; m. 8 Feb., 1725, at Albany, Sybrant Quackenbos.

     ii. Neeltie, bap. 30 June, 1706; spon.: Wouter Quakkenbosch, Jr., and Neeltje Quakkenbosch; d. 1775, unm. Neeltje Knickerbacker of Schaghtakakock, Albany County, made her will 26 March, 1775; proved 9 Oct., 1775, and recorded at Albany. In it she mentions Dirk T. Van Veghten and son Teunis, Cornelia, dau. of Igenas Kip, and her brother Teunis, Annatje, wife of Igenas Kip, and Annitje, wife of Lewis T. Viele, and her dau. Maria, Elezibeth, wife of John Fort, Neeltje, dau. of Harme Quackenbush, Annaitie Viele, dau. of Johannis Knickerbacker, and Margrita, dau. of Dirk T. van Veghten. Executors: Johannis S. Quackenboss and Dirck T. van Veghten (Fernow's *Calendar of Wills*, p. 228).

10   iii. Harmen, bap. 25 Dec., 1709; spon.: Kiliaan and Maria Van Rensselaer; d. 18 Sept., 1768, at Schaghticoke; m. about 1745, Rebecca De Wandellar.

11   iv. Wouter, bap. 19 Oct., 1712; spon.: Wouter and Cornelia Quackenbosch; d. 8 Aug., 1797, at Saratoga, N. Y.; m. 9 Jan., 1735, at Albany, Elizabeth Fonda.

12   v. Cornelia, bap. 21 Oct., 1716; spon.: Antony and Jannetie Bogardus; m. 29 Feb., 1744, at Albany, Teunis Van Vechten.

13   vi. Johannes, bap. 24 March, 1723; spon.: Nicol. and Maria Groesbeek; d. 16 Aug., 1802, at Schagticoke; m. 17 Feb., 1750, at Albany, Rebecca Fonda.

3. LAURENS² KNICKERBOCKER (Harmen Jansen¹), m. about 1707, Maryke Dyckman, b. about 1688, dau. of Johannes Dyckman* and Jannetie Viele. A curious chain of evidence leads to the location of Maryke Dyckman. She appears in 1724 at Linlithgo, N. Y., as Maritje, in 1731 at Germantown, N. Y., as Marike, in 1741 at Athens, N. Y., as Marytje, and in 1747 at Germantown, as Mariken, the full maiden name in no case being given, but on

___

* Johannes Dyckman, b. 1662; m. Jannetie Viele, dau. of Cornelis Cornelisen Viele and Suster, his wife, of Schenectady, the latter supposed to have been a Mohawk Indian woman. On 10 April, 1676, his mother bound him out to Major Abram Staats (Notary Papers, vol. I, p. 556). He was son of Johannes Dyckman and Maria Bosyns. Johannes Dyckman had been "first clerk" to the West India Company, he came out in 1651 and served as clerk and commissary at Fort Orange of Albany, but in 1655 was laid aside by insanity (Riker's *History of Harlem*, p. 545). He d. in Sept., 1672, and his wife, Maria Bosyns, in 1676. They had two children, Cornelis, b. 1647, who m. Jannetie, dau. of Dirck Claessen Pottbacker and Wyntie Roeloffs, and became the ancestor of the Bloomingdale branch of the family, and Johannes, b. 1662. Johannes was son of Joris Dyckman and Aeltie Poulus Root of Amsterdam, Holland.

5 Oct., 1766, Domine Fryemont received into the membership of the Dutch Reformed Church at Red Hook, N. Y., from the church on the Flatts "Louwrenz Knickerbocker and wife Maryke Dyk." Extensive research shows only one other occurence of the name of Dyk, namely when Jacob the five months old son of "Hannes and Engel Dyk" was baptised 19 April, 1738 at Athens. Hannes and Engel previously had children baptised at Linlithgo, but he is there called "Johannes Dyckman, Jr." Therefore it is evident that Dyk is equivalent to Dyckman. On the 24 Feb., 1723, Johannes Dyckman and Jannetje Dyckman, "echtelieden," or married people, became church members at Linlithgo. Johannes Dyckman m. Jannetje, dau. of Cornelis Cornelisen Viele of Schenectady, N. Y., and from her received land at the All Platts on which they lived but two years when the French and Indian massacre of 1690 happened. Cornelis Cornelisen Viele suffered great loss, for among the killed were his dau. Mary, the wife of Dowe Aukes, with her two children, and Mary Aloff, the wife of his son Cornelis; Arnout Viele, his grandson, was carried off alive to be held a captive for three years, but his dau. Jannetje with her husband and child escaped to Albany, later going to Dutchess County, but in 1715 removing to the Manor of Livingston. Johannes and Jannetje Dyckman had a son Johannes, bap. 11 May, 1690, at Albany, who m. Engel ——, and left descendants who settled at or near Linlithgo, N. Y., and a dau. named after her father's mother, undoubtedly born on the All Platts prior to the massacre and destined to become the wife of Laurens Knickerbocker, singularly her full maiden name only appearing once and then under the the the form of Maryke Dyk.

In 1715 Lawrence Knickerbocker was a member of a military company organized and under review at Oak Hill (*Claverack, N. Y., Centennial*, p. 45). An oath of abjuration and fealty was required to be taken by office holder in Dutchess County in 1729. Lowerens Knickerbacker, captain, was one of the signers (Edmund Platt's *History of Poughkeepsie, N. Y.*, p. 24). In 1723 he was taxed eighteen pounds and eighteen shillings (Smith's *History of Rhinebeck, N. Y.*, p. 45). He was a justice in 1735 (Platt's *History of Poughkeepsie, N. Y.*, p. 25). In 1750 he lived on Magdalen Island, an island in the Hudson River between the upper and lower Red Hook landings. The will of Elbert Harmensen Lieverse of New York City, lime burner, dated 15 June, 1750, proved 11 Oct., 1752, and recorded in Abstracts of Wills at New York City, vol. 18, p. 196, mentions his "wife's niece Catharine, the daughter of Lourens Knickebacker of Magdalen Island." The relationship is explained by the fact that Elbert Harmensen Liverse's wife Catharina Bogaert, and Lourens Knickerbocker's mother, Lysbeth Bogaert, were daus. of Jan Laurensen Bogaert and Cornelia Evertse. Catharina Liverse stood as one of the sponsors when her niece Catherine was bap. 19 Oct., 1731, at Germantown. In 1766 John Vosburgh and Cornelia, his wife, Lawrence Knickerbocker and Hans Jury Loundert, all of Rhinebeck precinct, in Dutchess County, of the one part, and Anthony Hoffman, of Kingston, Ulster County, and Zacharias

Hoffman of Rhinebeck, of the other part, agree to divide a certain tract of land lying adjacent to the south of the manor of Livingston, apparently belonging to them in common (Smith's *History of Rhinebeck, N. Y.*, p. 80).   Lourens Knickerbocker and Maryke Dyckman had the following children but their order is unknown:

- 14   i. Benjamin,' m. Aletteka Halenbeck.
- 15   ii. John, b. 1710; d. 10 Nov., 1786; m. (1) about 1732, Jacomyntje Freer; m. (2) 22 Feb., 1751, at Sharon, Conn., Jemima Owen.
- 16   iii. Harmen, b. 1712; d. 19 Aug., 1805; m. (1) about 1737, Catrina Dutcher; m. (2) Elizabeth ——.
- 17   iv. Elizabeth, d. 23 April, 1793, at Dover Plains, N. Y.; m. about 1739, Gabriel Dutcher.
- 18   v. Pieter, m. 17 Sept., 1742, at Kingston, N. Y., Marjerie Ben (Bain).
- 19   vi. Cornelis, m. about 1746, Eleanora Ben (Bain).
- 20   vii. Jannetje (Johanneke), b. 5 Nov., 1721; d. 18 March, 1799; m. 27 Dec., 1743, Silas Beldin.
-    viii. ——tje, a daughter, bap. 17 Oct., 1724, at Linlithgo; spon.: Jan and Tyssje Decker.
- 21   ix. Maritjen, m. 24 May, 1748, at Salisbury, Conn., Ruliff White.
- 22   x. Catherine, bap. 19 Oct., 1731, at Germantown; spon.: Martinus Hofman and Cathryn Luysze; m. 17 Sept., 1762, at Claverack, N. Y., William Van Alstyne.

4. JANNETJE' KNICKERBOCKER (Harmen Jansen'), b. in the Colony of Rensselaerwyck; m. (1) 22 March, 1704, at Albany, N. Y., Hendrick Lansing, Jr., b. there, son of Hendrick Gerritsen Lansing* and wife Lysbeth; m. (2) 6 March, 1709, at Albany, Anthony Bogardus, bur. there 14 April, 1744, son of Pieter Bogardus and Wyntje Cornelise Bosch (dau. of Cornelis Teunisen Bosch and Maritie Thomase Mingael).   Children bap. at Albany, except Wyntje, who was bap. at New York City, as follows:

- 23   i. Lysbeth,' bap. 5 Aug., 1705; spon.: Johannes Knikkelbakker and Lysbeth Lansing; m. 1722, Egbert Bratt.
-    ii. Wyntje, bap. 1 Sept., 1710; spon.: Elbert Harmense and Tryntje Van Brugh.
-    iii. Marya, bap. 10 Feb., 1712; spon.: Johannes and Annetjen Knikkerbakker.
-    iv. Pieter, bap. 21 May, 1716; spon.: Pieter and Sara Van Brugh.
-    v. Cornelia, bap. 3 Aug., 1718; spon.: Joannes Van Vegten and Susanna Bratt.
-    vi. Cornelia, bap. 11 Oct., 1719; spon.: Joannes and Anna Van Vegten.

---

* Hendrick Gerritsen Lansing was son of Gerrit Fredericksen Lansing from Hassell, near Swoll, in Overyssell, Holland, and Elizabeth Hendricks, who m. 2d Wouter Van Den Uythof of Albany, baker. Van Den Uythof m. again 14 Oct., 1691, Elizabeth De Lint, widow of Jacob Meesz Vrooman.

vii. Evert, bap. 10 June, 1722; spon.: Joh. Schoonmaker and Wyntje V. Vegten; bur. 23 July, 1746, at Albany.
viii. Anna, bap. 17 Feb., 1725; spon.: Jisse and Neelt Foreest.

5. CORNELIS[2] KNICKERBOCKER (Harmen Jansen[1]), bap. 6 Jan., 1692, at Albany, N. Y.; d. 30 March, 1776, at Sharon, Conn.; m. prior to 1722 Johanna Schut, probably dau. of Myndert Schut[*] and Sara Persen, bap. 7 March, 1697, at Kingston, N. Y.

In 1711 Harmen Knickerbocker deeded land in the south part of Amenia, N. Y., to Cornelius Knickerbocker, who in 1743 was living in Salisbury, Conn., on a farm which in 1748 he exchanged with Capt. John Sprague for land on Gay street north of Sharon near a pond called Knickerbocker's Pond, now Beardslee Pond (Isaac Huntting's *Little Nine Partners*, p. 366).

A tax assessment in Dutchess County in 1723 shows that Cornelius Knickerbacker was taxed eleven pounds and eleven pence (Smith's *History of Rhinebeck, N. Y.*, p. 46).

On 14 May, 1743, Cornelius Knickerbocker was one of the interpreters between the Indians Cabrickset and Tasawight, who were called to locate landmarks in the outline survey of Little Nine Partners made by Charles Clinton. In November Clinton and his men prepared to correct his Livingston "random line." They left the south bend of the Roelof Jansen for Nackawawick, the east end of the Livingston line, and spent the night at Cornelius Knickerbocker's who lived in that neighborhood. Again Knickerbocker was of service by helping show the Indian bounds of Nackawawick (Huntting's *Little Nine Partners*, p. 28).

Children of Cornelis Knickerbocker and Jonanna Schut:
　　i. Elisabeth,[3] bap. 7 Jan., 1722, at Kingston, N. Y.; spon.: Jonas de Longe and Blandina Peersen.
24　ii. William, m. Abigail ——. It is not proved that William belongs to this family, but the birth of his two daughters in Sharon, Conn., one being named Hannah, are suggestive of such a connection.
　iii. Johannes, bap. 22 May, 1731, at Saugertis (Katsbaan), N. Y.; spon.: Martinus Hoofman and Maria Schot.
　 iv. Debora, bap. 18 April, 1738, aged 9 months, at Athens, N. Y.; spon.: Hannes Knickerbocker and Jacomyn, his wife.
　　v. Cornelia, b. 20 Feb., 1740; bap. at Athens; spon.: Phil. Kuntz and Mar. Lis., his wife. She may have m. 12 May, 1765, at Sharon, Conn., Josiah Pettit. Josiah Pettit of Sharon and Rebekkah Ford of Amenia, N. Y., were m. 27 Aug., 1767, at Sharon.

---

[*] Myndert Schut m. before 16 Nov., 1694, Sara Janse Persen, dau. of Jan Hendricksen Persen and Annetje Matthys of Fort Orange, Albany. Annetje Matthys was dau. of Matthys Jansen Van Keulen and Margaret Hendricks of Fort Orange and Esopus. Myndert Schut owned a patent north of Malden in Ulster County. He was son of Willem Jansen Schut.
William Jansen Schut of Shawangunk, N. Y., m. Grietie Jacobs. In his will dated 6 May, 1706, proved 4 June, 1722, and recorded at Kingston, N. Y., he left his son Myndert 100 gulden.

6. CORNELIA[3] KNICKERBOCKER (Harmen Jansen[1]), bap. 21 July, 1695, at Albany, N. Y.; m. prior to 1716 Jan Vosburgh, son of Jacob Vosburgh and Dorothea Janse Van Aalsteyn. In 1723 he lived in Dutchess County and was taxed eleven pounds and eleven pence (Smith's *History of Rhinebeck, N. Y.*, p. 45). On 17 Oct., 1724, Jan and Cornelia Vosburgh became members of the church at Linlithgo, N. Y.; on 7 Sept., 1753, they joined the Dutch Reformed Church of the Flatts, near Nether Rhinebeck, N. Y., and on 5 Oct., 1766, were received into the membership of the Dutch Reformed Church at Red Hook, N. Y. In 1732 Jan Vosburgh was a supervisor in Kipsbergen, Dutchess County (Smith's *History of Rhinebeck, N. Y.*, p. 47). In 1755 John Vosburgh of the Precinct of Rhinebeck owned three slaves (above authority, p. 50).

Children of Jan Vosburgh and Cornelia Knickerbocker:

    i. Jacob,[4] b. 7 June, 1716; bap. 18 June, 1716, at West Camp, N. Y.; spon.: Peter and Gertroud Vosburg.

25   ii. Catharine, m. 30 Dec., 1747, at Rhinebeck, Jacob Hermans.

26   iii. Dorothea, m. Volkert Witbeck.

    iv. Everth, bap. 1735, at Germantown, N. Y.; spon.: Everth Knickerbocker and Maria Decker.

27   v. Marten, bap. 29 July, 1738, at Linlithgo; spon.: Reier Schermerhorn and Geertje Ten Eyck; m. 1766, Cornelia Gilbert.

7. EVERT[3] KNICKERBOCKER (Harmen Jansen[1]), bap. 3 Sept., 1699, at Albany, N. Y.; m. there 23 May, 1725, Geertruy Vosburgh, dau. of Jacob Vosburgh and Dorothea Janse Van Aalsteyn. In 1723 he resided in Dutchess County and was taxed seven pounds and seven pence (Smith's *History of Rhinebeck, N. Y.*, p. 46). In 1755 Capt. Evert Knickerbacker of the Precinct of Rhinebeck owned a slave named Maria (above authority, p. 50).

Children of Evert Knickerbocker and Geertruy Vosburgh:

28   i. Elisabeth,[4] bap. 21 Aug., 1726, at Linlithgo, N. Y.; spon.: Lour. Knickerbocker and Cath. Vosburgh; m. 12 June, 1747, at Rhinebeck Flatts, N. Y., Petrus Heermance.

    ii. Dorothe, bap. 29 June, 1729, at Kinderhook, N. Y.; spon.: Martin Hofman and Catrina Vosburgh; m. (1) 9 Nov., 1750, at Germantown, N. Y., her cousin Peter Martense Vosburgh, son of Marten Vosburgh* and Eytje Van Buren. In the marriage record she is called "Carlotta," but this is evidently meant for Dorothea. On 21 Oct., 1757, "Peter Martense Vosburgh and wife Dorothea Knickerbacker" joined the church at Linlithgo. She m. (2) before 1775 Dirck Wesselse Ten Broek, bap. 1 May, 1715, at Albany; d. on his bowery and was interred in the family

* Marten Vosburgh was baptised 31 Jan., 1697, at Albany; m. there 21 Oct., 1719, Eytje Van Buren, bap. 7 Nov., 1700, at Albany, dau. of Pieter Martensen Van Buren and Ariaantje Barents. Marten was son of Jacob Abrahamsen Vosburgh.

cemetery, eldest son of Samuel Ten Broek and Maria
Van Rensselaer. Dirck Wesselse Ten Broek m. (1)
28 June, 1743, at Kinderhook, Catharina, dau. of
Leendert Conyn and Emmetje Jannetje Van Alen,
and she was mother of his children. Dorothea
Knickerbocker appears to have had no children by
either of her husbands. "Dirck Ten Broek and
Dorothea Knikkebakker, his wife," stand as sponsors
for Dirck, son of Andreas Gardener and Barbel
Schmit, bap. 25 Dec., 1774, at Germantown. Ten
Broek several times represented the manor of Livingston in the Provincial Assembly. The Assembly
of New York, under the Constitution, was composed
of twenty-four members. They met at Kingston, 9
Sept., 1777, and the following month were dispersed
by the British troops. He was a member of this
session, as also of the second, which was held at
Poughkeepsie the year following. He continued to
to be Representative until 1783 (*History of Albany
and Schenectady Counties, N. Y.*, Howell & Penney,
p. 353). The bowery of his grandfather, Dirck
Wesselse Ten Broeck, with its tract of twelve hundred acres on the Roelof Jansen Kil, became his
property, partly by inheritance from his father, and
partly by purchase from the heirs of his uncle,
Tobias Ten Broek (*Ten Broek Genealogy*, p. 65).

29   iii. Cornelia, bap. 10 June, 1733, at Linlithgo; spon.: Jan
and Cornelia Vosburgh; m. 27 Feb., 1755, at Rhinebeck Flatts, her cousin, Isaac Vosburgh, bap. 5 Sept.,
1731, at Kinderhook; son of Pieter Vosburgh* and
Dirckie Van Aalsteyn.

8. PIETER[2] KNICKERBOCKER (Harmen Jansen[1]), bap. 19 April,
1702, at Albany, N. Y.; bans registered 16 May, 1725, at Kingston, N. Y.; m. Neeltjen Freer, bap. 15 May, 1696, at Poughkeepsie, N. Y., dau. of Abraham Freer and Echie Willems Titsoort;
m. 28 April, 1694, at New Paltz, N. Y. Pieter and his bride were
residents of Dutchess County.

Peter Knickabaker, labourer, was made a freeman in New
York City 15 May, 1740–1 (*Burgher and Freeman of New York*,
New York Historical Society Collections, 1885, p. 142).

On 12 April, 1774, the Common Council of the City of New
York ordered that "Peter Knickerbacker late a Cartman in this

------

* Pieter Vosburgh was bap. 22 May, 1686, at Albany; m. there 18 Feb.,
1717, his cousin, Dirckie Van Aalsteyn, bap. 26 May, 1695, at Albany, dau
of Lambert Jansen Van Aalsteyn and Jannetje Thomase Mingael. Pieter
was son of Jacob Abrahamsen Vosburgh.
    Jacob Abrahamsen Vosburgh m. Dorothea Janse Van Aalsteyn, dau. of
Jan Martensen, called "the Weaver," and Dirckien Hermans. Jacob and
Dorothea Vosburg were among the earliest church members at Linlithgo, N. Y.
Jacob was son of Abraham Pietersen Vosburgh, a carpenter and trader, and
owner of a saw-mill on Wynant's Kill, which he sold in 1674 to Wynant
Gerritsen Van Der Poel. In 1654, Pierson states that Abraham sent down 1,500
beavers.

City who is old and Infirm and unable to follow the Business of carting be Appointed to the Office of an Inspector of Cord Wood for the Coenties Slip, in the Room and Stead of Cornelius Van Horne, and he the said Peter Kniekerbacker is hereby Appointed to the said Office Accordingly, and that before he enter upon the Duties of said Office, he first take an Oath for the Due Execution of the same." (*Minutes of the Common Council of the City of New York*, vol. 8, p. 24.)

Pieter Knickerbacker and wife, Neeltie Freer, joined the church at Red Hook, N. Y., 30 Sept., 1775, with letters. Children:

    i. Elisabeth,⁸ bap. 29 May, 1726, at Kingston, N. Y.; spon.: Gysbert a Berg and Jannetjen Knickerbocker; d. young.

30 ii. Abraham, m. 28 Nov., 1754, at New York City, Geertruid Van Deusen. Abraham probably belongs to this family.

31 iii. Harmen Jansz, bap. 13 Jan., 1734, at Kingston, N. Y.; spon.: Jan Vosburg and Cornelia Knickerbocker; d. "1802;" m. 1777, Susanna Basson.

    iv. Elisabeth, bap. 7 Jan., 1739, at Kingston, N. Y.; spon.: Jacob Vosburg, Jr., and Dorothy Vosburg; probably m. 5 Nov., 1757, at New York City (license dated 2 Nov.), William Pasman.

(*To be continued.*)

INSCRIPTIONS IN MILLTOWN CEMETERY, SOUTHEAST, N. Y.

COPIED BY EMMA J. FOSTER AND JULIA R. LIVINGSTON.

(Continued from Vol. XXXVIII., p. 277, of the RECORD.)

Marvin, Rachel, wife of Nath'l Marvin, d. Nov. 27, 1810, aged 23 yrs.

Elizabeth, wife of Ichabod Marvin, d. Apr. 18, 1845, in the 60 year of her age.

Morris, Minerva, wife of Jachin Morris, d. April 25, 1831, in the 29 year of her age.

Thomas C., son of Jachin & Minerva Morris, d. Oct. 10, 1853, Æ. 23 yrs., 11 mo., & 2 ds.

Morehouse, Elizabeth, dau. of Andrew & Elizabeth Morehouse, d. July 22, 1839, aged 3 yrs., 3 mo. & 23 ds.

Northrup, Irving, d. Dec. 6, 1846, aged 4 mo. & 20 ds. Child of Wm. C, & Agnes Northrup.

Edwin, d. Dec. 9, 1846, aged 4 mo. & 23 ds. Child of Wm. C. & Agnes Northrup.

James, d. Oct. 4, 1855, aged 73 yrs., 2 mo. & 20 ds.

Susan, wife of James Northrup, d. Apr. 6. 1849, aged 63 yrs., 1 mo. & 14 ds.

Edwin, son of James & Susan Northrup, d. Feb. 16, 1812, Æ. 6 yrs., 18 ds.

Olmstead, Betsey, d. Sept. 29, 1836, in the 97 year of her age.
 James M., Born July 8, 1817, Died Oct. 5, 1847.
 Eunice, wife of James M. Olmstead, Born July 28, 1815, Died
  May 1, 1848.
 Polly, wife of Judson Olmstead, d. Sept. 23, 1854, in the 49
  year of her age.
 Nathan, departed this life, March 27, 1836, aged 55 yrs.
 Sally, wife of Nathan Olmstead, d. Oct. 29, 1854, aged 67 yrs.,
  10 mo. & 14 ds.
 Samuel H., son of Nathan & Sally Olmstead, d. Mar. 19, 1833,
  Æ. 21 yrs., 10 mo. & 14 ds.
 Ebenezer, d. Nov. 24, 1855, aged 46 yrs.
Paddock, David, d. June 21, 1818, aged 30 yrs.
 Electa, wife of David Paddock, d. Nov. 16, 1870, Æ. 76 yrs.
 Cyrus, son of David & Electa Paddock, d. Sep. 10, 1838, aged
  23 yrs., 6 mo. & 10 ds.
 David, son of David & Electa Paddock, d. May 25, 1818, aged
  8 mo. & 11 ds.
 Miriam, My Mother, d. Apr. 27, 1823, aged 79 yrs. & 11 mo.
 Anson, d. July 5, 1831, æ. 43.
 Lydia Langford, wife of Anson Paddock, Born 1792, Died 1873.
 Emily C., dau. Judah & Jane Paddock, d. Oct. 2, 1828, aged 2
  yrs., 9 mo. & 5 ds.
 Isaac, departed this life, June the 22nd, 1817, aged 25 yrs.
Palmer, Daniel, son of Joseph & Lydia Palmer, d. Apr. 2, 1841,
  Æ. 6 yrs., 5 mo. & 27 ds.
Penny, Darius, d. March 23, 1814, in the 42 year of his age.
Platt, William, d. May 26, 1839, aged 38 yrs., 5 mo. & 26 ds.
Purdy, Martha, d. Dec. 14. 1844, aged 20 yrs. & 6 mo.
 Mary, d. Feb. 3, 1844, aged 22 yrs. & 7 mo.
 William E., d. Aug. 7, 1843, aged 23 yrs. & 10 mo.
Raymond, Asa, d. March 31, 1846, aged 62 yrs., 3 mo. & 11 ds.
 Fanny, wife of Asa Raymond, d. Jan. 22, 1848, aged 60 yrs.,
  11 mo. & 16 ds.
Rice, Edward, d. Nov. 6, 1826, Æ. 61 yrs., 4 mo. & 4 ds.
 Lucy, wife of Capt. Edward Rice, d. March 23, 1826, Æ. 55
  yrs., 11 mo. & 7 ds.
 Henry, son of Capt. Edward Rice, d. Mar. 29, 1826, Æ. 22
  yrs., 1 mo. & 29 ds.
 Lewis, d. July 11, 1849, aged 53 yrs., 3 mo. & 6 ds.
Richards, Nathan, d. Feb. 15, 1839, aged 62 yrs.
 Cynthia, wife of Nathan Richards, d. Apr. 20, 1848, in the 72
  year of her age.
 Sally Betsey, dau. of Nathan & Cynthia Richards, d. Dec. 4,
  1844, aged 29 yrs.
 Ezra, d. Apr. 25. 1819, aged 68 yrs.
 Mary, wife of Moses Richards, d. July 4, 1868, Æ. 99 yrs.
 Moses, son of David B. & Delia Richards, March 11, 1833;
  March 11, 1839.
 Moses, d. March 3, 1824, aged 63 yrs.
 Abigail, wife of Charles F. Richards, d. March 23, 1825, aged
  25 yrs.

Rider, Nathan, d. Nov. 6, 1815, aged 25 yrs.
Ritch, John W., d. Aug. 16, 1841, in the 67 year of his age.
    Catharine, wife of John W. Ritch, d. Dec. 2, 1833, in the 49 year of her age.
    Delight, dau. of John & Catherine Ritch, d. Dec. 24, 1834, in the 26 year of her age.
Roberts, Selina, d. Oct. 22, 1837, in the 18 year of her age.
    Rufus, d. Aug. 10, 1825, aged 31 yrs.
    Benjamin, d. Nov. 16, 1823, aged 62 yrs. & 8 mo.
    Ruben, son of Benjamin & Abigail Roberts, d. March 12, 1814, aged 18 yrs.
Rockwell, Reuben, d. June 26, 1849, aged 80 yrs., 7 mo. & 21 ds.
    Cumphy, wife of Reuben Rockwell, d. Dec. 16, 1820, aged 50 yrs., 10 mo. & 26 ds.
    Esther, wife of Reuben Rockwell, d. Sept. 4, 1838, aged 59 yrs., 8 mo. & 22 ds.
    Rufus, d. Nov. 19, 1838, aged 26 yrs., 3 mo. & 21 ds.
    Clarissa, d. Oct. 27, 1818, aged 23 yrs. & 19 ds.
Rowland, Sophia, d. Aug. 6, 1820, aged 19 yrs., 10 mo. & 20 ds.
    Hezekiah, d. Apr. 29, 1819, aged 60 yrs., 3 mo. & 20 ds.
Russell, Ransom S., son of Ransom & Eunice Russell, d. Oct. 1, 1832, aged 4 yrs.
Sanford, Ahaz, son of Hezekiah & Betsey Sanford, d. July 21, 1813, aged 24 yrs. & 6 mo.
    Hezekiah, Esq., d. March 18, A.D. 1834, aged 72 yrs., 2 mo. & 12 ds.
    Zalmon, Esq., d. Apr. 30, 1809, aged 41 yrs., 8 mo. & 23 ds.
    Betsey, wife of Hezekiah Sanford, d. Aug. 22, 1844, aged 82 yrs., 9 mo. & 12 ds.
Sears, Seth, d. Aug. 2, 1809, in the 73 year of his age.
    Mary, wife of Isaac Sears, d. Apr. 11, 1821, aged 30 yrs.
    Isaac, son of Isaac Sears, d. Jan. 21, 1823, aged 2 yrs.
    Comfort, d. Dec. 24, 1827, aged 76 yrs.
    Eunice, wife of Comfort Sears, d. Jan. 23, 1839, aged 84 yrs.
    David H., d. Sept. 26, 1830, aged 35 yrs., 11 mo. & 7 ds.
    Isaac, d. Oct. 27, 1839, aged 67 yrs., 8 mo. & 25 ds.
    Priscilla, wife of Isaac Sears, d. Oct. 18, 1851, aged 72 yrs., 10 mo. & 21 ds.
    Samuel, d. Oct. 10, 1833, in the 57 year of his age.
    Phebe, dau. of Samuel & Phebe Sears, d. Apr. 6, 1819, aged 20 yrs.
    Deliverance, dau. of Samuel & Martha Sears, d. Sept. 25, 1819, aged 1 year.
    Benjamin, d. March 12, 1827, aged 90 years.
    Mary, wife of Benjamin Sears, d. May 26, 1814, aged 73 yrs.
    Heman, d. Aug. 18, 1817, Aet. 50.
Knowles, Capt., d. June 10, 1817, in the 79 year of his age.
    Seth & Rheumamah, The Graves of, he died May 1, 1819, Æ. 48, she died Dec. 9, 1813, Æ. 31.
    Ann Ophelia, dau. of Geo. E. & Mary Jane Sears, d. Aug. 31, 1841, aged 4 yrs., 9 mo. & 24 ds.
Selleck, Isaac, d. May 1, 1828, Aet. 66 yrs.

Selleck, Betty, wife of Isaac Selleck, d. Apr. 29, 1820, Aet. 51 yrs.
  Lucretia, dau. of Isaac & Betty Selleck, d. May 10, 1821, Aet. 32.
Smith, Nancy, Born April 21, 1788, Died March 15, 1850.
Stevens, Demmon, d. March 4, 1848, aged 61 yrs., 10 mo. & 26 ds.
  Rachel, wife of Demmon Stevens, d. Jan. 17, 1871, aged 80 yrs., 5 mo. & 21 ds.
Swords, Lebbeus, d. Oct. 20, 1848, Æ. 79 yrs. & 4 mo.
  Ruanah, wife of Lebbeus Swords, d. July 9, 1835, in the 70 year of her age.
  Eleanor G., dau. of Lebbeus and Ruamah Swords, d. Aug. 14, 1846, aged 35 yrs.
Townsend, Mary, dau. of Nancy Townsend, d. Aug. 1, 1834, aged 18 yrs. & 8 mo.
  Phebe,   e of Alonzo Townsend, d. Nov. 23, 1845, aged 36 yrswif
Trowbridge, Cornelia Ann, dau. of Phineas B. & Sally B. Trowbridge, d. Aug. 6, 1848, aged 17 yrs., 4 mo. & 5 ds.
  George P., son of Phineas B. & Sally B. Trowbridge, d. Apr. 15, 1845, aged 4 yrs., 8 mo. & 26 ds.
  William Henry, son of William C. & Mary E. A. Trowbridge, d. Jan. 12, 1840, aged 3 mo. & 28 ds.
  William, son of William C. & Mary E. A. Trowbridge, d. March 10, 1849, aged 5 mo. & 15 ds.
Turner, Mary, dau. of James & Betsey Turner, d. June 14, 1835, aged 15 yrs. & 4 mo.
Wanzer, Silvia D., wife of Henry B. Wanzer, d. Sept. 3, 1862, aged 24 yrs., 3 mo. & 13 ds.
Warring, Peter, d. June 27, 1849, aged 67 yrs., 6 mo. & 3 ds.
  Esther, wife of Peter Warring, d. July 16, 1831, Æ. 44 yrs., 7 mo.
Webb, Charles, son of Abraham & Polly Webb, d. Jan. 26, 1823, aged 10 yrs., 1 mo. & 21 ds.
  Abraham, d. Sept. 25, 1856, aged 76 yrs., 5 mo. and 12 ds.
Weed, Ithamar, Esq., d. Apr. 30, 1829, aged 73 yrs.
  Delight, wife of Ithamar Weed, Esq., d. Sept. 28, 1844, aged 83 yrs.
  Mary, dau. of Hart & Roxanna Weed, d. Feb. 14, 1807, aged 1 yr., also David, d. Dec. 2, 1808, aged 5 ds.
  Polly, dau. of Ithamar & Delight Weed, d. Feb. 2, 1819, aged 30 yrs.
  Elizabeth, d. May 8, 1832, Æ. 3 yrs., 10 mo. & 4 ds.
  William H., d. March 9, 1833, Æ. 2 yrs., 9 mo. & 14 ds.
  Pamela, d. Jan. 24, 1833, Æ. 11 mo. & 4 ds., three children of Hendrick & Polly Weed.
  Wm. Henry, son of Hendrick & Polly Weed, d. Sept. 26, 1828, Æ. 2 yrs., 7 mo. & 17 ds.
  Pamela, d. Feb. 16, 1809, in the 31st year of her age.
Wooster, George, son of John R. and Sally Wooster, d. July 23, 1829, Æ. 2 yrs., 11 mo. & 7 ds.
  Elizabeth Malvina, dau. of John R. & Sally Wooster, d. Dec. 14, 1840, aged 7 yrs., 3 mo. & 17 ds.

Wooster, Laura, wife of Sylvanus Wooster, d. July 19, 1812, aged
24 yrs.
Young, Archibald, d. May 14, 1822, aged 43 yrs.
Ava P., dau. of Archibald & Sophie C. Young, d. Sept. 29,
1819, aged 1 yr., 3 mo. & 14 ds.
Eber, Born July 4, 1798, Died Dec. 11, 1844.
Elkanah, son of Eber & Minerva Young, Born July 16, 1832,
Died March 21, 1835.

NEW YORK GLEANINGS IN ENGLAND,

Including "Gleanings," by Henry F. Waters, not before printed.

CONTRIBUTED BY LOTHROP WITHINGTON,

30 Little Russell St., W. C., London.

(Continued from Vol. XXXVIII., p. 206 of the RECORD).

George Forrester of the City of New York, Mariner. Will 4
August 1748; proved 14 February 1750/51. To William Holt of
New York, Vintner, my friend and executor, all shares in the
Sunderland, man of war, and the *Antelope*, privateer of New York.
Witnesses: Charles Gilmore, Peter van Vechter, John Bryant.

Busby, 45.

John Rush of New York in America, Hatter, and by God's
grace shall return thither again. Will 13 May 1743; proved 1
June, 1743. To my wife, now at New York, all my wearing
Apparell and Utensils and Stock in Trade that is now in my
possession in London, except the hatboxes, they to be sold and
the money to be sent her with £10 value in copper halfpence.
To Edward Daniel of Redmaid Lane, County Middlesex, Cooper,
£20. Rest to my son John and daughter Sarah when 21. Executor: said Edward Daniel. Witnesses: Ann Way, James Burn,
John Perry.

Boycott, 208.

Margaret White of East Greenwich, county Kent, Spinster.
Will 5 June 1766; proved 12 January 1767. All my copyhold
lands and Estate in Manor of Ealing otherwise Zeling, county
Middlesex, to my nephew Thomas White, son of my late deceased
Brother, Thomas White of Serjeants Inn, Esq. If he dies with-
out any issue, I give the said estate to my Nephew and two
Nieces, children of my late deceased Brother Francis White, who
are now living in New York in North America. To my servant
Martha Hopton, all my clothes, and £20. To my nephew
Thomas White, and Joseph Blisset £500 Old South Sea Annuity,
part of £800 standing in my name, in trust for my said servant
Martha Hopton. Residue and all reversions to said nephew
Thomas White, now living in Southampton. Executors: Nephew
Thomas White and Mr. Joseph Blisset of Six Clerks Office,
London, gentleman. Witnesses: A. Mole, Andw. Hatt, Walter
Vincent.

Legard, 31.

Enoch Stephenson, City of New York, Province of New York in America. Will 3 Febuary 1735/6; proved 1 December 1753. To my wife Catharine Stephenson, all my jewels, household goods, Negro Slaves, namely Maria and her son and daughter, Quaco and Sarah, Qua a negro Boy and Cato a negro girl. All the rest and residue of my estate real and personal to my wife Catherine Stephenson, and my children, viz: Enoch, Catherin, Isabella, John, and Richard, and to such child or children as may hereafter be born to me, share and share alike. If I die in New York, my executors to call in all my estates and to sell the house I b ugh of John Price, situated on Port Royal, Jamaica, and also two Lots of land I bought of David Jemison in King Street in Eastward part of New York. Executors and Guardians to my children: my wife Catherine, my brother Pennington Stephenson, at present residing in England, Peter Valet and Joseph Robinson, both of New York, merchants, and if my children should go to Jamaica during their minority, I appoint my friend Colln. Edwin Sandys their guardian there. Witnesses: Gulⁿ Verplanck, Abraham Van Horne, Junr., Willm. Hewtin.   Searle, 325.

Susannah Thurnam, widow and relict of Francis Thurnam, late of the City of New York, America, Merchant, deceased. Will 23 August 1758; proved 26 January 1760. To my daughter Elizabeth Thurnam all my wearing apparrell; if she die in infancy, between my two sisters in law, Elizabeth, wife of Nicholas Roosevelt, and Gertrug Thurnam, that is the silks and Linen, the calico and stuffs, to my Aunts Agnis Lockwood, wife of Joseph Lockwood, half, Grace Williams, wife of William Williams, one quarter, and Sarah Brown, wife of Isaac Brown, one quarter. My fee simple estates in England or America as follows: one half to my son Richardson Thurnam, and one half to my daughter Elizabeth. In case of death of both children without issue, I give four equal fifth parts to Brothers and sisters in law, Ralph Thurnam, John Thurnam, Elizabeth Roosevelt, and Gertrug Thurnam, and the remaining one fifth to my Uncle and Aunts, Joseph Lockwood, Grace Williams, and Sarah Brown. My leases in the City of London or elsewhere in England to my executors in trust for my son and daughter. Executors: Brother in law John Thurnam, of City of New York, Merchant, Nicholas Roosevelt, of the said City, Goldsmith, and Dirck Schuyler, of said City, Merchant. Witnesses: Thomas Pettit, Abraham Bussing, John McKesson. Proved by John Thurnam, reserving to the other executors.   Lynch, 40.

Mary Boudinot, living in parish of St. Giles in the fields, Middlesex, Spinster. Will 9 July 1712; proved 26 May 1716. To poor of the French Church called Greek Church one guinea. To my nephew Elias Boudinot, living in New York, one guinea, and to all his brothers and sisters one guinea each. To John Belin my nephew and to his daughter who is at Rotterdam one guinea. To James Belin, son of Allard Belin, my nephew, deceased, one guinea. To Mary Belin, my grandniece, daughter of Mr. James Belin and Jane Montague, the rent of 38 livres Tour-

nois French money upon a house at Marons Boat in the Province
of Xaintonge in France. To my grandnephew Allard Belin, mer-
chant in London, and to his sister Jane Mary Belin, £60 each.
Residuary Legatee and Executrix: My grandniece and god-
daughter Mary Belin, daughter of Mr. James Belin. Witnesses:
Stephen Brigand, Anthony Sion, Isaac Delpech, Not. Pub. 1712.
This is truly Translated out of French by me Isaac Delpech,
Notary Public.   Fox, 92.

Gilbert Burnet, Esquire, now in London, Eldest son of William
Burnet, late Governor of New York, deceased. Will 17 June 1762;
proved 21 June 1762. To my friend, Mrs. Jane Walton of Scotland Yard, Westminster, Spinster, all Interest Money now due to
me in Holland and America, or elsewhere, and all my personal
estate. To my son Thomas Burnet, now Apprentice to Mr. ——,
Apothecary, all the rest and residue of my real estate. Executrix:
said Jane Walton. Witnesses: Manuel Ielees, Richard Lovett,
Tolson Banting.   St. Eloy, 234.

Peter Wraxall, at present residing in City of New York. Will
10 September 1759; proved 13 February 1762. To my honoured
father and friend Mr. John Wraxall of Bristol in England £20.
To my sister Mrs. Ann Wraxall, by my father's first wife and my
own mother, £400. To my sister Mrs. Mary Wraxall of Bristol
£50. If Ann die before my decease, £300 of the above £400 to
my niece Elizabeth Wraxall, daughter of my Brother Richard
Wraxall, £100 to my said sister Mary. To my friend Sir William
Johnson, Baronet, £20. Life and Death are the indubitable
appointments of a Wise Righteous, and Benevolent God. To his
Mercy through the intercession and merits of my Lord and
Saviour Jesus Christ, I comitt my soul and my most beloved wife
and friend. I desire I may be buried without any kind of Ex-
pense which may border upon Ostentation. Executrix and
Residuary Legatee: Wife Elizabeth Wraxall. Secretary's Office
New York, 10 September, 1759. Anne Devisme, John Watts,
and Beverley Robinson, make oath to truth of depositions and
Elizabeth Wraxall is granted execution. [Signed] Geo: Banyar.
Anne Devisme, wife of Peter Devisme being a sister of Elizabeth
Wraxall, relict of Peter Wraxall.   St. Eloy, 86.

Sir Henry Moore of the Island of Jamaica, Bart, at this time
his Majesty's Governor in Chief of the Province of New York in
North America. Will 11 April 1769; proved 7 June 1770. All
my estates, real and personal in Jamaica and Great Britain, to
Henry Dawkins, Esquire, of Standlinch, County Wilts, Edward
Morant, Esquire, of Pilewell, County Hants, Edward Long,
Esquire, of Jamaica, sole Judge of the Court of Vice-Admiralty
in that Island, and John Gordon, Senior, of St. Mary's parish,
Jamaica, practitioner in Physic, in trust to pay my debts, and
then to my wife Catharina Maria Moore £600 per annum out of
my estate of Moore Hall, parish of St. Mary, as by marriage
indenture of 11 January 1750/51, and at her decease to my child,
John Henry Moore, and his heirs. To my daughter Susanna

Jane, now wife of Captain Alexander Dickson of H. M. 16th Regiment of Foot, £3000. Residue to my said son, whose guardian I appoint my wife Catharina Maria Moore. Witnesses: Fransis Child, Robt. Hull, Phil. Livingston, Junior.

Jenner, 237.

Christopher Billop, prisoner in the Fleet prison in the parish of St. Brides in the City of London, gentleman. Will 25 April 1724; proved 24 April 1725. My plantation in Bentley and Manor of Bentley and Mansion house, etc, in province of New York, upon Stratton Island I give to my daughter Mary, now wife of the Reverend William Skinner, Clerk, for life, and then to her heirs Male, in default to Christopher Farmar, second son of my son in law Thomas Farmar, he to pay £200 New York money to every daughter of said Mary Skinner, daughter Mary to leave to Christopher or whoever inherits, five good Feather beds, sheets, etc, curtains, and Vallences, pewter and woden ware for six people, Table linen, 5 pair Iron Dogs, five shovells and Tongs, five Chambers, Table in each romms. Seats used in that Country, Utensills for Dairy of ten Cows, Casks in Cellar for Cyder, four horses, six oxen fit for ploughs, ploughs, harness, etc, ten Milch Cows and Calves, three steers of three years old, four of two years, four Heifers of two years, ten yearlings a Bull of two years, ten Hogs of 12 months, two Sows and a Boar, 100 ewes and a Ram, Ten weathers of two years, and   , whoever inherits to take the surname [sic] of Billop without the mixture or addition of any other Surname whatever. If Christopher dies, to Thomas Farmar, third son; if he dies, to Brook Farmar, fourth son; if he die, to Robert Farmar, fifth son; if he die, to Samuel Farmar, sixth son; if he die, to William Farmar, seventh son. My plantation near Rareton River, known as Junions Land in province of New York to my daughter Anne Farmar, wife of said Thomas Farmar, and her heirs male excepting Jaspar Farmar, eldest son of said son in law Thomas Farmar, to whom I give only £20. Out of money due to me from Sr Alexander Rigby's, Knt, estate late deceased, amounting by this time to £5200, I give to Mr. James Fittar of London, Merchant, £200, and to my Nephew Thomas Billop of Deptford, county Kent, £500. To said William Skinner, clerk, £500. The residue after payment of my debts to the younger children of Thomas Farmar. To my Neice Hannah Booth, £50. Executors: James Fittar and Nephew Thomas Billop. Trustee: William Skinner. Witnesses: Tho. Frank, Wm Abell, Wm Abbott, John Baker, Edward Games. Memorandum 16 May 1724, Whereas but £20 given at first to Hannah, made £50 by testator. Witnesses, ditto.

Romney, 80.

Thomas Cooper of the parish of Matfellon als. White Chapel, county Middlesex, also Citizen and Merchant taylor of London. Will 1 February 1714/15; proved 1 February 1715/16. To my Brother Robert Cooper £125, a silver cup and silver poringer, also 15 shares in the Company for Smelting [written "selling" in first entries] down Lead with Pit Coal and Sea Coal, and after his decease 5 of the shares to Thomas Prigg, son of Robert and Anne Prigg, and 5 to Mary Payne his sister, wife of John Payne; also I give to him all money owing to me from John Fisher, Doctor in Colchester. To Thomas, son of Robert and Anne Prigg, deceased, 10 shares in aforenamed Company. To George Whitehead £5. To Thomas Pistow, Esquire, Hatter, £30. To Martha Collier, Wife of William Collier, Butcher, £10. To Elizabeth Bowing, wife of Edward Bowing of Boram, £5. To Ann Wilkinson, my servant, £5. To Thomas Pitstow, Esquire, and Mary Payne £40. To John Knight £10, all my shares in the said Company for Smelting down Lead and all my interest in the New Pensilvania Company, and all the rest and residue of my estate in England and New Yorke and East and West Jersey in America to Thomas Pitstow and John Knight, in trust for Mary Payne, wife of said John Payne. Executors: Thomas Pitstow and Mary Payne. Witnesses: Tho. Butler, Daniel White, Susanna Butler. Proved by the affirmation of the executors.

Fox, 22.

Ann Crookston, of the parish of Saint George in the East in the County of Middlesex, widow. Will 10 September 1750; proved 23 February 1753. To Eldest Son, Samuel Crookston of East Ham, Essex, Shipwright, 1s. To youngest son, John Crookston, now at Eastchester beyond the Seas, 1s. Rest to Granddaughter, Mary Ann Goadby, of St. George's, Spinster, executrix. Witnesses: Jane Armin, Jas Bennett.

Commissary of London,

Register No. 77 (1753–1754.)

William Mountgomery, late of New York. Will 1 September 1799; proved 16 July 1782. To loving friend, Margaret Mountgomery, daughter of Samuel Mountgomery, Merchant in Armagh, £50., if Mr. Andrew Thompson of Newry in Ireland has not paid the same, but if paid [not written above, sic] to trustees, etc. To Cousin, William Mountgomery, son to Mr. John Mountgomery, my silver watch, and after my brother Joseph, and James 2 bonds given up remaining part of rent and personal estate (except moities are in Mr. Lightbodys) to four brothers, John and Joseph, James and Robert Montgomery. If I die in Mr. Lightbodys' house, to Elizabeth Lgihtbody best bed etc. To Mrs. Agnes Lightbody 100 dollars, looking glass, candlestick, etc. To Margaret Mountgomery, daughter to Samuel Mountgomery, merchant in Armagh, my chinen bowel, not tricked, and diamond ring. Executors: Brothers, James and Robert Mountgomery. Witnesses: William Edmondson, Gabriel Lightbody. Will of said William Mountgomery, formerly of New York, but late of Newingdon Precinct in America. Proved by brother James of Armagh, executor, reserving to Robert.

Prerogative Court of Ireland,

Will Book No. 98 (1782), folio 68.

(*To be continued.*)

THE SKILLMANS OF AMERICA AND THEIR KIN.

By William Jones Skillman, Philadelphia, Pa.

(Continued from Vol. XXXVIII., p. 302, of The Record.)

99. Peter[6] Skillman (Gerardus,[5] Thomas,[4] Isaac,[3] Thomas,[2] Thomas[1]), b. March 5, 1787; d. April 29, 1831; m. Rebecca, dau. of Simeon Smith of near Mt. Airy, Hunterdon Co., N. J., (b. Oct. 13, 1783; d. Jan. 7, 1866); lived in Princeton. Children there born and reared, and the graves of nearly all are in the cemetery of that old college town.

  i. Ira,[7] b. 1807; d. May 1, 1835; m. Abigail ——. Had one dau., Irena Rebecca, d. Dec. 8, 1835, æ. 3 mos. and 8 ds.

  ii. Jared, b. 1810; d. Oct. 30, 1845; m. Eleanor, dau. of Thomas Benham, blacksmith, Princeton. Had: Rebecca, b. Nov. 10, 1844; d. Jan. 27, 1857. Widowed mother m. (2) Abraham Skillman (see No. 139), just returned from Ohio, where his first wife, Harriet Wainwright had d. in 1841, leaving six children; three more, Sarah, Daniel and Alice A. (now widow of George B. Carson, Somerville, N. J.) were added.

  iii. Charles, b. Jan. 23, 1812; d. May 7, 1855; m. Catharine, dau. of Thomas C. Thompson, of the old Mill at Kingston (see No. 8), then of Scudder's Mills, Mapleton (Aqueduct Mills). Had: 1. Fred'k V. D., b. July 13, 1844; enlisted Oct. 16, 1861, Comp. B, 1st N. J. V. I.; discharged for disability from wounds March 20, 1863; m. April 25, 1878, Sarah F. Renwick; Real Estate and Insurance, Jersey City. 2. Emma, b. June 7, 1866; m. Benjamin Spicer.

  iv. Peter, b. 1814; d. Oct. 3, 1847; m. Jane ——. Had: 1. Howard, b. Jan. 30, 1842; d. inf. 2. Ira, b. Sept. 19, 1844; d. young. Graves by their father's in Princeton cemetery.

  v. Maranda, b. May 26, 1817; d. 1839.

  vi. Eliza H., b. 1819; d. Dec. 17, 1890; m. James C. Burke; d. Dec. 1, 1884. Had: 1. William E., b. Oct. 2, 1850; druggist, Princeton; m. Kate W. Early, b. March 25, 1854; one son, Charles Lozier, b. Sept. 2, 1877; wife, Marian L. Turner, Brooklyn, N. Y., and their son, William L., b. Nov. 26, 1906. 2. James E., b. Aug. 9, 1854; d. Feb. 23, 1904; Savings Bank, Princeton; m. Annie Potts, Baltimore, b. Dec. 29, 1863; two children, Edmund P., b. Aug. 8, 1887, and Mary Early, b. May 9, 1890.

  vii. Rebecca, b. 1823-4; d. April 16, 1835.

  viii. Jacob Van Dyke, b. 1825; named for a maternal uncle; d. 1873, a farmer at Carlyle, Clinton Co., Ill. During the Civil War he and wife (no children) lived in St. Louis; she from Baltimore originally. Widow returned to St. Louis.

100. GERARDUS[6] SKILLMAN (Gerardus,[5] Thomas,[4] Isaac,[3] Thomas,[2] Thomas[1]), b. 1791; d. Dec. 28, 1864; m. (1) Mary Christie, d. Dec. 19, 1830; m. (2) Lydia Applegate (b. 1813; d. May 18, 1877). One of the best known citizens of Princeton, leading baker and confectioner there all his life; name Gerardus from Beekman ancestor, nearly always badly pronounced. Had twelve children, five by first wife, seven by second.

    i. Henry,[7] b. 1815; d. Dec. 11, 1831, æ. 16.
    ii. Edwin, b. 1818; d. Jan. 7, 1825; æ. 6 yrs., 11 mos.
    iii. Theodore, d. in young manhood; widow removed to Buffalo, N. Y.
    iv. Margaret, b. 1825(?); d. June 13, 1881.
    v. Amanda, b. 1828(?); d. April 7, 1886. These two sisters made their life home in Princeton, and their names are both on a single stone in the cemetery.
    vi. Kate, b. 1836(?); m. Rev. Gershom H. Nimmo, minister (Presby.) at Hartsville, Bucks Co., Pa., where he d. March, 1898.
    vii. Elizabeth, m. John Barclay, New York.
    viii. Garreta, unm.; no record.
    ix. Jane, unm.; no record.
    x. Nettie, b. Aug. 27, 1846; m. T. C. Jones; d. at Chanute, Neosha Co., Kansas, Sept. 15, 1879.
    xi. Gerardus, salesman in Maginnis' Bookstore, Princeton, 1876; no further record.
    xii. Mary Virginia, d. inf., May 15, 1856; buried in Princeton Cemetery.

101. MARY[6] SKILLMAN (Thomas,[5] Thomas,[4] Isaac,[3] Thomas,[2] Thomas[1]), b. Feb. 22, and bap. April 11, 1779, in Harlingen Ref. Dutch Church; m. John M. Nevius, probably of the seventh generation from Johannes Nevius, a schepin of New Amsterdam. Petrus, a grandson of the latter, a farmer, removed from Flatbush, L. I., to New Jersey, *circa* 1740, with four children, Peter P., Martin, David (see 95) and Wilhelmina. John M. was son of Martin Nevius and wife Sarah Stothoff. Family home was at Blawenburg. There were six children, all bap. at Harlingen.

    i. Sarah[7] Nevius, b. March 11, 1802; d. unm.
    ii. Eliza Ann Nevius, b. May 25, 1805; m. 1823, John Hartough; d. at home of son-in-law George Kershaw, at Harlingen.
    iii. Martin Nevius, b. Jan., 1809; lived at Ringoes, N. J.; m. (1) Ann Andrews; no issue; m. (2) Lizzie Kirkpatrick, dau. of Rev. Jacob Kirkpatrick, pastor (Presby.) from 1810 till his death in 1866 of the Ringoes Church at Pleasant Corners (now Larisons). Had one son.
    iv. Mary Nevius, b. Nov. 15, 1810; m. Peter Stryker of Blawenburg (see 44).
    v. Joanna Nevius, b. Sept. 15, 1815; never m.

vi. Catharine Nevius, b. May 8, 1821; m. James Van Zandt, one of the substantial farmers of Blawenburg.

102. HENDRICK[6] SKILLMAN (Thomas,[5] Thomas,[4] Isaac,[3] Thomas,[2] Thomas[1]), b. May 12, bap. May 28, 1780; d. 1849; m. Dec. 21, 1803, Heyltje Williamson; lived in the old homestead at Rocky Hill. Had:

i. Elizabeth,[7] b. Oct. 13, 1804; m. March 31, 1821, John A. Voorhees. Children: 1. Abraham, b. Sept. 27, 1822. 2. Henry, b. Oct. 8, 1823. 3. Sarah, b. March 21, 1828. 4. John, b. May 15, 1830. 5. Martin, b. Oct. 24, 1834. 6. William, b. April 24, 1838. 7. David C., b. Oct. 10, 1839. Joined by Conf. of Faith Harlingen Ref. Dutch Church, May 28, 1831. Lived at Blawenburg.

ii. Lucretia, b. Oct. 9, 1807; m. Van Doren Wyckoff; no issue.

iii. Ann, b. Aug. 26, 1817; m. John A. Staats; one child, d. inf.

iv. Jeremiah Williamson, b. Jan. 25, 1821; m. Mary Andrews. Had: 1. Catharine S., b. 1840. 2. William H., b. Feb. 14, 1846; m. Ann Elizabeth Stryker; five children; live on the Homestead at Rocky Hill.

v. Catharine Hageman, b. Sept. 29, 1823; no record.

103. JOHN[6] SKILLMAN (Thomas,[5] Thomas,[4] Isaac,[3] Thomas,[2] Thomas[1]), b. June 2, 1782; m. (1) Mary Ann, dau. of Alexander McCaraher (b. Aug. 9, 1787; d. April 26, 1834) and mother of his children; m. (2) 1836, Margaret Blackwell, widow of Dr. Reeves; she d. June 16, 1863, and is buried at Kingston on the hill.

i. Thomas,[7] b. Aug. 30, 1808; d. March 25, 1810.

ii. Thomas J., b. April 15, 1810; d. April 11, 1881; m. Sept. 8, 1835, Sarah Ann, dau. of John Stout and wife Sarah Hart, related to John Hart of Hopewell, Signer of the Declaration of Independence; general merchant of highest standing all his life at Rocky Hill, N. J. Had: 1. Mary Ann, b. 1836; d. inf. 2. Luther Stephens, b. Oct. 29, 1837; joined Comp. F, 30th Regt., N. J. V. I., Sept. 3, 1862, in Civil War; m. Mary E. Backus; two children, Thomas J., and Julia A.; Insurance Broker, Trenton, N. J. 3. Mary Frances, b. Aug. 8, 1850; m. Charles H. Voorhees; two children; live in Brooklyn, N. Y.

iii. James McC., b. May 28, 1812; d. April 9, 1814.

iv. Elizabeth A., b. June 12, 1813; d. July 25, 1880; m. May 7, 1834, Peleg H. Barker; general merchant at Kingston, N. J.; d. 1869.

v. Mary, b. Dec. 8, 1816; m. June 12, 1840, Isaac Vanderveer, Rocky Hill. Had: 1. Emma, d. inf. 2. Margaret, m. Judge John D. Bartine, Somerville, N. J. 3. Augustus, m. Evelyn M. Gaston. 4. George Van Dyke, m. Adelle Peters; four children.

vi. Henry J., b. Feb. 16, 1819; m. (1) Dec. 9, 1841, Anna Van Pelt; had Caroline, m. Amos Sutphen, Lower

Cross Roads, N. J.; m. (2) Feb. 11, 1846, Martha Van
Dyke; four children.

vii. James, b. Sept. 1, 1821; d. March 21, 1887; unm.
viii. Margaretta, b. March 26, 1824; m. Feb. 7, 1844, Henry
H. Van Dyke; d. June 10, 1897, leaving six children.
ix. Sarah, b. Feb. 9, 1826; m. William H. Cox. Had: 1.
James H. 2. Ella, m. Wallace Lanning. 3. Mary,
m. —— McCoy. 4. Luther.

104. THOMAS[6] SKILLMAN (Thomas,[5] Thomas,[4] Isaac,[3] Thomas,[2]
Thomas[1]), b. July 23, 1786; d. of Asiatic Cholera, June 9, 1833;
learned the printer's trade in Philadelphia and, 1803, went to
Lexington, Ky., established, 1824, the *Western Luminary* and
largest publishing house west of the Alleghanies; Elder in the
Presbyterian Church, and often delegate at the General Assembly; printer and circulator of religious books; m. 1813, Elizabeth,
dau. of Ebenezer Farrar of New Hampshire and wife Martha,
dau. of Gen'l Hugh Mercer, killed at the Battle of Princeton.
Her father and family had settled at Lexington in 1789. Surviving her husband nearly 40 years, she d. Feb., 1872, æ. 86.
Children:

i. Claudius Buchanan,[7] d. inf.
ii. Elizabeth, m. James Howard of Kentucky, who d. early.
Had one son, Thomas Skillman Howard; d. unm.
iii. Thomas, b. *circa* 1820; druggist in Lexington and d.
unm. about 1867.
iv. Henry Martyn, b. Sept. 4, 1823; d. March, 1902; m.
Oct. 30, 1851, Margaret, dau. of Matthew T. Scott;
graduate of Transylvania University (Med. Dept.),
Lexington, 1847; Prof. of Physiology, etc., therein;
also practitioner; Gov't Surgeon in Civil War; 1868,
Pres. State Med. Association. Had: 1. Matthew
Scott, and 2. Ethelbert Dudley; both d. in infancy.
3. Thomas T., b. 1860; d. 1896, unm. 4. Henry M.,
b. 1865; m. 1890, Laura, dau. of Avery and Amanda
(Frazier) Winston; two sons: 1. Henry Martyn, b.
1891. 2. Avery Winston, b. 1894.

105. ABRAHAM[6] SKILLMAN (Thomas,[5] Thomas,[4] Isaac,[3] Thomas,[2]
Thomas[1]), b. Oct. 27, 1788; d. Oct. 3, 1858; m. (1) Magdalen
Davis, Sept. 23, 1809. With her and their six children, all bap.
in the Harlingen Ref. Dutch Church, they removed, 1822, (she
dying the same year), to Lexington, Ky.; m. (2) Aug. 11, 1828,
Betsey Robb (b. 1800; d. 1873). Children:

i. Thomas,[7] b. Nov. 2, 1811; d. unm.
ii. William Davis, b. April 19, 1813; m. April 9, 1835, Elvira Taylor, Frankfort, Ky. Had: 1. Joseph, b. in
Monmouth Co., N. J., 1836 (see No. 51). 2. Magdalen D., b. 1838; m. E. A. Palpey, New Orleans. 3.
William D., b. 1840, Quincey, Ill. 4. Elizabeth R., b.
1843, Quincey; m. Charles Palpey, New Orleans. 5.
Ann McQuiddy, b. 1845, St. Louis, Mo.; family home
in the years following and where the remaining
children were born. 6. John T., b. 1847. 7. Abra-

ham H., b. 1849.   8. Richard D., b. 1851; m. Amanda
Orr; three children living.   9. Robert, b. 1853; d.
1891; m. 1880, Lizzie Herr; had Lucy, William R.
and Neil.   10. Henrietta, b. 1847; m. Neil McKin-
non; seven children; home in Toledo, O.

   iii. Henry, b. Feb. 9, 1815; d. unm.
   iv. Mary, b. Oct. 17, 1816; m. April 9, 1835, Dr. Charles H.
      Spillman, Lexington; settled at Harrodsbury, Ky.
   v. John, b. Nov. 29, 1818; d. young.
   vi. Ann, b. Sept. 8, 1820; m. Oct. 22, 1840, Merritt P. Lan-
      caster (d. 1895); merchant of Lexington; d. Feb. 24,
      1891.   Had: 1. Abraham B., b. 1841; m. (1) 1876, Susan
      A. Harris; three children; m. (2) 1897, Naomi Hill;
      three children.   2. Magdalen D., b. 1857; m. 1876,
      John Hull Davidson; two children.
   vii. Elizabeth, b. May 24, 1844 (alone to survive of mother's
      four children); m. April 21, 1874, Dr. John W. Scott,
      son of Matthew T. (see No. 104) and brother of Mar-
      garet.   Had: 1. John Skillman Scott, M. D.   2.
      Margaret Scott.

106. ELIZABETH[6] SKILLMAN (Thomas,[5] Thomas,[4] Isaac,[3] Thomas,[2]
Thomas[1]), b. March 9, 1790; m. Samuel Terhune, descendant of
Jan Terhune who was at New Brunswick as early as 1717, coming
from Flatlands, L. I.; originally from Nederland prior to 1657;
ancestor Albert Albertse Terhunen.   Their family home was at
Blawenburg, the children being bap. at Harlingen, the old
church.

   i. Thomas Skillman[7] Terhune, b. 1818(?); m. Mary Bo-
      gart, dau. of Joseph Skillman and wife, Maria Stry-
      ker (2nd cousins).   Had: 1. John Newton, b. Jan. 16,
      1843.   2. Emmeline, b. Aug. 16, 1845.
   ii. William Terhune, b. May 21, 1820.
   iii. Elizabeth Terhune, b. Jan. 20, 1822.
   iv. Catharine Aurelia Terhune, bap. March 18, 1823.
   v. Henry Terhune, b. Jan. 21, 1826.
   vi. John Terhune, d. a babe.

107. MARY[6] SKILLMAN (Abraham,[5] Thomas,[4] Isaac,[3] Thomas,[2]
Thomas[1]), b. Dec. 17, 1788; m. at Harlingen, Oct. 8, 1806, Leffert
Totten.   Their ten children were all bap. at Harlingen, the
family home:

   i. Abraham Skillman[7] Totten, b. May 12, 1808.
   ii. Maria Totten, b. Sept. 7, 1810.
   iii. Lucretia Totten, b. Nov. 8, 1812.
   iv. Levi Totten, b. Sept. 13, 1813.
   v. John Simpson Totten, b. May 7, 1817; m. at Neshanic,
      N. J., Sept. 20, 1840, Cornelia B. Packer; wagonmaker
      at Griggstown.
   vi. Joseph Totten, b. Oct. 30, 1818; m. —— Ganz.
   vii. Rachel Totten, b. June 25, 1821.
   viii. Sarah Joanna Totten, b. March 28, 1823.
   ix. Cornelius Waldron Totten, b. March 21, 1825.
   x. Catharine Elizabeth Totten, b. Dec. 17, 1827.

108. LUCRETIA[6] SKILLMAN (Abraham,[5] Thomas,[4] Isaac,[3] Thomas,[2] Thomas[1]), b. Oct. 3, 1790; m. Nov. 25, 1813, John R. Stryker; joined by Confession of Faith Harlingen (Ref. Dutch) Church, Aug. 4, 1831. Children bap. in Harlingen:

  i. Judith Ann[7] Stryker, b. July 28, 1816.
  ii. Ida Stryker, b. Nov. 18, 1818.
  iii. Abraham Skillman Stryker, b. Nov. 23, 1824.
  iv. Garret Stryker, b. April 25, 1833.

109. JOSEPH[6] SKILLMAN (Abraham,[5] Thomas,[4] Isaac,[3] Thomas,[2] Thomas[1]), b. Nov. 17, 1793; m. Nov. 30, 1816, Maria, dau. of Stephen Stryker (b. Oct. 22, 1797; d. Sept. 30, 1874); a farmer, being a ruling elder in the Blawenburg (Ref. Dutch) Church of which he was a charter member, having joined at Harlingen, Nov. 14, 1822. Children:

  i. Lucretia,[7] b. Oct. 11, 1817; d. Oct. 5, 1871, buried at
   Belle Mead; m. Kourt V. Sutphen. Had: 1. John,
   b. 1838. 2. Abraham S., b. 1839. 3. Anna M., b.
   1841. 4. Ida V., b. 1843. 5. Rachel, b. 1847. 6.
   Joseph, b. 1849. 7. Sarah, b. 1851.
  ii. Mary Bogart, b. July 26, 1819. (See No. 106.)
  iii. Jecoliah, b. July 28, 1821; m. Jacob Pettenger. Three
   children: 1. Abraham. 2. Alfred. 3. A daughter.
  iv. Sarah, b. 1822; m. Lewis Chamberlain, Reaville, N. J.
  v. Rachel, b. May 10, 1824; m. Levi Apgar, Tenton, N. J.
   Had: 1. John Gardner Apgar, b. Nov. 23, 1851.
  vi. Abraham J., b. March 26, 1825; d. 1907; m. Mary Van
   Dyke. Had: 1. Ezekiel Voorhees, Trenton, d. 1904.
   2. Edward Van Dyke, manufacturer, Trenton. 3.
   Rachel. 4. Mary Ella. The father a civil engineer
   and contractor, Trenton. From him Skillman
   station on the Bound Brook line of the Reading R.
   R. in N. J. got its name.
  vii. Catharine, m. Robert I., son of Dr. Cicero Hunt,
   Ringoes, N. J., and Annie Iredell, his wife, Hatboro,
   Pa., b. 1831; d. July 23, 1903. Their home in Philadelphia. Had: 1. Wesley, bap. in Blawenburg (Ref.
   Dutch) Church, June, 1859; d. inf. 2. Maria Louise.
   3. Annie Iredell.
  viii. Ann Cooper, m. Disbrough Bergen Voorhees, *circa*
   1856. Four children bap. in Harlingen.
  ix. Stephen Stryker, m. in Harlingen, Dec. 24, 1858, Harriet, dau. of Jacob Whitlock.
  x. Thomas, m. Dec. 19, 1866, Emily Schomp. Had: 1.
   Joseph A., b. 1868, and other children. Live at
   Skillman (Blawenburg), N. J.

110. CATHARINE[6] SKILLMAN (Abraham,[5] Thomas,[4] Isaac,[3] Thomas,[2] Thomas[1]), b. Dec. 2, 1804; m. Dec. 11, 1823, William Van Dyke. Their children were bap., three in Harlingen and three in Blawenburg, where the family home was.

  i. Abraham[7] Skillman Van Dyke, b. July 25, 1824.
  ii. Ralph (Roelif) Van Dyke, b. Dec. 5, 1825.
  iii. Anne Cornelia Van Dyke, b. Aug. 14, 1829.

      iv. Lucretia Van Dyke, b. Aug. 17, 1837.
      v. Peter Van Dyke, b. June 17, 1840.
      vi. John Berrian Van Dyke, b. Nov. 24, 1841.

111. THOMAS Q.[6] SKILLMAN (Issac,[5] Thomas,[4] Isaac,[3] Thomas,[2] Thomas[1]), b. Sept. 22, 1796; m. Dec. 8, 1816, Ann (2d cousin), dau. of Abraham Beekman Skillman and wife, Catharine Voorhees. With her, her mother and sisters (see No. 16) he came from Harlingen, N. J., *circa* 1820, to the Miami Valley, near Cincinnati, and there made their future home. Children:

      i. Abraham Nelson,[7] b. 1817 in N. J.; m. —— Hardenbrook. Reared a family.
      ii. Mary, b. in N. J., 1819; m. (1) Thomas Smiley; m. (2) Thomas Kirk, both of Ohio. No children.
      iii. Gitty Ann, b. 1821; mother's full name; d. unm.
      iv. Catharine, b. 1823; m. William Watson; removed to Northern Illinois. One son.
      v. Isaac, b. 1825; m. —— Winedge. Had large family, Logansport, Ind.
      vi. Lavinia, b. 1827; m. Dominicus Van Dyke Skillman (b. Oct. 8, 1824), son of Thomas B. Skillman (see No. 151).
      vii. Jacob, b. 1829; d. young.
      viii. Emory, b. 1831; m. —— Cameron. *Note:* John N. Skillman d. at Cripple Creek, Col., 1902. Had a son there named Emory, and Emory Skillman was an actor in N. Y. City in 1903. Were these the same?
      ix. Martin, b. 1833; m. and had a large family in Logan Co., O.
      x. Alva, b. 1835; d. unm.
      xi. Joanna, b. 1837; m. —— Combes; lives in Kansas.
      xii. Albert Firman, b. 1839; twice m., but no children; lives in Cincinnati, O.
      xiii. William Henry, b. 1841; d. inf.

112. JAMES Q.[6] SKILLMAN (Isaac,[5] Thomas,[4] Isaac,[3] Thomas,[2] Thomas[1]), b. Dec. 22, 1800; d. Oct. 13, 1851; m. Nov. 16, 1823, Ann Stryker (b. Sept. 20, 1805; d. May 18, 1856); graves at Clover Hill; blacksmith at Bridge Point (Harlingen); also farmer at Neshanic; nephew of Gertrude Quick of Roycefield, who m. Peter Nevius of Quick's Mills, and at her death left property to his four children, all bap. at Neshanic Church (Ref. Dutch). These children were:

      i. Cornelia,[7] b. May 26, 1826; m. Jan. 6, 1852, Stephen R., son of Thomas Hope, farmer of Hillsboro (Millstone), N. J.
      ii. Peter Stryker, b. Oct. 21, 1827; d. May 1, 1900; m. at Neshanic, Nov. 15, 1854, Sarah Gano (b. 1834), dau. of Stephen Gano, farmer. Had: 1. John Van Zandt, 2. Retta Van Zandt, twins, b. Feb. 25, 1863. 3. Lewis B., b. Sept. 2, 1866.
      iii. Margaretta, b. Dec. 23, 1833.
      iv. Isaac Nevius, b. Dec. 22, 1839; d. Sept. 10, 1851.

(To be continued.)

SOUTHOLD, N. Y., TOWN RECORDS, VITAL STA-
TISTICS FROM LIBERS D. AND E., IN THE
TOWN CLERK'S OFFICE.

CONTRIBUTED BY LUCY DUBOIS AKERLY, WITH NOTES.

(Continued from Vol. XXXVIII., p. 250 of the RECORD.)

REEVES. Catura Reeves Daughter of ye above named was born
The 21t of augt 1727.
Nathan Reeves Son of the above named was born The 8th of
augt. 1732.
James Reeves Son of ye above named was borne The 19th of
augt. 1736.
Thomas Reeves Son of ye above named was borne April ye
20th 1739.
Entd. January ye 29th 1739/40
pr Benj. Youngs Town Clerk.
BOOTH. William Booth was married to Hannah King the — day
of —— 1688.
Births.   William Booth son of ye above named was born May
ye 28: anno Dom. 1689.
Hannah Booth Daughter of ye above named was born feb-
ruary ye 22: anno Dom. 1691.
Samuel Booth Son of ye above named was born Iuly ye 15:
anno Dom. 1693.
George Booth Son of the above named was borne april ye 28.
anno Dom. 1696.
Mehetabell Booth Daughter of ye above was borne Octobr.
ye: 9th: anno Dom. 1699.
Constant Booth Son of ye above named was born Ianuary ye
8th anno Domni. 1701, & Departed this Life March the
27/1774.
Mary Booth Daughter of ye above named was borne augst.
ye 30th anno Domni. 1703.
Martha Booth Daughter of ye above named was borne
August ye 27th 1706.
Constant Booth was maried to Mary King the seven day of
October, 1725 & said Mary died 30 Aug. 1769.
William Booth Son of ye above named was born ye 23 of
novemr 1727.   Died ye 12 march 1760.
Samuel Booth Son of ye above named was born ye 27 of
feby. 1729/30.
John Booth Son of ye above named was born ye 9th of April,
1732.
Mary, Daughter of ye above named was born ye: 21: of July,
1736 and died 1793.
Hannah Daugter of ye above named was born April ye 4th
1739.

BOOTH. George Booth Son of the above named was born March th
30/1741 (and Died february the 4/1774.)

Joseph Booth Son of the above named was born May th
6/1743.

Constant Booth Son of ye above named was born March ye
3/1745/6 and Died November 19/1746.

Katherine Booth Daughter of the above named was Born
February 14/1748.

NOTE. BOOTH.—See *A Contribution to a Genealogy of the Family of
John Booth of Shelter Island, N. Y.*

YOUNGS. South Hold Septem? ye: 16: 1695. Benjn. Youngs
born about 1668 was married to Mary Grover and departed
this life in the year of i. Lord, 1742, the 29 of July & 75 of
his age.

Mary ye wife of ye sd. Benjamin Youngs departed this life
in ye year of our lord 1706: ye 4th day of november.

Births of their children.

Grover Yongs (written over Youngs) was Borne October the
third day Jn ye Yeare of our lord 1697 and departed this
life ye 25th Day of January 1739/40.

Experience Yongs was Borne novemr. the six day in ye
Year of our lord, 1699 and departed this life ye first Day of
Jany. 1733/34 being wife of Rev. Ebenezer Prime.

Mary Youngs Daughter of the above named was borne
August ye 2d day Jn ye Year of our lord, 1701 and De-
parted this Life ye 10 Day of Janvery 1768 being ye wife of
Rbt. Hempstead.

Benjamin Youngs Son of ye above named was borne march
ye 27th in ye Year of our lord 1703 and departed this life
ye 26th of Septr. 1729.

Deborah Youngs Daughter of ye above named was born
february ye: 14th Jn the Yeare of our lord 1704/5 and departed this Life ye 18 of March 1746/7 being the wife of
John Ledyard.

NOTE. See the *Youngs Genealogy*. Robert[4] Hempstead, son of Joshua[3]
(Joshua,[2] Robert[1]) and Abigail Bayley Hempstead, m. Mary Youngs; his
brother John, b. 1709, m. Hannah Salmon. Their father wrote *Hempstead's
Diary*.

COREY. Jsaac Corye was married to Sarah Ludly (written over,
might have been Ludlam, or Linde) in ye Year of our lord
1682.

Jsaac Corye Son of ye above named was borne January ye
first in ye Year: 1683/4 and Departed this Life in ye Year
of our lord 1699.

Sarah Corye Daughter of ye above named was born octobr:
23d in ye Year of our lord 1685. Ame Reed Daughter of
Sarah Corye had a Son Called Epenetus born the third
Day of february 1746/7.

David Corye Son of ye above named was borne Aprill ye: 16:
in ye Yeare of our lord: 1690 and Died October ye 30/1758,
aged 68 years 6 ms. & 3 Days.

COREY. Deborah Corye Daughter of ye above named was born
february: ye: fift in ye Yeare of our lord 1693.

Jonathan Corye Son of ye above named was borne Septr: ye:
7th day in the Yeare of our lord 1697.

David Corye was married to Mary Brush in ye Yeare of our
lord 1712 which Sd. Mary departed this life the 24 of
Decemr. anno Dom. 1720.

David Corey Departed this Life 30 Oct. 1758.

Deborah Cory Daughter of ye above named was born: 15th
Augt. 1714 and departed hir life November 26, 1787.

Mary Corey Daughter of the above named was: born 23 of
Novemr. 1726.

Martha Corye Daughter of ye above named was born 18 of
January 1718/19.

Sarah Daughter of the above was borne 15 of Decemr. 1720
& Died the 22 Sept. 1776.

Elisabeth Corye Daughter of the above named David Cory &
Ruth his second wife was born ye 20th of March 1723 the
said Ruth wife of ye Sd David Corye Departed this Life
february ye 7th day, 1739/40.

Ruth Cory Daughter of the above named was born october
ye 12, 1724 and departed this life the last day of January
1724/5.

David Cory Son of ye above named was born ye 30 of
Novemr. 1725 and departed this life the 27 of feby. 1731/2.

Ruth or Daughter of ye above named was born 5 of April
1726C y

Jasper Cory Son of ye above named was born ye 31 of
Decemr. 1728.

Zophar Cory Son of ye above named was born ye 15. of
novemr. 1730.

Ann Cory Daughter of ye above named was born ye 7 of
Septemr. 1732 and departed this life the Sept. the 25 day
1805—7 oClock a.m.

David Cory Son of ye above named was born ye 29. of June
1734.

Benjamin Corye Son of ye above named was born Augt ye:
14th 1736.

Abraham Corye Son of ye above named was born ye 22 of
August, 1739.

COREY. Abraham Corey was Born August ye 22, A.D. 1739.

Bathsheba his wife was Born Aprel ye 28, 1741.

They was Married November ye 12, A.D. 1761.

David Corey Son of the above was Born February 21, A.D.
1764.

Abraham Corey Son of the Above was Born November 14
A.D. 1766.

Jonathen Corey Son of the was Born March ye 21 AD. 1769.

Bathsheba Corey daughter of the above was Born April ye
5, A.D. 1772.

Mehetabel Corey daughter of the above was Born December
ye 26 A.D. 1779.

COREY. David Corey son of the above was maryed to Mildred
Hudgens in Virginia August 26 A. D. 1784.

NOTE. See *The Corey Family of Southampton and Southold, Long Island,
New York.*

YOUNGS. John Youngs Son of Christopher Youngs was borne
october ye: 21 (25?): in ye Year of our lord 1679.

WIGGINS. John Wiggens was married to Mary Harrod January:
14 in ye Year of our Lord 1701.
    Beirths.
John wiggens Son of ye above named was borne: March ye:
1: in ye Yeare of our Lord 1702 and departed this Life the
18 Decembr. In the Year 1768.
David wiggens Son of ye above named was born Aprill ye
28th in ye Year of our Lord 1704.
Mary wiggens Daughter of ye above named was borne ·
Decemr. ye 12th in ye year of our lord 1705.
Thomas wiggens Son of ye above named was borne: Decem-
ber ye 9th in ye Year of our lord 1707.
Hannah wigens Daughter of ye above named was borne:
April ye: 20th: 1709.

NOTE. When, or whence, this family came to Southold is unknown, but
Wiggens was a surname in Southwold, Eng. In 1662, George Warren and
others having refused to take oaths and subscriptions, John Wiggins, Edmund
Curtis, John Arnold and others were appointed to take the place of the non-
jurors.

CONKLING. Joseph Conklyng Senr. was married to Abigaill
Tuthill Novemr. ye   1690.
Joseph Conklyng Son of ye above named was borne august
ye 7th in ye Yeare of our lord: 1691.
John Conklyng Son of ye above named was borne octobr. ye
16th in ye Yeare of our lord 1694.

NOTE. It is greatly to be regretted that there is not a Conkling Genealogy
in print. Joseph [2] Conklyng, Sr., was doubtless son of Capt. John [3] Conklyng of
Hashamomack and d. 23 Nov., 1698; his son Lieut. Joseph, [4] above, b. 1691; d.
20 Jan., 1739-40, in his 49th year; m. Lydia Kirkland, who d. 29 Jan., 1743, ae. 57.
Their son Capt. Joseph Conkling m. Sarah Wickham.

PATTY. John Patty was married to Mary Chatfield March ye 12:
in ye Year of our Lord 1688/9.   ·
Edward Pattey Son of ye above named was borne february
the: 16: in ye Year of our Lord: 1690/1.
Elizabeth patty Daughter of ye above named was borne
aprill ye: 7th in ye year of our Lord: 1693.
David patty Son of ye above named was borne february: 23d
in ye year of our lord: 1695.
Mary patty Daughter of ye above named was borne may ye
7th in ye year of our lord 1697.
Elizabeth patty Daughter of ye above named was borne
June ye: 16th in ye year of our lord 1699.
Hannah patty Daughter of ye above named was borne march:
27th in ye year of our lord 1701.

NOTE. The surname Petty (or Patty) is found at Southwold, Eng. A
certain John Petty m. Susan Draper there, 16 Nov., 1628. He might have been

the ancestor of Edward Petty of Southold, L. I., whose sons John and Edward were b. 26 Nov., 1658. John prob. m. Mary Chatfield, and Edward, according to the late J. H. Petty of Amityville, m. Mercy, dau. of Rev. John Youngs and his first wife.

LANDON.   James Landon was married to Mary Vaill in May, 1707.
>   Mary Landon Daughter of ye above named was born novembr: 26th 1707.
>   Joseph Landon was borne to ye above named Decemr: ye: 18th 1708. Sd Joseph Landon Died 8 October, 1773.
>   James Landon Son of ye above named was borne august: ye: 5th 1711. (Another handwriting) to Salisbury, Conn.
>   Daniel Landon Son of ye above named was borne 7th day of January 1713/14. Removed to Litchfield, 1740.
>   Rachel Landon Daughter of ye above named was born ye: 12th day of octobr. 1716.
>   David Landon Son of ye above named was borne ye 8th July anno Dom. 1718. To Litchfield.
>   John Landon Son of ye above named was borne ye 21 July, anno Dom. 1720.

NOTE.   James Landon was doubtless son of Nathan and Hannah Landon, *see beyond.*
Samuel and Abigail (Wetmore) Bishop of Connecticut had a dau. Sarah, who m. James Landon, prob. James, Jr., above, b. 1711. He had a son Ashbel.
Daniel Landon above, m. (1) —— Fiske, Brooklyn; m. (2) Martha Youngs of Southold.
Rachel above, m. Samuel Moore.

DIMON.   Jonatn. Dimon was married to Sarah Solemon the 9th day of May in ye year of our lord Christ, 1710.
>   Births.
>   Jonathan Dimon Son of ye above named was borne feby. ye 12th day in ye year of our lord Christ 1710/11.
>   Sarah Dimon Daughter of ye above named was borne ye 12. of Septembr. Jn ye year of our lord Christ.
>   (Elmary Dimon Daughter of ye above named was borne & buried) preceding entry erased & and is in the same hand-writing as the following.
>   John & Elizabeth Son & Daughter of ye above named was born the 2 day of March in ye year 1715/16 and ye Sd John departed this life ye 10 day June in ye year 1716.
>   Mary Dimon Daughter of the above named was borne the 19 day of august 1718.
>   Ame Dimon daughter of the above named was borne the 14th day of Septembr. 1721.
>   Deborah Dimon Daughter of the above named was borne october the 12th 1725.
>   Jonathan Dimon Son of ye above named was born february ye 12th 1727/8.

GOLDSMITH.   Thomas GoldSmith was married to Abigail Booth.
>   Abigaill GoldSmith Daughter of ye named was borne ye 9th day of august in ye year of our lord 1710.
>   Richd. GoldSmith Son of ye above named was borne ye December the 5 day in the year of our lord 1711.

GOLDSMITH.   Joshua Gold Smith Son of ye above named was borne ye 26 day of June Jn ye Year of our lord Christ 1713.

Nathaniel Gold Smith Son of the above named was borne the first of Decemr. anno Domini 1719.

Thomas Gold Smith Son of ye above named was born ye 26th Septr. in the Year of our lord Christ 1726.

Elisha Gold Smith Son of the above named was born ye 8th of Sept. anno Domini, 1731.

KING.   John King was married to Catharine Osborne augt. ye: 22: 1704.

Mary King Daughter of ye above named was borne July ye 22 day in ye Year 1705 and Departed this Life August the 30/1769.

Joseph King Son of ye above named was borne Decemr. ye 27. in ye Year 1706.

Henry King Son of ye above named was borne Decemr. ye 19: in ye year 1708.

Constant King Son of ye above named was borne feb. ye 19: in ye year 1711/12.

Elexander King Son of ye above named was borne Septr. 18; in ye year 1713.

Elizabeth King Daughter of ye above named was borne April ye 17: in the year 1715.

Prosperous King Son of ye above named was borne ye 14th June in ye year 1717.

Benjamin King Son of ye above named was borne 26th day of June 1722.

NOTE.   Of the children above Henry, doubtless of Middletown, Conn., d. 24 Feb., 1748–9, ae. 40. He m. not Elizabeth Beebe as formerly supposed, but Mary, dau. of John Hamlin, 22 June, 1732. She m. 2d Saml. Merriman. Issue: Mary King, b. 1734; d. 1735; Henry, b. 1736; d. S. P. before March, 1760; Mary, 2d, b. 1738; m. Ephraim Fenno; John, b. 1739; d. 1746; Elizabeth, b. 1741; m. Jacob Whetmore, Jr.; Joseph, b. 1743; m. Jerusha Marsh.

Alexander King, b. 18 Sept., 1713, lived east of Water Mill, L. I., in 1776; m. Sarah Havens, and had: Alexander, Jr., and Benjamin, of Southampton Town; Patience, b. 1753; m. Elias Sears; Sarah, b. 1757; m. (1) Joseph Danforth; m. (2) Ambrose Seymour; Mary, who m. James Fostick; Abigail, single in 1790, and prob. another daughter who m. Wm. Cleaves.

Benjamin King, b. 26 June, 1722; m. Elizabeth King, 20 Nov., 1746, and had: Jerusha, b. at Southold, 20 Aug., 1747; Elizabeth, b. at Middletown, 17 Jan., 1748–9; Capt. Benjamin, b. 23 Sept., 1750; Capt. Henry, prob. bap. 3 Jan., 1753; d. ab. 1800; and a son d. 15 Nov., 1754. (See *Middletown Rec.* and *Mattituck Ch. Rec.*)

BROWN.   Edward Brown was married to Mary Martine.   Births.

Jane Brown Daughter of ye above named was borne ye 4 Janewary anno Dom. 1700/1.

Samuel Brown Son of ye above named was borne ye 4: august anno Dom. 1702.

Timothy Brown Son of ye above named was borne ye 11 march anno Dom. 1704/5.

Edward Brown Son of ye above named was borne ye 25 December anno Dom. 1707.

Mary Brown Daughter of ye above named was borne ye 29 April anno Dom. 1711.

BROWN. Eles Brown Daughter of ye above named was borne ye 23 Sept. anno Dom. 1714.

NOTE. This entire family are omitted in *Moore's Indexes*, and perhaps did not stay long in Southold Town.

CONKLING. Gideon Conkelyn was married to Hannah Tarbell. Births.
Hannah Conkelyn Daughter of ye above named was borne ye 13 September anno Dom. 1714.
Gideon Conkelyn Son of ye above named was borne ye 31 January anno Dom. 1715/16.
Mary Conkelyn Daughter of ye above named was borne ye 3d march anno Dom. 1716/7.
Martha Conkling Daughter of ye above named was borne ye 22 march anno Dom. 1718/9.
Phebee Conkling Daughter of above named was borne ye 4th march anno Domini 1720/1.
Jacob Conkling Son of ye above named was borne ye 11th day of June 1723.

NOTE. Gideon Conkelyn was doubtless son of Jacob² (John¹), of Hashamomack. Jacob's other sons were Jacob, Joseph, Samuel and John. Gideon, Joseph, Samuel and John were Youngs names, so possibly Jacob's wife Mary was a Youngs.

YOUNGS. Septr. 7th 1715 nathan Youngs was married to Deborah Corye.
Deborah ye Daughter of ye above named was borne April 22: 1716.
Mary ye Daughter of ye above named was born novembr. 10th, 1719.
Phebee Daughter of ye above named was born July 10th 1721.
Silas Son of ye above named was borne January ye 5, 1723/4.
Bethia Daughter of ye above named was borne augt. 24th 1726.

PECK. John Peck was married to Mary Horton ye 26th of June, 1701.
Jerimiah Peck Son of ye above named was borne March ye: 26: 1702 Mary wife of Sd. John Peck departed this life September ye: 9th 1702.

(To be continued.)

SOCIETY PROCEEDINGS.

REGULAR MEETING OF THE SOCIETY, NOVEMBER 8TH, 1907.

First Vice-President Clarence Winthrop Bowen in the Chair.
The following deaths were reported since the last meeting of the Society: Bowen Whiting Pierson, July 4, 1907; Francis Hartman Markoe, M.D., Sept. 13, 1907; Rev. Melatiah Everett Dwight, M.D., D.D., Sept. 14, 1907; Mrs. Willis L. Chaffee, Oct. 8, 1907.

The following resignations have been accepted by the Executive Committee: Frederick Aycrigg Pell, resigned Oct. 19, 1907; Mrs. Thomas H. Whitney, resigned Oct. 1, 1907; Diedrich Willers, a Corresponding Member for Seneca County, New York, resigned Oct. 16, 1907.

The Executive Committee reported the election of the following: Jacob Edgar Bookstaver, Annual Member, Binghamton, N. Y., proposed by John R. Totten; Ernest Christie Brown, Annual Member, 741 St. Nicholas Avenue, City proposed by Mrs. F. E. Youngs; Mrs. J. Wray Cleveland, Annual Member, 131 East 64th Street, City, proposed by John R. Totten; Miss Adelia A. Dwight, Annual Member, Waldorf-Astoria Hotel, City, proposed by Rev. John Cornell; Mrs. William A. Ewing, Annual Member, 134 West 58th Street, City, proposed by Mrs. Levi Holbrooke; Miss Julia Freeman, Annual Member, 25 Broad Street, City (assuming membership of father, late Gen. F. M. Freeman), proposed by John R. Totten; Adelos Gorton, Annual Member, Philadelphia, Pa., proposed by John R. Totten; Archer M. Huntington, Annual Member, 1083 Fifth Avenue, City, proposed by John R. Totten; Samuel Dayton Pierson, Annual Member, Geneva, New York (assuming membership of brother, late B. W. Pierson), proposed by John R. Totten; Mrs. Nottingham Taylor, Annual Member, Waldorf-Astoria Hotel, City, proposed by Rev. John Cornell.

Vice-President Bowen then introduced the speaker of the evening, Prof. Herschel C. Parker of Columbia University, who gave a most interesting lecture entitled "Canadian Alps," First Ascents and Explorations in the Mountains of British Columbia and Alberta. Which was illustrated by 120 beautifully colored stereopticon views.

REGULAR MEETING OF THE BOARD OF TRUSTEES, NOVEMBER 12TH, 1907.

Present: Messrs. Bowen, Drowne, Eliot, Field, Gibson, Morrison, Mott, Totten, Walker, Wilson and Wright. Regrets received from Mr. Goodwin.

Chairman, First Vice-President Clarence Winthrop Bowen, called the attention of the Board to the loss by death on Sept. 14, 1907, of our late President Rev. Melatiah Everett Dwight, M. D., and moved that a Committee be appointed to draw up suitable Resolutions regarding the services of Dr. Dwight to the Society and embodying the Society's appreciation of its loss; also that these Resolutions, together with those passed by the Executive Committee be engrossed and a copy sent to the family of Dr. Dwight and spread upon the minutes of this meeting as well as published in the January issue of the RECORD. He suggested as members of the Committee Messrs. Gen. James Grant Wilson, Tobias A. Wright and George Austin Morrison, Jr., with full power to carry the matter to completion. Carried.

The Chair called attention to the loss by death since the last meeting of the Board of two Trustees: Bowen Whiting Pierson and Rev. Melatiah Everett Dwight, M.D., and moved that nominations be made to fill these unexpired terms in accordance with the provisions of the By-Laws, also that these nominations be acted upon and vacancies filled by election at once. Nominations were duly presented of Howland Pell in place of Mr. Pierson, and Archer M. Huntington in place of Dr. Dwight, and these persons were unamiously elected.

The Chair then called attention to the vacancy existing in the office of President of the Society, and that nominations were in order to fill said vacancy.

Nominations were duly presented and seconded of Gen. James Grant Wilson and Clarence Winthrop Bowen. On motion the nominations were closed and Mr. Field appointed as teller. Mr. Field reported that seven ballots had been cast for Mr. Bowen and four for Gen. Wilson.

Gen. Wilson moved that the election of Mr. Bowen be made unanimous. Carried.

Attention was then called to the vacancy existing in the office of First Vice-President and Mr. Morrison nominated Archer M. Huntington. No further nominations were made and on motion nominations were closed. The Secretary was on motion authorized to cast one ballot and announced the election of Archer M. Huntington as First Vice-President.

5

The Treasurer's report was read, received and placed on file. He reported as follows:

Permanent Fund,	$ 250.00
Reserve Fund,	373.11
Building Fund,	80.00
General Fund,	445.33
	$1,148.44

On motion meeting adjourned.

REGULAR MEETING OF THE SOCIETY, DECEMBER 13TH, 1907.

President Clarence Winthrop Bowen in the Chair.

The President announced the appointment of the following Committees:

Auditing Committee: Ellsworth Everett Dwight, Evelyn Briggs Baldwin.

Nominating Committee: William Mattoon King, Chairman, Ellsworth Everett Dwight, Walter Lispenard Suydam, Marshall Clifford Lefferts, William Bunker.

The following death has been reported since the last meeting of the Society: Col. Henry Dudley Teetor, who died Nov. 19, 1907, at Lancaster, Ohio.

The Executive Committee reported the election of the following: George Byron Louis Arner, Annual Member, 1120 Amsterdam Avenue, City, proposed by Tobias A. Wright; Ellsworth Everett Dwight, Annual Member, 36 Franklin Street, Morristown, N. J., proposed by William Mattoon King; Willard Goldthwaite Bixby, Annual Member, 194 Hester Street, City, proposed by Mrs. F. E. Youngs; Palmer Heath Lyon, M.D., Annual Member, 519 West 162d Street, City, proposed by Mrs. F. E. Youngs; Henry Cole Quinby, Annual Member, 3 Nassau Street, City, proposed by Mrs. F. E. Youngs.

President Bowen then introduced the lecturer of the evening, Gustavus Charles Hanus, Commander U. S. Navy (Retired), Superintendent, who gave a very interesting lecture, entitled, "The Nautical School of New York City. Life on the Schoolship 'St. Mary' afloat and on shore, at work and at play, at home and abroad. The new Schoolship, the U. S. S. 'Newport.'" Illustrated by many stereopticon views.

HENRY RUSSELL DROWNE, *Secretary.*

CORRECTION.

THE family of Richard and Mary (Rowley) Cook of East Hampton, Conn., and Plainfield, N. Y., is incorrectly given on p. 206, Vol. XXXVII, of the RECORD. A lineal descendant of this pair has furnished revised data as follows:.

Richard[5] Cooke (Josiah,[4] Joshua,[3] Josiah,[2] Josias[1]), the youngest child of Josiah[4] and Hannah (Sparrow) Cooke, was b. at Middletown (now Chatham), Conn., May 17, 1753 (Hinman's *Early Conn. Settlers*, p. 701), though the inscription on his gravestone at Plainfield, N. Y., reads: "died Aug. 13, 1833, aged 82 years." He was a Revolutionary soldier, serving from May 19, 1778, to Jan. 1, 1782, in the company of Capt. Edwards Eells of Middletown, and was a pensioner in 1818 (*Connecticut Men in the Revolution*, pp. 172, 317, 641). His will, dated at Plainfield, Aug. 12, 1833, probated Oct. 8, 1833, mentions wife Susannah, eldest son Alvan, and youngest son Nathaniel, and no other children. One son d. before the father, and the dau. Lucy Alvord is not mentioned. Children: i. Lucy, b. Aug. 7, 1784; m. Oct. 11, 1804, Dea. James Hall Alvord; she d. at Winsted, Conn., Sept. 11, 1850. ii. Alvan, b. Dec. 15, 1786; m. Aug. 31, 1811, Lucretia Smith, b. Nov. 10, 1786; they lived in Plainfield, N. Y., and Johnstown, Wis., where he d. Jan. 27, 1856. iii. Florus, b. April 26, 1793; m. May 7, 1817, Mary Couch, b. June 6, 1796, in Meriden, Conn., dau. of John and Anna (Rice) Couch; she d. in Wallingford, Conn., June 7,

1881; the family settled in Plainfield, N. Y., where Mr. Florus Cooke d. April 26, 1819. They had an only child, Richard Florus' Cooke, b. Jan. 19, 1818, at Plainfield; d. at Philadelphia, Sept. 26, 1876. iv. Nathaniel, b. ——, 1794; m. Betsey Fuller, and d. Nov. 20, 1867, without children.

HOMER W. BRAINARD, Hartford, Conn.

NOTES.

SNOW.—Judd's *History of Hadley, Mass.*, p. 140, states: "Josiah (Snow), son of Josiah,' So. Hadley, m. (1) Dec. 8, 1757, Azubah Dickenson, m. (2) ——. Children by second wife."

James Henry of South Hadley, in will made March 6, 1767, mentions daughter, *Elisabeth Snow*, Hampshire Co. Prob. Rec. (at Northampton) Vol. XI, p. 14, and in a deed made by *Josiah Snow* of South Hadley, in Oct., 1765, he calls *James Henry*, his *father*, Hampshire Co. Deeds, Vol. VI, p. 506 (at Springfield).

Josiah Snow's first child was b. June 18, 1762, so it would seem that his second wife, mother of his children, was *Elisabeth Henry*, daughter of *James* (See *Hist. Hadley*, p. 68).   LOUISE TRACY.

VAN HOOK, SMIT AND CROSMAN FAMILIES. LAWRENCE VAN HOOK.—In Vol. X, p, 47, of the RECORD, it is erroneously stated that Lawrence Van Hook was "a Judge in New York." Research concerning this Lawrence Van Hook discloses that he probably died prior to 28 July, 1724, at Freehold, N. J., leaving a will dated 14 July, 1724, which was proved 14 Aug., 1724, at Perth Amboy, N. J. He m. (1) on 2 July, 1692, Johanna Hendricx of New York, who d. in 1693-4, leaving one child, Johanna, bap. 11 June, 1693; d. 1724, at Freehold, N. J. He then m. (2) probably about the latter part of 1694, Johanna Smit, dau. of Hendrik Barentse Smit of Boswyck, Long Island, by whom he had issue: Gerritje, bap. 29 Sept., 1695; d. in infancy; Gerritje, bap. 25 Dec., 1696; Arent, bap. 9 Oct., 1698; Hendrik, bap. 19 Feb., 1701; Isaac, bap. 22 Aug., 1703; Gerrittie, bap. 1 Oct., 1704; Benjamin, bap. 26 Jan., 1707; Maria, bap. 9 April, 1710; Francesca, bap. 31 Oct., 1714. All his children except Francesca were bap. in New York, but she was bap. in the Old Marlborough Church, near Freehold, Monmouth County, New Jersey.

Laurence Van Hook resided in the Province of New York as early as 1661, and at Boswyck about 1687, but returned to New York City prior to Sept., 1699, where he frequently held public office, viz.: as Constable, 29 Sept., 1689; High Constable, 29 Sept., 1700; Assessor for the Dock Ward, 29 Sept., 1705, reappointed 1706. He removed to Freehold, N. J., in the early spring of 1712, where he is described in various deeds recorded in the County Clerk's Office as a "bolter," as "of the City of New York, merchant," and as "of the County of Monmouth." He was a large land owner in the vicinity of Freehold, New Jersey, and also owned some land in Westchester County, New York. He served as "an Assistant Justice" of the Court of Quarter Sessions of Monmouth County, New Jersey, from 1714-1721.

ROBERT CROSMAN.—In Vol. XXII, p. 77, of the RECORD, John Crosman is given as the first ancestor of "The Crosman Family in America." This is an error as Mr. Baylies in his *History of New Plymouth*, Part 2, p. 286, mistook the name "John Greenman" for "John Crossman" in the list of the original purchasers of Taunton, Mass.

The original immigrant was Robert Crosman from Somertshire. England, who settled in Dedham, Mass., where he became a freeman in 1642. He m. there 25 May, 1652, Sarah Kingsbury, dau. of Joseph and Millicent Kingsbury, and had issue, his first child, Sarah, b. 1653, at Dedham. He removed to Taunton, Mass., in 1653, where he had eleven other children, descendants of whom still live in Taunton.

HENDRIK BARENTSE SMIT.—Hendrik Barentse Smit, m. Geertje Willemse, and his name apparently first appears on the records in the year 1655. The inventory of his estate is dated 6 Nov., 1690, and amounts to £16,407-10s-0d. His will appears in Book I, p. 236, Kings County. Registry.

Any further information concerning the above Laurence Van Hook and Hendrik Barentse Smit is earnestly requested.   J. HERON CROSMAN,
95 Elm Street, New Rochelle, N. Y.

QUERIES.

ABBOTT.—I would be glad to learn anything relating to James Abbott who came to Long Island about 1690(?), from Somersetshire, England. He is said to have married on Long Island and had five sons and two daughters. One of his sons, Benjamin, being the father of Rev. Benjamin Abbott (1732-1796), the noted M. E. minister of New Jersey. Date of birth and death, names of wife and daughters, and residence particularly desired.
A. S. ABBOTT, Bethel, Ohio.

KELSEY.—Wanted the parentage and ancestry of William Kelsey. I am told that in the year 1632 William Kelsey was a member of Rev. Thomas Hooker's congregation, in Braintree, Essex County, England. Mr. Hooker's flock was at that time in great trouble, their shepherd had fled to Holland to escape fines and imprisonment for non-conformity, and to enjoy the privilege of such a pastor they were willing to migrate to any quarter of the world. They turned their eyes to New England, hoping that if they could make a comfortable settlement there they might induce him to follow them. Accordingly they came to America in 1633 and "began to sit down" at Wollaston, a few miles south of Boston. But it was the policy of the colony to keep the population as much concentrated as possible, and by order of the Court they moved to Cambridge—then Newtowne—where they were known as the Braintree Company.   MARTENSE HARCOURT CORNELL,
Wappingers Falls, N. Y.

EARLY AMERICAN MERRITTS.—Wanted, date of births and deaths, names of parents and wives: Ezekiel, Newport, R. I., 1638; Edward, New York, 1701-10; George, Boston, 1 May, 1684; George, Perth Amboy, N. J., 1694; Henry, Scituate, Mass., 1628, d. 1652; Isaac, Bristol, Pa., 1684, wife Joyce Olive; John, Scituate, 1652; John, Grand Jury, New York, 1641; John, Captain, m. Sybil Ray, 1649; John, killed at South Deerfield, 18 Sept., 1675; John, taxed in Maryland, 1681; John, m. Catherine Guthrie, 1684; Nicholas, Salem, b. 1613, d. 1686, wife Margaret Sandin; Philip, Boston, b. 1662, d. 20 Sept., 1735, wife Mary; Richard, Charlestown, Mass., m. Mary Simmons, 12 Jan., 1685; Samuel, Kent Co., Md., 1708; Thomas, Delaware Bay, 1664-80; Thomas, Rye, N. Y., 1673-1721, second wife Abigail Francis; William, New York, Mayor, 1695, d. 1708.
DOUGLAS MERRITT, Rhinebeck, N. Y.

OBDER.—Wanted information as to the origin of the name Obder. One of the sons of Elijah Miles and Frances Cornell is Thomas Obder Miles, b. 1789, Long Island or Nova Scotia.   MISS G. C. MILES, 3231 Forrest Ave., Chicago.

PALMER.—Wanted in particular the parentage or ancestry of Samuel Palmer, b. in Westchester Co., N. Y., 1743; d. at Bloomingcove, Orange Co., N. Y., 1817; m. Sarah Pierce?

FLEWWELLING.—Ancestry of Sarah Flewwelling who m. Ajah Palmer, 1808?

VROOMAN.—Date and place of death of Abraham Vrooman, who m. Marytje Verplanck, 1735? E. COWING, 24 E. Bayard St., Seneca Falls, N. Y.

BOOK NOTICES.

COL. HENRY LUDINGTON. A MEMOIR. By Willis Fletcher Johnson, A. M., L. H. D. Printed by his grandchildren, Lavinia Elizabeth Ludington and Charles Henry Ludington. New York. The De Vinne Press. 1907. 8vo, cloth, pp. ix+235.

The first chapter of this memoir is taken up with the history of the Ludington name in England, and an account, in narrative form, of the American progenitors of Col. Henry Ludington. The last chapter contains brief notices of some later generations. The body of the work, therefore, is devoted to a study of the life and character of this worthy and efficient militia officer, and a large number of letters and other documents are given in full, thoroughly illustrating Col. Ludington's career. There are numerous excellent portraits and facsimiles, and an index. The compilation shows great care and research, and the make-up is in the usual satisfying manner of the DeVinne Press.

THE BARNES FAMILY YEAR BOOK. An annual publication issued under the authority of the Barnes Family Association. Compiled by Trescott C. Barnes, Secretary and Genealogist. Vol. I, 1907. New York. The Grafton Press. 1907. 8vo, cloth, pp. 64.

This is a sensible year book, composed entirely of Barnes genealogies, and with a good index. It contains accounts of some immigrant Barnes, and descendants of Thomas Barnes of Hartford, and Thomas Barnes of New Haven, of the Barnes Family of Long Island, and of Joshua of East Hampton. A novel idea is exploited in the Record of Ancestry, in which, as the basis for a Barnes Genealogy, the pedigrees of members of the Barnes Family Association are given. There are also obituaries and a department of Information Wanted. This practical form of family association report is worthy of imitation.

CLASS OF 1847. THE CENTENNIAL CLASS, COLLEGE OF NEW JERSEY, PRINCETON, N. J., NOW PRINCETON UNIVERSITY, consisting of brief biographies of its members from 1847 to 1907. Compiled by its Historian and Secretary, Henry B. Munn and Alfred Martien, Philadelphia. Printed for the class by Patterson & White Co. 1907. 12D, cloth, pp. 94.

Clad in its University colors, this little volume is a tribute to the glories of their *Alma Mater, Old Nassau,* and contains biographies and portraits of the faculty and class of that far-away year. Of especial interest to this Society, is the account of Mr. Seth Hastings Grant, a former officer of the Society, and author of its name.

ANCESTRY OF COL. JOHN HARVEY OF NORTHWOOD, NEW HAMPSHIRE. By John Harvey Treat, A. M. Boston. Privately printed. 1907. 8vo, cloth, pp. 47.

This volume is a good example of a favorite present-day form of genealogical printing, namely, to set forth the ancestors and descendants of some favorite or especially distinguished individual. Col. John Harvey was an original member of the New Hampshire Society of the Cincinnati, although at the time of signing its rolls he was a Lieutenant. He is represented in this Society by the compiler of this genealogy. The book is well printed and indexed.

FITZ RANDOLPH TRADITIONS. A Story of a Thousand Years. L. V. F. Randolph. Published under the auspices of the New Jersey Historical Society. 1907. 12D, cloth, pp. 134 and a chart.

In this interesting little brochure nothing more is attempted than, as is stated in the sub-title, to tell the story of the family for a thousand years. The author is convinced that the descent of Edward Fitz Randolph of Scituate, Mass., and Piscataway, N. J., is ·proven from Rolf the Norseman, and his argument for this conclusion is very interesting. The work is attractively bound and illustrated, having a number of English views. It has always seemed a pity that this family has, to such an extent, dropped the distinctive part of the surname, but this little work may inspire some of them to replace it.

SOCIAL LIFE OF VIRGINIA IN THE SEVENTEENTH CENTURY. By Philip Alexander Bruce, Richmond. Printed for the author by Whittet & Shepperson. 1907. 8vo, cloth, pp. 268. For sale by the Bell Book Company, Richmond, Va. Price, net, $1.50, postpaid, $1.60.

5A

Written in a straightforward and pleasing style, this work will be found of great interest to genealogists as well as students of social life and customs. Several chapters are devoted to the English origin of the higher planting class, and authorities are liberally cited. The great events of life, and its diversions, are treated of in separate chapters, and the book is a valuable addition to Virginiana.

MATTAPOISETT AND OLD ROCHESTER, MASSACHUSETTS. Being a history of these towns and also in part of Marion and a portion of Wareham. Prepared under the direction of a committee of the town of Mattapoisett. New York. The Grafton Press. 1907. 12D, cloth, pp. xii+424.

Thr various chapters in this history are by different hands, most of them, however, having been contributed by Miss Mary Hall Leonard and Mr. Lemuel LeBaron Dexter. There are about 150 pages of extracts from the Records, showing old Rochester soldiers and sailors, baptisms, marriages and lists of members of the Second Church, and other items. There are a number of good illustrations, and the index is well done. The work of this committee was in connection with the fiftieth anniversary of the setting off of Mattapoisett from Rochester, and the result of their labors is a very worthy volume.

THE SACKETTS OF AMERICA, THEIR ANCESTORS AND DESCENDANTS, 1630–1907. By Charles H. Weygant. Newburgh, N. Y. Journal Print. 1907. Quarto, cloth, pp. 553.

Simon Sackett of Newtown (Cambridge), Mass., who came with a wife and one son in the *Lyon* in 1630, and John Sackett of New Haven, his brother, passenger in the same ship, with one son, are the progenitors of the large and highly respectable family whose records are herein set forth. The compiler has been generous and wise enough to include daughter's descendants, and many prominent people are to be found among them. Hon. Hamilton Fish, John Alsop, the Lawrences, the Kings, and many other well-known names appear among the daughters' descendants. In the male line will be found many military and civil records of importance. In some cases, the ancestors of allied families are given. The type is good, and good judgment has been used in the printing. There is an excellent index. This work has been long awaited, and is a very useful addition to genealogical records.

WILLIS RECORDS; OR RECORDS OF THE WILLIS FAMILY OF HAVERHILL, PORTLAND AND BOSTON. By Pauline Willis. London. Printed by St. Vincent's Press. 1906. 8vo, half leather, pp. 115.

Part I is concerned with the Willis family. Part II deals with the allied families of Gammell, Ball, McKinstry, Leonard, Kinsman, May, Sewall and Phillips. A third part contains family letters, but these and the illustrations are only included in volumes sent to members of the family.

THE HISTORY OF ULSTER COUNTY, NEW YORK. Edited by Alphonso T. Clearwater, LL.D. Kingston. W. J. Van Deusen. 1907. 8vo, leather, pp. 712+xii.

A new history of Ulster County, especially one edited by Judge Clearwater, is sure to attract attention. Perhaps the most important additions which this work makes to our knowledge of the county, are the carefully edited and corrected military records. About one hundred and fifty pages at the end of the book are devoted to biographical notices, and there is a partial index. The illustrations are remarkably good, and the book is of a more practical size than most county histories, and is attractively and substantially bound.

GENEALOGICAL NOTES OF THE CARPENTER FAMILY, including the Autobiography and Personal Reminiscences of Dr. Seymour D. Carpenter. Edited by Edwin Sawyer Walker, A. M. Springfield, Ill. Illinois State Journal Co., Printers. 1907. 8vo, cloth, pp. xv+242.

These Carpenters are descendants of Heinrich Zimmerman, anglicized Henry Carpenter, who came from Switzerland and settled in Pennsylvania. The major part of the book contains, in interesting narrative form, the family history, and the autobiography of Dr. Seymour D. Carpenter, and these are followed by the genealogy in brief, in an appendix. Letters, biographies, and other miscellaneous matter follow, and there is a good index. Dr. Carpenter was born in 1826, and spent his early life near Lancaster, Ohio. His recollections of pioneer life, and the War of the Rebellion, in which he served as a surgeon, being mustered out in 1865 with the rank of Brevet Lieutenant-Colonel, are full of interest.

THE ANCESTRY OF JANE MARIA GREENLEAF, wife of William Francis Joseph Boardman, Hartford, Connecticut. William F. J. Boardman. Hartford. Privately Printed. 1906. 8vo, cloth, pp. 133.

This is a companion volume to *The Ancestry of William F. J. Boardman*, and is arranged in the same manner. Allied families in this work are: Jones, Cleveland, Hartshorne, Hibbard, Champion, Johnson, Nichols, Sumner, Toocker and others. A number of family portraits are properly included, and the index is unusually good.

COLLECTIONS OF THE CONNECTICUT HISTORICAL SOCIETY, VOLUME XI. THE LAW PAPERS. Correspondence and Documents during Jonathan Law's Governorship of the Colony of Connecticut, 1741–1750. Vol. I, October, 1741–July, 1745. Hartford. Connecticut Historical Society. 1907. 8vo, cloth, pp. xxxv+391.

The Connecticut Historical Society, having previously published the correspondence and documents covering Joseph Talcott's governorship of the State, continue their work with the papers of Governor Law, who succeeded Talcott. Law was Governor at the time of the Louisbourg expedition in 1745, and during the trying times which succeeded it, and proved himself able and efficient under difficult conditions. This volume contains, amongst other valuable records, several lists of colonial soldiers.

VITAL RECORD OF RHODE ISLAND. Vol. XVI. James N. Arnold. Providence. Narragansett Historical Publishing Company. 1907. Quarto, cloth, pp. lxiv+601.

Like the previous volumes of this series, the present one will be found of the greatest assistance to genealogists. It contains marriages from *The United States Chronicle* and *The Providence Semi-Weekly Journal*, and both marriages and deaths from *The American Journal, The Impartial Observer* and *The Providence Journal*. These notices relate to persons all over the United States, and should not be overlooked by those making any genealogical research.

WILLIAMSBURG, THE OLD COLONIAL CAPITAL. Lyon Gardiner Tyler, LL.D., President of William and Mary College. Richmond. Whittet & Shepperson. 1907. 8vo, cloth, pp. 285.

This very interesting work, compiled by an authority of President Tyler's standing, is most acceptable to the students of early conditions in Virginia. Nearly one hundred pages of this book are filled with the history of William and Mary College, whose beginnings are found very nearly three hundred years ago, although the charter was not signed until February 8, 1693. But aside from the college, much of interest must always surround the old capital of Virginia. It was one of the earliest English settlements on this continent; in the house of burgesses here it was that Patrick Henry offered his famous set of resolutions upon the Stamp Act; it was here that Bruton Parish was established in 1674, and it was to the old parish church that a Bible has just been given by King Edward VII, and a lectern by President Roosevelt. The book is illustrated with good taste and judgment, many old views and facsimiles being shown, and there is a good index. Its general appearance is excellent.

MONOGRAPH ON THE SOUTHGATE FAMILY OF SCARBOROUGH, MAINE.
THEIR ANCESTORS AND DESCENDANTS. Leonard B. Chapman. Portland,
Me. Hubbard W. Bryant. 1907. 8vo, cloth, pp. viii+60.

These records are the outcome of a series of articles entitled *Grandpa's
Scrap Book*, which appeared in the *Deering News* in 1900. Besides the
Southgate data, considerable material on the Bowne, Boyd, Browne, Lawrence,
Merrill and Smith families is presented here. Portraits of Bishop Southgate
and Dr. Southgate are included, with a view of "Dunston Abbey." Some
additional genealogical matter will be found in the Preface, and the index is
well made and practical.

GENEALOGY OF LAMB, ROSE AND OTHERS. Daniel Smith Lamb, A. M.,
M. D. Washington. Beresford, Printer. 1904. 8vo, stiff paper, pp. 100.

These are the ancestors of the compiler. The introduction gives a brief
historical review of the early settlements in which the ancestors dwelt,
followed by a list of counties in New Jersey and their principal towns in 1765.
The principal families treated of, are: Bates, Clement, Colliers, Cranmer,
Devinney, Hancock, Howard, Lamb, Matlack, Owen, Pennell, Rose, Stout and
Van Princess. There are indices of names and places.

THE GRAVES WE DECORATE. Storer Post, No. 1, Department of New
Hampshire, Grand Army of the Republic, Portsmouth, N. H. Prepared for
Memorial Day, 1907, by Joseph Foster, member Storer Post. With an Appen-
dix containing the list of graves and additional records prepared in 1893.
Portsmouth. John D. Randall, Printer. 1907. 8vo, pamphlet, pp. 20+76.

This is a careful compilation by Mr. Foster, formerly a Pay Director in the
Navy, now retired, who has for a number of years contributed genealogical
material to the common knowledge. His work will be found of the greatest
practical use. The names of the dead soldiers and sailors are given alphabetically under the names of their burial places, with service, rank or ship,
death, age and part of the cemetery in which they lie. This work of Storer
Post is worthy of emulation.

A CATALOGUE OF AUTOGRAPHS, BOOKS, MANUSCRIPTS, MEDALS, PEDI-
GREES, PORTRAITS, TRACTS AND OTHER MATTERS CONNECTED WITH THE
SEVERAL FAMILIES OF THE NAME OF BAKER, now in the possession of
Charles Edward Baker, Sherwhod, Nottingham, England. Nottingham. R.
H. Judd, Printer. 1907. 12D, pamphlet, pp. 32.

This comprehensive title fully explains the little work. The lists of
manuscripts ought to be of service to Baker genealogists, and the scheme of
collection seems a most commendable one.

A BRIEF HISTORY OF CHEMUNG COUNTY, NEW YORK, FOR THE USE OF
GRADED SCHOOLS. Ausburn Towner. New York. A. S. Barnes & Company.
1907. 12D, cloth, pp. ii+103.

While this history is written in a simple style for the purposes set forth,
its footnotes will be found of value from a genealogical standpoint. A re-
capitulation of important events by years will be found in the back of the book.

NICHOLAS MUNDY AND DESCENDANTS WHO SETTLED IN NEW JERSEY IN
1665. Compiled by Rev. Ezra F. Mundy of Metuchen, N. J. Lawrence,
Kansas. Bullock Printing Company. 1907. 8vo, cloth, pp. 160.

This work contains chiefly the record of Samuel, one of the sons of
Nicholas Mundy. The compiler encountered the usual difficulty met with by
those attempting New Jersey genealogy, but has succeeded in placing before
us considerable material on the family, which is now largely scattered throughout the West.

THE ANCESTRY OF WILLIAM FRANCIS JOSEPH BOARDMAN, HARTFORD,
CONNECTICUT. Being his lineage in all lines of descent from the emigrant
ancestors in New England. William F. J. Boardman. Hartford. Privately
printed. 1906. Quarto, cloth, pp. 419.

In this handsome ancestral memorial Mr. Boardman has apparently reached the apogee of his genealogical labors. Instead of dealing with each family name in a separate article, Mr. Boardman has arranged the work by generations, beginning with himself as generation number one. A second division of the book shows lines of descent from emigrant ancestors, and a third section contains charts. There are many excellent illustrations and a copious index.

IN OLDE NEW YORK. Sketches of old times and places in both the State and the city. Charles Burr Todd. New York. The Grafton Press. 1907. 12D, cloth, pp. 253.

A large portion of this volume was written twenty years ago and appeared in the *Evening Post* and *Lippincott's Magazine*, and is repeated with very little change because it describes types and conditions now passed away. This has its advantage, because the limited space allotted to this series, many things which were considered important twenty years ago would be slurred over in articles brought up to date. The author has a certain picturesqueness of style, and his accounts of persons and things are most realistic. Like *Mattapoisett and Old Rochester*, this is one of the Grafton Historical Series, edited by Henry R. Stiles, A.M., M.D.

WADHAMS FAMILY. A Genealogy of the Wadhams Family is being compiled by Harriet Wadhams Stevens (Mrs. George T.), 22 E. 46th Street, New York City. She would be glad to correspond with those interested.

ACCESSIONS TO THE LIBRARY.

September 9 to December 4, 1907.

DONATIONS.

Bound.

Boardman, William F. J.—Ancestry of Jane Maria Greenleaf. Ancestry of William Francis Joseph Boardman.
Bruce, Philip Alexander.—Social Life in Virginia in the Seventeenth Century.
Carpenter, Seymour D., M.D.—Carpenter Genealogy.
Chapman, Leonard B.—Southgate Family of Scarborough, Me.
Clearwater, Hon. A. T.—History of Ulster County, N. Y.
Curtis, Gen. Newton M.—From Bull Run to Chancellorsville.
Daughters of Holland Dames.—Record Book, 1907.
Goold, Nathan.—Maine Historical Collections, Series II, Vol. IX. Index. Collections, Vol. X Maine Society, Sons of the American Revolution, Portland, Me., Centennial.
Grafton Press.—Barnes Family Year Book. Mattapoisett and Old Rochester. In Olde New York. The Cherokee Indians.
Grant, Seth Hastings.—The Centennial Class of the College of New Jersey.
Hathaway, Charles R.—Report of the Temporary Examiner of Public Records, Connecticut, 1906.
Harris, Edward Doubleday.—James McKinney.
Ludington, C. H.—Colonel Henry Ludington.
Montgomery, Thomas.—Pennsylvania Archives, Series V, Vols. 1 to 8.
Mundy, Rev. Ezra F.—Nicholas Mundy and His Descendants.
Noyes, Charles Phelps.—Noyes-Gilman Ancestry.
Randolph, L. V. F.—Fitz-Randolph Traditions.
Rowlee, Prof. Willard W.—Lieutenant Heman Rowlee.
Smithsonian Institution.—Annual Report.
Society of Colonial Wars.—Addresses and Year Book.
Totten, John R.—Medical Directory of New York, New Jersey and Connecticut.
Towner, Ausburn.—Brief History of Chemung County, N. Y.

Treat, J. Harvey.—Ancestry of Col. John Harvey.
Tyler, Lyon G.—Williamsburg, Va.
Weygant, Charles H.—Sacketts of America.
Willis, Pauline.—Willis Records.
Woolley, Charles, Sr., and Charles Dod Ward.—Ward Genealogy, bound
  manuscript.

Pamphlets, Etc.

Americana Society.—American Historical Magazine.
Archivist, Ottawa.—Constitutional History of Canada.
Baker, Charles Edward.—Baker Family Catalogue.
Balch, William Lincoln, Sec'y.—Third Balch Family Reunion.
Boston Cemetery Department.—Report, 1906.
Brink, Benjamin M.—Olde Ulster.
Christman, F. W.—Palatine Records from the British Museum, manuscript.
Clark & Wilkins.—Concise Atlas of the World.
Congdon, G. E.—Waterman Year Book, 1905.
Corbett, John.—Watkins, N. Y., Express, 4 numbers.
Cornell, Rev. John.—Cornell Tombstone Inscriptions, manuscript.
Davis, Andrew McFarland.—Barberries and Wheat.
Dwight, Rev. M. E.—Genealogical Exchange.
Edwards, Rev. John Harrington, D.D.—Edwards Family.
First Reformed Church.—Church Tablet.
Foote, Edward Bond.—In Memoriam, Edward Bliss Foote.
Foster, Joseph.—The Graves We Decorate, 1907.
Hathaway, Charles R.—Report of the Temporary Examiner of Public Records,
  Connecticut, 1904.
Kimball, Sarah Louise.—Putnam's Historical Magazine, VII, 10.
Lamb, Daniel Smith, M.D.—Genealogies of Lamb, Rose and other families.
Lawton, Mrs. Thomas A.—Rhode Island Historical Magazine.
Locke, Arthur H.—Portsmouth and Newcastle Inscriptions.
Macy, W. A., M.D.—Memorial Notice of Dr. Edwin Cooper Dent.
Morrison, George Austin, Jr.—Records of Amity, Conn., I.
Myers, Edward—Tarrytown Argus, clippings.
Needham, Henry C.—Wales, Mass., Centennial.
N. Y. Genealogical and Biographical Society.—Subject Index to the Record,
  Vols. I-XXXVIII.
Quinby, Henry Cole.—New England Family History.
Totten, John R.—Association of Graduates, West Point, 1907. Official Register
  of Officers and Cadets, West Point. Our Race News Leaflet. Subscription
  to The Norwalk Hour.
Tracy, Dwight, M.D.—The Charles Larned Memorial.
Truax, Jas. R., Sec'y.—Schenectady County Historical Society Report.
University of Texas.—Bulletin No. 88.
Van Alstyne, Wm. B., M.D.—Pedigree of Mrs. Van Alstyne, manuscript.
  Van Valkenburg Tombstone Record, manuscript. Pedigree Chart of W.
  B. Van Alstyne, M.D., manuscript. Newspaper clippings.
Wendell Bros.—The Wendell System of Perpetual Family Records.
Willers, Hon. Diedrich.—The Old State Agricultural College, Ovid, N. Y.
Wyoming Historical and Geological Society.—History of the Society.

OTHER ACCESSIONS.

Acadiensis.
Albany County Records, Vol. 14.
American Catholic Historical Society Records.
American Monthly Magazine.
Annals of Iowa.
Bibliography of Vermont.
Bliss' History of Rehoboth, Mass.
Bradford, Mass., Vital Records.
Claremont, N. H. Gravestone Records.
Condit Family.
Connecticut Historical Society's Collections, Vol. XI.
Essex Antiquarian.

Essex Institute.
Franklin Mass., History.
Gargrave, Yorkshire, Registers.
Genealogist.
Grafton, Mass., History.
History of New Bedford Churches.
History of the Second Church, Hartford.
International Genealogical Directory.
Journal of American History.
Mayflower Descendant.
Middleboro, Mass., History.
Miscellanea Genealogica et Heraldica.
Moulton Family Annals.
New England Historical and Genealogical Register, and Register Index.
Ohio Archæological and Historical Quarterly.
Old Northwest Genealogical Quarterly.
Otsego County, N. Y., Biographical Review.
Palmer, Mass., History.
Pelham, Mass., History.
South Carolina Historical and Genealogical Magazine.
Terrington, Yorkshire, Registers.
Thompson's History of Long Island, 2 vols.
Virginia County Records, Vol. IV, Marriages.
Virginia Magazine of History and Biography.
Vital Records of Rhode Island, XVI.
Washington County, N. Y., Gazetteer.
William and Mary College Quarterly.
Yale Biographies, III, IV.
Yarmouth, N. S.
Year Books of Probates, IV, 3.

The New York Genealogical and Biographical Society WANTS, and will buy:

PEIRCE'S COLONIAL LISTS.
HOWLAND GENEALOGY.
HUBBARD'S STANSTEAD COUNTY, CANADA.
VERMONT HISTORICAL GAZETEER.—Vol. III.
POWERS' SANGAMON COUNTY, ILL., SETTLERS.
NEWPORT HISTORICAL MAGAZINE.—Index to Vol. IV.
RHODE ISLAND HISTORICAL MAGAZINE.—Vol. VII, Part 4.
WALDO'S HISTORY OF TOLLAND, CONN.
INDEXES TO WILLS AT TRENTON, N. J.
ROBERTSON'S POCAHONTAS DESCENDANTS.
NARRAGANSETT HISTORICAL REGISTER.—Vol. IX, Nos. 3, 4, and Index.
CONNECTICUT QUARTERLY.—Vol. I, No. 1.
AUSTIN'S ALLIED FAMILIES.
MASSACHUSETTS HISTORICAL SOCIETY'S COLLECTIONS.
RICE'S BIRTHS, MARRIAGES AND DEATHS IN WORCESTER, MASS.
BALCH GENEALOGY.
ALDEN GENEALOGY.
CONNECTICUT HISTORICAL SOCIETY'S COLLECTIONS.—Vol. I.
BAYLES' HISTORY OF WINDHAM COUNTY, CONN.
OUR ANCESTORS.—By Van Horne.—Vol. I, all after No. 2.
NEW ENGLAND NOTES AND QUERIES.—Vol. I, No. 3, and all after No. 4.
NEW HAMPSHIRE REPOSITORY.—Vol. I, Nos. 1, 2, 3; Vol. II, Nos. 2, 3, 4.
COLONIAL MAGAZINE.—Vol. I, all after No. 5.
NATIONAL MAGAZINE.—Vols. I–XV, inclusive; Vols. XVI, No. 4; XVII, Nos. 4, 5, 6; XVIII, all Nos.; XIX, Nos. 1, 4, 5, 6.

THE NEW YORK

GENEALOGICAL AND BIOGRAPHICAL

RECORD.

DEVOTED TO THE INTERESTS OF AMERICAN
GENEALOGY AND BIOGRAPHY.

ISSUED QUARTERLY.

April, 1908.

PUBLISHED BY THE
NEW YORK GENEALOGICAL AND BIOGRAPHICAL SOCIETY.

THE NEW YORK
Genealogical and Biographical

SAMUEL WARD

THE NEW YORK
Genealogical and Biographical Record.

| VOL. XXXIX. | NEW YORK, APRIL, 1908. | No. 2. |

SAMUEL WARD KING.

By George Austin Morrison, Jr., A.M., LL.B.

Samuel Ward King, the thirteenth Governor of the State of Rhode Island, was born on 23 May, 1786, at Johnston, Providence County, Rhode Island, and was the fifth child and third son of William Borden King and his wife Welthian Walton. He was a lineal descendant of Clement King, who appeared at Marshfield, Mass., in 1668 and removed to the Providence Plantations about 1687, where he died about 1690, leaving an eldest son John King, who had issue, a son Josiah King, who in due course had issue, a son William Borden King, the father of the future Governor. It is now clearly established that Clement Kinge, the first settler, was a son of Clement Kinge and Mary Raynor of St. Giles, Cripplegate, London, England, and a grandson of that Ralphe Kinge of Watford, Hertfordshire, England, who, in his will, dated 1 Aug., 1653, and proved 21 Nov., 1656 (P. C. C. Berkley 419), wrote in his own hand "and whereas my sonne Clement intended to make a will in writinge but the violence of his disease being so great he desired me not to have it perfected but said he would leave all to his wife's disposinge." Daniel Kinge, Gent. of Lynn, Mass., 1644, also mentioned in the will of his father, Ralphe Kinge, was an uncle of Clement Kinge of Marshfield. Through his mother, Mr. King was related to the Walton, Greene and Coggeshall Families, members of which held important and influential positions among the early Colonial settlers. Mr. King received his early education at the district school and for a short period was a student at Brown University, Providence.

He desired, however, to become a physician and as there was no medical schools in those days, he became the pupil and assistant of his relative, Dr. Peter Ballou, a learned and well established physician of Smithfield, R. I. After serving faithfully for some years, Mr. King received his certificate to practice medicine, dated 5 Aug., 1807, and signed by Peter Ballou, the original of which is still in the possession of his descendants.

Dr. King then started upon his career as a country doctor, but not finding that profession as lucrative as he expected, he

6

took the position of cashier of the Agricultural Bank of Olney-ville and served in that capacity for several years.

Upon the declaration of war with Great Britain in 1812, Dr. King volunteered as surgeon on a privateer schooner sailing from Providence on 3 Aug., 1812. This vessel was captured by a British ship on 20 Aug., 1812, and taken to Barbadoes, West Indies, as a prize of war, where the Captain, First-Lieutenant and Surgeon were paroled. The original parole permit issued to Dr. King is still preserved in the family and is dated Barbadoes, 4 Oct., 1812, and signed by "John Barker, Lt. R. N., Agent for Prisoners." From an endorsement on the back it appears that Dr. King was at this time 26 years of age, 5 feet 9¼ inches in stature, rather stout, with a long visage, fair complexion, light hair and blue eyes.

Dr. King must have either effected an exchange, or escaped shortly after the granting of parole, as his return to Providence is recorded in the *Providence Gazette*, on 19 Nov., 1812.

There is a family tradition that upon his return Dr. King re-enlisted and served as surgeon on the ships *Wasp* and *Hornet*, being on board the latter when she captured on 18 Oct., 1812, the British sloop-of-war *Frolic* off the coast of North Carolina, only to be taken in turn by the British a few weeks later. It is also stated that Dr. King was an eye-witness of the fight between the U. S. frigate *Chesapeake* and the British frigate *Shannon* off Boston harbor in June, 1813, and was called on board to assist the ship surgeon in attending upon Captain James Lawrence during his last moments and heard that commander's historic words of "Don't give up the ship."

Possibly it was in memory of this event that Dr. King called his first son, born in 1820, James Lawrence King.

At the end of the war he resumed his private practice at Johnston (Olneyville), Rhode Island, and was elected Town Clerk of Johnston in 1820, serving in that office continuously until 1843, when he declined a re-election. He was also appointed a Justice-of-the-Peace for Johnston in June, 1810, and again served in that capacity from May, 1818, to 1830. He was one of the Electors for Johnston at the 12th presidential election in 1832 when he and his three associates cast the vote for Henry Clay of Kentucky, for president, and John Sargent of Pennsylvania, for vice-president, both National Republicans. He further served as Inspector of Prisons from 1838-40, and as Clerk of the Court of Common Pleas in May, 1843.

Dr. King appears to have taken an active interest in politics early in life, and it was in 1839 that he reaped his reward for his devotion and efforts for sound government. During this year no choice for Governor and Lieutenant-Governor was had and Dr. King, then serving as first State Senator, became the Acting Governor.

In 1840 he received the Whig nomination for the office of Chief Magistrate and was duly elected Governor of Rhode Island by a majority of 1,311, the vote being Saml. W. King, 4,797; Thomas F. Carpenter, 3,418; scattering, 68; making a total of 8,283.

This vote of 4,797 cast for Mr. King was the largest polled since 1818, and also the largest ever given a candidate for Governor in the then history of the State. Dr. King was re-elected in 1841 by a majority of 2,585, the vote being Saml. W. King, 2,648; scattering, 63; making a total of 2,711; and again re-elected in 1842 by a majority of 2,648, the vote being Saml. W. King, 4,864; Thomas F. Carpenter, 2,211; scattering, 5; making a total of 7,080. It was during his last term as Governor that the celebrated outbreak known as the "Dorr Rebellion" took place and in order to clearly understand the causes of this war *in camera*, a brief statement of Rhode Island history becomes necessary.

The Colony of Rhode Island and the Providence Plantations—which later became the State of Rhode Island—had been governed for one hundred and eighty years under the Royal Charter secured on 9 July, 1663, from King Charles II, by the efforts of Dr. John Clarke, sent to the Court of St. James by the Colonists for this purpose. This charter—one of the most remarkable documents in the history of go ern en s, in that it granted liberty of religious thought and worship with a just civil government as opposed to the narrow and dogmatic charters of the Plymouth, Massachusetts Bay and Connecticut colonial governments—restricted the suffrage to those owing real property to the amount of $134 and to their eldest sons. During the course of time, however, the growth of population and the rapid influx of people from other countries and States, left almost two-thirds of the people without the power to vote, and as early as 1820 the subject of the reformation of the oligarchical form of government and the extension of the suffrage began to be agitated. In 1837 a champion of the people's cause appeared in the person of Thomas Wilson Dorr, a lawyer and politician of Providence, R. I., member of an old and highly respected family and a man of education and marked ability. Born a second son, Mr. Dorr was unable to vote at the general election and hence soon took the lead in the struggle to amend the Charter or frame a new State Constitution, granting more liberal suffrage. Mr. Dorr, as a Whig member of the Assembly from 1833–1837, repeatedly urged that the representation in the Legislature was unfair in that only one-third of the people held the voting power and that the City of Newport, with 8,000 inhabitants had six members, while the City of Providence with 23,000 inhabitants had only four.

His motions for a more liberal constitution were defeated, and despairing of securing the desired suffrage from a Whig Government and Legislature chosen by a minority of the population, Mr. Dorr changed his political principles, became a Democrat and resorted to popular agitation against the so-called autocratic land-holding class.

In the latter part of 1840, Dorr and his supporters organized the so-called "Suffrage Party," which on 17 April, 1841, held a political procession and mass meeting in Providence, where much turgid eloquence was indulged in and the press filled with attacks on those holding the voting power. Another mass meeting was held at Newport on 5 May, which was adjourned to meet at Providence on 5 July, 1841, where a call was directed for a State constitutional convention. An election of delegates was held on 28 Aug., 1841, who proceeded to meet at Providence on 4 Oct., and frame a form of Constitution, which was submitted to the people at a general election held the 27, 28 and 29 Dec., 1841. The Dorr party claimed that at this election 13,944 citizens, which number was not only a majority of the adult population of the State, but also a majority of those entitled to suffrage under the charter, voted to accept the new People's Constitution as that of the State.

There can be no question but that this constitutional convention, the constitution then framed, and the subsequent election to ratify same, were illegal.

The supporters of the government forthwith organized themselves into a so-called "Law and Order" Party, which was derisively called the "Landholders" Party by Dorr and his associates, who branded all opposed to their views and claims as "Aristocrats."

Realizing the serious nature of this popular movement and the necessity for some change in the voting qualification, the regular Legislature met on 6 Feb., 1841, and in turn called a Constitutional Convention, the duly elected delegates to which met in Nov. and adjourned until Feb., 1842. On this last date they agreed upon a form of Constitution, which was submitted to the people (entitled to vote under the old Royal Charter) on 21, 22 and 23 March, 1842, and rejected.

Meanwhile Governor King foreseeing that the rapid growth of the suffragist party and its revolutionary and rebellious attitude towards the established government would lead to serious trouble, on 4 April, 1842, sent a committee and two letters to President Tyler at Washington, stating "that Rhode Island was threatened with domestic violence," and asking for recognition and assistance in case of need. The President replied on 11 April stating that while he recognized the regular State Government, in his opinion the necessity for armed intervention by the Federal government had not as yet arisen, nor did it appear that the regular Government of Rhode Island was not able to cope with the situation; he therefore declined to interfere previous to an actual outbreak but promised if an insurrection should take place to come to the aid of the established government.

On 18 April, 1842, the so-called "Suffrage Party" held an election under the terms of the so-called "Suffrage" constitution, at which they chose Mr. Dorr, their leader, as Governor, and a Legislature composed entirely of his supporters.

The People's Assembly forthwith met for organization in Providence on 3 May, 1842, received Governor Dorr's inaugural message, remained in session for two days, during which they passed several unimportant acts, and then adjourned to meet in Jan., 1843. It never met again however, as later the movement was suppressed.

As soon as the rejection of the "Landholders" constitution was known, Governor King convened the General Assembly in extra session on 25 April, 1842, and they then passed an act known as the "Algerine Act," making it a misdemeanor, punishable by fine and imprisonment for any person to act as Moderator or Clerk at any election meeting, under the People's Constitution, and treason for any person to accept office under it. At the same time Governor King warned the militia to be ready for service at thirty minutes' notice.

The regular government in turn proceeded to hold the usual election under the charter, 20 April, 1842, and chose Samuel Ward King Governor for the third term.

Each government now claimed legislative power and while the regular government officers proceeded to organize at Newport on 3 May, the People's Party issued an appeal to arms and marching upon the State House in Providence attempted to seize the government offices. The "Law and Order" Party however, anticipating such action, had taken possession of the State House and barricaded the doors, so that Dorr and his friends could not effect an entry.

Matters now assumed so serious a look that many of Dorr's supporters hesitated to come into direct conflict with the governing powers and began to withdraw from his support and desert the party.

Governor King thoroughly alarmed at the situation once more despatched a committee with a letter to the President on 4 May, 1842, to which a second non-committal reply was made by the Washington authorities. On 17 May, 1842, Governor King was informed that an attempt would be made by the Dorrites to seize the State Offices and he immediately issued a Proclamation for the troops to repair to the State Arsenal and take up arms.

Meanwhile Mr. Dorr collected his forces, and on the evening of the 18 May, 1842, made an armed attempt to seize the State Arsenal at Providence, which was thwarted by the appearance of the troops, commanded by Governor King in person.

Mr. Dorr realizing the serious character of his attempt, and the consequences of its failure, fled to Connecticut, whence he set out for Washington to seek the sanction and support of the Federal authorities. Governor King immediately proclaimed $1,000 reward for his capture and punishment, at the same time writing the President on 25 May, setting forth the actions of the "Suffrage or People's Party," and stating that Dorr was actively engaged in raising forces in other States against the Government of Rhode Island.

The Federal Government however again declined to intervene in the matter on behalf of either party, and Mr. Dorr then returned to Rhode Island, stopping in New York on his way back, where he was cordially welcomed by the leaders of Tammany Hall and assured of their sympathy and support.

When Mr. Dorr reached the village of Chepachet, a small hamlet ten miles from Providence, in the Town of Gloucester, he was met by an enthusiastic crowd of his adherents, who acclaimed him as their rightful Governor and informed him that the mass of the people were prepared to fight for their rights under his leadership. Mr. Dorr thereupon promptly issued a proclamation, signed as Governor, convening a General Assembly at Chepachet.

Governor King in turn had been active, calling upon the law-abiding citizens for aid and again appealing to the Federal Government, stating that he feared "insurgents from abroad" were being called into the State by Dorr and his friends. Finally on 25 June, 1842, martial law was proclaimed and serious steps taken to put down the so-called rebellion.

On 28 June, 1842, a small gathering of about 300 men with arms and 5 cannon met at Chepachet and made a military demonstration in favor of Mr. Dorr, seizing and fortifying "Acote's Hill," but upon the appearance of the State troops and other citizens to the aggregate number of 3,000 or more, the Dorr forces retreated from the field, and Mr. Dorr realizing that his cause was lost, ordered his forces to disperse and fled to Connecticut and subsequently to New Hampshire, a reward of $5,000 being offered by the Rhode Island State authorities for his capture. Gov. King applied to both Governors of Connecticut and New Hampshire for the surrender of Mr. Dorr, but both declined to take any action against the so-called "traitor," their sympathies being doubtless with the democratic rule. Quiet was entirely restored in a few days, and while a number of arrests had been made and a small number of persons imprisoned for a short period, the court proceedings were soon quashed and the incident closed.

Thus terminated the so-called "Dorr Rebellion" without serious injury to persons or property, the only blood shed being the death of one Alexander Kelby, an innocent by-stander who was wounded when the troops fired a volley at Pawtucket village on 27 June, 1842, and who subsequently died of his injuries.

The Legislature in June, 1842, now fully alive to the necessity for concession and change in the suffrage, issued a call for a new Constitutional Convention, which met at Providence in Sept., but adjourned to East Greenwich where, on 5 Nov., 1842, a new Constitution and form of government was adopted, based upon the old charter but eliminating most of the objectionable features of the ancient form of government. This Constitution, duly submitted to the people, was almost unanimously ratified by them an now forms the present Constitution of the State of Rhode Island.

Samuel Ward King was thus the last Governor of Rhode Island under the old Royal Charter.

Mr. Dorr subsequently returned of his own will to the State in 1843, was arrested and tried at Newport for high treason and on 27 June, 1844, condemned to imprisonment for life at hard labor. He was released, however, under a general Amnesty Act in 1847 and restored to his civil rights in 1851. In 1854 his friends in the Assembly succeeded in passing an act reversing the judgment in his case but the Supreme Court declared such act unconstitutional. Mr. Dorr died 27 Dec., 1854, and one of his biographers states "he was a man of strict honor and integrity and high character and to good abilities joined an untiring patience and an indomitable will."

The publications and newspaper articles for and against the Dorrites are voluminous, but viewed with the clear and calm judgment which reflection and years ever bring to concensus of public opinion, is that although the principles advocated for more liberal suffrage were sound, nevertheless the method attempted in carrying out such reform was unconstitutional and dangerous to the underlying principles of State government.

The attitude and action of Governor King during the entire episode was marked by constant watchfulness for the general public welfare, firmness in upholding the lawful authority of the State and conciliation toward the opposing par . His use of the military forces was temperate and able, and hisytactful treatment of those of the "Suffragists" who were arrested, went far toward quieting party feeling and uniting the citizens into a law-abiding body.

Governor King was personally inclined toward a liberal interpretation of the charter and an extension of the voting power and it was due to his efforts in that direction that the new constitution was finally adopted. At the same time his sense of justice and right forbade any resort to violence for the purpose of forcing the illegally framed Dorr Constitution upon the State and he opposed this effort of the discontented element with all the resources at his command.

He was in his family and social life a man of peculiar charm of manner, a good conversationalist and possessed a well in-formed and retentive mind. His views upon questions of the day were liberal and founded upon well digested investigation, but he was tenacious of his opinion and direct in all statements of personal and political policies. Perhaps one of his most admirable qualities was a whole-hearted generosity and con-fidence in his fellow men, and it is said that he more than once returned to his country home without his coat, having given that garment to some unfortunate met on the road side.

Governor King was m. on 20 May, 1813, by Elder Elisha Sprague at Johnston, to Catherine Latham Angell, only child of Olney and Mary (Waterman) Angell, b. 6 July, 1795; d. 4 May, 1841. She was a lineal descendant on her mother's side of Frances, dau. of Lewis Latham, Falconer to King Charles I.

The children of Samuel Ward King and Catherine Latham Angell were as follows:

    i. Mary Waterman, b. 1 Dec., 1814; d. 26 March, 1815.
    ii. Mary Anna, b. 1 March, 1816.
    iii. Eliza Smith, b. 23 Jan., 1818.
    iv. James Laurence, b. 24 March, 1820.
    v. Charles Rollin, b. 8 May, 1822.
    vi. Samuel Ward, b. 4 Aug., 1824; d. 9 April, 1826.

vii. Maria Waterman, b. 30 Nov., 1826; d. 20 Aug., 1827.
viii. Catherine Maria Waterman, b. 29 June, 1828.
ix. Sarah Frances, b. 24 Dec., 1829; d. 22 July, 1830.
x. Frances Elvira, b. 26 July, 1832.
xi. Antoinette Louisa, b. 30 May, 1833; d. 8 June, 1835.
xii. Samuel Ward, b. 4 March, 1835.
xiii. Antoinette Welthian, b. 14 Jan., 1838; d. 18 Dec., 1839.
xiv. Child (unnamed), b. 1 May, 1841; d. 2 May, 1841.

Of these fourteen children, only seven reached adult age, and with the death of Charles Rollin King on 12 Jan., 1903, the male line of Governor King's family became extinct. After ending his last term as Governor, Mr. King retired from active life and d. on 21 Jan., 1851, at Providence, being buried in the private burial ground of the Kings at Johnston, R. I. A brief obituary of Governor King states: "The firm and conciliatory course pursued by Governor King did much to allay the bitterness of party strife and secure the satisfactory result which was at length reached in the settlement of the important questions which had agitated the public mind." . . . "Few men have enjoyed in their day to a greater degree the confidence of the public, and few men in their private lives have exhibited greater amiability and generous kindness of heart. In the troublous times of 1842 his conduct won the approbation of friends and conciliated his opponents and in his voluntary retirement he carried with him the respect and esteem even of those against whom he acted in seasons of unusual difficulties." The portrait of Governor King is taken from a very old painting, now in the possession of his descendants in Providence—and is said to be a good likeness.

THE SKILLMANS OF AMERICA AND THEIR KIN.

By William Jones Skillman, Philadelphia, Pa.

(Continued from Vol. XXXIX., p. 57, of The Record.)

113. Isaac N.[6] Skillman (Isaac,[5] Thomas,[4] Isaac,[3] Thomas,[2] Thomas[1]), b. Nov. 24, 1803; d. Sept., 1840; m. Jan. 15, 1825, Pamela, dau. of John Stryker and wife Elizabeth Hageman, he being one of the four children of John Stryker, killed at the Battle of Germantown (Rev. War), whose widow afterward m. John Skillman (see No. 36). The names and dates of bap. in Harlingen Church (Dutch Ref.) of these four are: 1. Garret, bap. 1769; 2. Ida, Feb. 28, 1771; 3. Abraham, Feb. 21, 1773, and John (above), Nov. 7, 1774. With two little girls Isaac and wife removed, 1829, from Neshanic, N. J., to Hamilton Co., O. (near Cincinnati). They had six children as follows:

i. Elizabeth,[7] b. Dec. 1, 1825; d. Aug., 1894; m. May, 1845, Elon Strong. Had: 1. Freeman, b. 1846; d. 1855.   2.

Hannah, b. 1848; m. 1870, Jonathan Skillman (see
No. 70). 3. Emily, b. 1852; m. 1875, Benjamin Hill.
4. Albert, b. 1853; m. (1) Nancy Pentacost; m. (2)
Mary Welch. 5. Lillie, b. 1855; m. 1874, Andrew
Norris. 6. Freeland Rodman, b. 1857; m. (1) Anna
Siebohm; m. (2) Amanda Welch. 7. Percy, b. 1860;
d. 1881. 8. Anna, b. 1863; d. 1885. 9. Sherman, b.
1865; d. 1906. 10. Zebulon, b. 1867.

ii. Sarah, b. July, 1827; d. May, 1903; m. (1) John Knox;
m. (2) Daniel Chidester. Had: 1. Janet, b. 1849.
2. Katharine, b. 1851; m. John Calanan. 3. John, b.
1853. 4. Anna, b. 1855; d. 1875.

iii. Edwin, b. Aug., 1832; d. 1870; m. 1859, Mary Wisbey.
No issue.

iv. Josiah, b. Dec., 1836; m. 1870, Lucy Calhoun. Had:
1. Nelson (now in Kansas). 2. Edwin. 3. Josiah. 4.
Anna. 5. Mary. 6. Ben. 7. Lucy. 8. Lillie. Served
in the war from April, 1861, to Sept., 1865, as a member of " Merrill's Horse," four years of the time in
scout duty. Has lived in Illinois since 1867.

v. Anna, b. Nov., 1838; m. 1865, Theodore Burns. Had:
1. Aletta, b. 1868; m. —— Knight. 2. Mary, b. 1873.
3. Theodore, b. 1882.

vi. Mary, b. Jan. 26, 1841; m. March 12, 1861, Leonard B.
Harris. Had: 1. Julia, b. 1863; m. 1905, R. S.
Beavens. 2. Minerva, b. 1865. 3. Elsie, b. 1867; m.
1891, Barton S. Hill. 4. Clinton, b. 1869; m. 1903,
Lillian Hedges. 5. Henry, b. 1871; d. 1899. 6.
Twins: Freeman, unm.; 7. Amy, b. 1873; m. 1895,
W. C. Perrine. 8. Clyde, b. 1876; d. 1900. 9. Edith,
b. 1879. 10. Bernice, b. 1881; m. (1) 1902, Edward
Ballard (d. 1904); m. (2) Harvey W. Dutcher, 1906.

114. JOHN N.[6] SKILLMAN (Isaac,[5] Thomas,[4] Isaac,[3] Thomas,[2]
Thomas[1]), b. Sept. 25, 1809; d. June 23, 1894, and with son
Thomas lies buried in Harlingen Churchyard at Belle Mead.
A large farmer at Post Town, now Plainville, N. J.; m. (1) Jan.
17, 1833, Sarah Moore (b. Dec. 10, 1814; d. May 13, 1853); m. (2)
Oct. 4, 1854, Hannah Van Middlesworth (b. April 7, 1824, and now
1907 living). Children: by first wife, seven; by second three:

i. Isaac,[7] b. Oct. 30, 1833; live at Canton, Fulton Co., Ill.
ii. Abraham, b. July 24, 1835.
iii. Joanna, b. March 11, 1837; d. Dec. 28, 1904; m. Peter
Sutphen, Neshanic, N. J. Had one dau., Mrs. William H. Huff of Belle Mead.
iv. John, b. Dec. 13, 1839; lives near Canton, Ill.
v. Thomas, b. May 18, 1842; d. March 28, 1888.
vi. Emily, b. Nov. 23, 1845; d. April 26, 1846.
vii. Theodore, b. Feb. 28, 1852; lives at or near Canton,
Fulton Co., Ill.
viii. George Martin, b. May 22, 1857; d. Feb. 4, 1886; m.
Anne Van Derveer.

ix. Charles V. M., b. May 20, 1859; m. Jan. 18, 1889, Sarah
J. Burniston (b. Dec. 26, 1862). Had: 1. George C.,
b. July 22, 1889.

x. Jessie Augusta, b. June 25, 1863; m. Dec., 1887, Jacob
K. Schwenger. Had: 1. George N., b. 1888.   2.
Frank C., b. 1890.   3. Ray D., b. 1893.

115. ISAAC[6] SKILLMAN (Jacob,[5] Thomas,[4] Isaac,[3] Thomas,[2]
Thomas[1]), b. March 3, 1792, at Three Mile Run, near New Brunswick, N. J.; d. at Litchfield, Ill., 1855; a wanderer, and had lived
in at least six States of the Union, New Jersey, New York, Michi-
gan, Missouri, Texas and Illinois; m. Dec. 27, 1816, Betsey Powell,
and *circa* 1818 removed to near Brockport, N. Y. Both wife and
he are buried at Litchfield. Children:

i. Peter Voorhees, b. at Three Mile Run, Oct. 17, 1817;
d. in San Francisco, 1892; m. but no children.

ii. Jacob T. B., b. Oct. 17, 1819, at Brockport, N. Y.; d. at
Romeo, Mich., 1895; m. 1853, Louisa Edgett; served
2½ years in 5th Mich. Cav., Army of Potomac.
Children: 1. William J., b. 1855; m. at Oakwood,
Mich., two children. 2. Cassius Clayton, b. 1857;
d. 1859. 3. Costella, b. 1860; m. —— Sutherland,
three children.

iii. Eleanor M., b. Oct. 19, 1821; d. at Irvington, Ill., 1897;
m. (1) —— Bryan; m. (2) —— Griffths.

iv. Sarah Ann, b. Sept. 22, 1823; m. —— Short. Had: 1.
James. 2. William. Home in Hillsborough, Ill.

v. Abraham D., b. Jan. 20, 1826; d. Chicago, 1899; com-
mission merchant; m. a cousin, Hannah Powell,
Romeo, Mich. Had: 1. Alice, m. and lived in
Boston, Mass. 2. Fred'k B., a dentist, Chicago.

vi. Isaac, b. July 8, 1828; Union soldier in Civil War;
never m.; drowned in Bear River, Utah, in going to
California, 1866.

116. JACOB TEN BROECK[6] SKILLMAN (Jacob,[5] Thomas,[4] Isaac,[3]
Thomas,[2] Thomas[1]), b. March 10, 1794; d. June 26, 1864; m. Nov.
14, 1822, Rachel Corey Ayres (b. April 2, 1798; d. May 17, 1883);
grad. at Union College, Schenectady, 1816, same class with
William H. Seward; licensed M.D., 1825; practiced in New
Brunswick thirty years. Children:

i. Sarah Amelia,[7] b. Sept. 2, 1823; d. Jan. 6, 1852; m.
Aug. 5, 1846, Charles Rudolph von Romondt, Prof.
in Rutgers College; later home in Washington, D.C.
Had: 1. Charles Diedrick, b. 1847. 2. Henry T. B.,
b. 1849; d. 1877.

ii. Anna Maria, b. Jan. 23, 1825; d. Feb. 3, 1895; m. Rev.
Charles Rudolph von Romondt, May 18, 1863; home
in Washington, D. C. Had: 1. Enos A., b. 1865; d.
1866. 2. Walter Middleton, b. 1867; d. 1868.

iii. Ellen Henrietta, b. April 5, 1827; d. 1835.

iv. Alanson Freeman, b. March 8, 1829; d. 1832.

v. Louisa Adeline, b. Feb. 27, 1831; d. 1832.

vi. Enos Ayres, b. Nov. 16, 1833; a grad. of Rutgers
College, 1851; m. Oct. 9, 1867, Alice Middleton; live
in Washington, D. C. Had: 1. Nettie Ayres, b. 1868;
d. 1870. 2. Nannie Van Dyke, b. 1870. 3. Julia M.,
b. 1874. 4. Alice M., b. 1875. 5. Eva Garnett, b.
1877; m. George Thorne. 6. Wesley Middleton, b.
1878; m. 1903, Fannie Hull Burnett, Washington.

117. ABRAHAM⁶ SKILLMAN (Jacob,⁵ Thomas,⁴ Isaac,³ Thomas,²
Thomas¹), b. March 11, 1796; d. Dec. 2, 1862; grad. at Princeton,
1819; took his M. D. 1823, and settled for life at Bound Brook; m.
at Trenton, N. J., March 7, 1827, Susan Emma Palmer (b. at
Yardleyville, Pa., 1803; d. March 31, 1870). Their children:

i. Joseph P.,⁷ b. May 19, 1832; in N. Y. City from 1852 to
date; merchant; appraiser in Custom House; m.
May 14, 1856, Elizabeth, dau. of Henry V. Shaddle,
N. Y. City; d. March 13, 1902. Had: 1. Julia, d. inf.;
2. Harry S. 3. Susan Emma, m. George Clark, two
children. 4. Lizzie S., m. (1) W. W. Brook, one dau.;
m. (2) Fred'k L. Colwell of Stamford, Conn.; d. Feb.
19, 1904.

ii. Charles Hamilton, b. Nov. 30, 1833; grad. of Rutgers
College, 1851; of Princeton Theol. Sem. 1854; his
one pastorate was of Presby. Church at Luzerne,
N. Y.; d. April 19, 1862; never m.

iii. Ellen Palmer, m. Lewis D. Cook, Bound Brook.

118. JOHN⁶ SKILLMAN (Jacob,⁵ Thomas,⁴ Isaac,³ Thomas,²
Thomas¹), b. June 27, 1800, eldest child of 2nd wife, Mary Hageman; d. 1865; m. Martha, dau. of Christoffel C. Beekman and
wife Mary Van Dyke of Six Mile Run, now Franklin Park, N. J.;
d. 1887; farmer and occupied the homestead or old-time Freling-
huysen parsonage farm at Three Mile Run. Had:

i. Theodore,⁷ b. 1834; m. 1859, Agnes, dau. of Abraham
J. Suydam. One dau., Jane S. Farmer, now living
in New Brunswick.

ii. John, b. 1836; d. unm., 1865; buried at Three Mile
Run.

iii. Mary, b. 1838; m. 1858, Augustus Van Zandt of Blawen-
burg (d. 1884); her home now at Lawrenceville,
N. J., with her four living children: 1. Irene. 2.
Russell. 3. Eugenia. 4. Hubert.

iv. Henry, b. 1845; m. Mary, dau. of Isaac W. Pumyea of
Three Mile Run. One dau., Cassie.

v. William, b. 1847; m. twice. Three children: 1. Leroy.
2. Laura. 3. Marion. Farmer at Blawenburg.

vi. Jacob, b. 1850; removed to Kansas and m. there.
Three children: 1. Martha B. 2. Edward. 3. John.

119. WILLIAM⁶ SKILLMAN (Jacob,⁵ Thomas,⁴ Isaac,³ Thomas,²
Thomas¹), b. Jan. 11, 1803; d. Aug. 23, 1872; m. April 28, 1829,
Maria, dau. of Frederick Davis and wife Margaret Hoagland of
Six Mile Run (b. March 8, 1812; d. Oct. 29, 1874); removed, 1839,
from Three Mile Run to Blackwell's Mills, near Millstone, N. J.
Children:

  i. **Margaret,**' b. April 13, 1832; m. Dec. 15, 1852, Bernard
    S. Voorhees (d. Dec. 17, 1896). Had: 1. William S., b.
    1853. 2. Margaret Anna, b. 1855; d. 1861. 3. Fer-
    dinand Schureman Schenck, b. 1857. 4. Eugene, b.
    1859; d. 1861. 5. Alice, b. 1867; m. 1896, Jacob
    Brogley. All but 1st live in New Brunswick; he in
    Brooklyn, N. Y.
  ii. **Mary,** b. June 6, 1834; m. June 11, 1854, Isaac B.
    Allen; d. May 19, 1884.
  iii. **Frederick,** b. Jan. 4, 1837; carpenter and builder; d.
    unm. at home in Jersey City, Nov. 11, 1897.
  iv. **Jacob,** b. Feb. 22, 1839; hardware dealer, Jersey City;
    m. in Neshanic, April 18, 1861, Jane Davis, dau. of
    Peter V. Davis, Town and County Clerk. Had: 1.
    William Edgar, 2. Peter Davis, twins, b. Sept. 1,
    1862; bap. in Neshanic Ref. Dutch Church, Aug. 29,
    1863.
  v. **William,** b. Jan. 31, 1841; m. Mary Lodge; removed
    (1872) to Pocahontas, Bond Co., Ill.

120. **MARY BEEKMAN**[6] **SKILLMAN** (Jacob,[5] Thomas,[4] Isaac,[3]
Thomas,[2] Thomas[1]), b. Aug. 26, 1804; m. 1829, Christopher B.
Voorhees; both joined by Confession Harlingen (Ref. Dutch)
Chu‸h, Nov. 6, 1834, and the following children are there on
record as bap. in infancy:

  i. **Jacob Skillman**[7] **Voorhees,** b. Sept. 20, 1830; went to
    Streator, La Salle Co., Ill., whither the family
    eventually removed.
  ii. **Martha Beekman Voorhees,** b. Sept. 20, 1833.
  iii. **Isaac Voorhees,** b. May 3, 1836; d. y.
  iv. **Isaac Voorhees,** b. Dec. 26, 1846.

Ellen in No. 41, *ante,* is Eleanor T. B. (Ten Broeck), m. Peter
Van Tine, and her sister Jane and husband lived and d. near
Millstone, and there two of their children lived. For record of
Aaron L. (Longstreet?), see No. *121.*

121. **THOMAS**[6] **SKILLMAN** (Jacob,[5] Thomas,[4] Isaac,[3] Thomas,[2]
Thomas[1]), b. May 27, 1808; d. Sept. 10, 1853; m. (1) Oct. 8, 1837,
Caroline Stringham, dau. of George Burret Raymond (N. Y. City)
and wife Susan Parker, Virginia, niece of Robert Fulton (b. June
29, 1807; d. March 19, 1845); m. (2) Ellen, dau. of Daniel Polhemus, Middlebush, descendent from the first of the name in
America, Domine Johannes Theodorus Polhemus, who in 1654
became first pastor of the Collegiate (Ref. Dutch) Churches on
L. I.; educated at Rutgers and took his M. D. at Col. Phys. and
Surg's, N. Y., 1830, and settled in practice at his birth-home,
near New Brunswick, N. J. Six children were by the first wife
and four by the second:

  i. **Thomas Henry,**' d. inf.
  ii. **Lucy,** d. inf.
  iii. **George R.,** b. 1836(?); m. Dec., 1858, Mary Lockwool;
    lives at Chester Pa.; eight children.

iv. Sidney, b. March 19, 1839; d. April 25, 1876; m. July 3, 1861, Susanna C. Watson. Had: 1. Olive Clifton, b. 1867. 2. Sidney, b. 1869.

v. Julia, b. at Three Mile Run, Nov. 8, 1840; m. May 16, 1860, Oliver Clifton Wilson, ship chandler 23 years, West St., New York City; d. April 10, 1896. Had: 1. Irene Clifton, b. 1861; d. inf. 2. Percey R., b. 1863; m. 1891, Louise Suydam, Baldwinsville, N. Y.; two children, Percey and Anna. 3. Ella Hall, b. 1865; m. 1898, William Burnside Peck, Boston. 4. Charles Sanford, b. 1866, m. 1900, Clara Anthony. 5. Olive Clifton (as preceeding at New Brunswick), b. 1867; d. inf. 6. Harriet, b. 1873; m. 1897, Henry Judson Chapin, N. Y. City. 7. Louise, b. 1878.

vi. Frank, b. April, 1842; d. Sept., 1886; m. Sarah Voorhees, Jersey City. Had: 1. George. 2. Ella. 3. Louise.

vii. William, b. Jan. 16, 1849; d. inf.

viii. Lydia, b. July 29, 1850; d. Sept. 3, 1851.

ix. Thomas Henry, b. Feb. 29, 1852; m. April 27, 1876, Annetta Vreeland; druggist, New Brunswick; no children.

x. Emma, b. March 29, 1853; d. inf.

*121.** Aaron[6] Skillman (Jacob,[5] Thomas,[4] Isaac,[3] Thomas,[2] Thomas[1]), b. June 23, 1810 (possibly the "L" in his name was for Aaron Longstreet); d. Aug. 21, 1869; m. 1831, Eliza Ann Van Nostrand, Six Mile Run (b. April 6, 1812; d. Dec. 1, 1895). The family in 1854, removed to Mt. Clemens, Macomb Co., Mich., where certain Beekmans, Skillmans and other N. J. families had early settled. The children were all b. at Three Mile Run:

i. Catharine,[7] b. Nov. 3, 1832.

ii. Abraham, b. Sept. 9, 1833; d. Feb. 17, 1885; two sons, both d.

iii. Mary Adaline, b. Feb. 25, 1835.

iv. Martin Luther, b. Aug. 21, 1838; two sons; live at Mt. Clemens.

v. Georgiana, b. April 26, 1840; d. Aug. 21, 1865.

vi. Isaac, b. June 19, 1842.

vii. Ann Eliza, b. April 15, 1844; d. July 3, 1876.

viii. George Washington, b. April 8, 1846; m. and lives near Sandusky, O.; one son living.

ix. Delphi, b. June 7, 1848.

x. Peter Van Doren, b. Dec. 15, 1851.

122. Abraham[6] Skillman (Cornelius,[5] Thomas,[4] Isaac,[3] Thomas,[2] Thomas[1]), b. Nov. 27, 1802, at Hopewell, N. J.; d. July 1, 1881, at Lambertville; m. March 1, 1827, Henrietta, dau. of David Stout, Assoc.-Justice Hunterdon Co., and after it was formed, 1838, of Mercer Co., N. J., b. May 31, 1804; d. Nov. 22, 1889; a farmer. Children:

---

* Some one (now unknown) kindly sent the author this family record (see No. 41).

i. Charles Augustus,' b. Dec. 16, 1827; m. March 2, 1854, Sarah A., dau. of Abraham Stryker Skillman and wife Sarah Williamson (see No. 93); grad. of Princeton, 1848; admitted to bar, 1851. Had: 1. Charles H., lawyer. 2. Mary, m. James S. Studdiford, Lambertville. 3. Carrie Disbrough, m. Samuel W. Cochran, druggist.

ii. Caroline, b. May 2, 1830; m. Feb. 7, 1856, William M. Jewell, merchant; d. Aug. 24, 1870. Had: 1. Charles A., b. 1857; M. D., Penn. Univ.; d. 1900. 2. Mary E., b. 1864; m. Joseph E. Baldwin, Florida, Judge.

iii. Ida Stryker, b. Feb. 12, 1832; m. Jan. 22, 1862, Dr. Edward P. Hawke, practiced at Blawenburg, then at Hopewell, and d. Dec. 12, 1898. Had: 1. Carrie. 2. William W., dentist, Flemington. 3. Edward S., physician, Trenton. 4. Henrietta, teacher, Fort Lee, N. J. 5. Mary Emma.

iv. Mary Emma, b. May 20, 1844; m. Oct. 18, 1864, Ralph Ege, b. Nov. 22, 1837, business man, Hopewell. Had: 1. Albert A. 2. Sarah. 3. Andrew Howard, d. 1891. 4. Ida Skillman. 5. Mary. The Ege's descend from Adam, migrant from Germany, *circa* 1748, who m. Margaret, dau. of Thomas Hunt. See Chambers' *Early German Settlers of N. J.*

123. PETER[6] SKILLMAN (Cornelius,[5] Thomas,[4] Isaac,[3] Thomas,[2] Thomas[1]), b. Sept. 15, 1808; in Med. pract. at Harlingen over 40 years; d. April 1, 1888; m. Nov. 28, 1833, Louisa, dau. of Abraham C. Beekman of Griggstown, and wife Rachel Cruser, dau of Major Cornelius Cruser of Harlingen; b. 1816; d. March 11, 1887; both buried at Belle Mead. Her father's second wife was Elizabeth Houghton, and his father was Christopher Beekman, and mother Martha Veghte; Gerardus, 1707, and Catharine Van Dyke were next before, preceeded by Christopher, 1681 (or Christoffel, *Dutch*), and Mary De la Noy; then came, 1653, the famous Gerardus of Flatbush, and Magdalen Abeel, and we reach the top of this line in America in Willem, 1623, and Catrina De Boogh (De Bow). Children of Dr. Peter and Louisa Beekman:

i. James Alfred,' b. Sept. 17, 1834; d. in N. Y. City, Sept. 12, 1874; U. S. Marine on board of man-of-war, *New Orleans;* buried at Belle Mead.

ii. Cornelius P., b. May 16, 1837; farmer at Harlingen; never m.

iii. Abraham B., b. June 28, 1839; m. Anna Moor, now deceased; a practicing physician at Bertram, Linn Co., Ia.; two children, Anna Louisa and Frances Rachel.

iv. John Calhoun, b. July 25, 1842; m. Mary, dau. of Jacob Van Derveer and wife Jane Stryker of Harlingen; a grocer in New Brunswick, N. J.

v. Rachel Adah, b. March 23, 1848; at home with her brother Cornelius in the homestead at Harlingen.

124. BETSEY[9] SKILLMAN (John,[8] Benjamin,[4] Isaac,[3] Thomas,[2] Thomas[1]), b. 1790(?); m. (1) Jacob Erwin, drowned in Delaware River, 1831; m. (2) John Beaumont (2nd wife) of New Hope, Pa. Children as follows:

    i. Elizabeth[7] Erwin. No record.
    ii. Margaret Erwin, m. —— Snook: No other Record.
    iii. Nelson Beaumont, New Hope, Pa., d. unm.
    iv. Jackson Beaumont, m. Miss Stuckert.
    v. Sarah Ann Beaumont, m. (1) an actor from whom she secured a divorce; m. (2) John Schenck, Pennington, N. J., a brother of the Rev. Noah Hunt Schenck of St. Anne's Church (Prot. Episc.), Brooklyn, N. Y.
    vi. Louisa Beaumont, m. Dr. Saba Pearson; one son George.
    vii. Harrison Beaumont, a physician, d. unm. *circa* 1898 in Philadelphia.
    viii. John Beaumont, m. Kate Bassoe.
    ix. William Beaumont, d. y.

(*To be continued.*)

THE TWO MARTHA GOODSPEEDS.

CONTRIBUTED BY MISS LOUISE TRACY.

In the course of tracing the ancestry of Martha Goodspeed, the wife of John Crosby of Lee, Mass., back to the emigrant ancestor, a curious error was discovered in the statement set forth in the work entitled *Notes on Barnstable Families* by Otis.

The data concerning the Crosby family stated that John Crosby, son of John and Mary Crosby, m. Martha Goodspeed of Barnstable, Mass., they having been published on 22 Aug., 1766, and m. on 26 Nov., 1766, by Nymphas Marston, Esq., in Barnstable. John Crosby with his wife and children removed to Lee, Berkshire County, Mass., in 1780, and in 1781 united with the Congregational Church there. Martha (Goodspeed) Crosby d. in 1812 at Lee, Mass., and her tombstone in the Lee Cemetery bears the following inscription:

*"In Memory of Mrs. Martha Crosby, wife of Mr. John Crosby, Sr., who died 25 May 1812 in the 71st. year of her age.

    Farewell all sublunary things
    I go to see the King of Kings."

From the age given on her tombstone it would appear that this Martha Goodspeed was b. 1741-2.

The record of the Goodspeed family contained in Otis' *Notes on Barnstable Families*, p. 404, shows that a Martha Goodspeed, dau. of James and Elizabeth (Fuller) Goodspeed, was b. on 31

* See *Crosby Genealogy* by C. C. McLean, pp. 3 and 4, and *History of Lee, Mass.*

July, 1741, at Barnstable, Mass., but Otis adds "She married on 12 June, 1760, Samuel Winslow of Hardwick."

A genealogical problem was at once presented as to whether the Martha Goodspeed, wife of John Crosby, was identical with that Martha Goodspeed who m. Samuel Winslow, or was an entirely different person, and whether she was a dau. of *James* Goodspeed or not.

An examination of the *Winslow Memorial* disclosed that Martha Goodspeed, wife of Samuel Winslow, was b. on 7 Feb., 1739, at Barnstable, Mass., and the *History of Hardwick, Mass.,* and the *History of Pomfret, Vt.,* confirmed this statement concerning the age of Martha (Goodspeed) Winslow. This birth date agreed with the birth date of a Martha Goodspeed, dau. of *Ebenezer* Goodspeed, given by Otis, p. 404, and thus clearly proved the existence of two of the name of Martha Goodspeed, both of Barnstable, Mass., born within a year or so of each other. Otis had erroneously allotted Martha, dau. of *James* Goodspeed, as the wife of Samuel Winslow, when his wife was clearly Martha, dau. of *Ebenezer* Goodspeed.

In order to make the proof of this error stronger, a letter was addressed to the town clerk of Pomfret, Vt., asking for a copy of the inscription on the tombstone of Martha (Goodspeed) Winslow. The town clerk in due course forwarded a letter which she had obtained from Mr. Walter E. Perkins, who had been making a study of Pomfret history for some years, which reads as follows:

Pomfret, Vt., August 10, 1907.

Mrs. E. P. Perkins, Town Clerk, Pomfret Vt.:

Respecting the inquiry of Louise Tracy of New Haven, will say, the grave of Martha Goodspeed, wife of Samuel Winslow, is at the Cushing Cemetery in Woodstock. The gravestone says: died March 9 1813, aged 74 years.

I have never seen the Winslow Genealogy, but here is what Samuel Winslow wrote: "I Samuel Winslow was born at Rochester april ye 6 Day old Stile A. D. 1735 my wife martha goodspede was born at Barnstable february ye 7 Day old stile 1739 we was marad at Barnstable june ye 12 New Stile A D 1760"

"My Mother Martha Winslow Departed this Life at pomfret on the Ninth Day March 1813 at 9 a clock A M hur age was seventy four years and eighteen days old after a short But Distressing sickness of (—?) Days of Lung fever She Diede with a Smile on Her Countenance she lived with us twelve years ten Munths into 3 Day

March 9 1813
Ebenezer Winslow her oldest Son"

Respectfully yours,
Walter E. Perkins.

This letter certainly settles the question as to *which* Martha Goodspeed m. Samuel Winslow.

RECORDS OF THE UNITED BRETHREN CONGREGA-
TION, COMMONLY CALLED MORAVIAN CHURCH,
STATEN ISLAND, N. Y.

BAPTISMS AND BIRTHS.

ABBREVIATIONS.

Sr.—Sister—A Communicant. M. M.—Married Man. M. W.—Married Woman.
Br.—Brother—A Communicant. S. M.—Single Man. S. W.—Single Woman.
Wid.—Widow.

(Continued from Vol. XXXIX., p. 32 of THE RECORD.)

DATE	PARENTS	CHILD	SPONSORS
1851.			
Oct. 5.	Carl Christian Frid-erick Deinmann Louise Johanna Catarina Reuter, his wife	Friderica Dorotea Cicilia	Germans now living at New Brighton
Nov. 6.	Benjamin Lydle &	George	
Oct. 10.	wife Ann, late Pierson, nee Fredericks of	Washing-ton	
1852.	Richmond		
Jan. 23.	Adam Fügel	Nathan	
Jan. 1.	Catharine Thum, his wife		
Feb. 8.	Heinrich Weid-	Carl Hein-	Germans, now at Port
1851.	muller	rich Chris-	Richmond. C a r l
Oct. 25.	Eliza Gerd, his wife	tian	Etsch, Heinrich Kaus, Christina
1852.			Hützel
March 3.	George Ebbits	George Pat-	
1847.	Serena Downs, his	ten	
b. April 27.	wife		
1845.			
b. Feb. 3.		Ann Wright	.
1849.			
b. Jan. 7.		Lucy	
1850.	All ch. of above		
b. Nov. 27.	parents	Harriet	
1852.			
April 4.	Dietrich Senne &	August	Living near 4 Corners.
1851.	wife Dorothea	Ernst Wil-	Christian Schiegel,
Nov. 29.	Krumdick	helm Chris-	August Senne, Ernst
		tian	Senne, Friedrich
1852.			Lange
April 4.	Ernst Senne	Diedrich	Johann Chr. Schiegel,
Jan. 4.	Gesine Schiegel, his wife	Friedrich Christian August	Diedrich Senne, Friedrich Senne, Friedrich Lange, August Senne

DATE	PARENTS	CHILD	SPONSORS
1852.			
April 23.	C h a r l e s Lewis	Charles	Both ch. bap. at house
1849.	Moelich	Frederick	of Isaac Housman
b. Sept. 5.	C a t h a r i n e Ann		
	Hausman, dau. of		
1851.	Isaac, his wife		
b. Feb. 12.		Elizabeth	
1852.	Same parents	Augusta	
April 29.	Abraham Vanduzer	John Hous-	
Jan. 9.	Eliza Ann, his wife	man	
1851.			
b. Jan. 6.	Joh Vanduzer	Peter	
	F r a n c i s Louisa	Winant	
	Roff, his wife		
b. July 10.	Jacob Vanduzer	Eveline	
1852.	Margaret, his wife		
b.	Isaac Vanduzer	Isaac Oliver	These 4 bap. at house
March 23.	Mary, his wife		of Sr. Sarah Van-
			duzer at Tompkins-
			ville
May 2.	Wm. Vroome	Ann Eliza	Living at Tompkins-
1851.	Catharine Egbert,		ville. Bp. at house
April 22.	his wife		of Sr. Vroome near
1852.			4 Corners
May 2.	Wm. Seawood	Elizabeth	At Port Richmond
March 13.	Ann Neats, his wife	Frances	

1852. BAPTISMS BY BERNARD E. SCHWEINITZ.

DATE	PARENTS	CHILD	SPONSORS
July 25.	Daniel Eidam	Elizabeth	Germans in Factory-
Feb. 8.	Margarita N e t e r -		ville. Bp. in D. Ref.
	man, his wife		Ch. at Port Rich-
			mond
Sept. 1.	Friedrich A. Dreyer	Carl Bruno	Bp. at house of gr.-
	of Brooklyn		father, Dr. Schmidt
	Augusta Henriette		
	Schmidt, his wife		
Sept. 5.	Andrew Soner	Anna Maria	Germans at Factory-
1851.	Clara Wagner, his	Clara	ville. Baptism at Mr.
Nov. 22.	wife		Rathyen's house in
1852.			Port Richmond
Sept. 10.	Joseph Jacobsmyer	Johann	Germans near Port
1851.	Anna, his wife	Christian	Richmond. Bap. at
Aug. 28.			parent's house when
1852.			very sick
Oct. 3.	James Hausman	Theodore	Living at Factoryville
1850.	Catherine B a u e r,	Adam	
June 24.	his wife		
1852.			
Oct. 3.	Jacob Fried'k Jackel	Magdalena	Living at Factoryville.
1850.	Eva Maria Sekin-	Rosina	Bp. at h o u s e of
Feb. 27.	ger, his wife		James Housman

DATE	PARENTS	CHILD	SPONSORS
1852.			
Oct. 3.	Thomas Sharrot	Alfred	Bp. at house of gr.-
Sept. 9.	M a r y Elizabeth		mother Mrs. Mary
	Voorhis, his wife		Vanderbilt
Oct. 17.	Paul Schmidt	Carl Henry	
June 5	Catharine Müller,		
or 11.	his wife		
Oct. 17.	Reinhart Koch	Anna Maria	Both Bp. in D. Ref.
July 31.	A n n a Catharina		Ch. at Port Rich-
	Walter, his wife		mond
Nov. 28.	Adolph Levando	Joseph	Bp. at Factoryville
1850.	Emma Schmidt, his		
b. Nov. 3.	wife		
1852.			
b. Sept 21.	Same parents	Elisabeth	" "
Dec. 1.	Bernard Alfrenk	William	Bp. at parents' dwel-
1850.	A n n a Myers, his	Henry	ling near Mariner's
b. April 22.	wife		Harbor
1851.			
b. 11 Oct.	Same parents	John	
1852.		Frederick	
Dec. 12.	Christian Bloch	Louise	Bp. at D. Ref. Ch. at
Dec. 14.	Rebecca Knief, his	Marie	Port Richmond
	wife		
Dec. 14.	Sarah Rodgers, wife of Capt.		Bp. at her home where
	W. Cole		she was confined by
			consumption
Dec. 14.	Capt. W. Cole	Jonah	
1844.	Sarah Rodgers, his	Rodgers	
Nov. 30.	wife		
1853.			
Jan. 9.	Jacob Mauer	John Jacob	
1852.	Catharine K e b e l,		
June 20.	his wife		
1853.			
March 6.	J o h a n n Heinrich	Johanna	Bp. in Ch. at Port
1852.	Knoch	H e n erika	Port Richmond
Sept. 13.	Martha Elisabetha	Juliana	
1853.	Penhart, his wife		
March 13.	Robert Summers	Sylvester	
1852.	S u s a n Ann Stil-		
Sept. 29.	well, his wife		
1853.			
March 27.	B. E. Schweinitz	Paul Bern-	Sr. Mary Connelz of
Feb. 23.	M a r i e Ottilie	hard	B e t h l e h e m, Pa.,
	Goepp, his wife		(absent), Br. L. H.
			Cortelyou & Eliza,
			his wife, Mr. & Mrs.
			Dettmar B a s s e of
			Brooklyn. N. Y., Br.
			John F. Bigler of N.Y

DATE	PARENTS	CHILD	SPONSORS
1853.			
March 27.	Heinrich Jansen	Heinrich	Bp. in Ch. at Port
Feb. 1.	Eden	Jansen	Richmond
	Cathrina Behrens,		
	his wife		
May 8.	Edward Holzhalb	Bertha	Bp. in Ch. at Port
1852.	Bertha Holzhalb,		Richmond
Dec. 28.	nee Motzer		
1853.			
June 19.	John Ahrens	Anna Maria	Anna Hattof, Maria
1852.	Margretha Als-		Alsguth. Bp. in
July 21.	guth, his wife		Port Richmond
1853.			
July 17.	Albert Hulsebas	Gesina Car-	Bp. in Ch. at Port
April 20.	Fredericka Caro-	olina	Richmond
	lina Feust, his wife		
May 15.	Daniel Torrance &	Alfred	
1852.	wife Sophia J.		
Nov. 6.	Vanderbilt, dau.		
	of Corn. Vander-		
1853.	bilt of N. Y.		
May 22.	Jacob Salbacher	Bertha	Bp. at parents' house
1851.	Barbara Shelling		at 4 Corners
Dec. 6.			
1853.			
Aug. 8.	Louis Ettlinger	Adolph	Germans
June 25.	Charlotte Abel, his		
	wife		
Sept. 2.	Maria Egbert [nee Simonson],		On her dying bed
	wife of Jacob Egbert of Tomp-		
	kinsville		
Sept. 25.	James Burger	Maria	
March 27.	Maria Jane Noble,	Ottilia	
	his wife		
Nov. 20.	James Coyne	Harriet	Both members of our
July 6.	Harriet Matilda	Matilda	church
	Thompson, his		
	wife		
Nov. 28.	Benjamin Lydle	Josephine	Bp. at Richmond in
Nov. 18.	Ann [Nancy] Fred-		house of parents
	ericks, his wife		
Dec. 2.	Cornelius P. Bird	Cornelia	At Tompkinsville in
1852.	Lydia Eliza Egbert,		presence of ch's.
April 12.	his wife		mother & gr.-
			mother Lydia Eg-
1853.			bert
Dec. 9.	Abraham S. Egbert	Cornelius	Bp. at parents' house
1852.	Mary Eliza Bird,	Bird	at Vanderbilt Land-
May 31.	his wife		ing
1853.			
Nov. 12.	Same parents	John	

DATE	PARENTS	CHILD	SPONSORS
1853.			
Dec. 11.	John Simonson of	Catharine	
1854.	Clifton		
Jan. 15.	Joshua Mercereau	Stephen	Living on South side
1852.	Sarah Ann Perine,	Henry	
Nov. 30.	his wife		
1854.			
March 13.	John Godfried Geb-	John God-	Germans. Godfried
Feb. 8.	hardt	fried	W. Gebhardt & his
	Catharine Christina		wife
	E h r h a r d t, his		
	wife		
March 13.	George Barth	John	Natives of Germany,
Feb. 21.	Elisabeth Schmidt,		now of New Brigh-
	his wife		ton Conn. Bp. at
			house of gr.-father
			John Schmidt, who
			was sponsor with his
			wife Catharine Gal-
			mer

1854. BAPTISMS BY A. A. REINKE.

DATE	PARENTS	CHILD	SPONSORS
Sept. 25.	John V. Egbert	Lemont	Living near Bound
Aug. 8.	Ellen Simonson, his	Williams	Brook, N. Jersey.
	wife		Bp. at Parsonage
Oct. 15.	James Wilson Shar-	Cornelia	Bp. at house of gr.-
Aug. 22.	rott	Frances	parents
	Agnes C a r o l i n e,		
1855.	his wife		
Jan. 7.	Robert Sommers	Lavina	
1854.	Sarah A. Stilwell,		
July 17.	his wife	.	
1855.			
April 11.	William Vroome	Wm. E m -	
1854.	Catharine M a r i a	mett	
Feb. 2.	Egbert, his wife		
1855.			
June 20.	A b r a h a m Van	Mary	Bp. at house of Mrs.
1854.	Duzer	Emma	S. Van Duzer
Dec. 12.	Elizabeth Ann Van		
1855.	Duzer		
June 20.	John Van Duzer	Peter	" " "
1853.	Louisa Roff, h i s	Winant	
Jan. 14.	wife		
1855.			
June 20.	Isaac Van Duzer	Jacob	Bp. at house of Mrs.
1854.	Mary, his wife	Theodore	S. Van Duzer
July 22.			
1855.			
June 20.	Jacob Van Duzer	John Jacob	" " "
1853.	M a r g a r e t Van		
Nov. 4.	Duzer		

7A

DATE	PARENTS	CHILD	SPONSORS
1855.			
July 1.	Jns. Pearce	Mary Jane	Both lately arrived
March 28.	Matilda Lunt, his wife		from London, Eng.
Aug. 20.	Jno. Schmidt	Catharine	Near Bull'shead
March 7.	Catharine Eulner, his wife	Margaret	
Sept. 30.	James Wood	William	
	Emily Britton, his	Henry	
1856.	wife		
Jan. 1.	James Coyn & his	James	
1855.	wife Harriet Ma-		
July 19.	tilda Thompson		
1856.			
April 13.	Cornelius P. Bird	Jane Louisa	Bp. at house of Mr.
1855.	Lydia Eliza Eg-		Wm. Vroome in
Sept. 23.	bert, his wife		Tompkinsville
1856.			
April 17.	Garry Vroome	Mary Anna	Bp. at house of Mr.
Feb. 23.	Mary Elizabeth		Christopher Vroome
	Martling, his wife		at Centreville
April 27.	Jacob Frettert	Frederick	
March 26.	Maria Steker, his	Jacob	
	wife		
		Magdalena	
Sept. 9.	Jacob Van Duzer	Wm. Oliver	Bp. at house of Mrs.
1855.	Margaret Van		Sarah Van Duzer at
Oct. 16.	Duzer		Quarantine
1856.			
Sept. 28.	George M. Root	Elliott	
1854.	Anna M. Van	Aymar	
July 15.	Duzer, his wife		
1856.			
Oct. 26.	Peter Hirschle	Heinrich	
Sept. 2.	Francesca Weber,		
1857.	his wife		
April 3.	Robert Barnes,	George &	Bp. at house of parents
April 1.	Louisa Ketteltas,	Elizabeth,	in presence of gr.-
	his wife	twins	parents & sisters
April 7.	Peter Anderson	Margaret	Bp. at parents' house
1855.	Waglom	Anna	in presence of ——
May 25.	Margaret Stilwell,		S. Summers & S.
1857.	his wife		Mersereau
April 12,	Anna, wife of Joseph Egbert, bap. in Ch. on occasion		
Easter.	of the confirmation of Sarah L. Cortelyou, Elizabeth		
	Simonson & Br. N. Britton.		
April 26.	Jacob Herman	Mary Ida	
1856.	Garretson of Cen-		
Jan. 11.	treville		
	Elizabeth Egbert,		
	his wife		

DATE	PARENTS	CHILD	SPONSORS
1857.			
April 26.	Alexander Littell	Ada Louise	
1856.	Hannah Jane Eg-	.	
July 27.	bert, his wife		
1857.			
April 18.	James Baker	Julia Ann	Bp. at house of gr.-
1856.	Elizabeth Burning-		mother
b. Oct. 6.	ham, his wife		
b. not		Sarah Eliza-	
given.		beth	
	Ch. of above parents	Joanna	
1857.			
Sept. 1.	Jno. Housman	Egbert	
1856.	Susan Haughwout,	Haughwout	
July 18.	his wife		
1857.			
Sept. 27.	George Vroome	Maria Ann	Bp. in parents' house
1856.	Elizabeth Taylor,		at Centreville
b. March 22.	his wife		
1857.			
b. March 27.		Leonora Walker	
Sept. 17.	Jno. W. Burbank	John Alfred	Both ch. bap. in sick
1847.	Anna Egbert, his		room of the mother,
b. July 9.	wife	.	in presence of wit-
1850.			nesses
b. April 9.	Same parents	Anna	
1857.			
Oct. 1.	Jacob Van Duzer	Lilian	Bp. at home of Mrs.
May 23.	Margaret Van Duzer		Sarah Van Duzer
Oct. 1.	Isaac Van Duzer	Daniel	
1856.	Mary Van Duzer	Clyde	
Oct. 10.			
1857.			
Oct. 15.	Geo. M. Root	Pierre Van-	
	Anna M. Van Duzer, his wife	derbilt	
Dec. 2.	Isaac Romer	Emma Jane	At house of parents
1847.	—— Noble, his		in New Dorp
b. Sept. 20.	wife		
1854.			
b. May 14.		Mary Matilda	.
1857.			
b. Feb. 21.	Ch. of above parents	Catharine Ann Elting	
1858.			
Jan. 25.	Geo. Washington	Geo. Wash-	
1849.	Blake	ington	
March 6.	Mary Ann Wood,		
	his wife		

DATE	PARENTS	CHILD	SPONSORS
1858.			
Feb. 2.	Henry Hilton	Edward	Bp. in house of parents
1850.	Ellen Banker, his	Banker	in 9th St., N. York
b. March 25.	wife		
1852.			
b. Jan. 10.		William	
1854.		McMurray	
b. April 21.		Cornelia	
1856.			
b. Jan. 13.		Josephine	
1857.			
b. June 12.	All ch. of above	Henry	" " "
	parents	Graham	
1858.			
April 4.	Isaac Swift of Cen-	S a r a h &	Bp. in Ch. at confirma-
	treville and ——	Emma	tion of Henrietta
			and E m e l i n e Eg-
			bert, C a t h a r i n e
			Vroom & Mrs. Julia
			Luby
May 23.	Abm. Egbert	Catharine	Of New Dorp
	Ann Egbert	Hannah	
Sept. 26.	Edward Wood	Mary	Bp. at house of gr.-
1857.	Catharine M a r i a	Augusta	p a r e n t s Cornelius
Aug. 23.	Egbert, his wife		Egberts
1858.			
Sept. 28.	Wm. H'y S m i t h	Mary Eliza-	Colored
1855.	Garrettson	beth	
Sept. 26.	Diana Spicer		
1858.			
Sept. 28.	Thomas Spicer	Ann Eliza	Colored
April 4.	Matilda Catharine		
	Spicer		
1857.			
b. in Aug.	John Garrettson	Margaret	Colored
	Jane Spicer	Ann	
1858.			
Dec. 8.	L a w r e n c e H.	James Wal-	Bp. at home of Stephen
	Bogart	nut	Martling after the
	S a r a h Catharine		wedding of Mr. Jas.
1857.	Bogart		Vreeland to M i s s
b. April 30.	Same parents	Stephen	[E. or C.] Martling
		Martling	
1858.			
Dec. 20.	Edward M. John-	John	Bp. at parents' house
May 30.	son, gardener at		on Mr. Newman's
	Mr. W. H. New-		grounds
	man's		
	Margaret Johnson		

DATE	PARENTS	CHILD	SPONSORS
1859.			
Feb. 27.	A m a n d e n s A.	Edward	Bp. at P a r s o n a g e.
Feb. 5.	Reinke	Jacob	Bp. by Rev. Alex-
	Ellen E l i z a b e t h		ander R. Thompson
	Rece, his wife		of D. Ref. Ch. at
			Stapleton. S p o n -
			sors—Br. & Sr. Cor-
			t e l y o u, Br. & Sr.
			Coyne, Br. Clement
			L. Reinke
Feb. 23.	Abraham Sharrott	Jno. W i l -	
1858.	Hannah Jane Shar-	liam	
Sept. 1.	rott		
1859.			
April 17.	William Vroome	Christopher	Bp. at house of Br.
1858.	Catharine Egbert,		Garry Vroome
April 11.	his wife		
	Garret Vroome	Sarah Eliz-	" " "
	Elizabeth Martling,	abeth	
1859.	his wife		
July 14.	Cornelius P. Bird	Susan Ann	
April 18.	L y d i a Eliza Eg-		
	bert, his wife		
July 14.	Benjamin S i m o n-	Helen	Both bp. in house of
1858.	son	Melissa	gr.-mother L y d i a
Sept. 24.	Adeline Egbert, his		Egbert
1859.	wife		
July 21.	A b r a h a m Van	Edward	
1858.	Duzer	Vanderbilt	
April 17.	Elizabeth Ann Van-		
1859.	derbilt, his wife		
Oct. 2.		Ann Lyle	Bp. at parents' house
1858.			
April 29.			
1859.			
Oct. 16.	Alexander Littell	Emma	Bp. at School house at
1858.	Jane Littell	Laura	Centreville a f t e r
Jan. 17.			evening service
1859.			
Nov. 3.	Ja es Cubberly	Walter	
Sept. 3.	Frances Crocheron,	Inman	
	his wife		
Nov. 14.	Samuel Farrow	Lucy Ann	Bp. at house of mother
1855.	Catharine E l i z a-		Sharrott, S. side
b. Dec. 25.	beth Farrow		
1858.			
b. July 25.	Same parents	Ida Lucretia	
1859.			
Nov. 20.	Robert Summers	Emily Etta	
1858.	Susan Summers		
Oct. 18.			

DATE	PARENTS	CHILD	SPONSORS
1859.			
Dec. 1.	Henry Hilton	Alexander	Bp. at their house in
July 25.	Ellen Hilton	Stewart	E. 28th St., N. Y.
1860.			
Jan. 23.	George Vroome married son of Christopher		
Feb. 5.	Edward M. Johnson	Jane	Bp. at parents' house
1859.	Margaret Johnson		at Mr. Newman's
Oct. 2.			
1860.			
April 29.	Jacob Van Duzer	Percival	Bp. at house of Mrs.
1859.	M a r g a r e t Van		Sarah Van Duzer
July 25.	Duzer		
1860.			
May 28.	George Vroome	Louis	Bp. at parents' home
1859.	Elizabeth Taylor,	Taylor	at Centreville
July 4.	his wife		
1860.			
June 24.	Thomas Luby	Mary	Bp. at Parsonage
Jan. 15.	Julia Luby	Elizabeth	
Sept. 9.	John Kadlitz	Cora	Residing n e a r Br.
April 2.	Elizabeth Kadlitz		Summers
Sept. 26.	James Vreeland	Jennie	
1859.	Elizabeth Martling,	Martling	
Dec. 21.	his wife		
1860.			
Oct. 8.	Wm. F. Butler	Adelaide	
Jan. 25.	Leah E l i z a b e t h		
	Johnson his wife		
Oct. 10.	Peter A n d e r s o n	Caroline	
1859.	Waglom		
July 22.	Margaret Stilwell,		
	his wife		
1860.			
Oct. 13.	Robert Barnes	Sarah	
1859.	Mary Louisa Barnes	Louisa	
April 8.			

BAPTISMS BY E. T. SINSEMAN.

DATE	PARENTS	CHILD	SPONSORS
1860.			
Nov. 17.	David Colon	David Ben-	Bp. at house of gr.-
1852.	Sarah Ann Colon	net	parents
July 12.			
1860.			
Dec. 27.	Alexander Littell	Clara	Bp. at house of Mr.
Jan. 25.	Hannah Jane Lit-	Adelaide	Edward Egbert at
	tell		Centreville
b. Aug. 23.	Edm. Crocheron	Leah Stout-	
	Lucretia Crocheron	enborough	
1861.			
Feb. 11.	August Brunholer	Carl August	
Jan. 30.	Elizabeth B r u n -		
	holer		

DATE	PARENTS	CHILD	SPONSORS
1861.			
March 6.	John Brindley Frances Brindley	John Tunis Frances	Bp. in sick-chamber of mother at Tompkinsville
1859. b. Aug. 3.	All ch. of above parents	Belle William H.	
1861. April 10. Jan. 19.	Edward Johnson Margaret Johnson	Elizabeth Secord	
Oct. 2. 1853. b. Nov. 11.	John Vanderbilt Sarah Vanderbilt	Eva Louisa	Bp. at house of Mr. Jacob Van Duzer in Tompkinsville
1855. b. Feb. 20. 1861.	Same parents	Charles Henry	
b. Feb. 23.	Jacob Van Duzer Margareth Van Duzer	Priscilla	" " "
1860. b. Nov. 12. 1861.	Isaac Van Duzer Mary Van Duzer	Henry Carey	" " "
b. March 2.	Abraham Van Duzer Elizabeth Van Duzer	Eliza Ann	" " "
May 12.	Bradley Woad Elizabeth Woad	Agnes	
Nov. 7. 1860. Oct. 25.	Albert Vroome Caroline Vroome	Martha Jane	Bp. at house of Will. Vroome, Centreville Sponsor, Maria Vroome
b. Nov. 24.	Benjamin Simon- son Sarah Adeline Sim- onson	Ecford Webb	Lydia Egbert
1861. b. Feb. 9. 1862.	William Vroome Catharine Vroome	Lydia	
Jan. 9. 1860. Sept. 10. 1862.	John Housman Susan Ann Hous- man	Caroline Houghwout	
April 1. 1861. Aug. 12. 1862.	James Coyne Harriet Coyne	Margaret	
April 13. 1861. Dec. 11. 1862.	William Taylor Emeline Taylor	Josephine Adelaid	
April 19. 1861. Sept. 17.	John Radlitz Elizabeth Radlitz	Ada Medora	

DATE	PARENTS	CHILD	SPONSORS
1862.			
July 1.	John Vanderbilt	John	Bp. at house of Mr.
1858.	Eliza Vanderbilt	William	Thomas Sharrott
Nov. 11.			
1862.			
July 1.	"Mary Clara, dau. of Eliza Van-		" " "
1860.	derbilt & Henrietta Vander-		
Dec. 19.	bilt [Thus in original Ch. book]		
1862.			
July 1.	Oliver Vanderbilt	Ann	" " "
1861.	Sarah Vanderbilt	Amelia	
March 23.			
1862.			
July 1.	Joseph Housman	Mary	" " "
1861.	Lydia Housman	Elizabeth	
Nov. 25.			
1862.			
July 4.	Carl Sebastian	John Henry	Mathew Oelmann,
June 16.	Kirch		Anton Rappeneker
	Christine Kirch		
July 6.	Edwin T. Sense-	William	Thomas Lueders,
March 21.	man	Ormsby	Elenore Lueders
	Sarah Lueders, his		
	wife		
July 29.	William Johnson	William	
June 30.	Charlotte Johnson		
Aug. 1.	Robert Barnes	Frederic	
July 26.	Mary Louisa Barnes		
Aug. 6.	George L. Reader	Christopher	Bp. at gr.-parents'
Jan. 27.	Cath. Reader	Vroome	house
Aug. 11.	George W. Vroom	Eliza Tay-	
1861.	Elizabeth S. Vroom	lor	
Dec. 21.			
1862.			
Aug. 11.	Peter Heal	Eliza	Bp. at Mrs. Swifts'
March 6.	Emma Heal	Swift	house
Oct. 19.	John Theodor. Zorn	Georgiana	Bp. by Eugene Lei-
Aug. 22.	Esther Ruth Eliza	Theodora	bert. Sponsors:
	Zorn	Jacobina	Sarah Leibert. Miss
			Alvina Schuman,
			Theodore Klein-
			knecht, by proxy
Oct. 28.	Christian Knoesel,	Catharina,	Charles Wolf, Catha-
Sept. 29.	Mr. Banker's far-	sick child	rine Rose. Bp. in
	mer		parents' house at
	Salome Knoesel		Freshkill by Eugene
			Leibert

MARRIAGES.

By Rev. H. Gambold.

1764. Dec. 27.	David Burger Anne Stilwell	In presence of about 30 persons in her mother's house at Old Town
1766. March 4.	Christian Jacobson Anne Vandeventer	
1771. Nov. 17.	George Colon Mary Limner	
1773. June 29.	Edward Beatty Eleanor Cortelyou	
1774. July 17.	Nathaniel Britton Catharine Colon	
1775. Jan. 15.	Lewis Ryerze Catharine Connor	
1777. Aug. 3.	James Egbert Elisabeth Martinoe Jacob Wood Elisabeth Nichols	
Dec. 28.	John Buskirk Jane Blaw	
1778. Jan. 21. Jan. 30.	Peter Selif Elisabeth Beglo "Peter Guyon [or Deyoung]" Catharine Ketteltass	
April 5.	Peter Haughwout Mary Martinoe	
April 5.	Cornelius Dugan Aletta Cousine	
May 20.	Stephen Wood Alice Simerson	
June 17.	Albert Journey Mary Perine	
Aug. 9.	Hezekiah Rickow Sarah Dennys	
Aug. 20.	Benjamin Appleby Sarah Van Pelt	
Aug. 26.	Jonathan Gage Elizabeth Medes	
Aug. 27.	Tucker Tabor Jane Love	
June 7.	John Bachus —— Brock	
Aug. 30.	Thomas Robinson Alice Hill	
Sept. 6.	Gager Freeman Catharine Simeson	
Sept. 11.	Elihu Wolly Sara Vansise	
Sept. 15.	Thomas Parker Eleanor Smith	

1778.	Joseph Sylva
Dec. 20.	Susanna Mitchell
Dec. 20.	Isaac Decker
	Ally Burbank
1779.	John Lisk
Jan. 1.	Sara Decker
Jan. 6.	John Dunham
	Elisabeth Oliver
Feb. 3.	Lewis Dunham
	Catharine Slegt
Feb. 9.	Joseph Beers
	Mary Barton
Feb. 28.	Abraham Bowlby
	Sara Lake
May 5.	Christopher Hevler
	Elizabeth Bront
May 9.	James Johnson
	Mary Wood
May 16.	Reuben Rickow
	Ann Thorn
May 17.	William Carroll
	Mary Chambers
May 26.	William Jeacocks
	Hannah Garrison
June 12.	Benjamin Prall
	Margaret Simonson
June 21.	Thomas Trot
	Sophia Romer
Oct. 18.	Thomas Batten
	Mary Hinslif
Oct. 31.	Nathaniel Britton
	Sarah Pugh
Nov. 7.	Daniel De Hart
	Elisabeth Mersereau
1780.	Stephen Mercereau
Jan. 23.	Sara White
Jan. 23.	William Biggs
	Hannah Beard
1779.	Peter Rednor
Nov. 20.	——
1780.	Robert Mesy
Feb. 13.	Margaret Daily
March 2.	Stephen Wood
	Joice Boyes
March 14.	John Innes
	Eleanor Smith
April 9.	Jonah Colon
	Elizabeth Zeller
May 6.	William Ellison
	Ann Hughs
May 8.	Hezekiah Marks
	Eleanor Callahoun

1780.	John Britt
May 15.	Catharine Hemmium
May 16.	Jesse Tabor
	Elizabeth Wood
May 31.	William Beser
	Eleanor Elland
July 3.	John Fortunate
	Sarah Britton
July 16.	John Hughs
	Ann Dobson
July 23.	Rulof Jacobus
	Lydia Van Syle
Aug. 25.	John Williams
	Tryphena Gold
Aug. 31.	Jacob Long
	Eliz. Fleming
1781.	John Tyson
Jan. 3.	Mary Housman
Jan. 16.	Eliphalet Jones
	Elizabeth Bogart
Feb. 16.	Jesse Keen
	Margaret Henly
Feb. 25.	John Mersereau
	Judith Poillon
March 15.	William Reed
	Elizabeth Waters
March 25.	Daniel Lewis
	Elizabeth Handlin
April 4.	Richard Webb
	Dorcas Bardine
April 3.	Joseph Stackhouse
	Sarah Anderson
April 15.	Nicholas Journeay
	Ann Garretson
April 22.	David Leaforge
	Catharine Seguine
April 29.	John Wood
	Caturey Ridgway
May 12.	Ashley Bowen
	Sarah Palmer
May 13.	Barney Slack
	Mary Cole
May 30.	Henry Parlee
	Rebeka Cole
June 3.	John Guyon
	Sara Ward
June 3.	Thomas Craddock
	Sarah Bedel
June 3.	William Granger
	Sarah Stuart
June 10.	Myles Gardner
	Eleanor Strickland

1781.		Amos Rooke
June	13.	Martha Mersereau
June	18.	John Mersereau
		Mary Taylor
June	18.	James Mitchel
		Margaret Wilson
Aug.	13.	John Segoin
		Catharine Jennins
Aug.	15.	Joseph Leake
		Frances Egbert
Aug.	15.	Peter Price
		Mary Spann
Sept.	2.	Henry Miller
		Elisabeth Garrison
Sept.	5.	Daniel Storer
		Catharine Androvette
Oct.	7.	Daniel Perine
		Lucy Holmes
Oct.	21.	John Garretson
		Martha Codmas
Nov.	8.	John Kruse
		Jemima Simonson
Nov.	20.	Peter Saunders
		Letta Skinner
Nov.	30.	Edmund Warner
		Jane Fitchet
Dec.	4.	Edward Egbert
		Mary Cortelyou
Dec.	6.	Henry Priester
		Elizabeth Romer
Dec.	18.	Adam Smith
		Hannah Barclay
Dec.	20.	William Thorn
		Anne Rickow
1782.		Duncan Kennedy
Jan.	14.	Mary Mann
Feb.	14.	Lewis Frazur
		Catharine Thorn
March	12.	John Egbert
		Mary Holmes
March	22.	Jonathan Parker
		Mary Paterson
April	8.	George McLeland
		Margery Teague
April	14.	Cornelius Mersereau
		Aultje Amerman
April	22.	Simon Meyer
		Ann Bush
April	23.	George Grey
		Mary Eldridge
April	28.	Peter Perine
		Ann Palmer

(*To be continued.*)

THE GREENE FAMILY OF PLYMOUTH COLONY.

RICHARD HENRY GREENE A.M., LL.B.,
Corresponding Member of the N. E. Historic Genealogical Society.

FOURTH GENERATION.*

10. DESIRE⁴ GREEN (Warren,³ William,² William¹), b. at Eastham, Mass., Jan. 14, 1735; m. Philip Goff† of Wethersfield, Conn., who was b. at Middletown, about 1727. She d. at Easthampton, Conn., April 22, 1767. He d. at Chatham, Conn., Oct. 27, 1779. Their children, b. at Middletown and Chatham, were:

    32   i. Mercy⁵ Goff, b. 1756; bap. Jan. 12, 1757.
    33   ii. Benjamin Green Goff, bap. Oct. 9, 1757.
    34   iii. Timothy Goff, bap. July 27, 1760.
    35   iv. Philip Goff, bap. Aug. 17, 1766.
    36   v. James Goff, bap. June 2, 1767 (record says 1776).

11. ELIZABETH⁴ GREEN (Warren,³ William,² William¹), b. and bap. at Middle Haddam, Conn., July 5, 1742. I was informed she m. Jeremiah Brainerd, but I think, that was an error, from the fact that another Elizabeth m. a man of that name.

12. BATHSHEBA⁴ GREEN (Warren,³ William,² William¹), b. and bap. at Middle Haddam, Conn., Oct. 23, 1743; m. Stephen Hosmer,‡ Oct. 3, 1763, who was bap. Feb. 19, 1744. Stephen and Bathsheba lived at Middle Haddam, Conn. Children:

    37   i. Stephen⁵ Hosmer, bap. Mid. Had., April 26, 1767.
    38   ii. Asa Hosmer, bap. Mid. Had., April 26, 1767.
    39   iii. John Budd Hosmer, bap. Mid. Had., June 5, 1768.
    40   iv. Ann Hosmer, bap. Mid. Had., April 12, 1772.
    41   v. Mary Hosmer, bap. Mid. Had., July 31, 1774.
    42   vi. Peter Hosmer, bap. Oct. 27, 1776; lost at sea.

---

* The first three generations was published in Vol. LVII, *N. E. Hist. & Gen. Register*, January, 1903.

† Philip Goff was descended from Philip¹ Goff, who settled in Wethersfield, Conn., before 1649. He built the first house in present Rocky Hill 1655. He was freeman Oct., 1669, and d. 1674. He left a widow Rebecca and five children.

Philip² Goff, second son and third child, b. 1653; m. Mrs. Naomi, widow of John Reynolds, and dau. of John and Ann Latimer, b. Wethersfield, Conn., April 4, 1648. He d. March 7, 1724-5.

Philip³ Goff, eldest child, b. 1685; m. Dec. 15, 1703, Mary, dau. of Thomas and Hannah Couch. He d. March 9, 1724-5. They lived at Knowle's landing, now Middle Haddam, 1720.

Philip⁴ Goff, b. Oct. 15, 1704; m. about 1725, Sarah ——. He was bap. Mid. Had., Sept. 13, 1741; she Sept. 19, 1742. They lived in the part of the town which was afterwards East Hampton.

Philip⁵ Goff, the eldest child, m. Desire Green.

‡ I was wrong in the former paper in calling him Caswell. He was son of Stephen Hosmer, b. April 24, 1711; Yale, 1732; d. 1751. Grandson of Rev. Stephen Hosmer, b. 1679; Harvard, 1699; first pastor of First Church, East Haddam, 1704, till his death June 16, 1749. His wife was Sarah Long of Boston, Mass. She d. Sept. 30, same year.

43   vii. Bathsheba Hosmer, bap. Mid. Had., Aug. 23, 1778.
44   viii. Matilda Hosmer, bap. Mid. Had., April 8, 1781.
45   ix.   Horatio Hosmer, bap. Mid. Had., Sept. 14, 1783.
46   x.   Euclid Hosmer, bap. Aug. 20, 1786; went to the West
            Indies.
47   xi.   Rozilly Hosmer, bap. June 20, 1790.
13. SARAH⁴ GREEN (Warren,³ William,² William¹), b. Dec. 27,
1723; m. Oct. 5, 1767, David Dimock,* b. Rocky Hill, 1745; moved
to Vermont, then Wyoming Valley, Pa, where his wife d. 1813,
then he moved to Montrose, Pa., and d. there Aug. 14, 1832. They
had:
48   i.   Infant, d. Oct. 13, 1775.
49   ii.   Infant, d. Nov., 1775.
50   iii. Mehetable Dimock, m. Jared Clark of Middletown and
            East Haddam.
51   iv.   Asa Dimock, b. May 27, 1776, Rocky Hill.
52   v.   Davis Dimock, b. Aug. 22, 1780.
14. WARREN⁴ GREENE (Warren,³ William,² William¹), b. Aug. 31,
1747; bap. Sept. 6, 1747; m. Lucy Brainerd, Nov. 1, 1770. She
was b. Chatham, Conn., Feb. 6, 1747-8, dau. of Nathan and Sarah
(Gates) Brainerd of Chatham. They lived in Chatham, then
Ashfield, Hampshire Co., Mass., then Richfield, Otsego Co., N. Y.
She d. Feb. 16, 1821; he d. June 28, 1824, at Richfield. Children:
53   i.   Child, b. Aug., 1771; bap. Feb. 16, 1773; d. Feb. 18,
            aet. 18 mo.
54   ii.   Levi Greene, b. 1772, Chatham; bap. Feb. 16, 1773.†
55   iii. Anson Greene, b. Jan. 3, 1774; bap. April 13, 1774.
56   iv.   Hannah Greene, b. May 8, 1776; bap. June 23, 1776.
57   v.   Brainerd Greene, b. May 8, 1778; bap. Oct. 18, 1778.
58   vi.   John Greene, b. Ashfield; bap. July 30, 1781.
59   vii. William Greene, bap. May 30, 1784.
60   viii. Warren Greene, bap. June 4, 1786.
61   ix.   James Greene, bap. J ne 15, 1788.
62   x.   Timothy Greene, b. Feb. 3, 1790; bap. April 10, 1791.
15. BENJAMIN⁴ GREENE (Warren,³ William,² William¹), bap. Middle
Haddam, July 2, 1749. He was perhaps the Benjamin Green

* David Dimock was descended from Thomas¹ Dimock, who came from
England, was freeman Dorchester, Mass.; removed to Scituate, then Hingham,
was freeman Plymouth Colony, Dec. 3, 1639; Deputy, Magistrate, Council of
War, and Lieutenant of the Militia. He m. at Barnstable, Ann Hammond of
Watertown, Mass.
   Deac. Shubael² Dimock, bap. Dec. 15, 1644; m. April, 1663, Joanna, dau. of
John Barsley, for second wife, and had five children, of whom Schubael was
one. He removed to Mansfield, Conn., and d. Oct. 29, 1732, in his 91st year.
   Schubael³ Dimock, b. Feb., 1663; resided at Barnstable, Mass; m. (1)
Bethna, dau. of John and Hope (Howland) Chipman; m. (2) Tabitha, dau. of
Melathia Lothrop, May 4, 1699. She d. July 24, 1727; he d. Dec. 16, 1728.
   Samuel⁴ Dimock, only child, b. May 7, 1702; m. Hannah, dau. of Jos. and
Hannah (Cobb) Davis, June 1, 1740; lived at Saybrook, Conn. Justice of Peace,
Lieutenant and Captain in Militia. Removed to Rocky Hill, Conn., and d.
during the war.
   David⁵ Dimock, in the text, m. Sarah Green.
   † A Capt. Levi Green, Westmoreland Pa., had a dau. Sarah, m. June 26,
1817, John Rockwood, b. July 7, 1782.

who served in Col. Jedediah Huntington's Reg., Conn. Continentals, on the Hudson River, July 15, 1780, until Dec. 9, 1780.

19. WILLIAM[4] GREENE (William,[3] William,[2] William[1]), was b. Middletown, Conn., March 8, 1771; bap. March 14, 1773, East Haddam, Conn. William[4] Greene was son of William[3] Green, who m. Jan. 25, 1770, Elizabeth Young, b. Aug. 26, 1733, dau. of Robert[3] Young, Jr.,* b. Dec. 11, 1696, in Eastham, Mass.; m. Oct 3, 1717, Elizabeth Pepper, b. July 11, 1698, dau. of Isaac and Apphia (Freeman) Pepper of Eastham. He removed to Middletown, Conn. His parents both d. when he was a child and he was sent to his uncle, Capt. James Green, to be brought up with his younger brother Enoch. He was first in a store at East Haddam Landing, then went to sea. He m. Oct. 26, 1791, at East Haddam, Indiana, dau. of Jehiel† and Temperance Tinker of that place. They had three children, who were bap. by Rev. Solomon

* Robert[2] Young, Sr., was b. Eastham, Aug., 1667; m. March 22, 1693–4, Joanna, dau. of Samuel and Lydia (Doane) Hicks of same place.
    Robert[2] Young was son of John[1] Young who came to Plymouth, Mass., from England, and m. Dec. 13, 1648, Abigail, dau. of Henry Howland, brother of John, the *Mayflower* Pilgrim.

    † John[1] Tinker came from England about 1637, m. (1) Sarah Barnes; she d. 1648; m. (2) 1651, Alice Smith; he d. Hartford, Conn., Oct., 1662.
    Amos[2] Tinker, 4th child, b. Lancashire, Mass., Oct. 28, 1657; m. Sarah, dau. of George Durant, June 1, 1682; he d. Lyme, Conn., 1730, aet. 73.
    Amos[3] Tinker, Jr., b. Lyme, Jan. 17, 1716–7; m. Lucy Lee, b. Lyme, June 20, 1699, dau. of John and Elizabeth Smith.
    Sylvanus[4] Tinker (Amos,[3] Amos,[2] John[1]), b. Lime, Dec. 9, 1730; m. (1) Abigail Olmstead, 1755; m. (2) Welthy Gilbert, 1781. One of his descendants was wife of Jeremiah Day, President of Yale. He was partner of Richard Green at East Haddam in the shipping business. He sold half the dock and storehouse at the Landing to Capt. James Green, Jan. 20, 1770.
    Phinehas,[4] eighth child, brother of the last, b. Feb. 6, 1634–5; m. Nov. 24, 1761, Charity Marshall (sister of Ruth, who m. Capt. James Green), b. Freetown, Mass., Nov. 6, 1738; he d. July 14, 1782; she d. April 21, 1802. Children:
      i. John Marshall[5] Tinker, b. 1763; m. Lovina Snow. Children:
          i. Clarissa,[6] b. 1800; m. Erastus Jackson.
          ii. Benjamin Snow, b. 1802; m. Mary Hopkins.
          iii. Sylvester, b. 1807; m. Catherin Kennedy.
      ii. Martin Tinker, b. 1767; m. Naomi Spellman. Child:
          i. Almyra, b. 1794; m. Carlos Gibbons.
      iii. Sylvester, b. 1772; m. Ann Staples. Child:
          i. James Green Tinker, b. 1797; m. Phebe Van Gorder.
      iv. Parthenia, m. 1806, Norman Fancher.
      v. Lucinda, m. —— Rowley.
      vi. Charity.
      vii. Olive, never m.
      viii. Lee, lived in Bozra and later in New York.
    Jehiel[4] Tinker (Amos,[3] Amos,[2] John[1]), b. Lyme, Nov. 11, 1741; m. Temperance ——. He lived in East Haddam in 1775; was appointed second lieutenant of the armed brigantine *Minerva*, Giles Hall was captain, and James Hopkins first lieutenant. She was 108 tons burden, 40 seamen and 40 marines. In 1776 Conn. fitted out three galleys, one at New Haven, one at New London, and one at East Haddam; this last built by Job Winslow, was commanded by Captain Jehiel Tinker, first lieutenant, David Brooks, second, Elias Lay, master, Calvin Ely. Captain Tinker also, at some time in the war, commanded a small privateer from East Haddam. I do not think he was killed in the service as some say, but he d. before 1799. After his death his heirs (Sept. 23, 1803), Henry and Almyra White, Temperance Tinker and

Blakeslee of St. Stephens Episcopal Church in 1804; in the baptismal record she is called "India, widow of Wm. Green." He
was lost at sea in the schooner *Polly* from New London, Conn., in
1801. Wilson Green, son of Capt. James Green, was with him on
this voyage, and he also was lost. Mrs. Indiana Greene m. Feb.
5, 1806, Gideon Burr.* She d. June, 1858, aged 87, and was buried
at Canaan, N. Y. Children:

   63   i. William Young⁴ Greene, b. July 20, 1792.
   64   ii. Russell Tinker Greene, b. June 26, 1794.
   65   iii. Sophia Indiana Greene, b. Jan. 11, 1798.

20. ENOCH⁴ GREEN (William,³ William,² William¹), b. May 8, 1772.
He came with his brother to East Haddam and was brought up
by Capt. James Green. He returned to Middletown afterwards,
where he was a member of the Second Congregational Church,
and Oct. 13, 1788, subscribed to an agreement to support the
ministry in that church. I have heard he removed to the
vicinity of Whitestone, N. Y., afterwards.

21. HANNAH⁴ GREEN (James,³† William,² William¹), b. March 14,
1755; bap. April 11, 1773, East Haddam, Conn.; m. Joseph
Hungerford. He went to Boston, 1775, on the Lexington Alarm.
She m. (2) Capt. David Pierson from Southampton, L. I., who
commanded a company in Col. Josiah Smith's 1st L. I. Regt., at
the battle of Long Island, Aug., 1776. She lived at East Haddam
the last of her life and d. July 2, 1833. She had two children
both by first husband:

   66   i. Hannah⁵ Hungerford, b. July 13, 1778.
   67   ii. Joseph Hungerford, b. 1781; never m.; d. Aug. 12,
           1816, aet. 35.

23. JAMES⁴ GREEN, JR. (James,³ William,² William¹), b. April 8,
1758; m. Mary Gelston, dau. of Deac. Maltby and Mary Gelston
of Bridgehampton, L. I. She was b. July 3, 1758. He was a sea
captain and d. at sea, Dec., 1784. Her elder sister Catharine was
wife of Gov. De Witt Clinton, Elizabeth was the first wife of
David Pierson who m. (21) Hannah⁴ Green above. The father,
Maltby Gelston, was b. March 20, 1723; m. Mary, dau. of Dr. Thos.
and Mary (Livingston) Jones, N. Y. He was son of Judge Hugh
and Mary (Maltby) Gelston, who was for twenty-one years Judge
of Court of Common Pleas, Suffolk Co., N. Y. When the British
overran Long Island, Deac. Maltby Gelston fled to East Haddam,
and occupied a house on the river bank, south of the present
Watrous and near the Boss Hubbard place; part of the foun-

Indiana Green sold to Richard Green "land of late Jehiel Tinker in Moodus
Landing, where the dwelling stands." Children:
       i. Almyra⁵ Tinker, m. Henry White.
       ii. Temperance Tinker, unm.
       iii. Indiana Tinker, m. Oct. 26, 1791, William Green, 4th.
   * Indiana Green Burr had: Henry A., Gideon and Clarissa Ann Burr; her
second husband d. Oct. 18, 1827, aged 76 years.
   † In the sketch of (9) James³ Green, there is an error which should be
corrected, it appears on page 8 of reprint. Speaking of Mary Drake, I should
have said *her mother was Hannah Moore, dau. of Deacon John Moore,* for she
was not a dau. of Henry Wolcott as has been said many times.

dation was visible some years since. It was afterward occupied
by Mrs. John Marshall (who was Elizabeth Winslow) and her
dau. Ruth. The foundation has now fallen into the river with
the ground about it.

24. WILLIAM⁴ GREEN (James,³ William,² William¹), b. Aug. 26,
1760; bap. March 14, 1773. Went into the navy, when young,
during the war of Independence. He never returned and it was
reported to his family that he was drowned trying to escape
from the prison ship in Wallabought Bay, N. Y. Harbor. The
Conn. ship-of-war, *Oliver Cromwell*, was ordered Dec. 5, 1777, to
enlist crews with all speed, under the rules of the Continental
Congress. Timothy Parker was made captain. She was built at
Saybrook, 1775. April 20, 1778, Parker reported prizes taken, the
Cyrus, 16 guns, the *Admiral Keppel*, 18 guns. In his report he
speaks of the merit of his officers in action, "keeping such
inexperienced young boys (as many of them were) to their
quarters, without the show of fear or noise or confusion." Hence
William then in his 18th year was not the only boy.

In a list* of prisoners committed to Forton prison, Eng., Oct.
13, 1777, appears the name "William Green, ship *Oliver Cromwell*." Another entry, same name, without vessel, later. The
History of New London, says, "the crew were released Aug.,
1779, they had been on prison ships *Jersey* and *Good Hope*."
Webb's statement published in the *N. Y. Gen. & Biog. Record*,†
says: "The *Cromwell* was not captured until 1781. The list of
Prison Ship Martyrs also has his name. He may have been in
England as a prisoner and sent back for exchange or other
reasons.

He had the example of his father who had gone to the war
and his teacher, Nathan Hale, the martyr, who lived with them
and was dead.

25. BENJAMIN⁴ GREEN (James,³ William,² William¹), b. East
Haddam, Aug. 31, 1762; bap. March 14, 1773; m. Betsey Bigelow,
b. June 14, 1768, Colchester, Conn., dau. of Jonathan‡ and Elizabeth (Otis) Bigelow, and grand-dau. of James Otis and Sarah
Tudor, his wife, dau. of Samuel Tudor. Benjamin Green d.
July 31, 1828. Mrs. Green d. July, 1855. Children:
  68   i. James⁵ Green, b. July 29, 1789.

---

* *N. E. H. & G. Register*, Vol. XXXIII, p. 37.
† Vol. XXIX, p. 221.
‡ Jonathan Bigelow was b. Aug. 10, 1740; m. 1758; d. Jan. 13, 1823; son of
Asa and Dorothy (Otis) Bigelow; Asa, son of Lieut. John and Sarah Bigelow;
John, son of Joshua and Elizabeth (Flagg) Bigelow; he was son of John and
Mary, dau. of John and Margaret Warren. Children of Jonathan and Elizabeth (Otis) Bigelow:
    i. Delight, b. Dec. 24, 1759; m. John Fisk.
   ii. Dorothy, b. Feb. 3, 1761; m. Lt. John Brown.
  iii. James, b. March 16, 1764; m. Anna Day.
   iv. Elsey, b. March 27, 1766; d. June 13, 1776.
    v. Betsey, m. Dec. 25, 1787, Benjamin Green.
   vi. Sarah Tudor, b. March 2, 1771; m. Roger Wing.
  vii. Eunice, b. June 3, 1773; m. Chester Bardwell.
 viii. Jonathan, b. Aug. 11, 1775; drowned 1793.

8A

69   ii. Ruth Green, b. Dec. 14, 1790.
70   iii. Betsey Green, b. Sept. 26, 1795.
71   iv. Harriet Green, b. April 30, 1800.
72   v. Benjamin Green, b. Jan. 2, 1803; d. unm.
73   vi. Hannah Green, b. Jan. 2, 1803.
74   vii. Sarah Wing Green, b. March 27, 1808.
75   viii. Anson Green, b. Aug. 14, 1810.

26. RICHARD[4] GREEN (James,[3] William,[2] William[1]), b. March 10,
1765, at East Haddam; bap. March 14, 1773; m. May 1, 1803, Sally
Webb,* of Saybrook (now Chester), Conn.   After his marriage
he moved into the Jehiel Tinker homestead, which he bought
Sept. 23, 1803, for $1,015.00 from the heirs Henry and Almyra
White, Temperance Tinker and Indiana Green.   This place containing 80 rods, is described in the deed as at Moodus Landing,
between Thomas Marshall, Joseph Atwood and Elijah Atwood.
It was beautifully situated at the top of the terraces on the upper
road, facing the river, a double colonial house, in which Richard
Green lived until his death, and there all of his children were
born.   It was the second house south of Captain James Green's
house where he was born.   The south wing of Maplewood Seminary, now being taken down, is remembered as it stood between
Eliphalet Bulkeleys and Aunt Piersons.   Richard Green was a
merchant and ship owner until he retired from business in 1814,
when he furnished the capital for the new firm " R. and T.
Green," managed by his younger brother Timothy.   He was
Tithing man, constable, surveyor of highways, selectman, and
many times moderator of town meetings.   In 1816 he was appointed to purchase land for the town.   He was captain of the
East Haddam South Company, 25th Regiment Conn. Militia, and
in that capacity marched his company in 1812 on an alarm to
New London.   This was in the second war with England.

Capt. and Mrs. Green always attended the First Church in
East Haddam, which was then called Uptown, now Little Haddam.   Captain Green d. at his home in East Haddam, Feb. 8,
1848, aet. nearly 83 years.   His widow removed to Brooklyn,
N. Y., where three of her sons resided, but after her only
daughter's marriage, she went with her to live in Danbury,
Conn., where she d. June 5, 1858, aged 78; her remains were
placed beside her husband's in Riverside Cemetery, East Haddam.   Their children, all b. at East Haddam, were:

76   i. Richard William[5] Green, b. March 28, 1804.
77   ii. Henry Green, b. Sept. 5, 1805.

---

* Sally Webb was dau. of Wm. Webb, b. Sept. 19, 1746, who m. Elizabeth
Hudson, dau. of Richard and Keturah (Goldsmith) Hudson, all of Sterling,
Southold, L. I., which he left when the British took possession after the Battle
of Long Island, in which he participated as a member of Joshua Young's Co.,
Col. Josiah Smith's Regiment. He d. Sept. 23, 1832. He was descended from
Richard[1] Webb, who came from England to Cambridge, Mass., 1626, m. Eliz.
Gregory, and d. at Stamford, Conn., 1656; John[2] and Ann Webb, Northampton,
Mass.; John[3] and Susanna (Cunliffe) Webb of same; Henry[4] Webb, b. Nov.
29, 1668, lived and d. Dec. 6, 1712, at Wethersfield, Conn.; m. Oct. 10, 1695,
Mary, b. Oct. 16, 1672, dau. of Sam'l Hurlbutt; Ebenezer,[5] b. Nov. 20, 1697,
lived Southold, d. 1776. Had Wm.[6] Webb, in the text.

78   iii. William Webb Green, b. March 29, 1807.
79   iv. James Wilson Green, b. March 20, 1809.
80   v. Sidney Green, b. Jan. 2, 1811.
81   vi. Frederick Warren Green, b. Aug. 16, 1813.
82   vii. Elizabeth Green, b. Aug. 28, 1816; d. Feb. 1, 1818.
83   viii. Sarah Ann Green, b. April 16, 1819.

27. ANN[4] GREEN (James,[3] William,[2] William[1]), b. East Haddam,
Feb. 13, 1768; joined the church June 5, 1796; m. Nov. 29, 1789,
Jared Spencer, son of Maj.-Gen. Joseph Spencer* and Martha,
dau. of Hezekiah Brainard, his wife. Jared was a twin, b. June 5,
1762; bap. Millington, July 25, 1762; graduated Yale, 1784, and
later admitted to bar and practiced till his death. He was captain 6th Regt. Militia. He perished in a snow storm Nov. 11,
1820; his wife d. Nov. 11, 1855, aged 87 years and 9 months.
Children:
84   i. Nancy[5] Spencer, b. May 29, 1791.
85   ii. Mary (Polly) Spencer, b. Sept. 12, 1793; d. Sept. 7, 1860.
86   iii. Lucretia Spencer, b. Sept. 12, 1793; d. April 26, 1858.
87   iv. Richard Green Spencer, bap. May 4, 1800.

29. OLIVER[4] GREEN (James,[3] William,[2] William[1]), b. East Haddam, Aug. 16, 1773; bap. Aug. 22, 1773; m. Dec. 10, 1797, at
Cheshire, Mass., Damaris Howe, b. Killingly, Conn., Oct. 6, 1779;
she was dau. of Isaac and Damaris of East Haddam. After
marriage they lived at Cheshire for a time and two of their
children were b. there. He was a blacksmith and had a forge
where the East Haddam bank stood later. Their residence was
adjoining on the north. He was Justice of the Peace and postmaster. He d. Jan. 2, 1848; she d. Oct. 27, 1866, and both were
buried at East Haddam. Children:
88   i. Nancy[5] Green, b. Aug. 25, 1799.
89   ii. Marshall Green, b. Sept. 7, 1800; d. Aug. 19, 1826.
90   iii. Son, b. and d. Sept. 10, 1802.
91   iv. Timothy Green, b. Nov. 2, 1803; d. March 2, 1814.
92   v. Oliver Green, b. Dec. 31, 1805.
93   vi. Lucretia Bacon Green, b. March 1, 1808.
94   vii. George Warren Green, b. June 28, 1810; d. Nov. 18, 1822.
95   viii. Edmund Harris Green, b. Dec. 10, 1812; d. California 1850.
96   ix. Mary Ann Green, b. Nov. 11, 1816.
97   x. Timothy Wilson Green, b. Jan., 1822; d. Oct. 15, 1822.

---

* Gen. Joseph Spencer was son of Isaac and Mary (Selden) Spencer, who
was son of Samuel Spencer of Millington, Conn., who was son of Sergeant Jared
Spencer of Cambridge, Mass., one of the first settlers of Haddam. Joseph
Spencer was Major of Colonial troops at Louisburg, 1757; Lieut.-Col. 1759, and
1760; he was General of Militia, Conn., 1775. He went with his brigade to
Boston, 1775, and Congress made him Brigadier-General, July, 1775; in Aug.,
1776, he was made Major-General of the Continental Army. He resigned, 1777,
but as General of Connecticut Militia, assisted Gen. Sullivan in R. I., Aug., 1778.
He was then elected to Congress from Conn. His family was large and have
been influential in many States of the Union.

30. TIMOTHY[4] GREEN (James,[3] William,[2] William[1]), b. East Haddam, July 3, 1776; bap. July 21, 1776; m. April 18, 1813, Mrs. Lucretia (Hathaway) Knowles, b. Feb. 4, 1779, Fairhaven, Mass., dau. of Samuel and Joanna (Gilbert) Hathaway of that place. He succeeded his father, who was the first postmaster, and lived in the brick house just north of the family homestead. He was lister, 1806–10; collector road tax, 1812; gauger, 1817; surveyor of lumber, 1818, and State Senator. He d. June 15, 1853; she d. March 31, 1856. They were buried in Riverside Cemetery, East Haddam. Children:

98   i. Maria Theresa[5] Green, b. April 21, 1815.
99   ii. Catherine Lucretia Green, b. Aug. 14, 1819.
100   iii. Timothy Franklin Green, b. Oct. 11, 1811.

(*To be continued.*)

THE KNICKERBOCKER FAMILY.

BY WILLIAM B. VAN ALSTYNE, M.D.

(Continued from Vol. XXXIX, p. 41, of THE RECORD.)

9. ELIZABETH[3] KNICKERBOCKER (Johannes Harmensen,[2] Harmen Jansen[1]), bap. 1 Nov., 1702, at Albany, N. Y.; m. there 8 Feb., 1725, Sybrant Quackenbos, bap. there 14 June, 1702, son of Adrian Quackenbos and Catherine Van Schaick. Children, bap. in Albany:

   i. Catharina,[4] bap. 5 Sept., 1725; spon.: Anth. V. Schayk and Cath. Quakkenbosch.
   ii. Anna, bap. 25 Feb., 1728; spon.: Piet. Quakkenbosch and Neeltie Knikkerbakker; d. y.
32   iii. Johannes, bap. in May, 1729; spon.: Jesse and Neeltie D. Foreest; m. 9 Dec., 1758, Jannetje Viele.
   iv. Adriaan, bap. 18 March, 1732; spon.: Adr. and Cathr. Quackenbos.
33   v. Annaatje, bap. 15 Jan., 1734/5; spon.: Harmen and Neeltje Knickerbakker; m. 1752, Lodovickus Viele.
   vi. Elizabeth, bap. 11 Sept., 1737; spon.: Johannis and Cornelia Knickerbakker; d. y.
34   vii. Harmen, bap. 6 Dec., 1738; spon.: Wouter and Elizabeth Knickerbakker; m. about 1764, Judith Morrel.
   viii. Neeltje, bap. 28 Feb., 1742; spon.: Johannes Knickerbakker, Jr., and Corna. Knickerbacker.
35   ix. Elizabeth, bap. 28 Feb., 1742; spon.: Anthony and Catharina Quackenbos; m. 28 May, 1762, at Albany, Johannis I. Fort.

10. HARMEN[3] KNICKERBOCKER (Johannes Harmensen,[2] Harmen Jansen[1]), bap. 25 Dec., 1709, at Albany, N. Y.; d. 18 Sept., 1768, at Schaghticoke, N. Y., aged 58 years, 8 months and 18 days; m. about 1745, Rebecca De Wandellar. On 27 Nov., 1751, Harmen

was ordained a deacon in the Dutch Reformed Church at Schaghticoke, N. Y.; in Nov., 1763, Jacob Viele succeeded him; on 20
Dec., 1767, he was appointed elder, and on his decease, his brother
Johannis was elected to the office. He is described as "a beloved
elder" in this church. "Harmen Knickerbocker of Schotta Coak,
Albany County, yeoman," made his will 12 Sept., 1768, proved
1 Nov., 1768, and recorded at Albany. In it he mentions his
nephew John, son of brother John Knickerbocker, sister Elizabeth Quockenbos, nephew Darieh Vanfactor and his sister
Hannah Kipp, brother Woughter Knickerbocker, sister Nealcha
Knickerbocker, cousin Hannah, wife of Cornelius Vanfaiter,
cousin Hannah, wife of Lewis T. Vieley, and cousin Hannah,
wife of Egmon Kipp. He wills real and personal property,
the latter including a silver teapot, six dozen spoons and six
dozen tablespoons. The executors were his brothers Woughter
and John Knickerbocker (Fernow's *Calendar of Wills*, p. 225). It
is evident that when Harmen made his will his wife and son
were dead. Child of Harmen Knickerbocker and Rebecca De
Wandellar:

    i. Johannes, bap. 25 May, 1746, at Albany; spon.: Johan-
        nes and Cornelia Knickkerbackker; probably buried
        2 Dec., 1747, at Albany.

11. WOUTER KNICKERBOCKER (Johannes Harmensen, Harmen
Jansen), 19 Oct., 1712, bap. at Albany, N. Y.; d. 8 Aug., 1797, at
Saratoga, N. Y.; m. 9 Jan., 1735, at Albany, Elizabeth Fonda,
bap. 4 July, 1711, at New York City, dau. of Isaac Fonda* and
Alida Lansing. Wouter Knickerbocker was for many years a
resident of Albany. Children, bap. at Albany:

  36   i. Anna, bap. 9 Nov., 1735; spon.: Hannes Knicker-
        bakker and Elizabeth Quackenbos; m. 10 Dec., 1757,
        Cornelius Van Vechten.
    ii. Isaac, bap. 20 Nov., 1737; spon.: Isaac and Alida Fonda.
  37 iii. Alida, bap. 20 Nov., 1737; spon.: Hendrik and Marytje
        Fonda; d. 17 Feb., 1819, at Schaghticoke, N. Y.; m.
        21 Oct., 1758, Dirk Van Vechten.
    iv. Elizabeth, bap. 25 March, 1739; spon.: Lucas and
        Rebecca Hooghkerk; d. y.
    v. Elizabeth, bap. 28 Sept., 1740; spon.: Abraham Fonda
        and Cornelia Knickerbakker.
    vi. Johannes, bap. 3 April, 1743; spon.: Wouter Groes-
        beek and Neeltje Bratt; d. y.

---

* Isaac Fonda, bap. 9 March, 1684, at Albany; m. there 3 Dec., 1708, Alida
Lansing, bap. there 3 July, 1685; buried there 23 March, 1748; dau. of Hendrick
Gerritsen Lansing and wife Lysbeth. He was son of Douwe Jelisen Fonda.
    Douwe Jelisen Fonda, d. 24 Nov., 1700; m. Rebecca ——. He owned land
at Lubberde land (Troy) in 1676. They were church members at Albany in
1683. He was son of Jillis Douwesen Fonda.
    Jellis Douwesen Fonda was in Beverwyck as early as 1654. He m. Hester,
perhaps the Hester Jansz who stands as sponsor in 1690 at the baptism of Anna,
dau. of Douw Jelisen Fonda. In 1664 Hester Douwese, assisted by her children Douw and Greetien, sold to Jan Coster Van Aecken two distiller's kettles
for four hundred guilders seewant, she being then probably a widow. In 1666
she was widow of Barent Gerritsen.

vii. Johannes, bap. 16 Nov., 1746; spon.: Harmen and
Neeltie Knikkaback.

viii. Rebecca, bap. 18 June, 1749; spon.: Harmen Knickerbacker and Rebecca Hooghkerk.

Wouter Knickerbocker had children buried at Albany 29 Nov.,
1737, 9 Oct., 1743, 16 July, 1747, and 26 Sept., 1752.

12. CORNELIA[9] KNICKERBOCKER (Johannes Harmensen,[8] Harmen
Jansen[1]), bap. 21 Oct., 1716, at Albany, N. Y.; m. 29 Feb., 1744, at
Albany, Teunis Van Vechten, bap. there 10 July, 1709; buried
there 27 June, 1756; son of Dirk Cornelisen Van Vechten* and
Margarita Harmense Luwes of Schaghticoke, N. Y. Children:

  i. Dirck,[4] bap. 17 Feb., 1745, at Albany; spon.: Benjamin
   Van Veghten and Catharina Wendel.

38 ii. Anna, bap. 4 Dec., 1748, at Albany; spon.: Joh. and
   Neeltje Knickerbacker; m. there 29 Jan., 1767, Ignas
   Kipp.

  iii. Margaritta, bap. 2 Jan., 1752, at Schaghticoke; spon.:
   Dirck Van Vechten and Elisabeth Van ——.

  iv. Johannes, bap. 23 Oct., 1755, at Albany; spon.: Harmen and Rebecca Cnikkerbacker.

13. JOHANNES[9] KNICKERBOCKER (Johannes Harmensen,[8] Harmen
Jansen[1]), bap. 24 March, 1723, at Albany, N. Y.; was m. there
17 Feb., 1750 (Schaghticoke Records), by Rev. Theo. Frieling-
huysen, to Rebecca Fonda, bap. 14 April, 1718, at Albany,
"daughter of Col. Nicholas Fonda† and Anna Marselis."

On 22 Nov., 1752, Johannes joined the Dutch Reformed
Church at Schaghticoke and there at various times he officiated as
elder and deacon. The church record states that he "died 16 Aug.
1802 aged 79 years," furthermore that "he was in the colonial
army and was appointed Colonel 20 Oct. 1775." Revolutionary
War records show that he was Colonel of the Fourteenth Regiment of Albany County Militia. The record states further that
his wife "died 8 Jan. 1800 aged 81 years" and her life is expressed
in the text "She was full of good works and alms deeds which
she did." In *Harper's Magazine*, vol. 54, p. 42, is a picture of
Colonel Johannes Knickerbocker and his wife reproduced from a

---

* Dirk Cornelisen Van Vechten, m. 5 Dec., 1703, at Albany, Margarita
Harmense Luwes, both b. and living in the Colony of Rensselaerwyck. She
was dau. of Harmen Livesz and Marretje Teunisz. He was son of Cornelis
Teunisen Van Vechten and Annetje Leendertse.

Cornelis Teunisen Van Vechten, alias Keesoom, of Papsknee, an island
below Albany, m. (1) in 1668, Sara Solomonse Goewey, daughter of Salomon
Abelsen; m. (2) Annetje Leendertse; m. (3) 3 June, 1689, at Albany, Maria
Lucase, widow of Jacob Claessen. Cornelis Teunisen Van Vechten was son of
Teunis Dirksen Van Vechten.

Teunis Dircksen Van Vechten with his wife, child and two servants came
to this country in 1638, in the *Arms of Norway*. He owned a farm at Greenbush, N. Y., in 1648. In 1663 he was referred to as "an old inhabitant here."

† Nicholas (Claes) Fonda, m. 16 Nov., 1716, at Albany, Annetje Marselis,
bap. there 30 June, 1689, dau. of Gysbert Marselis and Barbar Claasz Groesbeek. He was son of Douwe Jelisen Fonda and his wife Rebecca, both early
church members at Albany.

painting in the east room of the old Knickerbocker mansion at Schaghticoke. *Appleton's Cyclopædia of American Biography*, vol. 3, pp. 561 and 562, gives a clearer picture of Colonel Knickerbocker and a picture of his homestead.

Children of Johannes Knickerbocker and Rebecca Fonda bap. at Albany:

> 39   i. Johannes,⁴ bap. 24 March, 1751; spon.: Harmen and Rebecca Knickerbacker; d. 10 Nov., 1827, at Schaghticoke, N. Y.; m. 1 March, 1769, at Schaghticoke, Elizabeth Winne.
>
> 40   ii. Anna, bap. 11 March, 1753; spon.: Geysbert and Elisabeth Fonda; m. 5 April, 1771, at Schaghticoke, Abraham Viele.
>
> iii. Neeltie, bap. 24 Nov., 1754; spon.: Wouter and Neeltje Knickerbacker.
>
> iv. Elizabeth, bap. 24 Nov., 1754; spon.: Gerrit Marselis and Pollie Funda.

Johannes Knickerbocker had two children buried at Albany, one 4 March, 1756, and the other 2 Oct., 1757.

14. BENJAMIN³ KNICKERBOCKER (Laurens,² Harmen Jansen¹), m. about 1732, Aletteka Halenbeck.

5 Oct., 1766, Domine Fryemont received into membership of the Red Hook Reformed Church from the church on the Flatts Benjamin Knickerbacker and wife Aletta Halenbeek.

In 1766 Domine Kuypers made a register of the seats in the same church. Benjamin Knickerbocker paid 7s. for five places in seat number twelve. The five places may have been for himself and wife, his son and daughter-in-law and his grandson.

Benjamin Knickerbocker and Aletta Halenbeck may have had a child:

> 41   i. Laurentz,⁴ b. about 1733; m. Margerie Bain (Ben).

15. JOHN³ KNICKERBOCKER (Laurens,² Harmen Jansen¹), b. 1710; d. 10 Nov., 1786; buried at Lime Rock, Conn., said to be the first burial in that cemetery; m. (1) Jacomyntje Freer, bap. 4 Nov., 1711, at Kingston, N. Y., dau. of Abraham Freer and Aeche Willems Titsoort; m. (2) 22 Feb., 1751, at Sharon, Conn., Jemima Owen; b. and d. at Sharon, Conn.

The will of John Knickerbocker of Salisbury, Conn., is dated 5 June, 1785, proved 3 Jan., 1787, and recorded at Sharon, Conn. (Sharon Probate Records, Book F, p. 264). He wills his wife Jemima one-half the house and barn and the use of all his land adjoining the house known by the name of the Grant, during her life, also two cows, one horse and six sheep, firewood, necessary timber, etc., also one year's provisions, viz., meats and bread, and one-hundred weight of live swine. To his eldest son Abraham he gives thirty acres of feasable land and fifteen acres on the mountain; to his second son Lawrence, three acres and twelve acres, and to his fourth son Isaac fifteen acres adjoining that given Lawrence. To Harman's John, so-called, and my grandson, he wills twenty-five acres, with the house his father built. To his eldest daughter Mary Hogabome he gives one-half a lot of land Mr. McIntyre now lives on, joining easterly on Eben Hanchet's land and westerly on Widow Van Dusen's land, also land known as the Wite Pitch and to Jane Jackson he gives the other half of above said lot and pitch. To daughter Sary Griffin he wills all my land on the east side of the highway. The fifth son Solomon gets everything else not already given away, he giving to Harmon's three children, not before named in this will, viz., paying the boy Bartholomew £1.10, to Rachel and Thankful, twins, £1 to each when they are of age. He appoints Joseph Hanchet of Salisbury, and Jeremiah Hogaboom of Canaan, executors. The will is witnessed by Joseph Hanchett, Mary Valance and Aaron Jaqua.

The births of the children of John Knickerbocker, except Echie, are taken from the Salisbury, Conn., records:

42   i. Abraham,[4] b. 12 April, 1733; bap. 3 May, 1733, at Germantown, N. Y.; spon.: Jacobus and Anahke Decker; probably m. Jerusha ———. In the baptism the mother's name is recorded as Jacobaatche. This might have been a first wife of whom we have no record or a clerical error for Jacomyntje.

      ii. Echie, bap. 9 Feb., 1734, at Linlithgo, N. Y.; spon.: Jan and Tyssie Decker; probably d. y.; mother's name recorded as Jac———.

43   iii. Lawrence, b. 1 or 7 Sept., 1739, according to Salisbury records, but 1 Nov., 1739, according to the Athens, N. Y., church records when he was baptised; no spon.; probably m. Catharine ———.

44   iv. Harmon (Herman), b. 3 Jan., 1741/2, according to Salisbury records, but 13 Jan., 1742, according to the Athens church records, spon. to baptism being Herm. Knickerbocker and wife Catha.; d. prior to June, 1785; m. Thankful ———.

      v. Mary, b. 18 Dec., 1744; bap. 2 June, 1745, at Rhinebeck, N. Y.; spon.: Pettrus Knickerbocker and Meseri Penn; m. (Jeremiah) Hogabome.

     vi. Johanneke (Jane), b. 6 Aug., 1747; bap. 6 June, 1748, at Mount Ross,[*] N. Y.; spon.: Seilos and Johanneke Baldin; m. —— Jackson.

45 vii. Isaac, b. 17 June, 1750; bap. 15 Oct., 1750, at Linlithgo; spon.: Hendrick Schmit and Geertruy Frey; m. Hannah ———.

     viii. Sarah, b. 11 March, 1752; m. —— Griffin.

46   ix. Soloman, b. 12 Oct., 1754; m. about 1775, Anna Heath.

16. HARMEN[3] KNICKERBOCKER (Laurens,[2] Harmen Jansen[1]), b. 1712; d. 19 Aug., 1805, aged 93 years; m. (1) Catrina Duytcher,

---

* The first baptism in the Dutch Reformed Church of Greenbush in Livingston Manor; also known as Gallatin or Domine Vedder's Church, but now called Mount Ross.

b. 1712–21; d. 30 April, 1771, aged 5- years, dau. of Roelof De
Duidser and Jannetje Bressie; m. (2) Elizabeth ——, who d. 6
Sept., 1805, aged 77 years. "Herman Knickerbacker" and his
wives are buried in the family cemetery on the Belden farm
between Wassaic and Dover, N. Y. He lived opposite Mrs.
Joseph Belden's and where George N. Perry lived for many
years, the property now owned by William Rundall. The West
Side Cemetery is near the homestead.

A census of the slaves above the age of fourteen, taken in
1755 in the precinct of Rhinebeck, shows that Harman owned
two slaves, one of whom was named Tom. It is interesting to
note that Thomas, a negro man belonging to Hermanus Knickerbocker, was baptised 22 July, 1781, in the Presbyterian Church at
South Amenia, N. Y.

Harmanis Knickerbocker of Amenia Township, made his will
27 April, 1802, proved 11 Oct., 1805, and recorded at Poughkeepsie,
N. Y. (Book of Wills, vol. B, p. 550). In it he mentions wife
Elizabeth, sons Lawruence, Ruliff, John and Harmanis, daus.
Mary and Lydia, grandson Moses Butt and son Ruliff's son Cor-
nelius.

Children of Harmen Knickerbocker and Catrina Duytcher:

    i. Jannetje,⁴ bap. 20 April, 1738, aged 4 months, at
        Athens, N. Y.; spon.: Myndert Mynderse and Jan-
        netje, his wife; d. y.
    ii. Lauwrens, bap. 27 Jan., 1740, at Kingston, N. Y.;
        spon.: Petrus and Jannetjen Knickerbocker.
    iii. Janche, bap. 19 Sept., 1742, Rhinebeck-Red Hook
        (N. Y.) church records; spon.; Cornelis Knicker-
        bocker and Catharina Vosburgh; probably m. 4 April,
        1769, at Oblong, N. Y., John Crosswell. "Jane, wife
        of John Crofuell," d. 15 Feb., 1781, in her 39th year
        and is buried on the Belden farm.
47 iv. Rudolft, bap. 16 April, 1745, at Germantown, N. Y.;
        spon.: Jacob Vosburg and Elisabetha Knickerbocker;
        d. 28 June, 1807; m. 22 Dec., 1768, at Oblong, Cath-
        arine Dutcher.
48 v. Maritgen, bap. 28 Feb., 1748, at Germantown; spon.:
        Maritgen Knickerbocker and jury Segendorf; prob-
        ably m. 28 Jan., 1768, at Oblong, Joseph Gillet.
    vi. John.
    vii. Harmanis.
    viii. Lydia.

In the family cemetery on the Belden place is buried Mrs.
Catharine Knickerbacker, who d. 4 Sept., 1772, in her 19th year.
She may have been the young wife of one of Harmen's sons. In
that cemetery are also buried two sons of Lawrence and Mary
Knickerbacker, Samson, who d. 8 July, 1793, in his 5th year, and
Silas, who d. 27 April, 1806, in his 10th year.

17. ELISABETH⁵ KNICKERBOCKER (Laurens,⁴ Harmen Jansen¹), no
record of birth; d. 23 April, 1793, at Dover Plains, N. Y.; m.
Gabriel Dutcher, b. 2 Feb., 1720, at Tackkanick, N. Y.; bap. 10

April, 1720, at Lonenburg, N. Y. (New York City Lutheran
Church Records), son of Roelof De Deutser* and Jannetje Bressie.
Gabriel moved from Dutchess County, N. Y., to Salisbury, Conn.,
with his parents and there inherited his portion of the estate.
He returned to Dutchess County after 1759, but after his wife's
death in 1793, went to live with his son John at Cherry Valley,
N. Y., where he died.   His wife was buried in the old graveyard
at Dover Plains.   Children:

    i. Lauwrenz,⁴ b. 17 Jan., 1740; bap. at Athens, N. Y.; m.
        5 Nov., 1761, at Oblong, N. Y., Geertruy Wheeler.

    ii. Rulof, bap. 24 Aug., 1741, at Athens, N. Y.; "b. five
        weeks before at Camp;" spon.: Lour. and Marytje
        Knickerbacker, "the grandparents."

    iii. Mary, m. 8 Jan., 1765, at Oblong, N. Y., Edwardus
        Wheeler, formerly of Livingston's Manor. They
        had a son John, bap. 25 Dec., 1777, at Mr. Silas
        Belding's house (South Amenia, N. Y. records).   It
        is not proved that Mary belongs to this family.

    iv. Benjamin, bap. 29 Jan., 1744, at Germantown, N. Y.;
        spon.: Pieter Ben and Malche Knickerbocker. Ben-
        jamin moved to Dutchess County, later to White
        Creek, Washington County, N. Y., and finally to
        Shaftsbury, Vt., where he d.   He m. Thankful
        Benson. They had eight children for whose de-
        scendants see Ballou's *History of Milford, Worcester
        Co., Mass.*

---

* Roelof De Deutser, m. 17 Nov., 1700, at Kingston, N. Y., Jannetje Bressie,
dau. of Christoffel Bressie and Styntje Claes.   He d. 19 Jan., 1737, and his
wife d. 26 July, 1749.

The origin of the Dutcher family in this country is obscure. Two branches
appear at Kingston. The first represented by Machteltje Roelofse De Deutser,
who m. 19 Aug., 1683, at Flatbush, Long Island, Jan Hendricksen Oosterom,
and had children bap. at Bergen, Flatbush and Kingston. She was dau. of
Roelof Willemsen (Van Heerden) of Albany, New York City and Brooklyn,
and Willemptje Tyse, who m. (2) Jan Cornelisen Buys. The second branch
consists of the following De Deutsers:—Cornelia Janse, who m. prior to 1680,
Jan Wels; Cornelis, who m. prior to 1693, Leonora de Hooges, widow of Willem
de la Montague; Catharina, b. at Flatbush (Kingston), who m. 11 Feb., 1700, at
Kingston, Jan Rolan, widower of Judick Schirard; Dirick, b. at Hurley, who m.
19 Nov., 1699, at Kingston, Jannetje Bont; Roelof, who m. 17 Nov., 1700, at
Kingston, Jannetje Brussy; Barent of Tarrytown, N. Y., who m. (1) prior to
1701, Maritje Conkele, and m. (2) 29 Dec., 1717, Dirckje Smit, widow of Hen-
drick Lammersen; and David, b. in Esopus, who m. 19 Feb., 1714, at Kingston,
Elisabeth Deffenport. It is probable that they are brothers and sisters, for we
find them standing reciprocally as sponsors at baptisms of each others children,
and prominent among those children the names Johannes and Margrietje.
"John Williamson, ye Duitcher," took the oath of English allegiance in Ulster
County, 1 Sept., 1689, and "Cornelis ye Duitcher" failed to appear. Jan
Willemsen Brant and Grietje Cornelise had children bap. at Kingston: Willem,
22 Jan., 1662, and Tys, 24 April, 1681. Further research may prove that the
second branch of the Dutcher family are children of Jan Willemsen Brant and
that he is a brother of Roelof Willemsen previously mentioned.

For further particulars concerning the Dutcher family see *Our Colonial
Ancestors and Their Descendants*, by Henry Whittemore.

      v. Cornelius, bap. 24 May, 1746, at Germantown; spon.: Cornelius Knickerbocker and Ellaar Ben.

49   vi. Christoffel (Christopher), bap. 3 Jan., 1748, at Germantown; spon.: Christoffel and Gertraut Deutser; m. 9 June, 1768, at Oblong, N. Y., his cousin, Mary Belden, dau. of Silas Belden and Janetie Knickerbocker.

    vii. Catharina, b. 17 Sept., 1749; bap. at Athens; no spon.; may have m. William Woolcutt. They lived in Dover, N. Y., and had a son Sebastian, b. 13 Dec., 1748; bap. at South Amenia, N. Y.; spon.: John Wheeler and Ruth Samson.

    viii. Elias, m. 25 April, 1776, at Oblong, Mary Rose. They had children: Catharine, b. 21 Feb., 1777; John, b. 18 Aug., 1781, and Elizabeth, b. 18 May, 1783. It is not proved that he belongs to this family.

    ix. Jeany, m. 3 Feb., 1780, at Oblong, John Hoffcut. They lived at Dover and had children: Hannes Yeary, b. 4 Nov., 1780, and Elizabeth, b. 19 Oct., 1784. It is not proved that she belongs to this family.

50   x. John, b. 5. Jan., 1759, at Salisbury Conn.; d. 2 Dec., 1848; m. 17 May, 1779, Sylvia Beardsley.

18. PETRUS[3] KNICKERBOCKER (Laurens,[2] Harmen Jansen[1]), b. and residing in Dutchess County; m. 17 Sept., 1742, at Kingston, N. Y., Margerie (Meseri) Bain, b. in Dutchess County and residing in Kingston, N. Y.; bap. 18 Oct., 1719, at Kingston, dau. of Hugo Ben and Elisabeth Schot. Petrus lived near Mount Ross, N. Y. (Huntting's *Little Nine Partners*, p. 366). He and his wife were church members there prior to Nov., 1767, and he was appointed elder 4 May, 1770, and 20 May, 1780.

Children of Petrus Knickerbocker and Margerie Bain:

51   i. Marika,[4] bap. 4 Sept., 1743, Rhinebeck-Red Hook (N. Y.), church records; spon.: Cornelius and Jannetje Knickerbocker; m. 13 Oct., 1766, at Mount Ross, Johan Adam Dings.

52   ii. Philip, bap. 24 Feb., 1745, at Rhinebeck; m. 1 July, 1766, at Mount Ross, Anna Maria Dings.

53   iii. Laurentz, bap. 25 Oct, 1747, at Germantown, N. Y.; spon.: Johan Benn and Catharine Knickerbocker; m. (1) Maria Gertrude Snyder; m. (2) Nancy Race.

54   iv. Lisabeth, bap. 12 Nov., 1749, at Germantown; spon.: Hui and Lisabeth Ben; m. 30 Oct., 1769, at Mount Ross, Jacob Dings.

55   v. Petrus, b. 7 Nov., 1751; bap. at Rhinebeck Flatts, N. Y.; spon.: Pieter and Dorothea Vosburg; m. 18 Feb., 1790, at Claverack, N. Y., Rebecca Vosburgh.

    vi. Benjamin, m. and left descendants.

56   vii. James, bap. 20 July, 1755, at Mount Ross; spon.: Peter Ben and Hanna Lescher; m. 24 July, 1780, at Mount Ross, Maria Deunis.

57 viii. Majory (Margaret), bap. 8 May, 1757, at Linlithgo,
       N. Y.; spon.: James and Lisabeth Ben; m. Hugh
       Ray, New York State Marriage license dated 24
       May, 1775.
58 ix. John, bap. 12 May, 1759, at Mount Ross.; spon.: Jacob
       Hermanns and Catherina Vosburgh; m. 22 May, 1785,
       at Mount Ross, Anna Maria Kaus.
59 x. Hugh, bap. 30 Aug., 1761, at Linlithgo; spon.: Pieter
       Ben and Johanna Lesscher, his wife; m. 11 June,
       1786, at Mount Ross, Rachel Schram.

19. Cornelis[3] Knickerbocker (Laurens,[2] Harmen Jansen[1]), m.
Eleonora (Ellaar, Ellinar, Helena) Ben, bap. 7 Jan., 1722, at
Kingston, N. Y., dau. of Hugo Ben and Elisabeth Schot. On the
1 May, 1768, they became church members at Mount Ross, N. Y.
Cornelis Knickerbacker of North East Precinct made his will
7 Jan., 1774, proved 22 Jan., 1789, and recorded at Poughkeepsie
in Book of Wills, vol. A, p. 124. In it he mentions wife, son John
and daus. Caty, Catarina, Genne, Lana, Margree, Elizabeth, wife
of Benjamin Van Leuveren, and Mary, wife of Tobias Miller.
He appoints his wife and brothers Benjamin and Peter Knickerbocker executors. Children:
60   i. Elizabeth,[4] bap. 15 Feb., 1747, at Germantown, N. Y.;
       spon.: Peter Benn and Johanna Lescher; m. Ben-
       jamin Van Leuven.
61   ii. Marika, bap. 2 Oct., 1748, at Germantown; spon.:
       Peter and Meseri Knickerbocker; m. Tobias Muller
       (Miller).
     iii. Laurentz, bap. 3 Feb., 1751, at Linlithgo, N. Y.; spon.:
       James and Elisabeth Bean; probably d. young as he
       is not mentioned in his father's will.
62   iv. Johannes, b. 12 Nov., 1752; bap. at Rhinebeck, N. Y.;
       spon.: Jhan and Antje Ben; m. Susanna Pulver.
63   v. Cathrina, bap. 8 May, 1757, at Linlithgo; spon.: Ben-
       jamin Knickerbocker and Aletteka Halenbeeck, his
       wife; m. John Schermerhorn.
64   vi. Lena, b. 11 July, 1761; bap. at Rhinebeck Flatts, N. Y.;
       spon.: Johannes Van Wagenen and Geertrui Scott;
       m. Johannes Hilligass.
     vii. Margaretha, bap. 26 Aug., 1764, at Germantown; spon.:
       Philip and Maria Knickerbocker.
65 viii. Genne (Jane), m. Johannes Pulver.
66   ix. Cornelia, m. Simon Milius. Cornelia probably belongs
       to this family but is placed here without proof.

20. Janetie (Johanneke)[3] Knickerbocker (Laurens,[2] Harmen
Jansen[1]), b. 5 Nov., 1721; d. 18 March, 1799; m. 27 Dec., 1743,
Silas Belden, b. 13 Nov., 1717, at Wethersfield, Conn.; d. 9 April,
1787 (data from family records); son of Silas Belden and Abigail
Robbins. The house where Silas brought his bride stood in
what was called Dover, or more exactly the town of Washington,
at the foot of Plymouth Hill, on the left-hand side going up from
Dover. Their grandsons Lawrence and Silas began their married

lives in the homestead, but later Silas moved to the second house at the right of the foot of Plymouth Hill, on the right side of the road from Amenia. Lawrence remained and finally built a new house, moving the old one to the rear but with a space between them. A few months after the death of his wife, Louisa Ketcham Gregory, both structures were torn down. Tabor Belden (son of Joseph Belden and Eliphal Tabor) and his son Joseph built the present house on the lawn back of the old homestead further up the road and in the town of Amenia.

Silas Belden, Sen., of Charlotte Precinct, Dutchess County, made his will 20 Feb., 1786, proved 19 April, 1786, and recorded at Albany. In it he mentions wife Janetie, sons Silas and Lowrens, and daus. Mary, Jane and Elizabeth, and heirs of dau. Abegal and Katrine. He wills personal property and land in Charlotte Precincts, in Salisbury, Vermont, and in Canaan Township, Albany County. Executors, the wife, son Lourens and son-in-law Christopher Dutcher (Fernow's *Calendar of Wills*, p. 47).

Children of Silas Belden and Jane Knickerbocker:

67   i. Silas,[4] b. 9 March, 1745; bap. 2 June, 1745, Rhinebeck-Red Hook (N. Y.) Church Records; spon.: Benjamin and Maltgen Knickerbocker; d. 30 Sept., 1789; m. 17 Oct., 1765, at Oblong, N. Y., Dorcas Gillette.

    ii. Mary, b. 5 Nov., 1746; d. y.

    iii. Lorentz, bap. 25 Jan., 1747, at Germantown, N. Y.; spon.: Lorentz and Mariken Knickerbocker; d. y.

    iv. Laurentz, bap. 22 Feb., 1749, at Germantown; spon.: Benjamin and Catharina Knickerbocker; d. y.

    v. Lawrence, b. 18 Dec., 1750; d. y.

    vi. Mary, b. 23 Feb., 1751; m. her cousin Christopher Dutcher, bap. 3 Jan., 1748, at Germantown, son of Gabriel Dutcher and Elisabeth Knickerbocker. Either the date of her birth or that of the preceding Lawrence is wrong. We are inclined to think that the latter should be b. 18 Dec., 1748, and refers to a younger Lawrence.

68 vii. Abigail, b. 4 March, 1753; m. Clement Ray. She d. before Feb., 1786.

69 viii. Lawrence, b. 2 Sept., 1755; d. 20 Dec., 1832; m. 3 Oct., 1776, Susanna Wheeler.

    ix. Catherine, b. 7 Sept., 1757; m. 20 April, 1778, Pardon Burlingame. She d. before Feb., 1786, leaving children.

70 x. Jane, b. 25 April, 1762; m. David Morehouse.

71 xi. Elizabeth, b. 11 July, 1764; bap. 24 Aug., 1764, at their home at Nine Partners (South Amenia Records); m. Aaron Wilcox.

(To be continued.)

RECORD OF MARRIAGES BY ROSWELL HOPKINS, ONE OF HIS MAJESTY'S JUSTICES OF THE PEACE FOR THE COUNTY OF DUTCHESS, STATE OF NEW YORK.

1763, Dec.	8.	Samuel Cotten and Sarah Crouch.*
1764, Jan.	2.	Phillip Besee and Sarah Durham.
Jan.	12.	James Palmer and Deborah Spencer.
Feb.	19.	David Colin and Lucy Smith.
March	8.	Eliphalet Folliot and Elizabeth Dewey.
March	14.	Pane Atwill and Ruth Lamb.
June	18.	David Simons and Alice Abel.
July	8.	Nathan Mackwethy and Rachel Handy.
Nov.	4.	Gideon Spencer and Zerviah Buck.
Nov.	7.	George Sherman and Eunice Brown.
Dec.	12.	William Bradley and Lucretia Gates.
1765, Jan.	10.	Nathan Spicer and Abigail Mayhew.
April	22.	Josiah Cleaveland and Ruth Johnson.
May	16.	John Ollivett and Elizabeth Crouch.
		Ebenezer Case and Joannah Phillips.
June	13.	Samuel Johnson and Mary Penoyer.
Sept.	30.	Henry Fillemore and Mary Gillette.
Oct.	17.	Elias Shavilear,† Jr., and Sarah Ashley.
Oct.	23.	Abner Shavilaer and Deborah Wood.
Oct.	29.	Nathan Herrick and Mary Kidder.
Nov.	26.	John Seton and Leaneau Serenbergh.
Dec.	11.	Caleb Lamb and Anne Baliss.
1766, Jan.	12.	Samuel Behier and Deborah Cleaveland.
Jan.	16.	Abbel Ackley and Hannah Shavilear.
Feb.	5.	Edward Wheeler and Thankful Crippen.
		Samuel Wheeler and Chole Kidder.
April	10.	Benjamin Hopkins and Zereph Rudd.
July	6.	Joseph Germmond and Phebe Elderkin.
Aug.	21.	Ezra Murray and Hannah Gould.
Oct.	23.	James Bull and Anne Steward.
Nov.	20.	Daniel Shepherd and Mary Rudd.
Dec.	25.	Josiah Gale and Rachel Mead.
1767, Sept.	6.	Joshua Culver and Ruth Cook.
1768, Feb.	2.	William Bennet and Annah Buck.
May	5.	Benjamin Baker, Jun., and Mary Shavilier.
Sept.	15.	Isaac Willis and Martha Chapman.
Sept.	14.	John Tooley and Rhoda Egleston.
Nov.	2.	James Landon and Freelove Briant.
Dec.	26.	Elijah Park and Olive Brown.
1769, Feb.	23.	Ebenezer Carter and Lydia Holmes.
Dec.	18.	Thom. Pudney and Azubah Alger.

* The form written in the above record was as follows: "1. Dec. 8th, 1763, Then Samuel Cotten and Sarah Crouch was married together by me, Roswell Hopkins, Justice of the Peace." All the marriages were so recorded in the original manuscript record, but have been printed as above to save repetition.
† This is undoubtedly the English spelling of the French name "Chevalier."

1771, May	13.	John Benedict and Sussanah Allen.
June	13.	Jonas Standish and Sarah Stedman.
Sept.	12.	Jonathan Allen and Luise Lamb.
Dec.	1.	John Welsh and Susannah Spicer.
1772, Feb.	15.	John Pearl and Sarah Shepherd.
May	7.	Joseph Seger and Olive Calender.
May	31.	Joseph Avery and Deborah King.
July	26.	James Russel and Sarah Wells.
Aug.	16.	Daniel Hebbard and Mercy Pike.
Sept.	17.	Jonathan Autherton and Bathsheba Mead.
		Jared Gates and Sarah Pike.
Nov.	5.	David Buttolph and Anne Holmes.
Nov.	19.	David Gillet and Freelove Muxsun.
Dec.	27.	Isaac Lamb, Jun., and Abigal Fryal.
1773, Feb.	8.	William Herrick and Anna Goodrich.
Feb.	11.	Samuel Gale and Lydia Skinner.
Feb.	18.	Amos Parker and Lucy Culver.
March	8.	Michael McGee and Prudence Cammeron.
March	16.	Zachariah Dibble and Elizabeth Spencer.
Nov.	11.	Joseph Backus and Olive Park.
Dec.	28.	John Jones and Sarah Patterson.
1774, Jan.	31.	Michael McKay and Sarah Rowlee.
June	30.	Squire David and Mary Helme.
Sept.	8.	Joseph Delavergne and Sarah Gillet.
Nov.	3.	Samuel King and Lydia Hopkins.
Nov.	10.	Thomas Morey and Mercy Allen.
1775, Jan.	30.	Benjamin Webb and Sarah Holmes.
June	2.	Rufus Herrick, Jun., and Lydia Newman.
July	25.	Thadeus Gilbert and Patience Whipple.
1776, Jan.	25.	Jonathan Dunham and Elizabeth Holmes.
Feb.	15.	Timothy Tilson and Anne Adams.
March	17.	Samuel Holmes and Abigal Spalding.
April	18.	Samuel Chichester and Zerviah Osborn.
1777, April	3.	Elihu Paine and Mary Park.
April	20.	Ezra Thurston and Prudence Helme.
Dec.	31.	Benjamin Goodrich and Elizabeth Dunham.
April	24.	Isaiah Golding and Betsy Davis.
1778, April	2.	David Waters and Phebe Thurston.
Sept.	1.	Reuben Allerton and Louis Autherton.
Dec.	30.	David Rundel and Catharine Power.
1779, March	16.	Eliakim Hide and Lois Bates.
July	29.	Dan Crosman and Eunice Garnsey.
Aug.	9.	Daniel Hunt, Jr., and Hannah Miller.
Sept.	30.	Levi Cornwall and Lucy Ormsby.
Oct.	5.	William Butts and Rachel Lockwood.
Oct.	7.	John Bugbee and Elizabeth Lockwood.
1780, Jan.	20.	Simeon Cook, Jr., and Faith Barker.
		James Allen and Hannah Randel.
Nov.	2.	Robert Wood and Abigal Rudd.
		Daniel Hewett, Jun., and Hannah Miller.
1781, Feb.	13.	Joseph Ingersoll and Huldah Fisk.
April	26.	James Henderson and Martha Jane.
May	1.	Soloman Brown and Hannah Olmstead.

1781, May	7.	Alpheus Ingersoll and Sibel Adams.
	Oct.	18.	Benjamin Cook and Deborah Goodrich.
	Dec.	18.	King Mead and Anne Burris.
			Amos Evens and Anna Thurston.
1782, Jan.	16.	Thomas Pettigrove and Anna Willis.
	Jan.	27.	William Evens and Abigal Beebee.
	Feb.	21.	Nathan Rowley and Eunice Buck.
	Feb.	28.	Caleb Wadhams and Eunice Farr.
	June	6.	Ichabod Paine, Jun., and Tryphene Barker.
1783, June	26.	James Lloyd and Lucy Goodrich.
	April	10.	Ephraim Smith and Miriam Thurston.
	Sept.	17.	Elijah Goodrich and Rachel Lloyd.
	Nov.	4.	Caleb Raymond and Hannah Whipple.
	Dec.	21.	Oliver Pettibone and Martha Paine.
1784, March	3.	Nathaniel Pinney and Ann Eslestine.
	Aug.	10.	Edmund Palmer and Anne Lloyd.
	Sept.	9.	David Tryen and Mary Reosens.
	Nov.	11.	Jarvis Pike and Anne Mayo.
	Nov.	38.	Nathan Freeman and Cynthia Shepherd.
1785, Jan.	26.	Consider Wood and Mary Adams.
	March	17.	Nathan Holmes and Mary Paine.
	June	30.	William Andrews and Hannah Purves.
	Oct.	20.	Henry DeLavergne and Salomi Dunham.
	Dec.	30.	Israel Buck, Jr., and Rebecah Eldridge.
1786, Jan.	26.	James Smith and Ursilla Adams.
	March	5.	Abiram Howard and Olive Ransome.
	June	22.	Jehosaphat Holmes, Jr., and Patty Wells.
	July	5.	Elisha Crippen and Mary Goodrich.
	Nov.	—.	Benjamin Wood and Thankful Holand.
1787, Feb.	1.	Daniel Merritt and Phebe Akein.
	Feb.	18.	Conrad Chamberlain and Sarah Beardslee.
	April	20.	Abraham Ausin and Eunice Taylor.
	May	10.	Benedict Eldridge and Rhoda Shavilier.
	July	29.	Joseph Pinney, and Lydia Hebard.
	Sept.	2.	Daniel Hebard and Betsey Chamberlain.
	Oct.	11.	Gordon Moulton and Deborah Weeks.
	Nov.	20.	Ebenezer Garnsey and Silea Shavilier.
	Nov.	26.	Frederick Dillino and Joanna Doty.
	Dec.	6.	John Frinck and Hannah Hammond.
	Dec.	29.	John Dutcher and Matilda Luke.
1788, Jan.	15.	Frederick Powers and Ruth Penoyer.
	Jan.	17.	John Hall and Polly Butts.
	Jan.	24.	John Hanchet and Tiney Hamlin.
	March	12.	Jonah More and Martha Paine.
	Aug.	20.	Phillip Spencer and Sarah Hopkins.
	Nov.	10.	John McMurphy and Anne Wenn.
	Nov.	27.	William Bentley and Abeliney Shepherd.
	Dec.	16.	John Hill and Betty Bates.
	Dec.	18.	Philip Spalding and Sylvia Dunham.
	Dec.	28.	Frederick Goodell and Rhoda Garnsey.
	Dec.	29.	Ezra Miller and Mary Green.
1789, Jan.	1.	George Talbut Perry and Philomedia Holmes.
			Levet Howard and Deborah Carter.

1789, March 3. Ezra Gregory and Mary Mygatt.
    April 26. Joseph Fitch and Elizabeth Harris.
    May   5. Isaac Mygatt and Sarah Smith.
    June   4. Moses Smith and Waitstill Lassel.
    July 26. Joel Smith and Esther Benham.
    Oct.   7. Reuben Mayo and Sarah Atwill.
1790, March 28. David Bryant and Elizabeth Lounsbury.
    July 11. Ebenezer Owen and Mary Paine.
    July 26. Anthony Lloyd and Betsey Slassen.
    Aug. 26. Philip Tidd and Anne Freeman.
1791, April 3. John Morgan and Fanny Baker.
    Oct.   9. Isaac Reed and Hannah Pitcher.
    Nov. 21. Charles Stevans and Anne Hill.
1792, J l 17. Aaron Johns and Elizabeth Barnes.
1793, Feb. 2. Sampson Wood and Jude ——.
    Feb.   3. Thomas Adams and Unice Wheeler.
    Feb.   4. William Conner and Lucy Edwards.
    May   20. Silas St. John and Luise Fuller.
    July 11. Robert Parks and Lydia Herrick.
    Sept. 7. Abner Wood and Elizabeth Lathrop.
1794, April 23. David Parker and Susannah Teed.
    May   15. William Paine and Polly Smith.
    May   27. William Benson and Hannah Fills.
    Aug.   8. Thomas Barnes, Jr., and Polly Tyler.
    Sept. 18. Robert Hebard, Jun., and Mary Beardslee.
    Oct.   5. James Gerchan and Esther Anjevine.
1795, March 8. Bela E. Benjamin and Louisa Parks.
    March 7. Ebenezer Warner and Polly Enos alias Anne
               Smith.
    March 10. Ebenezer Carter, Jr., and Rachel Gillet.
    June 20. Andrew McFarlin and Sally Lord.
    Sept. 6. William Crandall and Jerusha Ashley.
    Oct. 13. Thomas Miller and Anne Sanford.
    Oct. 25. Gilbert Cornwall and Rhoda Bailis.
1796, April 23. Origen Hill and Abigal Smith.
1797, Jan.   5. Ebenezer Smith and Susannah Delamater.

SOUTHOLD, N. Y., TOWN RECORDS, VITAL STATISTICS FROM LIBERS D. AND E., IN THE TOWN CLERK'S OFFICE.

CONTRIBUTED BY LUCY DUBOIS AKERLY, WITH NOTES.

(Continued from Vol. XXXIX, p. 64 of the RECORD.)

PECK. The Sd John Peck was married to Martha Moore: May: 1703.
    John Peck Son to ye Sd John & Martha was borne ye 6th of
    June, 1704 and Departed this Life the 15 Iane. 1773. Easter
    wife to the Sd John Peck departed this Life the 7 March,
    1787.
    Bathsheba Peck Daughter of ye above named was borne
    february 1705/6.

9A

PECK.   Joseph Peck Son of ye above named was borne June 29th:
1708.

Harbert Peck Son of ye above named was borne October:
15th: 1709.

LANDON.   Nathan Landon died March 9, 1718, ae 54.   Hannah
his wife died (recent entry) Jany. 26: 1701: ae. 30.

Nathan Landon Son of Nathan & Hannah Landon was borne
In September ye 14th. day anno Domini 1696.

Samuel Landon Son of ye above Sd Nathan & Hannah was
borne ye 20th day of May anno Domini 1699.

Elizabeth Landon daughter of ye Sd. Nathan was borne Iune
12th: 1700 (or 1710).

NOTE.   Hannah, wife of Nathan Landon, was, according to a tradition at
Guilford, Conn., dau. of Stephen² Bishop (John¹), and his wife Tabitha, dau. of
Widow Parnel Wilkinson of Bermuda.   The name Parnel was in frequent use
in the Bishop family, and among Hannah's descendants.   Nathan and Hannah
Landon had children: Nathan above, Samuel and Eliza, who d. ——, and
doubtless James, and Hannah, who m. John Vail, ancestors of Bishop Thos.
Hubbard Vail of Kansas, and a child who d. in 1701.   If Elizabeth above,
was b. 1710, as Griffin's *Journal* asserts, she was not a dau. of Hannah above,
she m. Samuel Griffin.

For the other children of Samuel Landon below, see *A Partial Record of
the Landons of Southold.*

LANDON.   Samuel Landon was married to Bathia Tuthill, May 26,
1720(?).

The Sd Bathia was borne Decembr. 12th 1703, & Died 30
August 1761.

Henry Landon Son of ye Sd Samuel and Bathia was borne
October ye 30th 1721 & Died 27 Aug. 1735.

BOOTH.   Elisha Booth was married to Hannah Wilmot ye 27th
day of December, 1722. and he departed this Life Octobr.
28th 1725.

Elsha Booth Son of ye above named was borne ye 10th of oct.
1723.

Hannah Booth Daughter of ye above named was borne ye
29th day of Decembr. 1724.

Elexander Booth Son of ye above named was borne ye 24th
of may, 1726.

CURTICE.   Joshua Curtice was married to Mary Youngs daughter of
John Youngs & Mercy his wife ye eighth of September 1698.

Births.   The Sd Mary was borne December ye 4th 1676.

Mary daughter of ye sd Joshua Curtice & Mary his wife was
born ye 22 day of July 1699, about 3 in the morning.

•Ester Daughter of ye above named was born ye 24th of may
about 9 in ye morning 1701.

Joshua Son of ye above named was Born ye 1st february
1722/3: abt. 9 in ye morning.

Elisabeth daughter of ye above named was Born ye 30th
March, 1705 abt. one in the morning.

John Son of ye above named was Born ye 16th Octobr. 1707.

Caleb Son of ye above named was Born January ye 28th
1709/10.

Barnabas Son of ye above named was Born January ye 18.
1711/12.

Curtice. Benaiah Son of ye above named was Born January ye 22d. 1713/14.

A Son born to ye above named Ianuary ye 29th 1715/16, and departed this life the 25th of february following.

A Son to ye above named Augt. ye 17th, 1717, and departed this life the 13 october following.

Daniel Son of ye above named was born march ye 10th 1718/19; and departed this life february the 20th 1724/5.

Mercy Daughter of ye above named was born may ye 10th 1721.

Hempstead. Robert Hempstead born 1702, th 30 of Novembr.

Robert Hempstead was married to Mary Youngs Daughter of Benjamin Youngs, Esq. the 3d of June, 1725.

Sd. Mary was born ye 2 of August & Departed this Life the 10 of January 1768.

Robert Hempstead Esq. d. 5 March 1779.

Benjamin Hempstead was borne the 24th day of May, 1726. & was Drowned near Barbados on the 7th of feb. 1749/50, out of Sloop Stirling: Will: Moor master.

Abigail Hempstead daughter of the above named was borne ye 3d. day of february 1726/7.

(She m. 1st John Ledyard on the 6 May, 1750, children John, George, Polly & Fanny, m. 2d Dr. Micah Moore, children Julia who m. Matthias Case, Hannah, who m. Jona. Landin, Phoebe, who m. 1st —— Denison, 2nd —— Smith, 3d Joseph Wickham—she died 7 Mch. 1805. J. W. Case).

Elizabeth Hempstead daughter of the above named was born ye 7th day of december 1729.

Thomas Hempstead Son of the above named was born august th 13-1731.

Joshua Hempstead was born th 20 of July 1733.

Mary Hempstead   "   "   th 8 of Sebt. 1736.

Robert   "   "   "   ye 13 of Nov. 1738, & Died 24 august 1746.

Experience Hempstead was born the 5 of october 1740, & Died the 3 of November following.

Experience Hempstead was born the 6 of March 1741/2.

Deborah Daughter of ye above named was born ye 18 of may, 1744 & Died th 26 of august 1747.

The above named Robert Hempstead was married to his Second Wife the Widow mehetable Reeve the 19 of October 1768.

There Son Samuell Benjamin was Born the 18th of July, 1769, and Departed this Life the 18th of Decembr. 1772.

Mehetable Hempstead Daughter of ye above named was born the 15 of June. 1773.

Beebee. James Beebee of Southold was married to Susanna Babcock The daughter of Oliver Babcock of Westerly in ye Colony of Rhoad Jsland the 26th day of march anno Domini—1724.

James Beebee Son of ye above named James & Susanna was born January the 28th in ye year 1724/5 ye 5th day of ye week.

BEEBEE. Oliver Beebee Son of ye above named was born Septemr.
ye 23d 1726. the sixth day of ye week.

Mary Beebee Daughter of ye above named was born augt. ye
8th 1728. The 5th day of ye week.

Susanah Beebee Daughter of above named was borne ye 22d:
Day of June 1731. The 3 Day of ye week.

GLOVER. William Glover was maried to Deborah Lambert october ye 20th 1712 & Sd. Deborah Died the 4 of June 1773.

William Glover Son of ye above named William & Deborah
was born ye 3d day of Septr. Jn the Year 1713.

Deborah Glover Daughter of ye above named was born
march ye 15th 1715/16.

Sarah Glover Daughter of ye above named was born the 12th
day of march 1717/18.

. Daniel Glover Son of ye above named was born february the
20th 1719/20.

John Glover Son of ye above named was born Decembr. the
24th Day, 1721.

BROWN. Samuel Brown was married to Rebecka Beebee the 14th
of January 1712/13.

Mary Daughter of ye above named was born ye 14th of
December 1713.

Rebecka Daughter of ye above named was born ye 24th of
may, 1715.

Deborah Daughter of ye above named was born ye 17 of
Septembr. 1718.

Elisabeth Daughter of ye above named was born ye 10th of
March 1720/21.

Jonathan Son of ye above named was born ye 13 of May,
1723.

GEER. Oliver Geer was married to Elisabeth newbery the 10th of
June anno Domini 1731.

Vzziel Son of ye above named was born ye 22d Day of february 1731/2, The 3d day of ye week.

CONKLING. Henry Conkline was married to Temperance Bayley
the 16th Day of Ianuary 1716/17, & She departed this life
ye 25 of Febray 1739/40, & he Died the 25 Iuly 1753.

Henry Conkline Son of ye above named was born Octr. 13th
1717.

Benjamin Conkline Son of ye above named was born Sept.
29: 1719, & Departed this Life the 29 of July 1773.

John Conkline Son of ye above named was born March 22,
1720/1 & Died December th 24/1757 with the Small pox.

Temperance Conkline Daughter of ye above named was born
Sept. 12th 1722. (Sd. Temperance was married to Hennery
more November th 1/1744, and Died Novembr. 26/1758.

Elisabeth Conkline Daughter of ye above named was born
augt. 11th 1724.

Jonathan Conkline Son of ye above named was born Octr. 4th
1726.

Thomas Conkline Son of ye above named was born Septr.
10th 1728.

CONKLING. Deborah Conkline Daughter of ye above named was borne novembr. 1st 1732.

The above named Hennery Conkling was married to his Second Wife the Widdo mary Budd the 12 of May, 1742. (Sd mary Departed this Life 28 Iuly 1771, being then the wife of Sylvanus Davis.)

Hennery Conkling son of the above named Benjamin Conkling was borne July the 30/1754.

NOTE. Henry⁴ Conkling (John,³ Capt. John,² John¹), m. (1) Temperance² Bayley (Stephen¹), and m. (2) Widow Budd, dau. of Carteret Gillam. His son Benjamin was of Mattituck and m. Sarah ——, perhaps L'Hommedieu.

YOUNGS. Jsaac Youngs Son of Benj. Youngs Junr. was born april ye 12th 1708, Departed this Life th 26 of may, 1768.

Seth Youngs Son of ye above named was born ye 20th of feby. 1711/12 and Died In the year of our Lord Christ 1761, in Iune.

Joseph Youngs Son of ye above named was born Ianuary ye 1st 1714/15 and was Lost at sea.

Lidya Youngs Daughter of ye above named was born Ianuary ye 14th 1716/17.

Anna Youngs Daughter of ye above named was born march ye 30th. 1719.

Jsrael Youngs Son of ye above named was born Novemr. ye 11, 1721.

MOORE. Hennery Moore married to Temperance Conkling Novembr 1, 1744.

Temperance moore Daughter of ye above named was born th 9 october 1748.

Lydia moore Daughter of ye above named was born Novembr. 15, 1751.

Hennery Moore Son of ye above named was born November 5, 1753.

John moore Son of ye above named was born January 27/1756.

James Moore Son of ye above named was born february 25/1758.

CLEVES. David Cleves was married to Elisabeth moor feby. 14, 1727/8.

David Cleves Son of the above named was born Decemr. 9, 1728, and Departed this life may ye 1st 1731.

Joshua Cleves Son of ye above named was born March 4th, 1730/1.

David Cleves Son of ye above named was born feby. 6th 1732/3.

Beriah moor Cleves Son of ye above named was born Octr. 21, 1736.

Elizabeth Cleevs Daughter of ye above named was borne march ye 6th 1738/9. being Tuesday.

Deborah Cleeves Daughter of the above named was born June ye 29/1741.

Phebee Cleeves Daughter of the above named was born ye 19 of may, 1744.

YOUNGS. Samuel Youngs, late of Stanford was married to Rebecca Drown, of Southold, ye 13 of Septr. 1737.

YOUNGS. Samuel Youngs Son of ye above named was born ye 29th of July, 1738.

CONKLING. Jonathan Conkling was married to Elizabeth Hempsted 21 August, 1750.

Benjamin Hempsted Conkling son of the above named was born 28 May, 1751.

Jonathan Conkling Son of the above named was born Janvary ye 1, 1753.

Elisabeth Conkling Daughter of the above named was borne 29 march 1756.

Nathanael Conkling Son of the above named was born april 1758.

Desire Conkling Daughter of the above named was born 31 august 1763.

One child a Daughter born the 18 of march 1766 and Died ten (or two) Day old.

Deborah Conkling Daughter of the above named was born the 6 of august 1768, and Died the 19th august 1769.

MOORE. David Moore Son of Thomas Moore was born in the Year of our Lord 1713/November 25, the above named was married to Hepzibah Willmot the 30 day of Ianuary anno domini—1733/4.

the above named Hepzibah Willmot was born april the 6/1715.

David Moore Son of the above named was born Decembr. th 9/1734.

Hepzibah Daughter of the above named was born Decembr. th 12/1736.

Mary Daughter of the above named was born Iuly th 7/1739.

BooLah Daughter of the above named was born October th 2/1741.

Deborah Daughter of the above named was born Janvary the 17/1743/4.

LEEK. Philip Leek was married to Mary Wiggains avgust 11/1736.

Philip Leek Son of the above named was born Iune 10/1737. and Died Jvne 2/1738.

Hannah Leek Daughter of the above named was born October 30/1738 and Died oct. 6/1743.

Philip Leek Son of ye above named was born Jvne 27/1740.

Mary Leek Daughter of ye above named was born april ye 19/1741. and died October 20, 1743.

Submit Leek Daughter of ye above named was borne avgust 29/1744.

John Leek Son of the above Named was born March th 27/1747.

Mary Leek Daughter of the above named was born the 20 October, 1750.

BAXTER. Richard Baxter married to Hannah King the Daughter of William King, June ye 29/1740.

There Eldest Daughter Hannah was Born april 3/1741.

Bathshua Baxter was Born august the 4, 1742.

Svsanna there Daughter was born Janvary 21, 1743/4.

BAXTER. Richard Baxter Son of the above named was born
Janvary the 6/1746/7.

KING. James King Son of William & Bastrebee King was married unto Katharine Sheffield of South KingsTown In the
Colony of Rhoad Jsland on October the 30/1753.

Bathshua King Daughter of the above named was born the
4th of March, 1754.

James King Son of the above named was born ye 26 of
March, 1756.

Katherine King Daughter of the above named was born ye
14 of Avgust, 1758.

Abigail King Daughter of the above named was born ye 27
of Sept. 1760.

Mary King Daughter of the above named was born ye 11
of april 1763.

Hannah King Davghter of the above Named was born ye 28
of avgvst 1775.

SHEFFIELD. Robert Sheffield married to Svsanah King Davghter
of William & Bathsheeb King the 22 of Jvne 1749.

Svsanah Sheffeild Davghter of the above named was born ye
7 of Decembr. 1750.

Robert Sheffeild Son of ye above named was born ye 21 of
Janery 1752.

Second Son Robert Sheffield was born the 10th of avgvst
1753.

Bathshua Daughter of the above named born march the
16/1755.

DARROW. August the 8/1762 John Darrow was married to Mary
King Daughter of William King Juner.

Mary Darrow Daughter of the above named was born
Novembr. th 4/1763.

Elisabeth Darrow Daughter of the aboved Named was born
May th 11, 1766.

John Hanford, Son of the above named was born June the
15/1768.

BAYLEY. Benjamin Bayley Son of Stephen Bayley was Born
September ye 16: 1699, & he Departed this Life the 10
Novemr. 1770, and was married to Susanna Conklin November ye 19: 1723, then She was 20 Year old lacking: 18: day
(& she Died Novbr. 1./1769).

Susanna Bayley Daughter of the above named was Born
november ye 13:1724 on friDay about 10 a Clock at night.

Benjamin Bayley Son of the above named was Born Agust
ye 8th 1726 on monDay about foure a Clock in ye afternoon.

Stephen Bayley son of ye above named was Born fabruary
ye 23: 1728 about eleaven at night.

Mary ye Daughter of ye above named was Born June ye 20th
1730, and lived but about 8 months.

Jonathan ye Son of ye above named was Born Janaway ye
5th 1733 and lived about 7 year & 6 months.

Mary Bayley ye Daughter of ye above named was Born
December ye 25th 1734, a teusDay about 4 in ye morning.

BAYLEY. Dabro Bayley ye Daughter of ye above named was Born March ye 23th 1736 on tuesDay about 3 afternoon.

Gamaliel Bayley Son of ye above named was Born Januwary ye 16: 1738 a monDay about 2 in ye morning.

Lucretia Bayley Daughter of ye above was Born Iuly ye 31:th. 1740 a thursDay about 2 in ye afternoon, & Died the fovrth of Sept. 1773 being the wife of Joseph Peck.

Christian Bayley ye Daughter of ye above named was Born Janawary ye 4: 1743: about ten at night.

Jonathan Bayley ye son of ye above named was Born June ye 28: 1745 on friDay at aleaven at night.

Nathajel Bayley Son of ye above named was Born Janawary ye 9th: 1749: on monDay about a leaven a Clock.

Christopher Bradley Gran Son to ye above named was Born December ye 27: 1752, new Stile.

NOTE. Letters on the estate of Peter Christopher Bradley, were issued to his father-in-law Benjamin Bayley, 11 Nov., 1761. (*N. Y. Administrations.*)

Susannah, dau. of Benjamin Bayley m. Barnabas Horton.

BEEBE. Amon Beebee married to Anna Arnold March th 15/1763.

Said Amon Beebee was born 29 avgust 1739.

Anna Beebee Daughter of the above named born Jvne ye 6/1764.

Lucretia their Daughter Born March the 6/1766.

Amon Beebeee Born Iuly the 12/1768.

Benjamin Beebee Son of the above named was born 25 avgvst 1773.

Samuel Beebee Son of ye above named was born 19 Jvne 1774.

See *Beebee Genealogy.*

Liber E contains a few more records too recent for insertion here.

SOCIETY PROCEEDINGS.

JANUARY 10TH, 1908.

The Thirty-ninth Annual Meeting of the New York Genealogical and Biographical Society was called to order by the President, Mr. Clarence Winthrop Bowen on Friday evening, January 10th, at half past eight o'clock.

The Secretary then reported the deaths of the following members: Edward Braman, Annual Member, on December 31st, 1907; William Rhinelander, Life Member, on January 3d, 1908.

The Secretary further reported that the following Annual Members have been elected by the Executive Committee, viz.: George Byron Louis Arner, Richard Everett Dwight, Dr. William Kirby Dwight.

The annual reports of the officers and committees were then presented, read and filed as follows:—

The Secretary, Mr. Henry Russell Drowne, reported a membership of 9 Honorary, 127 Life, and 301 Annual Members, making a total of 437, being a a gain of 29 members, while the Corresponding Members number 102.

The additions to the Roll during 1907 were 4 Life, 42 Annual, and 11 Corresponding Members; while 2 have retired, 7 resigned and 11 died. Seven Regular Meetings were held in 1907 at which interesting papers were read.

The Board of Trustees held it inexpedient at present to accept the generous offer of Mr. Archer M. Huntington, of a building site adjoining the Library of the Hispanic Society.

The following amendments to the By-Laws were made, viz.: The Executive Committee was increased to five members; a Reserve Fund, the income of which could be used for the support of THE RECORD and the increase of the Library, was constituted; and the Publication Committee was increased to seven members.

During the past fiscal year Mr. Clarence Winthrop Bowen was elected President of the Society, Mr. Archer M. Huntington, First Vice-President, and Messrs. Warner Van Norden, Howland Pell and Archer M. Huntington, Trustees; Messrs. William Isaac Walker and William B. O. Field, Members of the Executive Committee, and Mr. George Austin Morrison, Jr., a member of the Publication Committee. Committees on Building and on Resolutions regarding the services and death of the late President, Rev. Melatiah Everett Dwight also were appointed.

The Chairman of the Executive Committee, Mr. John Reynolds Totten, reported in detail the present condition of the Society, the changes in the membership-roll, the subscribers to THE RECORD and the revenue derived from the Membership, THE RECORD and the Publication accounts; the compilation of a complete Subject-Index of the first 38 volumes of THE RECORD, the cost of which was generously defrayed by the late President, the Rev. Dr. Dwight; that the receipts from room-rents were greater than ever before, and that the sales of back numbers of THE RECORD. Pedigree Charts and Library Duplicates all showed a substantial increase over former years; that the Society received a total of $3,006.00 from Room and Hall rents, exclusive of the value of its own occupancy, whereas the entire adjoining building was rented for $2,100.00; that the total receipts for the year 1907 were largely in excess of the year 1906, indicating the increasing prosperity and importance of the Society; that an appeal for a Building Fund had resulted in contributions to the amount of $1,875.00, which had been invested to produce a satisfactory income; that an offer of $65.000.00 for the present building had been received and declined, and that tentative plans had been prepared for a new building for the Society.

The Librarian, Mr. John Reynolds Totten, reported that during the past year 301 books were purchased, 172 exchanged, 1,052 donated, making the total accessions 1,525, and the total volumes in the Library 15,498; that the visitors to the Library during 1907 numbered 1,742; that the new book cases had been placed in the Library and the books systematically re-arranged to provide for the expansion of the coming year.

The Treasurer, Mr. Hopper Striker Mott, reported the detailed financial statement that the total receipts of the Society were $11,471.85, being $4,315.81 greater than last year; that there were no liabilities, and that the equity on all property owned by the Society was $93,991.34, being an increase of over $20,000.00 for the past year.

The Necrologist, Mr. Josiah Collins Pumpelly, reported memorial notices on the deaths of the following members, viz.: Van Campen Taylor, John Aspinwall Hadden, Frank Sherman Benson, James Henry Smith, General Frank Morgan Freeman, David Wilcox, Bowen Whiting Pierson, Francis Hartman Markoe, M.D., Rev. Melatiah Everett Dwight, D.D., M.D., Mrs. Willis LaVerne Chaffee, Colonel Henry Dudley Teetor, Edward Braman and William Rhinelander.

The Registrar of Pedigrees, Mr. Winchester Fitch, being abroad, no report was submitted.

The Chairman of the Publication Committee, Mr. George Austin Morrison, Jr., reported that there were at present 298 subscribers to THE RECORD, a gain of 13 for 1907, and that the cost of the publication was $1,604.35; that it has been determined to maintain a standard size of about 300 pages of printed matter and 50 pages of index each year, and that at least one portrait plate and biography would appear in each number; that the late Rev. Dr. Dwight had personally assumed the expense of many extra plates and illustrations as well as the full Subject-Index, and his generosity and interest should be gratefully acknowledged, and that the aim of the Committee was the publication of genealogies and articles dealing particularly with the early history of the City and State of New York.

The Historian, Dr. William Austin Macy reported the data collected during the past year, with the list of donors and material received.

The report of the Nominating Committee was then read setting forth the names of those nominated for Trustees for the term 1908–1911, which was duly received and the election being held the following were elected, viz.: Clarence Winthrop Bowen, Henry Pierson Gibson, James Junius Goodwin, Warner Van Norden and Howland Pell.

The President then spoke in regard to the future of the Society, and Mr. Totten addressed the meeting as to the advisability of anticipating the future requirements of the Society and securing a desirable and permanent location and building for the Society.

After remarks by Messrs. Gibson, Field, Morrison and others it was on motion duly seconded

RESOLVED, that a vote of encouragement, appreciation and confidence be given to the Executive Committee in regard to the steps taken to secure a suitable and permanent site and building for the growing needs of the Society.

The President then introduced General James Grant Wilson, an Ex-President of the Society, who delivered an interesting address entitled "The Queens of Song."

On motion, duly seconded, a vote of thanks was tendered to General Wilson for his courteous services, and there being no further business the meeting was on motion, duly seconded, adjourned.

JANUARY 14TH, 1908.

A Regular Meeting of the Board of Trustees of the New York Genealogical and Biographical Society was held on Friday, January 14th, 1908, at 4.15 P. M., the President, Mr. Clarence Winthrop Bowen, being in the Chair.

Present: Messrs. Elliott, Totten, Mott, Wright, Gibson, Pell, Walker, Morrison Drowne, Field and Bowen.

The minutes of the last regular meeting were read and on motion, duly seconded, approved.

The Secretary then read a letter from Mr. Archer M. Huntington, which was on motion duly seconded placed on file and his resignation as First Vice-President, accepted with expression of regret.

The Annual election of Officers and Committees for the year 1908 was then held and the following were duly nominated and elected.

President: Clarence Winthrop Bowen; First Vice-President: William B. O. Field; Second Vice-President: Tobias Alexander Wright; Secretary: Henry Russell Drowne; Treasurer: Hopper Striker Mott; Librarian: John Reynolds Totten; Historian: William Austin Macy, M.D.; Necrologist: Josiah Collins Pumpelly; Registrar of Pedigrees: Winchester Fitch.

Executive Committee: Messrs. John Reynolds Totten, Chairman, George Austin Morrison, Jr., Henry Pierson Gibson, William Isaac Walker, William B. O. Field, the President and Treasurer Ex-Officio.

Publication Committee: Messrs. George Austin Morrison, Jr., Chairman, Henry Reed Stiles, M.D., Hopper Striker Mott, Tobias Alexander Wright, Josiah Collins Pumpelly and Edward Doubleday Harris.

Committee on Heraldry: Gen. James Grant Wilson, Chairman, Messrs. Charles Landon Jones and Charles Pryer.

Committee on Research: Mr. William Austin Macy, M.D., Chairman, Rev. John Cornell, for Southern Rhode Island, Messrs. George W. Cocks, for Long Island, John E. Stillwell, M.D., for Monmouth County, New Jersey, Alphonso T. Clearwater, for Ulster County, New York, Mrs. G. W. Smith, for Suffolk County, New York, and Windham County, Conn., Miss Lucy D. Akerly, for Suffolk County, New York, Messrs. Tobias A. Wright, for Washington County, N. Y., Edward Myers, for Westchester County, N. Y., William M. DuBois, for White Plains, N. Y., Mrs. Charles Dod Ward, for Oswego, N. Y., Mr. Rufus King, for Suffolk County, N. Y., William A. Macy, M.D., for Seneca County, N. Y., Evelyn Briggs Baldwin and Charles Landon Jones, for Litchfield County, Conn. The Corresponding Members for 1907 were re-appointed for 1908.

Mr. Totten then stated the urgent need for larger quarters and suggested the securing of a lot adjoining the present building for the erection of a new Society Building.

After a general discussion it was, on motion, duly seconded, Resolved that a Committee be appointed to examine, inquire and take into consideration the advisability of a new building and to report to the next meeting of the Board of Trustees.

The Chair thereupon appointed Messrs. Mott, Walker, Field, Morrison, Totten and Pell as such a Committee.

On motion, duly seconded, the Executive Committee were authorized to publish a list of Officers and Members, with a statement of the substance of the Reports of the Executive Committee, Treasurer, etc., for the year 1907.

The Treasurer then reported the financial condition of the Society to date.

On motion duly seconded the Publication Committee was directed to report at the next meeting the progress of the publications in THE RECORD of the Staten Island Church Records and the estimated cost of printing, indexing and binding a complete volume, to be known as Volume IV of the Society Collections.

On separate motions, duly seconded, the matter of Refreshments at the Regular Meetings of the Society was referred to the Executive Committee, with power, and the salaries for the year 1908 were adjusted and fixed.

The Chairman of Committee on Resolutions on the late Rev. Dr. Dwight then reported action had been taken, and presented the bound pamphlet of the engrossed resolutions and on motion duly seconded, the President and Secretary were directed to sign same and attach the seal of the Society and to forward the pamphlet to Mrs. Dwight.

There being no further business, the meeting was on motion duly seconded adjourned.

QUERIES.

DYCKMAN. — NAGEL. — POST. — BROWN. — Johannes[2] Dyckman (Jan[1]) of Kingsbridge, N. Y., whose dates according to a descendant were: b. 6 May, 1682; m. 2 March, 1701; d. 10 Dec., 1730; m. Deborah Nagel, b. 23 Feb., 1684; d. 1734. Who was the said Deborah Nagel? Was she not step-sister of Johannes Dyckman above, and dau. of Jan and Rebecca (Waldron) Nagel? Riker, however, said Jan and Rebecca's dau. Deborah Nagel m. Robt. Westgate. (See *Dutch Ch. Rec.*) Could not the said Deborah have m. Westgate in 1720, after the death of Johannes Dyckman, whose death above might have been 1703, instead of 1730.

Jan[1] Dyckman had a grand-daughter Ann Hedley, who m. Jacob Post, what relation was the said Jacob to Mary, dau. of Martin Post, who m. William Dyckman, and had sons William and Evert Dyckman, who went West many years ago.

The undersigned would like to communicate with any descendants of the said western William and Evert Dyckman, in the interest of a short account of the Dyckmans of Kingsbridge, which she is compiling.

Magdalena Dyckman m. before 1742 Evert Bruyn or Brown; Jemima Dyckman, her niece, m. another Evert Brown. What relation were these Evert Browns to each other? Wanted their ancestry and descendants.

L. D. AKERLY, 550 Park Ave., New York City.

KING.—John King of Mansfield, Conn., purchased land at Norwich, Conn., on 3 June, 1747, and later, as of Amenia Precinct, Dutchess County, N. Y., purchased other land at Norwich, Conn., on 1 Dec., 1767. He had known issue, a son William of Norwich, Conn., 1763, and a son John of Mansfield, Conn., 1760. John King (John) of Mansfield, Conn., m. 6 July, 1760, at Norwich, Conn., Elizabeth Birchard, dau. of Mr. Daniel Birchard, late of Mansfield, deceased, and had issue, b. at Mansfield, John, Elizabeth, Anne, Asa. Any information in regard to the ancestry of the first John King of Mansfield would be highly appreciated. There are indications that he may have been of kin to Hezekiah King of Mansfield, prior to 1725 (The Weymouth King Family), or perhaps of kin to The Northampton King Family.

GEORGE AUSTIN MORRISON, JR., 43 Cedar St., New York City.

KIP.—Catharine Kip, b. 8 Oct., 1790, in Ulster County, N. Y., was a dau. of John Kip. The date of his birth and the names of his father and mother is desired. He m. Christina Snook. What were the names of her parents and were they from Rhinebeck?

LOW.—WESTVAAL.—Jannetje Low m. Anthony Freer on 30 Oct., 1761. Who were her parents? Claartjen Westvaal of Minnisink m. Solomon Freer, 22 Sept., 1721. When was she b. and who were her father and mother? Was she a dau. of Johannes Westvaal who m. Maritie Jacobse Cool?

H. C. MC COLLUM, 1320 Williamette Boulevard, Portland, Ore.

MARCY.—Information is wanted concerning the ancestry of Dorothy Newell, wife of Hon. William Learned Marcy, Governor of New York, and Secretary of War under President Polk. Dates and places of her birth, marriage and death; her father's name, dates and places of his birth, marriage and death; her mother's name, and whatever is known of the Newell family of Southbridge, Mass., is earnestly desired.

EDSON.—I am compiling a genealogical account of the ancestors and descendants of Nathan Edson and his wife Mary Hall. Nathan was the son of Nathan, son of Samuel, son of Samuel, son of Samuel who came to Salem about 1639 from England; he was a soldier of the Revolution, and first settler of Stockbridge, New York. Any one having any information about any of the ancestors or descendants of . Nathan Edson are requested to communicate with me.   GEORGE THOMAS EDSON, Rumley, Van Buren Co., Ark.

MAYO.—I am compiling a brief history of the descendants of John Mayo of Roxbury, Mass., and of the Rev. John Mayo of Barnstable, Mass., and any facts and material of an historical or biographical nature, bearing on the use of this name will be highly appreciated, and all information gladly received in order to compile a full genealogical record.   CHESTER G. MAYO, U. S. N.,
Navy Yard, Brooklyn, N. Y.

MONNETT.—In *New York in the Revolution* appears the record of Anges Monett, as an enlisted man in the Orange County Militia (p. 255). Who can give any further information concerning him, his ancestors or descendants?

In " Report, State Historian, Col. Ser., Vol. II, p. 499, appears the record of Abraham Munnett (phonetic spelling was Monnett), as ensign 1738 in Capt. Thos. Van Pelt's Co. of Richmond Co. Militia, Richard Stillwell, Col. I am inclined to think he was a son of Isaac Monnett of Calvert Co., Maryland. Who can give any further information concerning him, his ancestry or descendants?

I am interested in any one of the name, as variously spelled: Monet, Monete, Monette, Monnet, Monnete, Monett, Monnett, Monnette, Munnett, Munnitt, Money, Maunay, etc.   ·   ORRA E. MONNETTE,
406 Merchant Trust B'ld'g, Los Angeles, Cal.

·   BOOK NOTICES.

THE BIBLIOGRAPHER'S MANUAL OF AMERICAN HISTORY, by Thomas Lindsley Bradford, M.D. Edited and revised by Stan. V. Henkels. Vol. I, A to E, Nos. 1–1,600, pp. 340; Vol. II, F to L, Nos. 1,601–3,103, pp. 349. Cloth, Royal 8vo. Press of Maurice H. Power, Philadelphia, Pa. 1907.

This work, which will ultimately reach five volumes, contains an account of all State, Territory, Town and County histories relating to the United States with verbatim copies of their titles and useful bibliographical notes, together with the prices at which they have been sold for the last forty years. The final volume will consist of two indices arranged alphabetically, one of short titles of authors, under the names of the States; the other of titles of subjects, localities, names of towns; the references in both these indices being to the number of the book in the author-title. This comprehensive list fills a long felt want among historians, librarians and collectors, and it is reasonable to predict will be the standard reference book on Americana for years to come. The subject matter evinces the greatest care and research and a through digest of all catalogues, lists and copyrighted publications, while the plan and scope of the work reflects the highest credit on the compiler and editor. No library of any pretension should be without this Manual and it should prove invaluable to those interested in historical subjects. The type, paper, composition and binding leave nothing to be desired and form practical working volumes, which deserve extensive patronage and success.

THE CHEROKEE INDIANS, with special reference to their relations with the United States Government, by Thomas Valentine Parker, Ph.D. Cloth, 12mo, pp. 116. The Grafton Press. 1907.

This small volume is a valuable addition to the Grafton Historical Series and in style, typography and binding fully up to the high standard set by these publishers. The treatment of the American Indian by the Federal Government has been the subject of so much ignorant and prejudiced criticism that any authoritative study of the problem will be more than welcome. The Cherokees being one of the "five civilized tribes," of a high order of intelligence and civilization, and largely Christians, are admirable examples of the application of Federal principals and policies to the Indian question. The work is well arranged, clearly and forcibly written, and evidences much research on the part of its author to establish his facts. It will be a valuable addition to literature already printed on this subject.

DUNHAM GENEALOGY. ENGLISH AND AMERICAN BRANCHES, by Isaac Watson Dunham, A.M. Cloth, 8vo, pp. 363. Press of Bulletin Print, Norwich, Conn. 1907. Full Index.

This work sets forth the general records of families named Dunham in England and the claim of specific descent of Deacon John Dunham from Sir John Dunham of Schrooby. The compiler asserts that "John Dunham, the emigrant," was identical with that "John Goodman," whose name appears as one of the signers of the Mayflower pact of 11 November, 1620, and that he adopted the Goodman name to escape religious persecution. This assumption appears to be unsupported by any substantial proof and is the more improbable in that no other signer of the pact used an "alias" or substituted a false name. Much time, labor and ingenuity has been expended upon tracing the Dunham descendants in America and the record appears to be complete and accurate. It is to be regretted that the system of indicating genealogical descent and indexing is one peculiar to Mr. Dunham and not the standard and accredited system. The book is illustrated with a cut of the Dunham Arms in colors and portraits of ancestors.

RECORD OF THE FARGO FAMILY, by John J. Giblin. Morocco, 12mo, pp. 32. Privately printed. Press of The American Bank Note Co. 1907.

A brief and well arranged genealogy of the descendants of Moses Fargo, and his wife, Sarah, who emigrated from Wales about 1680 and settled at New London, Conn. The spirit which prompted a descendant to collect and place in permanent printed form the genealogy of this early New England family should be highly commended as it preserves for all time a record of a family of commercial importance. The press work is excellent and the pamphlet is well bound and contains a full index of names.

SOME SPECIAL STUDIES IN GENEALOGY. I. AMERICAN EMIGRANTS— HOW TO TRACE THEIR ENGLISH ANCESTRY, by Gerald Fothergill. II. THE QUAKER RECORDS, by Josiah Newman, F. R. Hist. Soc. III. THE GENEALOGY OF THE SUBMERGED, by Charles A. Bernau. Cloth, 12mo, pp. 96. Press of Dunn Collin & Co., London. 1908.

For those unskilled in the intricacies of the English Record Offices this little work will prove invaluable, setting forth, as it does clearly and tersely, the successive steps to be followed in tracing our English forbears. It is astonishing to learn that a complete alphabetical list of all Quaker births, marriages and deaths from about 1650 down to the present time can be found at Devonshire House, whereby any Quaker descendant can in a few moments find his ancestry, if recorded. The chapter on the Genealogy of the Submerged, viz.: paupers, vagrants, tramps, bastards and removed families, is a revelation of a hitherto unexplored source of family history and in defence of such searching it may be quoted that one of the great-grandmothers of Queen Anne was only a poor bar-maid of a public house. This complete small book should be consulted by any one contemplating searching among the English records.

HERALDRY AS ART, by G. W. Eve. Cloth, 8vo, pp. 308. Full index. Published by B. T. Batsford, 94 High Holborn. Imported by Charles Scribner's Sons. Press of The Selwood Printing Works, Frame and London. 1907.

This work fills a long desired want and the author is to be highly complimented upon his simple, direct and scholarly treatment of an intricate science. Perhaps no art has suffered more at the hands of ignorant and unskillful craftsmen than the gentle art of tracing coat-armor. In spite of numerous treatises on the subject, the modern use of heraldry in architecture, painting, cermanics, decorations and sculpture has been lamentably bad, in part owing to the difficulty in acquiring a sound knowledge of the subject, and in part due to the inherent desire of modern workmen to improve or create new forms for what the ancient designers had developed into an exact science. Mr. Eve has not only recognized the inartistic results of modern heraldic decoration, but has set about pointing out the plain path to a revival of correct chivalric picture-painting and has compiled an admirable guide for future illustrators. His work is a "book beautiful" in selection and finish of type and in clearness of illustration—some of the cuts being almost as fine as engravings, and those illustrations made from his own design indicate artistic conception and feeling of a high order. The author's style is clear and terse, the lesson taught in the text being the more easily learned because the opinions are modestly advanced and courteously expressed. The book deserves liberal patronage and will be a most desirable addition to the collections of those bibliophiles interested in artistic subjects. •

GENEALOGY OF THE HILL, DEAN, PINCKNEY, AUSTIN, BARKER, ANDERSON, RHOADES AND FINCH FAMILIES, by Franklin Couch, LL.B. Cloth, small Quarto, pp. 129. Full index. Printed for private circulation by Newburgh Journal Co. 1907.

This comprehensive genealogy of seven prominent families, related to the Hill Family, was completed from data furnished by Mr. Uriah Hill, Jr., of Peekskill, N. Y., who was greatly interested in perpetuating a record of his forefathers for all time. It is an encouraging sign for future genealogical research in this State when one of such practical business life as Mr. Hill devotes his leisure hours to sustaining and advancing Mr. Couch in collecting such records as these. The line is traced in detail from Anthony Hill, an Englishman, born in Holland, who came to America in 1720, settled in New York City and eventually removed to Fox Meadows, now part of Scarsdale, Westchester Co., N. Y. The book is well printed, in legible type with good margins, and while the arrangement of heads of families does not show the full line of descent at a glance, yet the numerical system employed enables one to turn back to the preceeding ancestor with ease and despatch. The work should receive a welcomed place among the standard genealogies of New York State families.

HISTORY AND GENEALOGY OF THE HERNE FAMILY, from A.D. 1066 to A.D. 1907, by William T. Herne. Cloth, 8vo, pp. 753. Press of Examiner Printing Co., Independence, Mo. 1907.

Although the author of this work heads its title with the words "Brief History," the size of the volume and the voluminous data dealt with all bear witness to a marvelous amount of patience, industry and perseverance. As a record of William Herne, the London merchant, who came to America in 1680, and of others bearing the Herne name, whenever and wherever mentioned in Mss., State, County, Town and Family records, and newspaper of the day, this book will be found most complete and Mr. Herne is to be congratulated upon the successful result of years of study and research. It is profusely illustrated with wood cut portraits of the Hernes and their numerous descendants, and while the fact that it has no full name index and is not arranged according to genealogical methods will militate against its utility as a work of general reference, nevertheless it will be treasured by those whose families appear in its pages.

GENEALOGY OF THE JAQUETT FAMILY, by Edwin Jaquett Sellers. Revised Edition—Limited to 100 copies. Cloth, 8vo, pp. 226, Press of Allen, Lane & Scott, Philadelphia. 1907.

This record of an ancient Delaware Family, in type, press work, quality of paper and illustrations, attains a standard seldom reached in genealogical publications. The author traces his descent in unbroken lineage from Pierre Jaquet, citizen of Geneva, Switzerland, about 1500, who was the ancestor of Jean Paul Jaquet, the first of his name in this country, in the year 1654. The early records of this family when in Geneva and Nuremberg are given with extraordinary completeness and the expense, time and care which must have been devoted to searching for, examining and transcribing these Swiss and German records would seem enormous. The author has arranged the names upon a numerical plan, which is somewhat confusing to the average student of genealogy, and while this system lends itself to ready reference, when studied and thoroughly comprehended, yet its general utility is not to be compared with the standard plan, followed by the chief magazines and publications. An individual and thus necessarily limited system of indicating descent can never be consulted with ease and expedition by the general reading public, no matter how clear and perfect it may seem to its deviser. The book is fully indexed and well worth acquisition by those who desire a select library of genealogical publications.

LANE GENEALOGIES, Volume III, compiled by James Hill Fitts. Cloth, 8vo, pp. 439. The Nair-Letter Press, Exeter, N. Y. 1906. Full Index.

This is the concluding volume of the series and deals with the English Family of Lane settled at Rickmansworth, Hertfordshire, England, 1542-1758; Job Lane of Malden, Mass., 1649; James Lane of Casco Bay, Maine, 1650, and Edward Lane of Boston, Mass., 1657. The compiler, now deceased, has collected a valuable number of records, and after arranging the varied families—not necessarily related—has placed them in such genealogical form as to render the task of the future family historian in continuing the lines comparatively easy. The extracts from English wills of Lane are particularly interesting and the fact that from 1662-1816, or about one hundred and fifty years, the Job Lane family received an annual rental from the English estates, is an unparalleled instance in New England history. So few of the early Colonial families can make the connecting link with English ancestry of good yeoman stock that every additional work tracing origin in the Old Country is more than welcome. The book is the production of a scholar and merits the highest praise, not only for its accuracy and research, but for the admirable style of arrangement and letter press. It is well illustrated with portraits and pictures of the Lane kith and kin.

GENEALOGIES OF THE LEWIS AND KINDRED FAMILIES, edited by John Meriwether McAllister and Lura Boulton Tandy. Cloth, 8vo, pp. 416. Press of E. W. Stephens Publishing Co., Columbia, Mo. 1906. Full Index.

The authors of this interesting record frankly avow their desire to compile a genealogy of the Lewis Family of Virginia rather than a biographical record of their ancestry and have completed a work of value and utility. Every item of importance in public or private records has been secured and given its place in the pages of the book. The press work, paper and binding are excellent, without being extravagant, and the reading matter is tersely set forth. The arrangement of the lines of descent and the index are unusual, an individual system being used rather than a standard one. No matter how clear and simple such may be to the authors, it is difficult for the general student of genealogy and to this extent the usefulness of the book will be crippled.

MACOMBER GENEALOGY, by Rev. Everett S. Stackpole. Paper, 8vo, pp. 88. Press of The Journal Company, Lewiston, Me. 1907.

A well arranged genealogical record of John Macomber of Taunton, Mass., 1643, and his descendants, brother of William Macomber of Duxbury, 1638. The compiler has taken particular pains to trace the Revolutionary and Mayflower ancestry and his search among public and private records appears to be exhaustive. He further gives full notes upon those in England and Scotland bearing the Macomber name and a frank criticism and description of the several alleged Macomber coats-of-arms, which in most cases appear to have been made to order. His disavowal of all pretensions in regard to the right to coat-armor without ample proof of authority to bear same is encouraging in this age of sham pedigrees and impossible royal descents. Mr. Stackpole has gone to some expense in collecting and publishing this record, and his appeal for subscribers to the book deserves generous response, particularly as the contemplated genealogy of William Macomber of Marshfield, 1638, cannot be issued unless the sales of the present genealogy warrant the future volume. It is to be regretted that no present index has been printed, although the intention is to index both volumes, when the second volume is issued.

AN ABSTRACT OF A GENEALOGICAL COLLECTION, by Malcolm Macbeth. Volume I. Paper, Small Quarto, pp. 50. Press of Nixon-Jones Printing Co., St. Louis, Mo.

The idea of this preliminary publication is to place data so far collected before the public in such shape that members and kinsman of the Macbeth Family will be interested in correcting all errors and forwarding such additional information as they may possess. The names of a number of Huguenot families will be found on these pages, with facsimiles of original signatures, etc., and it is earnestly hoped that those related will make many additions to the compiler's store of genealogical history. The completed genealogy will contain over 55 portraits of ancestors, and about 75 pictures of houses occupied, monuments, tombstones, etc., and be issued in three volumes.

MEN OF AMERICA. A Biographical Dictionary of Contemporaries. Edited by John W. Leonard. Cloth, 8vo, pp. 2,188. Press of L. R. Hamersly & Co., New York. 1908.

The utility of this work cannot be questioned and the list of names appears to be a fairly representative one in view of the difficulty of choice involved. A number of like publications have been issued during the past few years and contain many prominent names omitted from the present work, so that the editor seems to have produced a selective rather than comprehensive book. The magnitude of his task, however, precludes perfection and the list of biographies will be welcome as a ready book of reference.

NEW ENGLAND FAMILY HISTORY, Vol. I, April 1, 1908, No. 4. Edited and published by Henry Cole Quinby, A.B., LL.B. Paper, Royal 8vo, pp. 42. New York. 1908.

This quarterly has undertaken to place in print the genealogical records of families of Maine and Massachusetts. Its pages will doubtless be devoted to printing the history of those early settlers, whose families have been less prominent and hence more neglected than the original Colonial leaders and their descendants. This purpose at once entitles it to a safe place upon the shelves of all historical-genealogical libraries and will result in the preservation of data rapidly becoming most difficult to secure. The magazine is well illustrated and printed and should do considerable work in the line selected.

NEW JERSEY ARCHIVES, First Series, Volume XXVI, Newspaper Extracts, Volume VII, 1768–1769, Edited by William Neilson. Cloth, 8vo, pp. 649. Full index. The Call Printing and Publishing Co. 1904.

A continuation of the publication of Documents relating to the Colonial History of the State, the present volume consisting of extracts from American Newspapers relating to New Jersey. No more instructive and valuable work could have been undertaken by the New Jersey Historical Society than this admirable digest of the Colonial press and its utility to future historians of New Jersey renders this series invaluable. The time and labor expended in searching and transcribing items from the contemporary journals, both local and foreign, must have been great and the decision as to the importance of the items must have required nicety of judgment and sound historical ability. The example set by the New Jersey Society should be followed by other State Historical Societies in regard to their own commonwealths, and funds expended in such research and publication cannot fail to yield a large return in membership and donations. These books are printed in clear, legible type and the pages bound for service, rather than ornament. The entire series, to which

Volume XXVI is a worthy addition, should be a delight to scholars and should be found upon the shelves of every library of any pretention throughout the United States.

COLLECTIONS OF THE NEW YORK HISTORICAL SOCIETY for the year 1900. Abstract of Wills. Volume IX. Cloth, 8vo, pp. 373. Printed by the Society, New York. 1901.

This fine publication is a continuation of the Series of Abstracts of Wills on file in the Surrogate's Office of the City of New York, and contains the Wills filed and proved from 7 January, 1777 to 7 February, 1783, with Letters of Administration from 17 January, 1779, to 18 February, 1783. The period covered by this volume is peculiarly interesting, embracing as it does the most important years of the Revolutionary War, and its subject matter proves beyond dispute that any impression that wills were not recorded during the struggle for liberty is erroneous. Both the British and the State Governments exercised probate jurisdiction during the war, the former covering New York City, Long Island, Staten Island and the lower part of Westchester County, while the latter covered the remaining part of the Province of New York. At the end of the War, Samuel Bayard, the last Royal Secretary delivered over to Lewis Allaire Scott, Deputy State Secretary, some 709 original wills, probate and administration papers, etc., and also the volumes of recorded wills. The record from Colonial to State Government is thus continuous and full, and this volume of the Historical Society should be a mine of information to those interested in the history and genealogy of the patriots and tories. The book is clearly printed, has an exhaustive index of names and is fully up to the high standard set by the Society in all its publications. Great praise should be accorded to Mr. William S. Pelletreau, the compiler, for his invaluable labors in this field.

GENEALOGICAL COLLECTIONS RELATING TO THE FAMILIES OF NOBLET, with some particular account of William Noblit of Middletown Township, Chester County (now Delaware County), Pennsylvania, U. S. A. Compiled by John Hyndman Noblit. Cloth, 8vo, pp. 400. Printed for private circulation by Ferris & Leach. 1906.

This is a most complete collection of data concerning the family records of those named Noblat, Noblot and Noblets of France; Noblet and Noblett of Great Britain; Noblet, Noblett, Noblit and Noblitt of America, illustrated by facsimiles of the several coat-armors used by the various families in France. 'Tho the name is an unusual one, Mr. Noblit has gathered together a mass of important material, and while he has made no attempt at genealogical arrangement, the gleanings are now preserved for all time and will prove a mine of information for future searchers in this field. Each French record is followed by its careful translation, and the style of arranging and printing this work is heartily to be commended, while a full index renders all references ready and time saving. The task of putting the different records into type was no light one and the entire appearance of the book reflects high credit upon the intelligence and artistic facilities of its compiler.

THE OGDEN FAMILY IN AMERICA, ELIZABETHTOWN BRANCH AND THEIR ENGLISH ANCESTRY, compiled by William Ogden Wheeler. Edited by Laurence VanAlstyne and Rev. Charles Burr Ogden, Ph.D. Cloth, Quarto, pp. 532. Full Index. Printed for Private Circulation by J. B. Lippincott Company, Philadelphia. 1907. With a Second Volume of 37 Charts showing Descent of Female Lines.

The lives of John Ogden, the Pilgrim, and his descendants, 1640–1906, inspired this magnificent work, one of the finest ever published in this country, and in searching out and arranging the historical and genealogical matter incorporated in the book the compiler, who unfortunately died before the completion of his task, erected an everlasting monument to his industry, ability and family pride. It is difficult to review the characteristics of this volume, when all it contains is admirable and beyond criticism. No less than 30 general illustrations and 54 portraits are incorporated in the family history and the diversity of type, intricate press-work, beautiful paper and margins all make it a masterpiece of composition. The genealogical system of arranging the names not only follows the most approved custom but in some regards is an actual improvement upon the standard arrangement—the ancestral chain, given after the name of each descendant having issue, showing the full line of descent at a glance and each descendant having his or her own number. Ancestors of any line can be turned to instantly. The index of names might have referred to the name number instead of the page number, and thus obviated some delay in looking down the page for the name, but this is a debatable improvement. The history of this family discloses a long line of patriots—many of whom held positions of the highest responsibility and trust in the community and none of whom were unworthy of perpetual record. This work is a model for all would-be family historians to follow and neither years nor progress in the art of book-making will make obsolete this volume or take from it the unique quality of being as perfect as human skill can make it.

ONTARIO HISTORICAL SOCIETY. PAPERS AND RECORDS. Volume VIII. Paper, 8vo, pp. 228. Published by the Society, Toronto. 1907.

This is a continuation of the admirable series of publications of this Society and the present volume is fully as interesting as the seven preceeding books. It contains well written articles on The Insurrection in the Short Hills in 1838; The Hamiltons of Queenstown, Kingston and Hamilton, and three papers on Kingston History, together with the Church Records of the Niagara Peninsular, Stamford and Chippewa, and Extracts from the Cummings Papers. The annals of early Canadian settlers are being rapidly gathered together and put into reference shape by this excellent Society.

PORTSMOUTH AND NEWCASTLE, NEW HAMPSHIRE, CEMETERY INSCRIPTIONS, by Arthur H. Locke. Paper, 8vo, pp. 44. Portsmouth, Privately Printed. 1907.

This interesting record consists of abstracts from some two thousand of the oldest tombstones in the cities of Portsmouth and Newcastle, N. H., and is supplementary to material already published in the *New England Register*. It completes the vital statistics of the early settlers of Portsmouth and its alphabetical arrangement of names, abbreviation marks of locality and form of printing attest to the time, labor and care of the compiler. It is due to the generosity and genealogical sense of such men as Mr. Locke that this country will in time have secured as complete a record of its early colonists as can be obtained at this late day.

SHAKERS OF OHIO. Papers concerning the Shakers of Ohio, with Unpublished Manuscripts, by J. P. McLean, Ph.D. Cloth, 8vo, pp. 415. Press of L. J. Heer Printing Co., Columbus, O. 1907.

It is somewhat paradoxical that any historical-genealogical record should be kept of a sect whose foundation principle was opposed to the perpetuation of the race. Nevertheless the story of the rise of the Shaker Communities in Ohio and their present decline and disintergration is interesting reading and the author has accomplished a fine task in collecting and printing these records, fast going to decay and destruction. Shakerism was promoted in this country by Ann Lee in 1779 at New Lebanon, Columbia Co., N. Y., where the parent community established itself and under the leadership and revelations of this extraordinary woman, claiming to be a manifestation of the second coming of Christ, the sect flourished and spread throughout the United States. The book is well illustrated with portraits, pictures of Shaker communities and homes, and will prove a mine of information to those interested in the growth and fall of a peculiar people.

HISTORICAL MANUAL OF THE CONGREGATIONAL CHURCH OF TOPSFIELD, MASS., 1663-1907. Cloth, 8vo, pp. 60. Published by the Church Press of A. T. Merrill, Topsfield, Mass.

This early Colonial church was organized in 1663 with the Rev. Thomas Gilbert as minister. The early town records, which also contained the church records prior to 25 March, 1659, were lost by fire, and the first volume of church registers commences in 1684, when the membership was 49, viz.: 22

males and 27 families. This little book, setting forth, as it does, the simple annals of a quiet parish, should be interesting reading to the descendants of the early founders and parishioners. The biographical sketches of the Ministry of the Church evince careful research and preparation and the book is a fit memorial of a religious establishment which did much to sustain and advance the early colonists of Massachusetts.

ENGLISH ANCESTRY OF GOVERNOR WILLIAM TRACY OF VIRGINIA, 1620, AND OF HIS ONLY SON, LIEUTENANT THOMAS TRACY OF SALEM, MASS., AND NORWICH, CONN., by Dwight Tracy, M.D., D.D.S. Paper, Quarto, pp. 31. Press of The Journal of American History, New Haven, Conn. 1908.

This pamphlet is of unusual interest in that it proves beyond peradventure that the English Pedigree of Tracy, printed in J. Britton's "Toddington" in 1840, is erroneous and incomplete, in setting forth that William Tracy, who married Mary, daughter of Sir John Conway of Arrow, Co. Warwick, died without issue. Britton was a leading English authority and without doubt compiled his genealogical chart of the Family of Tracy from ancient deeds, records and Heraldic visitations. His error is shown clearly by the early letters of William Tracy and records of the Virginia Co., wherein is mentioned his wife Mary, son Thomas and daughter Joyce, who married Captain Nathaniel Powell. This son Thomas is later identified with Lt. Thomas Tracy of Watertown and Salem, Mass., in 1636, and thus a long line of descendants can be linked up to an ancient and noble family in England, descended from Egbert, first Saxon King of England, 800–838 Anno Dominie. The evidence is indisputable and sets forth not only in reprints but in facsimile reproduction of the ancient documents the proof positive of the continuation of the line of William Tracy in Virginia and New England. Relation to English nobility and the right to bear coat-armor is so frequently assumed without the slightest proof save the statement of furnishers of ready-made pedigrees that Dr. Tracy's scholarly and exhaustive research should be a matter of pride to all his kin. The pamphlet is illustrated with a full page plate of the Tracy Arms, blazoned in proper colors, and a portrait of Dr. Tracy, together with excellent facsimile reproductions of ancient documents and pictures of the several manors and county seats of the family in England.

ANCESTORS OF REV. WILLIAM HOWE WHITTEMORE, Bolton, Ct., 1800, Rye, N. Y., 1885, and of his wife, Maria Clark, New York, 1803, Brooklyn, 1886, by William Plumb Bacon. Cloth, Quarto, pp. 124. Limited Edition. Press of Adkins Printing Co., New Britain, Ct. 1907.

The compiler has charted and traced back as far as possible the several ancestors of the Rev. Mr. Whittemore and his wife and set forth no less than 55 lines of descent converging in the two subjects of this work. Such method of genealogical record is of value and interest to the immediate family of the Rev. Mr. Whittemore, and from the publication of this interesting record it is hoped the compiler will be encouraged to devote a full genealogical volume to the Whittemore family only. The book is well printed but is not arranged according to the now well established and standard form insisted upon by the leading genealogical societies and the lack of an index of names must be deplored. The compiler frankly states that the arrangement of the work in his opinion renders an index superfluous but the utility of his work is thereby minim:zed and localized to individual members of the Whittemore family.

MR. THOMAS FLOYD-JONES has issued an 8vo, cloth, index to his "*Floyd-Jones Family*," reviewed in the April, 1907, RECORD.

MR. FREDERIC G. MATHER, compiler and editor of *New York in the Revolutio*: and the supplement to the same, is now engaged upon the story of the Refugees who crossed from Long Island to Connecticut in 1776. The story will include copies of all the original documents which Mr. Mather already has. He would, however, appreciate any information (more especially as to the return of the Refugees to Long Island, and the whereabouts of their descendants to-day) that descendants of the Refugees may have and are inclined to give. His address is, Stamford, Conn.

ACCESSIONS TO THE LIBRARY.
December 5, 1907, to March 13, 1908.
DONATIONS.
Bound.

Bacon, William Plumb.—Whittemore-Clark Genealogy.
Bowen, Clarence Winthrop.—Reminiscences of New Hampton, N. H.
Charles Scribner's Sons.—Heraldry As An Art.
Commissioner of Education.—Report.
Couch, Franklin, and Hill, Uriah, Jr.—The Hill Family.
Davis, Walter.—Old Records of the Town of Fitchburg, Vol. VII.
Dunham, Isaac W.—Dunham Genealogy.
Fargo, James Francis.—Fargo Family.
Fitts, Mrs. Mary C.—Lane Family, Vol. III.
Floyd-Jones, Thomas.—Index to Floyd-Jones Genealogy.
Gould, J. Porter.—Manual of the Topsfield Congregational Church.
Hamersly, L. R.—Men of America.
Hearne, William T.—Hearne History.
Heer, Fred. J.—Shakers of Ohio.
Henkels, Stan. V.—Bradford's Bibliographer's Manual of American History,
     2 vols.
Keep, Austin Baxter.—Holcombe Family Bible.
New York Mayflower Society.—Year Book.
Noblit, John Hyndman.—Noblet Genealogy.
Randall, F. E.—Randall Genealogy.
Sellers, Edwin Jaquett.—Jaquett Family.
Suydam, Walter Lispenard.—St. Nicholas Society's Year Book.
Tandy, Mrs. L. B.—Lewis and Allied Families.
Thacher, Mrs. George Winslow.—American Presbyterianism.
Wheeler, Miss Laura.—Ogden Family, Elizabethtown Branch, 2 vols.
Wright, Tobias A.—Mail and Express, with Index, 6 vols.

Pamphlets, Etc.

Arner, G. Louis.—History of the First Congregational Church, Jefferson, Ohio.
Ashton, N. H. E.—John Fraser, Botanist, manuscript.
Bacon, Horace S.—Lowell Historical Society's Contributions.
Bowen, Clarence Winthrop.—Magazine of American History.
Brink, Benjamin M.—Olde Ulster.
Burr, Hon. Tunis B.—Crab Meadow, Northport, L. I., Inscriptions, manuscript.
Cambridge Historical Society.—Publications.
Chamberlain, H.—Seneca Falls Historical Society's Report.
Chief of Bureau.—U. S. Navy and Marine Corps Register.
Corbett, John.—Schuyler County Chronicle.
Cornell, Rev. John.—Newspaper Clippings.
Dorrance, Miss Anne.—Wyoming Commemorative Association Proceedings.
Dwight, Rev. M. E.—Genealogical Exchange.
Dwight, Mrs. M. E.—Framed Etching of Rev. M. E. Dwight, D.D., M.D.
Edson, George Thomas.—Pedigree of G. T. Edson, manuscript.
First Reformed Church.—Church Tablet.
Green, B. Frank.—Clan Gordon of Scotland, manuscript.
Greve, Charles T.—Quarterly Publication, Historical and Philosophical Society
     of Ohio.
Haughwout, Rev. Lefferd, M.A.—Lefferts-Haughwout Letters, manuscript.
Holbrook, Levi.—N. E. Historical and Genealogical Register, January.
Holcombe, the late W. F., M.D., and Keep, Austin Baxter.—Souvenir of the
     Westchester Library and Reading Room.
Lefferts, Marshall Clifford.—Bijdragen tot de Geschiedenis van Overyssel.
Leonard, I. B.—Gowanda News, newspaper.
Macy, W. A., M.D.—Jacobus Nostrand's Syphering Book, manuscript. Benja-
     min Ferris' Note Book, manuscript.
Mercantile Library.—Report.

Missouri Historical Society.—Abstract of Malcolm Macbeth's Genealogical Collection, Vol. I.
Myers, Edward.—Historical Sketch of the Third Reformed Church, Albany.
New England Society.—Anniversary.
New York Public Library.—Bulletin.
Ontario Historical Society.—Report. Records, Vol. VIII.
Quinby, Henry Cole.—New England Family History.
Roe, Mrs. Charles.—Sohier Coat of Arms, framed.
Rowlee, W. W.—Ulster County Tombstone Inscriptions, manuscript. Rev. Orlo Bartholomew's Address, manuscript.
Salem Press Company.—Massachusetts Magazine, I, 1.
St. Mark's Church.—Year Book.
See, Mrs. Horace.—Coal Medal. Wilkesbarre Record. Jamestown Magazine. N. Y. Branch of the American Red Cross. World's Work.
Stackpole, Rev. Everett A.—Macomber Genealogy.
Steelman, Emma J.—Baptist Burying Ground, Cape May, N. J., manuscript.
Superintendent of Documents.—Check List, 3rd edition.
Suydam, Walter Lispenard.—Pedigree of Mrs. W. L. Suydam, Jr., manuscript. Report of the Daughters of the Cincinnati. Ceremonies at Fraunces' Tavern. Colonial Wars Banquet.
Terry, Miss.—Old Commercial Receipts, manuscript.
Thacher, Mrs. George Winslow.—N. E. Historical and Genealogical Register, 5 numbers. N. Y. Genealogical and Biographical Record, 14 numbers. Newburgh Historical Society's Papers, XII, XIII.
Totten, John Reynolds.—St. Thomas' Church Year Book. Our Race News Leaflet.
Tracy, Dwight, M.D., D.D.S.—Tracys in America. Arms of Tracy. Lieut. Thomas Tracy and "Widow Mason."
University of Vermont.—Catalogue.
Van Alstyne, W. B., M.D.—Newspaper clippings.
Vanderbilt, O. DeG.—Year Book, Princeton University, Class of 1906.
Virginia State Library.—Fourth Annual Report. Bulletin, I, 1.
Wallace, H. E.—Inskeep Genealogy, chart. Moorefield Examiner.
Washington, William Lanier.—Roster of the Virginia Society of the Order of the Cincinnati.
Weed, Edward Franklin.—Hollingsworth Genealogical Memoranda.
Woods, Henry E.—Report of the Public Archives Commission.

OTHER ACCESSIONS.
Acadiensis.
Albany and Schenectady Counties History.
Albany Conveyances, XIV.
American Antiquarian Society's Proceedings.
American Historical Magazine.
American Jewish Historical Society's Publications.
American Monthly Magazine.
Annals of Iowa.
Annals of Portsmouth.
Annals of St. Michael's Parish.
Archives of Maryland, 3 vols.
Augusta, Maine, History.
Berkshire County, Mass., Gazetteer.
Berkshire, England, Visitations.
Booth's History of New York City, 2 vols.
Brodhead's Delaware Water Gap.
Buffalo and the Senecas, 2 vols.
Burke's Report on Rhode Island.
Chautauqua County, N. Y., History.
Chittenden County, Vt., Gazetteer.
Commandery of the State of Pennsylvania, Loyal Legion.
Concord, N. H., History.
Connecticut Magazine.
Connecticut Valley History, 2 vols.

Descendants of Lewis Morris of Morrisania.
Dexter Genealogy.
Eastern Vermont History.
Eastport and Passamaquoddy.
Ellsworth Homestead.
Essex Antiquarian.
Essex Institute.
Fiske Family Papers.
Genealogist.
Guilford Portraits.
Harlem Commons History.
Hay Family.
Historic Homes on Long Island.
Historical Register of Pennsylvania.
Hough's History of Jefferson County, N. Y.
Index Library.
Jerseyman, 28 numbers.
Journal of American History.
Journals of Portland, Me.
Lossing's Field Book of the Revolution, 2 vols.
Machias, Me., History.
Massachusetts Soldiers and Sailors in the Revolutionary War, XVI.
Mather's Magnalia, 2 vols.
Mayflower Descendant.
McCormick Genealogy and Family Trees, 2 vols.
Meginness' Historical Journal, I.
Middlebury, Vt., History.
Monroe County, N. Y., Landmark.
Montgomery Co., Pa., History.
Montpelier, Vt., History.
N. E. Historical and Genealogical Register.
Niagara County, N. Y., History.
N. H. Genealogical Record.
N. J., Archives, 1st Se., Vol. XXVI.
N. Y. Churches, History of.
N. Y. Historical Society's Abstracts of Wills, IX.
Ohio Archæological and Historical Quarterly.
Old and New Monongahela.
Old Northwest Genealogical Quarterly.
Old Sands Street Church.
Old Westmoreland.
Pease Genealogy.
Pocahontas and Her Descendants.
Porter, Me., History.
Powers' Sangamon County Settlers.
Rusling Family.
St. Lawrence County, N. Y., Directory.
Sea Kings of Norway, 3 vols.
Some Pioneers of Washington County, Pa.
South Church, New Haven, History.
Stearns' First Church of Newark.
Steele's History of New Brunswick Church.
Thomas Mellon and His Times.
Thornhill, York, Parish Registers.
Tioga, Chemung, Tompkins and Schuyler County History.
Tompkins County, N. Y., Landmarks.
Tucker County, W. Va., History.
Union, Me., History.
Universities and Their Sons, 5 vols.
Va. Magazine of History and Biography.
Vincent's History of Delaware.
Washington County, Pa., History.
Wyoming, Pa., History.

OFFICERS

NOTICE

To Subscribers to "The Record".

Subscribers to "THE RECORD" are requested to notify the New York Genealogical and Biographical Society of any change in their addresses at any time, and especially changes during the Summer period; in order that the *July Issue of* "THE RECORD" may be delivered at their proper summer homes. Many RECORDS are delivered in July at City houses which are closed for the season and do not reach the subscribers on that account. For such failures of delivery this Society cannot be held responsible.

Subscribers desiring it, upon formal notice to this office, can have their July number of "THE RECORD" held for delivery with the October number, thus avoiding chance of loss on account of closed homes in the Summer.

THE NEW YORK
GENEALOGICAL AND BIOGRAPHICAL
RECORD.

DEVOTED TO THE INTERESTS OF AMERICAN
GENEALOGY AND BIOGRAPHY.

ISSUED QUARTERLY.

July, 1908.

PUBLISHED BY THE
NEW YORK GENEALOGICAL AND BIOGRAPHICAL SOCIETY,
226 WEST 58TH STREET, NEW YORK.

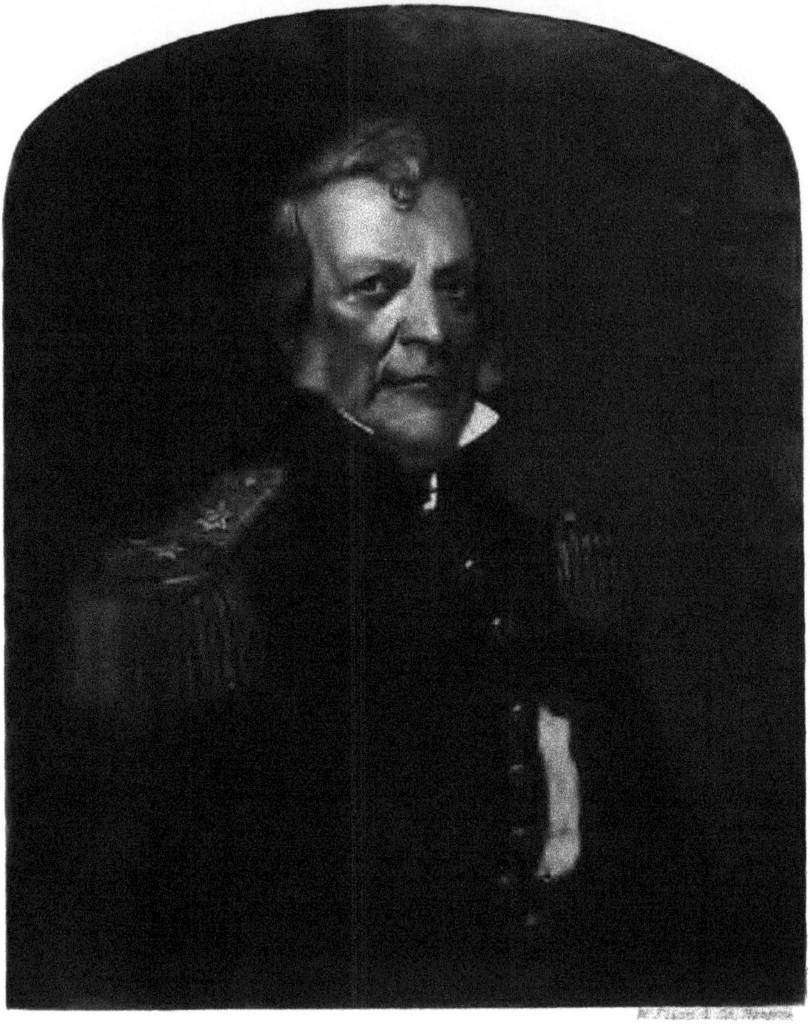

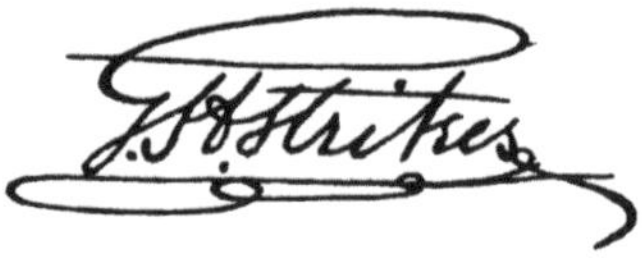

THE NEW YORK

Genealogical and Biographical Record.

| Vol. XXXIX. | NEW YORK, JULY, 1908. | No. 3. |

MAJOR-GENERAL GARRIT HOPPER STRIKER.

By Hopper Striker Mott.

The subject of this sketch was born in the mansion at Striker's Bay, which stood on an eminence overlooking the shores of "a certain cove," as the deed words it, at present 96th Street and Riverside Drive. He descended in the sixth generation from Jacobus Strijcker—the progenitor of the family in America—Magistrate of the Court of Burgomasters and Schepens, whose history has been heretofore told in this publication for January, 1907. The General's grandfather, Gerret Striker, for whom he was named, assumed the method of spelling his name which has been retained by the Manhattan branch of the family and differentiates it from the rest of the clan. He settled at the Bay in 1764 with his wife and son James, born Sept. 18, 1755, where he built his home.

The mansion stood on the edge of the line of British defence before and during the Battle of Harlem Heights. This locality was for long periods a hotbed of discord. For many years the residents of the district lived in daily fear and expectation of incursions and indignities. Mrs. Gerrit Striker whose husband had lately died (Sept. 17, 1775), opposed the enlistment of her son for these reasons, feeling with just cause that his assistance at this juncture would be needed. It is known that during the battle he used the family wagon to convey the wounded from the field and that the mansion was turned into a temporary hospital. Many soldiers of either side were cared for here with the aid of his mother. Twice the house was pillaged and finally all the live stock was driven off. Several skirmishes between the picket lines occurred on the immediate premises, in one of which a patriot and two Tories were killed in the lane which led from the Bloomingdale Road. These were buried near where they fell. Early in the struggle some officers were quartered in the house and at least one party of captives was billeted on the inmates, pending their removal to improvised prisons at the lower end of the Island. James Striker joined the American army, going to New Jersey where he enlisted as a member of the Light Horse Troop, 2nd Battalion of Somerset Militia, of which his relative in the same generation, John Stryker, was captain.   This troop formed part of Washington's forces and was present at the battles of Trenton, in Dec., 1776, Princeton, in Jan., 1777, Germantown, in Oct. of that year, and Monmouth, in June, 1778.   It was during his absence that these incursions occurred.   The place was again invaded by the enemy in 1781.   The slaves and servant men were driven off and the women compelled for days to cook and attend to the wants of their captors.

Yet a boy when his enlistment expired, a longing for home caused Striker, in the summer of 1780, to set out towards that goal. On reaching the ancestral habitation of his Captain, at Millstone, N. J., he was fitted out as a yeoman and in this disguise proceeded on his way.   At Tilly Tudlum, just north of Fort Lee, he succeeded in getting a boat wherewith he reached the shores of his mother's property "in the enemy's country."   Soon after his arrival he took out a license from the Secretary of the Province on Sept. 23, to marry Mary, dau. of Johannes and Wyntje (Dyckman) Hopper.   She lived only six years, dying at the age of twenty-six, on Sept. 20, 1786.   Her remains were deposited in the Hopper burial ground, at the southwest corner of Ninth Avenue and 50th Street.   Three children resulted from this union, viz.:

> i. Ann, b. Feb. 23, bap. June 25, 1781; d. unm. April 12, 1860.
> ii. Lavinia (Winifred), b. May 27, 1782; m. Jordan Mott, at Striker's Bay, Sept. 24, 1801; d. at "Mott's Point," March 16, 1862.
> iii. Garrit Hopper, b. March 29, 1784.

After James Striker's death the mansion became a tavern. In 1841 Joseph Francis was its landlord.   The years of his tenancy were memorable for the number of noted personages who assembled there.   Poe and his child wife, Virginia, spent the summers of 1843 and 1844 in a cottage near by which stood at 84th Street.   While he resided in Bloomingdale he wrote that that notable poem, *The Raven*, and it was his habit to wander down the declivity to the shores of the bay.   Often did he occupy a seat on Francis's piazza to enjoy the prospect and commune with his friends and familiars, of whom the names of Woodward, Morris, Willis, English, the author of *Ben Bolt*, and the lawyer-poet, William Ross Wallace, are recalled.   Trees of tremendous girth and height were on the ground, one of which, "a grand old elm," inspired Morris to compose that noble lyric, *Woodman, Spare that Tree*.   In 1837, wrote the poet, he caught a tenant of the property in the act of cutting it down for firewood.   "The old gentleman," with whom he was walking, asked the iconoclast what it was worth when felled, and ascertaining that ten dollars would prevent its destruction, paid the price and exacted an agreement in writing that it should be saved.   We have Morris's testimony that in 1862 it was still standing.

Under the tavern's successive bonifaces it became a noted resort for excursions, target-shooting, etc.   There was a dock and small station of the Hudson River Railroad on the grounds. The lawn fronting the river made a fine dancing floor, and at the rear of the house were found the targets. A well-known clergy-man is authority for the statement that here was a scene of sylvan beauty unsurpassed, and that he had never in his long life been in so entrancing a spot. The property was sold in June, 1856, and the house was destroyed by fire in the early sixties, when Robert Pennoyer was its landlord.

The youngest child and only son of the family passed his boyhood at his father's house and after an education which befitted his position, started his business career with money supplied by his grandfather. In 1801, at the age of seventeen, he was living at 181 Broadway. He was a merchant in 1833 at 55 Broad Street and in 1852 and 1853 the directory places his office at 78 Broadway with his son Garrit, although military headquarters continued to be his downtown centre, he having exhibited a marked aptitude for that career. An early bio-graphical sketch of him asserts that he had before his twenty-second year proved himself a good soldier and thereafter an efficient officer, panting for service and eager for the attainment of those laurels which can be earned alone in such employ. At the age of 26, he was commissioned Lieutenant in the 5th N. Y. Regiment, 2nd Brigade of Infantry, under Col. J. W. Mulligan, with rank from March 25, 1809. On the breaking out of the Second War with England he was assigned as Captain of the 4th Company in the 5th Regiment of Volunteers, Isaac A. van Hook having succeeded Mulligan in command. During the excited period of the fortifying of Bloomingdale Heights, while he was living at Striker's Bay, he attended the different calls of his home ward (the Ninth) and was active in obtaining subscriptions and laborers. Meetings were held in Rodger's Tavern, at 70th Street and Bloomingdale Road, which were attended by the neighbors in a united effort to hasten the erection of defences for the safety of their homes, that ward in which the work was carried on being the centre of active preparation. When not engaged in a military capacity Captain Striker lent the enthusiasm of his youthful endeavors to stimulating others, to seeing that the family horses did their proper share at the works and to collect-ing vegetables from the farm and attending to their distribution. His home was so near the line of defences that he passed much time during their construction on the gr nd, and with the assistance of his father's slaves, aided and abetted the progress of the work. The regiment to which he belonged was the last to be regularly designated by the Committee of Defence and it practically completed the works on Bloomingdale Heights.

On March 22, 1816, Striker was promoted to the rank of Major in the 82nd Regt., 3rd Brigade, commanded by Lieut.-Col. Joseph D. Fay, and in the regimental orders issued at this time, his former Colonel (van Hook) expressed himself in the warmest terms of Capt. Striker's "soldierly conduct and gentlemanly demeanor" while under his command. Promotion to the Lieut.-Colonelcy of the same regiment followed April 24, 1818. He reached the grade of Brigadier in 1828, and rose to the rank of Major-General in Feb., 1837.

The General commanded the 2nd Division of uniformed troops on Oct. 14, 1842, in the notable pageant that marked, amid great popular rejoicing, the completion of the Croton Water Works. In fact, he was a prominent figure in all the celebrations of his time, for example: the reception to ex-President Lamar of Texas, in 1840; the anniversary of the Battle of the Thames, Oct. 5 of that year, at which Gen. Harrison won renown, when he served as Grand Marshal of the parade and the ball at Harrison's inauguration March 4, 1841, at Washington Hotel. "The immense ball room, the most magnificent in the Union, was arrayed with all the taste and elegance which the unrivalled Dejonge could bestow," says the newspaper report of the affair. In April of the same year, he was aide at the funeral ceremonies in Harrison's memory, and was one of the committee at the reception to Charles Dickens and wife who reached New York, Jan. 20, 1842. In June, 1843, President Tyler visited the city on his way to the dedication of Bunker Hill Monument. The great parade was held on the day of his arrival. The steamboat *New Haven*, Capt. Vanderbilt, left Castle Garden wharf on the 17th and proceeded to Perth Amboy where the President was met and escorted to the city. During the funeral honors to Major-General Morgan Lewis, April 10, 1844, he was likewise conspicuous. Webster made his debut before the New York bar in the General's employ in May of this year.

A "grand military ball" was tendered to the General at the Apollo Rooms in 1846, at which he was presented with a service of plate, a gold medal and a pair of "Revolutionary boots." The *Sun* of April 4 reported that the beauty and fashion of the city graced the occasion. *London Punch* printed a facetious diatribe anent the boots, with a picture thereof, which filled a page of that noted periodical. The General was also prominent at the funeral solemnities over the death of Andrew Jackson, and at the great pageant on Oct. 19, 1847, at the laying of the cornerstone of the Washington Monument at Hamilton Square.

"Being the idol of the boys," says a chronicler, "the General's appearance with them in military costume on horseback was the signal for an unfailing ovation." His hair and eyes were as black as a raven's wing. He used to relate that he had lived in the Outward, in the 9th, 12th and 22nd Wards although he had never moved. The *Evening Express* dubbed him "gold snuff-box Striker" from his ostentatious manner of using that article. His speeches as reported were of a lively and spirited disposition, full of gracious raillery, good humored and witty withal. In his personal appearance he was immaculate. The *N. Y. Gazette* noticed the military ball, of which he was a manager, which was held at the N. Y. Theatre in the Bowery, Jan. 8, 1829, to celebrate the victory at New Orleans. This edict of fashion was laid down in the advertisement announcing the event: "Small clothes are considered as part of full dress for officers and citizens, but pantaloons, having been recently admitted as appropriate costume, will be approved." The General was a "decided but reasonable Whig" and served as Deputy Receiver of Taxes on the

Native American Ticket in 1844, and represented the 12th Ward in the Legislature in 1848.

On June 25, 1818, General Striker (t_hen Colonel) m. Eliza Bella, dau. of Capt. Alexander McDougal, of the British service, and his wife, Mary Elsworth of New York. They continued to reside at Striker's Bay until John Hopper, the younger, died the following year, when they removed to the latter's residence "Rosevale" on the Hudson at the foot of what later became 53rd Street. It was approached by the lane which his great-grandfather laid out from his homestead at the Bloomingdale Road and 51st Street, and which ended at the mansion. It took the the name of Striker's Lane thereafter. Entrance was obtained to the grounds through two stone posterns leading to a road which divided around a circle lying immediately before the house and led to the family barns and stables. The old place was set in the forest with gardens to the east, and on the west massive trees to the water's edge. Trees such as were not deemed to be found within miles of the city towered overhead. Majestic peacocks guarded the portal and strutted about in august grandeur. Looking from the broad veranda, a superb river view met the gaze, and in the immediate foreground one saw a goldfish pond, surrounded by a railing on which sat plump Muscovy drakes, which flew at one's approach and struck the water with a resounding splash. Descending the steps to and beyond the pond, winding walks under the trees and by rocks and wild flowers and bushes, finally brought one to the billiard house, where an old-fashioned table, so large as to leave barely space to promenade around it, occupied the lower story. Upstairs were garnered the fruits and nuts for winter consumption. Continuing the walk, still under grand natural trees and along narrow meandering paths, the bath-house was reached, situated in a cove over the sandy floor of which flowed a stream whose sources were the springs in the pond above. The old soldier was a man of taste and culture and the conservatories were his great pleasure. The name "Rosevale" was doubly appropriate, as a large share of the enclosed grounds were given to rose culture, the remainder being a valley sloping precipitously in places but generally gradually towards the river, the mansion itself being the line of demarkation.

Here the General maintained a boundless hospitality and dwelt some fifty years, constantly adding to the charms of his garden, his particular hobby. His numerous friends and admirers flocked around him and the abode was the centre of hospitality for leading men of the nation. On one of the window panes in the parlor appeared the names of Lafayette, Kossuth and Clay, scratched thereon with a diamond during their respective visits. "Old Bullion" Benton, Webster, Greeley, General Scott and other military celebrities, with a host of lesser lights, were welcome here. At the funerals of two of his distinguished friends during 1852 Striker acted as aide in the procession in honor of the obsequies of Clay July 20, and as pall-bearer for Webster he represented one of the then 31 States of the Union, Nov. 16. The

General was a conspicuous figure in the New York of his day, strikingly like his old friend Winfield Scott. It has been said of him that he united in his person the gentleman and the soldier, the high-spirited convivialist, the good husband, the tender father, the kind friend—in short all the qualities that were centered in the gentleman of the olden time. He departed this life at his home on April 15, 1868. The Rev. Dr. Hutton of the Washington Square Church and Domine van Aken of the Bloomingdale Reformed Church officiated at the ceremonies held there, when a vast concourse thronged the spacious mansion and lined the lane and the street as the procession passed. His remains were interred in Trinity Cemetery, where a plot had been prepared owing to the contemplated demolition of his ancestral church and the consequent abandonment of the family vault. At one of the last services held there, his funeral discourse was preached by Domine van Aken, which was published in full in the *Christian Intelligencer*. In recognition of his active participation in the construction of the defences on Bloomingdale Heights, the descendants of those who aided therein, as represented by the Daughters of 1812, inscribed his name on the tablet placed on Fayerweather Hall of Columbia University to commemorate the defences erected during that war.

THE SKILLMANS OF AMERICA AND THEIR KIN.

By William Jones Skillman, Philadelphia, Pa.

(Continued from Vol. XXXIX., p. 91, of The Record.)

125. Nicholas Veghte' Skillman (John,' Benjamin,' Isaac,' Thomas,' Thomas'), b. March 1, 1800; m. (1) Susan Howell; m. (2) May 30, 1830, Eliza Naylor (b. April 10, 1810). Had one child by first wife, seven by the second, all b. at Lambertville. N. J.:

    i. Lavinia,' b. 1825; m. John Scarborough and with him removed to Ohio.

    ii. Caroline, b. 1831; m. William Williamson. Had: 1. George, m. Margaret Martin. 2. Eliza, m. Horace Dean. 3. Harriet, m. William Hart.

    iii. Henry, b. 1832.

    iv. Mary Eliza, b. 1834; lives unm. at Lambertville, N. J.

    v. George, b. 1838; enlisted April 27, 1861, in Comp. I, 3d N. J. V. I. (3 months); m. Mary A. Wharton. Had: 1. Ellen. 2. Gaddis. 3. Milner. 4. Ada. 5. Harriet. 6. James. 7. Theodore.

    vi. Harriet, b. 1839; m. James Tomson. Had: 1. Caroline. 2. Florence. 3. William. 4. Lillian.

    vii. Nicholas Veghte, b. 1840; m. Annie Folie. Had: 1. Grantley. 2. Stella. 3. Eliza. 4. Nicholas. 5. Caroline, and 6. Florence, twins. 7. Percy. 8. William. 9. Maud. 10. Margaret.

viii. Theodore, b. 1842 (most of these birth dates are esti-
mates); m. Adelaide Holcombe. Had one dau., and
then removed to Kentucky.

126. BENJAMIN⁶ SKILLMAN (Thomas,⁵ Benjamin,⁴ Isaac,³ Thomas,²
Thomas¹), b. 1780, at Hopewell, N. J.; m. 1808, Catharine Green;
1st home in Philadelphia (1809), at 43 Vine St.; in 1818 at Ann St.:
"Catharine, wid. of Benjamin" in Directory down to 1869.
Children:

   i. Thomas Andrew,⁷ b. Nov. 2, 1809; d. 1886; m. Catharine Kline. Had: 1. Anna E., b. 1836; m. Joseph
Cowperthwait, one son, Dr. Edwin G., Philadelphia.
2. Thomas B., b. 1839; d. 1893; m. Kate J. Lomax,
two sons. 3. John G., b. 1842; m. Sophia Hitchcock,
four sons. 4.Theodore K., b. 1845. 5. William B., b.
1847; m. Louisa Foulke. 6. Joseph K., b. 1850; m.
Lottie Sterrett.
   ii. Rebecca, b. Sept. 23, 1811.
   iii. John Green, b. Oct. 3, 1813.
   iv. Elizabeth, b. June 7, 1815; joined on confession First
Church (Ref. Dutch), Philadelphia, 1831; m. J. Warren Coulston, Phila. bar (d. 1907); son of same name
and profession.
   v. Anna, b. Dec. 2, 1817.

127. ANDREW⁶ SKILLMAN (Thomas,⁵ Benjamin,⁴ Isaac,³ Thomas,²
Thomas¹), b. at Hopewell, 1787; d. at Baton Rogue, La., 1849;
educated at Princeton (not a graduate), and early went South; m.
Anne Sterling. Children:

   i. Annie,⁷ m. Calvin Routh, Natchez, Miss.; d. 1852.
Left: 1. Andrew Routh, Lake St. Joseph, La. 2.
Annie Routh, m. Allen Borrie, druggist, Natchez.
(See Dr. Stiles' *Hist. Ancient Wethersfield, Conn.*)
   ii. Edward, physician, d. 1848; left two daus. living on
the Red River, La.
   iii. Louisa, m. —— Lea, a widower, in New Orleans. Had:
1. Ann, m. Henry Salisbury. 2. Fannie, m. Henry
Hester, Supt. (1876) Cotton Exchange; and two sons
and two daus. besides.
   iv. Fannie, m. Dr. W. P. Walker; d. *circa* 1860. Large
family scattered over the South; a dau. and her
family at Port Hudson, La.
   v. Kate, m. (1) William Palmer, one son; m. (2) ——
Fuller; again a widow, and (1876) lived with son in
Washington, D. C.
   vi. Mary, m. 1849, John J. Ellet. Had: 1. Henry E. 2.
Thomas J. 3. Winthrop G. 4. Arthur. 5. Benjamin. 6. Alfred. 7. Annie. Home at Yazoo City,
Miss.
   vii. Sarah, m. Dr. David C. Price, St. Paul, Minn. Had
two daus. and one son.
   viii. Eliza B., m. Maj. J. J. Noah, Washington, D. C. Three
sons and one dau.

ix. Ursula Hunt, m. Augustine Lincoln (Baltimore). One
    son and two daus. in Washington. There the mother
    of this large family (long a widow) lived (1876). No
    later date here than that.

128. WALTER⁵ SKILLMAN (Thomas,⁵ Benjamin,⁴ Isaac,³ Thomas,²
Thomas¹), b. July 12, 1793, at Stoutsburg (Blawenburg), N. J.; m.
1819, Ura (Wilah, Ursula, Osseltje, Osie) Garrison (See No. 4),
dau. of Maj. William Garrison of Stoutsburg (Algernon, father of
Alfred Weart, Blawenburg, m. her sister); was a school teacher
and kept a general store at Stoutsburg, once a village. Children:

i. William Garrison,' b. 1820; d. 1880; m Sept. 14, 1847,
    Margaret West (d. 1896); came to Philadelphia 1844;
    merchant 1853. Had: 1. Anna, b. 1848; m. Robert
    H. Long. 2. Mary G., b. 1851; m. —— Taylor. 3.
    Evaline, b. 1857; m. —— Hollis. All widows later.
ii. Elizabeth Ann, b. 1822; m. Samuel A. French. They
    had one son, Garrison, Chicago, Ill., with whom the
    mother, a widow, lived.
iii. Andrew, b. 1824; never m.
iv. Ursula, b. Dec. 6, 1838; d. March 21, 1839.

Ursula Hunt (b. 1763) wife of Thomas (See No. 46) and mother
of Walter Skillman, *et al.*, was dau. of Edward⁴ Hunt (Jonathan,³
Edward,² Ralph¹), forebears in Hopewell of this extensive New
Jersey (and American) family.

129. SALLY⁶ SKILLMAN (see No. 47), dau. of Jacob, b. 1791, at
Kingston, N. J.; m. in Union, Broome Co., N. Y., 1817, John
Drake Mersereau (b. June 25, 1789; d. Aug. 2, 1866), eldest son of
Joshua Mersereau and wife, Barbara Van Pelt, and grandson of
John, a soldier with Washington at Trenton; of a pioneer
Huguenot family. (See *Baptisms of Ref. Dutch Church of Port
Richmond, S. I.*, Vol. XXXVII of THE RECORD.) Had eleven
children, the eldest, Aletta, b. April 26, 1818; the youngest, Han-
nah, b. Feb. 2, 1836, and nearly all m. in the region.

130. ELIAS SCUDDER⁶ SKILLMAN (Jacob,⁵ John,⁴ Jacob,³ Thomas,²
Thomas¹), b. 1798, at Kingston, N. J.; with the family removed,
1805, to Union, N. Y. (Susquehanna Valley). Next year returned
to Kingston relatives and went to school four years, returning at
17. Was named for Elias (second son of Lemuel Scudder and
wife, Margaret Longstreet of Princeton brother of writer's
maternal grandfather). In 1817 m. Barbara, dau. of Joshua Mersereau (sister of John), and wife Keziah Drake (b. Aug. 29, 1795;
d. March 7, 1857). He d. 1879. Children:

i. Gitty' (Margaret), b. Aug. 19, 1818; m. Abraham Day.
ii. Frederick, b. Nov. 20, 1819; m. Amanda Councilman.
iii. Caroline E., b. March 4, 1821; m. Peter Thom.
iv. David R., b. March 21, 1823; m. Mary Rounds; lived
    in Owego, N. Y. Had there (1893), the old family
    Bible with records in possession.
v. Elias S., b. Aug. 25, 1825; m. Mary Quin.
vi. John M., b. Jan. 17, 1827; m. Angeline Randal.

vii. Phoebe A., b. Dec. 8, 1829; m. Christopher R. Mersereau, who d. 1902.

viii. Joshua M., b. Oct. 20, 1833; m. Letta Barney.

ix. Jane, b. May 10, 1836; m. Uri Harper.

131.   JOHN⁵ SKILLMAN (Jacob,⁴ John,⁴ Jacob,³ Thomas,² Thomas¹), bap. in Kingston (N. J.) Church (Presby.), Nov. 22, 1795; d. 1856, in early home at Dryden, Tompkins Co., N. Y., whither he had removed from Union; m. *circa* 1817, Margaret Sharp ("Aunt Peggy"). Children:

i. Betsey,⁶ b. May, 1818; d. 1894; m. —— Cole; a widow living with daus. in Syracuse, N. Y. Eldest dau. ten years a missionary (1893) in Turkey (Macedonia); youngest son, Prof. Cole, Norwich University, Vt., then a student at Bonn (Germany).

ii. William F., b. 1820; home at Dryden.

iii. James, d. inf.

iv. John, home in Canada.

v. George, grocer, Camden, N. J.; d. 1900, widow surviving.   ·

132.   ABIGAIL⁵ SKILLMAN (sister of above), b. Dec. 19, 1799; bap. at Kingston Church (Presby.), as Abby Van Dine; d. July 27, 1872; m. James Harvey, Binghamton (d. 1872). Had six sons and four daus., all but three to grow up and marry, from Jacob, the eldest, b. May 15, 1821, to John M., the youngest, b. Dec. 3, 1841.

133.   DAVID COMFORT⁵ SKILLMAN (Abraham,⁴ John,⁴ Jacob,³ Thomas,² Thomas¹), b. at Kingston, N. J., Aug. 12, 1796; d. Oct. 13, 1875; came to Springfield, O. (journeyman tailor), and there m. 1818, Sarah, dau. of Sam. Carey. Miss Jane Comfort, dau. of the Kingston Minister (Presby.) for whom he was named, was a schoolmate of David and his sister Mary. Record here given by James R. in 1876, he and younger brother then living in Sparta, Wisc. Family dates estimated. Children:

i. America Minerva,⁶ b. 1819.

ii. Mary, b. 1821.

iii. John Quincey, b. 1823.

iv. David Francis, b. 1826.

v. Sarah, b. 1828.

vi. James Reed, b. 1830; home in Wisconsin.

vii. Philander, b. 1832.

viii. Eliza Martha, b. 1835.

134.   JAMES REED⁵ SKILLMAN (Isaac,⁴ John,⁴ Jacob,³ Thomas,² Thomas¹), b. at Kingston, Oct. 6, 1808; d. 1864; m. June 15, 1840, Rosetta Anderson (b. June 6, 1817; d. April 18, 1847; buried in Princeton Cemetery). Children:

i. Harrison Anderson,⁶ b. May 9, 1841; d. Nov. 8, 1895, in Kingston (N. Y.) City Hospital; a printer at Havre-de-Grace, Md.; enlisted Aug. 13, 1861, at Trenton in 4th N. J. V. I., and served through the war; discharged as captain, July 25, 1865. A printer then at Vineland, N. J.; then Gov't. proof reader at Washington, D. C.; later editor of *Daily True Ameri-*

can, Trenton; finally of *Kingston* (N. Y.) *Freeman*;
m. 1864, Carolyn Ellis, Trenton, N. J.   Had: 1.
Bertha.   2. Rosetta, Vineland, N. J.

   ii. Mary, b. 1844; m. Samuel Dean, Trenton.   Had:
     Laura, m. G. B. Woolston, Trenton.

  iii. Elizabeth Berrien, b. April 27, 1846; d. Dec. 24;
     buried at Princeton.

  iv. Charles Worrel, b. 1847; d. inf.

135. GEORGE⁶ SKILLMAN (Robert,⁵ Jacob,⁴ Jacob,³ Thomas,²
Thomas¹), b. in Baltimore, Nov. 13, 1803; d. 1863; m. Sept. 1, 1841,
Eliza Jane McLean, long d.   Children:

    i. Charles,⁷ b. June 29, 1842; m. Oct. 13, 1865, Laura V.,
     dau. of his uncle Robert.   Had: 1. Charles.   2.
     Robert.   3. Naomi.   4. Rose.   5. George.   A Balti-
     more family.

   ii. Robert, b. Feb. 11, 1849; lived in Canada.

  iii. John R. H., b. March, 1852; home at Norfolk, Va.

  iv. Hannah A., b. April 8, 1854.

   v. Ellis, b. May 20, 1856; lives in Canada.

136. ROBERT⁶ SKILLMAN (Robert,⁵ Jacob,⁴ Jacob,³ Thomas,²
Thomas¹), b. May 18, 1813, in Baltimore; m. Dec. 25, 1835, Naomi
S. Miller.   Children:

    i. George R.,⁷ b. Jan. 1, 1837; manufacturer; m. April 22,
     1858, Mary E. Pierce (d. Feb., 1904).   Had: 1. Geo.
     R., Jr., b. 1860.   2. Virginia, b. 1861.   3. Wm. P., b.
     1863; d. 1864.   4. Robt., b. 1865.   5. Mary E., b. 1866·
     6. Sarah A., b. 1869.   7. Wilbur F., b. 1872.   Physician,
     Baltimore.   Many grandchildren.

   ii. Ann H., b. Aug. 25, 1838; m. Sept. 9, 1856, Isaac H.
     Bozman.   Four sons.   Lives at Norfolk, Va.

  iii. Melissa N., b. April 15, 1840; m. (1) 1860, Joseph
     Franklin, d. 1868; m. (2) 1870, William L. Bryant.
     Five children.

  iv. Laura V., b. Aug. 5, 1847; m. 1865, Charles Skillman
     (cousin).

   v. Robertina, b. June 20, 1850; m. 1873, Ezekiel Jones.

  vi. Emma, b. March 23, 1854; m. 1872, James W. Keys.

137. JOHN⁶ SKILLMAN (George,⁵ Jacob,⁴ Jacob,³ Thomas,²
Thomas¹), b. *circa* 1796 (father b. probably 1773; see and correct
Nos. 18 and 52); m. Jan. 17, 1825, at Cooperstown, N. Y., Sarah
Ann, dau. of Alexander L. Stewart and wife, Sarah Lispenard,
dau. of Anthony Lispenard, who m. Sarah Barclay, Jan. 27, 1803.
Name as "John B. Skillman, merchant," is in the Directory (N. Y.)
from 1820; at his death (1827) as "editor and proprietor of the
Courier and Enquirer," which then passed into charge of Gen.
James Watson Webb, his brother-in-law.   Children:

    i. Lispenard Stewart,⁷ b. Nov. 20, 1825.   His father's
     name from both self and sister was legally dropped
     when the mother, a widow, m. Sept. 24, 1835, the
     Rev. Charles S. Stewart (second cousin), a missionary
     (1823-25) to the Sandwich Islands, and later, Chaplain

U. S. N. This arrangement was for oneness of name in two sets of children in the home of the grandfather and of the parents. The second marriage had no issue. Lispenard S. (above) m. Nov. 16, 1859, Mary Horton, and had: 1. Sarah Amelia, b. 1862. 2. Robert Lispenard, b. 1866.

   ii. Sarah Lispenard, b. 1827, a babe in arms at her father's death; m. June 15, 1851, Elihu Phinney of Cooperstown, long a ruling elder in the Presbyterian Church (d. Sept. 20, 1892, ae. 70), the widow surviving. Had one son, Alexander Stewart Phinney. This widow of John Skillman and mother of his two children is of the fifth generation in descent of Antoine L'Espinard (Anthony,[4] Leonard,[3] Anthony,[2] Antoine[1]), a religious refugee (1669) from Rochelle, France, making his home finally at New Rochelle, America, and giving rise to one of the largest Huguenot families in this country, and specially identified with the early life and interest of N. Y. City.

138. JACOB C.[6] SKILLMAN (George,[5] Jacob,[4] Jacob,[3] Thomas,[2] Thomas[1]), b. at Richmondville, N. Y., 1805; began business (hardware) at 155 Pearl St., N. Y., in 1826; later a merchant at Fort Plain, N. Y.; for a time member of the State Legis. for Schoharie. Long in dry goods trade, N. Y. City; m. Helen Bond. Children:

   i. John Edward,[7] b. 1837; fancy goods, N. Y., 1865; moved to South Bend, Ind., 1870; d. there 1905; m. Sarah V. ——, N. Y. City, 1861. Had: 1. Emma, d. 1900. 2. George W., b. 1863; bookkeeper, Collegiate Church (Ref. Dutch); m. Emma Spencer. Four children: 3. Robert. Two sons: 1. Robert. 2. Arthur.
   ii. George W., no record.
   iii. Robert E., fancy goods (1855), 7th Ave., N. Y. City.
   iv. Harriet.
   v. Isabelle, fancy goods, 745 6th Ave., N. Y., 1866; m. Enoch P. Breen.
   vi. Albert, in upholstery, N. Y., 1876.

139. ABRAHAM[6] SKILLMAN (Jacob,[5] Abraham,[4] Jacob,[3] Thomas,[2] Thomas[1]), b. June 15, 1795, at Kingston, N. J.; m. (1) 1824, in Clinton Co., O., Harriet Wainwright, also from N. J.; d. 1841; m. (2) Eleanor Benham (see No. 99); stage line proprietor. Had nine children, six by first wife, three by second:

   i. Jacob,[7] b. 1825; blacksmith, Loveland, O.; never m.
   ii. Peter, b. 1827; d. 1897; m. Ruth Roundabush. Had: 1. Flora, m. Chas. Andrews. 2. Anna, m. Theodore Reeves, St. Louis, two children. 3. Kate, unm. 4. Beulah, d. unm. 5. Frank, d. inf. 6. Ruthella, unm. 7. Abraham, b. 1877; a dentist; d. ae. 24.
   iii. James, lives at Blanchester, O.; m. Ellen Arnold. Had: 1. Edward A. 2. Ethel.

iv. Andrew, went 1849 to California; m. and had: 1. James.
2. Perry. 3. Eva.
v. Peregrine, home at Blanchester; m. Nancy Butz. Had:
1. Leonia, m. Adolph Gramlich. Shawneyville, O.
2. William V., druggist, Spokane, Wash. 3. Rose,
unm., Gano, O. 4. Laura, m. Charles Lupton. 5.
Grace, m. John Hines. 6. Bessie, unm.
vi. Hannah, m. David Comfort Bastido, Princeton. Early
Huguenot name on Staten Island and in N. J.
vii. Elizabeth, m. Alfred Benham, Princeton. Had: 1.
Edgar. 2. Alice. 3. Blanche.
viii. Daniel, lives in Alabama; no further record.
ix. Alice, m. George Corson; lives a widow with five
grown up children in Somerville, N. J.

140. WILLIAM J.[6] SKILLMAN (Jacob,[5] Abraham,[4] Jacob,[3] Thomas,[2]
Thomas[1]), b. Feb. 9, 1802; moved from Kingston, N. J., to Lan-
singburg, N. Y., 1825; brush manufacturer; m. 1826, Catharine
Wickmire, b. Sept. 15, 1801. Both long dead. Children:
i. Sarah E.,[7] b. Nov. 16, 1827; d. unm.
ii. William H., b. Oct. 22, 1829; d. March, 1902.
iii. Ellen, b. Dec. 19, 1831.
iv. Francis A., b. June 20, 1833.
v. Edward A., b. May 18, 1836.
vi. John J., b. Aug. 13, 1838; d. young.
vii. Charles E., b. Jan. 25, 1842.
viii. Albert W., b. Oct. 24, 1843; d. inf.
ix. George E., b. April 18, 1846; recently mayor of Troy,
N. Y.

141. GEORGE[6] SKILLMAN (Jacob,[5] Abraham,[4] Jacob,[3] Thomas,[2]
Thomas[1]), b. at Kingston, N. J., Nov. 14, 1811; d. Dec. 13, 1895,
Princeton; m. 1836, Susan Bennett of Bennett's Hill, New Brunswick, N. J. (b. Oct. 2, 1812; d. Dec. 26, 1884). Children:
i. George,[7] b. 1837; d. inf.
ii. Conover, b. 1841; d. inf.; both buried at Kingston.
iii. Amelia, b. 1843; m. 1866, Thomas E. Benham (d. 1898,
ae. 60). One son, William Leroy, d. 1891. Mrs. B.
d. April 29, 1905, leaving a precious memory as
foster mother (at Benham Hall) of hundreds of
students of theology in Princeton who now as ministers and missionaries are scattered over the world.
iv. John G., b. 1845; enlisted Oct. 15, 1861, in Comp. K,
9th N. J. V. I., and Jan. 18, 1864, reenlisted for the
war; m. 1868, Kate Baker. Five children, Princeton.
v. William B., b. 1847; m. 1873, Mrs. Maggie Ayers of
Hightstown, N. J. Three children.
vi. Josephine, b. 1849; m. 1882, Henry Kinsey, Princeton
(d. 1897). No children.
vii. Theodore, b. 1852; m. 1873, Mary Hawk, Cranbury,
N. J.; home in Princeton. Six children.
viii. Augustus Tracy, b. 1856; hardware dealer, Hightstown; m. Caroline Thom Embly of Philadelphia
(d. 1900). One dau., Annie, b. Sept. 24, 1888.

142. MARY ANN[6] SKILLMAN (see No. 54), dau. of William H., b. Sept. 9, 1806; d. Feb. 10, 1884; m. Neshanic, N. J. (life home), 1824, Nathaniel Foster (d. 1883). Had: 1. William, b. 1826; removed to Ohio, later to Kansas. 2. Jacob, b. 1827; after three years in the Civil War, from Ohio, settled at Lacon, Ill.; d. 1903. 3. Catharine, b. 1829; d. widow of Henry R. Wyckoff, Neshanic. 4. Sarah, b. 1831; m. 1851, Isaac Reed. Four children. 5. Ann Rebecca, b. 1834; m. 1854, Andew J. Cahill; lived at Dayton, O. Two children. 6. Andrew J., b. 1836; d. 1842. 7. Mary Scudder, b. 1838; m. Wm. Wolverton. One son, Nathaniel. 8. Matilda, b. 1840; m. George Conger, N. Brunswick, N. J. 9. John R., Three Bridges, N. J., State Senator for Hunterdon, b. 1844; m. 1871, Amanda Cole. One son, Wm. Winfield. 10. Josephine, b. 1846; d. 1849.

143. JACOB RUNYON[6] SKILLMAN (William H.,[5] George,[4] Jacob,[3] Thomas,[2] Thomas[1]), b. June 22, 1808; d. May 20, 1883; m. Dec. 14, 1831, Mary Scudder, dau. of Richard and wife, Jane, dau. of Capt. William Jones and Mary Pinkerton, Princeton (b. July 9, 1813; d. June 20, 1888). Graves of both are near their home, in churchyard at Pennington, N. J. (Presby.). Children:

   i. Catharine Jane,[7] b. Sept. 18, 1832; d. inf.
  ii. Henry, b. Sept. 28, 1833; d. Dec. 4, 1835.
 iii. William Jones, b. April 19, 1835; grad. of Rutgers College, 1860, and of N. B. Theo. Sem., 1863; for ministry, see Church Records (Ref. Dutch). Editor *Journal*, Sioux Falls, S. D., and *City and State*, Philadelphia; m. June 4, 1863, Susie Eleanor, dau. of Hartshorne Willett Gilliland (son of David Gilliland and wife, Eleanor Perine Willett, of South River region, N. J.) and Ann, dau. of Manuel Brown and wife, Susan Early; home at 44 Bowery in 1st N. Y. Directory, 1811. Children: 1. Mary, b. 1864; m. 1884, Frank M. Hatch, South Bend, Ind. 2. Willet Runyon, b. 1866; m. 1895, Ada Harrison, Orange, N. J.; home, Bedford Park, Bronx. Two boys. 3. Ernest Dumont, b. 1867; m. 1892, Marie Schaetzel, Sioux Falls, S. D. Two children. 4. Herbert, b. 1869; d. inf. 5. Regner, b. 1871 6. Anna Francesca, b. 1873; d. April 27, 1895. 7. Arthur D., b. 1875; m. 1906, Julia Early; home, Los Angeles, Cal.. One child. 8. Lionel Gilliland, b. 1877; m. 1902, Anna Watson Stone, Philadelphia (Wissahickon); home, East Elmhurst, N. Y. City (Queens). 9. Edith, b. 1879; d. inf.
  iv. Amanda, b. Jan. 11, 1837; d. Brooklyn, N. Y., 1899; m. Sept. 5, 1855, B. F. Murphy, Island of Cuba, who d. at Lima, S. A., Feb. 6, 1870. Had one dau., Frank, m. Will Hickman, N. Brunswick, N. J.
   v. Richard Scudder, b. Oct. 14, 1838; d. April 12, 1842.
  vi. Elias H., b. May 29, 1852; m. Ida Search, Dec. 15, 1875. One dau., Anna Blackwell, m. 1906, Wilson Hunt; live at Pemberton, N. J.

The father and mother in this home for most of their lives belonged to the old church (Ref. Dutch) of Six Mile Run (now Franklin Park) and the children, there baptized, were all b. at Ten Mile Run, Somerset Co., N. J.

144. WILLIAM R.[6] SKILLMAN (William H.,[5] George,[4] Jacob,[3] Thomas,[2] Thomas[1]), b. May 3, 1814; d. 1888; m. Nov. 11, 1835, at Kingston, N. J., Eliza Robison (b. 1814; d. 1892); wagonmaker; removed to Sangamon Co., Ill., 1838, to Chicago, 1847, and to Fairview, Fulton Co., 1862. Children:

    i. Joseph,[7] b. Jan. 15, 1842; joined Comp. H, 14th Ill. V. C. at Peoria, 1863; d. in a Maryland hospital, 1863; never m.

    ii. Elizabeth, b. Aug. 18, 1845; m. 1862, Louis Rabenau. Eight children living, Galesburg, Ill.

    iii. Kate, b. Sept. 8, 1848; d. June 5, 1903; m. Feb. 17, 1870, Henry M. B. Wilson, son of the Rev. A. D. Wilson, pioneer minister at Fairview, Ill., of the R. C. A., organizing and serving there (1838–1856) the first church (Ref. Dutch) west of the Allegheny Mountains. Had eight children, six living.

    iv. Charles C., b. in Chicago, Sept. 11, 1851; d. 1880; m. 1877, Nancy Abbot. Two children and widow surviving.

    v. William R., b. May 16, 1857; lives in Fairview, unm.

145. REBECCA[6] SKILLMAN (dau. in the family, No. 54), b. Aug. 25, 1816, named for grandmother, Rebecca Gracie; d. April 23, 1897; m. April 3, 1835, Charles Tindell (b. 1815, in Trenton; d. in California, 1858); home, N. Brunswick, N. J. Had: 1. Caroline Low, b. 1836; d. 1894; m. Aug. 22, 1860, Henry J. McDonald, major in Civil War in 11th Conn. V. I.; prisoner, 1864, at Salisbury, N. C.; home in Des Moines, Ia. 2. Abigail, b. 1837; d. 1841. 3. Samuel, b. 1839; d. 1841. 4. Charles H., b. 1841; m. 1872, Martha W., dau. of Rev. Dr. George R. Noyes, Prof. Heb. and Orient. Langs., Harvard Div. School, Cambridge, Mass. First in Unitarian and later in Prot. Epis. ministry; home in Boston, Mass. 5. Edward, b. 1843; m. 1869, Anna A. Dunn; coal dealer, N. Brunswick, N. J. 6. Harriet, b. 1845; m. 1878, Clarence S. Smith. 7. Anna A., b. 1847; m. 1866, Isaac Halstead. 8. Mary S. W., b. 1849; m. 1882, James P. Smith. 9. George W., b. 1852; d. 1854. 10. Howard Bishop, b. 1855; m. 1877, Martha Timmons.

146. JOHN R.[6] SKILLMAN (William H.,[5] George,[4] Jacob,[3] Thomas,[2] Thomas[1]), b. Feb. 18, 1821; m. April 16, 1842, Lucretia Huff (b. 1825; d. 1899); long a carriagemaker at Flemington; home now at Elizabeth, N. J. Of eight children only two surviving infancy:

    i. Peter H.,[7] b. Oct. 26, 1851; m. Nov. 20, 1872, Anna F. McCann. One child. Home in Elizabeth, N. J.

    ii. Sarah, b. Oct. 30, 1853; m. at Flemington, N. J., Nov. 23, 1871, Farley S. Taylor. Two children.

(To be continued.)

RECORDS OF THE UNITED BRETHREN CONGREGA-
TION, COMMONLY CALLED MORAVIAN CHURCH,
STATEN ISLAND, N. Y.

MARRIAGES.

ABBREVIATIONS.

Sr.—Sister—A Communicant. M. M.—Married Man. M. W.—Married Woman.
Br.—Brother—A Communicant. S. M.—Single Man. S. W.—Single Woman.
Wid.—Widow.

(Continued from Vol. XXXIX., p. 108 of THE RECORD.)

1782.		Peter Prall
May	19.	Elizabeth Ridgway
June	9.	Moses Van Namur
		Mary Legrange
June	12.	—— Telston
		Susan Newland
June	12.	John Ferris
		Mary Stilwell
June	13.	Richard Hately
		Mary Cole
June	23.	Peter Boost
		Mary Van Namer
June	3.	Jacob Vanderbilt
		Rachel Dennis
July	14.	Hugh Doyle
		Elisabeth Chambers
July	24.	Charles Murphy
		Catharine McBride
Sept.	14.	William Allen
		Martha Grimma
Oct.	7.	William Van Pelt
		Sarah Saunders
Oct.	9.	Isaac Baldwin
		Frances Kelly
Nov.	3.	Asher Codington
		Judith Taylor
Nov.	10.	James Butler
		Frances Butler
Nov.	24.	Abraham Stilwell
		Ann Ward
Dec.	1.	Thomas Gerrand
		Esther Smith
Dec.	1.	Garret Bush
		Elizabeth Van Namur
1783.		Henry Sleight
Jan.	23.	Catharine Butler
March	18.	John Wandel
		Susannah Latterette

1783.	Elias Van Winkel
March 25.	Lucy Price
April 15.	William Alexander
	Jane Allen
April 16.	Jacob Crocheron
	Ann Morgan
May 14.	Henry Barger
	Mary Tysen
June 11.	Daniel Ross
	Desire Bigilow
Aug. 7.	Abraham Lake
	Patience Berbank, widow
Aug. 10.	Laurence Cripps
	Susanna Fountain
Aug. 12.	Roger Flinn
	Johanna Barnes
Aug. 29.	John Ayre
	Elizabeth Smith
Aug. 30.	Zenophon Jewet
	Gertrude Garritson
Sept. 2.	George Adkens
	Abigail Ogles
Sept. 9.	Abraham Long
	Ann Rambel
Sept. 17.	Anthony Fountain
	Martha Crips
Sept. 25.	Nicholas Britton
	Judith Johnson
Oct. 6.	John Ingham
	Margaret Calcraft
Oct. 15.	Barent Simonson
	Anne Beatty
Oct. 26.	Austin Barton
	Rebeka Burbank
Nov. 19.	"John Byvank or Burbank"
	Elisabeth Decker
Dec. 28.	Timothy Wood
	Mary Blake
1784.	Joakim Stilwell
Feb. 15.	Susanna Scarret
Feb. 18.	John Van Pelt
	Judith Durant
Feb. 17.	Cornelius Fountain
	Elisabeth Vandeventer
May 7.	John Dorset
	Martha Cortelyou

By Rev. Jas. Birkby.

1784.	James Burdine
Aug. 3.	Elisabeth Egbert

By Rev. Frederick Moering.

1787.	John Garrison
May 31.	Elizabeth Connor
Sept. 20.	Cornelius Bedell
	Elizabeth Jacobson
1788.	John Jacobson
July 2.	Hilletje Bedell
Nov. 16.	Samuel Egbert
	Cathrine Smith
Nov. 17.	John Martino
	Jane Christopher
Dec. 17.	Jacob Cortelyou
	Elizabeth Corsen
1789.	Abraham Egbert
May 31.	Ann Martino
Dec. 23.	John Baker
	Charity Wandel
1790.	Samuel Smith
Jan. 3.	Elizabeth Perine
Jan. 16.	Francis Post
	Experience Marshall
Feb. 21.	Daniel Corsen
	Rebecca Martino
April 7.	Peter Fountain
	Claushea Spears
1791.	Richard Conor, Junr.
May 19.	Sophia Clausen
July 6.	Tunis Egbert
	Ann Burbank
Sept. 25.	Stephen Ketteltas
	Ardrae Britton
Oct. 30.	John Van der Bilt
	Elizabeth Taylor
1792.	Joseph Moore
Jan. 26.	Johanna Ward
Jan. 26.	William Williams
	Sarah Hooper
Feb. 19.	John White
	Mary Lockerman
March 25.	Elisha Kribbs
	Magdalene McLean
1793.	Benajah Martino
Feb. 4.	Hannah Decker

By Rev. Jas. Birkby.

1793.	James Lewis
Nov. 5.	Rebecca Collong
1794.	Jeremiah Baker
Feb. 2.	Sarah Butler
Feb. 3.	John Marshall
	Sussanna Swaim

1794.	Zedick Vincnant
Feb. 6.	Catherine Sefurde [or Lefurde]
Feb. 25.	Vincent Fountain
	Alice Jinnings
April 1.	Richard S. Cary
	Judith Bard
June 5.	Matthew Decker
	Mary Latterete
Sept. 25.	Isaac Symerson
	Elizabeth Barnes
1795.	John Britton
Jan. 1.	Rachel Burbank
"in 1794."	Rubin Symerson
	Phoebe Decker
1795.	Antony Fountain
Feb. 17.	Phoebe Thomson
Feb. 19.	Matthias Enyard
	Sarah Decker
March 5.	Peter Cortelyou
	Amey Hilliyard
March 22.	Richard Decker
	Mary Ann Kinsey
Aug. 3.	Thomas Vanderbilt
	Williga Symerson, from the north side
1796.	Christopher Parkinson
Sept. 24.	Phoebe Garritson. Md. at house of Henry Garritson, Esq.
Oct. 23.	Edward Egbert
	Sarah Phrol. Md. in the church
1797.	Jacob Lossier
May 2.	Sarah Beatty. In church
June 22.	John Chroson
	Catharine Ryerss. Md. at the house on north side
Oct. 22.	Henry Miller
	Elizabeth Barton

BY REV. FREDERICK MOERING.

Dec. 28.	John Beatty
	Elizabeth Lake
1798.	Abraham Decker
Jan. 20.	Cathrine Kinsey
Sept. 2.	James Burdine, widower
	Margret Oakley
Sept. 2.	Robert Anderson of N. Y.
	Mary Sargent
Nov. 10.	Niclas Depew of N. Y.
	Sussanna Seymourson of Staten Island
1799.	Daniel Lake
Jan. 17.	Ann Lockerman
Feb. 28.	John Merlin
	Cathrine Mitchel
March 19.	Niclas Depuy
	Cathrine Decker

1799.	Ord. Housman	
Aug. 4.	Mary Morgan	
Dec. 21.	Mathew Stevenson	
	Anne Drake	
1800.	Daniel Froom	
Jan. 19.	Martha Baker	
April 14.	George Colon	
	Billetje Lewis, widow	
Sept. 9.	John Morrel	
	Jane Jones	
Sept. 21.	Daniel Jones	
	Elizabeth Christopher	
Oct. 16.	Robert Journey	
	Sarah Cole	
Nov. 20.	Peter Van Pelt	
	Cathrine Glendinen	
1801.	George Shingles, single	
May 3.	Jemima Bredsted, single	
June 21.	David Vanamour [Van Namur?]	
	Elizabeth Mercereau	
Aug. 11.	Mathew Bennet	
	Rachel Burbank	
Aug. 23.	Jacob Bantea, single	
	Elizabeth Wood, single	
Aug. 29.	Nathaniel Frome, single	
	Mary Barton, single	
Sept. 22.	Abraham Mitchel, single	
	Margret Decker, single	
Oct. 14.	Gerrit Post, single	
	Margret Mercereau, single	
Nov. 16.	Aaron Simonson, single·	
	Elizabeth Mercereau, single	
Nov. 21.	James Warren, single	
	Elizabeth Mercereau, single	
Dec. 3.	John Corsen, single	
	Sussanna Enyard, single	
Nov. 29.	Richard Van Pelt, single	
	Elizabeth Donats, single	
Dec. 6.	Niclas Bush, single	
	Cathrine Van Pelt, single	
1802.	Cornelius Egbert, single	
July 28.	Naatje Housman, single	
Sept. 4.	John Burbank, single	
	Ann Egbert, single, dau. of John Egbert, Senr.	
Nov. 9.	Joseph Skerret, single	
	Elizabeth Lockerman, single	
Dec. 27.	Jeremy Baker, single	
	Deborah Hatfield, single	
1803.	John Hatfield, single. Md. by Rev. N. Brown, no min	
Oct. 1.	ister of any other church then on the Island	
	Catharine Bogart, widow, by maiden n. Van Pelt	

By Rev. Nathaniel Brown.

1803. Peter Mitchel, widower
Oct. 16. Sarah Baker, widow
Dec. 5. John Skerret, single
    Catharine Perine, single

1804. William Barton, single, son of Austin Barton & Re-
March 4.   becca, his wife, m. n. Burbank
    Lucy Egbert, dau. of John Egbert & Mary, his wife, by
        m. n. Holmes
March 29. John Journeay, single
    ——, single, from New York
Aug. 4. Charles Symonson, single
    Mary Vanderbilt, eldest dau. of Br. Cornelius & Sr.
        Phebe Vanderbilt
Aug. 18. Abraham Symonson, single
    Phebe Locker
Oct. 6. Peter Cozine, single
    Susanna Butler, single
Nov. 24. Richard Aroe, single
    Elizabeth Stilwell, single
Dec. 23. John Skerret, single
    Francis, by maiden name Rooks, widow

1805. Isaac Barton, single, son of Joseph Barton
Feb. 2. Catharine Colon, dau. of James Colon, Sr., deceased
April 1. Nicolas Vaucleve, single
    Mary Terret
Feb. 12. James Murray, single
    Susan Skerret, dau. of Richard Skerret
April 14. Isaac Burbank, single, son of Abm. Burbank
    Sarah Egbert, eldest dau. of Mary, dec., & Edwd. Eg-
        bert
    Tunis Egbert, single, youngest son of Edward & Mary
        Egbert, dec.
    Sarah Barton, dau. of Joseph Barton
June 9. Jeffries Alston, single
    Sarah Decker
Sept. 22. —— Morgan, single
    Francis Wynand, single
Oct. 2. Abner Johnson, single
    Salome Hedding
Oct. 13. Cornelius Beatty, second son of Edw. & Eleanore
        Beatty
    Ann Jacobson, eldest dau. of John & Hilletje Jacobson
Oct. 20 Richard Taylor, single
or 28. Dinah Swaim, single
Oct. 23. Ozias Alnsley, widower
    Elizabeth Johnson, widow
Nov. 9. Joseph Lake, single
    —— Morgan, single
Dec. 22. Michael Marsac, single
    Rachel Jinnings, single

· 1806.	Daniel Stilwell, single
Jan. 16.	Hanna Skerrett, single
March 2.	John Decker, single
	Mary Van Norman, single
March 2.	William Morgan, single
	Sabina Decker, single
March 22.	Jacob Breasted, single
	Lavina Totten, single
June 22.	William Beatty, single
	Mary Barger, single
July 6.	Richard Bedell, widower
	Hanna Van Pelt, widow, m. n. Pepperill
Aug. 7.	Peter Breasted, single
	Sara Crips, single
Aug. 12.	Abraham Lisk, single
	Jane Wandel, single
Oct. 23.	James Colon, single
	Charity Johnson, single
1807.	Abraham Hooper, single
Feb. 10.	Charity Stilwell, single, dau. of Abraham & Ann Stilwell. Md. in minister's house, in presence of John Marsh, John Dorset & others
April 30.	James Romer, single
	Mary Stilwell, single, dau. of Abm. & Ann Stillwell. Md. in presence of above & some others
June 28.	Daniel Lake, widower, son of Joseph Lake & wife
	Ann Flitcher, single. Md. in ch. in presence of Corn. Perine & Mary Fountain & others
Aug. 9.	Peter Van Pelt, widower. Md. in church in presence of James Skerrit, his sister & others
	Martha Wood, single
Aug. 1.	Cornelius Christopher, single. Md. in church in presence of their neighbors
	Sarah Pew, single
Oct. 11.	John De Fries [De Forest?], single
	Charlotte Vanderbilt, single, dau. of Corn. Vanderbilt & Phebe, his wife. Md. in church in presence of a number of people
Oct. 11.	Jack & Margaret, Blacks, md. by consent of their respective owners
Dec. 19.	William Drury, single, from Scotland
	Susan Stilwell, single, dau. of Joshua Stilwell & Susan Skerrit, his wife. Md. in minister's dwelling in presence of Danl. Guyon & some of Bride's relations
Dec. 22.	Barnet Depew, single
	Sarah Decker, single, dau. of Israel Decker & his wife. Md. in presence of bride's father & others in minister's house
1808.	—— Depew, single, brother of above
Jan. 23.	Elisabeth Decker, single. Md. in church in presence of Moses Wood & others

1808. Daniel Guyon, widower, son of James Guyon & Ann
March 12. Connor, dec.
   Elisabeth Young, widow, maiden n. Clawson. Md. at
   house of Richd. Connor, in his presence & his wife's
   Sophia Connor & her brother Reuben Clawson
March 13. John Fountain, single, son of Anthony Fountain & his
   first wife
   Margaret Holmes, single. Md. in church in presence of
   his Bro. Anthony, his uncle & aunt H. Crusers &
   others
July 7. Joseph Mersereau, single
   Sara Bedell, single, dau. of Richd. Bedell & his first
   wife whose maiden name was Elnesly. Md. in church
   in presence of Joseph Barton & others
July 9. John Decker, single
   Mary Burbank, single, dau. of Abm. Burbank & wife.
   Md. in church in presence of John Burbank & others
July 16. David Praul, single, father dec.
   Catharine Dorsett, single, eldest dau. of John & Martha
   Dorsett. Md. in house of John Dorsett in presence of
   Bride's parents & others
Aug. 20. John Jennings, single
   Catharine Skerret, single, dau. of Richard Skerret. Md.
   in church in presence of some near neighbors
Sept. 11. Abraham Van Pelt, single
   Mary Fountain, single, dau. of Vincent Fountain &
   wife. Md. in church in presence of some neighbors
Dec. 2. Odissa Shay, single
   Appolonia Mott, widow, m. n. Skerret. Md. in ch. in
   in presence of N. Froome, his wife & others
1809. Abraham Decker, single, son of Col. Decker & his wife
April 1. Ann Martino, single, third dau. of Steph. Martino &
   Elen., his wife. Md. in ch. in presence of bride's
   bro. & sister & neighbors
Oct. 22. John Burbank, widower, son of Abm. & his wife
   Ann Decker, single, dau. of Mathias & his wife. Md. in
   presence of Mr. Simonson & some neighbors in
   church
Nov. 5. David Decker, single, son of Mathias & his wife
   Catharine Decker, single, dau. of Mathias. Md. in
   presence of Mr. Taylor, Mr. Wood & others in church
Dec. 10. Abraham Simonson, single
   Ann Prall, single. Md. in church in presence of several
   neighbors from the Neck
Dec. 14. Hosea Alexander Rozeau, single, son of Peter Rozeau,
   Esq., & Mary, his wife
   Mary Morgan, single, dau. of Jesse & Cath. Morgan.
   Md. at Mr. Jesse Morgan's house in West Quarter in
   presence of parents of both parties & other relations
Dec. 23. Stephen Wood, single, son of Stephen Wood & his wife
   Ann Bodine, single, dau. of James Bodine. Md. in
   church in presence of friends and relations

1810. Abraham Merril, single

Jan. 14. Elisabeth Martino, single, dau. of Stephen Martino & Eleon., his wife. Md. in presence of some of their friends here in the laborers' room

Jan. 27. John Simonson, single, son of Simonson, dec.
Catharine Garretson, single, dau. of John, in whose house she was md. in presence of a number of friends & relations

Feb. 22. Lewis R. Marsh, single, lawyer, son of Ralph Marsh & Jennet, his wife
Margaret P. Dubois, single, dau. of Lewis Dubois & Elis., his wife. Md. here in the laborer's house

March 10. William Squires, single, son of —— Squires Taylor [tailor?] & wife
Lena Merril, single. Md. in minister's house in presence of bridegroom's sister & others

March 31. John Decker, single
Elisabeth Van Pelt, single. Md. in presence of neighbors in minister's house

Aug. 19. Robert Marsh, single, from Jersey State, son of Christopher Marsh & Ann, his wife
Rhoda Marsh, single, dau. of John Marsh & wife of Staten Island. Md. in West Quarter at Bride's parents' house, both parents and some relations being present

Sept. 27. Moses Van Pelt, single
Mary Upton, single. Md. in minister's dwelling, Peter Colon & some neighbors present

Sept. 29. Isaac Lewis, widower, son of late Lewis & Billetje, his wife [now Colon]
Rachel Marshall, single, both of Staten Island. Md. in in church in presence of neighbors

Oct. 14. John M'Cullagh, single, from N. Y.
Sarah Gibson, single. Md. in minister's dwelling in presence of bride's father & brother from here & others from N. Y.

Dec. 19. Joseph Sylvy, single
Elizabeth Skerret, single, dau. of Richard Skerret, both of St. Island. Md. here in presence of relations

1811. Anthony Fountain, single, son of Anthony Fountain & 1st wife [née Journey]
Feb. 16. Ann Egbert, single, dau. of James Egbert & Elizabeth, his wife, deceased. Md. in house of Br. James Egbert, he & family being present

Feb. 28. Abraham Winant, single
Hettie Dubois, single. Md. here in church in presence of Br. Bunninger from N. Y., & some neighbors

April 9. Nathaniel Bodine, single, son of John Bodine & Stat. Island
Maria Garretson, single, dau. of John Garretson & 1st wife, Elisabeth, née Conner. Md. at house of bride's father in presence of parents & other relations

1811.   Francis Morse, single, from England
May —.   Mary Pew, single, dau. —— Pew, dec. & wife of St.
          Island.   Md. in presence of some of bride's relations
          in minister's dwelling
June 29. Thomas Skerret, single, son of Richard & his wife of
          St. Island
          Martha Crips, single.   Md. in presence of their brother
          & sister here in church
June 29. Stephen Mott, single, son of John Mott & Appolonia,
          his wife, née Skerret, of St. Island
          Mary Mitchel, single, dau. of Peter Mitchell of St.
          Island & his wife, née Skerret.   Md. at same time as
          above
Sept. 18. Patrick Currant, single, from Ireland
          Jane Hunter, widow.   Md. in presence of some neigh-
          bors from Quarantine ground
Oct. 28. James Egbert, son of James Egbert & Elizabeth, his
          wife, maiden name Martino
          Sarah Merril, dau. of John Merril & wife of Staten
          Island.   Md. in presence of neighbors
Nov. 23. Aron Van Pelt, single, son of Van Pelt & wife of St.
          Island
          Sara Praul, single, dau. of John Praul & his wife, whose
          m. n. was Hilliard.   Md. at church in presence of
          relations
Dec. 23. Abraham Brasted, single, son of John Brasted of Staten
          Island, & wife Willempje Bratt
          Elsea Silvy, single, dau. of Joseph Griggs de Silva &
          Susan, his wife.   Md. in presence of relations
1812.   Cornelis Johnson, single, son of Nath. Johnson, dec., of
Jan. 2. S. Island, & his wife Eleonore, m. n. Vanderbilt
          Elizabeth Corsen, single, of Staten Island.   Md. in
          presence of relations
Jan. 28. Abraham Van Houten, single, from Elizabethtown,
          N. Jersey
          Catharine Grandine, single.   Md. in presence of re-
          lations
Jan. 29. David Barger, single, son of Henry Barger & wife
          Mary, by m. n. Tysen, both decd.
          Sara Cortelyou, single, second dau. of Jacob Cortelyou
          & wife Elisabeth, m. n. Corsen.   Md. in house of
          bride's parents, they & relations present
May 2.   Jacob Beatty, single, son of Edward Beatty & Eleonore,
          his wife, m. n. Cortelyou
          Eliza Cortelyou, single, oldest dau. of Jacob & Elisa-
          beth Cortelyou.   Md. in church in presence of most
          of the neighbors
May 10.   Stephen Martino, single, son of Stephen & his wife, m.
          n. Haughwout
          Charity Christopher, single, dau. of Peter Christopher
          & wife.   Md. in presence of some relations

1812.   John Bird, single, son of Anthony Bird
May 28. Susan Mitchel, single, dau. of Peter Mitchel & his first wife, dec. Md. in presence of some of their neighbors from Quarantine
May 25. John Fountain, single, son of Vincent Fountain & wife
            Jane Housman, single, dau. of Abm. Housman & his wife. Md. here in presence of some relations
Sept. 6. John Decker, single, son of Barnet Decker & his wife
            Ann Jones, single, dau. of J. Jones, dec., & his wife now a widow. Md. in presence of some friends from Quarantine
Sept. 18. Mathias Jones, single, son of Jones, dec., & Catharine, his wife
            Juliana Sylvy, single, dau. of Jas. & Susan Sylvy. Md. as above
Oct. 10. Jacob Housman, single, son of Abm. Housman
            Lena Cruse, single. Md. in presence of some friends from North side of Island
Nov. 1. John Baker, single, son of Andrew & Catharine Baker of Germany
            Elizabeth Prickett, also from Germany. Md. in presence of some friends
Dec. 17. William Winant, single
            Hannah Decker, single, dau. of Jacob Decker from the Manor. In presence of some neighbors.
1813.   John Lake, single
Jan. —. Sarah Prickett, single. Md. here in the house
Feb. 8. John Sebring, single, son of Widow Eliza Sebring of N. Y.
            Eliz. Taylor, single. Both from North Side of Island. Md. in presence of some neighbors
June 20. Peter Post, single, son of Francis & Experience Post
            Catharine Merrill, dau. of John & Frances Merrill
June 27. Isaac Housman, son of Abm. & Jane Housman
            Frances Van Namur, dau. of Aaron & Mary Van Namur
Nov. 24. John Christian Jacobson, single, 21 yrs., eldest son of John V. D. Jacobson, farmer on St. Island, & Hilletje, his wife. m. n. Bedell
            Catharine Connor, eldest dau. of Richard Connor, Esq., & Sophia, his wife, by m. n., Clawson. This marriage was by Rev. John C. Bechler at house of Richard Connor, Esq., in presence of friends & relations

By Rev. J. C. Bechler.

1813.   Jesse Laforge, single
Dec. 8. Catharine Pryor, single
1814.   John Decker, single, about 22 yrs., a waterman
Feb. 26. Ann Egbert, single, youngest dau. of late Edward Egbert. Md. in house of Mr. Isaac Burbank in the Manor in presence of some friends

1814.   James, ⎫ Blacks, belonging to Mr. Garrettson
March 25. Mary, ⎭   belonging to Mr. Edw. Perine. With
consent of their masters

April 30. Sam, ⎫ Blacks, belonging to Mr. Richd. Corson
Mary, ⎭   belonging to Mr. John Garrettson.
With consent of their masters

May   8. Simon, ⎫ Blacks, belonging to Mr. Abm. Fountain
Sally, ⎭   Mr. Ketteltas. With consent of their
masters

Oct.   1. Cesar & Saran, both about 22, belonging to Mr. Richd.
Freeling

Oct. 23. John Bodine, son of Vincent Bodine, farmer
Elisabeth Martino, dau. of Benajah Martino, at whose
house they were md. in presence of number of
friends

Oct. 26. Daniel Decker, single, son of Mathias & Mary Ann
Decker
Mary Lewis, dau. of James & Rebecca Lewis. Md. in
presence of friends

Nov. 12. Henry Seguine, single, weaver, son of John & Rachel
Seguine
Patience Brittain, dau. of John & Rachel Brittain.
Md. at parsonage in presence of friends

Dec. 26. Arthur Burbank, son of Abm. & Lena
Mary Ann Enyard, dau. of Mathias & Sarah

1815.   Matthew Decker, single, son of Matthew & Mary
Jan.   1.   Decker
Ann Colon, single, dau. of —— & Jane Colon

Jan.   3. William Decker, single, son of Barnet & Hannah
Decker
Rebekkah Ammeman, dau. of John & Elizabeth Am-
meman

Feb.   4. Peter Wood, single, son of James Wood
Sarah Ann Cortelyou, dau. of Peter & Amy Cortelyou

Feb. 11. Tunis Egbert, single, carpenter, son of Abm. & Ann
Egbert
Isabella Vanderbilt, single, dau. of John & Elizabeth
Vanderbilt

Feb. 12. Stephen Wood, single, farmer & carpenter, son of late
Joseph Wood & Ann, his wife
Ann Marsh, single, dau. of Richd. & Sarah Marsh

Feb. 20. Jesse Wynant, single, son of George & Elizabeth
Wynant
Catharine Wright, single dau. of Joshua & Catharine
Wright

March 26. Nathaniel H. Martin, single, son of Benjamin & Abi-
gail Martin of N. Jersey
Sarah Dorsett, single, second dau. John & Marth
Dorsett, at whose house they were married

(*To be continued.*)

THE KNICKERBOCKER FAMILY.

By William B. Van Alstyne, M.D.

(Continued from Vol. XXXIX, p. 125, of The Record.)

21. Maritjen[3] Knickerbocker (Laurens,[2] Harmen Jansen[1]), m. 24 May, 1748, at Salisbury, Conn., Ruloff White (Weit), b. about 1724, son of Joshua White[*] and Christina Dutcher. Their marriage is recorded on the church records at Germantown, N. Y., in 1748 (full date is not given), he being "son of Gasguve Weit" and she "daughter of Laurenz Knickerbocker." There is no such name as Gasguve, but it is interesting to note that Gzysyn and Mary Weydt have a child baptised 23 Nov., 1721, at Albany, N. Y., and that Gryphyn Wyet stands as sponsor there in 1722. The settlement of the estate of Jane Dutcher proves that Ruloff White was son of Joshua White and Christina Dutcher.

On the 21 March, 1767, Christiana White requested that letters of administration be granted on the estate of her mother Jane Dutcher, late of Salisbury, Conn., to her son Ruliff White. In the distribution of this estate the heirs of Kathren Knickerbocker have a share, no names being mentioned (Sharon, Conn. Probate Records, book 3, p. 190). Children baptised at Germantown:

    i. Maritgen,[4] bap. 24 July, 1748; spon.: Benjamin and Catharin Knickerbocker.

    ii. Christin, bap. 30 Jan., 1750; spon.: Herman and Catharin Knickerbocker; d. 23 June, 1818; m. Gabriel Dutcher, b. 16 June, 1747; d. 22 Oct., 1820.

22. Catherine[3] Knickerbocker (Laurens,[2] Harmen Jansen[1]), bap. 19 Oct., 1731, at Germantown, N. Y.; m. 17 Sept., 1762, at Claverack, N. Y., Willem Van Alstyne, bap. 10 Dec., 1721, at Albany, N. Y.; d. May 22, 1802, at North East, N. Y.; son of Thomas Van Alstyne and Maria Van Alen. Willem m. (1) about 1744, Christyntje Van Alen, bap. 16, June, 1723, at Kinderhook, N. Y., dau. of Stephanus Van Alen and Marya Muller.

William Van Alstyne probably lived on the farm inherited in 1760 from his father to whom it was granted in 1752 by John Van Rensselaer. It was described as lying between the Kinderhook Creek and the Claverack Creek.

On 1 May, 1772, William Van Alstyne of Claverack, yeoman, leased a house and shop and a fulling mill with mill dam and two acres of land to Thomas Avery of the same place, fuller, for

---

[*] Joshua Weyt (White), m. 24 Nov., 1720, "at the parsonage at Claverack, N. Y.," Christina Dutcher (New York City Lutheran Church Records). He was son of Willem Wit and Judith Meels, bap. 1 May, 1698, at Kingston, N. Y.; she was dau. of Roelof de Duidser and Jannetje Brusy, bap. 8 Aug., 1703, at Albany, N. Y. Roelof de Duidser and Jannetje Brusy were m. 17 Nov., 1700, at Kingston; she being dau. of Christoffel Brusy and Styntje Claes.

the term of seven years. Said Thomas was to have wood for his own fire, and also for "the press" from any part of said William's land.

In Aug., 1791, he bought a farm in Hillsdale, N. Y., of John Collier.

On 19 Oct., 1793, William Van Alstyne deeded as a gift to his son Lawrence a negro boy called Tom. The residence of both father and son was given as Hudson, but in Dec. of 1794, articles of agreement were entered into between Nicholas and Philip Hoffman of the one part, and William Van Alstyne of Columbia County, of the other part, wherein the party of the first part bind themselves to convey on the first day of April, 1795, unto the party of the second part a certain farm in the town of Amenia, in the county of Dutchess, which formerly belonged to Col. Brinton Paine, and was at that time in the occupation of Elijah Bryan, as overseer for the said Nicholas and Philip Hoffman. In the final division of the county into townships this farm came to lie in North East instead of Amenia.

On 12 July, 1799, William sold to his son Lawrence, also of Amenia, N. Y., the farm he had bought of Nicholas and Philip Hoffman.

William Van Alstyne was a captain in Col. Jeremiah Hogeboom's regiment which served during the Revolutionary War. His commission, dated 4 April, 1770, and signed by Cadwallader Colden, Governor of the Province of New York, is in the possession of the Holland Society.

He was buried in a small burying ground on the farm bought from the Hoffmans. His wife was also buried there but the tombstone has long ago disappeared. She survived her husband, for in her son Lawrence's will, made 2 May, 1806, he provides that his mother, Catharine Van Alstyne, shall have her support out of his estate, and at his house as long as she lives (*Lambert Janse Van Alstyne and Some of His Descendants*, by Lawrence Van Alstyne of Sharon, Conn.).

Children of William Van Alstyne and Catherine Knickerbocker:

    i. Thomas,[4] b. 18 Feb., 1765; bap. 24 Feb., at Claverack, N. Y.; spon.: Lambart Van Aalsteyn and Alettika Oosterhout, his wife; d. 10 Sept., 1838; m. Mabel Butler, b. 3 Jan., 1767; d. 13 Feb., 1831; dau. of Ezekiel Butler and Mabel Jones. Thomas was a clothier and moved from Hudson to Amenia, N. Y., soon after May, 1795.

    ii. Lawrence, b. 22 June, 1767; bap. 12 July at Linlithgo, N. Y.; spon.: Benjamin Knickerbocker and Aletteke Halenbeeck, his wife; d. 7 May, 1806, at North East, N. Y.; m. about 1788, Mary Murdack, b. 21 Aug., 1768; d. 13 Dec., 1836. He moved from Hudson to Amenia, N. Y., soon after May, 1795.

    iii. William, b. 31 Jan., 1770; bap. 12 Aug. at Claverack; spon.: William Van Ness, Jr., and Marytje Van

Alsteyn; d. 28 Jan., 1811; m. 10 Dec., 1797, Maria
Vosburgh, b. 1 June, 1776; bap. 9 June at Kinderhook; d. 13 March, 1820; daughter of Pieter Vosburgh and Fitje Van Hoesen. William was a clothier
and lived at Claverack, N. Y.

    iv. Mary, b. 6 Jan., 1773; bap. 10 Jan. at Claverack; spon.:
    Richard Ysselstean and Maria Van Alsteen, his wife;
    d. 15 April, 1863; m. 22 Feb., 1795, at Claverack,
    John Leggett, b. 23 Dec., 1770; d. 26 Jan., 1847; son
    of James Leggett and Catherine Reyn. They re-
    sided at Claverack.

23. LYSBETH³ LANSING (Jannetje,² Harmen Jansen¹), bap. 5
Aug., 1705, at Albany; m. 1722, Egbert Bratt, bap. 26 July, 1702,
at Albany; son of Antoni Bratt* and Willempje Teunis. Children baptised at Albany:

    i. Willempie,⁴ bap. 5 May, 1723; spon.: Barent and Wil-
    lempie Bratt; d. y.
    ii. Hendrick, bap. 4 Oct., 1724; spon.: Anth. and Jann.
    Bogardus; d. y.

---

* Antoni Bratt m. 9 Dec., 1685, at Albany, N. Y., Willempje Teunis, b.
1662; dau. of Teunis Teunisen Metselaar and Egbertje Egberts. He was son
of Barent Albertsen Bratt.
    Barent Albertsen Bratt m. Susanna Dircks, called Janse for her stepfather
Jan Jansen Bratt "de Noorman," dau. of Dirck Dircksen Mayer and Maritie
Post, the latter b. in Brazil. Maritie Post m. (3) 26 Nov., 1699, at Albany,
Eduwart Carbert, b. in England. Barent Albertsen was son of Albert Andriessen Bratt "de Noorman" and Annetje Barents Van Rotmers, natives of
Frederickstad, Norway, who left Amsterdam, Holland, 25 Sept., 1636, in the ship
The Arms of Rensslaerwyck, which arrived in Albany 7 April, 1637. They
settled on a stream just south of Albany which in consequence became known
as Norman's Kill, and here he laid out a farm and built a mill (N. Y. GEN.
AND BIOG. RECORD, Vol. XXXV, p. 45). Annetje Barents Van Rotmers d. in
1662, and on 10 July, 1663, her children gave to Storm Albertsen Van Der Zee,
her eldest son, power of attorney to collect property inherited from Pieter
Jacobsen van Rendsburgh (Rynsburgh), husband of Geesie Barents, their
maternal grandmother (Notary Papers at Albany, p. 347). This right enabled
Storm to sell a share in a house and lot at New Amsterdam inherited from his
mother and occupied by Burgomaster Allard Anthony. Geesie Barents was in
this country as early as 1642, for in June of that year Pieter Jacobsen, b. in
Rendsburgh (probably Rendsburg, a town of Prussia, in Holstein, on the
Eider), and "Gysje Pieters" (Pieters meaning wife of Pieter), both of Fort
Orange, made a joint will (Berthold Fernow's *Calendar of Wills*, No. 956) in
which real and personal property was left to her dau. "Annitje Alberts"
(Alberts meaning wife of Albert). In 1667 Geesie Barents was at Kingston,
N. Y., standing as one of the sponsors for Cornelia, dau. of Roelof Swartwout
and Eefgen Albertse Bratt.
    Albert Andriessen Bratt m. (2) Geertruy Pieterse Coeymans, widow of Ab-
raham Pietersen Vosburgh, but was afterwards legally separated from her.
Through her first husband she became ancestress of the Vosburg Family.
There were no children by her second husband. On 31 July, 1695, Geertruy
Vosburgh received from the heirs of Pieter Van Alen a grant of land on the
Kinderhook Creek, consisting of one-fourth that property called the Groot
Stuk and occupied by her for her eldest son Pieter, the grantee. This deed
was confirmed in April, 1713, by a quit claim deed. Albert Andriessen Bratt
d. 7 June, 1686.

    iii. Hendricus, bap. 7 Nov. 1725; spon.: Ant. and Jann.
        Bogardus; d. y.

    iv. Anthony, bap. 29 Jan., 1727; spon.: Barent and Wil-
        lempie Bratt; m. about 1751, Maria Van Alsteyn,
        bap. 27 July, 1729, at Albany; dau. of Jacob Van
        Alsteyn and Pietertje Van Iverin.

    v. Jannetie, bap. 7 Sept., 1729; spon.: Anth. and Jannetie
        Bogardus.

    vi. Hendricus, bap. 29 Dec., 1732; spon.: Ant. and Reb.
        Brat.

    vii. Willempie, bap. 31 Oct., 1736; spon.: B. and W. Bratt;
        m. 1764, Jacob Lansing.

    viii. Johannes, bap. 19 Oct., 1740; spon.: Evert and Cornelia
        Bogardus; d. y.

    ix. Johannes, bap. 4 Jan., 174/5; spon.: Harmen and
        Anatje Bogardus.

24. WILLIAM[3] KNICKERBOCKER (Cornelis,[2] Harmen Jansen[1]), m.
Abigail ——. Children b. at Sharon, Conn.:

    i. Abigail,[4] b. 28 Feb., 1748/9.
    ii. Hannah, b. 4 June, 1750.

25. CATHERINE[3] VOSBURGH (Cornelia,[2] Harmen Jansen[1]), m. 30
Dec., 1747, at Rhinebeck Flatts, N. Y., Jacob Heermance, bap.
23 Sept., 1716, at Kingston, N. Y.; son of Andries Heermance[*]
and Neeltje Van Wagenen. On 5 Oct., 1766, they were received
into the membership of the Dutch Reformed Church at Red
Hook, N. Y., from the church on the Flatts. Jacob Heermance
of Red Hook, made his will 9 March, 1784, proved 26 Sept., 1785,
and recorded in New York. In it he mentions eldest son Andreas
and sons John, Jacob and Martin, and daus. Cornelia, wife of
David Van Ness, Neeltje, wife of Peter Cantine, Annetje, wife of
Isaac Stoutenburgh, Jr., and Dorothea. Jacob Heermance lived
in and probably built the stone house at one time occupied by
Lewis Beckwith, west of Henry Benner's on the road from Henry
Cotting's to the river, near the post road (Smith's *History of
Rhinebeck, N. Y.*, p. 84). Children:

    i. Andres (Andrew), bap. 26 Dec., 1748, at Germantown,
        N. Y.; spon.: Andres and Nelgen Hermans.

    ii. Cornelia, b. 29 Dec., 1751; bap. at Rhinebeck Flatts;
        spon.: Jacob Vasburg and Cornelia Knickerbocker;
        m. David Van Ness. They lived at Red Hook in the
        house which became Stephen Holmes' Inn, later the
        home of Wilhelmus Benner (above authority, p. 84).

    iii. John.

    iv. Eleanor (Neeltje), m. Peter Cantine. From 1785 to
        1791 they lived in Upper Red Hook; later he kept a
        store at Barrytown Landing, and in 1798 followed
        the same pursuit at Hoffman's or Red Hook Land-
        ing (above authority).

    v. Jacob, b. 28 Feb., 1760; bap. at Rhinebeck Flatts;
        spon.: Folkert Witbeck and Dorothe Vosbug. Lived
        after 1792 where Peter Cantine lived.

vi. Anna, m. Isaac Stoutenburgh, Jr.   Lived at Red Hook.
vii. Martin, bap. 19 May, 1766, at Rhinebeck Flatts; spon.:
      Pieter Vosburg and Dorothea Knickerbocker; m. a
      dau. of Dr. Hans Kiersted.   Martin came into pos-
      session of his father-in-law's property at Red Hook
      where in 1793 he built the present brick mansion
      (above authority).
viii. Dorothea, bap. 11 Feb., 1770, Rhinebeck-Red Hook,
      N. Y., church records; spon.: Pieter and Cornelia
      Witbeck; m. Henry De Witt.   Lived at Red Hook.

26. DOROTHEA[3] VOSBURGH (Cornelia,[2] Harmen Jansen[1]), m.
Volkert Witbeck, probably bap. 10 Aug., 1718, at Albany, N. Y.; son
of Jan Witbeck and Agnietje Bronk, who were m. there 7 April,
1705.   On 5 Oct., 1766, they joined the Dutch Reformed Church
at Red Hook, N. Y., by letter from the church on the Flatts.
Children:

i. Joan (Jan),[4] bap. 20 April, 1747, at Germantown, N. Y.;
    spon.: Joan and Cornelia Vosberger.
ii. Cornelia, bap. 10 Dec., 1749, at Germantown; spon.:
     Johan and Agneten Witbeeck.
iii. Hermanus, b. 13 May, 1751; bap. at Rhinebeck Flatts;
      spon.: Jacob Heermanse and Catrina Vosburg.
iv. Pieter, b. 28 July, 1752; bap. as above; spon.: Andries
     Witbeek and Lena Van Vechten.

27. MARTEN[3] VOSBURG (Cornelia,[2] Harmen Jansen[1]), bap. 29
July, 1738, at Linlithgo, N. Y.; m. Cornelia Gilbert, New York
State marriage license, dated 19, Nov. 1766.   The following
children except Jan appear on the Rhinebeck-Red Hook church
records:

i. Jan,[4] bap. 20 Dec., 1767, at Germantown, N. Y.; spon.:
    Volkert Witbeck and Dorothea Vosburgh, his wife.
ii. William, bap. 21 May, 1769; spon.: Jacob Vosburgh
     and Maria Gilbert.
iii. Marten, bap. 13 Jan., 1771; spon.: Jacob Heermansen
      and Catharina Vosburg.
iv. Hannah, bap. 23 March, 1777; spon.: William and
     Althea Gilbert.
v. Jacob, b. 17 June, 1782; spon.: Johan and Aletta
    Sickles.

28. ELISABETH[3] KNICKERBOCKER (Evert,[2] Harmen Jansen[1]), bap.
21 Aug., 1726, at Linlithgo, N. Y.; m. 1 May, 1747, at Rhinebeck,
N. Y., Petrus Hermance, bap. 6 Sept., 1724, at Kingston, N. Y.;
son of Andries Hermance and Neeltje Van Wagenen.   Petrus
probably m. (2) 11 Nov., 1752, at Rhinebeck, Maria Van Wagenen,

---

* Andries Heermance, bap. 12 April, 1685, at Kingston; m. Neeltje Van
Wagenen, b, 17 April, 1692; daughter of Gerrit Aartsen and Clara Pels.
Andries lived at Rhinebeck, N. Y., and was son of Jan Focken Heermans from
Ruynen, Province of Drenthe, Holland, who m. 23 Aug., 1676, at New York
City, Engeltie Jans Bresteed, bap. there 29 Nov., 1654; dau. of Jan Jansen
Breestede and Marritje Andries.

bap. 20 Feb., 1732, at Kingston; dau. of Simon Van Wagenen and Maria Schepmoes.   Child bap. at Rhinebeck Flatts:

      i. Evert,* bap. 12 Oct., 1747; spon.: Evert Knicker-
      bocker and Geertruy Vosburg, his wife.

29.   CORNELIA* KNICKERBOCKER (Evert,* Harmen Jansen¹), bap. 10 June, 1733, at Linlithgo, N. Y.; m. 27 Feb., 1755, at Rhinebeck Flatts, N. Y., Isaac Vosburg, bap. 5 Sept., 1731, at Kinderhook, N. Y.; son of Pieter Vosburg and Dirckie Van Aalsteyn.   Children:

      i. Pieter,* b. 1 April, 1756; bap. at Rhinebeck Flatts;
      spon.: Pieter and Dorothea Vosburg.
      ii. Geertrui, b. 12 Oct., 1758; bap. at the Flatts; spon.:
      Evert Knickerbocker and Dorothea Vosburg.
      iii. Dirk, bap. 25 Jan., 1762, at Germantown, N. Y.; spon.:
      Marten Vosburg and Catryntje Knickerbacker.
      iv. Evert, bap. 5 May, 1765, at Linlithgo; spon.: Evert
      Vosburgh and Cornelia Witbeck.
      v. Jacob, bap. 10 June, 1768, at Kinderhook; spon·: Jacob
      and Dirkje Vosburgh.

30.   ABRAHAM* KNICKERBOCKER (Pieter,* Harmen Jansen¹), m. 28 Nov., 1754, at New York City, Geertruid (Gerretje?) Van Deursen, bap. 21 March, 1733, at New York City; dau. of Johannes Van Deusen and Geertje Minthorne.

Abraham Knickabaker, labourer, was registered as a Freeman of New York City, 6 May, 1760 (*Burghers and Freemen of New York*, New York Historical Society Collections, 1885, p. 194).

Children of Abraham Knickerbocker and Geertruid Van Deursen:

      i. Elizabet,* bap. 2 July, 1755, in Dutch Reformed Church,
      New York City; spon.: Harmen Knickerbocker and
      Elizabeth Van Deursen, young dau.
      ii. Abraham, bap. 14 March, 1759, as above; spon.: Har-
      manus Knickerbocker and Heyltje Ryt, widow of J.
      Ryt.   Abraham Knickerbacker, cartman, at a Com-
      mon Council held 30 March, 1784, was sworn and
      admitted as a Freeman of New York City and
      ordered to be registered (*Burghers and Freeman of
      New York*, p. 243).
      iii. John, b. 17 Sept., 1768, "about 2 o'clock Saturday;"
      bap. in First Moravian Church, New York City.

31.   HARMEN JANSEN* KNICKERBOCKER (Pieter,* Harmen Jansen¹), bap. 13 Jan., 1734, at Kingston, N. Y.; "d. 1802;" m. Susanna Basson.   Children:

      i. Ebert,* bap. 4 Nov., 1776, in St. Peter's Lutheran
      Church, Rhinebeck, N. Y.; spon.: Peter and Elisa-
      beth Hermanse; m. Sally Reit (Reick).
      ii. Gertge, bap. 28 Oct., 1778, as above; spon.: Wilhelmg
      and Gertraut Becker; m. Levi Pawling, b. 29 Jan.,
      1771; d. 12 Feb., 1858, at Staatsburgh, N. Y.; son of
      John Pawling and Marietje Van Deusen, his second
      wife.   Levi Pawling m. (2) 18 May, 1816, Hannah
      Griffing, dau. of Stephen Griffing and Elizabeth Uhl.
      He lived at Staatsburgh.

iii. Nelge, bap. 13 April, 1780, as above; spon.: Andreas and Maria Hermanse.

iv. Pieter, bap. 19 May, 1782, at Dutch Reformed Church at Rhinebeck; spon.: Georg Scherp and Rebecca Tedtor, his wife; "d. 1848;" m. 14 July, 1806, in the above Lutheran Church, Jane Montross.

v. Catharina, bap. 22 Feb., 1784, at Rhinebeck; spon.: Cornelis Elbendorf and Jacomyntjen Heermans, his wife.

vi. Magdalena, bap. 18 April, 1786, in the Lutheran Church at Rhinebeck; spon.: Johannes and Magdalena Statsch.

vii. Maria, b. 16 March, 1788; bap. in Dutch Reformed Church at Rhinebeck; spon.: Martynus and Maria Burger.

viii. Elizabeth, b. 5 March, 1792; bap. as above; spon.: Johannes Bergh and Elizabeth West.

32. JOHANNES SYBR.[4] QUACKENBUSH (Elizabeth,[3] Johannes Harmensen,[2] Harmen Jansen[1]), bap. in May, 1729, at Albany, N. Y.; m. there 9 Dec., 1758, Jannetje Viele, dau. of Teunis Viele and Maria Fonda. Of their children Maria, Peter and Adriaan were bap. at Schaghticoke, the others at Albany:

i. Elizabeth,[5] bap. 1 July, 1759; spon.: Seybrant Quackenhos and Neeltje Deforeest.

ii. Teunis, bap. 25 Oct., 1761; spon.: Teunis and Catharina Vile.

iii. Maria, b. 31 Oct., 1763; spon.: Lowis Viele and Annatje Quackenbush (mother's name Hannah Viele).

iv. Rebecca, b. 20 Nov., 1767; spon.: Abraham and Rebecca Slingerland.

v. Annetje, b. 1 Nov., 1 1769; spon.: Adriaan and Folkje Qwakkenbusch.

vi. Sybrand, b. 17 Nov., 1771; spon.: Wouter and Elisab. Knickerbakker.

vii. Peter, b. 30 June, 1774; spon.: John Y. and Geesje Viele.

viii. Adriaan, b. 1 March, 1778; spon.: Johs. Knickerbacker and Elisabeth Winne.

33. HANNAH[4] QUACKENBUSH (Elizabeth,[3] Johannes Harmansen,[2] Harmen Jansen[1]), bap. 5 Jan., 1735, at Albany, N. Y.; m. 1752, Lodovicus (Louis) T. Viele, bap. 30 Aug., 1725, at Albany, son of Teunis Viele* and Maria Fonda. Of their children Sybrand, Johannis and Catharina were bap. at Schaghticoke, N. Y., the others at Albany:

i. Maria,[5] bap. 24 Feb., 1754; spon.: Teuwnis and Maria Viele.

ii. Elizabeth, bap. 30 Jan., 1757; spon.: Seybrant and Elisabeth Quackenbos.

iii. Teunis, bap. 5 Aug., 1759; spon.: John and Catarina Viele; d. y.

iv. Teunis, b. 26 Jan., 1762; spon.: Teunis and Catharina Vile.

13

    v. Sybrand, b. 1 Sept., 1764; spon: John S. Quackenbos
and Jannitje Viele.

    vi. Stephanus, b. 3 Feb., 1767; spon.: John Viele and
Geesje Slingerland.

    vii. Johannis, b. 3 April, 1771; spon.: Harmen Quackenbos
and Judith Mabe.

    viii. Catharina, b. 31 Jan., 1774; spon.: Lewis P. and Catharina Viele.

34. HARMEN[4] QUACKENBUSH (Elizabeth,[3] Johannes Harmensen,[2] Harmen Jansen[1]), bap. 6 Dec., 1738, at Albany; m. there about 1760, Judith Morrell, bap. there 27 May, 1739; dau. of Daniel Morrell and Alida Dox. Of their children, Daniel, Elisabeth, Sybrand and Jacob were bap. at Albany, the others at Schaghticoke, N. Y.:

    i. Elisabeth,[5] bap. 20 Sept., 1761; spon.: Adriaan and
Elisabeth Kwakkenbush.

    ii. Sybrand, b. at Schaghticoke; bap. 29 Sept., 1763;
spon.: Sybrand Kwakkenbush and Anatje Vile.

    iii. Daniel, b. 27 Aug., 1765; spon.: Pieter and Elizabeth
Dox.

    iv. Johannis, b. 18 May, 1766; spon.: Johs. Quackenbush
and Jannitje Viele.

    v. Neeltje, b. 17 Aug., 1769; spon.: Louis and Maria Viele.

    vi. Jacob, b. 15 Nov., 1772; spon.: Samuel Marl and
Elisab. Knikkerbacker.

    vii. Catharina, b. 15 Jan., 1774; spon.: Pietertje Yates and
Dirk T. Van Veghten.

35. ELIZABETH[4] QU·KENBUSH (Elizabeth,[3] Johannes Harmensen,[2] Harmen Jansen), bap. 28 Feb., 1742, at Albany, N. Y.; m. 28 May, 1762 (both Albany and Schaghticoke records), Johannis I. Fort. Children bap. at Schaghticoke, N. Y., except Isaac and Petrus, who were bap. at Albany:

    i. Jacomyntje,[5] b. 7 Dec., 1766; spon.: Peter Beneway
and Marytje Fort.

    ii. Isaac, b. 25 June, 1768; spon.: Harmen and Lena
Ganzevoort.

    iii. Sybrand, b. 16 June, 1770; spon.: Hannis Quackenbos
and Judikje Morrel.

    iv. Catharina, b. 7 July, 1772; spon.: Louis and Maria
Viele.

    v. Johannis, b. 3 April, 1775; spon.: Johannes Quackenbos and Jannitje Viele.

    vi. Petrus, b. 4 Sept., 1777; spon.: Petrus and Marytje
Benneway.

    vii. Harmen, b. 20 July, 1779; spon.: Abraham Viele and
Annatie Knickerbacker.

(To be continued.)

---

  * Teunis Viele, bap. 28 Sept., 1702, at Schenectady, N. Y.; m. 12 Oct., 1724, at Albany, Maria Fonda, bap. there 7 Jan., 1700; dau. of Johannes Fonda and Maritje Loockermans, m. there 5 Dec., 1694. Teunis was son of Louis Viele and Maria Freer.

NEW BRUNSWICK LOYALISTS OF THE WAR OF THE AMERICAN REVOLUTION.

Communicated by D. R. Jack, Historian of the New Brunswick Loyalists' Society; Cor-Sect. of the New Brunswick Historical Society; Author Centennial Prize Essay, History of St. John; Editor Acadiensis etc.

Note.—The reference letter in the second column in the list of New Brunswick Loyalists indicates, it will be remembered, the source of the information from which the list has been compiled. The readers of the Record are requested to note the following additions to the schedule which appeared in the January, 1904, issue.

"P" Roll of Loyalists, etc., settled in Belle Vue in Beavor Harbor, Charlotte County, 10th July, 1784.

"Q" Muster of passengers on transport *Cyrus* on 21st Aug., 1783, upon her trip from New York to the Saint John River. On the 6th of Sept., she was at sea, and on the 14th of Sept., she was in the Saint John River. Copy of return furnished by H. A. Powell, Esq., of Sackville, N. B. (See *Collections of New Brunswick Historical Society*, No. 5, 1904, pp. 277-8-9.)

"R" New Brunswick Loyalists, 1709 in number, whose names appear in the Passamaquoddy section of Major General Campbell's Muster of Loyalists and Disbanded Soldiers, from an original copy initialed by Col. Edward Winslow—of the expulsion of the Acadians fame—compiled 1784 (see *Canadian History Readings* by G. U. Hay, said original copy being now the property of Ward C. Hazen of Saint John, N. B.). The names appearing in this compilation have been copied from the said original by the compiler of this record.

"S" Loyalists who settled on Kemble Manor, Saint John River, N. B., mentioned by Jonas Howe in his article upon that subject, (see *New Brunswick Magazine*, Vol. I, p. 157.

— This sign indicates that the individual was *less* than 10 years of age in 1783.
+ This sign indicates that the individual was a child but *more* than ten years of age in 1783.

(Continued from Vol. XXXIX., p. 16, of the Record.)

Name	Ref. Letter	From	Settled	Note
Pratt, Jacob	P		Beaver Harbour	
Pray, John	A		St. John	
Preble, Avis	C		St. Andrews	{ Possibly a descendant of Gen. Jedediah Preble, commander of Fort at Penobscot until 1764, whose son John was an early trader at Charlotte Co., N. B.
Prentice, David	A		St. John	
Preston, Thomas	B		"	
Pretty, Jasper	A		"	
Price, Rev. Walter	K		York Co.	Mason, Freeman St. J., 1790
Price, Peter	K N P	Pennsylvania	Penfield, Char. Co.	Episcopal minister
Price, Anne	P		Beaver Harbor	
Price, John	P+		"	} Probably family of Peter Price
Price, Mary	P—		"	
Price, Ruth	P—		"	

Name	Ref. Letter	From	Settled	Note
Price, George Webb	S		Kemble Manor	
Price, ——, widow	S		"	
Price, Allan	S		"	
Prince, John	K		Hampton	d. 1825
Priest, John	C I		St. Andrews	
Proctor, Joshua	A		St. John	
Proctor, Nathaniel	A		St. John	
Proser, Benjamin	B		Carleton	Freeman, St. J., 1785. Yeoman
Proud, James	A		St. John	
Prout, Thomas	A B		"	
Provost, Augustus	A		"	
Pryer, Edward	B		Carleton	
Puddington, William	A		St. John	
Purcell, William	A		"	
Purdy, Gilbert	A Q K	Westchester, N. Y.		Fisherman, Freeman, St. J., 1795
Purdy, David	A K	"		Capt. King's Am. Regt.
Purdy, Thomas (Perdy?)	Q			Probably husband & wife, & parents of Jonathan & Obadiah Purdy
Purdy, Eli zbeth "	Q +			
Purdy, Jonathan "	Q -		St. John	Fisherman, Freeman, St. J., 1795
Purdy, Obah "	Q		"	Cordwainer, Freeman, St. J., 1798
Purdy, Joseph, Jr	K		"	Drowned River St. J., 1844
Rhrdy, Samuel	K		"	d. St. J., 1841, Blockmaker, Freeman. St. J., 1793
Purdy, Henry	K		"	d. 1827, æt. 83
Putnam, Daniel	A	Worcester, Mass.	Fort Lawrence	2d son of Judge P., d. 1798, æt. 36
Putnam, Ebenezer		"	St. John	Judge Supreme Court, N. B., one of the giants of the Am. Col. Bar
Putnam, James	B K L	"	"	Son of above
Putnam, James, Jr	B		"	
Q				
Quantum, John	H		Charlotte County	Member Penobscot Association
Quigg, John	A		St. John	
Quill, Thomas	A		"	
Quinton, Hugh	A B	New Hampshire		Served in Old French War. Was in various encounters in Rev. War. Born Cheshire, N. H., 1741.

Name	Ref. Letter	From	Settled	Note
R				
Racey, Philip	B		Carleton	Member Cape Ann Association
Ramsay, Esther	I		Charlotte County	
Ramsay, William	R		Fredericton	
Rainsford, Andrew	K			Receiver-General of N. B.
Rankin, John	K N P	Pennsylvania	Pennfield	Members of a colony of Quakers who settled at Pennfield, named after Wm. Penn. Name of settlement originally Penn's Field
Rankin, Abram or Abraham	P K N	"	"	
Rankin, Roads	P		Beaver Harbour	
Rankin, Angus	G R		Schoodic Falls	
Rankin, Abigail	P		Beaver Harbour	Probably wife and children of Roads Rankin, above
Rankin, Anne	P+		"	
Rankin, Rebecca	P-		"	
Ranger, Tartolus	P		St. John	
Randolph, David	A		Beaver Harbor	d. 1828
Ranter, William	P		Carleton	
Rawrison, D. B.	B		St. Andrews	
Ray, Daniel	C		Kingston	
Raymond, Mary, widow	M	Norwalk, Conn.	Hampton	
Raymond, Stent	A	Darien, Conn.	Kingston, Kings Co.	Sisters to Silas R. above
Raymond, Samuel Rice	A	"	"	
Raymond, Mary		Norwalk, Conn.	Kingston	m. John Marvin 9 March, 1787
Raymond, Mercy		"	"	m. Eliz. C. Perkins 27 March, 1799
Raymond, Grace		"		m. James O. Betts 5 April, 1802
Raymond, Samuel	K M	"	Kingston, Kings Co.	d. 5 June, 1824, aet. 76
Raymond, Hannah		"		
Raymond, Silas	K	Darien, Conn.	Petersville	
Raymond, Thomas		"	St. John	
Readhead, William (Redhead)	C H		Charlotte County	d. 1835, aet. 76, Innkeeper & Freeman, St. J., 1785.
Redding, William	B		Carleton	
Redding, Henry	B			

Name	Ref. Letter	From	Settled	Note
Reece, Alexander	A		Cumberland Bay	Was lineal descendant of Welsh King Rees Ap Madoc
Reed or Reid, Alexander	A		St. John	Well-known merchant, d. 11 Nov., 1811
Reed, James	A K L		"	d. 1820, aet. 63. Mariner. Freeman, St. J., 1785. At his death King's Pilot
Reed, William	A		"	
Reed or Reid, Robert	A		Charlotte County	Gentleman, Freeman, St. J., 1790
Reed, John	I		"	
Reed, Abraham	I		"	Members Cape Ann Assoc'n
Reed, Stephen	I			
Reed, Robert	I K	New York	St. John	Mason, Freeman, St. J., 1785
Reed, William	I	New York	Charlotte County	Member Cape Ann Assoc'n
Reed, Leonard	K		St. John River	Lieut. King's Am. Regt.
Reeves, John	Q K		Sussex Vale, Kings Co.	Magistrate, d. at S., 1815, aet. 74
Regan, Jeremiah	A K	Pennsylvania	Pennfield	
Register, Daniel	K P		Beaver Harbor	
Rekeman, Albert	P		"	
Remington, Peter	P			
Remington or Rementon, Jonathan				
Remington, Gershom	C N	Pennsylvania	Penfield	d. 1835, aet. 80
Renshaw, Thomas	K N	"	"	
Renshaw, James	A A K		St. John	
Repley, James	K		"	
Reve, Anthony	A B		Carleton	Probably all members of one family
Reyᵗlds, Jesse	A		St. John	
Reynolds, Wm.	N			
Reynolds, Joshua	O			
Reynolds, Elizabeth	O			
Reynolds, Pine	O			
Richards, Jonathan	B		Carleton	
Richardson, John	K		St. John	
Richards, Charles	S		Kemble Manor	Ensign N. Y. Vols., Commission dated April 20, 1783

Name	Ref. Letter	From	Settled	Note
Rider, Stephen	A		St. John	⎫ Probably members of one
Rigby, John	C H		St. Andrews	⎬ family
Rikeman or Rickeman or Rekeman, Anthony				⎭
Rikeman, Eliz.	P		Beaver Harbor	
Rikeman, Eliz., 2nd	P		"	
Rinby, Maurice	P		"	
Risteen, Joseph	H		Charlotte Co.	Member the Penobscot Association
Ritchie, James	K		Carleton Co.	d. 1839, aet. 90
Riter, Hyronimus	A		St. John	
Ritter, Sperons (Riter Hyronimus?)	C		St. Andrews	
Robb, John	H		St. John	
Roax, Timothy	A		St. Andrews	⎫ Several of this name mentioned in
Roax, John	C H		"	⎬ records of All Saints Church St. Andrews. Name there spelled
Roax, Timothy, Jr.	H		"	⎭ Roix
Roake, Martha	P		Beaver Harbor	
Robinson, John	A L	Born Co. Derry, Ire.	St. John	
Robinson, Patrick	B		Newcastle, Grand Lake	Mariner, Freeman, St. J., 1785
Robie, Thomas	B		Carleton	
Robinson, Lawrance	C			
Robinson, Alexander	C H		St. Andrews	One of the Penobscot Association
Roberts, Stephen	I		"	Member Cape Ann Association
Robie, James			Charlotte County	⎧ d. 1833, aet. 77. Served in army of
Roberts, Zachariah	K	New York	Queens Co.	⎨ Sir Wm. Howe
Robins, Robert	P		Beaver Harbor	
Robertson, Christopher	A		St. John	
Robertson, Daniel	A		"	
Robertson, Duncan			Tabusintac	
Robinson, Beverly, the Younger	K	New York	St. John	A member famous "Black Watch" ⎧ Lt.-Col. Loy. Am. Regt. Grnd. Columbia Col., N. Y., m. Nancy, dr. of Rev. Henry Barclay, Rector of Trinity Ch., N. Y.

NAME	REF. LETTER	FROM	SETTLED	NOTE
Robinson, John	K L	New York	St. John	Brother to the last mentioned. Lieut. Loy. Am. Regt. Both he and his sons were prominent in early New Brunswick history
Robinson, John, of St. Andrews	K C D		St. Andrews	d. at St. A., 1807, aet. 53. Lydia, his widow d. at same place in 1820, aet. 55
Roden, Wm., Sr.	K		Portland	d. at Portland, N. B., 1839, aet. 91
Roden, Wm., Jr.	B		Carleton	
Rogers, Fitch	B	New Hampshire	St. John	Mariner, Freeman, St. J., 1795. Returned to U. S. Member of first City Council St. J., 1785. Freeman, St. J., 1785
Rogers,	A K	"	"	
Rogers, Patrick	A K	"	Sussex Vale	Esquire, Freeman, St. J., 1790 d. at S., 1821
Rogers, James	A K		St. John	
Rogers, Thomas	A B K		"	
Rogers, Ge.	A K		"	Yeoman, Freeman, St. J., 1785
Rogers, Richard	A		"	Yeoman, Freeman, St. J., 1785
Rogers, Henry	A			
Rogers, Elizabeth	A			
Rogers, Anthony	A			
Rogers, Anne	A			
Romsay, Edrd (Ramsay)	P		Beaver Harbor Charlotte Co.	Member Penobscot Association
Roe, W. L.	H			
Roome, Jacob	A B		St. John	Possibly sons of John Le Chevaller Roome of N. Y., a lawyer, who was a petitioner for grant of lands in Nova Scotia, July, 1783, and who sailed for Eng. same year. See Sabine, p. 241. Henry Roome, painter, and Jacob, saddler, were made Freemen, St. J., 1785
Roe, W. H.	A			
Rooke, Amos	A		Beaver Harbor	Probably children of Amos Rooke
Rooke, Fanny	P		"	
Rooke, George	P—		"	
Ross, John	P—		St. John	
Ross, Daniel	A		"	
Ross,	A			

(To be continued.)

GENEALOGICAL NOTES RELATING TO THE ENGLISH ANCESTORS OF THE YOUNGS OF SOUTHOLD, N. Y.

COMMUNICATED BY LUCY DUBOIS AKERLY.

One of the interesting characters of our Colonial history was the Rev. John Younges (Yonges), principal founder of Southold, the earliest town on the east end of Long Island.* He m. (1) Joan Herrington; m. (2) Mary Warren. The baptisms, marriages and burials given below and relating to the families of Herrington and Warren, have never before been printed, and are from a transcript of the Parish Register of Southwold, England, and are published through the courtesy of Rev. Epher Whitaker of Southold, N. Y., and Rev. Claude Hope Sutton, Vicar of Southwold, England.

John Yonge of St. Margaretts', Suffolk, ae. 35 yrs.,† and Joan, his wife, ae. 34, with 6 children, John: Tbo: Anne: Rachell: Mary & Josueph, were examined by the Commissioners, 11 or 12 May, 1637, being desirous to pass to Salem in New England to inhabit, & being forbyden passage, went not from Yramouth.‡

Nevertheless on 14:6:1637, Mr. John Younges was received as an inhabitant of Salem, Mass. How he became in 1640 the first minister at Southold, Long Island, and the central figure there, is too well known to be repeated here.§

Just what was intended by St. Margaret's, Suffolk, is hard to determine, probably the edifice at Reydon, and the mother church of St. Edmond's, Southwold, two miles distant; although there were apparently other St. Margaret's in Suffolk at the time, at Easton Barent, Ilkelshall, Heringham, Leiston and Lowestoft.

The father of Rev. John Yonges, Rev. Christopher Yonges, was inducted to the living of Reydon with Southwold, 14 Jan., 1611.‖

On the last day of Feb., 1611, a mandate was issued for inducting Christopher Yonges, Clerk, into the real possession of the Vicarage of Reidon, which position he occupied until his death in 1626. His will describes him as of Southwold, and he is interred in the chancel of the church there.

His widow Margaret, and six children survived him, five of whom came to America. Two children, Edward and Elizabeth Yonges, presumably the eldest of the family, were drowned on St. James day, 16—, in company with 30 others from Southwold in returning from Dunwich Fair.¶

---

* Whitaker's *History of Southold, N. Y.*
† His tombstone says he d. 24 Feb., 1671-2, in his 74th year.
‡ Hotten's *Passenger Lists.*
§ Moore's *Historical Address of 1890 ; Record*, IV, 6; X, 75, 152; XIV, 65; *Essex Inst. Hist. Coll.*, 2d Series, IX, 54; *Youngs Gen.*
‖ Wake's *History of Southwold.*
¶ *Institution Books* at Norwich; *Act Book* at Probate Registery, Ipswich; *Consistory Court Wills*, Norwich; Water's *Gleanings in England.*

There was early a chapel at Reydon, known as St. Margaret de Rissemere. Greatly do we deplore the loss of the early Reydon and Southwold Parish Registers with their priceless genealogies. That of Reydon now dates from 1712, that of Southwold from 1602.

The latter has the following: "1622, July 25, John Yonges, & Joan Herrington, widow," and the baptisms of their children John and Thomas in 1623 and 1625, respectively.

Their marriage license, 24 July, 1622, calls John, bachelor, and Joan, spinster. The bond was in Mr. Christopher Yongs.*

The original Southwold Parish Register, a long, narrow book, which the writer had the privilege of examining, reads distinctly, "Joan Herrington, widow." The writing is the same as for several years previously, an unusually clear hand, presumably that of the father of groom, Rev. Christopher Yonges, himself. At any rate, the entry was unquestionably made during his incumbency, and is therefore that to which we attach most weight.†

If a widow as seems probable, Joan was doubtless that Joan Jentilman, who m. at Southwold, 7 March, 1613, Robert Herrington. His son Robert was bap. 1 Oct., 1616, after which we hear no more of him.

Joan, dau. of William and Agnes Jentleman, was bap. 5 July, 1603; Robert, son of Margt. Herrington, the 2 Nov., 1607. If these parties were m. in 1613, they could not have been bap. as infants.

A Joan Jentilman m. Thomas Beaumont 14 Nov., 1628.

Margaret Herrington was buried 6 Dec., 1611.

William Jentleman was buried the 28 April, 1616. Letters of administration on the estate of William Jentilman of Southwold were issued 11 Feb., 1616 (qu. 1617?), to his widow Anne.

Thomas Jentilman (Jentleman) b. in Southwold in 1511, was Bailiff there in 1534, '72, '86, '96 and 1604, and d. 30 July, 1609.†

Probably Thomas, son of Rev. John Yonges was named after him.

Other Jentilman entries are:

1603: March 2, Thomas, son of James & Mary Jentleman, baptized.

Marriages:

1603, Feb. 6, Richard Jentleman & Susan Capp.
1605, Feb. 13, Richard Garrard & Martha Jentleman.
1606, Jan. 26, Thomas Carnell (Camell, Cornell?) & Mary Jentilman.
1608, April 6, John Mills & Agnes Jentleman.
    "   Sept. 8, Thomas Purt & Christian Jentleman.
1609, Sept. 10, William Gardner & Susan Gentilman.
1612, Oct. 12, Robt. Hachett & Elizabeth Jentleman.
1614, Jan. 2, Thomas Hunter & Susan Jentleman.

---

* *Marriage Licenses from the Official Note Book of the Archdeaconry of Suffolk*, at the Ipswich Probate Court.
    † The original meaning of spinster was descriptive of an occupation, and as such was sometimes used of married women.
    ‡ *N. Y. Gen. & Biog. Record*, April, 1904.

Burials:

1602, Sept. 12, Richard Jentilman.
"   Oct. 4, Margaret Jentleman.
"   Nov. 8, Mary Jentleman & Thomas, her son, buried together.
"   Dec. 4, Christian Ientleman.
"   " 24, Thomas Jentleman.
1603, July 10, Judith Jentleman.
"   " 20, Thomas   "
"   " 28, Margaret   "
"   Aug. 3, Toby   "
"   Sept. 5, Elizabeth Jentleman.
1606, May 8, Margaret   "
1607, Sept. 20, Martha, dau. of Mr. Jas. Jentleman & Martha, his wife.
1610, Aug. 18, Martha Jentilman.
1616, April 28, William Jentilman.

The name Jentilman was found at Dunwich, near Southwold. In the Church of the Grey Friars, one of those buildings "eaten by the sea," were entries of Jentilman in 1506 and 7. Mrs. John Jentleman was buried in 1511, John Jentleman in 1522, and Robert Jentleman in 1525.*

Letters of Administration were issued on the estate of John Jentleman of Southwoulde, to Richard Garrard, 13 April, 1622.

Under Herrington we find: Marriages:

1608–9, Feb. 27, Wm. Hunter & Margaret Herrington.
1609, Aug. 2, Stephen Herrington & Cecily Furth. Stephen Herrington was Bailiff in 1609, '12 and '19.
1609, Nov. 26, John Herrington & Awdry Harle.

Baptisms:

1611, June 4, Mary, dau. of John Herrington.
1615, May 14, Catharine, dau. of John & Awdry Herrington.
1618, May 28, Stephen, son   "   "   "
1621, June 17, Joan, dau.   "   "   "
(Joan, dau. of John Herrington was buried 7 June, 1633.)
1624, May 30, Elizabeth, dau. of John & Awdry Herrington.
1626, Oct. 29, John, son of John & Adre Herrington.
(1627, Jan. 15, child of John Herrington buried.)
1629, Sept. 6, Susan, dau. of John & Awdry Herrington.
1631, June 18, Mary,   "   "   "   "

1638, Jan. 23, Commission to Mr. John Goldsmith, clerk, Vicar of Raidon, cum Southoulde, & Philip Seaman, clerk, curate there, to administer the oath to Awdry Herrington, relict of John Herrington of Southoulde, deceased intestate, well and truly to administer his estate.

Letters of Administration were issued to the said Awdry, widow of John Herrington, 25 Jan., 1638.

1621, Sept. 9, Betres, dau. of Stephen & Betres Herrington, bapt.
1625, Sept. 25, Alice,   "   "   " Beatrice   "   "
1627, March 11, Thomas, son of Thos. & Alice Herrington.
1627, June 3, Elizabeth, dau. of William & Margaret Herrington.

* Gardner's *Hist. of Dunwich.*

1633, Sept. 29, William, son of William & Margaret Herrington.
Burials:
1609, April 1, Catharine Herrington.
1624, Aug. 29, Stephen Herrington, Sr.
1627, Sept. 17, Stephen Herrington.
    " Jan. 15, Mistress Herrington.
1629, Feb. 9, child of Thomas Herrington.
1636, Sept. 25, Susan Herrington.
    A marriage license was granted to Robert Burgis, widr., of Loestoft, & Alice Herrington, widow, of Southwolde, 26 June, 1630.

Letters of Administration were granted 26 May, 1632, on the estate of Judith Herrington, dec'd., late of Ippswich to her sister, wife of George Deathe.

Letters on the estate of William Herrington, late of Hintlesham, with a non-cupative will attached, were granted 29 June, 1632, to his relict Barbara.

The will of William Yonges of Lowestoft, 22 June, 1530, proved 7 March, 1530, names William Hocker of Lowestoft, executor.

William Yonge & Estabel Beelle were m. at Heacham, 11 Oct., 1558.*

Christopher Horne of Aylesham, mentions in his will, 4 March, 1602, his sister Johan Yonges, his nephew Christopher Yonges, the elder, and his sons, Christopher, John and William Yonges.

William Yonges of Great Yarmouth, in his will, 13 Sept., 1611, names his wife Dorothy, his daughters, but no sons, Brother Henry Yonges, Henry, son of his brother John Yonges, kinsman Augustine, Edmund and James Yonges.

The will of Thomas Yonge of Waybread, Suffolk, husbandman, 17 of King James, names wife Alice, dau. Elizabeth & fower other children, ffrancis, Thomas, Jonathan & Stephen Yonge. Cousin Roger Meene, executor, proved 6 March, 1619, at the Archdeaconry Court of Suffolk.

1619, Nov. 9, Letters of Administration were granted to Mary Yonge, widow of John Yonge of Stoake, deceased, on his estate.

The marriage license of William Yonges of Bungay, & Prudence Hoxton, widow, of Southwold, late of Solherton, was dated 29 Nov., 1622.

1631, Jan. 28, a Commission was issued to John Yonges & Mr. Nathaniel Roe, clerks, to administer oaths to Elizabeth Welche, widow & relict of John Welche of Northales, deceased, to well & truly administer the estate of the said John Welche.

1632, July 1, Thomas Yonge m. Amy Allyard.*

1632, Nov. 19. The will of John Yonges of ffelixstowe was proved.

1632, Jan. 14, Letters on the estate of Doratie Yonges of Stoake, with a non-cupative will attached. Administration to George Harvie, principal legatee.

* Phillimore and Johnson's *Parish Registers of Norfolk.*

1633, Nov. 15, Letters of Administration of —— Yongs of Oxford, to —— Daniel, mother of the deceased.

1636, Aug. 6, Will of Henry Young of Henley, proved.

That Yonges abounded in Suffolk is shown by the fact that in 1674, 46 Yonges households paid the hearth tax in the above county.

A small farm of 160 acres, near Wenhaston station, about seven miles from Southwold, was entailed for three generations and intended "to be kept in the family so long as there was a John Yonges."

The tenants were unable to hold it, and when the entail expired, the land was sold in Oct., 1901. Two of the owners, John Yonges, were buried at Wenhaston in 1868 and 1899 respectively.

The last owner, the third John Yonges, told the writer in 1903 that his grandfather probably came from Uggelshall, as they were obliged to settle the above estate there.

Thomas Warren (Warryn), merchant, was of Southwold. His will, 4 March, 1641, proved 13 Sept., 1645, names son Thomas, dau. Elizabeth, wife of Thomas Gooch of Southwold; two grandchildren, Mary Gardiner and Benjamin Youngs, children of his dau. *Mary, wife of John Youngs, now in New England;* dau. Margaret, wife of Joseph Youngs; dau. Christian, wife of Symon Barnard; son George Warren; son Robert Warren, deceased; son Thomas Warren and son-in-law Simon Barnard, executors. (Arch. Suff. Ipswich, Original Wills [1645], 120.)*

There appears to have been two families at Southwold, one of Thomas Warren, Bailiff in 1614, '20, '27, '33 and '38, and the other of Thomas Warne, who was buried 23 Jan., 1637.

Some of the Warne entries below were probably intended for Warren and written Warin.

"1602, June 7, Mary, dau. of Thos. & Mary Warne, baptized."

Mary, wife of Rev. John Youngs, of whose marriage dates we have no record, calls John Youngs her "last husband." She d. after 5 Nov., 1678, on Long Island, N. Y.†

"1604, May 23, Elizabeth, dau. of Thomas & Mary Warne, baptized."

"Elisabeth Warren m. Thomas Gooch 20 June, 1620," and had children christened: "Thomas Gooch, 6 May, 1621," and "John Gooch, 27 Oct., 1623."

Thomas Gooch, Sr., Thomas, Jr., John Gooch & others refused to take the oaths & superscriptions in 1662, & were discharged from being four & twenties.

1607, April 8, Robert, son of Thos. & Mary Warne, baptized.

1640, Dec. 7, Robert Warren buried.

1609, Oct. 18, Margt. (Martha erased), dt. of Thos. & Mary Warne, baptized.

---

* See *N. Eng. Hist. & Gen. Register*, April, 1898, and *N. Y. Gen. & Biog. Record*, April, 1904.

† *Southold Town Rec.*, II, 18.

1611, Nov. 11, Christian, d. of Thomas Warren, baptized. We have not the date of her marriage to Simon Barnard.

Christian was a favorite name in the Youngs family on Long Island. It was used at Southwold by the Jentlemans as well as by the Warrens.

1613, March 2, George, son of Thos. Waryn, baptized.

In 1662, Mr. George Warren, one of the Bailiffs, desiring time to consider the oaths & superscriptions imposed by Acts of Parliament, etc., is ordered to be discharged from being Bailiff, or from bearing any office in the corporation at Southwold, unless he subscribes to the said oaths before December 1st. Mr. Simon Bernard to officiate in his room.*

1613, Jan. 23, Margaret, dau. of Thomas Warne, baptized.

1632, Feb. 5, Joseph Yongs & Margt. Warren married. She was living at Southold, N. Y., 9 May, 1669, a widow.†

Her son Gideon Youngs was perhaps named after the Gideon of the next entry.

1616, June 5, Gideon Warne, son of Thos. & Margt. Waryne, baptized.

1618, Dec. 6, Deborah, dau. of Thos. & Mary Warne, baptized. Deborah Warren doubtless single in 1641.

1619, June 8, wife of Thos. Warren, buried.

1624, May 24, Catherine, dau. of Thos. & Mary Waryn, baptized.

1625, Jan. 13, Catherine, dau. of Mr. Thomas Warren, buried.

1640, April 7, Mary, wife of Mr. Thos. Warren, buried.

1644, Jan. 18, ulto, Mr. Thos. Warren, buried.

1615, Jan. 2, Thos. Stannard, servant to Thos. Waryn, buried.

1619, Feb. 14, John Warren & Alice Keble married. Their marriage license 12 Feb., 1619-20, describes them as both single, and of Reydon. Thomas Waryn, surety.‡ The Kebles of County Suffolk were an armorial family.§

1620, Nov. 24, John, son of John & Alice Waryn, baptized.

1621, March 4, Thos. son of John & Alice Waryn, baptized.

1624, June 14, Thos. son of John Waryn, buried.

1623, March 4, Alice, wife of John Waryn, buried.

1624, Nov. 5, John Waren buried.

1828, Oct. 7, Robert Bonnar & Elizabeth Waryn married.

1628, Dec. 21, Margt., dau. of Wm. & Susan Warren, baptized.

1662, Aug. 12, Thos., son of Thomas & Mary Warren, baptized.

1683, Feb. 6, Rebecca, dau. of John & Anne Warren, baptized.

1685, June 24, Elizabeth, dau. of John Warren, buried.

1685, June 24, Elizabeth, dau. of another John Warren, buried.

1688, Dec. 12, Thos. Warren & Martha Senor, of Sd., married.

1755, May 31, Martha Warne or Warren, wid., buried.

Letters of Administration on the estate of Christopher Warren of Hennesfield, dec'd., issued to his Relict, Anne, 4 Dec., 1631.

---

* Gardner's *Hist. of Dunwich.*
† *Southold Town Rec.*, I, 373.
‡ *Mar. Lic. from the Official Note Books of the Archdeaconry of Suffolk.*
§ Muskett's *Suff. Manorial Families.*

1633, Jan. 20, marriage license granted to Thomas Warren &
Ann Noaks of St. Matthew's (Ipswich?).

The marriage license of Thomas Warren & Judith Fisher of
St. Clement's, Ipswich, was dated 3 July, 1634.

Possibly Thomas Warren, the Southwold merchant, who d. in
1644, and John Warren, who m. Alice Keble in 1619, were
brothers, and sons of George Warren who was buried at Southwold, 14 Dec., 1614.

The Warren family furnished Bailiffs for Southwold Borough
at intervals from 1614–1662. According to the Parish Register
there, they seem to have resided in that town from 1611–1705.

In this connection it is gratifying to learn that the title deeds
of the Southwold Vicarage, at Queen Anne's Bounty Office in
London, show that the property, including a mansion and
enclosed piece of land, was sold in 1705, by the late widow of
of John Warren to John Thompson, whose heirs, lineal and
collateral, and others held it till 1829, when it was sold to the
Governors of Queen Anne's Bounty, and is now held by them in
trust for a Vicarage.

The " mansion " of the title deeds was built on the foundations
of an older house, in which are the cellars of the existing house.

There are two deeds, with the signatures of Mrs. Hannah
Knowles, formerly widow of John Warren, of Hannah Bohm, and
of Mary and Elizabeth Warren. The seals against the last two
names, are distinctive, and the same in both documents.

Warren, as a family name, comes from Normandy, whence
William de Warrenne came with William the Conqueror, and
whose daughter, Gundreda, he afterwards married. He was
greatly esteemed and trusted by his royal father-in-law.*

Burke's *General Armory* mentions 45 armorial families of
Warren, 2 of Warreyn and 2 of Warryn, and the particular one to
which Thomas Warren above, of Southwold, belonged is much
to be desired.

THE GREENE FAMILY OF PLYMOUTH COLONY.

RICHARD HENRY GREENE, A.M., LL.B.,
Corresponding Member of the N. E. Historic Genealogical Society.

(Continued from Vol. XXXIX, p. 116 of the RECORD.)

FIFTH GENERATION.

32. MERCY[5] GOFF (Desire[4] Green, Warren,[3] William,[2] William[1]),
bap. Jan. 12, 1757; m. Zaccheus Cook, Jr., Middle Haddam, Conn.,
Jan. 18, 1776, probably of the family of Henry of Mass., who had
three children who removed to Conn. John settled in Middletown, Henry and Samuel in Wallingford, Conn. His father d.
April 19, 1812, aet. 93, therefore b. about 1719, probably at Eastham, Mass. He signed a petition to Conn. Legislature, 1744,

* Burke s *Extinct and Dormant Peerages.*

about the church at East Hampton. Zaccheus Cook, Jr., was administrator on the estate of (33) Benjamin Green* Goff, and acted Sept., 1782, in the administration. He and his family removed to N. Y. State, I have not the town.

33. BENJAMIN* GREEN GOFF (Desire⁴ Green, Warren,³ William,² William¹), bap. Oct. 9, 1757. He was a soldier in Capt. Holmes Company of Col. Samuel Selden's Regiment, and private First Regt. Continentals from East Haddam, April 22, 1777, to April 22, 1780, when he was discharged. The history of Wethersfield says: he was killed June 24, 1781. He was then in the militia.*

34. TIMOTHY* GOFF (Desire⁴ Green, Warren,³ William,² William¹), bap. July 27, 1760. Went into the service in Lieut. David Smith's Company, Col. Thomas Belden's Regiment, April and May, 1777, served at Peekskill, N. Y. There was a Timothy Goff of Easthampton, Conn., m. Eveline, dau. of Elihu and Almyra (Wright) Cook, but I have not been able to identify him.

35. PHILIP* GOFF (Desire⁴ Green, Warren,³ William,² William¹), b. Aug. 17, 1766; bap. June 2, 1767; m. Oct. 19, 1787, Chloe Cole, dau. of Marcus and Phebe (Scovill) Cole; he was the eldest child of Ebenezer and Elizabeth Cole, who removed from Eastham, Mass., to Chatham, Conn., 1748, and d. 1752. Elizabeth Cole d. Feb. 19, 1794, aged 85. Ebenezer and Elizabeth had: i. Marcus; ii. Ebenezer; iii. Elizabeth; iv. Jerusha Cole. Philip Goff d. Oct. 23, 1823. Marcus Cole was in the French War, and in the Continental service, May, 1775, to Feb., 1778, when he was lieutenant in Huntington's Regiment of the line. Marcus and Phebe Cole had: i. Abner, b. 1754; m. Lydia Freeman, 1785; ii. Hendrick, m. Phebe Griffith; iii. Marcus, m. Sally White; iv. Phebe, m. Thomas Ackley; v. Reliance, m. Joseph Knowlton; vi. Chloe, m. Philip Goff; vii. Rebecca, m. Isaac Johnson; viii. Mary, m. Benjamin Leonard.

The U. S. census of 1790, under Chatham gives Philip Goff's family as consisting of two males over sixteen and one female; and Philip Goff, Jr., had in family one male over sixteen and two females. It would seem these were Philip, who m. Desire, and his son, Philip, Jr., who m. Chloe Cole.†

Philip and Chloe (Cole) Goff united with the church at Middle Haddam, July 18, 1790. This family removed from the neighborhood probably at the same time as Philip and Desire (Green) Goff, before 1800. Among my notes about Chloe Cole, I find

---

* There was a Benjamin Goff of Easthampton, m. Feb. 5. 1786, Abigail Brainard; they removed to Middle Haddam. They had: i. Benjamin, d. inf. ii. Niel, never m. iii. Phila, m. John Cole, and other children. The absence of the initial of the middle name makes me doubt the identity.

† Mr. H. B. Brainerd says: Philip Goff was b. about 1730, perhaps earlier; he was bap. at Middle Haddam, March 24, 1742, his grandfather, Philip (b. 1685), being alive, for his father is called Philip Goff, Jr. In records of Rev. John Norton, East Hampton, appears Philip Goff, d. Oct. 27, 1779, and Philip Goff's wife d. April 22, 1767. The first is the father-in-law of Desire; the latter is possibly Sarah (Atwell) Goff, his wife, tho' that is not certain.

these, b. Sept. 7, 1768, and d. Oct. 23, 1823. The future may explain them.

I have not been able to discover whether Philip and Chloe Goff had any children.

37. STEPHEN⁶ HOSMER (Bathsheba⁴ Green, Warren,³ William,² William¹), bap. Middle Haddam, Conn., April 26, 1767. He was the fourth of the name in direct line. Removed to Lebanon, Conn. Children:

101   i. Lavinia⁶ Hosmer.
102   ii. Stephen T. Hosmer.
103   iii. James Hosmer.
104   iv. William Hosmer.
105   v. Charles B. Hosmer.
106   vi. Mary Hosmer.
107   vii. John B. Hosmer.*

51. ASA⁵ DIMOCK (Sarah⁴ Greene, Warren,³ William,² William¹), m. July 5, 1794, Ruth Miller. He d. Dec. 18, 1833, at Dimockvill, Pa. Children:

108   i. Asa⁶ Dimock, Jr., b. April 5, 1795.
109   ii. Warren Dimock, b. April 30, 1796.
110   iii. Dorcas Dimock, b. Pittston, Pa., May 19, 1798.
111   iv. Shubael Dimock, b. Sept. 24, 1800.
112   v. John Green Dimock, b. Clifford, Pa., May 16, 1810; d. April 11, 1812.

52. DAVIS⁵ DIMOCK (Sarah⁴ Green, Warren,³ William,² William¹), m. June 5, 1797, Elizabeth Jenkins, b. Aug. 22, 1780. He d. Montrose, Pa., Sept. 27, 1854. He was a pioneer Baptist missionary, a leading man in Susquehanna Co., Pa. He was also a physician and associate judge. Children of Davis and Elizabeth Dimock:

113   i. Sarah⁶ Dimock, b. Feb. 2, 1799.
114   ii. Benjamin Jenkins Dimock, b. Feb. 16, 1800.
115   iii. Davis Dimock, Jr., b. Oct. 2, 1803.
116   iv. Betsey Dimock, b. Oct. 24, 1806.
117   v. Mary Jenkins Dimock, b. April 11, 1809; d. Jan. 16, 1819.
118   vi. Lydia Clark Dimock, b. July 6, 1811.
119   vii. Asa Green Dimock, b. Oct. 14, 1813.
120   viii. John Harding Dimock, b. Oct. 30, 1815.
121   ix. David Dimock, b. Oct. 31, 1818. Lost at sea May, 1839.
122   x. Gordon Zebina Dimock, b. Feb. 26, 1821.
123   xi. Shubael Dimock.

63. WILLIAM YOUNG⁵ GREENE (William,⁴ William,³ William,² William¹), b. East Haddam, Conn., July 20, 1792; bap. by Rev. Solomon Blakeslee, St. Stephens Church, 1804; m. Athens, N. Y., Sallie Obedience Hinman, b. Nov. 1, 1793, dau. of Edward† and

---

* There was a John Hosmer from Hartford in the Conn. Continental line, during the Revolution; he was a corporal; under the Act of 1818 he received a pension, at that time was living at New York.

† The Hinman family of Conn. is descended from Sergt. Edward¹ Hinman of Stratford, Conn., the first of the name in America. He appears there about 1651. He m. Hannah, dau. of Francis and Sarah Stiles. He was bap. in Eng-

Mercy Hinman, who were b. and d. at Athens. Wm. Y. Greene
d. at Natches, Miss., Sept. 23, 1818. His widow m. (2) Jan. 8, 1828,
Peter G. Coffin. She d. Feb. 4, 1834, and was buried at Athens,
N. Y., leaving by the second marriage one child, Uriah Hinman
Coffin, b. 1832. Peter G. Coffin d. Dec., 1856. Wm. and Sally O.
Greene had:

124   i. William⁶ Edward Greene, b. Aug. 17, 1812.
125   ii. Henry Augustus Greene, b. Dec. 6, 1814.
126   iii. Mercy Matilda Greene, b. Jan. 11, 1816; d. Feb. 19,
         1816.

64. RUSSELL TINKER⁵ GREENE (William,⁴ William,³ William,²
William¹), b. East Haddam, Conn., June 26, 1794; bap. 1804, at
same place and time as his brother and sister. He m. Sybil
Pratt who was b. at Canaan, N. Y., and d. at Athens, N. Y.
Mr. Greene m. (2) Dec. 21, 1826, Sarah Stiles Edwards, at
Plymouth, Pa. She was b. Oct. 30, 1807, at Cochecton, Sullivan
Co., N. Y. He removed to Jersey City, N. J., and d. there May 10,
1874. Mrs. Greene d. at same place Oct. 8, 1895. Children:

127   i. Almon W.⁶ Greene, b. 1816.
128   ii. Asaph Lorenzo Greene, b. Nov. 14, 1817, Hartford, N.Y.
129   iii. Matilda Ann Greene, b. Aug. 20, 1819.
130   iv. Julia Elizabeth Greene, b. Aug. —, 1821.
131   v. Henry W. Greene, } twins, b. Dec. 26, 1823.
132   vi. William S. Greene, }
133   vii. An infant.
134   viii. Sybil Pratt Greene, b. March 30, 1828, Plymouth, Pa.
135   ix. Clarissa Indiana Greene, b. Nov. 6, 1830, Canaan,
         N. Y.; d. Oct. 29, 1839.
136   x. Russell Edwards Greene, b. Sept. 26, 1832.
137   xi. Sarah Jane Greene, b. May 17, 1834.
138   xii. Emma Stitt Greene, b. Oct. 2, 1835.
139   xiii. Gideon Burr Greene, b. Sept. 29, 1837.
140   xiv. Arthur Seymour Greene, b. April 2, 1848, Hudson,
         N. Y.

65. SOPHIA INDIANA⁵ GREENE (William,⁴ William,³ William,²
William¹), b. Jan. 11, 1798, East Haddam, Conn. On Rev. Solomon Blakeslee's baptismal record, 1804, her name does not appear,
it reads: "India, wid. Wm. Green, William — Russel & —."
She m. April 23, 1815, Lyman Wait, Canaan, N. Y. He was b.
Oct. 26, 1796, and d. Jan. 25, 1840, Athens, N. Y. She removed
later to N. Y. City, where she d. April 25, 1895. Children:

---

land, Aug. 1, 1602; lived in Windsor, Conn., and d. Nov. 26, 1681, leaving four
sons and four daughters.
  Edward² Hinman, Jr., the youngest son, b. Stratford, 1672; m. Hannah
Jennings, b. July 25, 1678. dau. of Joshua, Jr., and Mary Lyon; d. Aug. 25, 1777,
the day she was 99 years old. He was one of the first Episcopalians in Conn.
They had 12 children.
  Ebenezer³ Hinman, b. Stratford, m. Obedience Jennings, June 4, 1739; she
was b. Aug., 1720, and d. Dec. 15, 1812. He d. Nov. 18, 1795, leaving 10 children.
  Edward⁴ Hinman, b. May 19, 1744; m. Dec. 26, 1790, Mercy Hinman
(Adam,⁴ Noah,³ Benjamin,² Edward¹), of Southbury, who was b. Dec. 26, 1756.
He d. June 2, 1834; she d. March 4, 1835. They had but one child: Sally
Obedience Hinman Greene above.

141   i. Jane⁶ Wait, b. Feb. 28, 1816.
142   ii. Clarissa M. Wait, b. May 3, 1818; d. July 15, 1819.
143   iii. William Seth Wait, b. May 7, 1820.
144   iv. Henry Lyman Wait, b. Feb. 8, 1822.
145   v. Emily Sophia Wait, b. April 1, 1825.
146   vi. Matilda Sally Wait, b. July 4, 1827.
147   vii. Lucretia M. Wait, b. Sept. 15, 1829; d. unm. Dec. 5, 1851.
148 viii. Henrietta E. Wait, b. Nov. 28, 1831.
149   ix. Edward Augustus Wait, b. Oct. 1, 1834.
150   x. Almira Ellen Wait, b. June 16, 1837.

66. HANNAH⁵ HUNGERFORD (Hannah⁴ Green, James,³ William,² William¹), b. July 13, 1778; m. Jos.* Spencer Brainerd of Hadlyme, Conn., May 24, 1800. They removed to Troy, N. Y., and Oct., 1808, to St. Albans, Vt., and he d. there Jan. 1, 1817. She d. Jan. 1, 1847. Children:

151   i. Joseph Hungerford⁶ Brainerd, b. Chatham, March 22, 1801.
152   ii. Hannah Brainerd, b. Jan. 12, 1803.
153   iii. Henry Lyman Brainerd, b. Troy, Jan. 18, 1806.
154   iv. Timothy Green Brainerd, b. Jan. 31, 1808.
155   v. George Brainerd, b. St. Albans, Feb. 9, 1810; d. March 2, 1810.
156   vi. George Brainerd, b. March 24, 1811.
157   vii. Ezra Brainerd, b. Dec. 18, 1813; d. Sept., 1814.
158 viii. Ezra Brainerd, b. Aug. 1, 1815.

68. JAMES⁵ GREEN (Benjamin,⁴ James,³ William,² William¹), b. July 29, 1787; m. Jan. 14, 1818, Sarah Ann Pierpont of Littlefield, Conn. Removed to Buffalo, N. Y. He d. there in Sept., 1848. They had one child:

159   i. James Pierpont⁶ Green.

69. RUTH⁵ GREEN (Benjamin,⁴ James,³ William,² William¹), b. East Haddam, Dec. 14, 1790, m. Feb. 25, 1827, John Warner Barber, who was b. Feb. 2, 1798, Windsor, Conn. He was descended from Thomas Barber who came to Windsor in 1635.† He was a widower having m. Harriet E. Lines, who d. March 17, 1826. After his second marriage he continued to live in New

---

* Jos. Spencer Brainerd. b. Dec. 7, 1776, ninth child of Deac. Ezra and Jerusha (Smith) Brainerd, who were m. Sept. 12, 1738; she was dau. of David and Dorothy (Brainerd) Smith. Jerusha was the ninth of thirteen children. David d. Oct. 11, 1811. Deacon Ezra Brainerd, Justice of the Peace, and many years member of Legislature, was son of Josiah, who was son of William and Sarah (Bidwell) Brainerd.

† Thomas¹ Barber came to America when about eighteen years old. He m. Jane ——, Oct. 7, 1640. They both d. in Sept., 1662.
  Josiah² Barber, b. Feb. 15, 1653, m. Abigail, dau. of Nathaniel Loomis, Nov. 22, 1677; she d. Feb. 9, 1700. He m. (2) Nov. 5, 1701, Sarah Drake, who d. Dec. 13, 1730. He d. Dec., 1733.
  Aaron³ Barber, b. July 20, 1697; m. Mary Douglas from New London Conn., Feb. 2, 1724.
  Elijah⁴ Barber, b. Jan. 11, 1744-5; m. Abigail Wood, Dec. 20, 1768.
  Elijah⁵ Barber, b. Oct. 24, 1769; m. Mary Warner, Jan., 1795, who d. Jan 20, 1839. He d. July 19, 1812. John Warner Barber in the text was their son.

Haven, Conn. Mrs. Ruth Barber d. Nov. 18, 1851. He was an engraver and publisher, his historical works are quite sought after, dealing in town histories of different States. John W. and Ruth Green Barber had:

- 160   i. Elizabeth Green* Barber, b. Nov. 20, 1827.
- 161   ii. Caroline C. T. Barber, b. May 23, 1829.
- 162   iii. John Barber, b. Nov. 5, 1830.
- 163   iv. James Barber, b. Aug. 10, 1832.
- 164   v. Harriet Barber, b. Feb. 27, 1835; d. June 24, 1862.

70. BETSEY* GREEN (Benjamin,* James,* William,* William*), b. Sept. 26, 1795, at East Haddam; m. Edmund Anson Wooding,* April 19, 1814. He was b. Woodbridge, now Bethany, Conn., son of Edmund and Anne (Peck†) Wooding of Woodbridge. Betsey was the first wife. They moved to Torrington Hollow in 1824. Was engaged in manufacture, first cotton, then clocks and locks. She d. April 23, 1825, near Oswego, N. Y., and was buried at Ransoms Mills, Tioga Co. He m. (2) Miss Pond. He d. Feb. 27, 1864, aet. 63. They had nine children. Betsey Green Wooding's children who outlived their infancy were:

- 165   i. Edmund* Wooding, b. Feb. —, 1815.
- 166   ii. Julius Wooding, b. Sept. —, 1816.
- 167   iii. James Wooding, b. Oct. 28, 1817.
- 168   iv. Anson Wooding, b. June 7, 1820.
- 169   v. Eliza Wooding, b. March —, 1825; d. Feb. 1830.

71. HARRIET* GREEN (Benjamin,* James,* William,* William*), b. East Haddam, April 30, 1800; m. Dec. 23, 1823, Geo. Nelson Blakeslee, b. Sept. 12, 1799, Plymouth, Conn.,‡ and d. Jan. 18, 1877; she d. Sept. 9, 1885, both at Waterbury, Conn. The children were all b. at Plymouth, now Thomaston, Conn. He was son of Samuel and Polly (Selkirk) Blakeslee. He was a farmer. They were both members of Trinity Episcopal Church. Children:

- 170   i. Geo. Pierpont* Blakeslee, b. Nov. 30, 1824.
- 171   ii. Julius Franklin Blakeslee, b. Dec. 4, 1825.

---

* This name is somewhat uncommon, it does not appear in *Savage's Genealogical Dictionary, Durrie's Index of Genealogies, 1886,* or the first fifty volumes of the *New Eng. Historic-Genealogical Register.*

† The Peck family were early settlers and residents in New Haven, Conn. Some have removed to Wallingford and other neighboring towns, but many are still in the city of New Haven. Eleazer was at Wallingford, 1670, and Jeremiah was m. at Waterbury, 1704, and d. 1751.

‡ There was a Thomas Blakeslee in Hartford as early as 1641. Samuel[1] was perhaps his brother, he was at Guilford, 1650; m. Hannah, dau. of Wm. Potter, and had eight children; d. 1672.

- i. John,[2] b. 1651; m. Grace ——; d. 1713.
  - i. John,[3] b. 1676; m. Susanna ——. Had: Daniel,[4] and 5 daus., all m. He d. 1751.
  - ii. Hannah (Sperry).
  - iii. Moses, settled in Waterbury; m. 1702, Sarah Benton. Had 14 children: 1. Moses; 2. Aaron; 3. Abner; 4. Jesse; 5. Job; 6. Sarah; 7. Dinah; 8. Hannah; 9. Phebe; 10. John; 11. Marah,
- ii. Samuel, Jr., b. 1662; m. 1684, ——; removed to Plymouth Conn., or as some say to Woodbury. They had 9 children.
- iii. Ebenezer. b. July 17, 1664; m. and had 8 children.

The ancestry of Samuel Blakeslee is probably among the foregoing.

172   iii. Harriet Evaline Blakeslee, b. Feb. 9, 1829; d. April 9, 1830.

173   iv. Louisa Evaline Blakeslee, b. Jan. 3, 1831.

174   v. Anson Green Blakeslee, b. Nov. 22, 1832; d. Feb. 21, 1846.

175   vi. Caroline Amelia Blakeslee, b. Jan. 15, 1834.

176   vii. Sarah Tuttle Blakeslee, b. Dec. 24, 1836; d. March 13, 1850.

177 viii. Edward Warren Blakeslee, b. July 24, 1840.

73. HANNAH[6] GREEN (Benjamin,[4] James,[3] William,[2] William[1]), b. Jan. 2, 1803, East Haddam; m. Aug. 28, 1825, Daniel Tuttle, b. 1803, son of Rev. Ezra* Tuttle of Patchogue, L. I. He d. of consumption, April 26, 1829; she d. March 11, 1855, Brooklyn, N. Y. Children:

178   i. Caroline Louisa[6] Tuttle, b. July 2, 1826; d. April 17, 1827.

179   ii. Mary Celestia Tuttle, b. Nov. 28, 1827; d. July 7, 1828.

180   iii. Daniel Green Tuttle, b. June 3, 1829; d. March 5, 1857. He was assistant editor *N. Y. Journal of Commerce.*

74. SARAH WING[5] GREEN (Benjamin,[4] James,[3] William,[2] William[1]), b. March 27, 1808; m. April 29, 1829, Silvester Tuttle, who was b. Sept. 5, 1806, Patchogue, L. I. Was in the hat business N. Y. City, then had an extensive coal business in Brooklyn. Mrs. Tuttle d. Sept. 21, 1846, at New York. He m. (2) May 2, 1849, Eliza Jane, dau. of Zelotes and Eliza (Atwater) Day,† b. June 27, 1823, of New Haven, Conn., and d. June 24, 1905, at her home 494 Bedford Ave., Brooklyn. She was prominent in St. Johns M. E. Church, the Eastern District Industrial Home, and other church and benevolent work. Children:

181   i. Chas. Henry Tuttle, b. April 30, 1830; d. July 10, 1831.

182   ii. Ezra Benjamin Tuttle, b. May 3, 1834.

183   iii. Sarah Jane Tuttle, b. Oct. 18, 1838; d. March 22, 1845.

75. ANSON[5] GREEN (Benjamin,[4] James,[3] William,[2] William[1]), b. Aug. 14, 1810, East Haddam; m. May 1, 1836, at New York, Lydia Foster Moore, who was b. Greenport, L. I., and d. there May 6, 1837. He m. (2) Mrs. Maria Blackman, who d. and he m. (3) at Commerce, Oakland Co., Mich., Nov. 25, 1859 Mary Louisa Farr, dau. of Joseph Gamble and Mary Ann (Tibballs) Farr of Pompey, N. Y. She moved after his death from Mich. to Hammondton, N. J. Children:

---

* A tradition in the Tuttle family places the first ancestor in Lynn, Mass. Ezra, b. Chelsea, Sept. 15, 1704, a mariner, was shipwrecked and settled at Patchogue, L. I. He was afterwards a Methodist preacher. His two sons, Daniel and Silvester, m. sisters, 73 and 74 in the text.

† Eliza Atwater Day was descended from David[1] Atwater, one of the first planters of New Haven, Conn.; through his son Jonathan,[2] b. July 12, 1656, and Ruth Peck, his wife, who had: Jonathan, Jr.,[3] b. Nov. 4, 1690, who m. (2) Martha Bradley, and had: Jeremiah,[4] b. Dec. 5, 1734; he was steward of Yale, m. Anna Mix, and had: Joseph.[5] b. May 27, 1790, m. Sarah Thomas. These were the parents of Eliza[6] Atwater, b. June 2, 1794, Mrs. Day in the text. Zelotes was son of Joel of New Haven, Conn. He m. Eliza Atwater, July 23, 1817.

14A

184.   i. Benjamin Anson⁶ Green, b. March 1, 1837, N. Y.; d.
       June, 1837.
185   ii. Matty Minnehaha Green, b. Feb. 17, 1862, Commerce,
       Mich.

76. RICHARD WILLIAM⁵ Green (Richard,⁴ James,³ William,² Wil-
liam¹), b. East Haddam, March 28, 1804; m. at New York City,
Aug. 7, 1828, Charlotte Gleason, dau. of Ebenezer Steele and
Prudence (Brainerd) Gleason, b. Farmington, Conn., June 2, 1806.
E. S. Gleason was b., lived and d. at Farmington; m. July 25,
1791, Prudence Brainerd, who was b. at East Haddam, July 31,
1774; d. June 8, 1811; dau. of Daniel Brainerd* and Prudence
Gridley, m. June 6, 1771. Mrs. Charlotte Greene d. July 3, 1829,
aged 22, and was buried in the First Church Cemetery, East
Haddam. R. W. Green m. (2) in 1834, Eliza Bulkley, who was b.
at Wethersfield, 1802; she d. at Philadelphia, Pa., Aug. 17, 1852.
Mr. Green was prepared for College by Dr. Parsons, but did not
enter, and in 1833 Yale gave him an honorary A. M. He came to
N. Y. in 1828, and taught school, removed to Philadelphia in 1832
and continued the profession of teaching until he d. Feb. 1, 1846.
His widow d. Aug. 17, 1852. He published *The Little Reckoner*,
an *Arithmetic, Algebra, Geometry, Grammar, Scholar's Companion* and *Revision of Valpy's Paley.* He was buried at Riverside Cemetery. One child:

186   i. Richard Gleason⁶ Greene, b. June 29, 1829, East Had-
      dam.

77. HENRY⁵ GREEN (Richard,⁴ James,³ William,² William¹), b.
East Haddam, Sept. 5, 1805. He was the second of the family to
come to New York, Oct. 1824, his brother William having come
in May, and all the family following at different intervals. He
and his brother William W., in 1826, started the firm of H. & W.
W. Green, grocers and shipping merchants; another brother,
Sidney, was taken in sometime after. After the crash of 1837,
they suffered from the failure and repudiations of southern
customers mostly at Mobile, where their vessels sailed, and they
were forced to suspend in 1842, but in time settled with every
one. He was paymaster in the militia, N. Y. City. Went to
California in 1849, and remained two years. He went into the
storage business, Todd Stores, Brooklyn, after his brother retired.
He was a member of the N. Y. Chess Club. He never m. and d.
at the residence of his nephew, R. H. Greene, 13 Orient Ave.,
Brooklyn, of pneumonia, April 16, 1886, universally respected and
regretted.

78. WILLIAM WEBB⁵ GREEN (Richard,⁴ James,³ William,² William¹), b. East Haddam, March 29, 1807; before he was 20 years
of age he was in business for himself in the City of New York,
and at forty-nine retired. He m. at 74 Beekman St., New York,

---

* The ancestor Daniel¹ Brainerd, b. Eng., settled Haddam, Conn., 1662;
had: Daniel² Brainerd, b. March 2, 1665; his son Daniel³ Brainerd, m. Susanna
Ventres, their son Daniel⁴ Brainerd, b. Feb. 24, 1722; d. Jan. 10, 1777; was the
father of Daniel⁵ Brainerd, who m. Prudence Gridley, 1771, and had: Prudence⁶
Brainerd, b. July 3, 1774; m. Ebenezer Steele Gleason, parents of Charlotte
Gleason Green in the text. See note 80, Sidney⁵ Green, below.

Aug. 10, 1836, Sarah Ann Todd, dau. of Col. Wm. W. Todd;* she
was b. June 21, 1813.   She was manager of the Graham Institute
for old ladies in Brooklyn, the Sanitary Fair, and Colored Orphan
Asylum, New York.   She was a devout Christian, uniting early
with the First Baptist Church, N. Y., and when her husband and
family united with the Washington Heights Presbyterian Church,
she united with them.   She d. in Brooklyn, while temporarily
away from her home at Fort Washington, N. Y. City, March 8,
1883.   Mr. Green was director of the Jackson Marine Ins. Co., the
Anchor Fire Ins. Co., Sherman & Barnsdale Oil Co., and president
of the Brooklyn Oil Co., and Green Island Oil Co., The North
Second St. and Middle Village R. R. Co. and treasurer of the
Brooklyn and Bushwick R. R. Co.   He was trustee of the Church
of the Pilgrims (Dr. R. S. Storrs), and the Washington Heights
Presbyterian Church (Dr. Chas. A. Stoddard), where he was also
chosen an elder, but his modesty prevented his acceptance.   When
he was 20 years old he was commissioned ensign (Dec. 24, 1827) of
the 10th Regt. of Infantry, N. Y., promoted lieutenant Sept. 20,
1828, and captain Sept. 10, 1833; he declined further promotion.

Capt. Green was elected for two terms, 1852-5, Alderman
from the First Ward (Brooklyn Heights), and Associate-Judge,
City Court.   He was a Whig, Native American, afterwards Union
and Republican.   His first vote was for John Quincy Adams,
Republican, his father and grandfather had been Federalists, but
that party was dead.

Alderman Green returned to New York after retiring from
business in 1856.   He was a member of the N. Y. Historical
Society, Society of the Sons of the Revolution, and War of 1812.†

He was the first one to whom his son imparted his plan to
organize the Mayflower Descendants, but when the meeting took
place, he was in his last sickness.

He lived at the time of his death, Dec. 30, 1894, at 235 Central
Park, West, and was buried in his mausoleum at Riverside
Cemetery, East Haddam, Conn.   Children:

187   i. William Todd[6] Greene, b. Jan. 2, 1838; d. May 16, 1847.
188   ii. Richard Henry Greene, b. June 12, 1839.

79. James Wilson[5] Green (Richard,[4] James,[3] William,[2] William[1]),
b. March 20, 1809; came to New York from East Haddam; m.
May 1, 1832, Catharine A. Whitney of Albany, N. Y., b. July 27,
1812; lived N. Y. City, then Richmond, Ind., for seven years,
then N. Y. until May 1, 1846, then Brooklyn, N. Y., where his
wife d. Aug. 21, 1849; she was dau. of Selleck and Betsey (Knapp)
Whitney.   Selleck was b. Stamford, Conn., June 28, 1779-80; m.
Jan. 26, 1805-6, Betsey, dau. of Jas. and Mary (Hubbell) Knapp.
He was son of Daniel and Hannah (Selleck) Whitney (see *Whit-
ney Genealogy*); she was dau. of Peter and Martha (Whiting)
Selleck.

* See *Todd Genealogy*, N. Y., 1867, also Appendix in same; *Duffie Family
Roosevelt Family, Herring Family and Dodge Family*.

† For other ancestry of W. W. Green see *Winslow Memorial, Webb
Genealogy* and *Magna Charta Barons and Their Descendants*.

While in Richmond, Ind., he was President of the village. Mr. Green m. (2) Mrs. Grace Hollister of Buffalo, N. Y.; she d. 1877. He was a lawyer, and active in politics; he and his brother William were members of the Order of the American Flag (Know Nothings) when James Harper was elected Mayor of New York, 1844, by the Native Americans. Mr. Green was editor of the *American Republican*, the party organ. He was elected, by the Republicans of New York, Councilman, 1864, '65 and '66, the last year he was chosen chairman. He d. Jan. 12, 1890, at Buffalo, N. Y., while on a visit to his dau. Anna Katherine Rohlfs. Children:

189   i. Sarah Elizabeth[6] Green, b. N. Y. C., Feb. 28, 1833; never m.; d. Jan. 18, 1906.

190   ii. James Frederick Green, b. N. Y. C., Jan. 11, 1835.

191   iii. Sidney Harper Green, b. Richmond, Ind., July 16, 1843.

192   iv. Anna Katherine Green, b. Nov. 11, 1846, Brooklyn, N. Y.

193   v. Henry Ward Beecher Green, b. July 22, 1849; d. Sept. 5, 1849.

80. SIDNEY[5] GREEN (Richard,[4] James,[3] William,[2] William[1]), b. at East Haddam, Jan. 2, 1811. When he came to New York his brothers Henry and William took him into their business, changing the firm name to Green & Co. He lived in Brooklyn and m. there Mary Gleason Deming, dau. of Frederick* and Mary (Gleason†) Deming of that place, May 12, 1846; she was b. in Litchfield, Conn., May 8, 1815. He was cotton merchant and broker, director of Union Bank, N. Y., also director and cashier

---

* John[1] Deming, the ancestor, m. 1637, Honor, dau. of Richard and Alice (Gaylord) Treat.

Daniel[2] Deming, b. Wethersfield, about 1652; m. Mary ——, 1678.

David[3] Deming, b. July 20, 1681; Harvard College, 1700; m. Mary Brigham; was ordained 1715, and preached at Medway, Mass.

David[4] Deming, b. Aug. 24, 1709, Middletown, Conn.; m. Mehitable, dau. of Henry and Mehitable (Rowley) Champion.(a)

Julius[5] Deming, b. April 16, 1755, N. Lyme, Conn.; m. Aug. 7, 1781, Dorothy, dau. of Henry and Deborah (Brainard) Champion.(a) He served in the army under Col. Champion in the commissary department, and moved to Litchfield.

Frederick[6] Deming, b. Oct. 4, 1787, Litchfield, Conn.; m. Mary, dau. of Ebenezer Steele and Prudence (Brainard) Gleason, July 19, 1813; she was b. May 15, 1796. He d. Sept. 13, 1860; she d. March 31, 1869, both at Brooklyn, N. Y. He was president of the Union Bank, N. Y.

† Thos.[1] Gleason, the ancestor, was at Watertown, Mass., 1652; Charlestown, 1662; m. Susanna ——.

Isaac[2] Gleason, b. 1654; lived at Enfield, was in the Falls fight, 1676, and d. 1698.

Isaac[3] Gleason, b. 1687; m. 1712, Mary, dau. of John Prior.

Isaac[4] Gleason, b. 1715; m. Sarah, dau. of Ebenezer Steele of Farmington.

Ebenezer Steele[5] Gleason, bap. Dec. 6, 1767; m. July 19, 1813, Prudence Brainard. They had: Mary[6] Gleason, b. May 15, 1796; m. Frederick[6] Deming, and Charlotte[6] Gleason, b. June 2, 1806; m. Richard W.[5] Green.

(a) Henry[1] Champion, the ancestor, of Saybrook, Conn., 1647.
Thomas[2] Champion, b. April, 1656; m. Aug. 23, 1682, Hannah Brockway.
Henry[3] Champion, b. May 2, 1695; m. Mehitable Rowley, dau. of Moses, and gr.-dau. of Moses and Elizabeth (dau. of Capt. Matthew Fuller) Rowley of East Haddam, Conn. Henry and Mehitable Champion had: Mehitable,[4] who m. David[4] Deming, and Col. Henry,[4] b. Jan. 19, 1720; m. Deborah Brainard, and had Dorothy[5] Champion, who m. Aug. 7, 1781, Julius[5] Deming, son of said David[4] Deming.

of the Marine Bank. He was trustee of the church of the Pilgrims (Rev. Dr. Storrs), Brooklyn. He d. at his residence, Monroe Place, Jan. 20, 1878; she d. Nov. 21, 1888. Children:
194   i. Mary Deming⁵ Green, b. Brooklyn, Feb. 6, 1848.
195   ii. Frederick Deming Green, b. Brooklyn, July 3, 1850.
196   iii. Ella Champion Green, b. May 8, 1852, Brooklyn.
197   iv. Clara Louisa Green, b. Dec. 28, 1855; d. Dec. 28, 1855.
198   v. Sidney Green, b. Dec. 19, 1856, Brooklyn.
81. FREDERICK WARREN⁵ GREEN (Richard,⁴ James,³ William,² William¹), b. East Haddam, Aug. 16, 1813. He was a merchant in his native town, and succeeded his uncle Timothy Green as postmaster, which office he held until 1845, when he removed to Brooklyn, N. Y. He manufactured cotton twine, later was engaged in the Brooklyn Oil Co., and finally was president of the National Storage Co., N. Y. He m. Mary Gardner Morgan, May 1, 1838; she was b. Sept. 24, 1815, dau. of Avery* and Jerusha (Gardner) Morgan of Colchester, Conn. She d. June 14, 1871. He d. April 5, 1870, in Brooklyn; both buried at East Haddam, Conn. Children:
199   i. Mary Lydia⁶ Green, b. Oct. 30, 1841, East Haddem.
200   ii. Eliza Bulkeley Green, b. Aug. 17, 1843; d. Oct. 12, 1844, East Haddam.
201   iii. Frederick Morgan Green, b. May 16, 1845, Colchester, Conn.
202   iv. Caroline Amelia Green, b. Sept. 18, 1847, Brooklyn, N. Y.
203   v. Morgan Henry Green, b. Feb. 5, 1850; d. Dec. 16, 1850.
204   vi. Henry William Green, b. April 13, 1853.
205   vii. Richard Avery Green, b. March 2, 1855; d. July 21, 1879.
83. SARAH ANN⁵ GREEN (Richard,⁴ James,³ William,² William¹), b. April 16, 1819, East Haddam. Some years after her father's death her mother and she moved to Brooklyn, N. Y. She m. Nov. 16, 1854, Samuel Canfield Wildman, who was b. March 16, 1811, Danbury, Conn., son of Fairchild and Mary (Canfield) Wildman. He united with the Congregational Church, Sept., 1831; was a farmer and director of the Danbury Bank. He m. (1) Sept. 3, 1835, Laura A. Bostwick, who was b. Aug. 29, 1812, and d. March 25, 1853. She had Mary, Samuel, Edgar and Laura, all deceased, only the last married. He d. 1894. Since then Sarah G. Wildman lived alone in Danbury until her death, April 18, 1908, aged 89 years. Children:
206   i. Fannie Louise⁶ Wildman, b. Feb. 21, 1856; d. June 6, 1856.

* James¹ Morgan, the ancestor, was b. in Wales 1607; came to Roxbury, Mass., 1640; m. Mary Hill; his son John,² m. (1) Rachel Dimond; m. (2) wid. Williams, dau. of Lt.-Gov. Wm. Jones, and gr.-dau. of Theophilus Eaton. William,³ b. 1693, eldest son of John, m. Mary, dau. of Capt. James Avery, Jr. Their eldest son, William, Jr.,⁴ b. June 17, 1723; m. Temperance Avery, and had: Wm. Avery⁵ Morgan, m. Lydia Smith. Their son Avery,⁶ m. Jerusha, dau. of Col. Jonathan Gardner. Mary Gardner⁷ Morgan, their fifth child, m. F. W. Green, in the text. Jonathan Gardner was son of John of Gardiner's Island; he m. Jerusha Stark, dau. of Silas and Jerusha (Hyde) Stark. (Vide *Morgan Gen.* and *Hyde Gen.*)

207   ii. Henry Green Wildman, b. Nov. 29, 1858.

84. NANCY[5] SPENCER (Ann Green,[4] James,[3] William,[2] William[1]), b. May 29, 1791, East Haddam; m. Oct. 27, 1819, Thomas Bunce of Middletown, Conn., a descendant of Thomas, of Hartford, 1640. Two children, neither m., and both d.:

208   i. Jared[6] Bunce.
209   ii. Nancy Bunce.

87. RICHARD GREEN[5] SPENCER (Ann Green,[4] James,[3] William,[2] William[1]), bap. May 4, 1800, East Haddam; m. Sept. 4, 1825, Sophia Lake; he lived in Canada and d. July 29, 1834. I am ignorant of this family.

88. NANCY[5] GREEN (Oliver,[4] James,[3] William,[2] William[1]), b. Cheshire, Mass., Aug. 25, 1798; m. Dec. 11, 1816, Horace Hayden,* b. 1786, son of Nehemiah, b. Dec. 4, 1755, and Sarah (Sill) Hayden of Essex, Conn. They lived in East Haddem. He was a merchant and ship builder. She d. July 3, 1822. He m. (2) Oct. 3, 1824, Esther (Beebe) Paine of Southold, L. I. He d. Aug. 18, 1840.† Children:

210   i. Nehemiah[6] Hayden, b. March 29, 1819.
211   ii. Nancy Green Hayden, b. Oct. 29, 1820.
212   iii. Horace Hayden, b. May 28, 1822.

92. OLIVER[5] GREEN (Oliver,[4] James,[3] William,[2] William[1]), b. East Haddam, Dec. 31, 1805; m. Sept. 21, 1839, at St. Louis, Mo., Georgian Marguerite Rohr; she was b. May 20, 1818, at Frederick, Md., dau. of George (b. April 25, 1793; d. Nov. 4, 1877) and Catharine (Koontz) Rohr; she d. Aug. 18, 1866, St. Louis, Mo. He was a manufacturer of vinegar, liquor and boat stores, and merchant. He d. at St. Louis, Sept. 27, 1875. Two children were b. Boonville, Mo., the others all in St. Louis. Children:

213   i. Cora Willey[6] Greene, b. Jan. 16, 1841.
214   ii. Katharine Henrietta Greene, b. April 12, 1843.
215   iii. Mary Alice Greene, b. Jan. 21, 1846.
216   iv. Evelyn Adelaide Greene, b. March 19, 1848.
217   v. Georgian Lucretia Greene, b. Jan. 6, 1851.
218   vi. Fannie Raiford Greene, b. May 6, 1854.
219   vii. Edward Marshall Greene, b. May 6, 1854; d. Feb. 1, 1855.
220   viii. Oliver Herbert Greene, b. Oct. 19, 1857.

93. LUCRETIA BACON[5] GREEN (Oliver,[4] James,[3] William,[2] William[1]), b. March 1, 1808, East Haddam; m. June 19, 1831, Dr. Sidney Brainerd Willey, b. Stafford, Conn., March 14, 1807, son of Calvin and Sally (Brainerd) Willey; Calvin was son of John Willey, b. 1741 (son of Benajah and Rachel Dutton Willey); m. April 30, 1767, Elizabeth, dau. of John and Elizabeth (Winslow) Marshall, the latter was b. Feb. 9, 1741, sister of Ruth Marshall (Mrs. James Green). John Willey was of Litchfield, Conn. Calvin was b. at

---

* John[1] Hayden was b. at Lyme, Conn., about 1700; his son was Nehemiah,[2] who had Uriah,[3] b. Jan. 10, 1732; m. Dec. 2, 1754, Ann Starkey, d. Nov. 24, 1808. Nehemiah,[4] b. Dec. 4, 1755, m. Sara Sill, d. May 29, 1791; they had Horace Hayden who m. Nancy Green.

† The children of Horace and Esther Hayden were: Geo. W., Wm. Henry, Jane M., Henrietta, Luther and Sarah Sill Hayden.

East Haddam, Sept. 15, 1776, he lived in Tolland Co., was Representative nine years, State Senator, two years, Judge of Probate, Presidential Elector, and 1825–1831, U. S. Senator. He d. Aug. 23, 1858. Lucretia Green Willey d. Nov., 1887. Dr. Willey graduated at Yale, 1828, and in medicine, 1831, practiced medicine in Brooklyn, N. Y., and d. April 13, 1853. Children:

221   i. James Marshall[6] Willey, b. March 25, 1832.
222   ii. Oliver Green Willey, b. May 15, 1835; d. Jan. 13, 1855.
223   iii. Sidney Brainerd Willey, Jr., b. Jan. 10, 1837; drowned June 28, 1847.
224   iv. Sarah Lucretia Willey, b. Sept. 17, 1841.
225   v. Sidney Brainerd Willey, b. Nov. 15, 1852.

96. MARY ANN[5] GREEN (Oliver,[4] James,[3] William,[2] William[1]), b. East Haddam, Nov. 11, 1816; m. Daniel Brainerd Warner, b. East Haddam, March 24, 1807, son of Daniel and Nancy (Brainerd) Warner. He was Brigade-Major and Inspector of Artillery, Conn. Major Warner has been Postmaster and Town Clerk, East Haddam; Rep. in Conn. Legislature, 1850–1, State Senator, 1852–3, President of Senate, 1853. He was ship builder and merchant, East Haddam; firm in later years D. B. Warner & Son. He d. Feb. 25, 1891; his widow d. Feb. 23, 1896. Children b. East Haddam, except first, b. Clinton, Mich.:

226   i. Nancy Lucretia[6] Warner, b. May 17, 1837; d. Jan. 19, 1838.
227   ii. Charles Belden Warner, b. July 28, 1839.
228   iii. Mary Green Warner, b. Aug. 7, 1842.
229   iv. Sidney Brainerd Warner, b. Dec. 5, 1848.
230   v. Georgian Lucretia Warner, b. April 3, 1852.
231   vi. Antoinette Louisa Warner, b. Sept. 22, 1854.

98. MARIA THERESA[5] GREEN (Timothy,[4] James,[3] William,[2] William[1]), dau. of Timothy and Mrs. Lucretia (Hathaway) (Knowles[*]) Green, was b. in East Haddam, April 21, 1815, was educated at Dr. Joseph Emerson's Seminary at Wethersfield, and m. in East Haddam, Oct. 14, 1840, Frederick William Shepard, M.D., of Essex, Conn. She removed to Hartford with three of her children soon after her husband's death, but was making her home in Saybrook at the time of her own death, which occurred in Hartford, May 4, 1883. Dr. Shepard, who was b. in Plainfield, Conn., March 18, 1812, was the son of Job Shepard, farmer, of Plainfield, and Azubah Clark of Saybrook, and was descended through a line of Plainfield and Concord, Mass., farmers from Ralph Shepard,[†] who came from Stephney, England, to Boston in 1635. Frederick W. was brought up in Saybrook, was graduated at the Yale Medical School in 1834, and practiced his profession for a brief period at Gale's Ferry, Conn., and for the remainder of his life at Essex, where he d. May 2, 1860. The children of Dr. and Mrs. Shepard, all b. in Essex, were:

---

[*] By her first marriage Mrs. Timothy Green was mother of Philo Knowles, a sea captain, who d. of yellow fever in the Gulf of Mexico; and Augusta Freeman Knowles, who lived in the family with her half sisters and brother until she m. late in life, Daniel W. Norton, a prominent citizen of Suffield, Conn.

[†] A small volume on *Ralph Shepard, Puritan*, was privately printed in 1893, by Ralph Hamilton Shepard of New Haven, N. Y., son of the late Sidney Shepard of Buffalo, N. Y.

232   i. Maria Green⁴ Shepard, b. April 14, 1842.
233   ii. Catherine Tyler Shepard, b. May 22, 1844; d. May 6,
          1846, Essex.
234   iii. Frederick Job Shepard, b. Jan. 23, 1850.
235   iv. Charlotte Lewis Shepard, b. Aug. 17, 1854.
236   v. John Woodruff Shepard, b. July 18, 1858.

99. CATHARINE LUCRETIA⁵ GREEN (Timothy,⁴ James,³ William,²
William¹), b. East Haddam, Aug. 14, 1819; m. Captain Henry
Selden Tyler, b. Haddam, Nov. 19, 1815, son of Selden and
Sarah (Randall) Tyler. They lived at East Haddam, Conn.,
Brooklyn, N. Y., and Brighton, Pa., where he d. Sept. 19, 1859.
He was a sea captain. She lived in Hartford, Conn., the latter
part of her life and d. there Sept. 26, 1887. Children:

237   i. Kate Green⁶ Tyler, b. May 12, 1848, East Haddam.
238   ii. Henry Whitney Taylor, b. March 6, 1850, East Haddam.
239   iii. Francis Tyler, b. Nov. 11, 1856, Brooklyn, N. Y.; d.
          April 16, 1857.

100. TIMOTHY FRANKLIN⁵ GREEN (Timothy,⁴ James,³ William,²
William¹), son of Timothy and Lucretia (Hathaway) (Knowles)
Green, was b. in East Haddam, Oct. 11, 1821, was educated at
Bacon Academy, Colchester, and after a brief engagement in the
manufacture of rubber goods in Colchester went West, spending
the greater part of his life in Malden, Ill., in lumber and grain
business. He served during the Civil War in the 139th Illinois
Volunteer Infantry. His last years were passed as clerk in the
Pension Office at Washington. He was prominent as a Sunday
school worker and as a Mason, and in Washington he was a deacon
and a much beloved member of the First Congregational Church.
He did a great deal of missionary work, had charge of a church in
Kansas for a year. He was a member of the Masonic Veterans
and of Pentalphia Lodge; State lecturer, editor of the *Mystic
Star*. He was a fine musician and belonged to many musical
clubs during his life, but especially used his talent in Christian
service. He m. in New London, Conn., Dec. 30, 1845, Sarah Maria,
dau. of Lemuel and Maria Ann (Dowd) Raymond, b. May 25,
1824. He d. in Washington, Feb. 14, 1895.* Mrs. Green d. in
Malden, Ill., Aug. 27, 1896. Their children were:

240   i. Caroline Amelia⁶ Green, b. Nov. 8, 1846, East Haddam.
241   ii. Timothy Franklin Green, b. Oct. 14, 1849, East Haddam.
242   iii. Catherine Maria Green, b. Dec. 29, 1854, Colchester,
          Conn.; d. Jan. 29, 1860, Malden, Ill.
243   iv. William Raymond Green, b. Nov. 9, 1856, Colchester.
244   v. Charles Dudley Green, b. Nov. 26, 1860, Malden.
245   vi. Henry Sidney Green, b. Aug. 17, 1864, Malden.
246   vii. Sarah Ann Green, b. Aug. 20, 1868, Malden.
247   viii. Ida Augusta Green, b. Dec. 3, 1869, Malden.

---

* Mr. Green was a great favorite in his native town, which was shown
when he was called to preside at the Centennial celebration of the church, in
Oct., 1894. He contracted a cold at that time, which resulted in his death a few
months afterwards. Mrs. Green was b. in Norwich, Mass. (now Huntington).
The family moved from there to Stockbridge, Mass., and thence to New
London, Conn.

RECORD OF MARRIAGES

By Ephraim Hubbell, Justice of the Peace in the North
Society of New Fairfield, at the Time of all the
following Marriages, but now the Town of
Sherman, Conn.

From Wm. A. Eardeley-Thomas.

1746, Oct. 12. Joseph Eastman & Phebe Henrise, both of New Fairfield, Conn.

Oct. 20. Joseph Congar & Hannah Pepper, both of New Fairfield.

1747, July 23. Joshua Cosens & Susannah Ellit.

Oct. 23. George Derle & Abiah Ginks.

1748, Feb. 28. William Browning & Patience Mosher.

April 4. Daniel Mosher & Ann Inwitt, both of the Oblong.

April 30. Saml Arnold & Dorithy Comstock.

May 2. Nathan Nobles of New Milford & Mary Gray of New Fairfield.

Nov. 7. Benjam Wells & Sarah Atwood.

Ebenezer Seley & Eliner Barns.

1749, Jan. 5. Samuel Cary & Susanna Page.

Oct. 12. John Maps & Lediah Cossons.

1750, Jan. 17. John Bennit & Abigil Hollister.

1751, March 11. Ebenezer Wright & Mercy Leach.

June 27. Job Lake & Desire Ginnins.

Dec. 5. Abraham Heneris & Elizabeth Wonzer.

1752, Oct. 11. William Makfield & Betty Jenk.

Oct. 24. Ebenezer Seleye & Hannah Hungerford.

Nov. 25. Amos Leach & Deborah Wonzer, both of New Fairfield.

1753, April 11. Gideon Prindle of New Milford & Lottis Towner of New Fairfield.

1754, June 13. Joseph Vaughan & Rebecca Towner, both of New Fairfield.

Oct. 31. Enoch Stilson of New Milford & Freelove Stilson of New Town.

1755, Sept. 23. David Wellow & Hepsibah Hubbell, both of New Fairfield.

1753, Oct. —. Robart Nicols & Anne Hurd.

1755, Nov. 27. Nehemiah Bardsle & Sarah Bardsle.

1756, July 13. David Barnum & Anna Towner, both of New Fairfield.

Feb. 5. James Pardee & Anna Wheeler.

Dec. 9. Saml Gregory & Abigail Hall of New Fairfield.

1757, Jan. 4. Silas Hill & Sarah Leach.

1757, March 16. Benjamin Barss & Abigail Barrit, at ye Meet⁻
ing House in yᵉ South Society.

  May 3. Hezekiah Olde of Stratfield & Rebak Bardsle of
New Fairfield.

  Aug. 25. Thoˢ Northrup & Joanna Leach, both of New
Fairfield.

1758, Feb. 7. Thoˢ Knap of Norfolk & Lowis Bass of New
Fairfield.

1759, April 28. Henery Burchance & Zurviah Hall, both of New
Fairfield.

1760, Jan. 17. Ephraim Quimby of Pattin(?) & Elizabeth Pepper of New Fairfield.

  April 2. John Leach & Martha Wonzer, both of New
Fairfield.

1761, May 14. John Maine of Stoning Town & Hannah Prindle
of New Fairfield.

1762, Feb. 8. Ephraim Leach & Dorithy Benit, both of New
Fairfield.

  Feb. 10. Mr. Peter Eastman & Esther Laine.

  March 11. Nathan Barnum & Lois Wheeler, both of New
Fairfield.

  Nov. 9. Nathaniel Hays & Lydia Mapes.

1763, Jan. 19. David Prindle & Jemima Leach of New Fairfield.

  Feb. 22. John Smith & Zurviah Page, both of New Fairfield.

  April 25. Gaions Smith & Keziah Gage.

1765, Oct. 30. Enoch Peck & Mary Graves of New Fairfield.

  Nov. 7. David Stevens & —— Barnum, both of New
Fairfield.

  Dec. 11. Shadrach Hubbell & Hannah Moger, both of
New Fairfield.

1766, Jan. 22. Simeon Leach & Elizabeth Prindle.

  Jan. 28. Abell Hollister of New Fairfield & Abigail
Chambers of New Town.

  June 11. Jonathan Hollister & Elizabeth Wording.

  Aug. 31. Amos Hoigg & Lydia Hoigg.

  Sept. 11. Ebenezer Stevens & Silence Barnum, both of
New Fairfield.

1767, Nov. 8. John Prindle & wid. —— Leach.

1768, June 7, Joseph Morgan & Mary Page.

1769, April 11. John Sturdivent & Joanna Conger.

  Sept. 3. William Thorn & Matha Hoigg.

1770, Nov. 1. Edward Ritchards & Lidea Page.

1771, Nov. 13. Samuel Marsh of New Milford & Merriam Leach.

1772, March 2. John Marsh of New Milford & Abigail Wonzer
of New Fairfield.

  July 9. John Leach & Hannah Page.

  Dec. 3. Amasa Hungerford & Elizabeth Seelye.

1773, Jan. 21. Timothy Barnum & Thankful Hollister, both of
New Fairfield.

1773, Jan. 26. Ruben Cran (or w) of Ridgefield & Mary Touner of New Fairfield.

April 15. Abel Cozer & Mary Moger, both of New Fairfield.

1774, Oct. 4. Eleazer Bennidict of Danbury & Ruth Hollister of New Fairfield.

Nov. 24. Caleb Pitts & Esther Sturdivent.

Dec. 19. John Gould of Fairfield & Elizabeth Sturdevant of New Fairfield.

1775, Feb. 2. Joel Conger & Anna Hollister, both of New Fairfield.

Feb. 17. Enos Peck & Anna Marsh, both of New Fairfield.

1776, Jan. 1. Ichabod Leach of New Fairfield & Ruth Marsh of New Milford.

July 3. Zephen^h Briggs & Patience Nuton, both of New Fairfield.

Oct. 25. John Page of Williams Town & Rebecca Porter of New Fairfield.

1777, March 3. Jeremiah Hackston & Rhoda Akins, both of Dutchess County.

May 27. Seth Barnum of Danbury & Abigail Bass of New Fairfield.

Sept. 14. Nathaniel Howland & —— Akin, both of Oblong.

Sept. 27. George Higgins & Patience Mapes, both of New Fairfield.

1778, Feb. 4. Mr. Jonathah Page & Johanah Northrup.

Feb. 26. Nathan Turrill of New Milford & Dorithy Phelps of New Fairfield.

April 9. Paul Wildman of Farming Town & Phebe Eastman of New Fairfield.

Oct. 29. Jeams Gregory & Lowis Rindle, both of New Fairfield.

Nov. 1. Willm G. Hubbell & Abigail Hyat.

Dec. 22. James Read of Judea & Martha Smith of New Fairfield.

1779, Dec. 9. Stephen Pepper, jr., & Esther Wonzer.

Dec. 16. Barnard Carpenter & Mabell Grannis.

Dec. 26. Joseph Barlow & Esther Orsborn.

1780, March 30. James Hazard & Martha Gold.

July 22. Nathaniel Fuller & Deborah Moger.

Sept. 11. Barnibas Wileman & Lowis Page.

1781, March 7. Elijah Conger & Martha Leach.

May 6. William Smith & Silence Pepper, widow.

Aug. —. Samuel Cook & Polly Wright.

Oct. 16. Capt. Joseph Giddings & wid. Elisabeth Kelley.

Oct. 30. —— Harvey & wid. Cone.

Nov. 1. Zadack Pratt & Hannah Pickit.

1782, March 19. Abel Lampher & Hannah Knap.

1783, Feb. 6. Jabiz Elwell & Dorcas Barnum.

July —. (torn) & Hannah Row.

Sept. 18. Rosill Lamphear & Elizabeth Lamphear.

1783, Sept. 20. Willm Gold & wid. Pitts.
(torn) Morrison & Hannah (torn) of Newbury.
1783, (torn) 25. Amos Hubbell & Lucy Holms.*
    " John Orsborn & Betsey Hollister.
1784, Feb. 19. Pownal Deming & Abigail Hubbell.
  April 12. Alex^{dr} Stuart, Esq., & wid. Zurviah Wright.
  Jan. 11. Ruben Cran (or w) & Rua Day.
  Aug. 12. Seth Gorham & Mille Dunk.
  Nov. 18. Seth Pepper & Azuba Leach.
  Dec. 28. John Durgee & Hannah Conger, both of New Fairfield.
1785, April 14. Amos Northrup & Zurviah Hungerford.
  April 15. John Hendrick & Anne Barnum.
  April 20. John Leach, Jr., & Uranah Hall.
  April 20. Ethel Burns & Griswold Hunt of New Milford.
  April 20. Henery Hatch & Amanda Hubbell.
  Sept. 28. Eliakim Andrus & Aniss Nickerson.
  Oct. 10. Stephen Benitt & Elizabeth Leach, both of New Fairfield.
1786, Jan. 8. Alfred Brunson of New Milford & Hannah Ackley.
  Jan. 19. —— Elliott of Dover & Liviney Stewart of New Fairfield.
  Feb. 28. Samuel Godfree of Fairfield & Clarice Fairchild of New Fairfield.
  March 13. Jacob Odle of Manchester & Rebecca Erbs (or Erls) of New Fairfield.
  May 1. James Quimbe & Hannah Burduff.
  May 25. Samuel Underhill of Dosset & Annis Barns.
  June 21. Charles Barns & Mercy Leach.
  June 22. John Benedict of Danbury & Rhamah Phelps of New Fairfield.
  June 29. Willm French & Lucee Hatch of New Fairfield.
  Oct. 30. John Worner & Abigail Stevens, both of New Milford.
  Nov. 12. Asa Brunson of New Milford & Elizabeth Hatch of New Fairfield.
  Nov. 13. Abraham Seeman of Dover & Lucindiah Gidgions of New Fairfield.
  Nov. 22. Nath^{el} Loomis of Washington & Anna Moger of New Fairfield.
1787, Feb. —. Seth Scovel & Abiah Conger of New Fairfield.
  March 25. Elihu Steuart & Eunice Wright, both of New Fairfield.
  April 12. Amos Leach & Helind Pepper of New Fairfield.

* Amos Hubbel, who m. 1783, Lucy Holms, was a son of Ephraim Hubbell, the Justice of the Peace, who m. the foregoing 144 couples, and before his marriage had been a soldier in the Revolution. His widow, in making application for pension in 1838, sent to the Pension Office at Washington, the original record of the foregoing marriages to prove her own marriage. In 1878, the Pension Office returned the said original record to the New Fairfield Town Clerk, and in April, 1885, they were in his safe, but have since disappeared.

1787, April 19. Eph^m Conger & Experience Eastman.

June 27. Rusel Wing of Quaker Hill & Nancy Fields of New Fairfield.

July 1. Jobe Hurlbut & Margit Hungerford, both of New Fairfield.

1788, Jan. 10. Hubbard Barlow & Polly Hubbell, both of New Fairfield.

Feb. 10. Henery Stevens of Fredrikburg & Experience Hatch of New Fairfield.

Feb. 17. Isaac Northrup & Urana Hubbell of New Fairfield.

Feb. —. Gabriel Sherwood & Johannah Sunderlin of New Fairfield.

April 13. Hail Lum of New Milford & Mary Prindle of New Fairfield.

1790, Feb. 18. William Bostwick & Mary Bearns of New Fairfield.

Nov. 7. Daniel Leach & Lois Lacey, both of New Fairfield.

Nov. 7. Gideon Draper & Dircus(?) Hollister, both of New Fairfield.

Nov. 22. Abraham Talman & Ollive Dugliss of Fishkills.

1791, Jan. 25. Ebenezer Hollister & Phebe Pepper, both of New Fairfield.

NEW YORK GLEANINGS IN ENGLAND,

Including "Gleanings," by Henry F. Waters, not before printed.

CONTRIBUTED BY LOTHROP WITHINGTON,
30 Little Russell St., W. C., London.

(Continued from Vol. XXXIX., p. 46 of the RECORD).

Edward Amhurst of Annapolis Royal in America, Esquire, but now residing in Cecil Street in the Strand in the County of Middlesex. Will 5 June, 1754; proved 25 June, 1754. All to my wife Mary Amhurst of Annapolis Royal. Executors: my wife Mary Amhurst and my friends Phillip Bromfield and Thomas Blanure of Lombard Street, London. Testator being seized with a paralytic stroke put his mark. Witnesses: E. Winniett, J. Morgan, F. Monson.   Penfold, 157.

William Cosby, Esq., Governor of New York and New Jersey in America. Will 9 March 1735-6; proved 3 July, 1739. The tract of land purchased of the Germans called the Manor of Cosby on both sides of the Mohaeke River in Albany County to

15

my two sons William and Henry. One third part of my lands in Rochester in Ulster County and the mines there to my wife Grace Cosby and the other two parts to my said two sons. My House and ground in Soho Square, London to my wife. My house at St. Leonards Hills and lands adjoining to my wife for life and at her decease to my son William. Residuary Legatee and Executrix: My wife Grace Cosby. Witnesses: James De Lancey, John Felton, Charles Williams, Will Cosby, Joseph Murray.   Henchman, 145.

Abraham Duane, Commander of his Majesty's Sloop, the *Beaver*. Will 3 January 1767; proved 28 August 1767. Sole Legatee and Executor: my Brother Cornelius Duane of the City of New York in North America. Witnesses: Richard Wells, David Hunter, George Dawford. Proved by William Neate, attorney for Cornelius Duane now residing at New York in North America.   Legard, 303.

Augustine Gordon of St. Johns Wappen, county of Middlesex, Chyrurgeon being now bound out in a voyage to sea. Will 2 November 1705; proved 8 December 1712. All my lands and estate in America I give to my wife Margarett for life and then at her decease to my son William Gordon. Residuary Legatee and Executrix: my wife Margaret. Witnesses: Joseph Haden in Wapping, Margaret Mearillon in Wapping near the Hermitage, Ephraim Bromwich, Scrivener in Virginia Street.

                                               Barnes, 235.

Hector Mackenzie, late of the Town of Bath on the Cohorton River in the County of Steuben and state of New York in the United States of North America, but now living at No. 63 Hatton Garden, county Middlessex, Esq. Will 16 October 1802; proved 5 August 1807. To William MacCra of Cree Bridge in County of Kirkubright, Galloway, Esq., and Daniel Wilson Davison of Clements Inn, Gentleman, all lands in the County of Steuben, opposite Mud Creek, formerly surveyed for Benjamin Patterson, two lots in Township No. 4, formerly surveyed by William Kersey, land in Township No. 5, surveyed by William Kersey for Hector Mackenzie which were confirmed by indentures made in September 1800 between Charles Williamson of Bath and me, also tract of land in Township No. 6 abutting on Crooked Lake, by an indenture made by Peter Faulkener of East Town in Pennsilvania, also land from William Dunn of Bath and land from Charles Cameron, also a messuage in Morris street in Bath, land from Finlay McClure, and all my money and goods in trust for my wife Diana, during her lifetime, and then after her decease for my children, to be equally divided among them when 21. Executors in trust of my will and guardians to my children: the said William McCra and Daniel Wilson Davison. Witnesses: F. Gogerly 2 Mount Roe, Lambeth, Elizabeth Mackenzie, Wandsworth Road, H. M. O. Mackenzie, same place.

                                               Lushington, 685.

William Smith. Will March 5 1755; proved 3 May, 1756. To James Skinner Esq. Sir, immediately after my decease its my desire that you and Mr. Adrian Philips become possessors of my shallop *Charming Peggy* of Bonacord. I charge my estate with the payment of two hundredweight of refined wax to Doctor Robert Jeffreys, ditto to Mr. Tobias Lisle. What Mr. Lewis Voss is indebted to me I forgive him. To "Crony 12 cans of such money as he chooses." My slave Angella I make free and give her for her sole use my slave man Thomas and my slave woman Domingo. I give my slave woman Tombang to Leestia, Rest of my goods to be remitted to Johnson and Fothergill, Merchants of London for the benefit of my friends. Executors: Governor Mr. Skinner and Mr. Adrian Phillips and all accounts depending between you (Mr. Skinner) Mr. Louree and my self I refer to you settling. At Bracoe Port in presence of Robert Jefferys, Daniel Crony.   Glazier, 150.

THE SANDS FAMILY.

CONTRIBUTED BY F. C. L. BECK.

The following record, apparently made by Joshua Sands, one of the early merchants of the City of New York, appears upon an old paper now preserved by one of his descendants, and will be of interest to the many members of that named family, who now reside in this city. The notes contained in parenthesis do not appear in the ancient paper but were from the records of St. Ann's Church, Brooklyn, N. Y., or elsewhere among family papers:

Josh* Sands, youngest son of John Sands of Queens County, Long Island, b. at Cow Neck, the 12 day of Oct., 1757; confirmed by Bishop Provoost, 20 Oct., 1791. (Died in Brooklyn, Sept. 13, 1835.)

Ann Ayscough, daughter of Dr. Richard Ayscough of the City of New York, was b. in New York the 5 day of Jan., 1761; confirmed as above. (Died in Brooklyn, July 17, 1851.)

Josh* Sands and Ann Ayscough were m. by the Rev. Mr. Moffatt at the house of Col. Wm. Malcolm, Wallkill, County of Ulster, on the 9 day of March, 1780. (Their children were:)

Ann Moore Sands was b. at Rhinebeck, in the County of Dutchess, on the 1 day of Jan., 1781; bap. by Mr. Moffatt; confirmed as above. (Married Fanning Cobham Tucker, July 11, 1804; d. ——, 1833.)

Richard Ayscough Sands was b. at Dr. Van Wyck's at Fishkill, Monday the 7 of April, 1783; bap. by Mr. Moffatt. (Buried St. Ann's Church, March 12, 1818.)

Grace Sands was b. in New York the 29 day of Nov., 1784; was bap. the 19 day of Dec. following, by the Rev. Mr. Beach; godmothers: Mrs. Moore, Mrs. Maher; godfather: Mr. Wm. Malcolm; d. Feb. 13, 1793, at 8 o'clock, a. m.

Elizabeth Sands was b. in New York the 20 day of Sept., 1786, and was bap. Sunday, the 15 day of Oct. following, by the Rev. Mr. Beach; godmother: Mrs. Malcolm. (Married Edward Trenchard, U. S. N., Feb. 3, 1814.)

William Malcolm Sands was b. March 9, 1788, at Brooklyn, in Kings County, and was bap. by the Rev. Mr. Wright, on Sunday the 30th following; godfathers: General William Malcolm, Mr. Peter McDougall; godmother: Mrs. Malcolm. (Married Elizabeth Breese; d. May 12, 1866.)

Sarah Ann Sands was b. Saturday, 27 day February, 1790, at Brooklyn, Kings County, and was bap. by the Rev. Mr. Wright, on Sunday, 21st day March following; Richard Moore Ayscough, godfather; Mrs. Barron and Miss Latouche, godmothers. (Married Thomas March, Sept. 28, 1808; buried St. Ann's Church, Nov. 28, 1860.)

Matilda Caroline Sands was b. at Brooklyn (K. C.), on Monday, March 5, 1792, and was bap. 29, s^d m^o, by the Rev. Mr. Rattoon; godmothers: Miss Fanny Malcolm, Miss Matilda Cruger; go a e, Mr. James Cornwall. (Buried St. Ann's Church, Ma$\mathfrak{ddththo}$,r1822.)

Joshua Rattoon Sands was b. at Brooklyn, May 13, 1795, and bap. by Rev. Dr. Nesbitt; spon.: Elijah D. Rattoon and H. Sands. (He m. (1) Mary Stevens; (2) Harriet Stevens; (3) Eliza Ann Crook.) (Died 1883, Rear-Admiral, U. S. N.)

Grace Augusta, b. 28 Feb., 1797. (Married Joseph Henshaw.)

Samuel Bayard Malcolm, b. 12 July, 1799. (Married Madaline Middagh, Nov. 9, 1825; buried Sept. 17, 1832.)

John Cornwall, b. 31 July, 1801; d. 14 Jan., 1804.

Harriet Ayscough, b. Oct. 10, 1803; d. unm.

SOCIETY PROCEEDINGS.

MARCH 10TH, 1908.

A Regular Meeting of the Board of Trustees was held on Tuesday, March 10th, 1908, at 4.45 P. M., the President being in the Chair.

Present: Messrs. Bowen, Drowne, Eliot, Gibson, Morrison, Mott, Totten and Wright.

The minutes of the last stated meeting were read, and on motion, duly seconded, approved.

The Secretary then read a letter from Mrs. Helen M. Dwight thanking the Society for the engrossed memorial of the late President Dwight, and also a letter of Mr. Archibald Rogers, withdrawing his resignation.

WITH PROFOUND SORROW THE NEW
YORK GENEALOGICAL AND BIOGRAPH-
ICAL SOCIETY ANNOUNCE THE DEATH
OF THE HONORABLE GROVER CLEVE-
LAND, HONORARY MEMBER, ON JUNE
24, 1908.

The Treasurer then read a statement of the several funds to date and reported the purchase of one New York City 4½% Bond, debited to the Permanent Fund.

On motion, duly seconded, it was resolved that the invested portion of the Reserve Fund be transferred to the Building Fund, increasing said fund to about $4,000.00.

The Chairman of the Executive Committee then reported the recent changes in some of the tenants of the building, and as Chairman of the Building Committee, reported that owing to the fact that only $3,900.00 was available in cash to finance a transaction of some $65,000.00; that the present annual rental value of the new property would be about $2,750.00, and the total estimated cost of maintenance and interest would be $4,012.32, acquiring the adjoining premises would result in an annual deficit of $1,262.32, which would have to be met by the Society. It was accordingly the unanimous opinion of the Committee that no steps be taken to acquire the adjoining premises until the available cash assets be increased to $20,000.00. He further read a letter from the real estate agent in regard to the method of acquiring the adjoining premises and financing the operation by mortgages.

On motion, duly seconded, it was resolved that the report and recommendations of the Building Committee be accepted and adopted.

The Chairman of the Publication Committee then stated that Volume IV of the Society Collections would soon be completed and the Publication Committee were authorized to expend up to $600.00 in issuing same.

The President then announced the proposed speakers and their subjects for the March, April and May meetings of the Society.

On motion, duly seconded, it was resolved that the next regular meeting of the Trustees be postponed from the second Tuesday to the third Monday in May, and there being no further business, the meeting was on motion, duly seconded, adjourned.

MARCH 13TH, 1908.

A Regular Meeting of the Society was held on Friday, March 13, 1908, at 8.30 P. M., the President being in the Chair. The Executive Committee reported the election of the following Annual Members:—Henry Trumbull Bronson, George Austin Morrison, Leon Nelson Nichols, Mrs. Elwood Osborn Roessle.

The President then introduced Mr. William Macdonald, Ph.D., LL.D., Professor of American History at Brown University, who proceeded to address the meeting on the subject of "John Neal, Literary Critic."

At the close of the lecture, it was on motion, duly seconded, resolved that the thanks of the members and guests present be extended to the speaker for his entertaining and instructive lecture, and there being no further business the meeting was on motion, duly seconded, adjourned.

APRIL 10TH, 1908.

A Regular Meeting of the Society was held on Friday, April 10th, 1908, at 8.30 P. M., the President being in the Chair. The Executive Committee reported the election of the following Life Member:—Henry Richard Taylor; and of the following Annual Members:—Murray Whiting Ferris, Edmund Hendricks, Jefferson M. Levy, Mrs. Charles Stewart Maurice, Robert C. Ogden, Edward Truex Platt, Jordan Jackson Rollins, Henry Woodward Sackett, Laurence Eugene Sexton, Arthur Outram Sherman and Robert Talmadge.

The President then introduced Mr. William Webster Ellsworth, who addressed the meeting on the subject of "Arnold and André, the Story of the Treason," illustrated with stereopticon views.

At the close of the lecture it was on motion, duly seconded, resolved that the thanks of the members and guests present be extended to the speaker for his interesting and instructive lecture, and there being no further business the meeting was on motion, duly seconded, adjourned.

15A

MAY 8TH, 1908.

A Regular Meeting of the Society was held on Friday evening, May 8th, 1908, at 8.45 o'clock. Mr. Tobias A. Wright, the Second Vice-President being in the Chair.

The Executive Committee reported the election of the following members:—Life Members: Gustav Amsinck, James Benedict, Edward Motley Weld. Annual Members: Mrs. Albro Akin, Rev. John Betts Calvert, D.D., Heth Lorton, Edward Bunnell Phelps, Maj. Harmon Pumpelly Read, Arthur Charles Rounds, Philip Henry Waddell Smith, William Alexander Smith, Charles Wadhams Stevens, Mrs. Thomas S. Strong, Erastus Theodore Tefft, Allen Mason Thomas, M.D., Theodore Newton Vail, Mrs. Schuyler Van Rensselaer, Mrs. William Leslie Van Sinderen, George Henry Warren, John I. Waterbury, Mrs. Levi Candee Weir, Alexander McMillan Welch, Horace White, Richard Henry Williams, Lucius Kellogg Wilmerding, Edwin Dean Worcester. Corresponding Member: Henry Judson Galpin, to represent Chenango County, New York.

Miss Mary V. Worstell, the speaker of the evening was then introduced and gave a lecture on "The Signers of the Declaration of Independence," illustrated with stereopticon views.

At the conclusion of the lecture, the thanks of those present was extended to the speaker for her interesting and instructive talk. There being no further business, the meeting was on motion, duly seconded, adjourned.

MAY 18TH, 1908.

A Joint Meeting of the Board of Trustees and of the Executive Committee was held on Monday, May 18, 1908, at 4 P. M., the President being in the Chair.

Present: Messrs. Bowen, Eliot, Field, Gibson, Morrison, Mott, Pell, Totten, Van Norden, Walker and Wright.

The minutes of the last stated meeting of the Board of Trustees and of the Executive Committee were respectively read and on motions, duly seconded, respectively approved.

The Treasurer then read a statement of the financial condition of the Society to date, upon which current appropriations were based, and the Publication Committee was authorized and instructed to prepare the Index for Volume XXXIX of THE RECORD when complete. The regular monthly accounts were then read, audited and approved, and the Treasurer authorized to pay same.

The resignation of Lewis D. Burdick, as Corresponding Member for Chenango County, New York, was received and accepted with regrets.

On motion, duly seconded, it was resolved that Life Membership and Entrance Fees to the amount of $520.00 be transferred to the Permanent Fund.

The Chairman of the Executive Committee then reported the leases entered into with new tenants in the building and the terms thereof, the statement of membership, showing a gain of 30 for the five months of the fiscal year, amounting to the sum of $825, and a statement of THE RECORD subscriptions and monies derived therefrom; a statement of the room and hall rents received; a statement of full sets and back numbers of THE RECORD sold; a statement of Dutch Church Marriages and Baptisms sold; a statement of RECORD Subject Indices sold; a statement of Pedigree Charts sold, and of Duplicates of the Library sold, all of which in detail were annexed to the minutes of the meeting. He further requested that the Treasurer be authorized and instructed to transfer to the Building Fund, the 4 U. S. Steel Bonds, 20 shares of U. S. Rubber 1st Pref. and 4 New York City 4½% Bonds, aggregating $4,400.00, and to the Permanent Fund the U. S. Steel Bond and 3 New York City 4½% Bonds, aggregating $800.00, which was on motion, duly seconded, so ordered.

He stated that the total invested funds then amounted to $5,200.00, netting the Society an annual income of $316.50.

The question of the present securities, consisting of bonds and stocks, being proper investments for the funds of the Society being discussed, it was the unanimous opinion of the Trustees present that such investments were proper and legal under the Charter of the Society, inasmuch as the sums invested were not specifically donated or acquired as guardianship or testamentary trust funds.

The Chairman of the Executive Committee then reported certain alterations and improvements to the building, and certain negotiations with prospective new tenants, which were approved and left to his discretion.

It was on respective motions, duly seconded, resolved that the Society do not acquire the copy of Records of First Baptists Church at Fleming, New York; that the Society present the California Genealogical Society with the last 5 volumes of THE RECORD, as a gift to build up the new collection of that Society; that the Treasurer pay all fixed charges and current expenses during the summer, as audited and approved by the Chairman of the Executive Committee; that the office and library be closed on Saturdays at 1 P. M. during the months of June, July, August and September, that the summer vacations of the Assistant-Librarian and of the Curator be the same as last year; that the library be closed for cleaning during the vacation of the Assistant-Librarian, and that the Editor of THE RECORD be a committee of one to examine into and report in regard to publishing a continuation of the Dutch Church Records of New York City, from 1800-1850.

There being no further business, the meeting was on motion, duly seconded, adjourned.

OBITUARY.

POSTLEY, COL. CLARENCE ASHLEY, of 817 Fifth Avenue, New York City, son of Gen. Brooke Postley, was born in New York, Feb. 9, 1849. He was elected an Annual Member of The New York Genealogical and Biographical Society Nov. 13, 1903. He died May 28, 1908. His wife and a daughter survive him. He was graduated from West Point in 1870, and was assigned to the Artillery branch of the army. Saw service in Florida in 1870-1872. Was Assistant-Professor of Mathematics at West Point, 1873-1878. Resigned from the service in 1883, with the rank of Lieutenant of Artillery in the Regular Army. He also served on the staff of his father with the rank of Colonel of Engineers. In 1874 he married Margaret Sterling of Bridgeport, Conn. This lady's ancestry dates back to the earliest Colonial days of Connecticut, and her family has always been one of the most substantial in the State. Colonel Postley was not engaged in any business, his time being occupied in the care of his father's estate. He possessed a valuable library, relating largely to the military history of this country. He was an enthusiastic yachtsman. Was at one time Commodore of the Larchmont Yacht Club and was the recipient of a large number of prizes for victories in many yacht races. He was also a member of nearly all the leading yacht clubs as well as the Union League, University, Manhattan, Riding, Players, United Service and the Country Club of Westchester County. He was also a patron of the Metropolitan Museum of Art. He resided a great deal in Paris and was on here for a short visit when he died.

STONE, COL. WILLIAM LEETE, A.B., A.M., LL.D., an ex-member of The New York Genealogical and Biographical Society, died on Thursday, June 11, 1908. He was a member of this Society during the year 1896. Amongst the publications of which the late Col. Stone was a collaborator in translation and which work was of great genealogical interest was the translation of the Dutch Records of New York City, and it may be of interest to state that his associates in this literary production were all members of The New York Genealogical and Biographical Society. Three of his most important works were: *The Life and Times of Sir William Johnson, Bart; Burgoyne's Campaign and St. Ledger's Expedition*, and *History of Washington County, New York*.

QUERIES.

MARIS.—Among the first settlers of Hudson and Bergen Cos., N. J., appears the name of Jury Maris—*an Englishman.* Jury Maris also owned land at Schraalenburgh. In 1723 (16 April) a Jurran Morris was requested by Cornelius Haring and Barent Nonel (both of Tappan), executors of the will of John Hart of Woodbridge, N. J., to examine said will. On church records of Hackensack, N. J., and of Tappan, N. Y., are the baptisms of the children of Jurian Maris and Freda Hause Harty (she bap. N. Y., 26 Aug., 1671). Can any one give parentage of above Jury (Jurie, Jurran, Jurian) Maris? His descendants all call themselves Morris.   CATHARINE T. R. MATHEWS,
Croton-on-Hudson, N. Y.

ROWLAND.—Wanted, the ancestry and parentage of David Rowland, b. 1762; d. 1843; buried near Fabius, Onondago Co., N. Y. Was he a son of David Rowland to whom, with others, the township of Sharon, N. Y., was granted on Feb. 12, 1767. He m. (1) Anna ——; m. (2) Zarviah Whipple, dau. of Isaiah and Eunice Whipple of Alexander, Genesee Co., N. Y., and had issue, a son Harry, who m. Mary Ann Parkerson, dau. of William(?) and Mary A. (Tompkins) Parkerson of Stony Point and Haverstraw, N. Y. Any information as to his brother or sister, as well as names of ancestors will be greatly appreciated.   GRACE M. ROWLAND, 502 Bee Building, Omaha, Neb.

SEELEY.—Fanny Seeley who d. in 1834; m. Joseph Bennett, b. Dec. 31, 1783, in Newtown, Conn.; d. in 1862. Can any one give me the names of the parents of Fanny Seeley.

BENNITT—FORD.—Thomas Bennitt or Bennett, b. Nov. 9, 1732, at Newtown, Conn.; d. Feb. 7, 1836; m. Sept. 29, 1772, Mollie Ford, who d. Aug. 9, 1814. Who were the parents of Mollie Ford?
Thomas Bennitt built over the Hoosatonic River a bridge known as the "Bennitt Toll Bridge." Tradition states that Patriot troops were allowed to pass over this bridge *without paying* toll. I would be glad to know if there is any historic proof of this tradition.   V. V. H., P. O. Box 536, New York City.

ERRATA.

HEARNE GENEALOGY.—In Vol. XXXIX, No. 2, p. 142 of THE RECORD, under Book Reviews, the name of the family should be printed "Hearne," that being the usual and correct spelling.

LANE GENEALOGIES.—In Vol. XXXIX, No. 2, p. 143 of THE RECORD, under Book Reviews, name of printer should be "The News-Letter Press, Exeter, N. H. 1903."

BOOK NOTICES.

THE ANTI-RENT WAR, by Albert Chapman Mayham. Cloth, Small Quarto, pp. 89. Press of Frederick L. Frazee, Jefferson, N. Y. 1906.

The attempt of Stephen Van Rensselaer to eject certain tenants in the Townships of Bern, Westerlo and Renneslaerville, Albany County, N. Y., and on "Blenheim Hill" from the lands owned by Patroon Van Rensselaer, because of non-payment of rent is the theme of this small book. The author tells the story of the anti-rent agitation of 1839–1846 in a clear, conversational style, which makes pleasant, as well as instructive reading. How the trouble of John A. King of Jamaica, Long Island, with his farm tenants on Blenheim Hill arose, and how they were settled has been hitherto almost an unknown chapter in the land history of the State of New York, and the author is to be heartily congratulated in placing the facts and persons engaged in this mimic war so vividly before the reading public. Clear type and excellent wood-cut illustrations make the work attractive and a desirable acquisition to both large and small libraries.

THE ANCESTORS OF ABNER BRUSH AND LAURA (HUBBARD) BRUSH, by Mrs. Chauncey H. Brush. Boards, 12mo, pp. 58. Privately printed. 1908.

This small brochure traces the descendants of Thomas Brush of Huntington, Long Island, N. Y., who owned a lot at Southold prior to 1653, and gives in narrative forms the genealogical details of their family history. It is more of a memorandum than a genealogy, but it is interesting reading and the notes are of value. The idea of tracing out and describing the several family bibles is excellent and worthy of being followed in more pretentious works.

THE CLARK FAMILY GENEALOGY, by Dr. A. W. Clark. Cloth, 8vo, pp. 149. Press of The Mirror-Recorder, Stamford, N. Y. 1907.

While this work purports to be a comprehensive genealogy of the Clark Family in the United States, it is practically only a record of the descendants of Randall and Dorothy (Tucker) Clark and Hazard and Eunice (Clark) Clark, carried out in the female as well as the male lines. A mass of disconnected data is included in the work, much of which has little or no reference to the families of Clark traced out. The compiler appears to have levied tribute upon various standard Clark Genealogies already published, without giving the authors any credit or notice for the extracts. Notably pages 72 and 78 are taken verbatim from *The Clarke Families of Rhode Island*, the standard work on this Rhode Island family—which unfortunately was not copyrighted. This abstracted material Dr. Clark has actually copyrighted in his book as if it was from original research—'tho it is the usual courteous custom in such cases to acknowledge the source of such wholesale extracts.

There are a number of errors and inaccuracies in the data—notably the descent of Timothy Clark, b. 29 March, 1719, stated on p. 13 to be a son of Timothy and Sarah (Richardson) Clark of Stonington, Conn., 'tho actually a son of John and Lydia (Andrews) Clarke of Stonington, who is assumed to be a son of Timothy and Sarah (Robbins) Clark of Bristol and Stonington, Conn., as the compiler admits in his introduction on p. 5. There is not the slightest proof that this Timothy Clark was in any way related to the great Clark family of Westhorpe, Co. Suffolk, England, which by the by Dr. Clark states came from Bedfordshire—an error which he found and copied from Austin's *Rhode Island Dictionary*—and which Austin some time past acknowledged to be a mistake.

The compiler frankly admits the basis for this work in the introduction, and the authority of the sources of his record may well be questioned by skilled and accurate genealogists.

The book appears to be a loose compilation of Clark facts and records already printed in other works, gathered from examination of printed works in libraries and historical societies rather than from the original records, and taken without acknowledgment or reference to the authors. Its utility will be confined to the recent generations of the particular branches of the Clark Family dealt with, viz.: that of Blenheim Hill, who hold an annual reunion and desire to see their names in print. The work is well printed and illustrated with wood cuts, but the index is not exhaustive.

THE COOPER AND ALLIED FAMILIES OF DETRICK, DOBELL, DOBINS, DOWDY, GILMORE, GREENE, HANNA, HENRY, LYMAN, MILLER, MILLS, MOORE, MORRIS, MOSS, RAWLING, RODECKER, STANTON, WILLETT, YOUNG, AND UNVERSAW, by W. F. Cooper. Paper, 8vo, pp. 16. 1906. Privately printed.

This small pamphlet is merely a convenient statement of the data gathered concerning the families set forth above. It is arranged alphabetically and not chronologically and hence will not be easy to consult save by those members of the Cooper family who know their own descent. It is evidently the intention of its author to elaborate and place in final genealogical form the valuable information here collected, but for the present the utility of the material published will be confined to a small and special circle. The line commences

15B

with Apollos Cooper of London County, Virginia, who lived in Revolutionary times and served in that war as a second lieutenant, and the record of his descent is carefully traced out.

THE DOBYNS-COOPER AND ALLIED FAMILIES OF BALLOU, BRAMBLE, COULTER, CREDIT, DUVAL, HENRY, KEMP, LAREW, LYON, NORWOOD, PERRY, PIERCE AND TAYLOR, by Miss Aurelia Anna Pierce Ballou and W. F. Cooper. Pàper, 8vo, pp. 31. No index. Press of State Printers, Lansing, Mich. 1908.

The object of this pamphlet is to give those of the name interested an early opportunity of using the material therein digested and to arouse interest and bring forth further information on the subject in hand. Edward Dobyns, born England on December 7th, 1747, was the first immigrant to settle in Culpeper Co., Virginia, prior to the Revolutionary War. His numerous descendents are set forth, with brief biographical sketches of the more prominent members of the family and many useful genealogical facts are collected for future reference. The spirit which prompted the compilers to record their family history is to be commended and every effort of this kind will render the task of future genealogists not only more easy but more accurate.

THE ELGIN BOTANIC GARDEN, its later history and relation to Columbia College, The New Hampshire Grants and The Treaty with Vermont in 1790, by Addison Brown, A.B., LL.B., LL.D. Cloth, 8vo, pp. 57. Full Index. Press of The New Era Printing Co., Lancaster, Pa. 1908.

The fact that Dr. Alexander Hosack in 1801 purchased land opposite the present Cathedral at Fifth Avenue and Fiftieth Street, developed it into a garden called the Elgin Botanical Garden, which he subsequently sold to the State in 1811. is little known even to many who pride themselves of their knowledge of early New York History. The garden did not flourish and in 1814, when Columbia College obtained the grant of lands embracing this small botanical experiment, it was suffered to go to ruin and decay. Owing to some doubt as to the intent of the Legislature in conveying the ground occupied by the garden to Columbia College, Judge Brown prepared this little sketch, clearly pro   that the grant to Columbia was not made in compensation for her land claims in Vermont or for any loss or injury to the College through the treaty of 1790.

The sketch shows much research, and the subject is happily treated by its author, who has brought a clear and judicial mind upon what has always been a somewhat obscure point of State history.

While the book has more historical than genealogical value, it contains a brief but admirable biography of Dr. Hosack and many items useful to searchers for the annals of some of the early New York families.

MAJOR WILLIAM FERGUSON, by Charles Beatty Alexander, LL.D. Cloth, 8vo, pp. 70. Limited edition. The Trow Press, New York. 1908.

This is a brief memorial of Major William Ferguson, born in Armagh, Ireland, son of Usher and Mary Ferguson, member of the American Philosophical Society, and officer in the army of the Revolution and in the army of the United States, and deals with his military career during the War of the Revolution and a subsequent campaign against the Indians, in which he met his death. The facts of his life as gathered from his letters and other memoranda are tersely set forth and make a valued record of one of the early patriots, who laid down his life for the privileges of freedom and the land of his adoption.

The little book is beautifully printed in large type on Italian hand-made paper and is a worthy tribute by a descendant to the valor and virtue of his ancestor.

JENKINS FAMILY BOOK, being a partial record of the descendants of David Jenkins and notes of families intermarried with them, by Robert E. Jenkins of the Chicago Bar. 1904. Cloth, small 8vo, pp. 213. Privately printed. No Index.

The compiler of this little book frankly states that he considers the tracing out of his maternal lines of quite as much importance as those on the paternal side and devotes much space to the maternal ancestry of Robert Jenkins of Clark Co., Missouri, the Ancestors of Maria (Raymond) Jenkins, the Masters Memoranda, and the Logan Memoranda. It is presumed that these allied families have never before been genealogically traced. David Jenkins came from Wales before 1700 and settled in the Great Valley of Chester Co., Pa., where comparatively little is known of him, but he left a sturdy line of children who have carried the name down to the present time. The book is not arranged according to genealogical standards, nor is it indexed, but has been compiled evidently from a desire to place in available printed form such facts as are known to its author and thus give a working medium for the future family historians. Any record is better than none and apart from the special interest to those appearing in its pages, the value of this book lies in its straightfoward statement of the family line and branches.

THE FAMILY OF LEETE, by Joseph Leete, Chevalier de La Legion D'Honneur, South Norwood, Surrey, in conjunction with John Corbet Anderson. Crushed Levant, Quarto, pp. 211. Second Edition. Revised and Enlarged. Press of Blades, East & Blades, London. 1906.

This beautiful volume contains the genealogical cronicle of the English family of Leete, whose ancestor was John Leete of Eversden, Co. Cambridge, and also incidently records a number of other Leete families, notably of Oakington, Co. Cambridge, of Governor William Leete of Guilford, Conn., the American branch, of the Irish branch, of Nicholas Leate, Alderman of London, and of the De Lettes of France. The author seems to have made an exhaustive search in the English Counties for records of all bearing his name from the earliest time and with a view to making a lasting memorial of his ancestry, has arranged and printed this great collection, with numerous pedigree charts and illustrations of ancient Mss. and places and persons of note. Undeterred by the great cost of such a search he has spared no expense in the publication, and the beauty of the paper, press work, type, illustrations and binding, would be difficult to surpass.

An honest pride in an ancient and honorable lineage has been stimulated by a praiseworthy desire to give to all of this name the results of many years' research, and the spirit which prompted so generous an action cannot be too heartily commended. The volume is unique not only as a family record but as an artistic publication, and those libraries or societies possessing copies of this valuable work are to be congratulated. Mr. Leete should feel assured of the thanks and appreciation of all future generations claiming descent from this English country family.

LYON MEMORIAL: Families of Connecticut and New Jersey, including records of the descendants of the immigrants Richard and Henry Lyon of Fairfield, Conn., with a sketch of "Lyons Farms" by S. R. Winans, Jr. Illustrated with maps and fully indexed. Edited by Sidney Elizabeth Lyon, Louise Lyon Johnson and A. B. Lyons, M.D. Cloth, 8vo, pp. 453. Press of William Graham Printing Co., Detroit, Mich. 1907.

The above book forms publication No. II, of the Lyon Genealogies, and in it is suggested the theory that the progenitors of these early New England Lyons were of the Scotch blood and related to the present family of Bowes-Lyon. The impression of an ancient seal of the lion rampant in a lozenge on the will of Samuel Winans of Elizabeth, N. J., dated 13 June, 1744, goes far toward establishing the above theory of descent, as the testator was a brother-in-law of Ebenezer Lyon of Lyons Farms. The idea and character of these Lyon compilations is excellent and in view of the destruction of many of the early records, perhaps the only accurate method of tracing a particular genealogy is to hunt out all early Colonial families of the name and trace them down to present time. Such material, well digested and indexed, may enable many families and descendants to link up their lines, who otherwise would be groping in the dark and unable to avail themselves of records not only unknown to them, but inaccessible because of distance. The Memorial is a valuable contribution to the genealogical shelves of libraries and historical societies, and reflects high credit upon its editors.

LYON MEMORIAL: NEW YORK FAMILIES. Edited by Robert B. Miller and A. B. Lyons, M.D. Cloth, 8vo, pp. 539. Fully indexed. Press of William Graham Printing Co., Detroit, Mich. 1907.

This volume forms one of a series of contemplated publications tracing all available records and information concerning the several Lyon families established in New England prior to 1650. The original prospectus contemplated only a single volume but the immense mass of data discovered soon extended the work into three sections, viz.: I. The Descendants of William Lyon of Roxbury, Mass., and of Peter and George Lyon of Dorchester, Mass. II. The Descendants of Richard and Henry Lyon of Fairfield, Conn.   III. The present book, which traces those descendants of Thomas Lyon of Rye, once of Fairfield, Conn., who form the allied New York families of the name. The work is supplemented by an introduction by Dr. G. W. A. Lyon on the English Lyon families and illustrated with maps and facsimile reproductions of interesting ancient manuscripts.

Thomas Lyon of Rye married a granddaughter of Gov. John Winthrop of Salem, Mass., and left a number of interesting letters addressed to his Winthrop relatives, all of which have fortunately been preserved by that family. The style of composition and handwriting of these ancient letters indicates their writer to have been a man of education and gentle birth, and while the modesty of the compilers of this record, in not claiming coat-armour and descent from titled forebears is to be commended, there is every reason to believe that these Lyon colonists were of ancient and honorable lineage.

The book has been compiled and printed in a direct, workmanlike manner, without useless digressions upon or assumptions of any vague family traditions and will be hailed as the authoritative work on this family.

THE NEW YORK OF YESTERDAY. A descriptive Narrative of Old Bloomingdale, by Hopper Striker Mott, with 78 illustrations, diagrams and maps. Fully indexed. Cloth, 8vo, pp. 597. Limited edition of 500 copies. Published by G. P. Putnam's Sons. The Knickerbocker Press, New York. 1908.

This fine publication had for its primar object the perpetuation of the History of The Bloomingdale Reformed Church, organized 1805, and incorporated 1806 as the Church at Harsenville, but fortunately the author was impelled to extend the work to a general historical and genealogical description of the entire district—a section of Manhattan Island but little mentioned in the many works descriptive of the growth of the great City of New York.

The book is divided into chapters respectively dealing with Bloomingdale, its boundaries, families, farms and landmarks, as well as its war history. Harsenville, and the Harsen Family; the First Consistory of the Church and the subsequent development of that house of religious worship; the Old Time Families; Reminiscences, Vital Statistics, being the registrar of Marriages and Baptisms, with exhaustive Indices; Appendices, containing transcripts of important documents, facsimile signatures, etc.

An immense amount of time, patience and labor must have been expended not only in collecting the material for this work but in digesting and arranging it. The author has shown a keen critical sense and a nice discrimination in utilizing many facts of minor importance to bring into greater prominence the vital annals of the district and the arrangement and narration of the data concerning the old time Bloomingdale families, shows him to possess not only sound genealogical methods, but a happy style of narration as rare as it is desirable in works of this character. Apart from the natural interest of his facts, the author has made a book of agreeable and easy reading, one that disguises dry historical data under a fluent descriptive style—and with the exception of the bare church vital records there is not a dull page in all the volume. The illustrations are wonderfully good, not only in subject and selection but as wood-cut reproductions, and evidence an exacting taste. The book is beautifully printed in large type with ample margins and the style of composition and arrangement leaves nothing to be desired. As a graceful tribute to its subject it is bound in blue, white and orange, the Dutch colors. This exhaustive work is worthy to grace the shelves of every public and private library of prominence in this country, and from the standpoint of a work of reference no library, that contains an historical department, should be without the book.

HISTORIC HOMES AND INSTITUTIONS AND GENEALOGICAL AND FAMILY HISTORY OF NEW YORK, by William S. Pelletreau, A.M.   Cloth, 8vo, 4 Vols., pp. 1479.   Illustrated.   The Lewis Publishing Co., New York.   1907.

The idea of publishing a work dealing with the genealogical history of the early settlers of the City of New York and their descendants is praiseworthy and such a collection, if properly selected and correctly set down would have filled a long felt want.   Unfortunately the author falls short of the standard such a book exacts and whether from commercial necessity or lack of nice discrimination, has filled up the pages with uninteresting annals of unimportant families.   In a number of cases the ancestor described has been foreign born and only lived in this city a comparatively few years, and his influence in advancing the renown of the Empire City might be measured by his subscription to a work publishing his name and portrait.

In the last ten years a number of publications of this character have been exploited and their utility, accuracy and value are open to grave doubt. Biographies of the unimportant and genealogies of the uninteresting are becoming a drug on the library shelves, and the time is rapidly approaching when the leading historical and genealogical societies must exercise a judicious selection in accepting new works of this character.   The books are well indexed and clearly printed but the glazed lead paper makes them heavy and unwieldly and the binding is bad.   The entire publication—both as to the quality and quantity of its subject-matter, letter-press, style and illustrations is commercial and cheap.

A PORTER PEDIGREE, being an account of the ancestry and descendants of Samuel and Martha (Perley) Porter of Chester, N. H., who were descendants of John Porter of Salem, Mass., and Allan Perley of Ipswich, Mass.   Compiled by Miss Juliet Porter, Worcester, Mass.   1907.   Paper, 8vo, pp. 161.   Indexed. Privately printed.

The compiler states that this volume is only the fore-runner of a more complete genealogy and has been printed to call forth further data and to ascertain whether the family interest is such as will warrant a publication in more permanent form.   The work of collecting the records has been carefullly done and the transcripts of wills, deeds, inventories, etc., appear complete and accurate. Dealing as it does with the families of Perley, Dodge, Herrick, Smith, Grover, Barney, Trumbull, Dresser, Howe, Thorley, Dana, Peabody, Andrews and Foster, comparatively small space has been alloted to each line, but a mass of valuable data has been printed and it is hoped that the compiler will receive substantial encouragement to continue her work.   The book is printed in large, distinct type, but the numerical arrangement of names is not standard and will only be clear to the compiler.   It is strange that family historians cling to an individual numerical arrangement.   Doubtless it is a method saving of labor, but one of small value to the general searcher, and seriously handicaps a book intended for general circulation.

THE CONTINENTAL CONGRESS AT PRINCETON, by Varnum Lansing Collins.   With a Portrait of General Washington, engraved by Sidney L. Smith. Cloth, 8vo, pp. 295.   Full index.   The University Library, Princeton, N. J.   1908.

The thanks of all the students of American history are due to the Princeton Historical Society for the publication of this scholarly work, dealing with important and little known episodes of the Revolutionary War.   The story of the mutiny of the Pennsylvania Troops of the Line in June, 1783, the consequent flight of the Continental Congress from Philadelphia, and the five months sojourn of that body at Princeton, together with the description of congressional life in its official and unofficial sides in the little academic town makes delightful reading. The author shows a keen appreciation of his subject, a nice discrimination in setting forth his facts in due order and a comprehensive grasp of the value and importance of his documentary data. The chapter describing the great debate on the location of a permanent federal residence is of peculiar interest. The letter-press, paper and wood-cut illustrations are in excellent taste and the work is assured of a permanent place in the list of desirable Americana.

PURMORT GENEALOGY, by Rev. Charles H. Purmort, D.D. Cloth, 8vo, pp. 148. Indexed. Press of The Homestead Co., Des Moines, Ia. 1907.

This interesting work traces out nineteen generations—the first nine of which are in England—of a family bearing an unusual name. The name is clearly of a French origin and doubtless was originally "Pour Morte" or "for death." The first immigrant in America was Philemon Portmort or Purmort, first teacher in 1635 of what is now known as the Boston Latin School. While the compiler must perforce assume that Joseph Purmort of New Castle, New Hampshire, whose descendants are fully compiled in the work, was a grandson of Philemon above, yet the ground of this presumption is almost as strong as if sustained by actual recorded data. The book represents years of research and reflects high credit upon its author, whose modesty in presenting this well-printed and illustrated work to students of genealogy is much to be commended. It is to be hoped that the book will bring forth much more data of valud and that its author may be the one chosen to put a second edition into circu ation.

VITAL RECORDS OF RHODE ISLAND, Vol. XVII, Providence Phenix, Providence Patriot and Columbian Phenix—Marriages, A to R, by James N. Arnold. Cloth, Quarto, pp. 599. Press of Narragansett Historical Publishing Co., Providence, R. I. 1908.

The new volume of this fine record of Rhode Island births, deaths and marriages, is fully up to the earlier publications of this series, not only in interest but in general style of press work and binding, and is admirably indexed as to names and localities. It covers the period 1802–1832, bridging over the period from Revolutionary to comparitively modern times and including the vital annals during the War of 1812. The patience, pertinacity and courage which Mr. Arnold has brought to his stupendous task arouses the greatest admiration, and as the work approaches its conclusion and wins a deserved financial success, no praise will be too great for this valuable genealogical record. It is hoped that Mr. Arnold will be inclined to take up the ancient burial ground records as well as a Digest of all the Wills and Administrations in Rhode Island from the earliest date of settlement to 1850. This would complete and make perfect the genealogical history of Providence Plantations.

HISTORY OF SAINT MARK'S CHURCH, New Britain, Conn., and its predecessor, CHRIST CHURCH, Wethersfield and Berlin, by James Shepard. Cloth, 8vo, pp. 707. Full Indices of Subjects and Persons. Press of the Tuttle, Morehouse & Taylor Co., New Britain, Conn. 1907.

This work is an exhaustive history of two important Episcopal parishes in Connecticut, introduced by a comprehensive statement of church history in America and in the State of Connecticut.

While the subjects of this work were not the largest or most important churches in Connecticut, yet their ministers were men of learning and repute, and among their congregations were those who have advanced the importance of the State of Connecticut and sustained her record of a God-fearing and observing Commonwealth. Full records of baptisms, marriages and burials are printed in the pages and the biographies of the successive ministers show painstaking research and accuracy.

The collection of facts for such a volume requires not only unlimited patience, but a mind naturally bent toward historical research and nice skill in arranging and placing in narrative form data voluminious enough to daunt the most enthusiastic antiquarian. Mr. Shepard has admirably completed the task and the memorial history does credit to its author and these early religious establishments.

In spite of its bulk, the book is readily handled, and owing to its excellent type and quality of paper, and 42 fine illustrations, it deserves a place on the shelves of every important historical society.

THE WHITMORE GENEALOGY. A record of the descendants of Francis Whitmore of Cambridge, Mass., 1625-1685, by Jessie Whitmore Patten Purdy. Cloth, 8vo, pp. 158. Indexed. Press of Pengelly & Broth, Reading, Pa. 1907.

The foundation of this work was the Whitmore Genealogy, compiled by Hon. William H. Whitmore in 1855, and the present volume carries down the earlier compilation to date. It is confined almost exclusively to a strict genealogical table of descent, with the few biographical facts tersely set forth, and forms a complete and concise family record of this branch of the name in America. The accuracy and arrangement of the facts shows patience and ability, and in style of press work, quality of paper and binding, the book will rank with the best productions of its kind. Essentially a genealogy, it should win a permanent place among kindred standard works.

THE WOOLSON-FENNO ANCESTRY, AND ALLIED LINES WITH BIOGRAPHICAL SKETCHES, by Lula May (Fenno) Woolson and Charles Amasa Woolson of Springfield, Vt. Cloth, 8vo, pp. 143. Illustrated and Indexed. Privately printed. Press of T. R. Marvin & Son, Boston, Mass. 1907.

This work traces back the ancestors of the authors, paternal and maternal, to the original immigrants into the Colonies, some twenty-five heads of families each, and thus is of a specific rather than general value. It is admirably arranged and contains much biographical data of rare interest but is in no sense a complete Woolson or Fenno genealogy. As a record of lineal descent from some fifty ancestors, the book merits the support and approval of the present representative family, and the authors have acquitted themselves well in tracing their intricate pedigree back to original sources. It may be said that too little importance has been made of collecting the annals of ancestral every day life—many genealogists confining themselves to a bald table of descent and accurate but meagre pedigrees. The authors of this work, however, have collected all possible material concerning each ancestor, and the result is a happy improvement on many works of this character. The book is beautifully printed on fine paper and makes a handsome volume.

ACCESSIONS TO THE LIBRARY.

March 14 to June 15, 1908.

DONATIONS.

Bound.

Alexander, Charles Beatty.—Major William Ferguson.
American Historical Association.—Report, Vol. II, 1905.
Baldwin, Evelyn Briggs, and American Baking Powder Association.—The Baking Powder Controversy.
Barnes, Charles Wheeler.—Historic Homes and Family History, 4 vols.
Bascom, Robert O., Sec'y.—N. Y. State Historical Association, Proceedings.
Brown, Addison.—New Hampshire Grants.
Brush, Mrs. Chauncey H., and Baldwin, Evelyn Briggs.—Ancestry of Abner and Laura (Hubbard) Brush.
Clark, Dr. A. W.—Clark Family.
Green, B. Frank.—Nevill Family, manuscript.
Jenkins, Mrs. R. E.—Jenkins Family Book.
Leete, Joseph.—Leete Family.
Lyon, A. B., M.D.—Lyon Memorial, Vols. II, III.
McFarland, H.—Descendants of Daniel McFarland.
Mayham, Albert C.—Anti-Rent War.

Princeton University.— Continental Congress at Princeton.
Purdy, W. T. H.—Whitmore Genealogy.
Purmort, Rev. C. H., D.D.—Purmort Genealogy.
Shepard, James.—History of St. Mark's Church, New Britain, and Christ
  Church, Wethersfield, Conn.
Stockton, Rev. Elias Boudinot.—Compendium of Censuses, N. J.
Suydam, Walter Lispenard.—Ecclesiastical Records, State of New York, 2 vols.
Van Alstyne, W. B., M.D.—Report of the State Engineer, New York, 1906,
  2 vols.
Ver Planck, William Gordon.—Proceedings at the O'Gorman Banquet.
  O'Briens of Machias, Maine.
Woolson, Charles Amasa.—Woolson-Fenno Ancestors.
Young, Ver Planck & Prince.—New York City Directories, 9 vols. Indexes
  to New York Conveyances, 21 vols. Notices of Pendencies of Actions,
  8 vo s.
Youngs, Mrs. Florence E.—English Clergy Directory, 1906.

Pamphlets, Etc.

Allen, John K.—George Morton of Plymouth Colony.
Brink, Benjamin M.—Olde Ulster.
Calhoun, Col. J. C.—Captain John C. Calhoun.
Cooper, W. F.—Cooper and Allied Families. Dobyns-Cooper and Allied
  Families.
Cornell, Rev. John.—Ancestry of Rev. John Cornell, pedigree chart, manuscript.
Corwin, Rev. E. T.—Reply of Rev. Joannes Megapolensis. The Amsterdam
  Correspondence.
Davis, Andrew McFarland.—John Harvard's Life in America.
Dorr, Mrs. Julia C. R.—W. Y. R., A Book of Remembrance.
Drowne, Henry Russell.—Surnames of the United Kingdom, I.
Dwight. Rev. M. E., D.D.—Genealogical Exchange.
First Church, Passaic.—Church Tablet.
Harvard University.—Official Register.
Heilbrig, Richard E.—The German-American Collection in the New York
  Public Library.
Holbrook, Levi.—Philadelphia North American.
Hoy, David.—Class of Eighty-Eight, Cornell University.
Macy, W. A., M.D.—Nova Scotia Hospital, 50th Report.
Mead, Spencer P.—Index, Mead Genealogy.
Myers, Edward.—Yonkers Loan Exhibition. Manuals, Congregational Church,
  Stanwich, Conn. Greenburgh Presbyterian Church, clippings. Requa
  and Knapp Families, clippings. Historic Bronx Borough.
Nichols, Mrs. L. E.—Dyckman Burial Ground, manuscript.
N. Y. Bible Society.—Report.
N. Y. Hospital.—Report.
N. Y. Public Library.—Bulletin.
Porter, Miss Juliet.—A Porter Pedigree.
Purdy, W. T. H.—Sarah Thorne White Memorial.
Quinby, Henry Cole.—New England Family History.
Spelman, Wm. C.—Class of Sixty-One, Williams College.
Suffolk County Historical Association.—Year Book.
Truax, James R., Cor.-Sec'y.—Schenectady County Historical Society's Report.
Ver Planck, William Gordon.—Hobart College Catalogues. New York of the
  Future. New England Society, Anniversary, 1903-1904. Columbia Uni-
  versity Quarterly, IV, 2. Discourse Before the Brooklyn Institute Law
  Department. Ancestry. Irish Scots and the Scotch Irish. Irish Rhode
  Islanders. The American College Against Plutocracy. Citizen's Union.
  Addresses of the Bar Association to Nicholas II. First Aid to the Injured,
  Report Association for the Protection of the Adirondacks. Alleged
  Toryism of the Clergy. Four Centuries of Conflict.
Wallace, H. E., Jr.—Moorefield Examiner.
Ward, Henry Alson.—Richfield, Otsego County, N. Y., Vital Records, manu-
  script.
Williams College.—Bulletin.

OFFICERS

NOTICE
To Subscribers to "The Record"

Subscribers to "THE RECORD" are requested to notify the New York Genealogical and Biographical Society of any change in their addresses at any time, and especially changes during the Summer period; in order that the *July Issue of* "THE RECORD" may be delivered at their proper summer homes. Many RECORDS are delivered in July at City houses which are closed for the season and do not reach the subscribers on that account. For such failures of delivery this Society cannot be held responsible.

Subscribers desiring it, upon formal notice to this office, can have their July number of "THE RECORD" held for delivery with the October number, thus avoiding chance of loss on account of closed homes in the Summer.

that he has recently removed to more commodious Chambers in London and largely increased his staff of Searchers, enabling him to give promptest attention to all genealogical queries.

ADDRESSES

ENGLISH	AMERICAN	CABLE
11 CLIFFORD'S INN	P. O. BOX 44	ELMLEA
FLEET STREET	SOUTH FREEPORT	LONDON
LONDON, E. C.	MAINE	(Adams or W. U. Code)

THE TUTTLE COMPANY

PRINTERS AND BINDERS

11 & 13 Center St., Rutland, Vt.

ESTABLISHED 1832

Special attention given to Genealogies and Town Histories, under supervision of an expert proof-reader and genealogist

Composition, Presswork, Binding at less than city prices. Expenses low, and 76 years experience

Correspondence solicited direct with customer. References given and required. Write us for prices if you are planning to publish a family history

TOBIAS A. WRIGHT

PRINTER AND PUBLISHER OF

Family Histories, Genealogical Records, Etc.

IN BOOK, PAMPHLET OR CHART FORM

ALL WORK SUPERVISED AND PROOFS READ BY A GENEALOGIST

150 BLEECKER STREET, NEW YORK

Five doors west of Sixth Ave. Elevated Station at Bleecker Street

THE NEW ENGLAND

HISTORICAL AND GENEALOGICAL REGISTER

Published quarterly in January, April, July, and October, by the New England Historic Genealogical Society.

Each number contains not less than ninety-six octavo pages of matter concerning the History, Antiquities, Genealogy and Biography of America.

Begun in 1847, it is the oldest historical periodical now published in this country. Vol. 63 begins in January, 1909.

Terms of subscription, three dollars ($3.00) per annum, in advance, beginning with January. Current single numbers, 75 cts. Advertising rates on application.

THE NEW YORK

GENEALOGICAL AND BIOGRAPHICAL

RECORD.

DEVOTED TO THE INTERESTS OF AMERICAN
GENEALOGY AND BIOGRAPHY.

ISSUED QUARTERLY.

October, 1908.

OCTOBER, 1908.—CONTENTS.

THE RECORD is issued quarterly, on the first of January, A
July and October. Terms: $3.00 a year in advance. Subscript
should be sent to   THE RECORD,
                                     226 WEST 58th STREET, NEW YORK, T

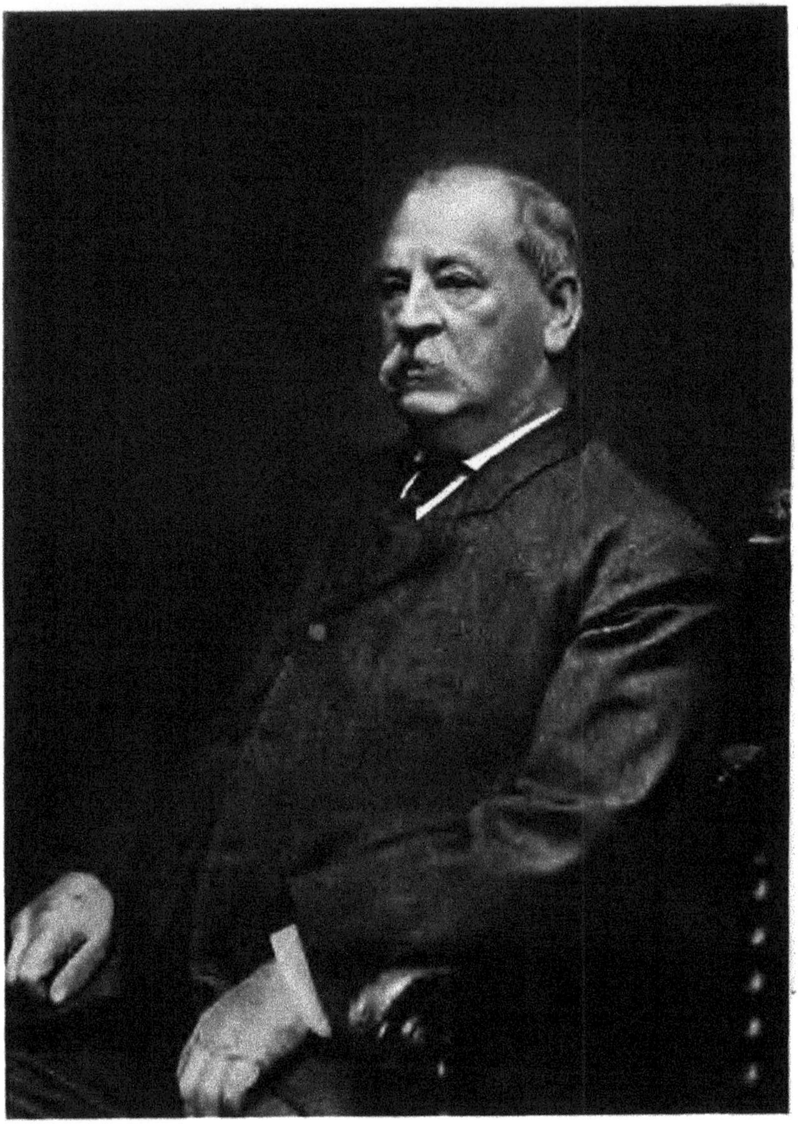

Grover Cleveland

THE NEW YORK
Genealogical and Biographical Record.

| VOL. XXXIX. | NEW YORK, OCTOBER, 1908. | NO. 4 |

GROVER CLEVELAND.

By Lyman Abbott.

A biography of Grover Cleveland will not be expected by the readers of the RECORD. Such a biography would involve an account of at least four important episodes in our National history, and an adequate account of either one of these would be impossible within the limits of a magazine article. This is rather an appreciation than a biography, and is written by one who might probably designate himself by the once familiar phrase of a Cleveland Republican. For from my first boyish activities in the Fremont campaign I had been until 1882 a persistent though sometimes a disgrunted Republican. Like many other Republicans I was opposed to the reconstruction policies of the Radicals; to the partnership between the Federal Government and the railways which resulted in the Credit Mobilier scandals; to the development of the doctrine of protection into a species of bargaining legislation favorable to special interests; to the corrupt doctrine "To the victor belongs the spoils" unsuccessfully concealed by defenses that were not even plausible. The administration of President Arthur, though better than was expected, seemed to me and to others a politician's administration. And when a factional fight in the Republican party in New York State,—a fight not between opposing principles but between opposing spoilsmen—issued in 1882 in the nomination of good men by nefarious means, I welcomed the nomination of Grover Cleveland by the Democratic party as an opportunity to rebuke and resist pernicious tendencies within the party with which I had affiliated ever since my first vote in 1860 for Abraham Lincoln. Mr. Cleveland was elected by a majority of upwards of 150,000 votes over all other candidates; not because he was a Democrat, but because he was Grover Cleveland, and by his administration of the Mayoralty in Buffalo had illustrated the policy which he afterwards interpreted in the now well-known phrase "A public office is a public trust." The doctrine has never been more happily phrased,

16

and by no man in public office since George Washington's time had it been more consistently and courageously illustrated.

This administration of the State compelled a reluctant Democratic machine to nominate him for the Presidency in 1884 against James G. Blaine, the plumed knight of the Republican party. I do not here raise the hotly disputed question concerning Mr. James G. Blaine, who was at once the most admired and the most contemned statesman of his era. But I was among those who regarded his nomination as a victory of the corrupt elements in the Republican party, and followed Henry Ward Beecher out of the Republican ranks, though not into the Democratic ranks. Mr. Cleveland was elected in that campaign of 1884 by the votes of men one of whom aptly described himself as an independent in municipal politics, a Republican in State politics, and a Democrat in National politics.

There are times when all questions of policy take a second place, overshadowed by the struggle of the humbler, less brilliant, but most essential virtues to assert themselves. Such was the period in American polictics from 1882 to 1892. Mr. Cleveland stood for the virtues of truthfulness in promise and profession, honesty in administration, and economy in public business. The two characteristic American admirations—that for brilliance in speech and action and that for rugged honesty in both,—were appealed to by the Presidential conflict of 1884, and the enthusiasm for honesty won. Mr. Cleveland's administration was not brilliant, but it was honest. It may not have been the administration of a great statesman—on that question opinions may differ; but it certainly was not the administration of a wily politician—on that question opinions will not differ. It was a business man's administration and it appealed to the business men of the Nation by its integrity, its sanity, and its business conservatism. Perhaps his most distinguished service to the Nation, it was certainly his first, was his practical adoption of what had before been a much praised and little practised theory, the merit system applied to public appointments. He added 30,000 posts to the Civil Service list, making a total number of competitive places of 86,000. Others had preceded him in elucidating the theory, but he was the first to reduce the theory to practice; and though the country has since carried the principle still further, it has never receded from the standard he set.

It was characteristic of Mr. Cleveland to mean what he said and to say what he meant. He had been elected in 1884 upon a platform which pledged the party to tariff reform. The tariff was not reformed. And in the Fall of 1887 he threw down a challenge to the special interests in a message which pledged him and so pledged the party if it re-nominated him, to a tariff for revenue only. This message was criticised at the time as impolitic. Perhaps it was. The Democratic party lost the election, probably in consequence of that message. But he did not lose the respect of his countrymen, and in the next succeeding campaign, that of 1892, he was elected on the issue which he had so clearly raised. The Wilson bill, as introduced into the House, was a consistent revenue tariff bill; but when it issued from the Senate, after it had been manipulated by the representatives of certain special interests, it was neither a consistent revenue nor a consistent protective measure. That Mr. Cleveland allowed it to become a law, though without his approval, has always seemed to me one of the mistakes of his political life; though it is to be said that other issues, of more immediate and pressing importance, had meantime arisen to justify Mr. Cleveland's reluctance to engage in a tariff controversy with Congress. However that may be, the Democratic party has never recovered from the injury inflicted on it by the refusal of the Democratic Senators to carry out in good faith the policy to which the Democratic platform pledged the party. Sixteen years have passed and Senator Gorman is dead; and still Independents like myself, who ardently desire a tariff for revenue only, while we have little hope of radical tariff revision from the Republican party, have even less from the politicians who gave the country the mongrel legislation known as the Wilson-Gorman bill.

There is no space here to discuss the perplexing currency problem which confronted President Cleveland's second term, and agitated it so fiercely in the campaign which immediately followed. It is difficult even to state the problem so that readers of different political opinions will understand it alike. There were many in the country who believed with President Walker of the Massachusetts Institute of Technology, that by an International Agreement a parity of values could be maintained between gold and silver, that in this way both could be made a common standard of values, and that such a common standard would result in less fluctuation of values than would result from any single standard, whether gold or silver. When it was found impossible to secure such an International Standard, a natural division arose among those who believed in International bimetallism, some urging a gold standard, some an attempt to secure such parity of value by National legislation alone. Those of us who believe, as I do, that National bimetallism would have been bimetallism only in name, that it would really have meant for the United States silver monometallism, and that it would have inflicted untold disaster upon the country, and especially upon the agricultural and laboring classes, must ever recognize the indebtedness of the Nation to Mr. Cleveland for the rugged defiance with which he faced popular clamor, both within and without his party, in his belief that a gold standard was the only honest standard. Even those who do not agree with him in that opinion, and were most bitterly hostile to him at the time, have, almost without exception, come to recognize the purity of his motives and the courage of his political action.

With the exception of Mr. Debs and his associates, the leader of the strikes then, the leader of the Socialist party now, the country has come also to recognize and approve the courage of his course in dealing with the famous Pullman strike in the summer of 1894. At that time the issue was somewhat confused. The irritating injustice of the Pullman Company, which laid all the burden of the hard times on the wage earners and none of it on either the stockholders or the higher salaried officials, created a sympathy for the strikers, which their boycott of perfectly innocent parties, and their acts of lawless and inexcusable violence, turned to sympathy against them, so that the general public had little inclination to side with either the Pullman Company or the strikers. But what I wrote in 1894 I may here repeat as an expression of the public sentiment outside the immediate battle field: "Rioting is not so dangerous to American civilization as compromising with rioters. * * * The battle field is not the place to debate delicate questions of rank and precedence; and we are in the midst of a battle. It is a time for men of all parties to sustain the President in using all the power which his law officers affirm that he possesses in enforcing law and punishing crime." It was much easier to write these lines than to act upon this principle. Mr. Cleveland in acting upon this principle, and in using the power of the Federal Government to put down mob violence, enforce law, restore order, and protect persons and property, in spite of the indifference, not to say the opposition, of both the city and the State authorities, rendered a service in checking the rising spirit of lawlessness in this country which the country hardly appreciates even yet. It may be added that it is doubtful whether even Mr. Roosevelt, Republican as he is, has done more to commend to the people of the United States the doctrine of the New Federalism—the doctrine that all the power which the Federal government possesses is to be employed whenever it is necessary to conserve those interests which are common to all the people of the Nation—than Mr. Cleveland, Democrat as he was, did in using the Federal powers to protect the United States mail and Interstate Commerce from the violence of local mobs.

All men have the defects of their qualities. If the diplomatic temperament leads its possessor at times to blur the line which separates tactful from untrue utterances, the honest temperament sometimes leads its possessor to declare his purpose in language which is needlessly offensive. This was in my judgment the only defect, though the very serious defect, in Grover Cleveland's famous Venezuelan message. Whether this was due to Mr. Cleveland or to his Secretary of State, Mr. Richard Olney, history does not know—it can only guess. A long drawn out boundary dispute between Great Britain and the irritating State of Venezuela threatened to issue in open war, and that in turn to result in bringing part of that Central American Republic under British sovereignty. That this would be in flat contravention of an American policy which Great Britain had been the first to recommend to us, but which is popularly known as the Monroe doctrine, is indubitable. It was wholly in accordance with our traditions to propose to Great Britain to arbitrate the question, and when she refused, to investigate the issues involved for ourselves that we might determine what course we would pursue. But it was neither courteous nor wise to announce beforehand that if Great Britain did not accept the results of such an investigation, the

United States would "resist by every means in its power, as a wilful aggressor upon its rights and interests, the appropriation of any lands or the exercise of any governmental jurisdiction over any territory which, after investigation, we have determined, of right, to belong to Venezuela." No doubt in this utterance Mr. Cleveland meant what he said, but it was a case in which it would have been better had he said less than he meant. That his message did not lead to a rupture of friendly relations between the two countries, if not to open war between them, is due not to the wisdom of Mr. Cleveland's language, but to the self-restraint of the English government and the English people.

Since his retirement from the Presidency and from active politics in 1896, Mr. Cleveland has been widely known as America's most distinguished private citizen. His life has been quiet; his inclination has been to retirement; his public service has been mostly confined to occasional utterances, always in favor of the highest and best ideals in our National life. His interest in education was indicated by his active work and wise counsel as a Trustee of Princeton College; in the welfare of the common people by his consent to act as Trustee in the reorganization of the Equitable Life Assurance Society; in National affairs, by his willing co-operation with President Roosevelt in the latter's successful endeavor to save the country from the disastrous consequences which a continuance of the great coal strike of 1902 would have inevitably brought upon the country.

Mr. Cleveland was essentially a product of American Democracy. Like Abraham Lincoln, our greatest President, like Chief Justice Marshall, our greatest Judge, he had not a college education. He was what men call a "self-made" man. His only schooling was such as he received in a public school, as clerk in a village store, as assistant to his uncle in a brief piece of literary compilation, and subsequently as clerk in a law office. From 1880, when he was elected Mayor of Buffalo, to 1892, when he was elected President of the United States, his political promotions were rapid and were never due to political chicanery nor to demagogic arts, but to popular appreciation of his character. But if he had not educational advantages, he had a good inheritance. From his English ancestry he derived, along with a lack of imagination, which was his most serious intellectual deficiency, an indomitable will, an aggressive honesty, a transparent truthfulness, a courage that never quailed, and a habit of vigilant and tireless industry; qualities that constitute the best characteristics of English blood. If he was neither an astute politician nor a great statesman, he was an honest business man. Charged with the business affairs first of a City, then of a State, finally of a Nation, at a time when nothing was so much needed in order to expose crookedness in public life as an example of its opposite, that example Mr. Cleveland furnished without a taint of that self-conscious showing forth of virtue which is the essence of Pharisaism. His name is an honorable addition to the Annals of America and his life is an example and an inspiration to its young men.

16A

ABSTRACTS OF INSCRIPTIONS

ON SOME OF THE OLDER STONES IN THE BURIAL GROUND ADJOINING THE DUTCH CHURCH, HOPEWELL, DUTCHESS COUNTY, N. Y.

Copied April 19th, 1899, by MISS HELEN W. REYNOLDS, of Poughkeepsie, N. Y.

Ida Schenck, wife of Isaac Adriance, d. July 2, 1804, in her 74th year.

Isaac Adriance, d. April 15, 1799, aged 76 years, 11 m., 18 days.

Goris Storm, d. Dec. 8, 1790, aged 66 years, 7 m., 13 days.

Mary Storm, wife of Goris Storm, d. April 29, 1806, aged 69 years, 9 m. 23 d.

Tunis Brinckerhoff, d. J—— 13th, 1790.

Lorine Griffin(?), wife of Rem Adriance, d. —— 17th, 1813, aged 52 y., 9 m., 21 d.

Catherine Storm, wife of Rem Adriance, d. April 3, 1800, aged 41 y., 5 m.

Theodorus Adriance, d. May 15, 1817, aged 66 y., 10 m., 8 d.

Hilliche Adriance, d. June 24, 1832, aged 75 y., 1 m. 22 d.

Diana Hogland, wife of Rem Adriance, d. May 11, 1812, aged 65 y. & 12 days.

Rem Adriance, d. April 3, 1795, aged 46 y., 10 m., 19 d.

Sarah, wife of Thomas Humphrey, d. Sept. 7, 1794, aged 36 y., 3 m., 15 d.

Thomas Humphrey, d. Feb. 19, 1804, aged 49 y., 9 m., 19 d.

Letitia Van Wyck, wife of Isaac Adriance, d. Dec. 6, 1762, aged 33 y., 10 m., 27 d.

Tamer Dennis, wife of Zachariah Flagler, d. April 11, 1795, aged 20 y., 8 m., 16 d.

Zachariah Flagler, d. Feb. 21, 1824, aged 54 y., 9 m., 26 d.

Catherine Hasbrouck, wife of Zachariah Flagler, d. April 15, 1862, aged 87 y., 10 m., 24 d.

Dinah, widow of Daniel Hasbrouck, d. March 5, 1827, aged 77 y., 3 m.

Ralph Philips, d. May 26, 1813, aged 84 y., 9 m., 10 d.

Barbara Philips, born Nov. 10, 1733, d. Sept. 12, 1820, aged 87 y.

Sarah Polhemus, widow of Rudolphus Swartwout, d. March 5, 1820, aged 94 y., 2 m., 12 d.

Thomas G. Storm, d. Feb. 26, 1830, aged 59 y., 7 m., 23 d.

Maria Shear, wife of Thomas G. Storm, d. Aug. 17, 1856, aged 82 y., 9 m., 17 d.

Thomas I. Storm, d. Jan. 29, 1847, aged 80 y., 2 m., 7 d.

Cornelius Wiltsie, d. May 5, 1821, aged 64 y., 3 m., 5 d.

Helena Strachan, d. June 20, 1799, aged 31 y., 4 m., 13 d.

Catherine Roughbeen(?), wife of John S. Brinckerhoff, d. Sept. 15. 1783, aged 22 y.

Elizabeth, wife of John Waldron, d. March 7, 1783.

Catherine, wife of Benjamin Moore, gentleman, of N. Y., d. June 8, 1781, aged 60 y.

Anne Monfort, wife of Abraham Shear, born Sep. 1, 1753, d. ——.

NEW BRUNSWICK LOYALISTS OF THE WAR OF THE AMERICAN REVOLUTION.

COMMUNICATED BY D. R. JACK, HISTORIAN OF THE NEW BRUNSWICK LOYALISTS' SOCIETY; COR.-SEC'Y. OF THE NEW BRUNSWICK HISTORICAL SOCIETY; AUTHOR CENTENNIAL PRIZE ESSAY, HISTORY OF ST. JOHN; EDITOR ACADIENSIS ETC.

NOTE.—The reference letter in the second column in the list of New Brunswick Loyalists indicates, it will be remembered, the source of the information from which the list has been compiled. The readers of the RECORD are requested to note the following additions to the schedule which appeared in the January, 1904, issue.

"P." Roll of Loyalists, etc., settled in Belle Vue in Beavor Harbor, Charlotte County, 10th July, 1784.

"Q." Muster of passengers on transport *Cyrus* on 21st Aug., 1783, upon her trip from New York to the Saint John River. On the 6th of Sept., she was at sea, and on the 14th of Sept. she was in the Saint John River. Copy of return furnished by H. A. Powell, Esq., of Sackville, N. B. (See *Collections of New Brunswick Historical Society*, No. 5, 1904, pp. 277-8-9.)

"R." New Brunswick Loyalists, 1799 in number, whose names appear in the Passamaquoddy section of Major General Campbell's Muster of Loyalists and Disbanded Soldiers, from an original copy initialed by Col. Edward Winslow—of the expulsion of the Acadians fame—compiled 1784 (see *Canadian History Readings* by G. U. Hay, said original copy being now the property of Ward C. Hazen of Saint John, N. B.). The names appearing in this compilation have been copied from the said original by the compiler of this record.

"S." Loyalists who settled on Kemble Manor, Saint John River, N. B., mentioned by Jonas Howe in his article upon that subject, (see *New Brunswick Magazine*, Vol. 1, p. 157.

— This sign indicates that the individual was *less* than 10 years of age in 1783.
+ This sign indicates that the individual was a child but *more* than ten years of age in 1783.

(Continued from Vol. XXXIX., p. 192, of the RECORD.)

NAME	REF. LETTER	FROM	SETTLED	NOTE
Ross, Alex.	F H		Didgeguash	
Ross, Edward.	C H		St. Andrews	
Ross, Daniel.	C C		"	
Ross, Henry.	C H		"	
Ross, John.	C C D			
Ross, Thomas.	C H K	Falmouth	Grand Manan	Mariner, d. 1804
Rose, William, Sergt.	D		St. Stephen	
Rose, ———.	Q —			
Roswell, John (Rosenell?).	B		Carleton	
Rothbun, Joseph.	K M	Rhode Island	Kingston, Kings Co.	
Rouse, David.	A		St. John	
Row, William.	F R		Didgeguash	
Ruckle, Francis.	B		Carleton	
Ruland, Joanna.	A		St. John	

Name	Ref. Letter	From	Settled	Note
Rulofson, Rulof	K		Hampton	d. at H., 1840, aet. 86. Magistrate
Rumbold, Thomas	B		Carleton	
Rundell, Charles	P		Belle Vue, Beaver Har.	
Rundell, Simthy	P		"	
Rupert, Christopher	A		St. John	
Russel, Cornelia	O+			
Russel, Jane	O—			
Russell, James	C H		St. Andrews	d. at St. J., 1808, aet. 73
Russell, Joseph	K P		St. John	
Russell, Ruell	P		Belle Vue, Beaver Har.	⎫
Russell, Eliz.	P—		"	⎬ Probably all members of one family
Russell, Molly	P—		"	⎭
Russell, Martha	A		St. John	
Ruthsen, Duncan	A			
Rutton, Mary	O			
Rutton, William	O			
Ryan, John	A K		St. John	⎰ King's Printer for N. B., d. Nfld., 1847, Freeman, St. J., 1785
Ryan, William	A		"	⎱ Cooper, Freeman, St. J., 1785
Ryan, Michael	C H		St. Andrews	
Ryan, John	D		St. Stephen	
S				
Sagurby, Nicholas	A		St. John	Member first vestry All Saints Ch.
Salt, Maurice	C D		St. Andrews	d. 1821, aged 86
Salkin, John	K A		Mace's Bay, Char. Co.	
Santeevoix, Joshua	A	Pennsylvania	St. John	
Sanders, Edward	I		Charlotte County	
Sands, Edward	K		St. John	
Sanger, Eleazer	P		Beaver Harbor	⎰ Merchant, Freeman, St. J., 1786.
Sanger, Hannah	P		"	⎱ Major Militia. Alderman, St. J.
Sarbutt, George	D		St. Stephen	Coroner, d. 1803, aet. 43

Name	Ref. Letter	From	Settled	Note
Sargent, Mary..............	I		St. David, Char. Co.	Probably all members of one family connection. The writer cannot now find any trace of the name in Charlotte Co. annals. Possibly like others, they applied for land from speculative reasons, but never fulfilled conditions of grant by residing thereon
Sargent, Samuel............	I		"	
Sargent, Samuel, Jr.........	I		"	
Sargent, Solomon...........	I		"	
Sargent, Solomon, Jr.......	I		"	
Sargent, David.............	I		"	
Sargent, Andrew...........	I		"	
Sargent, Peter.............	I		"	
Sargent, Valentine.........	I		"	
Sarvenear, James..........	A		St. John	
Saunders, John, Hon........	K	Virginia	Fredericton	Freeman, St. J., 1785. Gentleman. d. at F. 1834, æt. 60. C. J. of N. B. Was Capt. Queen's Rangers and an eminent lawyer
Saunders, John, of New Jersey..	K	New Jersey	Hampton	
Savelle, Jesse..............	I K	Providence, R. I.	St. David, Char. Co.	Officer of Customs at Providence. Brother to Jesse Savelle. It is said that these men, Jesse and Thomas, lived and died at Gloucester, Mass., not fulfilling the conditions under which land had been granted to them in N. B.
Savill, Thomas.............	I		"	
Savage, William...........	A K		St. John	d. at Maugerville, N. B.
Sayre, Rev. John..........	A K	Fairfield, Conn.	St. John	
Sayre, Rev. James.........	A K	New York	"	Brother to Rev. John S., returned to U. S. and was rector at Newport, R. I. 1786 to 1788: d. at Fairfield, Conn., 1798, æt. 53
Sayre, John, Jr...........	A K	Fairfield, Conn.	St. Andrews	Son of Rev. John Sayre
Scallion, Matthew..........	C H		St. John	
Schofield, Major...........	A		"	
Schonewolf, Charles........	A		"	
Scott, Robert..............	A		"	
Scott, Edmund.............	A K	{Tryon, now Montgomery, Co., N.Y.	"	
Scott, James..............	R F H		Charlotte County	
Scott, James..............	R		"	d. St. J., 1804, æt. 56
Scott, Holiday.............	C		St. Andrews	
Scott, James, Jr...........			"	
Scott, John...............	C R F		Charlotte County	

Name	Ref. Letter	From	Settled	Note
Scott, James	C	Waterbury, Conn.	Kingston, Kings Co.	d. at K., 1809
Scovil, Rev. James	K	"	St. John	Alderman, St. J.; d. at Granville, N.S., 1825
Scovil, Ezra	K	"	"	Merchant, St. J., d. there 1822
Scovil, Daniel	K			d. St. J., 1820, aet. 61
Scribner, Joseph	A K	Norwalk, Conn.	Kings Co.	
Scribner, Hezekiah	K M S	"	"	
Scribner, Elias	K M	"	"	d. St. J., 1837, aet. 77
Scribner, Thaddeus	K M	"	"	d. St. J., 1822, aet. 69
Scribner, Thomas	K		St. John	
Schureman, Philip, or Schurman	A K	New Rochelle, N.Y.	"	Tailor, Freeman, St. J., 1785
Seaman, William	A K	Dutchess Co., N.Y.	"	
Seaby, or Scoby, William	A K			
Sealy, Juston	B L	Staten Island, N.Y.	Carleton	d. 1785
Seaman, Benjamin	K L		St. John	Alderman, St. J., and Provincial Treasurer
Seaman, Richard	K	Ducthess Co., N.Y. New York?	"	
Seaman, John	K M			
Seaman, Hicks	K		Sheffield, Sunbury Co.	d. at Sheffield, 1841, aet. 84
Sears, Thatcher	A K L	Norwalk, Conn.	St. John	Descendant of Rev. Peter Thatcher of Boston, Mass. Freeman, St. J., 1785
Secord, William	A		"	
Seely, Seth	A K M	Stamford, Conn.		d. Carleton, 1833, aet. 88
Seely, Ebenezer	A K	Connecticut	St. George, Char. Co.	d. St. G., 1838
Seely, Stewart	K		St. John	
Seely, Seth, Jr	M K	Stamford, Conn.		d. St. J., 1852, aet. 85. Son of Seth Seely, above
Seeley, Orange	P		Beaver Har., Char. Co.	
Segee, John	K		New Maryland	d. 1835
Sellars, Robert	F R		Didgeguash, Char. Co.	
Senior, Bartholomew	A		St. John	
Servanier, James	K		"	Sold his grant of 200 acres, Dec., 1795
Sewell, Jonathan, Sr	B K	Massachusetts	"	Lt. 3rd Bat. N. J. Vols, d. St. J., 1803
Sewell, Jonathan, Jr	B K	"	"	Attorney-Gen. of Mass., prior to Rev. Chief-Justice of Lower Canada. Son of J. S., Sr.

Name	Ref. Letter	From	Settled	Note
Sewell, Sen.	B K	Massachusetts	St. John	{ Son of J. S., Sr., Solicitor-General of Lower Canada, d. at Montreal, 1832. Father and two sons were very famous men
Seymor, Thomas	A		"	
Shambier, Levis	A		Carleton	
Sn, Diel	B		"	
Shanks, James	B K		St. John	{ Lt. Prince of Wales Am. Vols. Freeman, St. John, 1785
Sharp, John	A		St. John	Shipwright, Freeman, St. J., 1785
Shaw, Moses	A		"	
Shaw, Jhn	A		"	
Shaw, Grge	B		Gl ton	{ Possibly the same mentioned by Sabine, Vol. II, p. 279
Shaw, ifs	B K	Newtown, L. I.	"	Tanner, Freeman, St. J., 1785
Shaw, John	C		St. Andrews	{ Officer of the Queen's Rangers, m. Nancy Goslin of Newtown in 1783
Shearman, Adrian	A		St. John	
Sheldon, John	A			
Shelton, Jeremiah	K		Portland	{ Officer in Loyalist Corps; d. 1819, aet. 64
Shepherd, William	A	Pennsylvania	St. John	
Sheppard, Joseph	C I		St. Andrews	
Sheppard, Samuel	C I	"	St. John	
Sherwood, Justus	A		"	
Sherwood, Adriah, or Abijah	A		St. John	d. Kings Co., 1836, aet 84
Sherwood, Jonathan	A		"	
Sherwood, Andrew	B		Carleton	
Shew, William	B		"	
Shields, David	C H		St. Andrews	
Shields, John	C H		"	
Shonnard, Peter	A		St. John	
Shonnard, Frederick	A		"	
Shortley, William	I		St. David, Char. Co.	
Sheppard, Richard	I		"	
Sheppard, Jacob	I		"	
Sheppard, Benj	I			
Sheppard, Thomas				
Sheck, Christopher	K		Sussex Vale	{ Carpenter. Freeman, St. J., 1785, d. at S., 1841. aet. 86

NAME	REF. LETTER	FROM	SETTLED	NOTE
Sherman, [?]be	K	Boston, Mass.	Sunbury Co.	{ Lt. Royal Fen. Americans. Drowned at Burton, Sun. Co.
[?]ea, Ephraim	P		Beaver Har., Char. Co.	No trace of this name found in early Char. Co. history. See note after Sargeant family in this issue of the RECORD
[?]ea, Oliver	P+		"	
[?]ea, Daniel	P+		"	
[?]ea, Sybell	P+		"	
[?]ea, Ruth	P+		"	
Shelea, Mary	K M	Dutchess Co., N. Y.	Kings Co.	
[?]y, Nathan	H		Charlotte Co.	
Shipton, Francis	A		St. John	
[?]in, Drummond	P		Beaver H., Char. Co.	
[?]in, Sarah	A		St. John	
Simpson, [?]Nad	C D		St. [?]	
[?]in, [?]Mel				
Simp[?]so, Sarah (Dibble)	A		St. John	Tailor, Freeman, St. J., 1785
Sickles, [?] bn	A		"	
S[?]s, William	A		"	
S [?]lbs, Daniel	C		St. Andrews	
Sickles, Daniel, Jr.	C		"	
Sighensparker, John	H		"	
Simmons, James	K		[?]e Co.	
Simonds, James	H	Boston?	St. John River	{ In 1776 embarked at Boston for Halifax, N. S.
Simmonds, William	I		Charlotte Co.	
Sims (Sime?), Robert	P		St. David, Char. Co.	
Sinclair, Robert	A		Beaver Har., Char. Co.	
Sinclair, George	C D K	Bucks Co., Penn.	St. John	
Sivany, Miles	A		St. John [?]	
Skelton, William	K		Long Island, Queens Co.	d. at L. I., 1836
Slaight, Henry	K M	Rhode Island	Kings Co.	{ d. 1852, leaving numerous descendants
Slip, John	K	Massachusetts		
Sloat, Abraham	B		[?]n	
Slocum or Slokum, Ebenezer				
Slocum, Eleazer				
Small, John				

Name	Ref. Letter	From	Settled	Note
Small, Thomas...	B K	New Hampshire	Carleton	d. at Belville, Ont.
Smith, John...	A K	New York	St. John	d. at F., 1834, aet. 83 Freeman
Smith, Wm...	A K		Fredericton	
Smith, Nathan...	A K	Rhode Island	St. John	Surgeon Loyalist Regt. St. John, 1785 son Nathan
Smith, William Howe...	A	"	"	
Smith, John J...	A		"	
Smith, Richard...	A		"	
Smith, Samuel...	A		"	
Smith, J...	A		"	
Smith, G rge...	A			
Smith, Jacob...	A K	New York	St. John River	Capt. de Lancey's 1st Batt. Was in garrison and was wounded at Ninety-Six; d. 1837, aet. 88
Smith, Thomas...	A K	New Hampshire	St. John	Goldsmith. Freeman, St. J., 1785
Smith, ...	K	Ridgefield, Conn.		
Smith, Wm., Jr...	A K M		St. John	
Smith, ...iel...	A	Connecticut		
Smith, James...	A K	New York	St. John	d. 1834, aet. 70
Smith, Rufus (M. D.)...	A		"	d. 1844. Was practicing physician upwards 50 yrs.
Smith, ...	A		Wind Co.	
Smith, Priscilla...	A			
Smith, ...	A K		...ville, Sun. Co.	Capt.-Lt. de Lancey's 2nd Batt.; d. at M., 1803, aet. 67
Smith, Shubal...	A K		St. John	
Smith, Robert...	A K		Fredericton	Magistrate, d. at F., 180, aet. 69
Smith, ...(Capt.)...	C D H K	Massachusetts		d. G. M., July, 1836, aet. 87
Smith, Bowen...	K		...Bac	d. at S., 1836. Son of ... Josiah Smith of Pe ...le, Ms.
Smith, Joseph...	C		St. Andrews	
Smith, James...	F R		Didgeguash, Char. Co.	
Smith, R...	I		St. D ...ad, Char. Co.	
Smith, Richard...	I			d. 1829, aet. 77
Smith, ...ert...	K		Queens o.	Magistrate, d. 1833, aet. 73
Smith, Elijah...	K		"	d. 1834, aet. 84
Smith, John...	K		Kings Co.	"A staunch Loyalist;" d. at W., 1842, aet. 85
Smith, Michael...	K		W...k, Car. Co.	

Name	Rep. Letter	From	Settled	Note
Smith, Adam	P		Belle Vue, Beaver Har.	
Smith, Francis	P		"	
Smith, John	P		"	
Smith, Andrew	P		"	
Smith, Jerard	P		"	
Smith, Freeman	P		"	
Smith, Hannah C.	P		"	
Smith, Hannah	P		"	
Smith, Mary	P		"	
Smith, J. C.	P—|			
Smith, Rebecca C.	O			
Smith, William	O			
Smith, Rachael	O			
Smith, Thomas	R		Charlotte Co.	
Smith, Duncan	R		"	
Smith, Jane	K		St. John	d. St. J., 1820, member Loyal Art.
Smiler, Samuel	H		Charlotte Co.	
Smose, George	D		St. Andrews	A vestryman All Saints Ch., St. Andrews
Smy, Richard	C		"	
Smythe, John	A K	New York	St. John	
Sneeden or Sneden, Robert	O K		St. John	
Sniffen, Shovel	O		"	
Snow, Benjamin	A K		St. John	Educated at Dartmouth College. School teacher. Freeman, St. J., 1785
Snow, John	A		"	Tanner, Freeman, St. J, 1785
Snowden, Randolph	B		Carleton	
Snyder, William	H		Charlotte Co.	
Snyder, Martin	K N	Pennsylvania	Penfield	
Solomon, John	C H		St. Andrews	A Quaker
Southick, Daniel	K		St. John	Printer. Pub. Royal Gazette at St. J. Was in 1792 Dep. Postmaster Gen. of N. B. Freeman, St. J., 1785
Sowers, John A.	I		St. David, Char. Co.	
Sower, Christopher, 3d.	I	Germantown, Penn.	"	
Spears, Ebenezer	I			
Spaulding, Rueben				
Spaulding, Reuben, Jr.				

Name	Ref. Letter	From	Settled	Note
Speakman, William	A K	Georgia	St. John	d. St. J., 1820, aet. 73 / Carpenter, Freeman St. J., 1785
Spear, John, or Spiers	A K		"	
Spence, James	A K		"	
Spence, Robert	A			
Spence, William	K		Hampton, Kings Co.	"Accumulated a large estate;" d. at H., 1821, aet. 74
Spencer, Samuel	C		St. Andrews	Elected vestryman All Saints Ch., St. Andrews, 13 April, 1789
Spencer, Wm	H		Charlotte Co.	
Spicer,	O			The first three of name of Spicer here mentioned were probably children of Ebenezer and Elizabeth Spicer. Ebenezer Spicer, Freeman, St. J., 1785
Spicer, Thomas	O			
do., William	O			
Spicer, Ebenezer	A Q		Springfield, Kings Co.	
do., Elizabeth	Q		St. John	d. at S., 1812, aet. 82
Spragg, Ebas	A		"	
Spragg, Caleb	A K			
Spragg, Richard	A K			
Sprage, Ms (Sprague?)	E H		Didgeguash, Char. Co.	Settled on his grant in 1789 and left in 1796
Sprick, Frederick	A K		St. John	
Springer, William	A K			
Sproul,	A			
Sproule, George	K S	Long Island, N. Y.	Fredericton	Surveyor-Gen. of N. B. and M. L. C.
Squire, Eleakin	P		St. John	
Squiers, Richard, or Squeirs	A K			
Squiers, Seth	K M	Stratford, Conn.		Grocer, Freeman, St. J., 1785 / Seth Squires with his wife and six children and Seth, Jr., arrived in transport Union at St. J., in spring of 1783
Squiers, Seth, Jr	K M	"		
Stackhouse, Joseph	B		Carleton	
Stackhouse, Robert	B		"	
Stanton, Benjamin	A K L	Rhode Island	St. John	d. at C., 1831, aet. 76. Housekeeper. Freeman, St. J., 1795 / His son was first male child born of Loyalist parents in St. John. Blacksmith, Freeman, St. J., 1795
Stanwood, Jonathan	I		Charlotte Co.	
Starkey, Jacob	P		Belle Vue, Beaver Har.	
Stanley, Thomas	A		St. John	
States, Margaret	A		"	

NAME	REF. LETTER	FROM	SETTLED	NOTE
Sterling or Stirling, Jonathan..	A K	Maryland	St. Mary, York Co.	Survivor wreck transport *Martha.* Capt. Maryland Loyalists; d. at St. M., 1826, aet. 76
S?s or Stevens, Sh lal..	A K			d. 1826, aet. 74. Tailor, Freeman, St. J., 1785
Stephens, Solomon..	A K		Kings Co.	
Stephens, Simon..	A		Musquash, St. John Co.	d. at M., 1819, aet. 66
Stephens, David..	A		St. John	Surveyor, Freeman, St. J., 1785
S?s, ?w ..	A K		"	
Stephens or Stevens, John..	A K	Charlestown, Mass.	"	Grad. Har., 1766, d. 1792
Steel, John..	A		"	Tailor, Freeman, St. J., 1785
St art, W?l kr..	A		"	Probably Walter Stewart, Yeoman, Freeman, St. J., 1785
Stewart, James..	A K		"	Officer Loyalists Corps, d. at Nashwaak, 1837, aet. 82
Stewart, Isaac..	A K		"	
Stewart, John..	A L		"	d. 9 July, 1791, aet. 38. Buried old Loyalist Graveyard, St. John.
Stewart, Peter..	A		"	Freeman, St. J., 1785
Stewart, Mordecai..	A		"	
Stern, David..	A		"	
Stewart, Hugh..	C R		St. Andrews	In 1798, Colin Campbell was adm. of est. in Char. Co. of Allen Stewart, deceased, and Duncan Stewart, "formerly lieutenant of the 74th, and now or late of His Majesty's Regiment of Foot, residing in Glasgow."
Stewart, Duncan..	C		"	
S?t, Stinson..	C H		"	
Stewart, ?s..	C H		Charlotte Co.	
Stewart, William..	E F H		"	
Stewart, James..	E F H R		"	
Stevens, William..	C		St. Andrews	
Stevenson, William..	D		St. Stephen	
Stewart, Al ander..	F R		Charlotte Co.	
Stewart, Allen..	F R		"	
Stewart, Ge..	F		"	
S?s, S?l..	I		St. Jhn ?s	
S?t, J ms..	K		St. ?s 6.	
Stewart, William..	K		" ?e 6.	
Stewart, William..	R			Merchant, d. at Cheltenham, Eng.; 1840, aet. 79. Freeman, St. J., 1785
S?, ?s..	R			Many years a pilot at St. A.
Stewart, John..	R			

(To be continued.)

RECORDS OF THE UNITED BRETHREN CONGREGA-TION, COMMONLY CALLED MORAVIAN CHURCH, STATEN ISLAND, N. Y.

MARRIAGES.

ABBREVIATIONS.

Sr.—Sister—A Communicant.	M. M.—Married Man.	M. W.—Married Woman.
Br.—Brother—A Communicant.	S. M.—Single Man.	S. W.—Single Woman.
	Wid.—Widow.	

(Continued from Vol. XXXIX., p. 178 of THE RECORD.)

1815.
April 16. Benjamin Sibell, single, son of John & Sarah Sibell
Frances Wynant, single, dau. of Daniel & Sarah Wynant, all of this Island. Md. at Parsonage

April 16. Aaron Saffin, son of William Saffin
Mary Wynant, single, dau. of Daniel & Sarah Wynant

May 13. Joseph Lockman, widower
Locky Cears, single, dau. of Elias & Jane Cears, both decd

May 27. Thomas Miller, son of Henry Miller, weaver, & wife decd.
Mary Haughwout, dau. of Wynant Haughwout, Esq., & Mary, his wife

Aug. 12. Nicholas Crocheron, single, 19(?) yrs., son of Nicholas Crocheron, Esq., & Ann, his wife
Ann Elizabeth Guyon, single, near 18 yrs., dau. of Danl. Guyon, Esq., & Frances his 1st wife. Md. at house of Danl. Guyon in the Neck

Oct. 4. Tom. a negro of Mr. John Fountain's, about 23
Sal, " of Mr. Barnt Lake, " 18. With consent of masters in writing

Oct. 7. Richard Skerrit, 21 yrs., son of James & Ann Skerret
Mary Mott, dau. of James & Appolonia Mott. Md. in house of Mrs. Appolonia Mott

Oct. 9. James Sharp, son of Wm. & Elizabeth Sharp. A young man living on North side of Island
Jane Cruser, dau. of John & Jemima Cruser of this Island. Md. at Parsonage

Nov. 22. William Stillwell, single, son of Abraham & Ann Stilwell
Lavina Simonson, single, dau. of Silas & Ann Simonson

Dec. 9. Matthias Haughwout, son of Francis & Hester Haughwout
Susan Ann Roff, dau. of Joseph & Catharina Roff

Dec. 23. Abraham Egbert, tanner & currier, son of Abraham & Ann Egbert
Ann Burbank, dau. of Jacob & Ann Burbank

Oct. 26. William Prawl, farmer, son of Danl. Prawl
Ann Egbert, dau. of Tunis & Ann Egbert

17

1816.   Thomas, } Blacks, belonging to Mr. John Seguine
Jan. 7.   Eliza, } belonging to Mr. Jeremiah Simonson

March 30. Tunis Egbert, single, blacksmith, son of John & Mary
Egbert

Margaret Crocheron, single, dau. of Richard & Jane
Crocheron

May 4.   William Blake, single, about 21 yrs., eldest son of
William & Ann Blake

Elizabeth Wood, single, dau. of Timothy & Mary Wood

June 2.   Abraham Noble, single, weaver, son of Daniel Noble,
dec., & Esther

Catharine Morgan, single, dau. of William Morgan, dec.,
& Mary, his wife. Md. in presence of friends & relations

"   Tom, } Blacks, belonging to Mr. Henry Crouse
Ana, } belonging to Mr. Nichs. Burgher

June 8.   Cornelius Sleight, son of Jacob & Jane Sleight

Mary Ann Butler, dau. of Nathaniel & Sophia Butler

Oct. 6.   Lewis Ryerze, son of Orris Ryerze, dec., & Sarah, his
wife

Catharine Decker, dau. of Richard & Mary Ann Decker

Oct. 20. Abraham Merrill, single, blacksmith, son of Abm. &
Mary Merrill

Eleonor Merrill, single, dau. of John & Elizabeth
Merrill. Md. in the church

Oct. 31. Oliver Decker, single, son of Abm. Decker & Mary, his
wife, decd.

Hannah Simonson, single, dau. of Barnet & Sarah
Simonson in whose house they were married

Dec. 2.   Gerrit Post, single, son of Abraham and Mary Post

Elizabeth Blake, single, eldest dau. of Wm. & Ann Blake

Dec. 23. Jacob Van Pelt, single, son of Samuel, decd., & Sarah
Ann Van Pelt

Mary Simonson, single, dau. of Joseph & Rebecca
Simonson, in presence of witnesses

1817.   John Blake, single, son of William & Ann Blake
Jan. 1.   Mary Van Name, dau. of Aaron & Cath. Van Name.
Md. in presence of friends at Parsonage

March 29. Egbert Merrill, single, son of John & Elizabeth Merrill of this Island

Mary Jones, dau. of Abm. Jones, decd., & Mary, his
wife. Md. at Parsonage in presence of friends

April 20. Michael Van Name (or Namur), single, son of Moses,
decd., & Mary Van Name (or Namur)

Gertrude Martha Cortelyou, youngest dau. of Jacob,
decd., & Elizabeth Cortelyou. Md. at house of
mother in presence of friends.

June 11. Samuel Coddington, single, son of David Coddington
& Elizabeth, his wife, m. n. Randolph

Catharine Jacobson, single, dau. of John V. D. Jacobson,
Esq., & Hilletje Bedell, his wife. Md. at parents' house

1817. John Winant, single, from North side of Island, son of
July 7. Simon & Sarah Winant
Martha ——, dau. of Barnet & Mary Jones, a widow
Aug. 27. Jeremiah Winant, son of John & Sarah Winant
Ann Crocheron, single, dau. of John, decd., & Sophia
Crocheron. Md. at Parsonage

By Rev. G. A. Hartman.

1817. Samuel Egbert, single, son of John & Mary, his wife,
Nov. 15. m. n. Holmes
Betsey Blake, dau. of John & Polly Blake
Dec. 13. Peter Sisk, single, son of John & Sarah Sisk, m. n.
Decker
Mary Wright, single, dau. of Thomas & Cath. Wright,
m. n. Blake. Md. at Parsonage.
Dec. 25. Elias Butler, single, son of John Butler and Polly
Kingston, his wife
Charlotte Van Pelt, single, dau. of Samuel V. Pelt &
his wife, Sally, by m. n. Housman. In presence of a
few friends at the Parsonage
1818. Joseph Lake, single, son of Joseph & Maria Lake, m. n.
Jan. 31. Coursen
Ann Jane Tuthill, dau. of Israel & Elizabeth Tuthill,
by m. n. Janer. Md. at parsonage in presence of
John Locker & Maria V. Namur
March 8. Terrence R. Ryers, single, son of Orris & Sarah Ryers
Ellen H. Decker, single, dau. of Matthias & Lydia
Decker
April 18. Abraham Seguine, single, son of John & Rachel
Seguine
Elizabeth Simonson, single, dau. of Joseph & Rebecca
Simonson. Md. at parsonage in presence of Wm. H.
Fountain & Lydia Seguine
May 11. Saul, } Blacks, belonging to Peter Decker
Louisa, } free woman. Md. in Ch. by per-
mission in writing from Mr. Decker
Aug. 23. Peter Van Pelt, single, son of David & Ann Van Pelt
Rachel Haughabout, single, dau. of Peter, dec., & Han-
nah, his wife. Md. at Parsonage, John Selenf &
Eliza Housman, witnesses
Sept. 8. James Wood, widower, son of Abraham, decd., & Ruth,
his wife
Esther Prue, single, dau. of Revd. Elias & Esther Prue.
Md. at Parsonage. All of this Island
Dec. 15. James Egbert, Sen., widower, son of Tunis & Ann
Egbert
Martha Egbert, m. n. Burbank, widow of Abraham
Egbert, shoemaker. Md. at bride's residence in
presence of their children & others

Dec. 26. Jacob Harzen, single, of Elizabethtown, N. Jersey, son of Cornelius & Ann Harzan of York Island

Margaretta Perine, single, dau. of Abm. & Sarah Perine, at whose house they were md. in presence of friends

1819.
Jan. 7. Jonothon Merril, single, son of Richard Merril & Martha, his wife, m. n. Hooper

Maria Egbert, single, dau. of James Egbert, Sen., & wife Elizabeth, by m. n. Martinse. Md. at house of Bride's parents in presence of friends

Oct. 2. Vincent Fountain, single, son of Vincent & Else Fountain

Catharine Butler, single, dau. of Isaac & Cath. Butler, both decd. Md. at Parsonage in presence of bride's brother Vincent Butler

Oct. 12. Abraham Tyson, single, son of Richard Tyson, widower

Ann Housman, single, dau. of Aaron Housman & wife Mary, by m. n. Morgan. Md. at Parsonage in presence of Richard Johnson, Rebecca Courson. By Rev. Benj. Mortimer of N. Y.

Oct. 25. Richard Tyson, widower

Elizabeth Cortelyou, widow. Md. at her dwelling. No other parties present but the clergyman, G. A. Hartman

Dec. 14. John Davis, son of John Davis, decd., & Sally, his wife

Jane Wood, dau. of Richd. & Cath. Wood. Md. in presence of Peter Johnson & Lucy Rodgers

Dec. 14. George Van Pelt, son of Peter & Mary Van Pelt

Ann Moore, dau. of James & Catharine Moore. In presence of John Van Pelt & James Moore, brothers to bride & bridegroom

1820.
Jan. 1. Abraham Van Duser, single, son of Daniel V. Duzer & Ann, his wife

Jane Vanderbilt, single, dau. of Cornelius Vanderbilt & Phebe, his wife. Md. at Parsonage, number of friends present

Jan. 4. Robert Wilson, free colored man

Nellie Simonson, free colored woman, etc.

Jan. 22. Moses Decker, single, son of Samuel Decker & Rebecca, his wife, by m. n. Decker

Lenah Pugh, single, dau. of Nicholas Pugh & Caty, his wife, by m. n. Decker. Md. in presence of Lydia Decker & James, bro. of bridegroom

March 18. Abraham Stilwill, son of Abraham & Caty Stilwill, dec., N. side of Island

Mary Scharret, dau. of John & Mary Sharret. In presence of Nicholas Daniels, Gitty Stilwill and Susan Ann Sharret

May 12. Daniel Jones, son of Barent Jones & Mary, his wife

Jane Banta, dau. of Jacob & Eliza Banta. Md. at Parsonage in presence of Bedell Johnston & Jane Wood

| 1820.
April 3. | John, } Blacks, belonging to Mr. Abm. Praul
Charity, } belonging to Mrs. Ryersz |

1820.
April 3. John, } Blacks, belonging to Mr. Abm. Praul
Charity, } belonging to Mrs. Ryersz

May 14. ThomasJohnston, } Blacks, belonging to JohnFountain
Sally Peterson, } free, residing with Mr. Dubois

May 20. James Scharrot, son of James & Hannah Scharrot
Jane Jennings, dau. of Lambert Jennings & Mary, his wife, decd. Md. at Parsonage in pres. of Richd. Johnston, Nancy White

May 24. David Cannon, son of Thomas & Betsy Cannon
Margaret Cannon, dau. of Isaac & Elizabeth Cannon. d. at Parsonage

June 3. Harry, } Blacks, belonging to Jesse Oakley
Tenor, } belonging to Mary Seguine. By permission of their masters

June 15. James Moore, single, son of James & Catharine Moore, m. n. Perine
Sarah Cannon, single, dau. of John & Ann Cannon. Md. at Parsonage in pres. of Joseph Shaddock & Martha Ann Taylor

July 4. Daniel Martling, single, son of Benjm. Martling & Elizabeth, his wife
Mary Blake, single, dau. of Edwd. Blake & Mary, his wife. Md. at house of Daniel Guyon, Esq., in presence of James Salter & Ann Martling

Nov. 5. John Egbert, single, son of Abraham & Nancy Egbert, m. n. Martinoe
Lydia Seguine, single, dau. of John Seguine & Rachel, his wife, m. n. Mitchell. In pres. of Abm. Bird & Lenah Perine

Nov. 18. John Cannon, single, son of John & Ann Cannon
Dinah Swaim, dau. of John & Martha Swaim. Md. at house of Mr. Martinus Swaim near Richmond

Nov. 26. Daniel Wood, single, son of Stephen Wood & Diodema, his wife, m. n. Housman
Deborah Mott, single, dau. of James & Appolonia Mott, by m. n. Scharrot. Md. at mother's house in presence of John Scharrot & Susan Ann Scharrot

Dec. 6. John Goodheart, single, residing near Woodbridge, N. Jersey, son of Christopher Goodheart & Sophia, his wife
Tabitha Merril, dau. of Richard Merril & Marth, his wife, m. n. Hooper

1821.
March 22. Daniel Buskirk, son of Philip Buskirk & Phebe, his wife, m. n. Tucker
Hannah Cannon, dau. of Andrew Cannon & Polly, his wife, m. n. Wright. Md. at Parsonage in presence of Benjamin Bedell & Judah Wright

June 3. Aaron Johnson, single, son of Daniel & Margaret ns n
Elisabeth Praul, single, dau. of Peter & Abigail Praul. In presence of James Colon & wife, the sister of Mrs. Johnson

17A

1821.
June 23. Peter Burbank, single, son of Abraham Burbank & Lenah, his wife

Hannah Butler, single, dau. of James Butler & Catharine, his wife. In presence of Newton Post & Eliza Herrington

June 23. Newton Post, single, son of Francis Post & Experience, his wife, decd.

Eliza Herrington, single, dau. of William Herrington & Betsey, his wife. Md. at Parsonage, in pres. of Peter Burbank & Hannah, his wife

July 21. Thomas, } Blacks, belonging to Col. Nicholas Burger
Maria, } belonging to Mr. Denyse D. Denyse.
Md. by consent of their masters

Sept. 26. Cornelius Van Name (or Namur), son of Aaron Van Name & wife Catharina, by m. n. Bartholew

Rebekah Coursen, single, dau. of Danl. Coursen & his wife Rebekah, m. n. Martinoe. Md. at Parsonage in pres. of Abraham Martling & Mary Courson

Oct. 31. Peter Woglom, single, son of Simon Woglom & wife Elisabeth, m. n. Dubois

Susan Simonson, single, dau. of Arthur Simonson & Harriet, his wife, m. n. Prickett. Md. at Parsonage

Oct. 18. Jacob Johnson, single, son of Jacob Johnson & Betsey, his w., m. n. Haughabout

Ann Burbank, single, dau. of John Burbank & his wife Ann, m. n. Egbert

Dec. 8. Peter Post, son of Garrit Post & Winie, his wife, by m. n. Bush

Mary Bartholew, dau. of John Bartholew, decd., & Mary, his wife, by m. n. Palmer. Md. at Parsonage

Dec. 19. Jacob Rozeau Cropsy, single, son of Hermanus Cropsy & w. Elizabeth, m. n. Rozeau

Elizabeth Cortelyou, dau. of Peter Cortelyou & Amy, his wife, m. n. Hilliard. Md. at bride's parents' house

Dec. 30. Bill, belonging to Mr. Parkinson at Old town

Dine, free Black. Md. by permission of master

1822.
March 30. Stacy D. Kenison, single, son of Stacy Kenison & Elizabeth, his wife, decd.

Maria Bush, single, dau. of William & Ann Bush, m. n. Van Namur. Md. at parsonage

Aug. 28. John Van Pelt, single, son of Peter Van Pelt & his wife, by m. n. Colon, dec.

Susan Christopher, single, dau. of John & Elizabeth Christopher, in presence of Jacob van Cleef & Catharine Wood at Parsonage

Sept. 10. John Crocheron, single, son of Abraham Crocheron & Jane Coursen, his wife

Patience Egbert, dau. of Tunis & Ann Egbert, m. n. Burbank. Md. at Parsonage

Oct. 2. Capt. Moses Mills, son of Revd. John Mills & Jemimah, his wife
Mrs. Mary Brintley, dau. of Oliver & Sarah Taylor. Md. at Parsonage

Nov. 3. Anzell Hill, son of Ephraim & Sarah Hill
Lenah Perine, dau. of Cornelius & Magdalen Perine at Quarantine. Md. at house of George Van Pelt in presence of Rev. Mr. Mortimer & number of friends

Nov. 30. John Miers, son of Derick & Mary, his wife
Martha Van Cleef, dau. of Daniel & Anletchy Van Cleef. Md. at Parsonage

Nov. 13. Joshua Mercereau, single, son of Stephen & Elizabeth Mercereau
Maria Sharrot, dau. of John & Catharine Sharrot, m. n. Perine. Md. at her father's house

Dec. 25. James Johnson, widower, son of Edward & Polly Johnson, m. n. Sharrot
Ann Martling, dau. of John & Cath. Martling. Md. at Parsonage

Dec. 26. Thomas Jackson, } Blacks, belonging to Col. Burger.
Judy Crockeron. } free. By his written permission.

1823. Merrel Hilliard, single, son of John Hilliard, Esq.

Jan. 2. Eliza Coursen, single, dau. of Richard Coursen & wife m. n. Egbert. In presence of father & friends

Jan. 2. Harry Swaim, } Blacks, by permission of their re-
Eliza Barnes, } spective masters, John V. D. Jacobson & Geo. Western Barnes, Esq.

Feb. 15. Daniel Jackson, } Colored, by permission of their
Mary Seely, } master Edward Perine

March 23. John Van Duser, single, son of Daniel Van Duser & Ann, his wife
Sarah Vanderbilt, single, dau. of John & Elizabeth Vanderbilt, m. n. Taylor. Md. in church

April 9. Daniel Mersereau, single, son of Stephen Mersereau
Ellen Maria Lozier, dau. of Jacob & Sarah Lozier, m. n. Beatty

May 11. Jacob Van Cleef, son of Daniel & Letty Van Cleef
Catharine Wood, single, dau. of Timothy Wood

May 17. Jacob Bush, son of Nicholas Bush & Caty, dec.
Mary Cairns, dau. of John & Harriet Cairns

May 17. Aaron Drake
Ellen Decker, dau. of Barnet & Catharine Decker

May 24. Peter Van Pelt, single, son of Jacob & Catharine Van Pelt
Elizabeth Decker, dau. of Barnet Decker & Catharine, his wife

June 4. Aaron Saffin, widower, son of William
Widow Eliza Foot, dau. of William & Sarah ——. Md. at Parsonage

June 8. James Britton, son of John & Rachel Britton
Frances Sylvy, Richard & Hester Sylvy. Md. at Parsonage

1823.   Jesse Paulus, single, son of Cornelius & Sophia Paulus
June 8.   Sarah Simonson, single, dau. of Joseph & Rebekah
         Simonson. Md. at Parsonage.
June 19.   John Wood, single, son of Stephen & Deina (or Demah?)
         Wood
         Mary Vroom, single, dau. of Christopher & Mary Vroom
July 19.   Edward Vanderbilt, single, son of John & Elizabeth
         Vanderbilt
         Mary Ann Egbert, single, dau. of Cornelius Egbert,
         dec. Md. at Parsonage
Oct. 4.   Ebenezer Davis, son of Ebenezer & Rachel Davis
         Elizabeth Merrell, dau. of Abraham & Ann Merrell.
         Md. at Parsonage
Oct. 18.   John Taylor, son of Abraham Taylor & Catharine, his
         wife
         Grace Thatcher, dau. of Charles & Elizabeth Thatcher,
         decd. Md. at Parsonage
Oct. 29.   John Dorsett, single, son of John and Martha Dorsett
         Ellen Connover Cropsy, dau. of Nichs. & —— Cropsy,
         m. n. Winant
Dec. 13.   Abraham Martling, son of John & Catharine Martling
         Elizabeth Wright, dau. of Thomas & Catharine, his wife
1824.   Richard Decker, single, son of Richard & Mary Ann,
Jan. 6.   his wife
         Eliza Egbert, dau. of Joseph & Jane Egbert, m. n.
         Martling
April 4.   Paris M. Davis, son of Richard & Sarah Moore Davis
         of N. Y.
         Eliza Jane Lake, dau. of Richard & Mary Lake of
         Staten Island. Md. at Parsonage in presence of Mrs.
         Price, the bride's sister & her husband
May 9.   Henry Kruser, son of John & Miami Kruser
         Ellen Simonson, dau. of Arthur & Mary Simonson.
         Md. at church
June 13.   Jacob Vreeland, single, son of George & Rebecca Vree-
         land
         Betsy Lockman, single, dau. of Joseph & Jane Lock-
         man. Md. at Parsonage
June 16.   John Barron, single, son of Joseph & Fanny Barron of
         Woodbridge, N. J.
         Mary Connor, single, dau. of Richard Connor, Esq., &
         his wife Sophia, m. n. Clawson. Md. at bride's
         parents
June 22.   Vincent Bodine, single, son of Vincent Bodine, dec., &
         his wife, by m. n. Blake
         Mary Ann Burbank, single, dau. of Isaac & Sally Bur-
         bank, m. n. Egbert. Md. at Bride's parents
Aug. 15.   Abraham Bird, single, son of —— & Martha Bird
         Susan Ann Perine, dau. of Cornelius Perine & wife.
         Md. at Parsonage

1824. Israel Decker, son of Israel & Leah, decd., Decker
Sept. 22. Catharine Bartholen, dau. of John & Mary Bartholen.
Md. at Parsonage in presence of Abraham Decker &
Mary Coursen

Sept. 29. Daniel Stilwell, single, from Long Island
Hester Silvy, dau. of Richard & Hester Silvy, by m. n.
Taylor. Md. at Bride's parents

Oct. 23. Barnt Seaman, } Colored, belonging to Daniel W. Lake
Margaret Price, } & md. by his permission

Nov. 18. Edward Barnes, single, son of John & Margrett Barnes
Maria Merrill, single, dau. of Mr. Abraham Merrill.
Md. at Parsonage

Dec. 11. Cornelius Egbert, single, son of Abraham, dec., Egbert
& Nancy, his wife, m. n. Martinoe
Maria De Pugh, dau. of Nicholas & Catharine De
Pugh. Md. in presence of friends

Dec. 18. Daniel Simonson, son of John & Phebe Simonson
Sally Ann De Pugh, dau. of Abraham & Mary De
Pugh. Md. in presence of Capt. Edward Perine &
Mrs. Eliza C. Hartman

Daniel Jackson, } belonging to Mr. Edward
} Colored, Perine
Ann ——, } widow, belonging to Mr.
Edward Beatty. By consent of their masters

Charles, } Colored, a freeman
Sarah, } residing at James Egbert, Jr.

1825. Richard Connor, single, son of Richard Connor, Esq.,
Jan. 6. & Sophia, his wife, by m. n. Clawson
Sarah Egbert, single, dau. of Janes Egbert & Elizabeth,
his wife, m. n. Martino. Md. at Bride's parents in
presence of friends

Jan. 8. Matthew Decker, single, son of Abraham Decker, decd.,
& Catharine, his wife
Eliza Cole, single, dau. of Richard Cole & Ann, his
wife, both decd. Md. at house of Joseph Egbert in
presence of friends

March 17. John Wood, widower, parents deceased
Catharine Jacobson, widow, dau. of Richard & Sophia
Conner, m. n. Clawson. Md. at Mr. Conners in
presence of friends

March 23. James Garretson, } free, Colored.
Ann Winet, }

April 7. Abel Cannon, son of John & Ann Cannon
Catharine Moore, dau. of James & Catharine Moore.
Md. at Parsonage

April 17. John Davis, single, of Mass., son of Jacob Davis &
Harriott (Reed), his wife
Susan Ann Scharrot, dau. of John Scharrot & Mary,
his wife. Md. at house of Abm. Stilwell, North side

1825.   Cornelius Egbert, son of John Egbert & Mary (Holmes),
June 5.   his wife
     Catharine Lake, dau. of Barnet Lake, decd., & Cath.,
     his wife. Md. at the bride's mother's

June 16.   Lawrence Crips, and aged widower
     Polly Lake, single, dau. of William Lake. Md. at Parsonage

July 2.   Henry Garretson, } Colored, free
     Mary Lawrence, }   belonging to Mr. Simon Perine

July 16.   Thomas Disosway, } Colored, both free, residing with
     Diana Clarkson, }   Hermanus Guion, Esqr.

July 30.   Abraham Decker, single, son of Israel & Rachel Decker
     Catharine Maria Pryor, single, dau. of Andrew &
     Elizabeth Pryor

July 31.   Cornelius Marston, son of John & Deborah Marston
     Mary Butler, dau. of James & Catharine Butler. Md.
     at Parsonage. In presence of John Laferge &
     Matilda Marston

Sept. 4.   George Avery, son of Geo. Avery, decd., & Grace, his
     wife
     Catharine Crips, dau. of James & Sally Crips. Md. at
     Parsonage in pres. of Lewis Mitchell & Ann Simonson

Nov. 1.   John N. Tooker, single
     Maria Jacobson, dau. of John V. D. Jacobson, Esqr., &
     Hilletje, his wife. Md. at house of Mr. Jacobson in
     presence of large number of friends

Nov. 20.   John Merrell, single, son of Abm. Merrell, dec., & Ann,
     his wife
     Margarett Housman, single, dau. of Abm. Housman &
     Hester, his wife. Md. at Parsonage

Nov. 27.   William Ross, son of William Ross
     Margrett Simonsen, dau. of Reuben & Jane Simonson, m. n. Decker. Md. at Parsonage

Nov. 30.   Abraham Housman, son of Abraham Housman & wife
     Margarett Bodine, dau. of James Bodine & Margarett,
     his wife. Md. at house of Mr. Bodine

Dec. 15.   Barzillai Burr, of New Jersey
     Ann Beatty, dau. of John & Elizabeth Beatty. Md. at
     house of Mr. Beatty

1826.   Garret Ellis, son of Garret & Mary Ellis
March 18.   Susan Butler, dau. of Nathaniel, decd., & Sophia Butler,
     his wife

April 2.   Edward Merrell, single, son of John & Elizabeth Merrel
     Catharine Shields, single, dau. of Thomas & Ann
     Shields. Md. at house of Mr. Bogart in the Manor

June 14.   Gabriel Martino, son of Benajah & Hannah Martino,
     m. n. Decker
     Eliza Catharine Martling, dau. of John & Dorcas Martling, by m. n. Laforge. Md. at house of parents

1826. James McLaughlin, single
July 27. Caroline Jaques, residing on North side of Island. Md.
    at Parsonage in presence of John M. Tooker & Israel
    Jacobson
Aug. 5. Samuel Johnson, ⎫   by permission of his mas-
         ⎬ Colored, ter, Judge Mercereau
    Hagar Thomas, ⎭   free
Aug. 16. Benjamin Praul
    Ellen Beatty, dau. of Edward & Eleanor, dec., Beatty.
    Md. at Parsonage
Oct. 11. John La Forge, son of David La Forge, dec., & Ger-
    trude, his wife, m. n. Martling
    Cornelia Simonson, dau. of John Simonson, dec., &
    Nancy, his wife. Md. at Parsonage   ·
Nov. 21. Walter Wendel, single, son of Peter & Sarah Wandel
    Ann De Puy, dau. of John & Ann DePuy. Md. at
    Parsonage
1827. Ellis Mundy, son of Joshua & Phebe Mundy
Jan. 6. Sarah Ann Egbert, dau. of Tunis Egbert & Sarah, his
    wife, m. n. Barton, in whose house she was md.
Feb. 5. Stephen McIntosh, son of Charles & Margarett Mc-
    Intosh
    Mary M. Marsac, dau. of Michael & Rachel Marsac, m.
    n. Jennings, in whose house she was md.
Feb. 18. Richard Johnson, son of James & Phebe Johnson
    Susan Van Pelt, dau. of Peter & Margaret Van Pelt
March 24. David Wood, son of James Wood, dec., & Elizabeth,
    his wife
    Eliza De Puy, dau. of Nicholas & Cath. De Puy. Md.
    at Mr. De Puy's in presence of friends
March 24. Winant Haughabout, son of Peter & Ellen Haughabout
    Sarah Britton, dau. of John & Rachel Britton. Md. in
    church in presence of friends
March 29. Capt. Benson Seaman, son of Wm. & Elizabeth Sea-
    man of N. Y.
    Eliza Jacobson, dau. of John V. D. Jacobson, dec., &
    Helletje, his wife. Md. at house of Samuel Cod-
    dington at N. Y.
April 22. Nathan Decker, son of John & his wife, dec.
    Mary Ann Bedell, dau. of James & Esther Bedell. Md.
    at Parsonage
April 22. Israel De Puy, son of Nicholas & Elizabeth, his wife,
    dec.
    Eliza Ann Decker, dau. of Abm. & Mary Decker, dec.
    Md. at Parsonage at same time as above
May 6. Matthew De Pugh, son of John De Pugh & Ann, his
    wife, dec.
    Maria Simonson, dau. of John & Phebe Simonson.
    Md. at Parsonage in pres. of Walter Wendel & his
    wife

1827.
June 23.
John Merrell, son of Thomas Merrell, dec., & Magdalen, his wife

Elizabeth Davis, widow, dau. of Abraham Merrell, dec., & Ann, his wife. Md. in presence of number of friends

Aug. 2.
Adam A. Doyle, formerly of Chambersburgh, Penna., son of Robert Doyle, dec., & Elizabeth, his wife

Catharine Merrell, dau. of John T. Merrell & Eliza, his wife. Md. at Parsonage

Aug. 22.
Daniel Butler, son of Isaac & Catharine Butler

Eliza Egbert, dau. of Cornelius Egbert, decd. Md. at Parsonage

Oct. 17.
James Mussentine, of Philadelphia, son of John & Margaret Mussentine, dec.

Catharine La Forge, widow, dau. of John & Susan Pryor. Md. at the Parsonage

Nov. 24.
John Decker, son of John & Martha Decker

Sarah Alston, dau. of Japhet & Sarah Alston. In presence of Abm. Decker & Eliza Christopher

Dec. 10.
James Beatty, son of Edward & Eleanor Beatty, dec.

Ann M. Bryant, dau. of David & Jane Bryant. Md. at house of the mother in N. Y.

Dec. 23.
Cornelius Vanderbilt, son of John & Betsy Vanderbilt

Eliza Martling, dau. of Benjamin & Elizabeth Martling, both dec. Md. at Parsonage

Dec. 31.
Peter Van Pelt, son of Richd. Van Pelt, dec., & Elisabeth, his wife

Betsy Butler, dau. of James & Catharine Butler. Md. in presence of friends at Parsonage

1828.
Jan. 15.
David Moore, single, son of James & Catharine Moore, m. n. Perine

Mary Ann Barton, single, dau. of —— Barton & Lucy, his wife, m. n. Egbert. Md. at house of her gr.-father John Egbert

Feb. 14.
Israel Wood, son of William Wood, dec., & his wife

Mary Parker, dau. of Nathaniel & Sally Parker. Md. at parents' house

March 6.
John Freeman, } Colored
Mary Prue,   }

May 11.
George W. Chambers, son of Wm. & Mary Chambers, dec.

Hannah Simonson, dau. of John & Ann Simonson. Md. at Parsonage in presence of friends

May 18.
Lewis Mitchel, single, son of Peter Mitchel & Sarah, his wife

Mary Boram, John & Sarah Boram, both dec. Md. at Parsonage

May 18.
Abraham Sharrot, son of John & Mary Sharrot

Margaret Housman, dau. of Benjamin & Letty Housman

1828.
Aug. 3. Benjamin Price, son of Elias Price & Esther, his wife
Jane Blake, dau. of John & Mary Blake. Md. in presence of a number of friends

Aug. 10. Joseph R. Heath, widower, from N. Y., son of Simon A. Heath & Eliza, his wife
Sarah Egbert, widow, dau. of Richard & Martha Merrell

Sept. 7. James Sharrot, Senr., son of Richard Sharrot, Senr., gatekeeper at Quarantine
Mrs. Van Cleef, widow. Md. at Parsonage, a number of friends being present

Sept. 11. Abraham Praul, single
Isabella Beatty, dau. of Edward & Eleanor Beatty, both decd. Md. at house of Benjamin Praul

Nov. 29. William Egbert, son of John Egbert, Senr., & his wife, decd.
Mary Ann Lake, daug. of Widow Catharine Lake at whose house the marriage took place

Dec. 14. Elias Price, single, son of David Price & Ruth Ellen, his wife
Polly Menee, dau. of Peter Menee & Sally, his wife

Dec. 31. Charles D. Wood, widower, son of James & Ann Wood
Elizabeth Jones, single, dau. of Abm. Jones, dec., & Elsy, his wife

1829.
Feb. 18. James Wood, single, at the Long Neck, son of John & Mary Wood
Abbey Ann Simonson, single, dau. of Reuben Simonson & Jane, his wife. At whose house they were married

March 2. William Winnings, widower, from N. Y., son of Wm. & Isabella Winnings, dec.
Ann Simonson, dau. of Joseph & Rebekah Simonson. Md. at Parsonage in presence of friends

May 30. Joseph Bedillion, } Colored, formerly of N. Jersey
Eliza Peterson, } formerly at G. W. Barnes

May 30. Aaron Fardon, } Colored, at Judge Seguine's
Hannah Jackson, } sister to Bedillion's wife

Nov. 15. John W. Burbank, single, son of Jacob & Ann Burbank, by m. n. Wandell
Gertrude Egbert, single, dau. of Abm. Egbert, dec., & Ann Martha, his wife. Md. in minister's dwelling

Dec. 30. Stephen Squire, widower
Martha Egbert, widow. In presence of Moses Egbert & wife in whose house they were married

Dec. 25. John Emmot to Maria Andee, Colored, living at Mr. Parkinson's

1830.
Feb. 3. Abraham Garretson, single, son of Col. John Garretson & Elizabeth, his wife, m. n. Conner
Eliza Sanders, single, dau. of Peter & Eliza Sanders. In presence of Peter Dorsett & Jane M. Betts

1830.   Joseph Christopher, single, son of Joseph & Elizabeth
May   4.   Christopher
             Maria Martino, single, dau. of Stephen Martino, dec.,
             & Eleanor, his wife. In presence of Holmes Egbert,
             Ellen Haughabout & Eliza C. Hartman
May 26.   Daniel Mersereau, single, son of Daniel & Ann Mersereau
             Lucretia (Christiana?) Sharrot, single, dau. of John &
             Catharine Sharrot
July 15.   Augustus Luckenbach, age 24, single, son of Samuel &
             Sarah Luckenbach of Bethlehem, Penn.
             Matilda Jacobson, 17 yrs., dau. of John V. D. Jacobson
             & Hilletje, his wife. Md. at house of Samuel Cod-
             dington, Esq., in presence of number of friends
Oct. 24.   Joseph Egbert, single, son of Abm. Egbert, dec., &
             Ann, his wife
             Eliza Fountain, single, dau. of Anthony Fountain, Jr.,
             & Nancy, his wife. Md. at church
Nov. 10.   Andrew B. Decker, single, son of Jeseph Decker &
             Catharina, his wife
             Patience Crocheron, widow, m. n. Egbert. Md. at
             house of her mother, Mrs. Ann Egbert
1831.   James Beatty, son of Thomas & Susan Beatty of N. J.
March 22. Maria Housman, dau. of Richard & Judith Housman
             of this island. Present, Edwd. Johnson, Jr., & Maria
             Housman
June 16.   Mathias Decker, son of David Decker & Catharine, his
             wife, m. n. Decker
             Jane Decker, dau. of John Decker, dec., & Ann, his
             wife. Md. at house of bride's mother
June 18.   John Simonson, widower, son of Arthur & Mary
             Simonson
             Rachel Baker, dau. of Jeremiah & Debby Ann Baker.
             In presence of Wm. S. Brown & Mary Burbank
Aug. 14.   Charles Barbour, single, son of Edward & Margrett
             Barbour
             Eliza Christopher, single, dau. of John Christopher &
             Elizabeth, his wife, both dec.
Oct.   8.   James Simonson, son of Abm. Simonson, dec., & Susan-
             nah, his wife
             Catharine Butler, single, dau. of James Butler & Cath.,
             his wife, dec. In presence of Eliza Ann Morgan &
             Jacob Mersereau
1832.   Stephen Martling, son of Garret Martling & Mary
March 15. Wood, his wife
             Mary Ann Bodine, widow, m. n. Burbank. In presence
             of Br. Edward & Nathan Housman
             Barnt Siebern, wid., to Delia Jackson, Colored
Oct. 14.   Abraham M. Steward, single, son of Thomas Steward,
             dec., & Hanneh, his wife
             Mary Ann Burgher, single, dau. of Mathias Burgher &
             wife. In presence of Jacob Garretson & Margaret
             Ann Tyson

1833.
May 26.

John C. Thompsen, son of John E. Thompsen, dec., grocer of Tompkinsville, & Mary Lake
Elizabeth Johnson, dau. of Anthony & Fanny Johnson. In presence of Ephraim & Addria Johnson

July 17.

Edward Burbank, single, son of Isaac & Sally Burbank, by m. n. Egbert
Jane Britton, single, dau. of Nathaniel & Mary Britton, m. n. Bodine

Aug. 1.

John Burgher, single, son of Mathias & Hannah Burgher, m. n. Tyson
Elizabeth Stilwell, single, dau. of Daniel & Hannah Stilwell. Md. in presence of friends

Dec. 29.

Abraham Bodine, son of James & Margaret Bodine, dec.
Abby Ann Kinsy, dau. of Benjamin & Susan Ann Kinsy. In presence of John Kinsy, her brother, & of Ann Merrel. Md. in church

1834.
Jan. 8.

Edward Johnson, single, son of Edward & Mary Johnson, m. n. Sharrot
Hannah Housman, dau. of Richard & Judith Housman. Md. at Parsonage in presence of Jeremiah & Judith Turner

Jan. 12.

Daniel Haughwout, single, son of Francis & Esther Haughwout
Jane Jones, dau. of Abm. & Alice Jones. At parsonage in pres. of Jacob Winant, Presilla Jones

Feb. 13.

Capt. Jacob H. Vanderbilt, son of Cornelius Vanderbilt, dec., late of this Island
Euphemia M. Banta, dau. of Wiart Banta, dec., & Sylva, his wife, of N. Y., where they were md. in presence of friends

May 21.

Samuel Lesher.   Both from Germany now at Tompkinsville
Elizabeth Nedicker.

May 26.

Leonhart Wilhelmin.   Both from Germany now at Tompkinsville
Catharine Maurer.

June 22.

Elias Price, son of Rev. Elias Price of Methodist Ch. & Hester his wife
Mary Ann Lake, dau. of Joseph & Mary Lake

Aug. 13.

James Thompson, son of Robert Thompson & Susan, his wife, dec.
Charity Guyon Romer, dau. of James & Mary Romer. Md. at parent's house in presence of friends

Sept. 27.

Jacob Housman, son of Benjamin Housman & Mary, his wife
Susan Robbins, dau. of Nathaniel Robbins, dec., & Mary, his wife. In presence of John & Mary Ann Haughabout

Nov. 4.

Dennis Sullivan, single
Elizabeth Vanderbilt, dau. of Capt. John Vanderbilt & Celia, his wife. Md. in presence of friends in dwelling of her parents at "town Point," New Jersey

Nov. 19.

James Egbert, son of James Egbert, dec., & Sally, his wife
Eliza Decker, dau. of Abm., dec., & Ann, his wife

1834. Nov. 19.	William Francis Post, single, son of Francis Post, dec., & Sarah, his wife Martha Ann Egbert, dau. of James Egbert, dec., & Sally, his wife. Md. at Parsonage
Dec. 26.	George Lentz. Both from Germany now at Tomp- Magdalen Jacky. kinsville
Dec. 30.	Israel O. Dissasway, single, son of Israel R. Dissasway & Ann, his wife Lucretia Jacobson, youngest dau. of John V. D. Jacob- son, & Hellethay, his wife, both dec. Md. in presence of friends
1835. June 14.	William Townsend, single, son of John & Sarah Townsend Dorcas L. Martling, single, dau. of Peter & Elizabeth Martling. Md. at dwelling of bride's parents in pres. of friends
March 26.	Tunis A. Egbert, widower, son of Abraham & Ann Egbert, dec. Charlotte De Foreest, widow, m. n. Vanderbilt. In presence of Mrs. Catharine Prall & Eliza C. Hartman
Sept. 3.	Abraham Lockman, single, son of Richard Lockman & Catharina, his wife, dec. Matilda Britton, single, dau. of Cornelius Britton & Jane, his wife, dec. Md. in presence of Hamilton & Ann Britton, in Parsonage
Oct. 12.	Oliver Martin, single, son of Moses Martin, dec., & Nancy, his wife Sarah Ann Vanderbilt, single, dau. of Capt. John & Presilla Vanderbilt of Elizabeth, Town Point, N. J. Md. in presence of a large number of friends
Oct. 14.	Abraham Vanpelt, single, son of David & Ann Vanpelt Ellen Maria Dorset, single, dau. of John & Martha Dorset, both dec.
Nov. 1.	Abraham Tyson, single, son of Peter Tyson & Mary, his wife, dec. Elsie Jane Haughawout. Md. in presence of some friends in dwelling of minister
Nov. 23.	James Livingston Lynch, single, son of James & Rachel Lynch Olivia Ann Marsac, dau. of Michael & Rachel Marsac. Md. at house of Bride's parents
Nov. 23.	William Thomas, son of Thomas & Elizabeth Thomas, dec. Mary Ann Hilyer. At same time as above
Dec. 5.	Williamson Decker, son of Reuben & Maria Decker, both dec. Mary Bonnel, dau. of Enos & Rachel Bonnel. Md. in minister's dwelling in presence of John Baker & Eliza Bonnel
Dec. 16.	Barnet Jones, son of Daniel & Elizabeth Jones Sarah Hatfield, dau. of James & Sarah Hatfield, both dec. In minister's dwelling in presence of Thomas Christopher & Elizabeth Jones

(*To be continued.*)

THE HOPPE-HOPPEN-HOPPER LINEAGE.

By Hopper Striker Mott.

I.

Long before the first of the name set foot upon New Netherland's soil, this family was rich, prominent, powerful and, as a consequence, much respected at Amsterdam. Its history harks back to ancient times in Holland where the name was spelled both Hoppe and Hoppen, a custom the pioneer in this country continued.

From *Beschryvinge Van Amsterdam* door Casparus Commelin, 1691, these data are derived:

Jan Claesz van Hoppen was Schepen of Amsterdam in 1469, '74, '79, '81, '83, '88, Councillor of the City 1483, Burgomaster, 1490, '91, and again Schepen 1494, '98, 1500, '02. Another Jan Claesz van Hoppen, doubtless his grandson, was Councillor of Amsterdam in 1549, Burgomaster the same year, Schepen 1554, again Burgomaster in 1560, '61, '64, '66, '67, '69, '71, '72, and Orphan Master in 1562, '63, '65, '68, '70, '73, in September of which latter year he died and was succeeded by Gerbrand Klaesz Banning. On one of the windows of the Old Church at Amsterdam is written, as translated from Vol. I, p. 426:

"This Church pane has been presented to the church by Jan Claasz van Hoppen, who has been Burgomaster, Schepen and Councillor of the City, who having been accused of being favorable to the new religion and subsequently taxed with being a heretic, was, by his Confessor, as a punishment for his conversion, ordered to proceed to Rome and there to purge himself, where (apparently on account of letters by the clergy from here, they knowing that he was a rich man) he was condemned as a penance to present this window to the Church, which seems to make known what is written on a sheet over his head, floating from the Bishop's staff:

Nemo Laeditur Nisi se ipso.

Besides, he was condemned not to drink anything but water during an entire year, but on his trip hither from Rome the use of water became very irksome and he returned to Rome and requested the Pope, because the water in this country was unhealthy without having been boiled in hops, to be permitted to boil some hops in his drinking water, which (those in Italy not knowing this to be beer) was permitted him, thus having been able, owing to this use, to mitigate his penance."

This pane of the Salutation of Maria was made by —— Digman. The Hoppe Coat-of-Arms is seen on this pane; he, Hoppen himself, lies buried in front of this pane, in the chancel of the Holy Virgin, as shown by a certain tombstone whereon the said Coat-of-Arms is also to be seen.

At page 550 it is related: "On the day of the Visitation of Our Lady we are bound annually to give every patient in our

18

Hospital a clear white loaf of bread and a pint of wine which has been donated by Jan Claesz van Hoppen and Styn his wife. On the 13th of September we are bound, on account of Jan Claesz Hoppen, to give the patients a meal consisting of boiled meat and wine; and in case the same be fishday, then fish shall be served as is proper."

Page 554: "Jan Klaesz van Hoppen was a regent of the Guesthouse or Hospital in 1511. Jan van Hoppen was a regent of the above hospital in 1547."

"But before commencing to preach, the Pastor Jan Aartsz prepared a Remonstrance to be delivered to the Burgomasters, as had been also done at Haerlem, which Jan Pietersz Reaal had delivered by a certain sailor, Pieter van Grieken, at the house of Jan Claasz van Hoppe, Burgomaster. But he refused to accept it, so that on July 30 the messenger had to deliver it at the City Hall, in the Little Tower."

Page 992: "Aug. 26, 1566. The Resolution (concerning the people of the new religion or protestants) was published throughout the town by the sound of the trumpet, in the presence of the Burgomaster Jan Klaasz van Hoppen, of Adriaan Paauw, Arent Brouwer and Egbert Roeloffz."

Page 1005, 1566, *circa* December. "When now the Colonel, in accordance with the Prince's [William the Silent] desire, retained the *privileges* accorded to the militia, everything turned out right and the militia men were invited to the house of the presiding Burgomaster Jan Claasz van Hoppe, who admonished them to observe harmony and to keep the above compact and rules. In the meantime the Prince took leave and departed via Haarlem for Antwerp. Since that time also the six chief Captains were not much troubled thereafter."

Page 1014, April 5, 1567. "In accordance with the above *privileges* the choice of delegate from among the City militia is confirmed by Burgomasters Joost Buik, Jan Klaasz van Hoppe and Hendrik Cornelisz."

Page 1019, May 5, 1567. "With approbation of the Court, Harman Roodenbug and Adriaan Reyniersz Pauw were charged to go with Burgomaster Joost Buyk to Antwerp and to request the Duchess [of Parma] not to station a garrison [Spanish] in the city. But arriving at Rotterdam they met Burgomaster Jan Klaesz Hoppe, who came from Antwerp and intended to return to Amsterdam, with orders to go back to Antwerp within four days and to reply to the question whether or not those of Amsterdam were inclined to accept a garrison. But the envoys, continuing their journey by carriage, met about eighty or a hundred ships with soldiers who were already ascending the Yael for Gouda and further to Amsterdam."

The following individuals are presumably of the same family: From 1666 to 1668 Dr. Cornelis Hop was pensionary [chief law councillor or Corporation attorney] of Amsterdam.

In 1678 Dr. Pieter Hop and in 1680 Dr. Cornelis Hop were Secretaries of the same city.

Cornelis Hoppesack was in 1655, Regent of the Poor House in Amsterdam, and from 1648-1663, Regent of the Poor House on the Old Side [of the City].

Gysbert Michielse Hoppesack was a Regent of the Old Men's and Women's House from 1634-1639.

Jan Hendrikz Hoop was a Regent of the Insane Asylum in 1615.

Jan Hendriksz Soop from 1611-1638 was Regent of the same Asylum.

Jacob Hop was, in 1690, City Advocate or Corporation Counsel of Amsterdam, and in the same year Cornelis Hop was one of the Twelve Secretaries of that city.

Vol. II, p. 1027. "On Feb. 16, 1569, Jan Cornelisz Kettelaer was imprisoned and Hendrik in de Hoppesack was summoned to the Hague [both for having embraced Protestantism]."

Hoppers was the name of a castle or Noble House in Friesland, in the village of Hemelum, under the district of Hemelumer-Oldevaart and Noordtwolde, in the quarter of Westergoo, says *Tooneel der Vereenigde Nederlanden*, (Scenery of the United Netherlands) by François Halma, Leeuwaarden, 1725.

In *de Vroedschap* (Town Council) *van Amsterdam*, 1578-1795, Vol. I, pp. 39, 258, are found these data:

"Jan Claesz van Hoppen was Schepen and Register at Amsterdam in 1549, Burgomaster in 1560. His daughter, Wijburch Jansdr. van Hoppen m. Jacob Jacobsz. Bennigh, son of Jacob and Maria Jacobsdr. Verheyen, Register 1578-1581, chosen Deputy of the Guard (Schutterijen) May 27, 1578, Schepen 1578, Cloth Merchant, Warden of the Cloths, 1580. Buried O. K. (Old Calender) Aug. 7, 1581. Their daughter Agnieta Jacobsdr. Bennigh, b. 1561, became first wife, July 20, 1596, of Dr. Sebastiaen Egbertsz, alias Sabastiannus Egberti, who was Register 1602-1618, appointed Governor of Maurits, Nov. 3, 1618, Schepen, 1593, Burgomaster 1606-8, Commissioned to the Council 1609-1611, High Professor of Anatomy in the Atheneum Illustre at Amsterdam 1595, Doctor of Medicine resident in 1596 in the Convent of the Eleven Thousand Virgins, in 1606 at the Old Side Cemetery and upon his death in Kalverstraat. His collective wealth and that of his two lamented wives at his death was florins 206,000. He was the son of Egbert Meynertsz and Diewer Jacobsdr., was born 1563 and buried O. K. April 16, 1621."

The Memoirs of one Joachim Hopper are often quoted. In *William of Orange* by Ruth Putnam (N. Y., 1895) at Vol. II, p. 122, is found: "Joachim Hopper was a learned Doctor of Laws, a Fleming, a Catholic and a Nationalist—that is, he was loyal to Philip, but wished the Spanish to be withdrawn. In 1566, he went to Spain to give the King information on the affairs of the Netherlands and remained there as representative of the Provinces. His counsel to Philip to permit an interregnum at this crisis, shows how little he understood the situation at home. As a practical man of affairs he was considered very effective. On March 18, 1577, Granville wrote: 'The letter seems to be very odd and evidently from the forge of poor Sieur Hopperus, who did

not write the best French in the world, God pardon him. He
was learned, but knew little of business, as can be plainly seen.'"

La Nouvelle Biographie Generale, Vol. 25, states he was born
at Sneeck in Friesland, Nov. 11, 1523. He received the degree of
Doctor in 1553 and forsook the profession of teaching the following year, on his appointment as a member of the Grand Conseil
de Malines. When the Spanish Government undertook the
creation of a University at Douay, he was put in charge of its
formation. Called to Madrid in 1566, he became Privy Councillor to Philip II, and Chancellor of Affairs of the Low Countries.
He was more moderate than the other ministers of that monarch
and was the author of numerous noted books and Mss. He died
at the capital, Dec. 15, 1576. *Vide* also Motley's *Rise of the Dutch
Republic*, Part II, Chap. V; Part IV, Chap. IV.

Christiaen Hoppe, born 1621, at Amsterdam, studied at Helm-
stadt and in 1647 became Lutheran preacher at Enkhuizen. In
1656, he removed to Haarlem and in 1660 was called to his native
city where he died in 1670. After 1652 he devoted himself to ed-
ucating young men for the ministry. A sermon written by him,
though only of six pages, 4to, was published for the fourth time
in the year 1710, forty years after his death.

SOME COLONIAL HOPPERS.

Three brothers, natives of County Durham, England, settled
in Flushing, L. I., *circa* 1675. About the year 1700, they appear
to have removed to Gloucester County in the vicinity of the town
of Woodbury, N. J. Here they dwelt for several generations but
the nearness of a metropolis, and their frequent intermarriage
with Philadelphia families, led to their gradual removal until now
none of the name are to be found near Woodbury. Tradition relates that the brothers were John, Robert and Christopher. The
first and third individuals appear in the *Documentary History* as
residents of Flushing in 1698, but only the descendants of John
can be traced in succeeding generations. No doubt the destruction of the records of that town in 1789 have deprived us of much
information. The descendants of John are found widely scattered. Although this line has been supposed to have been
Quakers, the early Friends' Records in Flushing and Westbury
do not contain the name.

Robert Hopper had land in Burlington, N. J., in 1683, and is
described in the records as of Scarborough, County of York, England. As this county adjoins Durham, the suggestion is raised
that he might have been one of the three brothers. He was a
seafaring man and made voyages, as master of the ship *The
Providence* between Scarborough and Philadelphia in the year
above written. His only daughter, or heir, died in England *circa*
1701.

Capt. James Hopper, born in Chester, England, was the owner
in New York City of vessels in the merchant service, 1793. He
and his brothers were sons of William H. Hopper. This seems
to be a distinct family from the other New York lines, and descendants now reside at Utica.

A prominent family of the name in Maryland which is represented by many branches, traces its ancestry to early times. They have been designated as the Eastern Shore Hoppers in distinction from the descendants of the Maryland branch of the Long Island and Woodbury lines. As early as 1676, Capt. William Hopper was a member of the Legislature, representing Queen Anne's County.

Hoppers appear to have early settled in Virginia and from there spread through western and southern states. These came from Ireland or England

Another line descended from William, John, Hugh and Alexander who came with their parents from the north of Ireland in 1753 and settled in the Newberry District, South Carolina. Some of these subsequently located in Alabama.

Descendants of a settler of the name who emigrated from Wales to South Carolina about the time of the Revolution and later removed to Kentucky, now live in Indiana. One Robert Hopper of Ireland, and settled in Fayette County, Penn., prior to that war, is now represented in the Western States. He is said to have had a brother in Maryland, which suggests a possible connection with those of the Eastern Shore.

John and Sarah Hopper who were married in London in 1773, were in Philadelphia in 1787, and have descendants in New York and Florida. Sarah was of Herefordshire and some of their issue were born in England and some in Philadelphia.

Savage's *Genealogical Dictionary* gives Daniel Hopper of New Haven in 1654, with the suggestion that it was intended for Hooper, and in the Rhode Island Census for 1774, is Henry Hopper of South Kingston, with six in family, four males and two females. These records indicate that there were early individuals of the name in New England. Some of the traditions of the Durham Hoppers, state one of the brothers located there.

Fragmentary records of other families of the name have been found in various places and may denote other lines than those enumerated. It is of ·

THE HOLLAND HOPPERS

that this article relates. Riker's *History of Harlem*, p. 432, states that this family " of good Dutch antecedents, are descended from Andries Hoppen, who, with his wife, Geertje Hendricks, emigrated hither in 1652. He was enrolled in 1653 in the burgher corps at New Amsterdam and granted the small burgher right in 1657, when he owned considerable property in the city; but this honor he survived little more than a year." Tradition gives the date of arrival as 1620. The pioneer sometimes added, as a middle name, the designation Willemszen, denoting that he was the son of Willem and wrote his name both with and without the final " n." He never lived in Harlem and is mentioned as above because he was the great grandfather of Yallass Hopper, who resided in that section at a much later date. It was not until the fourth generation that the termination "r" became regularly affixed, a concession required to fit the English pronunciation.

18A

A general trader and freighter, Hoppe's headquarters were at the capital. He traded in peltries, brick, timber, stone, dry goods, shoes, earthenware, seawan, tobacco and occasionally even sold a boat. With his yacht or sloop, he not only ascended the North River as far as Fort Orange, but also made trips to the north (the Dutch possessions in present New England) either for his own account or with cargoes belonging to others. It happened more than once that this enterprising trader, in order to be able to buy in a favorable market, mortgaged some of his property as security for large quantities of merchandise purchased by him. Often he appeared before the Worshipful Court of Burgomasters and Schepens, either to prosecute claims against unwilling or tardy debtors, sometimes also to protect himself against too previous or unreasonable creditors, at other times to force those who sold him merchandise to live up to the conditions of the sale.

From the little that the records contain about him, we learn that he was a strenuous, pushing, enterprising merchant ready to go with his "yacht" wherever there was a call for his services where there existed a demand for the commodities which New Amsterdam was able to supply, or where there was an offer of certain goods the Capital needed. He was a typical New Amsterdam merchant and though not nearly so wealthy as many among them, was the peer of any in enterprise, probity and business sagacity. Well-to-do for those days, he owned a number of parcels of real estate, besides his "yacht" and stock in trade.

He bought a plot of land in the City, Nov. 11, 1655, from Pieter van den Linden, described as a lot east of the Company's five houses, bounded west by Hendrik Kip, southerly close on the Old Fiscal's Kitchen. (Hendrik van Dyck, who retired as Fiscal in 1652 to be succeeded by Cornelis van Tienhoven.) So large and small, wide and long as according to the patent thereof to said Pieter van den Linden of March 26, 1646.

This property was on the north side of Bridge Street, between Whitehall and Broad (*Vide* Valentine's *Manual*, 1861, 582). This was probably used for warehouse purposes because at the time it stood very near the East River shore.

Hopper also owned a house and lot on the east side of Broadway, north of Beaver Street. In 1657, the next lot adjoining on the north was used by Jacob Leendertsen of Lubec, the southern boundary of which was described as being Hopper's lot (*Vide Ibid*, p. 592). Andries Hoppe's house, Oct. 25 of this year, was on the Broadway, says *Year Book*, 1900, Holland Society, and bounded north by that of Gysbert Imbroeck, east by the sheep meadows, south by Gerrit de Miller, and west by the aforesaid *Heere wagh*. It is further located Feb. 8, 1663, as being east of Heere Straat and adjoining on the south that of Adam Hardenbroock, present husband of Annetje Meinders, late widow of Ensign Dirck Barensen Smitt.

On Oct. 12, 1655, the principal burghers subscribed or were taxed for certain amounts towards needed repairs to the public works. Some offered to contribute in money, others in labor or in kind. Among the latter was Hoppe, who volunteered to furnish two cargoes of stone. He lived only six years after his arrival in the new country, and yet his name is conspicuous in the annals of the period.

Shortly before his death he entered into a contract with Jacob Jansen Stoll to purchase Bronck's Land (Morrisania). This property contained 250 morgen (500 acres) and was known to the Indians by the name of Ranachque. It is supposed that Jonas Bronck, the original owner, was killed by them in 1643. Governor Kieft granted this land Oct. 4, 1644, to Arendt van Curler who had married Bronck's widow and who transferred it to Stoll July 10, 1651. At the session of the Court of Jan. 29, 1661, Geertruyt Andries, said Stoll's widow, brought action against Geertje Hendricks, widow of Hoppen, for the payment of 400 guilders, balance due for the purchase of land and houses, according to contract, under hand, between their deceased husbands, and in addition two cows.

The defendant answered that as the plantiff could not deliver the sold land free from Indian claims and return the 1300 tiles which had been removed from the house, she should be non-suited and condemned to pay to her (defendant) the 2400 guilders already paid on account.

The court decided that Mrs. Hoppen should pay the balance demanded and that a due conveyance and deed should be delivered to her. In reference to the tile " she must demand them from those who enjoyed them." The deed was thereupon executed by Matthues de Vos, plaintiff's attorney and is of record bearing date Dec. 19, 1662.

Pending the conclusion of this matter, the widow Hoppen had intermarried with Dirck Gerritszen van Tright, van Buuren, May 8, 1660, and with his " approbation and consent " transferred the property to Harman Smeeman of " Comoonepau on the Maine," on the same day she had taken title. Said Smeeman, one of the earliest settlers of Bergen and a magistrate there in 1661, conveyed the land in question " for a valuable consideration" to Samuel Edsall on Oct. 22, 1664, and Governor Nicolls issued a royal patent to him therefor on the same date. Bolton's *Westchester* says that Capt. Richard Morris, the next possessor, must have purchased from Edsall *circa* 1670. The property was conveyed by letters from Governor Andros to Col. Lewis Morris, second proprietor of Morrisania, March 25, 1676.

During certain sessions of the Court held in 1665 and 1666, Thomas Hall, as attorney of Christiaen Davitsen, essayed to prove that his client had purchased of Andries Hoppen one half of the land, and that Geertje Hendricks, the widow, had sold the whole of it to Smeeman without consent and so Hall humbly craved judgment of restitution. On June 20, 1665, he demanded that she be required to give security for any judgment obtained, on the ground that she had no fixed domicile in the city. She asserted she had a house and lot there, which proved a satisfactory answer. On the trial she produced an award of arbitrators (Johannes van Burgh, Marten Cregier, Allard Anthony and

Nicholaes Bayard) dated July 24, 1665, showing that Davitsen had resold the land to her. The jury, composed, among others, of Isaac Bedlow, Gulian Verplanck, William Bogardus, Walter Salter and Johannes de Peyster, decided that the sale made in presence of the arbitrators should remain in full force. Plaintiff appealed June 6, 1666, but on Sept. 17, all parties appeared before Nicolaes Bayard and declared that they had mutually agreed "about the difference which was risen about Bronck's Land" and requested him to enter judgment "to the end that all proceedings at law in this case should seize."—*Minutes* of the Court.

The widow Hoppe's second husband, although called van Tright in the New York records, was known as van Duyn in New Jersey. He removed from Flatbush, L. I., where he was born, his father Gerret Cornelise van Duyn being the common ancestor of the family, to Bergen where he settled and died in 1686. He bought land in 1662 from Governor Stuyvesant on the Saddle River. His children wrote their names van Dien. Among his issue was Gerret van Dien, who married Vroutie Verwey and lived west of the above river. Winfield's *Land Titles of Hudson County*, p. 101, cites the confirmation of the above Dutch grant of 1662 in Dirck Gerritse on May 12, 1668, by "Philip Carterett Esq., Governor of the Province of New Cesarea or New Jersey," and relates that previous to his death he had sold the land to Baltus Barentsen van Kleek. He received the purchase money but before the transfer was completed, died leaving a widow, Gerten Hoppe and son Garret van Dien, then living in Hackensack. These completed the sale Oct. 13, 1686.

Hoppe died in December, 1658, leaving five children. Their mother appeared before the Orphan Masters, Dec. 11th, and stated that her husband had died intestate but had appointed as guardian of the children, Cornelis Aarsen and Lambert Huybertsen Mol, who were thereupon ordered to inventory the estate. She plead that, until she remarried, she was not obliged to produce an inventory and was informed that "the custom of fatherland" required it and that she should agree with the guardians as to the amount which she should set apart to each child. The guardians were reminded that the eldest child must remain with the mother. On March 5, 1659, they reported that an agreement had been made "about a settlement on the children of their paternal inheritance" and that 1000 florins (200 florins for each child) had been allowed. Jacobus Vis and Isaac Kip were appointed, April 29, 1660, to take a copy of the inventory "in order to settle their inheritance upon the children."—*Minutes* of the Orphan Masters.

These minutes at p. 138, give the names of the five children as Catrina, Wilhelmus, Hendrick, Matthys and Adolf. Riker states that there were only four and names the fourth Matthys Adolfus. His information was doubtless obtained from the Dutch Church records wherein only four are mentioned and where can be found the baptism and marriage of said Matthias Adolphus. No child named Adolf appears either there or in the Hackensack records whither all the children removed with their mother.

(*To be continued.*)

THE KNICKERBOCKER FAMILY.

By WILLIAM B. VAN ALSTYNE, M.D.

(Continued from Vol. XXXIX, p. 186, of THE RECORD.)

36. ANNATJE[4] KNICKERBOCKER (Wouter,[3] Johannes Harmensen,[2] Harmen Jansen[1]), bap. 9 Nov., 1735, at Albany; d. 30 Dec., 1809; m. 10 Dec. 1757 (both Schaghticoke and Albany records), "Col. Cornelius Van Vechten" of Schaghticoke, N. Y., bap. 9 Feb., 1734-5, at Albany; d. 31 Oct., 1813; son of Harmen Van Vechten and wife Elizabeth. Harmen Van Vechten, bap. 16 Feb., 1704, at Albany, was son of Dirk Cornelisen Van Vechten and Margarita Harmense Luwes. A sketch of Col. Van Vechten and the following children are given in the *Van Vechten Genealogy*:

    i. Harme,[5] b. 14 Jan., 1761; bap. 13 June, 1761, at Albany; spon.: Barent and Cathalyntje Van Buren; d. 19 Sept., 1762.

    ii. Elizabeth, b. 19 Aug., 1763; bap. at Albany; spon.: Wouter and Elizabeth Knikkerbakker; d. 10 Nov., 1767.

    iii. Marytje, b. 9 Dec., 1765; bap. at Albany; spon.: Gerrit and Alida Visscher; d. in her 94th year at Lansingburgh, N. Y.; m. Enoch Leonard.

    iv. Elizabeth, b. 23 Dec., 1767; bap. at Albany; spon.: Wouter and Elisabeth Knickerbakker; d. 10 May, 1769.

    v. Elisabeth, b. 18 Aug., 1770; bap. at Schaghticoke; spon.: Wouter and Elisabeth Knickerbacker; d. 13 April, 1840; m. Rev. Samuel Smith.

    vi. Harme, b. 1 March, 1772; bap. at Albany; spon.: Dirk and Alida V. Vegten; d. 26 May, 1859; m. 10 Jan., 1793, Catherine Wendell, b. 24 June, 1772; d. 21 July, 1830. He lived on a farm between Coverville and Bemis Heights, Saratoga Co., afterwards moved to Schuylerville where he died.

    vii. Rebecca, b. 9 Sept., 1773; bap. at Albany; spon.: Dirk and Alida Van Vegten; m. 6 Sept., 1792, Garret Wendell.

    viii. Lucas, b. 1775.

    ix. Margarietje, b. 16 Oct., 1776; bap. at Schaghticoke; spon.: Harmen Fort and Elizabeth Van Vechten; d. 12 Sept., 1777.

    x. Walter, b. 10 Dec., 1779; d. 1 April, 1860; m. (1) wid. Outhout; m. (2) Anna Van Vechten, b. 30 July, 1789; d. 18 April, 1856, dau. of Judge Abraham Van Vechten of Albany.

37. ALIDA[4] KNICKERBOCKER (Wouter,[3] Johannes Harmensen,[2] Harmen Jansen[1]), bap. 20 Nov., 1737, at Albany, d. 17 Feb., 1819,

at Schaghticoke, N. Y.; m. there 21 Oct., 1758, Dirk Van Vechten,[*] bap. 15 May, 1737, at Albany, son of Harmen Van Vechten and Elisabeth his wife. Of their children the first four were baptised at Albany, the others except John at Schaghticoke:

   i. Elizabeth,[*] bap. 21 Jan., 1759; spon.: Wouter and Elisabeth Knickerbacker.

   ii. Alida, bap. 14 Nov., 1761; spon.: Wouter and Anatje Knikkerbakker. Mother's name "Annetje Knikkerbakker."

   iii. Harmen, b. 7 Aug., 1765; spon.: Cornelis V. Vechten and Elisabeth Vile; d. Oct., 1848; m. 28 Dec., 1784, Nellie Kettle.

   iv. Wouter, b. 2 July, 1768; spon.: Johs. and Elisabeth Knickerbacker; d. 20 March, 1820; m. 11 Jan., 1788, Jane Fonda, d. 25 Jan., 1829.

   v. Cornelis, b. 13 Feb., 1771; spon.: Dirk I. and Pieterje Van Veghten; d. 2 Dec., 1837; m. 15 May, 1791, Maria Groesbeck, b. 15 June, 1775; d. 24 Jan., 1871.

   vi. John, b. 29 May, 1773; d. 6 April, 1843; m. 21 May, 1794, Maria Knickerbocker, b. 23 March, 1777, at Schaghticoke, dau. of Johannis Knickerbocker, Jr., and Elisabeth Winne.

   vii. Dirk, b. 22 Dec., 1775; spon.: Peter Viele and Elisabeth Fonda.

   viii. Derkje, b. 11 Feb., 1778; spon.: Corns. Van Vechten and Annatje Knickerbacker; m. 19 May, 1792, William Winne Knickerbocker, b. 9 May, 1773, at Schaghticoke, N. Y.; d. 1846, son of Johannis Knickerbocker, Jr., and Elizabeth Winne.

   ix. A dau., m. —— Becker. Lived at Amsterdam, N. Y.

38. ANNA[4] VAN VECHTEN (Cornelia,[3] Johannes Harmensen,[2] Harmen Jansen[1]), bap. 6 Dec., 1748, at Albany, N. Y.; m. there 29 Jan., 1767, to Ignas Kipp of Schaghticoke, N. Y. He was appointed elder in the Dutch Reformed Church at Schaghticoke, 18 Dec., 1788, and 12 Dec., 1782. Children bap. there, except Margarita:

   i. Sara,[4] b. 19 Aug., 1769; spon.: Philip and Lena Van Esch.

   ii. Margarita, b. 27 Oct., 1772; bap. at Albany; m. Harmen J. Groesbeck, bap. 28 Feb., 1765, at Schaghticoke, son of John H. Groesbeck and Maritje Viele.

   iii. Neeltje (Cornelia), b. 19 Jan., 1777; spon.: Abraham Viele and Anatje Knickerbocker.

   iv. ——, b. 1783; spon.: Johs. Knickerbacker and Elisabeth Winne.

   v. Jacob, b. 29 May, 1788; spon.: Hans W. Groesbeck and Anatje Devenport.

   vi. Teunis.

[*] A sketch of Derrick Van Vechten and the above children are given in the *Van Vechten Genealogy.*

39. JOHANNES⁴ KNICKERBOCKER, JR. (Johannes,³ Johannes Harmensen,² Harmen Jansen¹), b. 29 Jan., 1751; bap. 24 March, 1751, at Albany, N. Y.; d. 10 Nov., 1827, at Schaghticoke, N. Y., aged 76 years, 9 months and 19 days; m. 1 March, 1769, at Albany (Albany and Schaghticoke church records) "Elizabeth Winne, dau. of Capt. William Winne * and Maria De Frondelac of Albany," b. 6 April, 1752; bap. 12 April, 1752, at Albany; d. 10 Nov., 1828, it is said, at the same moment and hour as her husband. Johannes inherited the homestead at Schaghticoke. The house, a substantial brick structure, is still standing and contains many of the relics of olden times. Near by is the family cemetery and back of the mansion stands an aged tree around which it is said the Indians met to discuss war and peace. His wife joined the Dutch Reformed Church at Schaghticoke, 13 June, 1769, and he followed her example 9 June, 1771. Here he officiated at various times as elder and deacon. In 1792 he was a member of the State Legislature. John Knickerbocker, Jr., during the Revolutionary War was a private in the Albany County Militia (Land Bounty Rights), Fourteenth Regiment. He did not enter the service until after his father had resigned, and then entered the same regiment which his father had formerly commanded. The children of Johannes Knickerbocker and Elizabeth Winne were bap. at Schaghticoke, except Willem:

    i. Harmen,⁵ b. 17 Dec., 1769; spons.: Johs. and Rebecka Knickerbocker; d. young.
    ii. Willem, b. 11 Dec., 1771; bap. at Albany; spon.: Willem and Marytje Winne; d. young.
    iii. William Winne, b. 9 May, 1773; spon.: Willem and Marytje Winne; d. 1846, at Schaghticoke, aged 73 years. "Colonel William W. Knickerbocker" m. 19 May, 1792, at Schaghticoke, Derrica Van Vechten.
    iv. Rebecka, b. 3 May, 1775; spon.: Johs. Knickerbocker; m. 5 Aug., 1792, at Schaghticoke, John Bradshaw.
    v. Marytje, b. 23 March, 1777; spon.: William Winne and Marytje Dewandelaar; m. 21 May, 1794, at Schaghticoke, John Van Veghten.

---

*William (Willem) Winne was bap. 22 April, 1716, at Albany, son of Daniel Winne and Dirkje Van Ness; m. Maria De Frondelac, called Maria De Wandelaar on the Albany Church records, probably bap. 25 Dec., 1715, at Albany, dau. of Johannes De Wandelaar, Jr., and Lysbeth Gansevoort of Schaghticoke, N. Y. Daniel Winne, son of Pieter Winne and Tanaatje Adams, m. 16 March, 1698, at Albany, Dirkje Van Ness, dau. of Jan and Aaltie Van Ness. Daniel Winne of Rensslaer Manor, yeoman, made his will, 18 Jan., 1750-1, proved 2 March, 1757, and recorded at Albany. In it he mentions wife Dirckie and nine children, one of them being William. Pieter Winne was b. in the city of Ghent in Flanders; m. (1) Aechie Jans (by whom he had Pieter Pietersen Winne, b. 1643, lived in Esopus and m. Jannetje Alberts); m. (2) Tanaatje Adams, b. in Leeuwarden in Friesland, by whom he had twelve children. Pieter and Tanaatje Winne made a joint will, 6 July, 1684, proved 22 Feb., 1695, (Albany County Wills, Book I, p. 44). In 1677 he bought one half of Constapele's Island, and the same year a saw-mill in Bethlehem, Albany County, N. Y. He was Commissary or Magistrate of Bethlehem, Leeuwarden, the capital of Friesland is ten miles from the sea though once it lay on the shores of a deep bay.

vi. Harmen (Hermen), b. 20 July, 1779; spon,: Abraham
Viele and Annatje Knickerbacker; d. 30 Jan., 1855,
at Williamsburg, N. Y. Hermen, m. (1) Arietta
Lansing; m. (2) Rachel Wendel; m. (3) Mary Buel.
Rachel Wendel, dau. of John H. Wendel of Albany,
d. 29 July, 1823. He was a lawyer and lived at
Schaghticoke where he dispensed such generous
hospitality that he became known as " Prince of
Schaghticoke." There is a tradition to the effect
that a clause in the Knickerbocker grants provides that the holder of the title to a certain tract
of land must entertain the Mayor and Commonalty
of Albany once a year, and this agreement was carried out strenuously. He was elected to the 11th
Congress as a Federalist and served from 22 May,
1809, till 3 March, 1811. In 1816 he was chosen to
State Assembly and also filled the office of County
Judge. He is alluded to by Washington Irving in
the *Knickerbocker's History of New York* as " My
cousin, the congressman," and when Mr. Irving visited Washington he introduced him to President
Madison as " My cousin Diedrich Knickerbocker,
the great historian of New York." It was this inti-
mate friendship which was the origin of Irving's
humorous history of New York under the *non de
plume* of Diedrich Knickerbocker (Appleton's *Cyclo-
paedia of American Biography*, Vol. 3, p. 562; *N. Y.
Genealogical and Biographical Record*, Vol. 34, p. 1,
onward). His son, Right Reverend David Buel
Knickerbacker, D. D., Bishop of the Episcopal
Diocese of Indiana, was b. 24 Feb., 1833, at Schaghticoke, d. 31 Dec., 1894, in Indianapolis. He graduated
in June, 1853 from Trinity College, and during the
next three years studied at the Episcopal Theological Seminary in New York. He then went out to
Minnesota as a Missionary of the Episcopal Church
and began his labors among the Indians. He became Rector of a church in Minneapolis where he
remained until chosen Bishop of Indiana (*Year Book
of the Holland Society of New York*, 1895).

vii. Derckje, b. 17 June, 1781; spon.: Gerrit Winne and
Anatje Viele; d. young.

viii. Derkje (Derica), b. 27 Jan., 1783; spon.: Gerrit Winne
and Anatje Viele; m. 8 March, 1801, at Schaghticoke, Evert Van Allen, bap. 30 Aug., 1772, at Kinderhook, N. Y.; d. 14 Aug., 1854, at Defreestville,
N. Y., son of Abraham E. Van Allen * and Mary

* Abraham E. Van Allen was b. 25 June, 1750; bap. 15 July, 1750, at Claverack, N. Y., and d. before 1 April, 1816, when his widow gave power of attorney
to James Vanderpoel "to correct her third as widow of Abraham E. Van Allen."
He m. 16 March, 1771, at Kinderhook, Mary Fryenmoet, dau. of Rev. Johannes
Casparus Fryenmoet and Lena Van Etten and had nine children, of whom

Fryenmoet. Evert was a famous surveyor and civil engineer, as civil engineering was understood in those days. Howell's *History of Albany County*, says that he was the surveyor who laid out the most part of the City of Albany. He also did much work for the State and others in Jefferson, Lewis and St. Lawrence Counties. They had eleven children, one being the mother of Admiral Van Reypen. Evert was the principal legatee of his uncle and aunt, John E. Van Allen, the Congressman, and Anne Fryenmoet, dau. of Domine Fryenmoet, and is sometimes said to have been adopted by them.

ix. Johannis, b. 7 Dec., 1783; spon.: Joannes Knickerbacker and Rebecka Fonda; probably m. Rachel Visscher, dau. of Nanning H. and Alida Visscher of Waterford, Saratoga Co., N. Y.

x. Annatje, b. 19 Oct., 1786; spon.: Abram Viele and Anatje Knickerbacker; m. 27 Feb., 1805, at Schaghticoke, John De Foreest, Jr.

xi. Elisabeth, b. 17 Aug., 1788; spon.: William Van Antwerp and Rebecka Knickerbacker; m. John William Groesbeck, bap. 18 Oct., 1785, at Schaghticoke, son of William Groesbeck and Sara Viele.

xii. Neeltje, b. 12 June, 1790; spon.: William and Marytje Knickerbacker; m. Jacob T. E. Pruyn.

xiii. Cathalyntje (Kathlyne), b. 23 Aug., 1792; spon.: Gerrit Van Antwerp and Sara Kip; d. at age of 44 years,

---

Evert was the eldest. His mar. lic. bond calls him "tailor." Abraham was son of Evert Van Allen.

Evert Van Allen was b. about 1715, but the precise date of his birth or baptism nowhere appears. He was son of Johannes Van Alen and Sara Dingman, and Sara in her will (vid. Calendar of Wills number 1806, probated 1746) mentions her son Evert. He m. Margarita Fitzgerald and had seven children, of whom John E. was the eldest and Abraham E. was the second. Evert was dead in 1769 when his brother Jacobus made his will.

Johannis Van Allen is called "my eldest son" in his father's will, but the date of his birth or baptism is not found. He m. 3 July, 1697, at Albany, Sara Dingman, dau. of Adam Dingman and Aeltie Jacobse Gardiner. They appear to have had 10 children. He took the "test oath" in 1699, "lives to ye southward of Albany." On 22 Feb., 1677-8, he bought a lot on North Pearl Street, Albany. On 30 Nov., 1702, he signed the certificate in favor of Paulus Van Vleck, precentor of the Congregation at Kinderhook, and in consequence was summoned before the council at New York and received "a caution to be more careful in future." In 1716 he was a member of the consistory of the Reformed Dutch Church at Kinderhook. He was son of Lourens Van Alen.

Lourens Van Alen was in Kingston as early as 1669, later he is found at Albany and Kinderhook; he d. in 1714. He m. Elbertje Evertse, only child of Evert Luycase Backer, one of the original patentees of Kinderhook, and through her the entire interest in the Kinderhook (otherwise known as the De Bruyn) Patent passed into the Van Alen family. Lourens was closely related to "Pieter van Haelen, van Uytrecht, shoemaker," who came to New York in the *Vergulde Bever* in May, 1658, and lived at Kingston and Albany, but whether his younger brother has not been determined. The family name is probably derived from Haelen, an ancient town in Belgian Limburg.

Rev. H. Van Allen of Utica, N. Y., who is collecting material for a Van Allen Genealogy has kindly furnished the above lineage.

at Waterford, N. Y.; m. 18 Nov., 1810, John L. Viele,
b. 6 June, 1788, at Pittstown, N. Y.; d. 19 Oct., 1832,
at Albany, son of Ludovicus Viele * and Effie Toll.
John L. Viele of Waterford, N. Y., was educated at
Union College, served in the War of 1812, became an
attorney at law in 1808, counsellor in the Court of
Chancery in 1814, was New York Senator in 1822,
'26 and '29, Judge of the Court of Errors, and Regent
of the University of New York. Their son was Gen.
Egbert L. Viele, b. 17 June, 1825, at Waterford; d.
22 April, 1902, at New York City; m. there 3 June,
1850, Teresa, dau. of Francis Griffin and Mary Sands.

xiv. Abraham, b. 7 April, 1796; spon.: Abraham and Hanna
Viele; m. (1) Laura Sturges; m. (2) Mary Ann Hale.

40. ANNATJE⁴ KNICKERBOCKER (Johannes,³ Johannes Harmensen,² Harmen Jansen¹), bap. 11 March, 1753, at Albany, N. Y.;
m. 5 April, 1771, at Schaghticoke, N. Y. (New York State mar.
lic., dated 10 Sept., 1770) Abraham Viele. On 5 June, 1771, Annatje joined the Dutch Reformed Church at Schaghticoke.
Children bap. at Schaghticoke:

   i. Johannis,⁵ bap. 20 March, 1774; spon.: Johs. Knicker-
      backer and Rebecka Fonda.
  ii. Eva, b. 27 June, 1779; spon.: Jacob Viele and Eva
      Fort.

41. LAURENTZ⁴ KNICKERBOCKER (Benjamin,³ Laurens,² Herman
Jansen¹), b. about 1733; m. Margerie Bain (Ben). They appear
to have had an only child:

   i. Benjamin,⁵ bap. 4 Nov., 1753, at Germantown, N. Y.;
      spon.: Benjamin Knickerbocker and Letge Halen-
      beek his wife.

42. ABRAHAM⁴ KNICKERBOCKER (John,³ Laurens,² Harmen Jans-
sen¹), b. 12 April, 1733, at Salisbury, Conn.; bap. 3 May, 1733, at
Germantown, N. Y.; probably m. Jerusha ——. Children:

   i. Molly,⁵ b. 21 Oct., 1762, at Salisbury, Conn.
  ii. Jane, bap. 23 Oct., 1764.

---

* Ludovicus Viele, bap. 17 Oct., 1742, at Schenectady, N. Y.; m. Effie Toll,
bap. 15 Jan., 1749, at Schenectady, dau. of Simon Toll and Hester De Graaf.
He was son of Jacob Viele, bap. 21 June, 1719, at Schenectady; m. 4 July, 1742,
at Albany, Eva Fort, bap. 25 Jan., 1724, at Schenectady, dau. of Abraham Fort
and Anna Barber Clute of Schaghticoke. Jacob was son of Lodovicus (Lewis)
Viele of Schenectady and Schaghticoke as early as 1708 (Pearson), m. 12 Oct.,
1697, at Kingston, N. Y., Maria Freer, b. 1676, at Hurley, N. Y., dau. of Hugo
Frere and Marie Haye, his first wife. Lodovicus Viele was son of Pieter Cornelisen Viele and Jacomyntje Swart, dau. of Teunis Cornelisen Swart and Elisabeth Lendt or Van der Linde. Pieter Cornelisen Viele settled in Schenectady
where in company with Elias Van Gyseling he purchased Bastian De Winter's
bowery in 1670. He d. in 1688, and two years later during the massacre at
Schenectady, his widow and children escaped to Albany. Jacomyntje Swart
m. (2) Benony Arentsen Van Hoek; m. (3) Cornelis Vinhout. Pieter Cornelisen
Viele is said to have been son of Cornelis Cornelissen, b. 1622, in Utrecht; m.
26 Nov., 1645, at New York City, Aeltje Colet, widow. (*New York Genealogical and Biographical Record,* Vol. 34, p. 2.) In 1668 he paid for the use of the
" large pall " for the funeral of his wife who d. at Albany.

Both children bap. 23 Oct., 1764, at Salisbury, Conn., by Rev. Thomas Davies, A. M., an Episcopal minister.

43. LAWRENCE[4] KNICKERBOCKER (John,[3] Laurens,[2] Harmen Jansen[1]), b. 1 or 7 Sept., 1739, according to Salisbury, Conn., records, but 1 Nov., 1739, according to Athens, N. Y., church records; probably m. Catharine ———. Children, b. at Salisbury:

    i. Samuel,[5] b. 12 Jan., 1762.
    ii. Elizabeth, b. 16 March, 1764.
    iii. John, b. 19 Nov., 1766, in New Canaan.
    iv. Salmon(?), b. 28 Feb., 1773.

44. HARMON (HERMON)[4] KNICKERBOCKER (John,[3] Laurens,[2] Harmen Jansen[1]), b. 3 Jan., 1741/2, according to Salisbury, Conn., records, but 13 Jan., 1742, according to Athens, N. Y., church records where his baptism is recorded; m. Thankful ———. In addition to the children mentioned in their grandfather's will, Abraham and Lawrence are called children and heirs of Harmen Knickerbocker (Sharon Probate Records, Book G, p. 97). Children:

    i. John,[5] b. 15 Sept., 1766, at Salisbury, Conn.
    ii. Bartholomew.
    iii. Abraham.
    iv. Lawrence.
    v. Rachel, } twins.
    vi. Thankful, }

45. ISAAC[4] KNICKERBOCKER (John,[3] Laurens,[2] Harmen Jansen[1]), b. 17 June, 1750, at Salisbury, Conn.; may have m. Hannah ———. The following children are copied from the Salisbury, Conn., records:

    i. Cornelius,[5] b. 9 May, 1774.
    ii. Jeremiah, b. 1 April, 1776.
    iii. Reuben, b. 9 Aug., 1781.
    iv. Hannah, b. 20 Jan., 1783.

A son d. May, 1788, and was buried at Lime Rock, Conn.

46. SOLOMAN[4] KNICKERBOCKER (John,[3] Laurens,[2] Harmen Jansen[1]), b. 12 Oct., 1754, at Salisbury, Conn.; m. Anna Heath, dau. of Bartholomew Heath and Mehitable Crippen of Sharon, Conn.

On 22 Oct., 1789, according to agreement between the heirs of John Knickerbocker of Salisbury, that part of the real estate willed to Solomon was distributed among the other heirs. (Book E, Probate Records, p. 267.)

On 12 Jan., 1799, Solomon Knickerbocker and Anna, his wife, of the town of Freehold, County of Albany and State of New York, sell to Thomas Heath of Sharon, land in Sharon, Conn., set off by heirship from the estate of Bartholomew Heath, deceased, our father. (Land Records Book 12, p. 398.) The following children, except Hannah, were b. at Salisbury:

    i. Hannah,[5] d. 15 Sept., 1776, aged 16 months; bur. at Lime Rock, Conn.
    ii. David, b. 7 Aug., 1777.
    iii. William, b. 4 Aug., 1780.
    iv. Walter, b. 7 Aug., 1782.

v. Althea, b. 2 Feb., 1785.
vi. James, b. 19 May, 1787.

47. RULIFF (RULEF)⁴ KNICKERBOCKER (Harmen,³ Laurens,² Harmen Jansen¹), bap. 16 April, 1745, at Germantown, N. Y.; d. 28 June, 1807, aged 62 years; m. 22 Dec., 1768, at Oblong, N. Y., Catharine Dutcher, who d. 26 Dec., 1792, aged 51 years. The Kingston, N. Y., church records give Catrina, bap. 12 July, 1741, dau. of Johannes de Duytser and Catharina Bogardus, and Catalyntje, bap. 4 Jan., 1741, dau. of David DeDuitscher and Pietronelle Van Fredenburg. Rulef and his wife are buried on the Belden farm between Wassaic and Dover, N. Y. They lived at Dover. Children:

72   i. Tobias,⁵ bap. 30 Jan., 1773, Rhinebeck-Red Hook (N. Y.), records; spon.: Tobias Miller and Moriken Knickerbocker; d. 3 May, 1850, aged 77 years and 7 months; bur. in a small enclosure on the Belden farm on the west side of the road, between Wassaic and Dover; wife's name unknown.

73   ii. Cornelius, b. 1775; d. 12 Sept., 1850, aged 75 years; bur. near his brother Tobias; m. Susannah Nase.

    iii. Mary, b. 13 Feb., 1778; bap. at South Amenia, N. Y.; spon.: Hannes and Mary Woolsey.

    iv. Dorcas.

    v. Sarah.

48. MARY⁴ KNICKERBOCKER (Harmen,³ Laurens,² Harmen Jansen¹), bap. 28 Feb., 1748, at Germantown, N. Y.; probably m. 28 Jan., 1768, at Oblong, N. Y., Joseph Gillet, who d. 25 Oct., 1770, in his 30th year. Father and son are buried in a cemetery on the Belden farm between Wassaic and Dover, N. Y. Children, bap. in the Presbyterian Church at South Amenia, N. Y.:

    i. Joseph,⁵ bap. 20 June, 1769, at Widow Gillet's; d. 18 Nov., 1769, aged 10 months and 9 days.

    ii. Mary, bap. 30 Sept., 1770.

49. CHRISTOPHER⁴ DUTCHER (Elizabeth,³ Laurens,² Harmen Jansen¹), bap. 3 Jan., 1748, at Germantown, N. Y.; m. 9 June, 1768, at Oblong, N. Y., his cousin, Mary Belden, of Nine Partners, N. Y., dau. of Silas Belden and Janetie Knickerbocker. Christopher bought a large tract of land extending from the top of Chestnut Ridge at Dover Plains, N. Y., to the Ten Mile Run. He not only carried on an extensive farm but erected a flour mill on the Ten Mile River. They had at least the following children:

    i. Silas,⁵ bap. 10 Aug., 1777, at South Amenia, N. Y.; spon.: Silas Belding, Jr.

    ii. A dau., b. 8 Feb., 1779; bap. 28 March at South Amenia.

    iii. Lawrence, m. Jane Nasse.

50. JOHN⁴ DUTCHER (Elisabeth,³ Lawrence,² Harmen Jansen¹), b. 5 Jan., 1759, at Salisbury, Conn.; d. 2 Dec., 1848; m. 17 May, 1779, Sylvia Beardsley, b. 10 Oct., 1763; d. 14 Jan., 1844; dau. of Johiel Beardsley and Hannah Griffin. John Dutcher moved to

Dover, N. Y., and thence to Cherry Valley, Otsego County, N. Y. Children:

    i. Elizabeth,' b. 18 May, 1780; d. 8 June, 1780.

    ii. Christopher, b. 25 April, 1781; d. 23 April, 1845; m. 2 June, 1803, Martha Sloan, b. 3 May, 1784; d. 3 Jan., 1875.

    iii. Gabriel, b. 5 May, 1783; d. 21 May, 1849; m. Peggie McKillup.

    iv. Hannah, b. 26 April, 1785; d. 10 Jan., 1862; m. (1) —— Fitch; m. (2) Simon Gray.

    v. Johiel, b. 24 April, 1787; d. 14 Jan., 1822; single.

    vi. Sylvia, b. 2 March, 1789; d. 5 Nov., 1865; m. William Goodell.

    vii. Sally, b. 31 July, 1791; d. 21 March, 1842; m. William Knapp.

    viii. Pacefor Carr, b. 3 Jan., 1794, at Cherry Valley; d. 18 Feb., 1867; m. 31 Dec., 1821, Johanna Low Frink, b. 2 July, 1802; d. 7 Sept., 1881, at Roseboom, N. Y., within a mile from where she was born, dau. of Stephen Frink. He purchased a farm in Springfield, N. Y., but in 1846, removed to Seneca, N. Y.

    ix. Mary, b. 2 March, 1796; d. 16 Feb., 1882; m. April, 1821, John McKillip, b. 1790; d. 24 Dec., 1845.

    x. John, b. 1 Dec., 1797; d. 22 March, 1859.

    xi. Keziah, b. 14 March, 1800, at Cherry Valley; d. 4 Oct., 1878; m. 28 April, 1822, Benjamin Davis, b. 5 Oct., 1795, at Burlington, N. J.; d. 25 March, 1860.

    xii. Joseph N. (Dr.), b. 9 Sept., 1802; d. 1873; m. Louisa Spafford.

    xiii. Deborah White, b. 15 Aug., 1804; d. 24 Oct., 1868; m. 25 Sept., 1825, William Davis, b. 6 April, 1801; d. 22 July, 1876.

(To be continued.)

THE SKILLMANS OF AMERICA AND THEIR KIN.

By WILLIAM JONES SKILLMAN, PHILADELPHIA, PA.

(Continued from Vol. XXXIX., p. 166, of THE RECORD.)

147. HIRAM⁶ SKILLMAN (William H.,' George,' Jacob,' Thomas,' Thomas '), b. Oct. 23, 1823; d. Jan. 31, 1894; m. Jan. 16, 1844, Catharine Huff (yet living, 1907), sister of Lucretia (No. 146), at Elizabeth, N. J. Children:

    i. John R.,' b. 1848; Engineer; m. (1) Maggie Smith, 1868. By her had five children: 1. Lizzie. 2. Levi. 3. Charles (of Raritan, N. J.). 4. Kate. 5. Gertrude (of Plainfield). He m. (2) Sophia Du Shannick, 1885, and had: 6. Henry George. 7. John Harvey. 8. Cora. Family now of Garwood, N. J.

ii. David H., b. 1852; m. and lives in Elizabeth; has three
boys; carpenter and builder.
iii. James Harvey, b. 1855; weaver; unm. at Plymouth,
Mass.
iv. William Dilts, b. 1857; m. —— Sherwood; one dau.;
also a weaver of Plymouth.
v. Ella, b. Feb., 1861; m. John Matthews; three boys and
two girls.
vi. Wesley, b. 1864; never m.; with Cent. R. R., N. J.
vii. Edgar, b. Feb., 1867; m. —— Button; machinist at
Hartford, Conn.

148. THEODORE[6] SKILLMAN (Samuel,[5] Samuel,[4] Benjamin,[3]
Thomas,[2] Thomas[1]), b. at Kingston, N. J., March 4, 1800; d. 1842;
m. (in Pennsylvania) Oct. 23, 1819, Catharine Albright, sister of
"Polly" (see No. 68), who m. William. She was b. June 15, 1803;
d. May 28, 1886. Family home, Lockland, Hamilton Co., O.
Children:
i. Mary Ann,[7] b. Sept. 25, 1820; m. John Turner. Had:
1. John. 2. Henry. 3. Jane. 4. Maria.
ii. Anna, b. Dec. 12, 1821; d. April 10, 1892; m. —— Parsons, and had one dau., Drusilla.
iii. John, b. June 11, 1824; m. Julia Bigum. Had: Mollie.
iv. Hiram Newton, b. 1826; m. 1849, Eliza Palmer. Had:
1. Chas. Wesley. 2. John Wellington. 3. Alice.
4. William Edwin. 5. Albert Nelson. 6. Irvin
Bingley. 7. Luella. 8. Henry. 9. Flora.
v. Isaac, b. 1827; m. May 30, 1850, Martha Ann Bachelor.
Had: 1. Theodore Suel. 2. Louisa. 3. Hannah.
4. Belle. 5. Cassius M. 6. Orrin Grant.
vi. Margaret, b. 1829; m. —— Sullivan and had seven
children, all living in 1901.
vii. Louisa, b. Feb. 1, 1832; m. William Bachelor; three
children, all m. and living in Hamilton, O.
viii. William, b. Feb. 8, 1834; d. Jan. 10, 1880; m. but no
children.
ix. Jacob A., b. 1836; d. 1873; m. but childless.
In this single Lockland Family are 57 of the Skillman name,
or 102 all related, Dec. 2, 1901.
149. JOHN[6] SKILLMAN (Benjamin,[5] Thomas,[4] Benjamin,[3] Thomas,[2]
Thomas[1]), b. in Kingston, N. J., Sept. 21, 1790; d. 1870; m. Aug.
17, 1815, Susan Hollingshead, elder sister of Hetty (see No. 50)
and of Ann who m. John Scudder (writer's uncle) who removed
1847 from Princeton, N. J., to Maysville, Ky. Children:
i. George,[7] b. Nov. 20, 1816; d. 1818.
ii. Charles, b. April 7, 1818; d. inf.
iii. Edward, b. 1820; d. 1893; coal dealer, Harlem, N. Y.,
1863; two sons: 1. James, b. 1845, Pocomoke City, Md.
2. Archibald A., Williamsbridge, N. Y.; m. and has
one dau.
iv. Caroline, b. April 3, 1822; d. Oct. 9, 1823.
v. Archibald A., b. 1824; printer, Nassau St., N. Y., 1847;
in California, 1848, half-owner of *Pacific News*, San

Francisco; later, editor and proprietor of *Eureka Sentinal*, Nev.; d. 1900; m. (1) 1845, Elizabeth Hicks, Princeton; one son, James Carnahan, Allegheny, Pa., b. 1846; six boys and four girls; m. (2) 1857, Mrs. Sarah Black, nee Baker, Princeton; one son, Edward A., b. 1858, "Sentinal," Nev.

vi. Hettie H., b. Jan. 16, 1828; d. inf.

150. SAMUEL[6] SKILLMAN (Samuel,[5] Thomas,[4] Benjamin,[3] Thomas,[2] Thomas[1]), b. at Kingston on farm given by Lemuel Scudder to eldest son, Richard, *circa* 1783 (writer's grandfather); d. 1847; m. 1803, Sarah, dau. of William Hight, Princeton; lived and d. at Harlingen. Children:

i. Aaron,[7] b. 1804; d. 1869; m. 1827, Mary A. Van Pelt (b. 1808; d. 1860); shoemaker, Six Mile Run. Had: 1. Catharine, b. 1828; d. 1834. 2. Sarah, b. 1831; m. Dr. Lucien King; one dau., Emma. 3. Abraham V. P., b. 1834; d. inf. 4. James Romeyn, b. 1836; d. inf. 5. John Stryker, b. 1838; m. 1865, Mary, dau. of Simon Wyckoff, Pleasant Plains, N. J.; three daus. Home, Brooklyn; business in N. Y. City.

ii. Randall, b. 1806; m. 1833, Maria Stryker; lived at Post Town (Plainville), N. J. Had: 1. John, b. 1834. 2. Margaret, b. 1836. 3. Jane, b. June 11, 1838; m. Benjamin Hageman, Fairview, Ill. 4. Sarah, b. 1840. 5. David B., b. 1845. 6. Mary, b. Aug. 15, 1849. All but John bap. at Harlingen (Ref. Dutch) Church. Later the family removed to Illinois.

iii. James, m. March, 1841, Eliza Wood at Neshanic; lived at Harlingen. Had three children.

iv. David Bayard, b. 1812; m. Jane Williamson; a shoemaker, N. Brunswick, N. J. Had: 1. John, d. inf. 2. Sarah, m. Jacob N. Outcalt. 3. David. 4. Augusta.

151. THOMAS B.[6] SKILLMAN (Thomas,[5] Thomas,[4] Benjamin,[3] Thomas,[2] Thomas[1]), b. May 31, 1800, at Kingston, N. J.; d. Hamilton Co., O., March 15, 1896, oldest man of the region; m. Feb. 13, 1822, Jane Van Dyke. Children:

i. Thomas,[7] b. 1823; m. 1843, Mary Davis, and d. six weeks later, April 17.

ii. Dominicus Van Dyke, b. 1824; m. (4th cousin) Lavinia, dau. (see No. 111) of Thomas Q. Skillman, large farmer adjoining.

iii. Sarah Jane, b. 1827; m. (1) 1844, William Sater; two children, Amanda and Charles; m. (2) 1854, Casper Gearhardt; three daus., Allie, May, and Mattie.

iv. Mary Ellen, b. 1830; d. unm., June 23, 1897, of melancholia.

v. William R., b. 1833; d. 1891; m. Sarah C. Carroll, now living (1905) in Cincinnati; no issue.

vi. John, b. 1836; d. 1859 from an accident.

vii. Charlotte, b. 1838; m. May 17, 1857, Ezra Wetherbee (d. Sept. 11, 1894); two children.

viii. George, b. Nov. 17, 1840; d. Jan. 21, 1841.
  ix. Katharyn, b. May 28, 1842; m. May 15, 1867, William
      V. Sater, Bevis, O. Children: 1. Alma. 2. Stanley.
      3. Clifford.
   x. Annice, b. June 27, 1847; m. Nov. 11, 1869, Frank A.
      Wetherbee, Transit, O. Had: 1. Albert. 2. Clara.
      3. Goldie.

152. ALFRED⁸ SKILLMAN (Isaac,⁷ Thomas,⁶ Benjamin,⁵ Thomas,⁴
Thomas¹), b. 1803, near Princeton, N. J.; d. April 11, 1847; m.
1830, Sarah, dau. of Jacob Parker and wife Susan Sutphen. Home
at Kingston. Children:
    i. Phineas Withington,⁹ b. 1831; farmer at Rhode Hall.
   ii. Joachim, b. 1833; Sept. 18, 1861, joined Co. B., 9th
       N. J. V. I.; discharged July 12, 1865.
  iii. Archibald Alexander, b. 1836.
   iv. Hannah, b. 1840; d. Aug. 14, 1847.

153. JOHN SCUDDER⁸ SKILLMAN (Joseph,⁶ Thomas,⁵ Joseph,⁴
Thomas,³ Thomas¹), b. 1791; d. 1836; m. Dec. 26, 1810, Mehitable
Fanning; d. 1834. Both buried at Aquebogue, L. I. (W. of the
church). Children:
    i. Ida Harris,⁹ b. 1811; m. 1830, George Lee.
   ii. Joseph Hazzard, b. 1813; lived at Greenport, L. I.; d.
       1868; m. Emeline Chase. Had three daus. and one
       son.
  iii. John Scudder, b. 1816; lived at Hartford, Conn.; d.
       1887; m. Oct. 3, 1837, Nancy Hunt. Had: 1. John
       H. 2. Mary J. 3. Frances A. 4. Joseph Hazzard,
       b. 1848. 5. Hiram S. 6. Mehitable F.
   iv. Mary J., b. 1818; m. 1842, the Rev. William Tobey.
       No children.

154. JANE⁸ SKILLMAN (sister of above), b. 1786; m. 1814, Samuel
Griffing (b. 1788; d. 1856); was from Cutchogue, L. I.; taught
school at the Wallabout; then was a grocer in New York, later a
a prosperous up-town lumber dealer. Had six children, only two
arriving at maturity.

155. THOMAS⁸ SKILLMAN (Francis,⁷ Thomas,⁶ Joseph,⁵ Thomas,⁴
Thomas¹), b. 1791, at the Wallabout in the old Skillman home;
early a deacon in the church on Joralemon St. (1st Ref. Dutch);
in 1835 removed to a farm in Chenango Co., N. Y. (Smithville);
d. 1841; m. 1816, Catharine Onderdonk. Children:
    i. Francis,⁹ b. Sept. 1, 1817, in the old home on the Walla-
       bout site, now occupied by the U. S. Naval Hospital;
       d. Sept. 7, 1898, at Roslyn, L. I., on the farm given
       him in his youth by his grandfather Onderdonk; a
       J. P. for 24 consecutive years; Member of N. Y. As-
       sembly (1st District) 1867-8; m. (1) 1842, Sarah Ann
       Schenck (d. 1864); m. (2) 1865, Josephine D., dau. of
       Horatio Gates Onderdonk (b. 1835; d. 1906). Had
       an only dau., Elizabeth O., b. 1871; m. 1907, Samuel
       H. Andrews, Brooklyn.
   ii. Eliza B., b. 1820; d. July 31, 1827.
  iii. Joseph Onderdonk, b. 1825; d. inf.

iv. Joseph Onderdonk, b. 1827; d. 1872; home at Jamaica, L. I.; deacon in church there (Ref. Dutch); m. March 17, 1858, Gertrude Van Sicklen. Had: 1. Mary C., b. Dec. 21, 1858. 2. Ida Kouwenhoven, b. 1860; d. 1879. 3. Joseph Hegeman, b. July 16, 1863.

156. John[6] Skillman (Francis,[5] Thomas,[4] Joseph,[3] Thomas,[2] Thomas[1]), b. March 2, 1797, on the Wallabout; d. 1865; from a boy was a member of First Ref. Dutch Church, Brooklyn, and like his father, long a ruling elder therein; inherited the homestead farm which he sold about 1835; First Pres. of City Bank, Brooklyn; m. (1) March 13, 1828, Catharine Newberry (b. 1794; d. 1838); m. (2) Nov. 26, 1839, Mary K. Duffield (b. 1808; d. 1883). Of seven children only three survived infancy:

  i. John Moon,[7] b. 1831; never m.; paymaster in U. S. Navy; d. suddenly at Mobile, Jan. 13, 1865.
  ii. Anna, b. 1833; d. at Claverack, 1865; m. July 9, 1857, the Rev. Acmon P. Van Giesen, descendant of Rynier Bastiansen Van Giesen who came to America previous to 1660 from Holland; graduate of N. Y. University, 1849, and of N. B. Theo. Sem., 1852; pastor of the First Church (Ref. Dutch) of Poughkeepsie, N. Y., for nearly 40 years; d. there 1906; served at Catskill, Brooklyn, and Claverack Churches (Ref. Dutch). Two daus. survive.
  iii. Mary Emily, b. Feb. 14, 1835; d. Feb. 14, 1841.
  iv. Catharine Newberry, b. 1840; m. Henry M. Curtis.
  v. Emily Maria, b. May 16, 1842; d. May 10, 1870.
  vi. Mary Duffield, b. Aug. 25, 1844; d. Nov. 7, 1848.
  vii. Francis, b. Sept. 5, 1847; d. Aug. 9, 1849. Interments are all in Greenwood.

157. Thomas[6] Skillman (Thomas,[5] Thomas,[4] Joseph,[3] Thomas,[2] Thomas[1]), b. Dec. 12, 1789; d. 1876?; m. (1) Nov., 1813, Abigail L'Hommedieu (b. 1791; d. 1847; m. (2) Sept., 1848, Rosanna Barber (b. 1825; d. 1859); removed 1823 from Aquebogue to Chenango Co., (McDonough); a large and prosperous farmer. Children by Abigail, seven, by Rosanna, four:

  i. Jesse Carr,[7] b. 1814; m. May 16, 1837, Anna Youngs (b. 1818). Home at Troupsburgh, N. Y. Had ten children.
  ii. Benjamin L'H., b. 1816; m. June, 1838, Lucy I. Nichols; d. 1873. Had eight boys and three girls.
  iii. Albert R., b. 1819; m. 1843, Cordelia Beckwith. Had: 1. Thomas. 2. Harmanus, b. 1847. 3. Elsie, b. 1853.
  iv. Sarah, b. 1822; d. 1856; m. 1843, Samuel Beckwith.
  v. John, b. 1827; m. 1854, Clarinda Philley. Home at Zumbrota, Minn. Had six boys and one girl.
  vi. Josiah, b. 1830; d. 1864; m. Harriet Fairchild.
  vii. Mary, b. Aug. 8, 1833; m. Harmanus Beckwith.
  viii. Rachel, b. June 26, 1851.
  ix. Thomas W., b. June 20, 1852.

x. Nancy, b. May 22, 1854.
xi. Alfred H., b. June 13, 1857.

158. JOSIAH⁶ SKILLMAN (Thomas,⁵ Thomas,⁴ Joseph,³ Thomas,²
Thomas¹), b. 1794; d. 1854; removed about 1820 from N. Y. City
(a carpenter) to Chenango Co., and became a farmer; then for
sake of health went to Baltimore; m. 1819, Catharine Thomas.
Five children d. inf.; the rest are of record as follows:

    i. Griffith,⁷ b. 1820; d. unm., 1855.
    ii. Jane, b. 1822; m. George Brunson, Oswego, N. Y.
    iii. Joseph F., b. 1824; d. 1873; m. 1849, Lucretia Welch.
        Had 10 children. Live at Magnolia, Md.
    iv. Hannah, b. 1825; m. 1845, Samuel C. Hush.
    v. William, b. Sept. 27, 1835; no record.
    vi. Caroline, b. 1840; m. 1857, John A. McPherson.
    vii. Sarah, b. 1846; m. June, 1863, Noah Underwood. Fam-
        ily mainly in Baltimore or environs.

159. JOSEPH⁶ SKILLMAN (Thomas,⁵ Thomas,⁴ Joseph,³ Thomas,²
Thomas¹), b. 1802; d. 1875; a carpenter with Josiah in N. Y. City,
but became an extensive farmer in Chenango; lover of singing
and long chorister in Baptist Church (and member); m. 1828,
Miranda Carpenter. Had:

    i. John C.,⁷ b. 1829; m. 1854, Mary B. Philley and six
        children were theirs, five daus. and one son.
    ii. Jerusha, b. 1831; m. 1857, Theodore H. Fitch.
    iii. Elsie, b. 1833; m. 1862, Ephraim Loomis. No children.
    iv. Fred'k A., b. 1835: m. 1858, Eglantine Wait. Had two
        boys, Elmer and Frank M.
    v. Joseph Hudson (twin with Josiah who d. inf.); b. 1838;
        m. 1866, Lettie B. Cline; Member N. Y. Assembly,
        186–; prosperous farmer and man of affairs. Two
        children: 1. Ida May, b. 1867. 2. Henry Elwyn, b.
        1870.
    vi. Francis M., b. 1840; d. Oct. 19, 1864, of wounds re-
        ceived Sept. 6, at the battle of Winchester, Va.
    vii. William H., b. 1846; home and wife but no children at
        Leavenworth, Kan.

160. FRANCIS MARTIN⁶ SKILLMAN (Thomas,⁵ Thomas,⁴ Joseph,³
Thomas,² Thomas¹), b. at Aquebogue, L. I., 1812, and a lad of 12
removed with family to Chenango Co., N. Y.; lamed by accident
he became a teacher and farmer; m. 1837, Julia A. Chappell (b.
1815; d. 1879); removed 1856 to Mazeppa, Minn., and took up land;
elected to State Legislature, 1858; d. 1886. Children:

    i. Evander,⁷ b. 1838; enlisted in 1861 in Co. G., 3d Minn.
        V. I., then was 1st. Lieut and Q.-M. in 113th U. S.
        Col. Inf.; discharged April 10, 1866; m. 1865, Electa
        C. Lont. Had five boys. Home, Livingston, Mont.
    ii. Elsie, b. 1840; m. (1) 1857, J. O. Wilcox; d. a soldier,
        1864; m. (2) 1869, T. F. Sturtevant; lives a widow
        with one child, Nellie, in Red Wing, Minn.
    iii. Milon, b. 1842; served in Co. B., Brackett's Bat., Minn.
        Cav.; then in Indian service; discharged June 1,

1866; m. July, 1867, Mary Southwell (now dead); one son, Herbert, b. 1872. Home, Tyndall, S. D.

iv. Frank, b. 1844; 1st Lieut. Co. K., 113th U. S. Col. Inf.; resigned Oct., 1865; m. 1867, Lizzie Hopkins. Had four children. Druggist, 1880-90, at Valley Springs, S. D. Home now on a ranch near Oregon City, Ore.

v. Phil, b. 1845; enlisted 1861; later was 2d Lieut. Co. A., 113th Col. Inf.; mustered out, April 10, 1866; m. 1878, Fannie A. Rawson; lawyer; City clerk, Red Wing, Minn. (5 years); Mayor (3 terms), Aberdeen, Dak.; removed 1890, to Olympia, Wash. Children: 1. Fannie C. 2. Philip A., U. S. N., highest record as gunner in the entire service. 3. Katherine R.

vi. Sarah, b. 1847; m. 1868, Stephen O. Lont. Home, Waterbury, Conn.

vii. Ida, b. Jan. 18, 1850; d. April 13, 1871.

viii. William B., b. 1851; m. 1878, Mary E. Annible. Two boys, Charles A. and Edward. Home, Hollywood, Los Angeles, Cal.

ix. Charles Nelson, b. 1855; m. 1877, Julia Prescott. Two boys, Roy and Guy. Home, Big Timber, Mont.

x. James H., b. 1859; lives unm. with Elsie at Red Wing, Minn.

xi. Nellie E., b. 1862; m. Lynn Merrick. One son, Albert. Home, Alleghany City, Pa.

161. JOSEPH[6] SKILLMAN (Joseph,[5] Joseph,[4] Joseph,[3] Thomas,[2] Thomas[1]), b. on Chambers St., N. Y., Sept. 24, 1804; with his brother, Abraham B., in hardware business, 1839; also in basket trade, 1844; removed to Scotch Bush, Montgomery Co., N. Y.; m. 1832, Maria L. Anderson. Children:

i. Catharine,[7] m. John B. Hyatt.

ii. Josephine, m. Charles Lockwood and lived in Montgomery Co., N. Y.

iii. Joseph, lived unm. in Brooklyn. Nothing clear. Was this the man crushed in doing his duty by the falling of a chimney on him at the Ocean Mills Fire, 208 Fulton St., N. Y., Feb. 8, 1861, and buried in Greenwood with all the honors of the Fire Department for heroism? Newspapers of the time glow with praise of him, but is this the Joseph? Who knows?

162. ABRAHAM B.[6] SKILLMAN (Joseph,[5] Joseph,[4] Joseph,[3] Thomas,[2] Tnomas[1]), b. in New York City, Jan. 8, 1806; lifelong in hardware trade, his brothers along with him; many years at 271 Greenwich St.; m. Catharine Heroy. Children:

i. Martha B.,[7] d. Oct. 6, 1875.

ii. Isaac Brower, clerk, 1878; dealer in Glassware, 1886.

iii. George Augustus, no record.

iv. James Henry, no record.

163. JOHN[6] SKILLMAN (John,[5] John,[4] Joseph,[3] Thomas,[2] Thomas[1]), b. in Brooklyn (Bushwick), March 21, 1819; dealt in books as "Skillman & Lane," 400 Pearl St., 1840-41, and "John Skillman," 1842; m. (1) 1840, Sarah Ann Devoe; two daus.; m. (2) Dec. 3,

1846, Caroline Sevoe, stepdau. of —— Cadet, and by her were four additional children:

    i. Susan Frances,' d. inf.
    ii. Sarah A., b. Sept. 30, 1842; d. 1868.
    iii. Caddie, b. May 5, 1848; d. Sept. 28, 1867.
    iv. Susanna Gardner, b. 1849; d. Feb., 1851.
    v. Susanna Church, b. 1852; m. April 24, 1872, Edgar
        Halliday.
    vi. John Henry, b. 1855; drowned Jan. 5, 1864.

164. JOSEPH HENRY ' SKILLMAN (John,' John,' Joseph,' Thomas,' Thomas '), b. at Bushwick (Brooklyn), Dec. 19, 1837; d. May 2, 1890; m. 1873, Anna Stebbins. Children:

    i. Henry Christopher,' b. July 23, 1874.
    ii. Edwin Joseph, b. July 6, 1876.
    iii. May, b. June 14, 1883; d. inf.
    iv. Ethel, b. Feb. 4, 1885.
    v. Ralph Francis, b. May 17, 1889.

LORDS OF MANORS OF NEW YORK.

WITH A PREFACE ON THE ARYAN AND SEIGNEURIAL ORDER OF THE EMPIRE IN AMERICA.

BY THE VISCOUNT DE FRONSAC.

In 1540, Charles, Count of Hapsburgh, Grand Duke of Austria, King of Spain and Emperor of the Romans, extended the Seigneurial Order of the Empire over America, of which entire continent he had become absolute master.

To this Order, as a nobility, were admitted the Founders and Defenders of the Empire in America, to hold lands incorporated into lordships, or seigneuries, hereditarily with personal representation in the Emperor's Council in the various provinces where their seigneurial holdings extended; and as a class, even if bereft of lands and function by revolution and disaster, to constitute in their remotest generations a class of honor and precedence like the noblesse-de-race of old Europe.

The first and highest title of this Seigneurial Order he bestowed on Colan, grandson of Christopher Columbus (the Duchy of Veragua) with the additional rank of hereditary Vice-Admiral.

On the dismemberment of this great Empire of Charles by treaty and distribution, the rights of succession of rank and property of these families were continued by international agreement and the Seigneurial Order was continued by their establishment and added to by each succeeding monarchy. Thus the Dutch created their Patroon-Lords in New Netherland and when that passed to the British King Charles II, he added to them in Seigneurial succession the Lords of the Manors of New York, while in Carolina he created a special list of Seigneurial titles, such as Landgrave to rank with Earl, Cacique to rank with Viscount, and Baron and Lord of Manor. His brother, King James, VII (II), later on countersigned Lord Baltimore's addition of the Lords of the Manors of Maryland.

Already the Kings of France in Canada and Louisiana had followed after King James, VI's Baronets of Nova Scotia, with Seigneurial rank in the Dukes, Marquises, Counts, Barons and Seigneurs of that country—the highest of which was the Duke of Arkansas bestowed on John Law, finance minister of France and principal founder of Arkansas.

Then when all these degrees, concessions and rights passed by treaty under the sovereignty of King George, III, by the Treaty of Paris of 1763, they were expressly secured to the families who had won them by their nobility, valor and merit. So from monarch to monarch by treaty and treaty, the imperial titles and sovereignty of the Emperor Charles in America were passed on until they finally devolved on the Kings of Great Britain and Ireland, with the chiefship of the Seigneurial Order of the Empire.

The Revolution in America (1776-83) and the formation of the United States has not been deemed to have abrogated the Seigneurial honors of families residing in the states which were these former provinces of the Empire, any more than it destroyed the peerage rights of the family of Lord Fairfax of Virginia.

To assert, maintain and obtain recognition of these rights before the Court of the Empire, as well as to preserve the Aryan purity of succession of these families, caused their principal descendants to reorganize the Seigneurial Order of the Empire in 1880 (first established in America by the Emperor Charles in 1540) to which they added the name of Aryan. In 1908, by the generosity of the Baroness Dorchester, Greywell Hill, Winchfield, England (Chief of one branch of the Order), the dies of the decoration were paid for and made by Spink, 17 and 18 Piccadilly, London (maker to the King and for the Order of the Garter). They were approved by the Herald's College and by the Earl-Marshall of England (Duke of Norfolk), and are to be worn by those descendants in the male line of the family name of the above mentioned families on registration in the Aryan and Seigneurial College of Arms, Viscount de Fronsac, Herald-Marshall, London, Ontario, Canada.

The feudal and titled families of New York—Lord-Patroons, etc.,—who are eligible to this only Court, recognized and imperially founded order in America, are the following:

SCHUYLER, LORD OF BEVERWYCK.

Philip Piertersen Schuyler in 1650 was made Lord-Patroon of Beverwyck. His son was the first Mayor of Albany (1686-94). Arms: Vert, issuing from a cloud, ppr. a cubet arm in fesse, vested azure, holding in hand a falcon, close, ppr. Crest: a hawk, close ppr. Seigneurial Coronet.

KYP, LORD OF KYPSBURG.

Isaac Kyp, in 1688, was Lord-Patroon of Kypsburg. He was descended from Ruloff de Kype, a Norman Seigneur whose barony was near Alencon, France. Isaac came to New York in 1657 and was succeeded by his descendants, Jacob and Hendricks Kyp. Arms: Azure, a cheveron or, between two griffins sejant confrontee; in chief a dexter hand couped argent. Crest: a demi-griffin argent, holding in paws a cross, gules. Seigneurial Coronet.

SMITH, LORD OF ST. GEORGE'S MANOR.

Col. William Smith received the lordship of St. George's Manor at Brookhaven, Suffolk County, New York, in 1693. His son William was Judge of the Supreme Court and died in 1767, whose son William was Chief Justice and Royal Councillor up to 1782. He was averse to Republicanism and wrote a historical summary of the times. He settled in Canada and was Judge at Quebec after 1783. The family were from Hingham Fenn, Northampton, England. Arms: Or, on a cheveron gules, between three crosses-crosslet fitchee sable, three bezants. Crest: out of a ducal coronet or, an Indian goat's head argent, eared sable, bearded and attired of the first. Seigneurial Coronet.

EVANS, LORD OF FLETCHER MANOR.

Capt. John Evans was made by the King Lord of Fletcher Manor in 1694. The family is of Norman origin, descending from Richard, son of Payne de Avenes who came to England in 1194. Arms: Azure, a griffin passant, and a chief, or. Crest: a griffin passant, or, beaked, fore legged and ducally gorged, azure. Motto: "Durate." Seigneurial Coronet.

VAN COURTLANDT, LORD OF VAN COURTLANDT MANOR.

Stephen Van Courtlandt, by Royal patent, was Lord of Courtlandt Manor in 1697. It contained 83,000 acres. His ancestor Stephen, of South Holland, was a man of considerable importance in 1610, whose son Oloff came to New York in 1649, as a free-holder. Oloff was father of Stephen, the first Lord, who was Mayor of New York and a Royal Councillor in 1677, from whom descended Col. Philip Van Courtlandt, Lord of the Manor in 1783. The Manor house is yet possessed by the family whose rights of noblesse and representation are in the Aryan and Seigneurial Order of the Empire. Arms: Argent, the wings of windmill sable, voided of the field, between six etoils gules. Seigneurial Coronet.

LIVINGSTON, LORD OF LIVINGSTON MANOR.

Robert Livingston, by Royal patent, was Lord of Livingston Manor of 120,000 acres in 1686, who traced through Rev. Alex. Livingston of Sterling, 1590, to the Livingstons, Earls of Calendar in Scotland. From him descended several noted judges and jurists. Arms: 1st and 4th argent, three cingfoils gules within a royal tressure vert; 2nd and 3d sable a bend between six billets or. Crest: a demi-hercules, wreathed about head and middle holding club erect in dexter hand and in sinister a serpant ppr. Motto: "Si je puis." Seigneurial Coronet.

Gardiner, Lord of Gardiner Manor.

Col. Lionel Gardiner in 1639, by Royal patent, was made Lord of Gardiner Manor, Gardiner's Island. The Manor contained 3,300 acres. Most likely the family descends from William Le Gardiener who possessed estates in Rutland, England, in 1202. The name occurs in the XIII in Yorkshire, and in the following century in Wilts and Somerset. Arms: A cheveron, ermine, between two griffins' heads in chief and a cross pattée, argent in base. Crest: A pelican, sable, vulning itself, gules. Motto: "Deo non fortuna." Seigneurial Coronet.

Morris, Lord of Morrisania.

His Excellency, Lewis Morris, who had been Royal Governor of New Jersey in 1638, was by Royal patent in 1697, made Manorial lord of Morrisania. His son Lewis and his grandson Richard, Lords of the Manor in succession, were also both judges in admiralty. He descended from William Morris, Lord of Tinturn Manor, Co. Monmouth, England. The family originated with the Norman name of de St. Maurice, and the fief in Normandie existed in 1180. Isabella, John and Margerie Morice are recorded in England in 1272. Arms: 1st and 4th gules, a lion, ramp. regard. or; 2d and 3d three torteaux in fesse. Crest: A castle in flames, ppr. Seigneurial Coronet.

Philippse, Lord of Philippsebourg.

Hon. Frederic Philippse, by Royal patent in 1693, was made Lord of the Manor of Philippsebourg containing 1500 square miles. He was a Royal Councillor in the Province of New York and was born at Balsward, in Friesland. His son Frederic was a great leader in the Province and married a daughter of the Royal Governor. He was succeeded by his son, Col. Frederic, who left ten children, while of his daughters, Mary married Col. Beverley Robinson and Susan married Col. Morris. Arms: A demi-lion issuant of a ducal coronet, argent, crowned or. Crest: the same. Seigneurial Coronet.

Paine, Lord of Sophy Manor.

John Paine about 1666 was by Royal writ made Lord of Sophy Manor, Prudence Island, near Rhode Island. He was born in 1601 and first settled at Ipswich, Massachusetts, where in 1647-9, he was a Deputy to the General Court. He was proprietor of a fine estate and was the ruling elder and treasurer of Essex County for eighteen years. His first wife was Ann, daughter of

John Whiting of the Manor of Hudleigh, Suffolk, England. He was succeeded in manorial lordship by his son John. His other son, Robert, graduated at Harvard and was living in 1701. The family descends from Robert Payen of Normandie, 118-98, from one offshoot of whom were the Baronets Payne. Arms: Paly of six argent and vert; on a chief azure three garbs, or. Crest: A lion, ppr. supporting a sheaf of wheat. Seigneurial Coronet.

PELL, LORD OF PELLHAM MANOR.

Thomas Pell in 1666, by Royal writ, was made Lord of Pellham Manor. He was grandson of John Pell and Margaret Oberland whose father, Rev. John Pell was rector of Southwick, Sussex, England, 1590. His son obtained an addition to the Royal patent of lordship in 1687 whose original extent was 9,166 acres. The first ancestor of the family was Radulphus Pele of Normandie, 1180. From him Robert, son of Robert le Pele was settled at York, England. From the same source came also the Peels of Yorkshire and Lancaster, ancestors of Sir Robert Peel, one time minister of England. Arms: Ermine, on a canton azure, a pelican or, vulned, gules. Seigneurial Coronet.

BILLOPP, LORD OF BENTLEY MANOR.

Capt. Christopher Billopp received from the King in 1687 the lordship of Bentley Manor of over 2,000 acres, southwest part of Staten Island. He had been an officer in the Royal Navy. His only daughter married Mr. Young Farmer. The son by the marriage on inheriting the manorial lordship took the name of Billopp. The manor was the meeting place for Lord Howe, Dr. Franklin, John Adams and Edward Rutledge in 1778, in a fruitless undertaking to end the hostilities between the British provinces and the Parliamentary usurpation in England. Farmer-Billopp entered the British Army and became Colonel. His estates were confiscated by the Revolutionary Party in America in 1782 and he settled in New Brunswick where he became President of the Provincial Council. His descendants yet retain their Seigneurial honors. Arms: Vert, an eagle displayed argent, armed and langued gules. Crest: A wolff sejant regardant, argent vulned on the shoulder, gules. Motto: "Sublimiora Petamus." These arms were borne by the family of Biddulph since 1583 (ancestors of the Billopps), when they held the manor of Biddulph in Staffordshire, England. A Seigneurial Coronet is added for their manorial rank.

PAUW, LORD OF PAVONIA.

Michael Pauw in 1630 was Lord-Patroon of Pavonia. He was formerly of Holland and of a noble Dutch family. Descended from the same source was M. de Pauw, reader to King Frederic the Great of Prussia. Arms: Empaled, 1st, argeant, a paon with feathers displayed, ppr. 2ndly, azure, a granade stemmed and leaved, or. Seigneurial Coronet.

DE VRIES, LORD OF PAVONIA MANOR.

D. P. de Vries in 1636 received through the Pauw family the hereditary lordship of Pavonia Manor. He was formerly of Amsterdam, Holland. Arms: Azure, a cheveron between three ears of corn argent. Seigneurial Coronet.

MELYN, LORD OF PAVONIA HALL.

Cornelius Melyn was possessed of Manorial rights and patroonate lordship of the domain of Pavonia Hall, Staten Island in 1640. The family which had also English branches in the name of Mellen, was derived from Malins or De Malines in Flanders. The Lords of Malines descended from Bertold, living in 800, were established as Advocates or Protectors of Malines by the Bishop of Liege. They were Cavaliers of the Holy Empire in 1721. Arms: Gules, three pales vair, as recorded in their native city of Antwerp, to which is added the symbol of their rank. A Seigneurial Coronet.

MAYHEW, LORDS OF MAYHEW MANOR.

Matthew Mayhew, by royal writ became Lord of Mayhew Manor, Martha's Vineyard, in 1685. He was of a scholarly and distinguished ancestry, descended from Thomas Mayhew, gent., born in 1591 in England, and a passenger to Watertown, Massachusetts, in 1631. The latter was Deputy to the General Court (1634–44). He removed to Martha's Vineyard in 1647, where he was governor for the proprietors and preached to the Indians. His first wife was Martha Parkhurst, and his second, Grace, widow of Thomas Paine. He was father of Matthew, the first Lord of the Manor, and of Thomas, a judge of the Court of Common Pleas. Arms: Argeant, on a fesse sable between three roses, gules, a lily of the first, which arms were borne by their predecessor Richard Mayhew, Bishop of Hereford (1504–16), to which is added the Seigneurial Coronet.

MAYHEW, LORD OF TYSBURY MANOR.

Thomas Mayhew, judge, etc., brother of Matthew, first Lord of Mayhew Manor, received by Royal writ the Manor of Tysbury, adjoining Mayhew Manor, in 1671. Arms: same as above.

WYLLYS, LORD OF WYLLES MANOR.

The Hon. Samuel Wyllys (Welles), Secy. of the Colony of Connecticut, by Royal writ became Lord of Wyllys Manor in 1675, which included Plum Island. He was born in Warwickshire, England, in 1638. He came to Connecticut and was a magistrate in 1654. His wife was a daughter of Gov. Haines. His father, George, was one time Gov. of the Province, whose eldest son, George, remained in England in charge of the family estate of Tenny-Compton. Gov. Wyllys was also a commissioner to the Congress of the United Provinces held at Albany. The family descends from Effric de Welles, who held the fief of

Welles or Wellis in Normandie in 1180. Lord Samuel Wyllys was succeeded by his son Hezekiah, who was Secy. for the Colony (1712–34). His son and successor, Lord George Wyllys (married the daughter, Eliz., of Rev. James Hobart), was Colonial Secy. (1734–96), which office continued in this manorial family up to 1809, when it was held by Lord George Wyllys. Arms: Argent, a cheveron between three mullets, gule. Crest: A falcon expanded, ppr., belled, or. Seigneurial Coronet.

FLETCHER, LORD OF FLETCHERTON.

Col. Benj. Fletcher, Royal Governor of New York in 1692, by Royal writ was made Lord of Fletcherton Manor. He was descended from Robert Flechier, Normandie, 1198. Adam le Flechier came to England, 1272, from whom descended the Baronets Fletcher and Fletcher, Lord of Saltown in Scotland. Col. Fletcher was son of William Fletcher of Low Bashir Manor, Westmeath, Ireland, by wife Abigail, daughter and heiress of Henry Vincent of London. His son and successor, Lord Benj. Fletcher, is mentioned in connection with the Province of Pennsylvania where some of the family reside. Arms: 1st and 4th sable a cross flory between four escallops, argent: 2nd and 3d, azure, a cheveron between three quarterfoils slipped, argent. Crest: An arm in armor embowed holding in gauntlet an arrow, ppr. Motto: "Per Augustum." Seigneurial Coronet.

LOVELACE, LORD OF PAVONIA VILLA.

Col. Francis Lovelace, Royal Governor of New York in 1670, by Royal writ was Lord of Pavonia Villa, Staten Island. He was a son of Sir Richard, Baron Lovelace, of the Manor of Hurley. His relative, John Lovelace, succeeded him as Lord of the Manor and was also Royal Governor of the Province in 1708. He married Lady Ann Wentworth, daughter of the Earl of Cleveland, who was created Baroness Wentworth in her own right. She was ancestress of the Earl of Lovelace and Lord Wentworth. The peerage of Lovelace became extinct in 1736, but rights of representation in the Aryan and Seigneurial Order devolve on the next nearest colateral. Arms: 1st and 4th gules, on a shief indented argent, three martlets sable for Lovelace: 2nd azure, on a saltire engrailed argent, five martlets sable for Hingham: 3rd on a saltire argent, a rose of Lancaster for Neville. Crest: On the trunk of a tree, vert, an eagle displayed argent. Supporters: Two pegasi pourpre. Seigneurial Coronet.

PALMER, LORD OF CASSILTON MANOR.

Capt. John Palmer in 1687 by Royal writ became Lord of Cassilton Manor of the North part of Staten Island. In 1681 he acquired a large tract of land in Somerset Co., New Jersey. He was member of the Council of the Gov. Sir Edmund Andros, and had come from England with the commission of Chief-Justice. The name Palmer meant a Crusader. In England four of these families had a Norman origin. The Palmers of Lincoln, those of

York, those of Northampton, and those of Hants and Sussex. Arms: Or, on a cheveron gules, five acorns of the field. Seigneurial Coronet.

HEATHCOTE, LORD OF SCARSDALE MANOR.

Col. Caleb Heathcote by Patent Royal was Lord of Scarsdale Manor, 21 March, 1701. He was son of Gilbert of Westerfield, Derbyshire, and brother of Sir Gilbert, Lord-Mayor of London. He married Martha, daughter of Col. William Smith, a manorial lord of Long Island and former Governor of Tangiers. Lord Heathcote was Surveyor-General of the Province, and Mayor of New York in 1711. One of his daughters married James de Lancey, Lieut.-Gov. of the Province. Arms: Ermine, three pomeis charged with a cross, or. Crest: On a mural crown, a pomen between two wings displayed, ermine. Seigneurial Coronet.

VAN RENSSELAER, LORD OF RENSSELAERWYCK.

De Heer Kilieen Van Rensselaer was Lord-Patroon of Rensselaerwyck before 1637. He was a pearl and diamond merchant, and one of the Directors of the Dutch West Indian Company. His patroonate lordship extended in Albany and Rensselaer Counties. He died in 1645 and was succeeded by his son Kilieen, who married Marie Van Courtlandt. At his death in 1701, his sons Jeremiah and Stephen were the succeeding Lords of the manor. The latter died in 1747 and was succeeded by Stephen, who married Catherine Livingston. He died in 1764. His son, Gen. Stephen Van Rensselaer, born 1764, Lieut.-Gov. of New York, 1795–8, was Major-General 1812–15. By his first wife, Margaret Schuyler, he had Stephen, his successor, and other children by second marriage. Arms: 1st gules, a cross ancré argent: 2nd argent, a fesse embattled, voided, sable: 3d argent, three antique crosses, azure: 4th or three cheveronals sable. Motto: "Niemand Zondes." Siegneurial Coronet.

CHAMBERS, LORD OF FOX HALL.

Thomas Chambers, by Royal writ in 1667 became Lord of Fox Hall, near Kingston. The family is Norman and trace direct to Robert de la Chambre who held lands in feudal tenure in Worcestershire, England, in 1345. Arms: Argent, a cheveron sable, surmounted by another ermine between three chambers placed transverse of the escutcheon, of the second, fired, ppr. Seigneurial Coronet.

ARCHER, LORD OF FORDHAM MANOR.

John Archer, of Royal patent, was made Lord of Fordham Manor, 13 Nov., 1671. His father and grandfather were named John also, the latter of whom married Eleanor Frewin, and was son of Humphrey Archer, gent, born 1527. John, the first lord of the manor, was succeeded by his son John who married in New York in 1686, Sarah Odell. Their son Samuel was the third lord of Fordham Manor. The family trace to William Arcuarius, general of bowmen, Haunts, England, 1086, whose son Fulbert L'Archer witnessed a charter of Geoffrey de Clinton, time of King Henry, I. Arms: Per pale gules and azure; three arrows or, barbed and feathered argent. Crest: A dragon's head issuant of a mural crown of the last and third. Seigneurial Coronet.

LLOYD, LORD OF QUEENS MANOR.

—— Lloyd became Lord of Queens Manor by Royal assent in 1679. It was situated on Long Island. This family was of noble Welsh origin. Arms: Gules, a lion or. Crest: A bird rising, or. Seigneurial Coronet.

There may have been other manorial grantees or possessors of that Seigneurial dignity and rank. Fuller information is sought of these founders and defenders of the Empire in America so that all families thus entitled may appear in the forthcoming book, *Baronage of the Empire*, soon to be issued in England. All such information should be sent to the Viscount de Fronsac, London, Ontario, Canada.

OBITUARY.

WANDELL, TOWNSEND, lawyer, Annual Member, elected Jan. 12, 1900, was killed in a railway accident at Bologna, Italy, June 28, 1908, aged 60. Mr. Wandell was a bachelor; his father was Judge Benjamin Coe Wandell; his home was at 157 East 83d Street, where he lived with his brother Francis L. and his sister Miss Josephine Wandell. His office was at 51 Chambers Street. He was a graduate of the Columbia College Law School in 1865, and in his law practice his uprightness of purpose and trustworthiness of character gained for him the confidence and trust of many clients who placed the entire charge of their estates in his hands. His friend, J. S. Voorhees, in a letter to the press pays him this beautiful tribute: "Everyone loved and respected him, and they could not help loving him for he was true, honest and just. He had a kind word for every one. The world is better for having known Townsend Wandell and though his self-sacrificing earthly career is ended, his pure upright example will live and inspire others for good." Mr. Wandell was a member of the Union League, Club, the Sons of the Revolution, the Holland Society, the St. Nicholas Society, the Metropolitan Museum of Art, the New York Historical Society, New York Genealogical and Biographical Society, Phi Beta Kappa, Delta Kappa Epsilon, the Dwight Alumni Association, and the Columbia Law School Alumni. He was trustee and manager of the New York City Church Extension and Missionary Society of the Methodist Church, and manager of the New York Deaconess Home and Training School. The funeral services were held in the Madison Avenue Episcopal Church, Friday, July 24, 1908.

QUERIES.

WALDRON—VERMILYE.—Was Maria Goverts, wife of Resolved Waldron of Amsterdam, the mother of Resolved Waldron, Jr., the Harlem, N. Y., settler? Wanted proof that the said Resolved Waldron, Jr., and Johannes Vermilye, another Harlem settler, were entitled to use coat-armor, and the blazon of their arms.

SMITH.—Caleb Smith. the third of his name, in line, m. Hannah, dau. of Jacobus Dyckman, 26 Jan., 1804. Who was the mother of the said Caleb Smith; was he of the Tangier Rock or Bull Smith; what was his line back to the founder of the Smith family on Long Island; and what was the day and month of Caleb's death in 1858?

DYCKMAN. Who was the mother of the celebrated Staats Morris Dyckman? Riker's *Revised History of Harlem* gives him as son of Jacob and Tryntje Benson of Spuyton Duyvil, or Harlem, and m. to Eliza *Corne*. Bolton says he was the fifth son of Jacob Dyckman of Phillipsburgh, and m. Eliza *Kennedy*. His true parentage and dates of birth for himself and his wife are desired.

The marriage date of Jacob and Tryntje (Benson) Dyckman is asked for, and a dated list of their children: *Samson, Staats Morris, Benjamin, Jacobus John, Garret, Wm. Nagel, Maria, Catalina, Jane,* and perhaps *Jacob*.

Riker says John above, m. Aletta Goetchins, but members of the family say he m. Mehitable Westcot. Which is correct?

The will of Deliverance Conkling in 1762, names his dau. Deliverance Conkling, wife of Jacob Dyckman. Who were Jacob's parents? Could he have been son of Jacob and Tryntje Benson above?

Is Mr. D. Waters Dyckman a descendant of the Long Island family of Waters, and if so, how?

The above is asked for in the interest of a Dyckman Chart now being compiled.   LUCY D. AKERLY.

BOOK NOTICES.

OUR AMERICAN BARCLAYS, by Cornelia Barclay Barclay. Cloth, small Quarto, pp. 80. Limited edition, privately printed. The Grafton Press, New York. 1908.

This little work is filled with interesting details concerning the early members of the ancient Barclay Family of Albany, N. Y., so many of whom were loyalists at the time of the Revolutionary War. The information is largely imparted in the form of conversational letters addressed to the children of the compiler, with additional chapters on the early English and Scotch families of the name, the Saxon "de Berkeleys" and the Rev. Thomas Barclay, the first of his family in America, together with copies of various epistles written by and to members of his family. It is probable that the Rev. Thomas Barclay, who only took clerical orders at the late age of forty years, was allied to the Barclays of Fifeshire, Scotland, and was possibly a son of Sir Robert Barclay, Bart. of Pierston, County Fife, by his second wife Barbara Deas(?). Positive proof of this fact is lacking, but a skilled searcher in Scotland has produced many documents pointing to this origin of the family and the clue is well worth serious investigation. So much new and valuable data has been collected by Mrs. Barclay beyond the meagre facts hitherto known, that it is hoped a complete genealogy of this interesting Tory family will soon be published in the standard form and arrangement. In the meantime the compiler is to be congratulated upon putting the family history in so compact and readable a form, the book being beautifully printed in large clear type, with wide margins, and the paper and binding up to the high standard set by its publishers.

THE DESCENDANTS OF JAMES COLE OF PLYMOUTH, 1633. Also a record of the families of Lt. Thomas Burnham of Ipswich, 1635; Lt. Edward Winship of Cambridge, 1635, and Simon Huntington, England, 1635, with a complete record of the Cole, Coole and Coule families of America in the Revolution, By Ernest Byron Cole. The Grafton Press, New York. 1908. Cloth, Quarto. pp. 435.

There is some mention of the family before the emigration to America, but it is best known by the fact that the hill where the Mayflower pilgrims were

20

first buried is known as Cole's Hill, since James Cole, who came to Saco, Maine, in 1632, and one year later located at Plymouth, lived on a grant of ten acres including this first burial ground. His descendants are traced to the tenth generation and their children. To this is added the three families named on the title page, and other Cole families in America, which are only briefly given, as will be seen when seven families cover that number of pages. The Revolutionary records fill about fifty pages, and an index in three columns of eighteen pages, completes a book which shows industry and will be sought by many.

THE CANTRILL–CANTRELL GENEALOGY, by Susan Cantrill Christie. Cloth, Octavo, pp. 271. Full Index. The Grafton Press, New York. 1908.

This is the first complete record of the descendants of Richard Cantrill, a resident of Philadelphia prior to 1689, and of the earlier Cantrills in England and America, and in subject matter, arrangement, and beauty of print and binding reflects high credit upon the family historian and the publishers. It is the first genealogy of this family, one of the oldest in America, to be published and represents ten years constant and faithful labor. The name can be clearly traced to the original family of Cantrill or Cantrelle in France, and a brief history is given of the early Cantrills in England, Ireland and America. No claim is made to the arms or early lines of ancestry, however, unless there is absolute proof of right or relationship, and this frank attitude of the compiler cannot be too highly commended, as the general tendency of the family historian is toward assuming the arms of a distinguished ancestry, without the slightest right or reason. No less than 2127 desecendants are traced out and praise should be awarded the workmanlike manner of arrangement, which follows the best and most modern practice in genealogical manuscripts. The book is sure to become a work of reference and no large genealogical library can afford to be without a copy. A word of praise should also be said in behalf of The Grafton Press, the publishers, for its careful preparation and publication of the manuscript and the great skill and taste displayed. In this age of indifferent printing of inaccurate genealogical matter bound up in the cheapest form, it is refreshing to find a book of this character and style.

ADDITIONAL CONTRIBUTIONS TO THE HISTORY OF CHRIST CHURCH, HARTFORD, CONN., with the Records of Baptisms, Confirmations, Communicants, Marriages and Burials, 1760–1900. Volume II. Cloth, Octavo, pp. 517. Full Index. Press of Belknap & Warfield, Hartford. 1908.

This splendid transcript of the records of one of the most important churches in Hartford fitly crowns the compilation of the history of this parish, so well related in the first volume, previously reviewed in the RECORD. Church registers are dry reading save to those engaged in hunting up the lost generations of their name, yet these records are filled with many interesting details due to the untiring energy of Mr. George E. Hoadley, a member of one of the oldest families in the parish. By searching old magazines and newspapers, county and private graveyards, and by means of extensive inquiries and correspondence, Mr. Hoadley was able to add many items of incalculable value to the annals of the church. A marked feature of this volume is the exhaustive index, showing at a glance the place, number and character of the record concerning each name. The press work and binding is in keeping with and fully up to the standard of Volume I, and these volumes will have an important share in perpetuating the history of the early Connecticut churches.

DORCHESTER DAY. Celebration of the 277th Anniversary of the Settlement of Dorchester, 1630–1907, by James H. Stark. Cloth, Royal Octavo, pp. 117, with Index. Press of Municipal Printing Office, Boston. 1907.

The custom of celebrating the original founding of early Colonial towns is growing and will result in inciting civic pride and stimulating a desire to learn more concerning the historic progress of the New England cities. The more interest aroused among the descendants of the early settlers the greater harvest will result from the unearthing of private records and documents of priceless value, hitherto unavailable because of ignorance or indifference. This book was created by the efforts of the Dorchester Historical Society and contains the addresses and proceeedings which marked the four annual celebrations of Dorchester Day from 1904-1907. It is well printed and illustrated with portraits and pictures of old landmarks and spots of historic interest, and will be a pleasant reminder to those who took part in honoring their native town.

ANDREW ELLICOTT, HIS LIFE AND LETTERS, by Catharine Van Cortland Mathews. Illustrated, Cloth, Octavo, pp. 256 with Index. The Grafton Press, New York. 1908.

With the exception of a few brief statements in the histories of several other allied families, a short biographical sketch in Stuart's *Civil and Military Engineers of America*, and a few stray newspaper articles, no adequate account of Major Andrew Ellicott's career has been published before the present work. The book has been prepared from many valuable private papers, letters, diaries and documents in the possession of his descendants relative to the surveys and plans of the District of Washington and is doubly welcome as a full, fair and final biography of one of the ablest civil engineers this land has produced, and as a timely tribute to one, who, with Major L'Enfant, planned and laid out the City of Washington, the capitol of the United States. It would be impossible in a few brief lines to do justice to the many and vast surveying tasks accomplished by Mr. Ellicott, but when it is stated that he laid out the Baltimore and western boundary of Pennsylvania in 1785, made the first measurement of Niagara in 1790, laid out the road to Presqu' Isle Fort in 1793-95, and the Florida boundary, the ability and activity of the man commands the respect of the nation. He was the son of Joseph and Judith (Bleaker) Ellicott, whose direct ancestor was that Andrew Ellicott, who came from Devonshire, England, in 1731, to settle in Bucks County, Pa.

His father was an expert clockmaker, whose strong mathematical bent of mind undoubtedly endowed his talented son with the love of the exact sciences. The numerous extracts from private dairies and the copies of his letters incorporated in the book give a vivid picture of his career and in this way the author has cleverly made her talented subject tell his own story. His literary style is excellent, the text being clear, simple and flowing, so that the readers' interest is kept up with the progress of the work and he arrives at the close all too soon and with keen regret. The art of biography is difficult in that the personality of the writer is ever struggling with the character of the subject—it may be unavoidably—and the result is too apt to prove a personal and prejudiced criticism, rather than an impartial life history. In this work, however, the authoress has confined her words to description rather than comment, with a result as happy for her subject as it is creditable to herself. The illustrations are superior in tone and finish, the typography distinct and restful and the dress of the volume appropriate in quiet taste to the Quaker attributes of its hero. It is a book for the libraries of book-lovers as well as the general public and deserves every success.

A HISTORY OF THOMAS AND ANNE BILLOPP FARMAR AND SOME OF THEIR DESCENDANDTS IN AMERICA, by Charles Farmar Billopp. Cloth, Octavo, pp. 125. Full Index. The Grafton Press, New York. 1907.

The family of Farmar was early established at Sanciton, Co. Oxon, England, and Major Jaspar Farmar of County Cork, Ireland, first arrived in America in the ship *Bristol Merchant*, on September 9th, 1685, bringing with him his sons, their families and twenty servants. He settled on a tract of 5,000 acres purchased from William Penn, embracing all of "Farmars or Whitemarsh Township, Philadelphia County, South of Shippack Road."

His grandson, Thomas Farmar, Chief Justice of Supreme Court of New Jersey, son of Jaspar Farmar, Jr., the husband of Anne Billopp, daughter of Captain Christopher Billopp of the Royal Navy, was the founder of the branch of the family whose descendants are set forth in this work. Many of these descendants were officers in the English Army, and the annals of the family show a long line of distinguished men. The material has been ably treated by the compiler and his work evidences great research, accuracy and ability. The method of arrangement is somewhat confusing, and renders the tracing of any descendant difficult to one unfamiliar with the family lines, but this must be attributed to the narrative style which the author uses and to the wealth of interesting detail which fills the pages. The illustrations of Coat Armor, portraits and pictures of manor houses, as well as the entire style of the volume is in excellent taste and the work will make a valuable addition to select genealogical libraries.

FAMILY RECORDS OF THE DESCENDANTS OF GERSHOM FLAGG (born 1730) OF LANCASTER, MASS., WITH OTHER GENEALOGICAL RECORDS OF THE FLAGG FAMILY DESCENDED FROM THOMAS FLAGG OF WATERTOWN, MASS., AND INCLUDING THE FLAGG LINEAGE IN ENGLAND, by Norman Gershorn Flagg and Lucius C. S. Flagg. Cloth, Octavo, pp. 173, with Index. Privately printed. 1907.

In collecting and compiling all Flagg records in New England, whether of those of the name directly related, or of those as yet unplaced, the authors have undoubtedly preserved information which in a few years more might have been difficult if not impossible to secure. With all these facts before them future family historians can more readily exercise the process of selection and elimination so necessary in the compilation of an accurate and complete genealogy. Thomas Flagg, baptized at Whinberg, Norfolk, England, 1615, who sailed for America in 1637, when twenty-one years of age, and settled at Watertown, Mass., was the founder of the main American line of the name and from him sprang a long line of descendants. The compilers have made the dry facts of descent interesting by adding many excellent photographs of members of the family and their homes, and when possible have inserted short biographical sketches. The book shows an earnest spirit of research, a careful and accurate selection of the important facts contained in the town, county and court records, and a comprehensive arrangement of the subject. It is to be regretted that the system of nomenclature is special rather than standard, but this must in a measure be attributed to the fact that the compilers are not trained genealogists, and hence have sacrificed general utility to the public to an individual system with which they are familiar. What is easy to them through custom of usage may be extremely intricate to the general searcher, and as time saved is the essence of success in a long hunt for family pedigrees, any new and original method of indicating descent, requiring special education, is always condemned by skilled genealogists. The press work, paper and binding of the book is in excellent taste, and as an authoritative work the book is well fitted for extensive reference.

THE GRAFTON MAGAZINE OF HISTORY AND GENEALOGY, a Quarterly Publication, Vol. I, No. 1. June, 1908. The Grafton Press, New York. 1908.

The appearance of a new magazine devoted to historical and genealogical subjects is always weclome for a number of manuscripts, family histories and unpublished records are constantly coming to light, and it will soon be impossible for the older and well established periodicals to print even those deserving of record. The time is rapidly approaching, however, when a nice discrimination must be exercised, not only by the libraries in accepting genealogical works but by the magazines in filling up their numbers. Pages devoted to long lines of descent, without historical or biographical notes, soon grow uninteresting and "histories of the unimportant" are becoming a drug on the genealogical market. For this reason much care should be exercised in selecting and publishing material of this nature, and it is a pleasure to note that this first number of the Grafton Magazine is filled with good reading and with articles of literary value. May it have a successful and prosperous career in its chosen field and do its part in arousing and maintaining the interest and wholesome pride of all worthy descendants of the early settlers of this land.

JOHN HARVARD'S LIFE IN AMERICA OR SOCIAL AND POLITICAL LIFE IN NEW ENGLAND IN 1637-1638, by Andrew McFarland Davis. Paper, Octavo, pp. 45. Cambridge, John Wilson & Son, University Press. 1908.

The author deals with a single year of John Harvard's life and from scanty facts at hand, has framed a strong picture of the man and his time. Strange as it may seem, scarcely any information can be had concerning the celebrated founder of Harvard University, and much of his history in the Massachusetts Colony must be supplied from documents relating to his contemporaries and companions in Cambridge. Even the will in which he wrote his "immortal bequest" of his library and fortune to Harvard College has disappeared. The author has the happy faculty of so clothing a mere skeleton of a biography with living words and phrases, as to make it most interesting reading and in a sense conveys the impression of possessing more details of the Cambridge scholar's life than he has actually gleaned. The work will be a welcome addition to the little collection of biographies and histories of one whose early gift to learning will continue to bear fruit for hundreds of generations yet unborn.

THE ANCESTRY OF ROSALIE MORRIS JOHNSON, DAUGHTER OF GEORGE CALVERT MORRIS AND ELIZABETH KUHN, HIS WIFE, by R. Winder Johnson. Second Volume. Cloth, Quarto, pp. 87. Full Index. Privately printed, Philadelphia. 1908.

The English and Flemish ancestors of the subject of this work are clearly set forth in a series of pedigree charts prepared from Heralds Visitations, Town and Church Records and family documents, and the compilation evinces much learning and attention to detail. This style of genealogy, tho comparatively rare in this country, is one which enables the searcher to note at a glance the source of birth and in fact may be called a " map of descendants." The ancient Flemish records must be a mine full of facts concerning many of the early immigrants to this country and in tracing such portions as affect his kin, the compiler will aid and encourage other families of Flemish descent to make the effort of locating their ancestors beyond sea. Alliances with the family of Peter Paul Rubens, the great artist, and with the Stier Family of Antwerp are well worthy of perpetuation in record form and of a pardonable pride among their living descendants. The intricacies of descent have been tersely set forth and beautifully arranged by the compiler who shows a fine genealogical sense and confines his facts to simple, direct statement, without going into collateral speculations and digressions. The paper and printing of the work is worthy of admiration and imitation and it was a happy thought to add the facsimiles of family signatures from original documents in the Antwerp archives.

MIDDLETOWN UPPER HOUSES. A History of the North Society of Middletown, Ct., 1650–1800, with genealogical and biographical chapters on early families and a full genealogy of the Ranney family, by Charles Collard Adams, M.A., Secretary, Treasurer, etc. Cloth, Octavo, pp. 847. The Grafton Press, New York. 1908.

This book begins with an account of the first settlements in Connecticut prior to 1651, when Mattabeseck (1653 Middletown) was made a town. Upper Houses was finally called Cromwell in 1851. The history of this place is full and interesting. The descendants of Thomas Ranney occupy the pages from 143 to 505. Brief genealogies follow of Bulkely, Butler, Clark, Doolittle, Edwards, Eells, Gaylord, Gridley, Hall, Hubbard, Hurlburt, Keith, Kelsey, Kirby, L'Hommedieu, Prout, Riley, Sage, Savage, Smith, Stocking, Stow, Treat, Warner, White, Wilcox, and Williams families. The book throughout is profusely illustrated. A three column index of fifty-eight pages concludes the volume which will prove satisfactory to many. It would have been preferable to have the genealogies follow the approved plan adopted by the Register and Record but nevertheless the work is welcome.

CONSANGUINEOUS MARRIAGES IN THE AMERICAN POPULATION, by George B. Louis Arner, Ph.D. Paper, Octavo, pp. 99. New York, Columbia University. 1908.

The subject of intermarriages among kin is ably treated by the author, who has grouped the more striking features of such alliances into seven chapters,

20A

and while he does not claim an exhaustive statistical examination of the question, he has clearly set forth such principles as should be deduced from the material available. Although the pamphlet is not of a genealogical nature yet it will prove of value to those who study the history of families and by calling the attention of genealogists to this phase of social life, may result in valuable facts and discoveries. The author's style is clear and logical and his work shows much erudition.

GEORGE MORTON, OF PLYMOUTH COLONY, AND SOME OF HIS DESCENDANTS, by John K. Allen. Paper, Royal Octavo, pp. 43. Privately printed. 1908. Full Index.

The first known record of George Morton was in the Dutch Church Records of Leyden, Holland, and describes him as "merchant, from York in England, accompanied by Thomas Morton his brother and Roger Wilson, his acquaintance,' and married to Juliana Carpenter, maid from Bath in England, accompanied by Alexander Carpenter, her father, and Alice Carpenter, her sister, and Anna Robinson, her acquaintance. The marriage took place "23 July—2 August, 1612." He came to Plymouth in the ship *Anne* during the latter part of July, 1623, was a brother-in-law of Gov. William Bradford, and was probably the author of "Mourt's Relation," the first publication of information about the adventure of the Pilgrims. Nothing indicates his original place of residence in England, and his English ancestry has never been authoritatively traced, but the author has followed down the first four generations in America with great accuracy and has continued certain branches down to the tenth generation. The arrangement and treatment of this genealogy is altogether admirable, following as it does, the best principles of recording descent and clearly and concisely setting forth the link without going into collateral branches and unnecessary detail. The paging, printing and type used show the taste of a trained genealogist, and the sole regret is that the pamphlet is not bound in cloth for the greater preservation of its valuable contents.

TWO CENTURIES OF NEW MILFORD, CONN., an account of the Bi-Centennial Celebration of the founding of the town, held June 15, 16, 17 and 18, 1907, with a number of historical articles and reminiscences. Prepared under the direction of the Historical Committee by various citizens of New Milford and by the editorial department of the Grafton Press. Cloth, Octavo, pp. 307. Index. The Grafton Press, New York. 1907.

The selection of special writers to deal with the different subjects of interest in the history of the early towns, appears to be a wise method of collecting into one volume historical matter which could not be compiled by one author without great labor and research and credit is due to the editorial department of The Grafton Press, for inaugurating this method of arranging and preserving town and county histories. John Noble in 1707 erected the first log house in what was to be later New Milford, and by 1712, he and his son had been joined by twelve other families. Later John Read laid claim to this land but after no less than fifteen lawsuits, finally abandoned the struggle and removed to Redding. Thereafter the new town flourished and the names of Boardman, Taylor, Noble, Gaylord, Bostwick, Canfield, Baldwin, Griswold, Sherman, Sanford, Mygatt, Marsh, Hine and Turrill appear among the prominent settlers. Its most celebrated citizen was Roger Sherman, whose career during the War of the Revolution was conspicuous for sound legal sense and patriotism. The book is divided into two parts, the first relating to the ancient history of the town, the war records, the old houses and cronology, etc., and the second to the Bi-Centennial exercises. The illustrations consist of portraits of prominent citizens and some of the points of interest in the town, and are admirable half-tones, while the entire appearance of the book reflects credit upon its publishers, whose enterprise merits commercial success.

NEW JERSEY ARCHIVES. First Series, Volume XXVII. Newspaper Extracts, Vol. VIII, 1770–1771. Edited by William Nelson. Cloth, Octavo, pp. 713. Full Index. The Press Printing and Publishing Co., Paterson, N. J. 1905.

This volume continues the good work of collecting into referable shape the newspaper items concerning the State of New Jersey, and in no way falls behind its predecessors in the series. It contains many references to the celebrated Non-Importation Agreement, by which the people pledged themselves not to use or import English goods, until the tea and sugar taxes were removed; to the "Horseneck or Indian" Purchase and to the East Jersey Proprietors attempt to enforce their claims to the lands; to the British Garrisons at Elizabeth, Perth Amboy, New Brunswick and Freehold; to the Stage lines; to runaway servants and slaves, etc., and to hundreds of other minor facts, appearing in notices, advertisements, letters, etc. This material will prove invaluable to future State historians, for no surer evidence of the minds and motives of people is to be had, than the items contained in the newspapers of the times. The press work and binding is simple but effective and this book is uniform with the other volumes of the series.

NEW JERSEY ARCHIVES. Second Series, Volume III. Newspaper Extracts, Vol. III, 1779. Edited by William Nelson. Cloth, Octavo, pp. 786. The John L. Murphy Publishing Co., Trenton, N. J. 1906.

This volume chiefly relates to the progress of the War of the Revolution, of which the most notable episodes dealt with are the Battle of Minisinck; Col. Sincoe's dash on New Brunswick; the Lee-Laurens duel; the depreciation of the currency; the Governor Livingston and Sir Henry Clinton correspondence; the British raid on Elizabeth; and the raids of the Loyalists on the so-called "New Jersey Volunteers;" and the events at Washington's Headquarters at Middlebrook. Mingled with these war reports are the usual advertisements for sales of real estates, recovery of runaway slaves, eloping wives, and trade notices. In brief, the volume is a running diary of the men, time and places of 1779, and contains much valuable and curious information. In conjunction with the First Series, which deals with the Colonial period, the Second or Revolutionary Series, will fill out the annals of New Jersey, a State which was one of the most active and important battlegrounds in the struggle between the large landed proprietors and the small village tradesmen, and which as stragetic ground was alternately occupied by British and Patriot troops for many years of the war. This Series of Volumes of New Jersey History are all important and should be found in every Library of any size in the United States.

JOHN WATTS DE PEYSTER, by Frank Allaben. Cloth, Octavo, Two Volumes, pp. 660, with Index. Frank Allaben Genealogical Co., New York. 1908.

Perhaps there was no more interesting period in the constructive history of New York than that between the years 1820 and 1880, when the times, the customs, the manners and the populace all underwent those mighty changes which have brought about the present growth of the Imperial City. The late General dePeyster was a prime mover in many of these progressions and until his death remained one of the most interesting links between past and present New York. Of ancient and most honorable lineage, of kin to some of the best representative families in this State, possessed of an independent fortune and a generous income, of marked intelligence and ability, he early in life devoted himself to the study of military affairs, and by his sound advice and energetic efforts effected wide reforms in the Militia and Fire Department of the State of New York. For these services he was rewarded with the rank of Brigadier-General, and later breveted Major-General by the Legislature of the State of New York.

As an author of numerous monographs on a great range of subjects and as a military critic of the battles of the Revolutionary and Civil War, his writings always commanded the respect and attention of those interested in such subjects. Mr. Allaben is admirably fitted for the task of being his biographer, not only for his special genealogical knowledge, but for his ability to digest and put together the countless facts of interest found in the private diaries and writings of Mr. dePeyster. He has, when possible, made the General relate in his own language the important facts in his career and thus permitted the man to be his own defender and the reader his own critic. A complete biography of General dePeyster's writings is annexed to the second volume, as well as a full index, which greatly adds to the value of the work as a book of reference. The portraits and other illustrations are clear and well chosen and the publication merits the approval of the general reading public.

THE SANXAY FAMILY AND DESCENDANTS OF REV. JACQUES SANXAY, Huguenot Refugee to England in 1685, by Theodore F. Sanxay, A. M., LL.B. Cloth, Quarto, pp. 217, with Index. Privately printed, New York. 1908.

The name of Sanxay is unusual and can be traced back to the beginning of the Christian Era. Its Latinized form is Sensacus (A. D. 936) or Sancium, and there is a town in France, called Saxay, in the Province of Pitow, which existed as early as 300, A. D., but all indications go to prove that the family name existed before the town was established. Of several families of the name in France, that of Pierre Sanxay of Saintes, Pastor of a Reformed Church in 1569 is the first that can be traced of the present English family of the name. He was probably of gentle, if not noble birth, and the records of his church, commencing October, 1570, are still preserved. The compiler has traced out several branches in France and the main branch in England, from which springs the American branch, being descended from Rev. Jacques Sanxay, refugee to England in 1685, and pastor of St. Olaves Church, Exeter, England. The lines are clearly and fully established and the author has cleverly arranged his extensive facts in the smallest possible space. The research for the work must have been difficult and expensive, dealing as it does with ancient French notarial records, and the compiler exhibits a sound genealogical sense in his collection of family history. The type and fine paper used in this work leaves nothing to be desired, and it is an acquisition to the shelves of those interested in family research.

COLONIAL FAMILIES OF THE UNITED STATES OF AMERICA, in which is given the history, genealogy and armorial bearing of Colonial Families who settled in the American Colonies from the time of the settlement of Jamestown, 13th May, 1607, to the Battle of Lexington, 19th April, 1775. Edited by George Norbury Mackenzie, LL.B. Cloth, large Octavo, pp. 730. Full Index. The Grafton Press, New York. 1907.

The aim of this work is to make a complete and reliable record, devoted exclusively to those American families whose Colonial ancestors laid the foundations of the Republic, and the editor has brought to this monumental task great research, learning and ability, not only in tracing out his material from a mass of documentary data and traditional dicta, but in arranging and condensing his facts into reasonable bulk. Necessarily many of the pedigrees displayed in this volume, must have been supplied by the heads of the families interested and it would have been impossible for the editor to verify all the facts claimed, not only as to the right to bear coat-armor, but as to the original ancestor named and his location in Old England. Vast as is the difference between statement and proof of descent, the chasm is still more wide between bearing arms by right or by tradition. The desire of all good republicans for heraldic devices is after all an innocent vanity, and perhaps the strongest proof of our descent from the English commoners lies in the American Social classes so "dearly loving a Lord."

The editor of the work has wisely avoided the pitfalls of his task in accepting, without comment, those few claims which must try even the strongest genealogical faith, and simply records the pedigrees sent, leaving the reader the privilege of taking the claim with a grain of salt. The greatest value of the work lies in those pedigrees compiled *since* the date of arrival of the original ancestor in this country and such charts seem to be full, accurate and admirably arranged. The printing of the work follows the best English traditions and the type, paper and wood cuts of the arms all are worthy of this fine publication. The bulk of the families named are from the Southern Colonies and it is hoped that in the projected future editions of the work attention and space will be devoted to more of the New Englanders who are "armigers" of record.

The book contains an immense amount of genealogical information and for this reason should become a standard reference work on the book shelves. It will undoubtedly bring forth many more facts concerning the families dealt with from its readers and critics, who thus may aid in solving those genealogical problems which have caused and continue to cause so much controversy.

THE ASSOCIATION OF DESCENDANTS OF ANDREW WARD, January, 1907. Paper, 12mo, pp. 12. And REPORT OF THE PROCEEDINGS AT THE UNVEILING OF THE ANDREW WARD MONUMENT, FAIRFIELD, CONN. Paper, Octavo, pp. 26.

These pamphlets relate to the Annual Meeting, Officers and Members, and general information concerning the Society of Descendants of this early Connecticut settler and gives a brief biography and a description of the monument erected to his memory on the 13th June, 1907.

They form an appropriate record of the honor paid to an early Colonial magistrate by his numerous descendants.

LOOMIS FAMILY. A complete revision of the Loomis Genealogy, edition of 1875, by Dr. Elias Loomis, is now in the course of preparation. It will contain important discoveries made by Prof. C. S. Hoppin, Jr., in regard to the English ancestry of the family from the Church Records at Haxted, England, extending back to 1540, and will contain much new material concerning the American branches of the family, brought down to date, and numbering over 12,000 names of persons born Loomis, verified descendants of the pioneer Joseph Loomis. Any one who may be interested should communicate with Mr. Elisha L. Loomis, Pres. Loomis Genealogical Association, Berea, O.

ACCESSIONS TO THE LIBRARY.

June 16 to September 10, 1908.

DONATIONS.

Bound.

Allaben, Frank.—John Watts de Peyster.
Christie, Mrs. Susan Cantrill.—Cantrill-Cantrell Genealogy.
Flagg, Norman G.—Flagg Family Records.
Goodwin. James J.—History of Christ Church, Hartford, Conn., Vol. II.
Grafton Press, The.—Our American Barclays. History of Thomas and Anne (Billopp) Farmar. Two Centuries of New Milford, Conn. Middletown Upper Houses. Life and Letters of Andrew Ellicott. Descendants of James Cole of Plymouth. Colonial Families.
Johnson, R. Winder.—Ancestry of Rosalie Morris Johnson, Vol. II.
Merritt, Douglas.—Dunlap's History of New York. Sabine's Loyalists. Documentary History of the Church in Connecticut.
Morrison, George Austin, Jr.—New York Society, Sons of the Revolution, Year Books for 1893, 1896, 1899. Annual Report State Historian, N. Y., Vol. I. Bontell's English Heraldry. Cussan's Handbook of Heraldry. New Paltz Church Records. Hazard Family. Heitman's Register. Baird's Huguenot Emigration to America. Military Papers of Daniel D. Tompkins, Vol. I. St. Nicholas Society's Advance Sheets. Society of Colonial Wars, Constitution, Addresses and Year Books.
Murray, Harold G.—Record of the Class of 1893, Princeton University.
New York State Library.—Van Rensselaer Bowier Manuscripts.
Sanxay, Theodore F.—Sanxay Family.
Shedd, Mrs. G. V.—Records of the First Church, Preston, Conn.
Stark, James H.—Dorchester Day.
Swartwout, William Merrill.—Swartwout and Ketelhuyn Chronicles.

Pamphlets, Etc.

Bacon, Edwin F., Ph.D.—Tombstone Inscriptions, Lourens, N. Y., manuscript.
Betts, C. W.—Royal Lineage of Charles C. Betts, manuscript.
Brink, Benjamin.—Olde Ulster.
Commissioner of Education.—List of Publications of the American Bureau of Education.
Cornell, Rev. John.—Ancestry of Rev. John Cornell, pedigree chart.
Corporation Counsel, The.—Vice-President Clinton's Funeral Honors.
First Reformed Church.—Church Tablet.
Genealogical Society of Pa.—Collections, III, 3.
Grafton Press, The.—The Grafton Press Magazine, I, 1.
Harris, Edward Doubleday.—The Suffolk Association of Congregational Churches and Ministers. Biography of Ezekiel Cheever. Robert Roxby. Records Congregational Church, East Hampton, Conn. Moore Chart. Genealogist's Note Book. Historical and Genealogical Department, Literary Era. Old Ipswich. Reports of the Secretary of State and State Librarian, Conn. Report of Commission of Public Records. Josiah Harris of East Machias, Me. Genealogical Exchange, 4 vols.
Historical and Philosophical Society of Ohio.—Quarterly Publication.
Holbrook, Levi.—N. E. Historical and Genealogical Society's Proceedings.
Holden, J. A.—History of Chestertown Presbyterian Church. Chestertown Presbyterian Church Centennial.
Horton, Byron Barnes.—Horton Family Year Book.
Jennison, H. L.—Ancestry of Harrie Lee Jennison, Pedigree Chart.
Junkin, Francis T. A.—Genealogical Chart of Alexander and Allied Families.
Morrison, George Austin, Jr.—General Society, Sons of the Revolution, Directory, 1905. Supplement to N. Y. Society, S. R., Year Book, 1899.
Muskett, Joseph James.—Suffolk Manorial Families, II, 10.
N. C. Historical Society.—James Sprunt Historical Monograph.
N. Y. Public Library.—Bulletin.
Quinby, Henry Cole.—New England Family History, II, 6.
Reynolds, Miss Helen.—Dutchess County Tombstone Inscriptions, Manuscript.
Strippel, Henry C.—Albany Authors. Rev. J. G. Van Slyke's Anniversary Address. Historical Address, Kingston, N. Y.
Taulman, Joseph E.—Ancestry of Parker Harmanus Taulman, Pedigree Chart.
Turner, Rev. C. H. B.—Clippings.
Van Ommeren, C.—Vragen-Antwoorden.
Virginia State Library.—Bulletin, III.
Ward, Rev. George K., Sec'y.—Association of the Descendants of Andrew Ward Second Triennial Reunion. Unveiling of the Andrew Ward Monument.
Yale University.—Obituaries of Graduates.

OTHER ACCESSIONS.

Appendix to A List of Parish Registers.
Connecticut Census of 1790.
History of Cortland County, N. Y.
Holland Society's Year Book, 1906.
Index Library, Part 112.
Irish Settlers in America.
Maine Census of 1790.
Massachusetts Census of 1790.
Minutes of the Orphan Masters of New Amsterdam, II.
N. E. Historical and Genealogical Register Index, IV, 2.
New York Census of 1790.
N. J. Archives, 1st Series, Vol. 27, 2nd Series, Vol. 3.
Pedigree Register.
Pope's Pioneers of Maine and New Hampshire.
Register Connecticut Society Colonial Dames.
Registers of St. Martin's, Fenny Stratford.
Rhode Island Census of 1790.
Royal Descents; Scottish Records.
South Carolina Census of 1790.
Year Books of Probates, IV, 4.

INDEX OF NAMES IN VOLUME XXXIX.

Groesbeck, Margarita Kipp, 278
  Maria, 278
  Maritje Viele, 278
  William, 281
Groesbeek, Barbar Claasz, 118
  Maria, 36
  Nicol., 36
  Wouter, 117
Grogan, Jas., 9
  Louisa (Eloisa L.) Hoffman, 9
Grover family, 229
  Mary, 59
Guion, Hermanus, 262
Guinup, Sarah, 9
Guthrie, Catherine, 68
Guyon, Ann Connor, 174
  Ann Elizabeth, 253
  Catharine Ketteltass, 105
  Daniel, 174, 257
  Danl., 173, 253
  Elisabeth Clawson Young, 174
  Frances, 253
  James, 174
  John, 107
  Peter, 105
  Sara Ward, 107
Gysberts, Neeltje, 35
Gysbertse, Neeltje, 35

Hachett, Elizabeth Jentleman, 194
  Robt., 194
Hackston, Jeremiah, 215
  Rhoda Akins, 215
Hadden, John Aspinwall, 137
Haden, Joseph, 218
Hageman, Benjamin, 287
  Elizabeth, 84
  Jane Skillman, 287
  Mary, 87
Haines, gov., 297
Hale, Mary Ann, 282
  Nathan, 113
Halenbeck, Aletteka, 38, 119
Halenbeeck, Aletteka, 124
  Aletteke, 180
Halenbeek, Aletta, 119
  Letge, 282
Hall family, 305
  Abigail, 213
  Giles, 111
  John, 128
  Mary, 140
  Polly Butts, 128
  Thomas, 275
  Uranah, 216
  Zurviah, 214
Halliday, Edgar, 292
  Susanna Church Skillman, 292
Halma, Francois, 271
Halstead, Anna A. Tindell, 166
  Isaac, 166
Hamersly, L. R., 148
Hammond, Ann, 110
  Hannah, 128
Hamlin, John, 63
  Mary, 63
  Tiney, 128
Hanchet, Eben, 120
  John, 128
  Joseph, 120
  Tiney Hamlin, 128
Hancock family, 72
Handlin, Elizabeth, 107
Handy, Rachel, 126
Hanna family, 225
Hanus, Gustavus Charles, 66
Hardenbroock, Adam, 274
  Annetje Meinders Smitt, 274

Hardenbrook, ——, 57
Haring, Cornelius, 224
Harmense, Elbert, 38
Harmensz, Lysbet, 33
Harle, Awdry, 195
Harper, James, 208
  Jane Skillman, 161
  Uri, 161
Harris, Amy, 85
  Bernice, 85
  Clinton, 85
  Clyde, 85
  Edith, 85
  Edward Doubleday, 73, 138, 310
  Elizabeth, 129
  Elsie, 85
  Freeman, 85
  Henry, 85
  Josiah, 310
  Julia, 85
  Leonard B., 85
  Lillian Hedges, 85
  Mary Skillman, 85
  Minerva, 85
  Susan A., 55
Harrison, Ada, 165
  gen., 156
Harrod, Mary, 61
Harry, negro, 257
Harsen family, 228
Hartshorne family, 71
Hart, Harriet Williamson, 158
  John, 53, 224
  Sarah, 53
  William, 158
Hartman, Eliza C., 261, 266, 268
  G. A., 255, 256
Hartough, Eliza Ann Nevius, 52
  John, 52
Harty, Freda Hause, 224
Harvard, John, 232, 304, 305
Harvie, George, 196
Harvey, —— 215
  Abigail Skillman, 161
  America Minerva, 161
  —— Cone, 215
  David Francis, 161
  Eliza Martha, 161
  Jacob, 161
  James, 161
  James Reed, 161
  John, 69, 74
  John M., 161
  John Quincey, 161
  Mary, 161
  Philander, 161
  Sarah, 161
Harzen, Ann, 256
  Cornelius, 256
  Jacob, 256
  Margaretta Perine, 256
Hasbrouck, Catherine 242
  Daniel, 242
  Dinah, 242
Hatch, Amanda Hubbell, 216
  Elizabeth, 216
  Experience, 217
  Frank M., 165
  Henery, 216
  Lucee, 216
  Mary Skillman, 165
Hately, Mary Cole, 167
  Richard, 167
Hatfield, Catharine Van Pelt Bogart, 171
  Deborah, 171
  James, 268
  John, 171
  Sarah, 268

Hathaway, Charles R., 73, 74
  Joanna Gilbert, 116
  Lucretia, 116, 211, 212
  Samuel, 116
Hatsche, Elizabeth Georgiana, 32
  George, 32
  John, 32
Hatt, Andw., 46
Hattof, Anna, 96
Haughabout, Betsey, 258
  Ellen, 263, 266
  Hannah, 255
  John, 267
  Mary Ann, 267
  Peter, 255, 263
  Rachel, 255
  Sarah Britton, 263
  Winant, 263
Haughawout, Elsie Jane, 268
Haughwout, ——, 176
  Betsy, 25
  Daniel, 267
  Esther, 267
  Francis, 253, 267
  Hester, 253
  Jane Jones, 267
  Lefferd, 148
  Mary, 253
  Mary Martino, 105
  Matthias, 253
  Peter, 105
  Susan, 99
  Susan Ann Roff, 253
  Wynant, 253
Hauseman, Martha Swaim Butler, 32
Hausman, Catharine Ann, 94
  Catherine Bauer, 94
  Isaac, 94
  James, 94
  Theodore Adam, 94
Havens, Sarah, 63
Hawk, Mary, 164
Hawke, Carrie, 90
  Edward P., 90
  Edward S., 90
  Henrietta, 90
  Ida Stryker Skillman, 90
  Mary Emma, 90
  William W., 90
Hay, family, 150
  G. U., 14, 187, 243
Haye, Maria, 282
Hayden, Esther, 210
  Esther Beebe Paine, 210
  Geo. W., 210
  Henrietta, 210
  Horace, 210
  Jane M., 210
  John, 210
  Luther, 210
  Nancy Green, 210
  Nehemiah, 210
  Sara Sill, 210
  Sarah Sill, 210
  Uriah, 210
  Wm. Henry, 210
Hays, Lydia Mapes, 214
  Nathaniel, 214
Hazard, family, 309
  James, 215
  Martha Gold, 215
Hazen, Ward C., 14, 187, 243
Heal, Eliza Swift, 104
  Emma, 104
  Peter, 104
Hearne, 224
  family, 148
  William T., 148
Heath, Anna, 120, 283
  Bartholomew, 283
  Eliza, 265

Mesereau, Hannah, 160
   Jacob, 266
   John, 107, 108, 160
   John Drake, 160
   Joseph, 174
   Joshua, 160, 259
   Judith Poillon, 107
   Keziah Drake, 160
   Lucretia Sharrot, 266
   Marieta Gifford, 28
   Martha, 108
   Mary Taylor, 108
   Phoebe A. Skillman, 161
   S., 98
   Sally Skillman, 160
   Sara Bedell, 174
   Sara White, 106
   Stephen, 106, 259
Meserole, Cornelia Titus, 7
   Elizabeth Titus, 7
   Sarah, 7
Mesy, Margaret Daily, 106
   Robert, 106
Metcalf, Melatiah, 1
   Samuel, 1
Metselaar, Egbertje Egberts, 181
   Teunis Teunisen, 181
Meyer, Ann Bush, 108
   Simon, 108
Meynertsz, Diewer Jacobsdr, 271
   Egbert, 271
Middagh, Madaline, 220
Middleton, Alice, 87
Miers, Derick, 259
   John, 259
   Martha Van Cleef, 259
   Mary, 259
Miles, Elijah, 68
   Frances Cornell, 68
   G. C., 68
   Thomas Obder, 68
Millus, Cornelia Knickerbocker, 124
   Simon, 124
Miller, family, 225
   Abraham E., 18
   Anne Sanford, 129
   Catharine, 21
   Elisabeth Garrison, 108
   Elizabeth Barton, 170
   Elizabeth Titus, 8
   Ezra, 128
   George Albert, 18
   Hannah, 127
   Henry, 108, 170, 253
   Jane Simonson, 18
   Mary Green, 128
   Mary Haughwout, 253
   Mary Knickerbacker, 124
   Naomi, 162
   Peter, 8
   Robert B., 228
   Ruth, 201
   Thomas, 129, 253
   Tobias, 124, 284
Mills, family, 225
   Agnes Jentleman, 194
   Eliza Ann, 28
   Eliza Ann Egbert, 30
   Eliza Egbert, 26
   Gilbert Tunis Egbert, 30
   Jemimah, 259
   John, 26, 28, 30, 194, 259
   Mary, 26
   Mary Elizabeth Vanderbilt, 28
   Moses, 259
   Moses Newel, 26
Mingael, Jannetje Thomase, 41
   Maritle Thomase, 38
Minthorne, Geertje, 184

Mitchel, Abraham, 171
   Cathrine, 170
   James, 108
   Lewis, 264
   Margret Decker, 171
   Margaret Wilson, 108
   Mary, 176
   Mary Boram, 264
   Peter, 172, 177, 264
   Sarah, 264
   Sarah Baker, 172
   Susan, 177
Mitchell, Lewis, 262
   Peter, 176
   Rachel, 257
   Susanna, 106
Mix, Anna, 205
Moelich, Elizabeth Augusta, 94
   Catharine Ann Hausman, 94
   Charles Frederick, 94
   Charles Lewis, 94
Moering, Frederick, 169, 170
Moffatt, rev. mr., 219
Moger, Anna, 216
   Deborah, 215
   Hannah, 214
   Mary, 215
Mol, Lambert Huybertsen, 276
Mole, A., 46
Monett, Anges, 140
Monfort, Anne, 242
Monjean, C., 12
   Emma J. Tytus, 12
Monnett, Abraham, 140
   Isaac, 140
Monnette, Orra E., 140
Monson, F., 217
Montague, Jane, 47
Montgomery, James, 50
   John, 50
   Joseph, 50
   Robert, 50
   Thomas, 73
Montross, Jane, 185
Moor, Anna, 90
   Elisabeth, 133
Moore, family, 225
   Abigail Hempstead Ledyard, 131
   Ann, 256
   Benjamin, 242
   Boo Lab, 134
   Catharina Maria, 48, 49
   Catharine, 256, 261, 264
   Catharine Perine, 257, 264
   Catherine, 242
   David, 134, 264
   Deborah, 134
   Hannah, 112, 131
   Henry, 48
   Hennery, 133
   Hepzibah Willmot, 134
   James, 133, 256, 257, 261, 264
   Jane, 24
   Johanna Ward, 169
   John, 112, 133
   John Henry, 48
   Joseph, 169
   Julia, 131
   Lydia, 133
   Lydia Foster, 205
   Martha, 129
   Mary, 134
   Micah, 131
   Phoebe, 131
   Rachel Landon, 62
   Samuel, 62
   Sarah, 85
   Sarah Cannon, 257

Moore, Susanna Jane, 48, 49
   Temperance, 133
   Temperance Conkling, 133
   Thomas, 134
Morant, Edward, 48
More, Hennery, 132
   Jonah, 128
   Martha Paine, 128
   Temperance Conkline, 132
Morehouse, Andrew, 42
   Elizabeth, 42
   David, 125
   Jane Belden, 125
Morey, Mercy Allen, 127
   Thomas, 127
Morgan, ——, 172
   Ann, 168
   Avery, 209
   Cath., 174
   Catharine, 254
   Eliza Ann, 266
   Fanny Baker, 129
   Francis Wynand, 172
   J., 217
   James, 209
   Jerusha Gardner, 209
   Jesse, 174
   John, 129, 209
   Joseph, 214
   Lydia Smith, 209
   Mary, 13, 171, 174, 254, 25
   Mary Avery, 209
   Mary Gardner, 209
   Mary Hill, 209
   Mary Page, 214
   Rachel Dimond, 209
   Sabina Decker, 173
   Temperance Avery, 209
   William, 173, 209, 254
   William, jr., 209
   Williams Jones, 209
   Wm. Avery, 209
Morrel, Jane Jones, 171
   John, 171
   Judikje, 186
   Judith, 116
Morrell, Alida Dox, 186
   Daniel, 186
   Judith, 186
Morice, Isabella, 295
   John, 295
   Margerie, 295
Morris, ——, 154
   family, 225
   Catharine, 21
   Elizabeth, 26
   Elizabeth Kuhn, 305
   George Calvert, 305
   Jachin, 42
   Jurran, 224
   Lewis, 150, 275, 295
   Minerva, 42
   Richard, 275, 295
   Susan Philippse, 295
   Thomas C., 42
   William, 295
Morrison, ——, 216
   mr., 65, 138, 139, 220, 222
   George Austin, 221
   George Austin, jr., 65, 74, 77, 137-139, 151, 233, 309, 310
   Hannah ——, 216
Morse, Francis, 176
   Mary Pew, 176
Mortimer, rev. mr., 259
   Benj., 256
Morton, George, 232, 306
   Juliana Carpenter, 306
   Thomas, 306

25

Lightning Source UK Ltd.
Milton Keynes UK
UKHW011539020119
334817UK00008B/413/P

9 780282 999902